ALSO BY HOWARD STERN

Private Parts
Miss America

HOWARD STERN

COMES AGAIN

SIMON & SCHUSTER

New York London Toronto Sydney New Delhi

Simon & Schuster
1230 Avenue of the Americas
New York, NY 10020

First Simon & Schuster hardcover edition May 2019

SIMON & SCHUSTER and colophon are registered trademarks of Simon & Schuster, Inc.

For information about special discounts for bulk purchases, please contact Simon & Schuster Special Sales at 1-866-506-1949 or business@simonandschuster.com.

The Simon & Schuster Speakers Bureau can bring authors to your live event. For more information or to book an event, contact the Simon & Schuster Speakers Bureau at 1-866-248-3049 or visit our website at www.simonspeakers.com.

Interior design by Silverglass

Manufactured in the United States of America

10 9 8 7 6 5 4 3 2 1

Library of Congress Cataloging-in-Publication Data is available.

ISBN 978-1-5011-9429-0
ISBN 978-1-5011-9431-3 (ebook)

Interviews have been edited for clarity and length.

Endpaper photo: Preparing for the "Howard Stern Birthday Bash" at New York City's Hammerstein Ballroom, January 2014. (Photo by JD Harmeyer)

CONTENTS

Introduction 1

Or: How Simon & Schuster Bamboozled Me into Doing Another Book

INTRODUCTION

Or: How Simon & Schuster Bamboozled
Me into Doing Another Book

It's been over twenty years since my last book, and I vowed I would never do this again. The experience was miserable for me. Writing a book is extremely hard work—the kind of work that was required of me in college when writing a paper analyzing Ingmar Bergman and Federico Fellini movies. (I was a communications major with a minor in journalism, and I graduated one of those cum laudes—magna or summa, I can't remember which.) What made writing books even more grueling was my obsessive-compulsive disorder. I've struggled with OCD my whole life, and if you want to torture someone with OCD, just make them write a book. They will obsess over every single word, endlessly deliberate over each comma and period. It is excruciating. For the past two decades, publishers had been after me to write a third book, but I didn't want to subject

myself to all that pain and suffering, and besides, I had enough going on with my radio show and the few years I spent judging on *America's Got Talent*, so the answer was always no.

So why did I do it? Because Simon & Schuster handed me a finished copy. Tricky bastards.

Here's what happened. In April 2017, I agreed to take a meeting with this guy Jonathan Karp, number one top muckety-muck at Simon & Schuster. A mutual acquaintance, Vinnie Favale—at the time vice president of late night programming for CBS—had put him in touch with my longtime agent, Don Buchwald. Like I said, I usually shot down publishers, but I googled Jonathan and something in his impressive résumé grabbed my attention. Before joining Simon & Schuster, he'd worked for another publisher, where he started his own imprint that only released twelve books a year. While most big publishers put out hundreds of books a year, Jonathan had decided to do just a dozen— one book a month—focusing on projects he passionately believed in and putting the full force of marketing and publicity behind them. This was speaking my language. I had always been disappointed that publishers were so academic and didn't think of a book in the same way one might think of the opening of a movie. Book promotion had a lot of showbiz catching up to do. Apparently, Jonathan agreed with me. "Sure," I told Don, "I'll meet with him." I had zero intention of doing a book, but I figured it'd be an interesting conversation.

Jonathan came over to my apartment. (Though I'd take the meeting, no way was I leaving the house for it.) He walked in with a finished copy of this book you are holding in your hands—an actual bound version, with a cover and everything.

"You don't have to do a thing," he said. "We want a book of your best interviews, and we took the liberty of putting it together to show you how easy it is and how little work you'll have to do."

Crazy, right? I was impressed and flattered. I've been wined and dined in my career, and after spending so many years hustling and striving it is always enjoyable when someone tries to convince me to come work for them, but this took it to a whole new level. Surely no one in the

> ## FREE MONEY. NO WORK. I'VE ALWAYS DREAMT OF SUCH A WONDERFUL OCCURRENCE.

history of publishing had ever gone to so much trouble to get a dude to write a book. It was intoxicating and appealed to my ego, and at the same time addressed all my concerns about another literary effort. Free money. No work. I've always dreamt of such a wonderful occurrence. In fact, many years ago when the religious right was raising millions of dollars from their base to try and force me off the air, I would think, "If they just took that money and paid me not to broadcast, we would all be happy and everyone could get on with something more important than banning penis jokes." So when I held this lovely book in my hands, I was psyched. Just put my name on this and I'm going to get paid? C'mon, let's go.

I showed the book to my wife, Beth, hoping she might be impressed to find me emerging from my office with a finished tome. She would marvel at the brilliance of her husband who could crank out masterpieces at speeds only known to the Flash and Superman. In her eyes, I would be a regular Howard Dostoyevsky. Of course, she looked at the book, turned to me, and said, "What's going on here?" She was having none of it. She knew a scam was afoot.

I went ahead and signed the contract anyway. What do they say? Whenever something seems too good to be true, it probably is. Well, it was.

Jonathan had suggested I could just flip through the finished book and tweak it here and there, maybe write a little intro. One afternoon I sat down in my office to put in what I expected would be just a few hours of work. Not months, not days—hours. Suddenly, reality crept in. "These aren't really my *favorite* interviews," I thought. "Uh-oh. I don't really *love* the picture on the cover. Oh no. Hold it— wouldn't it be way more interesting if I could craft a book not only featuring my interviews, but one in which I write about my experiences in broadcasting? What if I could explain to some aspiring radio personality the art of the interview, offer a primer on my approach, chronicle how it has evolved over the years? Forget a little intro. What if I wrote an introduction for *every* interview—shared what I was thinking at the time and what I thought looking back now?"

Oh no, here we go again with the OCD—those nasty thoughts that were going to screw up the simplicity of all this. I ended up throwing out that finished book and starting from scratch. I would look in the trash and say to that book, "Curse you! Why aren't you good enough for me?" My agent, Don, told me I was overthinking it, and perhaps he was right, but I couldn't

put out a book that didn't authentically represent me and my journey.

So here we are . . . two years later. You now hold in your hands two years of work and labor. Perfection—or as close to it as I can come. That's my problem: everything has to be perfect. And since we're talking about the art of interviewing, let's go ahead and call that rule number one: Nothing is casual. Everything requires work, research, and thought. Agonize. Take it seriously. Don't leave it up to someone else, and don't phone it in. There is no such thing as a shortcut if you are going to turn in good work. If I ever enjoy the process, I know I have somehow produced something worthless. I've prided myself on putting energy and time into everything I do, and this book has been no different. I ended up devoting way more of my life to this than anyone thought would be required. I invested so much in it that I'm sure I will never ever go through this again. I swear I mean it this time.

My hat is off to Jonathan Karp. That whole concept of handing me a finished product worked. It got me to sign on and agree to write a book, even though this in no way resembles what he brought me— except for the binding. What a smart plan: show him the end result and we'll lure him in like the fish that he is.

Yet there is another reason I decided to do this book. It wasn't just Jonathan's craftiness, it was the timing of it. Had he come to me with the book idea now, I'm not sure I would be receptive to it, but around the same time he came to meet with me at my apartment, I was in the middle of dealing with a serious health scare, which I've never talked about until now.

I never mentioned it on my show, which is hard to believe, because there's nothing I won't talk about on the radio. My instinct is to blurt out everything on the air. I've turned my show into a confessional, and often my best material arrives when I force myself to go past my desire to keep things private. This time I said no to that urge. I just wanted to forget this whole thing, and until now only a handful of people knew about it.

On Wednesday, May 10, 2017, I missed a day of work, and I remember the date exactly because I never miss work. Even when I was on the air in Detroit, I would drive through ten feet of snow to get down to the radio station. It didn't matter. I got to work every day.

Apparently my perfect attendance did not go unnoticed. I missed this one day on the radio, and it turned into bigger news than the return of Jesus H. Christ. There were so many stories in the press. "It's like he disappeared! What's going on?" Reporters were even calling my parents' house. What was I, five years old? They were checking in with my mother as if I

had missed school, and I was surprised that anyone cared that much.

The show was off the air that Thursday and Friday for a scheduled vacation. For the next week there was all this weird speculation that something was wrong. Then I showed up that Monday, and I just made fun of it. I said I couldn't believe people were making such a big deal out of this, and that I was just sick with the flu.

I was lying.

About a year before, in 2016, I had gone for my annual physical. Same doctor I go to all the time. I'm used to him saying, "Everything's good. You take really good care of yourself. I wish all my patients were like you."

This time he said to me, "Everything's go—" Then he did a double-take at my chart and said, "Whoa, whoa, whoa."

I said, "What's 'Whoa, whoa, whoa'? You're scaring me."

"Nothing too alarming," he said. "It's just your white blood cell count looks a little bit low. Let's do another blood test in a month."

A month went by and we rechecked it, and it was even lower. The doctor said, "Look, I don't want you to worry, but why don't you see this doctor at Sloan Kettering."

"*Sloan Kettering?*" I said. "That's the cancer place!"

The Sloan Kettering doctor did *another* blood test and my white blood cell count

||||||||||||||||||||||||||||||||||||||||||||||||||||||||||||||||||||||||||||||||||||||||||||||||||||||||||||||||||||||

"CERTAINLY I KNOW THAT LOSING MY HAIR WOULD NOT BE THE WORST PART OF CHEMO, BUT JUST IMAGINE MY FACE WITH A BALD HEAD. NOT A PLEASANT THOUGHT. . . . WHEN IT COMES TO LOOKS, I QUOTE THE JAY-Z SONG: I HAVE NINETY-NINE PROBLEMS WITH MY FACE, BUT MY HAIR AIN'T ONE.

||||||||||||||||||||||||||||||||||||||||||||||||||||||||||||||||||||||||||||||||||||||||||||||||||||||||||||||||||||||

was even lower than the last time. This doctor said, "Well, there's nothing we need to do right now, but if it gets any lower, we could always give you a round of chemo."

"*Chemo?!*" I said. "Oh my God. This is crazy."

He said, "I just wanted you to know there are some things you can do, and we can treat this."

"Treat *what*?" I said. "What are we talking about?" Then I thought better of it. "Actually don't tell me that. I want to be kept in the dark." I'm so paranoid about my health. If I start googling, I'll go into a tailspin.

He said, "I want you to come for a blood test every month."

When you go for a blood test at Sloan Kettering, you're actually in with people who are getting chemo. The atmosphere was intense, life and death, as they were testing my blood for changes. I was in a panic, I was angry, and I was thinking, "This is it. This must be how I go. This isn't supposed to happen to me. My grandfathers had long lives, and my parents are in their nineties. This can't be happening."

There is a wonderful man I got to know over the years named Dr. David Agus. He's an expert in cancer, teaches at the University of Southern California, has written a few bestselling books, and was Steve Jobs's doctor. Just a fabulous guy. I contacted him and told him what was going on with me.

Without missing a beat, Dr. Agus said, "Do you eat a lot of fish?"

"Yeah," I said. "My wife, Beth, and I are into animal rescue, and we stopped eating meat. We even stopped eating poultry. So in order to get protein, I eat fish, like, twice a day."

He said, "Go get your mercury level checked."

I got my mercury level checked and it was through the roof. Normal is around seven. Mine was in the thirties. I cut down on fish, and my mercury level began to drop. After a few months my white blood cells went up. I was so relieved that Dr. Agus thought of this. If not for him, I might have been at Sloan Kettering hooked up to a slow drip of chemo and deprived of my Samson-like mane. Certainly I know that losing my hair would not be the worst part of chemo, but just imagine my face with a bald head. Not a pleasant thought. My hair has always been the lone redeeming quality of my appearance. Hardcore fans know I have really nice feet, but what good does that do me? No one ever sees those. I need my hair. When it comes to looks, I quote the Jay-Z song: I have ninety-nine problems with my face, but my hair ain't one. Despite whatever rumors you might have heard, I don't wear a wig and I don't use dye. A full head of dark, luscious curls is the only natural gift I've ever possessed, and I wasn't ready to give it up, so needless to say I was incredibly grateful to Dr. Agus.

He said to me, "I want to give you some peace of mind. If you ever get out to California, I've got a facility where we can do a full body scan on you, and you'll know for sure you're doing well."

Up until then, Beth had no idea what was going on. I didn't tell her about those monthly blood tests at Sloan Kettering. I didn't want her to worry, so I would just disappear for a while and go over to the hospital. With my gigantic ego, I was sure

> **THE KIDNEY SPECIALIST LOOKED AT THE MRI, SAW THE SPOT, AND SAID, "YOU HAVE TO GET THIS THING REMOVED. THERE'S A NINETY PERCENT CHANCE IT'S CANCER."**

she would wonder why I wasn't home. Good reality check: she had no idea I was gone. When Dr. Agus suggested going to California, I finally explained everything to Beth. We both figured Dr. Agus was simply being cautious and looking to reassure me. We always enjoy going to California, so we looked at it as an opportunity to visit friends, like Jimmy Kimmel and his wife, Molly. A couple months later we flew out, and I got the scan.

"Everything looks great," Dr. Agus said. "But when you get back to New York, go and get an MRI, because on your kidney there's a little spot. Sometimes these little benign cysts develop, and they can burst, and it makes it impossible to get a clear look. I don't think it's anything but get the MRI just to be safe."

I went back to New York and got the MRI. Dr. Agus called me and said, "I don't want to scare you, but I'm going to send the MRI over to a kidney specialist that I know. I want him to take a look at it." This is why I love Dr. Agus so much. He is so thorough and conscientious.

The kidney specialist looked at the MRI, saw the spot, and said, "You have to get this thing removed. There's a ninety percent chance it's cancer."

So much for peace of mind. Now I was *really* flipping out. They told me the surgery was a simple procedure. They would make seven incisions in my abdomen. That didn't sound so simple to me. The survival rate for something like this is high when they catch

THOSE HOURS WERE TERRIFYING AND MOVED SO SLOWLY. WHEN I'M ON THE RADIO, TIME FLIES, BUT IN THE HOSPITAL ROOM EVERY MINUTE FELT LIKE AN ETERNITY.

it early. I went ahead and scheduled it right away. I wanted it out of me.

I chose not to talk about it on the air. One of the things about being on the radio is, if you mention anything, people start to call in with all sorts of similar stories. "Kidney surgery? Oh, yeah, my brother went in for that . . ." And the stories never end well. The person always dies. The power of suggestion is something that overtakes me. I'm very susceptible to this kind of amateurish speculation. I didn't want to hear any of that.

My personality is that I block stuff out. I'm rather stoic, but I have to tell you, I was scared. My co-host, Robin Quivers, had just been through treatment for cancer. What she experienced was a nightmare—chemo, radiation, operations. Her original surgery took around twelve hours. When she went in for that, I kept calling the doctor for updates. I cried at the thought I might be losing Robin.

She is not only a loving and giving human being but someone who I am deeply connected to. How many professional relationships have lasted thirty-eight years, especially in broadcasting? How many times have you heard those rumors that your local friendly morning show actually

all despise each other? When I first got into radio I was alone and scared. I knew the day I met Robin I had a newfound inspiration to go and explore innovative ideas and concepts because I had a true friend who had my back. She more than anyone is my courage on the air. It would be impossible to describe my feelings for her and I am blessed and lucky that we ended up together.

Besides Beth, Robin was one of the few people I told what was going on. I also told my daughters, though not until I had scheduled the surgery. I didn't want to scare them. They were very worried yet so supportive and a tremendous comfort to me.

I decided I would do my show in the morning, and go in for surgery in the afternoon. That way I wouldn't miss work, but then the surgeon called and said, "I can take you in earlier." So I had to cancel the show at the last minute, and that's what caused the avalanche of newspaper articles.

The surgery took a couple hours, and after it was over and I woke up from the anesthesia, the doctor walked in and said, "The surgery went great. We'll have the results in a few hours."

Those hours were terrifying and moved so slowly. When I'm on the radio, time

> ❝ **AS YOU START TO GET OLDER AND YOUR BODY BEGINS TO BREAK DOWN, IT DOES GET YOU THINKING ABOUT YOUR LEGACY, ABOUT WHAT YOU'LL LEAVE BEHIND, ABOUT WHAT YOU'RE PROUD OF.**

flies, but in the hospital room every minute felt like an eternity.

The doctor finally came back in.

"Great news," he said. "It was just a tiny little cyst."

It was nothing.

Nothing was wrong with my kidney.

The sense of relief was orgasmic, but the thought that I had gone through all of this for nothing really screwed with my head. I was so angry at myself for once again being overly neurotic about my health.

I had to stay in the hospital overnight. The next day there were all those articles about how I missed work. It became a big thing in the media, and it seemed to me they were implying that I had done something horribly wrong by missing one day. I was lying in my hospital bed wearing one of those gowns where your ass hangs out thinking, "Are you kidding me? I might have had *cancer*."

I went back in to work Monday morning and every day after, but that surgery knocked me on my ass. It really walloped me. I had seven scars from the incisions, and it took me a full year to get back to feeling normal, to get to the point where I could start moving around comfortably.

I remember saying to Robin, "My God, I don't know how you did it." I looked at her with new respect. Compared to her experience, I felt like I had no right to complain, but Robin really understood what I was going through.

It wasn't just the pain, it was the fear. I never had any kind of health scare, and I certainly never spent a lot of time thinking about my death. Even now part of me feels that way—like there's no way the world could continue without me—but as you start to get older and your body begins to break down, it does get you thinking about your legacy, what you'll leave behind, what you're proud of.

I'm not proud of my first two books. I don't even have them displayed on my bookshelf at home. I think of them, and of the interviews I did with my guests during those first couple decades of my career, and I cringe. I was an absolute maniac. My narcissism was so strong that I was incapable of appreciating what somebody else might be feeling.

I have so many regrets about guests from that time. I asked Gilda Radner if Gene Wilder had a big penis. Great question. Drove her right out the door. George Michael's band Wham! Everyone I worked with said, "Whatever you do, don't ask them if they're gay. Do *not* ask them if they're gay." Within twenty seconds, I asked them if they were gay. Eminem came on the show once then never again. Same with Will Ferrell.

Possibly my biggest regret was my interview with Robin Williams. When Robin came on the show in the early nineties, I spent the entire time badgering him about how he had divorced his first wife and remarried his son's former nanny. I was attacking the guy, and he was justifiably furious with me. Years later, I realized I finally needed to apologize. I had already done this with some other people. I called them and tried to make amends. Some were gracious. A radio guy I had been awful to said, "You know what, man? I'm so glad you called. I actually felt bad for you that you were carrying around so much bitterness and ugliness inside, and I'm happy you don't have that anymore." Others were angry. A famous comedian I had bashed said to me, "I appreciate that you called, but I don't know if I could ever forgive you. I had to go through a lot of misery, because your fans were brutal." I didn't know what Robin's reaction would be. He could have hung up on me. He could have cursed me out. I had to do it. It took me twenty years to work up the nerve. I was in the midst of tracking down his phone number, and the next day he

died. I'm still filled with sadness over his loss and remorse for my failure to reach out sooner.

Telling Carly Simon how hot she was for a half-hour or spewing sex questions to Wilmer Valderrama—this ultimately led to nothing. It wasn't good radio. It was meaningless. It was just me being self-absorbed and compulsive about asking something that would provoke and antagonize. Those weren't really interviews. They were monologues. Instead of a conversation, it was just me blurting out ridiculous things. I had some real issues.

Then I started going to a psychotherapist.

This was in the late nineties. I had no idea how therapy worked. The only thing I knew about it was what I saw in movies and on television, where people would just sit there and tell stories. So that's what I did. My first session, I sat down in the chair and began telling the therapist anecdotes as if I was on the radio. I hit him with all my favorite routines. I did a thorough and involved set on the Stern family tree, complete with impressions of my family. I put together a few minutes on marriage, then moved into the pressures of the radio business, and closed with the trials and tribulations of raising a family.

After I was finished with my stand-up, the therapist instead of applauding said, "There's nothing funny going on here. Quite frankly, some of this stuff sounds pretty sad." My first response was to get defensive. Who was he to say that? I could tell that story and laugh. I had done it many times. Gradually, after a few more sessions, I realized he was right. He was the first person who ever said to me, "I take you seriously." I had always been hungry for someone to confide in like that, but I had pushed away my hunger. That's often what people who are traumatized do. In order to protect themselves, they act like nobody else matters. They tell themselves they don't need anyone.

The irony is that I've always had an appreciation for others in my work. Yes, it's called *The Howard Stern Show*, but I'm at my best when I have a bunch of people around me, when I can call on them and collaborate. Whether it's Robin or my producer Gary Dell'Abate or our jack-of-all-trades (sound effects, impressions, and so much more) Fred Norris; the staff of incredible writers and brilliant engineers; my front office, including chief operating officer Marci Turk and senior vice president Jeremy Coleman; my agent, Don Buchwald, and my executive assistant, Laura Federici; my bosses and the sales department at SiriusXM—I consider everyone a part of the team. What we do is like music, in a way. It's like a symphony. That is truly how I've always seen myself: as an orchestra conductor.

Yet that generosity of spirit didn't extend to my guests. I should have treated them as talented soloists and welcomed them to join in our performance. I was just too afraid that the audience would be bored when they didn't get their fix of outrageousness—as if some quiet notes would have destroyed the concerto. Everything had to be one loud, crashing crescendo.

Initially, I went to therapy twice a week. Then the therapist had me up it to three times. Eventually he recommended I make it four. I thought, "Man, I didn't know I was *that* screwed up." I was reluctant to make such a big commitment, but I did it. I completely gave myself over to the process.

The more I went, the more that translated into how I interviewed my guests. I found myself changing my approach because I had experienced what it was like to have someone genuinely interested in my life. Therapy opened me up and enabled me to appreciate how fulfilling it was to be truly heard. That led me to the thought: "You know, somebody

> **YES, IT'S CALLED *THE HOWARD STERN SHOW*, BUT I'M AT MY BEST WHEN I HAVE A BUNCH OF PEOPLE AROUND ME, WHEN I CAN CALL ON THEM AND COLLABORATE. . . . WHAT WE DO IS LIKE MUSIC, IN A WAY. IT'S LIKE A SYMPHONY. THAT IS TRULY HOW I'VE ALWAYS SEEN MYSELF: AS AN ORCHESTRA CONDUCTOR.**

else might actually have something to say. Let's just sit here and listen and not make it all about you."

At first, not making it about me was difficult. I had to learn to say no to myself. *Stop talking. Start listening. Let someone else shine and have a moment. Trust that the audience will remain there.* Saying no, disciplining that narcissistic part of myself that needs constant attention, was not as simple as it sounded.

What made my maturation even more challenging were the parameters of terrestrial radio—how success was solely defined by ratings. It was so competitive on the dial. Every station was fighting for the same advertising dollars, and the advertisers naturally went with whoever had the highest ratings. The ratings service measured every fifteen minutes. They tabulated how many people were listening through each quarter hour. It wasn't merely the size of a broadcaster's audience that got them high ratings, it was how many fifteen-minute blocks they could drag their audience through.

This became a science to me. I obsessively watched the clock, and as I saw the quarter hour coming up I would typically blurt out something so random and whacked out that I knew it would keep my listeners tuned in. This strategy obviously didn't lend itself to doing serious interviews. When I would have a guest, I would think, "If this person goes into

> ## I THOUGHT, "WHAT IF I COULD LISTEN TO MY GUESTS THE WAY MY THERAPIST LISTENS TO ME?"

a long explanation about something, if they're droning on about their latest project, my ratings will drop off." While my crazy behavior could mostly be attributed to my personal issues, it was also somewhat methodical. It was job security. I had young children to think about. I had a mortgage and car payments, just like my listeners.

Having success only made it worse. When I reached number one in the ratings, there was nowhere to go but down. If I wanted to keep my job, my ratings couldn't dip in the slightest. At least, that's how I saw it in my pessimistic view of the world. This was an unrealistic assessment of the situation. A few ratings points here and there weren't going to be a game changer. However, I wasn't about being realistic. I wanted to dominate. I put constant pressure on myself. It was a miserable way to live.

As I continued with therapy, I became increasingly frustrated. I was trying to grow as a person, and I was eager to bring that same growth into my work. I was excited to have real conversations. I thought, "What if I could listen to my guests the way my therapist listens to me?" I did the best that

> 66 **WHEN YOU'RE ABLE TO DO THE MOST SHOCKING THINGS YOU CAN THINK OF, THEN NOTHING IS SHOCKING ANYMORE. YOU CAN'T BE A REBEL IF THERE AREN'T ANY RULES.**

I could, but the format of terrestrial radio just wasn't conducive to that.

This wasn't the driving force behind my move to SiriusXM in 2006. The driving force was getting away from the FCC and also the excitement of building a brand-new business. The money wasn't bad either. The added bonus was that it allowed me to fully embrace this new, more mature interview style. If listeners didn't like it, they could turn to one of Sirius's other channels. Rather listen to grunge? Turn to Lithium. Want show tunes? Try On Broadway. I didn't see these other channels as competing with me, the way I did on terrestrial radio. I looked at all of Sirius as my universe. As long as people were listening to Sirius, I was satisfied. That really freed me to experiment.

When I first got to Sirius, people thought I was going to be even more X-rated than I'd been on terrestrial radio, since I didn't have to worry about the FCC and government censorship. That was my plan at first. Starting out, we did crazy segments, like a "Crap-tacular," for example, where we weighed a man's doody. He'd win prizes if he made a certain

amount of excrement. Can you believe it? You can do that on satellite radio. You can do it all day. What I soon realized is that when you're able to do the most shocking things you can think of, then nothing is shocking anymore. You can't be a rebel if there aren't any rules. Instead, the most shocking thing I could do was to grow, to change, to go somewhere fresh, to boldly go where no man had gone before—like at the beginning of *Star Trek*.

The problem was at first Gary had a hard time booking guests to do serious interviews. Hollywood publicists still saw me as a lunatic. They didn't know I'd been going to therapy and was trying to change. It took a while to convince them. One thing I think helped was the four years I spent as a judge on *America's Got Talent*.

There were many reasons I decided to do *AGT*. For starters, I had just bought a whole new John Varvatos wardrobe and I needed to show it off. Number two, I had calculated the risk of being a ratings failure and it wasn't high. The show was on in the summer—our only competition was reruns—and it already had a built-in audience. It was also a relief to be a part of an ensemble. The show was the main draw, not the judges. Before my experience with therapy, this would have been a reason *not* to do the show. Like a moth to a flame, I would have craved the spotlight. I would have demanded to be the focus. In light of the work I'd done on myself, it was a welcome change to play more of a supporting role. I was as anxious to try that on as I was to try on my new John Varvatos shoes. (By the way, lest anyone reading this think JV is slipping me a couple bucks under the table for these mentions, let me assure you that's not the case. I just like his clothes. Although what a great idea to sell advertising in one's book. Maybe next time.) I was additionally excited about working on such a large-scale production. I'd spent most of my career in toilet bowl radio stations where it was a one-person operation. There were times when I'd literally be working a tape recorder with my feet while using my hands to splice and edit. *AGT* had a crew of hundreds. It was thrilling to be a part of such a juggernaut. And though the previous seasons had been filmed in Los Angeles, the producers were willing to move the entire operation to New York to accommodate my radio schedule. It was also the realization of a childhood fantasy. Growing up, I wanted nothing more than to be a game show host. Gene Rayburn of *Match Game*, Bill Cullen of *To Tell the Truth*, Wink Martindale of *Tic-Tac-Dough*—these were all radio guys and professional announcers I loved. They were hired for TV because they had such a smooth presentation and delivery. They looked relaxed and appeared to be having so much fun. I thought it would be the greatest to have one of those long microphones and make snarky comments to contestants. Serving as a judge on *AGT* reminded me of that.

However, my principal motivation for joining the show was to shift the American public's perception of me. I thought, "How surprising and unpredictable would it be to see someone with my hard-ass uber-dude image on a feel-good prime-time network TV show?" Just when people believed they knew me, I'd prove they didn't.

It didn't take long to discover how successful I'd been in changing attitudes. After my first season on the show, I was in a restaurant with Beth when random moms and dads approached our table and asked if their kids could sit on my lap for photos. In just one summer, I'd gone from being America's Nightmare to Santa Claus. Though this was my objective, it felt very awkward. I had become accustomed to being thought of as Attila the Hun. It had become a protective shell that allowed me to keep my true self at a distance. Throughout my career I had put myself in uncomfortable situations, from dressing in women's clothing on the *Late Show with David Letterman* to donning the infamous ass-baring Fartman costume on the MTV Music Video Awards to concealing my face in elaborate makeup to impersonate Michael Jackson on a pay-per-view New Year's Eve special. Yet appearing unguarded and undisguised on *AGT* might have been the most uncomfortable I had ever felt.

I think publicists and their A-list clients responded to seeing this more vulnerable side of me. These days we have so many celebrities who want to do the show that we have to book them months in advance. They're also impressed by how prepared I am for these interviews. I have a team that does exhaustive research on each guest. They spend weeks searching for every morsel of information they can find. They compile it all, I study it closely, and then I write down an agenda of the questions I want to ask. Wherever I go, I carry a small wallet pad with a pen. I also have a waterproof pad in case I need to jot something down in the shower. You never know when a good idea is going to come. You have to be ready at any moment to capture it. By the day of the interview, I'll have roughly ten pages of notes and questions.

My memory is strange. If I read something, I don't retain it. If someone tells me that same thing, I remember it verbatim. So a few minutes before the guest walks into the studio, a member of my team, Jon Hein, will stand in front of my console and read my notes back to me. He regurgitates everything I've written down and all of the research, every word of every page. Instantly I've got it memorized. Very rarely do I even look at my notes during an interview. I have no idea how this works. Maybe that's why I'm in radio: everything with me is auditory. I don't want to analyze it too much, for fear I'll somehow jinx it and lose these superpowers. But I swear, when a guest walks in I know their complete life story as if it were my own.

Gary has told me that when he's watching the monitor in his office, there's

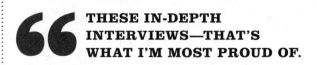

THESE IN-DEPTH INTERVIEWS—THAT'S WHAT I'M MOST PROUD OF.

always a point in every interview that I'll hit on something that causes the guest's face to change—as if they're thinking, "How in the hell do you know *that*?" Like in my interview with Jon Stewart when I shocked him by revealing the punch line to one of the first jokes he ever told onstage. Their realization that I've put in so much time and effort has a lot to do with why they're so willing to open up to me.

I also suspect guests like doing the show for the same reason I liked going to therapy. These are some of the most famous people in the world. Usually they go on a daytime or late-night talk show and they have five minutes to plug their movie or album or book and tell a couple of well-rehearsed stories.

With me, they have an hour, hour and a half—and no commercial breaks. That's the beauty of satellite radio. If I don't want to take a break, I don't do it. If the interview is going well, I'm not stopping. And if it's *not* going well, I can keep plugging away until it is. I also think that since I have let my guard down my entire career and been honest about myself—my insecurities and my anxieties and, yes, my small penis size— they are encouraged to be honest as well. They can express themselves in something more than a sound bite. By the end of these conversations the audience doesn't see them as one-dimensional celebrities anymore. They see them as regular people no different from themselves. We're all the same screwed-up, complex, beautiful human beings.

These in-depth interviews—that's what I'm most proud of. It's one of the things I want to be remembered for before I die of a noncancerous cyst. I want my show to be funny, irreverent, but also touching. I do this for anyone who has to commute for an hour and a half to their job and finally pulls into the parking lot but doesn't want to get out of the car. *That's* what I want to be my legacy. And that's another reason why I let Simon & Schuster push me into doing this book.

Perhaps my main motivation is my three wonderful daughters: Emily, Debra, and Ashley. I am over-the-top proud of them, and I've always wanted them to be proud of the work I've done on the radio—and on myself. Each of my daughters is unique, and their brilliance and charm continue to enlighten me. I'm lucky to be their father. Girls, I love you. Thank you for making me a dad, and being kind, sweet, and perfect. This one's for you.

The interviews collected here represent my best work and show my personal evolution. But they don't just show *my* evolution. Gathered together like this, they show the evolution of popular culture over the past quarter century: from Madonna

to Lady Gaga, Paul McCartney to Ed Sheeran, David Letterman to Stephen Colbert, Rosie O'Donnell to Ellen DeGeneres, Joan Rivers to Amy Poehler, Jay-Z to Kendrick Lamar, Barbara Walters to Anderson Cooper. It's not just the evolution of entertainment but of society as a whole. You have Harvey Weinstein and Bill O'Reilly rejecting (as they continue to do even now) any sexual impropriety, and you have Lena Dunham and Amy Schumer talking openly about their own sexual assaults. Then there is the late Chris Cornell talking about opioid addiction, and Leah Remini talking about Scientology, and Kim and Khloé Kardashian talking about how to make it as a reality star.

Speaking of reality stars, obviously the biggest shift in society has been watching the host of *The Apprentice* become president of the United States. Donald Trump has been on the show dozens of times over the years, in the studio as well as calling in, and he is hands-down one of the best guests I've ever had. He's everything you want out of an interview: funny, unfiltered, and willing to speak his mind. We were friendly off the air, in the rare times we would run into each other at some event in Manhattan. For example, once Beth and I wound up sitting next to him and Melania courtside at a Knicks game. You can see the paparazzi photos online. The way we are laughing and leaning in close it looks like we're best buddies and planned the whole evening together. The truth is we both took advantage of free tickets and wound up sitting next to each other randomly. I've never had Donald over to my place for dinner or vice versa. If we had been close friends off the air, he might have confided to me that he was actually serious about wanting to be president.

In my naivete, I figured like everyone else that this was no different from the other times he flirted with running: it was just a publicity stunt. I never thought he was genuinely interested in the job. I was sure that once he became front-runner for the Republican nomination, he would drop out. That's what I did when I ran for governor of New York in 1994 on the Libertarian ticket. My platform was only three issues, all of them traffic-related:

1. Eliminate the tolls for Jones Beach and the Southern State Parkway, because if you've been battling rush hour traffic to and from work all week and you want to go to the beach with your family on the weekend, you shouldn't have to wait for hours to get through a tollbooth.
2. Reinstate the death penalty and fill in the potholes with the crispy remains of all those executed.
3. Do construction on major roads at night so as not to snarl morning and evening commutes.

The public responded positively to these ideas. Some polls were showing me with 15 to 20 percent of the vote in a three-way race. That freaked me out. Me as governor? That wouldn't have been good for the state. I didn't know what I was talking about. I also realized that I would have to share my tax returns, and I didn't want to make that information public. It wasn't like I was afraid voters would discover a money laundering scheme for Russian oligarchs or strange payments to porn stars. I just didn't feel like letting my plumber know that I had a good year and now he had license to charge me triple for a dripping faucet. My candidacy was a goof, and so I quickly bailed. When Donald started winning primaries, I thought he would, too. Between Trump Tower and Mar-a-Lago, he had such a fun, stress-free life that it made no sense to me why he would exchange that for the pressure of running the country. And Lord knows he didn't want anyone looking at his tax returns. I still have no idea how he managed to avoid that.

Now here he is sitting in the Oval Office and flying around on Air Force One. Two years into his first term, I'm still trying to wrap my brain around it. I feel like I'm living in an alternate reality. Back in the early nineties when I was working on a script for the Fartman movie with J. F. Lawton, the screenwriter of *Pretty Woman*, he came up with Donald Trump as the story's villain. Fartman would save New York when Donald tried to put up condos in Central Park. Had we not abandoned the project, I would have asked Donald to play himself, and I'm sure he would have agreed. I don't recall him ever turning down a cameo. I bet Donald is just as stunned by what happened as I am. I don't think he believed he would win. Caught off guard by the mood in the country and the acceptance of his message, he decided to carry on as long as the impossible kept happening.

Do I support Donald's politics? I'm often asked this question. As my listeners know, I don't like talking about my political beliefs on the air. It's not because I'm worried I'll drive away SiriusXM subscribers who disagree with me. It's because I'm not well versed enough in politics. It's not one of my areas of expertise. I'm the guy who wanted to fill in potholes with the ashes of dead convicts! By the way, my attitude on the death penalty has totally changed in light of how many people have been wrongly executed. That's specifically why I don't like talking politics: my positions are constantly changing, and that's actually the single most important rule of being successful in radio, ahead of "nothing is casual"—have a definite opinion. What the opinion is doesn't matter. You just need to have a strong one and back it up. You can't be wishy-washy, which is what I am when it comes to casting my ballot. I've voted both Republican and Democrat, and I was a Libertarian candidate. As for my vote in the 2016 presidential election, I'll go into that later, in the chapter on Hillary Clinton. Bottom line, my political views are not good radio.

No matter how you feel about what Donald has done so far in his time as president, I think everyone can agree that his slow and steady transformation from a personality to a politician is damn fascinating. That's why I scoured through the archives and included a bunch of my interviews with him. I didn't do it to make fun of Donald or to make him look bad. His metamorphosis is on full display. In one of the early interviews, in 1997, he's calling a Miss Universe winner "an eating machine." By the last interview, in 2015, he refuses to rate Megyn Kelly's hotness on a scale of one to ten. "In the old days, I wouldn't have minded answering that question," he says, "but today I think I'll pass." That morning it became official: a phenomenal radio guest died and a presidential contender was born. Donald hasn't appeared on my show since.

My conversations with him also show my transformation as an interviewer—my shifting interest from his sexual exploits to his political ambitions. Once he was named the Republican nominee and later elected president, several of these discussions were unearthed by news outlets and subjected to endless commentary. My conversations with Donald Trump have become an important part of American history—believe me, I'm as shocked as you are—and so they deserve to be recorded in book form.

Excluding these conversations with Donald, I've provided introductions to each interview in the book so you can see what I was thinking at the time and what I think now, looking back.

If you're a SiriusXM subscriber, you might have heard some of these interviews before—either live on channels Howard 100 and Howard 101 or on our new app. (A huge thanks to the good folks at SiriusXM for creating an environment where I could do long-form interviews and for being so supportive of my career and this book.) But it's an entirely different experience reading them rather than listening to them. There is wisdom and laughs and so much more that I didn't catch during the original interviews.

There's no greater example of this than my discussion with Mike Tyson about the hunger of drug addiction.✦ When we talked, I was so caught up in the moment that I didn't fully appreciate his profundity and eloquence. As I read back over Mike's words, for the first time I could empathize with what drug addicts go through. (He also told of his own connection to Robin Williams, a revelation that wound up making headlines.)

These conversations are so inspiring. There is a lot to learn from these people, from their climb to success. If they all have one thing in common, it's that climb. The climb is everything. To hear how someone overcomes ridiculous odds and makes it—it never gets old. If you're having trouble finding motivation in life and you're looking for that extra kick in the ass, you will discover it in these pages.

One of the questions I'm most frequently asked is, "Of all the interviews you've ever done, which are your favorites?" It wasn't easy to choose. There have been nearly 1,500 of them in the thirteen years since I joined SiriusXM, plus a few thousand more going back earlier in my career. I took this process very seriously. I spent two years working on this book, with the invaluable help of many on my team as well as at Simon & Schuster—especially Sean Manning, my editor and alter ego on this project, who was there every step of the way. Hundreds of hours of audio were transcribed into more than a million words. I carefully reviewed that massive slab of material and whittled it into what you now hold in your hands.

As you'll see in these pages, there has been a lot of personal growth since my last two books. My view of the world has matured. Oh, don't worry, I still love the most base and juvenile forms of humor: sex talk, fart jokes, ridiculously silly phony phone calls, and of course the mysterious and often misunderstood "queef." I still take great delight in lengthy discussions with Ronnie the Limo Driver on whether squirting is pee and endless debates about who qualifies as a member of the Wack Pack. No chance your hero has become too highbrow, but I have found a comfortable and meaningful place in the universe.

✦ **For more on this from Mike Tyson, turn to page 528.**

These changes I speak of throughout the book have moved me in a meaningful and most needed direction that I never would have expected. Empathy, emotional openness, and a genuine curiosity about the beauty in the world have begun to develop. Allowing myself to be dependent and vulnerable is new to me. I feel reborn, liberated, free to be Patricia Marie. (An inside joke for my regular listeners. I promise there won't be too many of those. Patricia Marie is the real name of Wack Pack member Tan Mom, and she made a song . . . oh forget it. Just buy a subscription to SiriusXM already. Regular radio has too many commercials and you can't curse and it's time you just signed up. Stop being so cheap.) The hard-ass pose I've tried to maintain just doesn't work for me anymore. That posture was useful when I was young. It provided an almost impenetrable shell that protected me from feeling need. If I denied my own humanity, I would not go hungry for human kindness, touch, and most important love. It was a safe world but a lonely one—a kind of prison. So finally, after many years, I began to tear down some very well-constructed walls. I needed to do that if I was going to have a successful marriage with Beth, my best friend for the last nineteen years, as well as a deeper and more loving relationship with my fantastic daughters. I once needed solitary confinement but I was now willing to leave the safety of my incarceration and take a step outside.

The journey has been hard, but some really exciting experiences have blossomed because I was willing to dip my toe into new waters. I discovered an interest in not only other people but other passions besides radio: watercolor painting, sketching, photography, chess, and most of all a devotion to animal rescue. These pursuits provided new ways to reach out to the world, which I had kept shut out for so long. All of this has led to a richer, more satisfying existence, and all of this brought me to the idea of this book.

So here it is: book number three. I'm so proud of this book. Do me a favor and throw out the other two. Pretend you're a character in *Fahrenheit 451* and burn them. Here it is: *Howard Stern Comes Again.* A book about conversation. A conversation that, even though it's overheard by millions of people, can still be revealing and intimate.

Madonna

MARCH 11, 2015

Back in the early nineties I had a TV show on New York's WOR. I was up against *Saturday Night Live.* We only had a $50,000 budget, compared to the millions they spent, but we regularly beat them in New York. Then one week Madonna came out with the video for "Justify My Love." There was this huge uproar. MTV refused to play it.

That really pissed me off. This was pre-Internet, so there was no other way for people to see it. That week we achieved a blockbuster rating without having to write as many sketches. We just played the video in its entirety. In the two years I did that TV show, it was one of the highest-rated episodes.

We were always trying to get her on the radio show. When people ask Gary, "How long did it take you to book Madonna?" he says, "About thirty years." When she finally agreed to do it, we had to push the show back an hour to accommodate her schedule. That's the only time I've ever done that. There aren't many people I would do that for. That's how important it was to have Madonna on. (Any celebrities out there who are reading this and thinking of coming on the show, please don't make me do this again. I love all of you, but I have my routine. I need my lunch at a certain time. I need my nap at a certain time. I have everything planned to the exact minute. I'm at my best early in the morning. I fade out by eleven o'clock. There's no gas left in the tank. "It's over, Johnny," as the great Richard Crenna said in the first Rambo movie while trying to talk Sylvester Stallone down from killing everyone.)

She was as great a guest as you'd expect her to be. Totally candid. She talked about her childhood in Michigan and her early career struggles when she got to New York. She even revealed her relationship with Tupac Shakur, which made a lot of news. I don't think she ever talked about that before. But the thing I most appreciated was what she had to say about shocking people and causing controversy.

Obviously that's something I can relate to. When I look back now, it's very clear that Madonna was a kindred spirit. We were both pissing off religious groups, and fighting censorship, and pushing against America's puritanical boundaries. It would've been great to call her up and say, "Geez, I'm going through a nightmare. How are you getting through this? How do you deal? What's it like for you?" Maybe she could've helped me. Maybe I could've offered some comfort to her too. Unfortunately, at that time, I couldn't see her as an ally. I couldn't see her at all. Where my head was back then, I was just so competitive and angry, and I had a very negative attitude toward anyone.

Which is why it ended up being a good thing that it took so long to get her on the show. When it finally happened, I'd been through years of therapy and I could have that type of substantial conversation with her. I have a tremendous amount of respect for Madonna. I'm staggered by what she has achieved, and I was honored to speak to her.

Howard: Let me gaze upon you. Wow! Come on in, you look great. We are so excited you're here. I was just reading your credentials.

Madonna: My credentials?

Howard: Three hundred million albums sold. That's pretty damn amazing. Are you neurotic like me and you go, "It doesn't matter I sold three hundred million albums or I had a big radio audience, I worry about how to continue this whole party"?

Madonna: Yeah, I don't focus on my accomplishments, I focus on things I haven't done yet. Extremely neurotic.

Howard: Why do you think that is? Is there a part of you that doesn't believe that you made it? Do you still see yourself as this little girl from this small town?

Madonna: My manager always says, "Stop acting like you don't have any money." But it's just ingrained in me. I've got to work.

Howard: Is that because you grew up with no money?

Madonna: Yeah, I grew up with no money and a big family and a hardworking father and I had to work a lot to do simple things. Like if I wanted to take a dance class, my dad said, "Well, go get a job, I'm not paying for it."

Howard: I have the same affliction. I even say to my kids, "Oh, I have to work, I have to work." And they go, "Well, you've made enough money." I go, "No, I feel like I'm running out of money."

Madonna: It's not just I feel like I'm running out of money, it's also I like to do things. I like to be productive. I like to be creative.

Howard: Elvis, the Beatles, Michael Jackson, and you—that's the highest-selling artists of all time, which to me is phenomenal.

Madonna: That's good company.

Howard: That really is good company. And you are the only woman in that whole group.

Madonna: I'm practically the only one alive.

Howard: I interviewed Billy Joel and he said he sometimes pinches himself. He can't believe it. There's a handful of artists that can actually still sell stadiums and do all of that, and he's one of them. He's like, "Yeah, of course I go out and sing. I have to. It would be almost weird not to."

Madonna: He's hardwired.

Howard: You know him at all?

Madonna: I do. I mean, I don't *know* him. I met him once.

Howard: Is that a great part of fame? Having fabulous friends, getting to meet everyone?

Madonna: I do get to meet everyone but they don't necessarily become friends. Celebrities are really weird around other celebrities. They're actually quite shy.

Howard: You don't have a lot of celebrity friends?

Madonna: I don't.

Howard: Those relationships are hard to maintain?

Madonna: Yeah, because everybody is busy working.

Howard: Don't you also think that it's hard to be friends with you because you're so successful and that even other successful people want to be the star in the room? They want to be the one that draws the attention. Don't you think that sometimes?

Madonna: Possibly. I haven't really analyzed it. I certainly think that happens when it comes to relationships. Celebrities hooking up with celebrities is pretty rare.

Howard: When you get into the Rock and Roll Hall of Fame, does that mean anything to you? Do you get excited about that or do you sit there and go, "This is such bullshit"?

Madonna: I think I'm somewhere in the middle. I know it's an honor, but at the end of the day I don't really care about awards and those kinds of things. I care about how I live my life, how I treat people and if I raise good children.

Howard: You love being a mother?

Madonna: I do love it. It's also exhausting.

Howard: It is. When you went to adopt your children, the world gave you such shit for this. I remember being on the radio and going, "Why the hell would somebody want to prevent a kid who doesn't have parents or a home and someone wants to give them a good life?" Was that mind-boggling to you when you went through that?

Madonna: It crushed me. I have to say, it was one of life's great disappointments.

Howard: You didn't give up, though. You kept pressing.

Madonna: I went through the adoption and then I adopted another child. So I did keep on, but it was really a bizarre experience.

Howard: When that kind of pressure comes on you—and you've had pressure in your career. You go out, you do a video, and the Catholic Church is after you.

Madonna: Like I get excommunicated? That's happened three times, by the way. It's okay.

Howard: That type of pressure . . .

Madonna: I don't care about the pope. I

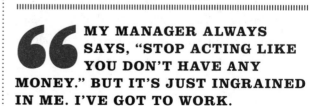

MY MANAGER ALWAYS SAYS, "STOP ACTING LIKE YOU DON'T HAVE ANY MONEY." BUT IT'S JUST INGRAINED IN ME. I'VE GOT TO WORK.

don't care what the Vatican thinks—that I'm, like, Catholic material or not. That's cool with me. But I find it really strange that people gave me a hard time for adopting children.

Howard: It's amazing. I didn't even understand their arguments. I truly didn't. Do you think people generally perceive you as a person they're against? It seems to me you're always fighting a battle with people, and it just sucks. It just has to be exhausting. I would crawl into a hole.

Madonna: I have certainly wanted to crawl into a hole, and that was one of those moments. Are you asking me why people give me a hard time?

Howard: They do, though, don't they? Here's the question, Madonna. People think you're doing something to shock them. And people think that when I'm on the radio I'm trying to shock them. That's what they think my goal is.

Madonna: Sometimes you are. I mean, you certainly have in the past, and so have I.

Howard: But do you believe that you're shocking?

Madonna: I think that thinking for yourself and having a strong opinion and going against the grain is shocking to most people, certainly in my business.

Howard: But are you shocked when people are shocked by you? Aren't you going out there just to entertain them? You want to make people feel good, you want to sing a song, you want to dance, you want to entertain them. But then they're being

shocked by you—I'm shocked that anyone can be shocked by anything I say.

Madonna: We live in a very puritanical country, you do understand that. Killing is okay, but . . . When I did "Like a Virgin," when I performed it live for the first time, actually my shoe fell off onstage. I had come down on the wedding cake, and my shoe fell off, and I was like, "Oh, shit, I can't dance in one shoe"—can I say "shit" on the air?

Howard: Yeah.

Madonna: I was like, "How am I going to play this out?" So I just dove for it on the ground. And when I dove for it my dress went up and my butt was showing. Everyone is showing their butt now, but back then nobody saw anyone's butt, and I didn't know my skirt was up. So I proceeded to sing the song laying down on the ground. I was just making the best of the situation, which is what I do. Like when I got yanked off the stage by my cape the other day. I'm hardwired to just keep going. After I got offstage during that performance, my manager was white as a ghost. He looked at me and said, "Do you know what you just did?" I said, "Yeah, I sang a song and I lost my shoe onstage." And he was like, "No, your butt was showing for the entire song. Your career is over."

Howard: And did you believe him?

Madonna: How would I not? I felt really bad, but I didn't do it on purpose.

Howard: Yeah, but there's a panic setting in. "I'm going to lose everything. I'm trying so hard here. I didn't mean to be controversial."

Madonna: No, I'm not like that. I wasn't that apologetic. I was just like, "Fuck it, I made a mistake."

Howard: You don't go somewhere and cry and say, "I just lost my career"?

Madonna: No.

Howard: See, I was just terrified all the time because I was told I was going to lose my career.

Madonna: I think that when that happens to you year after year, decade after decade, you just . . . it's just noise. At this point it's noise. People just like to give me shit.

Howard: You were just growing up—I'm going back to when you were a little girl.

Madonna: I'm still growing up.

Howard: Aren't we all? You are from a large family, and it's pretty legendary that you had a rough childhood and your mother died. When your mother dies and you're five years old, it's a black hole in your heart and that never goes away. And the fact that you have kids . . . how do you learn how to be a mother if you've never had a mother?

Madonna: That's a good question. I think you just learn as you go, and I try to be the mother that I didn't have. I try to be all those things that I wanted. I try to be nurturing, I try to be their friend, and I try to be there for them. I try to give them advice. Sometimes I make mistakes. Sometimes things don't go the way I plan, and I ask my sister for her advice because she was raised by my grandmother and she is a good mother.

THINKING FOR YOURSELF AND HAVING A STRONG OPINION AND GOING AGAINST THE GRAIN IS SHOCKING TO MOST PEOPLE.

Howard: Your father raised you, essentially?

Madonna: Yeah, when he wasn't working.

Howard: Your father married the housekeeper?

Madonna: Yeah.

Howard: And when that happened, she was your stepmother. You hated her. You couldn't stand her.

Madonna: Okay, you're going there. You're just going there, Howard.

Howard: I am. I'm curious, because to me this is fascinating. If you're not comfortable going there, I'll leave it.

Madonna: I'm with my psychoanalyst right now.

Howard: You are. Get on that couch.

Madonna: I'm on the couch. It was three years later. I was almost six when my mom died. So I was almost nine when my dad remarried. And she was our housekeeper for a bit, but she disappeared. It's a long story.

Howard: You mean she left you?

Madonna: This is like a soap opera. She was pregnant, but she went away to have the baby. It was somebody else's. Then she showed back up and my dad said he was marrying her. We were really shocked by it because we were still mourning and grieving my mother's death, which my father never spoke about.

Howard: He never sat you down and said, "Your mother died and this is—"

Madonna: No, he never said, "How do you feel about it?" We never had a group hug. We never had a cry. My father is very stoic and old-school, and I think he was devastated too. I don't think he had words for his pain.

Howard: My mother lost her mother when she was nine. Living with a woman who had lost her mother was maybe the most difficult thing. Sometimes I felt I had to be her father. It was a very difficult thing for me. That's why I asked you about it. That's why I was so curious about it, because I know how difficult that is. But I get two completely different pictures of you as a kid. One is of a rebel. At school you would be the kid who would hang out with the gay dance teacher. And then you were also the valedictorian or something. You were the super student. You got straight As.

Madonna: Well, I was smart, but I didn't socialize really. I didn't have friends.

Howard: Why do you think that was?

Madonna: Because I just thought everyone was an idiot. I always felt like an outsider growing up. I think a lot of it has to do with the fact that I didn't have a mother and I was the eldest daughter, so I had a lot of responsibilities. There was not a lot of free time in my life. It was school, come home, housework, help with dinner, do your schoolwork, clean the house, take care of the little kids, blah-blah-blah. My

house was not a fun place to bring people to, number one. Number two, we first grew up in Pontiac [Michigan], which was a very racially mixed, mostly black environment. We went to Catholic schools and we wore uniforms, and that was normal life to me. Then when I went to high school, we moved to a suburb. It was all white and we were living above our means.

Howard: Did you feel out of place in a white community?

Madonna: I did. And because now I didn't have a uniform, I was aware that my clothes were not as cool as everybody else's or as nice as everyone else's. I'd wear the same clothes every day. I just didn't fit in. I just felt like I was with rich people, and I felt out of place. I felt like they were members of country clubs and they had manicures and they wore nice clothes and I didn't fit in. I felt like a country bumpkin, and I was resentful because I didn't fit in, because I felt people were judging me all the time. I chose not to socialize with people.

Howard: You graduated early from high school, right?

Madonna: Yeah.

Howard: And then you decided to go to New York, which is really freaky.

Madonna: No, I went to the University of Michigan for a year and I was a dance major.

Howard: The way you saw your future and your way out of Michigan was you were going to be a professional dancer. You never even imagined you'd be a singer, right?

Madonna: No.

Howard: Isn't that weird?

Madonna: Very weird.

Howard: And then you go to college and some teacher says to you, "Hey, why don't you go to Alvin Ailey and go dance."

Madonna: No, he said, "You're too good for this. You don't need this. This is an environment for people who don't know what they want to do with their lives. Go. Go to New York."

Howard: So when you came to New York . . . the story I heard was you get off the bus, you have thirty-five dollars or something in your pocket. You're wearing your winter jacket in the summer. You get off the bus and you don't even have a place to live. And some dude walks up to you and asks you why you're wearing your winter coat. You talk to him and he says, "Come live on my couch." And you lived on his couch.

Madonna: Kind of.

Howard: Can you imagine?

Madonna: I know. The angels were protecting me. I met him at the flea market. I was just wandering around the streets. I actually took a taxi into the city. It was my first plane ride and my first taxi ride. So I said, "Take me to the center." He dropped me off at Times Square. You can imagine me looking up at all these skyscrapers and all the crazy people and the homeless people. Times Square was very different at that time.

Howard: I want to make this point because people think this shit happens overnight. It doesn't, and it's hard.

Madonna: Yes.

Howard: And it's not really luck. It's a lot of hard work.

Madonna: Sweat and tears.

Howard: So you come to New York to become a dancer. You're living on some guy's couch.

Madonna: He only allows it for, like, five days max.

Howard: How do you make money?

Madonna: I started going to auditions and I got into some dance companies, got a partial scholarship to the Alvin Ailey school. And then I started just making little bits of money. I was taking jobs. I did everything. I worked at Dunkin' Donuts. I got fired from the Russian Tea Room for wearing fishnets. I was the coat-check girl. I'm like, "You can't even see my legs. I'm behind a door."

Howard: But it's your nature to say, "Fuck you, I'm going to wear fishnets."

Madonna: It was just my nature to do the opposite of what people told me to do.

Howard: Did you explain to them you were Madonna?

Madonna: I wasn't Madonna then.

Howard: They didn't recognize you.

Madonna: They didn't see the future.

Howard: Did you find comfort in a friend like Michael Jackson? Because he's on par with you, in the sense that he's sold a lot of records, and wherever you go people are taking pictures of you and the whole thing. I remember you went to the Academy Awards with him. He was your date. Was he someone that you could reveal yourself to and really talk to?

Madonna: Well, I could certainly relate to him on many levels—many of the things that you've brought up. But he was also a very shy person and he grew up in a very different way than I did. He was famous since he was a child, and I think he never really had a childhood and he was painfully shy. So we didn't have a relationship that was so much about me revealing myself to him. It was more about trying to . . . like, making fun of the crazy world that we were working and living in, you know what I mean?

Howard: So he wasn't a guy you could sit there and talk to and treat him like someone who you could confide in. That wasn't him?

Madonna: To a certain extent. But we didn't talk about our childhoods. I think he felt eternally tortured by people. I think Michael was never happy with the way he looked. It was hard for him to look into people's eyes, and it was important for me to let him know that I wasn't judging him.

Howard: Do you like Letterman? I watched those old interviews, and I can't tell if you like him or you're just kind of annoyed.

Madonna: That's how I flirt with people.

Howard: Is that the flirt?

Madonna: Yeah.

Howard: Oh, it seems contentious and uncomfortable.

Madonna: Well, one time I was mad at him, when I said the f-word a lot. But the rest of the time was good.

Howard: You were really mad at him?

Madonna: I was in a weird mood that day. I was dating Tupac Shakur at the time, and the thing is he got me all riled up about life in general. So when I went on this show, I was feeling very gangsta. ✦

Howard: I didn't know you dated Tupac Shakur. That's shocking to me. That's never been out there, I don't think.

Madonna: I think people know if you're in the know.

Howard: I kind of know everyone you dated.

Madonna: Really? Well, give me the list, baby.

Howard: All right, you ready? Warren Beatty.

Madonna: Okay, everybody knows that.

Howard: As an observer, I thought you were really in love with him.

Madonna: I was.

Howard: Yeah, I thought that was love. You cared about him.

Madonna: I did.

Howard: With those breakups, do you go into a funk? Can a guy wreck you?

Madonna: Super-personal interview, my goodness.

✦ **For more on this from Snoop Dogg, turn to page 530.**

Howard: I know. I do need to know this thing.

Madonna: Why?

Howard: I don't know. I'm curious. I'd like to know you get your heart broken.

Madonna: Have you heard my new record? There are a couple of songs about heartbreak. Of course I've had my heart broken many times.

Howard: Wait, I was naming the people you've dated. Sean Penn.

Madonna: Well, I married Sean. And I married Guy Ritchie. So I was in love with them, of course.

Howard: Do you see a psychiatrist?

Madonna: I used to.

Howard: Do you ever question why your marriages can't stay forever? Or do you just not believe in that?

Madonna: Why they didn't work?

Howard: Yeah, why they didn't work.

Madonna: I did. I figured it out.

Howard: What's the answer?

Madonna: I'd rather not go into that. That will be revealing things about those other people, and I don't think that's—I take responsibility too.

Howard: The relationships were bad. They went bad.

Madonna: No, they just weren't right in the end. I mean, I didn't want to stay unhappy

> **MICHAEL WAS NEVER HAPPY WITH THE WAY HE LOOKED. IT WAS HARD FOR HIM TO LOOK INTO PEOPLE'S EYES, AND IT WAS IMPORTANT FOR ME TO LET HIM KNOW THAT I WASN'T JUDGING HIM.**

and miserable. It's very hard if you're an artist and a creative person and a woman, a strong independent female, to be in a marriage with a man who isn't threatened by that and is comfortable with all the things that I stand for and what I do. Some guys just want someone to stay home and take care of the kids. And that's valid.

Howard: But that's not you.

Madonna: No.

Howard: And it's never going to be you.

Madonna: No.

Howard: Do you drink?

Madonna: Not much. But I'm pretty fun when I'm drunk.

Howard: You are?

Madonna: Yeah, because usually I'm very in control.

Howard: What do you mean, you're fun when you're drunk? What happens?

Madonna: You're going to have to stick around and find out.

Tracy Morgan

AUGUST 16, 2016

I got turned on to Tracy Morgan by Jimmy Kimmel. Jimmy is a fan of the show, so he campaigns for people he wants to hear. He wrote me a bunch of times and said, "You have to get Tracy on your show. He'd be so great." I respect Jimmy's opinion, and he was absolutely right. The first time we had Tracy on was around 2007. The guy is just a home run every time. He's the guest who probably requires the least amount of work on my part because it almost doesn't matter what you ask him, he's got his own agenda.

Over the years we got to know each other, mainly from seeing each other at Knicks games. One of the perks of being famous is I get to sit in the front row. I'm not a huge basketball fan, but I love sitting there and watching a game. It's such a treat. Even more so when Tracy is there. He'll do his own play-by-play and yell out advice to the players. It's hysterical. ESPN should seriously hire him to do play-by-play on their broadcasts.

In June 2014, Tracy was in a horrendous accident. A Walmart tractor-trailer plowed into a Sprinter van carrying him and a few other comics. One of them, James McNair, was killed, and Tracy was airlifted to a hospital. He was in a coma for two weeks. I was really worried, and I was hearing all sorts of things. Someone would say he had no brain function and was being fed through a tube. Someone else would say he was getting better. I didn't know what to believe. From time to time I would reach out through a card or a note, but I never heard back.

Gary kept checking with Tracy's publicist, who is also Jimmy Kimmel's publicist. We weren't trying to get him on the show. We just wanted an update on his condition. The publicist kept saying Tracy was going to be okay, and promised that when he was ready to talk about what happened, it would be with us. It took about two years. Then we got a call from the publicist: "He's ready."

This interview was really emotional. Physically Tracy was healed, but I had never seen him so vulnerable. He cried a couple times, and he kept talking about God and his purpose on the planet. You could tell he was very moved by everyone who'd tried to reach out to him and all the love and support he'd received. If there was a blessing in the accident, it was that he realized people really do care about him.

Howard: An old friend to the show. On many, many times. We all know he had a horrible accident. But he's back. He's back. Let me look at you.

Tracy: I love you, Howard.

Howard: My brother. Are you all right?

Tracy: I feel like I tapped into something, man. A lot of love and goodwill out there for me. And I tapped into it.

Howard: I was so upset, and I couldn't get in touch with you.

Tracy: I wasn't talking to nobody, man. I wasn't in the state of mind for that. I didn't even know how to spell my name. I could barely talk, and my feet—I was in the wheelchair for six months with my feet like this, man [*uses hands to show how feet were angled*]. I wasn't ready for none of that.

Howard: The thing that freaked me out the most that I read, and tell me if this is true: after you came out of your coma—you were in a coma for almost eight days, am I correct?

Tracy: Yeah, like, nine and a half.

Howard: When you opened your eyes, you could not see. You were blind for—

Tracy: Five days.

Howard: For five days. Did they think that maybe your vision wouldn't ever come back?

Tracy: They didn't know. These are neurons in your brains that are destroyed, and it takes time to heal. They're still healing now. This nurse, Laurie, stayed with me every day, all day, from when I first came out of the helicopter. She's the one that cut my bloody clothes off of me. My wife went back home to get some clothes, because they had a hotel across the street. She says she was getting clothes, and then the phone rang, and Nurse Laurie said, "He's up. And he's asking for you." So she just rushed back to the hospital with my son, and I was blind. I was touching her face.

Howard: From what I read, you say you don't even remember the accident. You don't remember any of the details, nor do you want to.

Tracy: I was gone. They keep you in a dark room, so you don't stimulate your brain. So the swelling goes down. I just feel fortunate. You say, "You are blessed." I was blessed when I was born. We all are blessed.

Howard: No, you are blessed because doctors gave you less than a 2 percent chance of living. I mean, this is serious stuff.

Tracy: Well, God gave me a second chance.

Howard: He did. I'm really curious: When you come that close to death and the actual incident happens, do you feel any pain?

Tracy: What my wife said is that I'd try a couple times to get up in the bed. I didn't even know my femur was pulverized. I got a titanium rod in my leg for life, from my knee to my hip.

Howard: Wow.

Tracy: And the trauma to my head was kind of bad. I broke every bone in my face. My face was this big.

Howard: But you don't feel any pain when the actual accident happens?

Tracy: No, no. You don't even know you're there.

Howard: Your brain shuts down.

Tracy: That's what the brain does. It goes into protection mode. And you don't want to remember it.

Howard: Tracy, everyone wants to know: When did you jerk off for the first time?

Tracy: Oh my God.

Howard: When did it happen?

Tracy: That was going on in the hospital.

Howard: Really?

Tracy: All I do is masturbate. I beat my dick like it owes me money. My dick got a restraining order out on my hand. I woke up one morning and my dick was dialing 911. My heart machine started going off one day, and they started running to my room and they opened the door. I was there beating my dick.

Howard: Is that really true?

Tracy: Yeah, it's true.

Howard: Beating off relaxes you.

Tracy: You're going to beat off the pain.

Howard: God bless you, Tracy. I love you. I want to be serious for one second. I love you, and I want you to know: I was so fucking worried about you. Because at first I was like, "How serious is this?" And when I got word from a couple of people who are on the inside, they said, "Man, this is the real deal. He might go."

ALL I DO IS MASTURBATE. I BEAT MY DICK LIKE IT OWES ME MONEY. MY DICK GOT A RESTRAINING ORDER OUT ON MY HAND.

Tracy: I was gone.

Howard: Then I didn't hear from anybody for a while. I kept calling people, and I tried reaching out to you. Listen, you had your hands full. But I'm just so happy you're with us. You're just such a funny guy, and you're such an upbeat kind of guy. I remember sitting with you at a Knicks game, and you were carrying on like a lunatic. And I went, "This guy isn't doing this to get paid right now. He's just having a good time."

Tracy: Howard, let me tell you something, man. It's going to take more than eighteen wheels to get that away from me. I still have a lot to do.

Howard: Was it hard to be funny again?

Tracy: I was worried. I had other things on my mind. It was beyond show business in the beginning. It was life and death. I was looking at my daughter. My daughter was young. She was ten months old when it happened.

Howard: What were you in, a limo or in one of those big vans?

Tracy: I'm in the Sprinter. If we weren't in that, we would have been squashed like accordions. I didn't know the dude was up for twenty-eight hours. I didn't know that until a week later.

Howard: The guy who was driving the Walmart truck. That's a real danger in our country, actually. A lot of truck drivers—

Tracy: Cell phone use and all those things. So many distractions while you're driving. I am pissed. I didn't like that.

Howard: A lot of truck drivers are up for a tremendous amount of hours.

Tracy: You can't do that.

Howard: No.

Tracy: It cost a good man his life.

Howard: You're a very spiritual man. And you believe that when you were in the coma, you saw your father. Your father died when you were nineteen.

Tracy: I don't know if I was in the coma— in or out. I just remember that vision. Like a dream or whatever.

Howard: What did he say to you?

Tracy: He was not ready. He was not ready for me. And I just was crying.

Howard: You wake up and suddenly you're in the hospital. You can't walk. You can't move.

Tracy: I remember those days laying on the hospital bed and just looking out the window at night. I was looking out the window one particular night when it was raining. I was laying in the hospital bed about two in the morning. And I was just looking out the window.

Howard: When you can't walk and your memory's all fucked up from the accident and you can't speak, you have to literally go into years of therapy. You're probably still in physical therapy, am I correct?

Tracy: Yeah.

Howard: So you have to learn how to walk again.

Tracy: But it's the mental or emotional— that crash turned me into an emotional wreck. To anybody out there listening,

> **MY WIFE SAID THAT THE FIRST THING I SAID TO HER, I WHISPERED IN HER EAR, "THERE'S FREEDOM OUTSIDE THOSE DOORS." BECAUSE I WANTED TO GET OUT OF THE HOSPITAL.**

you try to get hit by a truck going that fast at eighty-five thousand pounds. Watch what it would do to you. It's going to turn you into a wreck. My wife said that the first thing I said to her, I whispered in her ear, "There's freedom outside those doors." Because I wanted to get out of the hospital.

Howard: Do you think you'll become an inspirational speaker? Is that in your future?

Tracy: Me? If I do anything, I'd give them my sense of humor. That's the gift He gave me. I tell people in interviews all the time. They want to talk about my material. I say, "It's like what Bruce Lee said in *Enter the Dragon*. 'It's like a finger pointing the way to the moon. Don't focus on the finger or you're going to miss all that heavenly glory.'"

Howard: Tracy Morgan is back.

Tracy: You know why I love coming on this show? Because I get to be so immature, talking about pussy and all. I like to talk more about money, but that got to be on the low-low. Walmart would sue the shit out of me, because they're confidential.

Howard: I read $95 million.

Tracy: The only ones that know what's in my pocket are my two girls.

Howard: Is it smart to tell your wife what you got from Walmart?

Tracy: Where's she going? I'm not getting married again. You know, in court there's no taxes come out. Child support can't even fuck with me. You get all of it. Only thing that comes out is the lawyer's fee.

Howard: Are you investing this money that you got, whatever the amount is? What are you doing with it?

Tracy: I got some money on the streets.

Howard: No, come on. What are you doing? You know what you ought to do? Grow a beard and get one of these farms like Jon Stewart.

Tracy: I might finance a couple of movies. I don't know.

Howard: But you're not going to blow the money?

Tracy: I don't care what people say. I'm going to buy a Ferrari.

Howard: You got servants and stuff going on?

Tracy: I ain't paying for no servants. I can make my own burger cheese sandwich. I'm from the hood, man. I'm from the projects.

Howard: Do you have an elevator in your house?

Tracy: Yeah.

Howard: Oh, shit.

Tracy: Yeah.

Howard: And a bowling alley?

Tracy: A basketball court, all that. I got a big movie theater. I won't leave my house, never. I'm chilling.

Howard: You're goddamn right.

Tracy: But it's all for my family. All I need is $1,500 in my pocket and a new pair of sneakers. That's all I need.

Howard: Any black people in your neighborhood?

Tracy: I told my brothers, "So you have your eyes on my neighborhood? I'm going to call the cops on you my motherfucking self, because you got no business here, goddamn it."

Howard: Do the cops hassle you? Do they say, "Oh, there's a black man"?

Tracy: They love me now.

Howard: They know it's you?

Tracy: They know. They love me.

Howard: You look good. Are you working out too?

Tracy: Yeah, I work out. I'm doing it right this time. I've got a second chance.

Howard: You're a fucking sex symbol.

Tracy: Yeah, I'm a sex symbol, but my daughter's three years old. I'm trying to be there for her.

Howard: But doesn't she need some black friends? In that whitey neighborhood aren't there just too many white people for her to find her identity?

Tracy: No, she doesn't have any problem with white people. With me, I'm not going to raise her with white and black. We're not going to raise our daughter that way. That's nuts. That's not the way me and her momma did. My wife is biracial, but I don't see that. I only see my wife. My mother-in-law's name is Christy Wollover, whiter than you. And I love my mother-in-law. That's mines. When I see my mother-in-law and my wife and my daughter standing right there—all that belongs to me. So if you don't want to lose a toe or finger, walk away, because I'm going all out for mine.

Howard: I love you. I really truly do. I'm so goddamn happy you are alive and doing well. I just appreciate you so much. And I'm glad I

> ## "I'M DOING IT RIGHT THIS TIME. I'VE GOT A SECOND CHANCE.

got to say that to you today, because I've been waiting to say it for two years.

Tracy: Thank you. I love you, Howard.

Howard: I'd blow you if your dick wasn't so big.

Jerry Seinfeld

JUNE 26, 2013

Whenever Jerry came on the show in the early days, I was super adversarial. Back then, I couldn't properly be a fan of anyone. As my style and perspective started to evolve, it became important to me to get a second chance with certain people. Jerry, being the saint that he is, gave me one.

I was so curious about his process. How does he write material? Is he constantly thinking about it? Is he on *all the time*? It was like being able to ask Picasso, "What kind of paint do you use? What brushes? How do you approach a canvas?" I wanted to treat Jerry the same way I would a great painter or filmmaker or chess player. What's the key to it all? Maybe some young comedian out there would be listening and say, "*That's* how you do it."

I think Jerry was absolutely flattered and impressed that I had that level of interest. He loved the experience. A few weeks later, he invited me to his home for dinner, and he said, "I have to tell you, I've never gotten so much feedback. Everyone in the world comes up to me about this interview. Everyone."

I said, "The reason, Jerry, is because you really spelled it out. It was a primer on how to be a comedian. You gave a master class."

And then he said, "I can never come on your show again."

"Why?" I asked.

"Because," he said, "it was so perfect. We could never do better than that interview."

This comment really upset me. I thought, "You mean I don't get rewarded for doing a good job and getting it right? Why am I being punished?" But that's so Jerry. That's his MO. He turned down more than a hundred million dollars to do one more season of *Seinfeld*. He felt he had reached perfection, and he wanted to go out on a high note. In this interview, he talks about walking away from *Seinfeld* and his uncanny sense of timing, but for me the standout moment is what he says about never being able to be fully present with anyone—even his wife and children. I think it is the most authentic and honest answer anyone has ever given me. It's something I relate to. I sometimes struggle to be completely in the moment, because I'm constantly thinking about the radio show and searching for material. For Jerry, this isn't a problem. For me, it's exhausting. I have given up a huge chunk of my life being Howard Quixote on a quest to find the next funny thing. But I do believe that is what it takes to be on top of your game in comedy. That's what it truly requires to be great. That's what Jerry's level of commitment is: he's always looking for the joke. So for any aspiring comics reading this, you might want to think twice before you attempt to make a living at it.

Howard: I was thinking about your new show, because I watched it, and I love it. I love the one with Letterman you just did. It is called *Getting Coffee with Comedians.*

Jerry: No, that's not what it's called.

Howard: Oh, I mean, *Getting in the Car with Comedians.*

Jerry: No, you're going to get it right, because that's why I'm here.

Howard: It's called . . . *Cars Getting Coffee.*

Jerry: No.

Howard: *Cars Drinking Coffee.*

Jerry: Oh my God. This guy.

Howard: It's called *Comedians in Cars Getting Coffee.*

Jerry: Thank you.

Howard: All right. So in that show, I was thinking about it, you're interviewing comedians, but you could never really go back and do another sitcom, because the feeling would be, "How could I ever top *Seinfeld*?"

Jerry: It's guaranteed. You can't top it.

Howard: You can't.

Jerry: You can't even get close to it.

Howard: It's iconic. Everything was lined up, everything was perfect. The casting was right.

Jerry: I'm not arrogant and stupid enough to think I did that. I know that I got caught in a perfect storm. Me and Larry fit together perfect. And then the cast.

Howard: Settle that for me right now. Larry David. He was 50 percent. He was your partner in this.

Jerry: Yeah.

Howard: But he never was on camera.

Jerry: Right.

Howard: And people always debate, "Well, gee, Larry really never got enough credit. Jerry, well . . ."

Jerry: Aw, really?

Howard: Yeah, it's like you were the front man.

Jerry: Who has these conversations that you would hear?

Howard: I have it with other people who are in the industry. You don't think he regrets not being on the show?

Jerry: No, no. At that time, he really was out of that mode of wanting to be in front of the camera. He really was writing, and thinking about writing, and really wanted to be a writer.

Howard: How did you know to team up with him?

Jerry: Because in comedy, as you know, it's about the bar, and you're waiting to go on. And you wait mostly. You're there all night. You get there at eight, you're going on, you hang—it's a long hangout, right? You know this. So you talk with a lot of guys and you go over to a guy, you start talking to him. And certain guys, it's funny right away. You're talking and all of a sudden, in two minutes, you hit into something hilarious.

Howard: Did you respect him as a stand-up comedy guy?

Jerry: Yes, I did.

Howard: You liked his act?

Jerry: I loved it.

Howard: And he never really caught on with his act the way you did?

" LARRY GOES, "THIS IS WHAT THE SHOW SHOULD BE. TWO COMEDIANS JUST MAKING FUN OF STUFF AS THEY WALK AROUND DURING THE DAY."

Jerry: Stand-up takes a lot of work, a lot of talent, and an equal measure of temperament. You have to have the right temperament.

Howard: Like going on the road and not letting that get to you?

Jerry: No, no. It's onstage. You have to have the resilience and that kind of energy onstage.

Howard: Right. And Larry didn't have that mechanism?

Jerry: He was a little fragile onstage. If it wasn't going well, which most of the time it's not—

Howard: He fell apart?

Jerry: Well, it's a tough thing. You're judged.

Howard: Why do I think it was so easy for you? I feel like a lot of things went right for you onstage, not wrong. Things didn't go wrong for you. You just had a way of—

Jerry: I had a flair for it.

Howard: And so when Larry was sitting at the bar with you, you guys start to talking. You say, "Hey, we gotta write this sitcom together."

Jerry: No, I had this meeting at NBC where they said, "[talent manager] George Shapiro sent a note to [NBC executive]

Brandon Tartikoff." This is how the show started. I apologize if you've heard all this before. It's an old story. George Shapiro sent a note to Brandon Tartikoff. One sentence: "Call me a crazy guy, but I have a feeling Jerry Seinfeld's going to be doing a TV series on NBC." I had been on *The Tonight Show with Johnny Carson* for nine years. Nobody at NBC, nobody, not one person after nine years of going on *Carson* three and four times a year, and killing, nobody said, "Why don't we talk to this kid? Maybe . . ."

Howard: Why do you think that was? Isn't it weird?

Jerry: Really? Why? Because network television companies struggle with the entertainment field. They struggle to create entertainment. It's a struggle for them. They're not good at it.

Howard: You think?

Jerry: Have you watched TV?

Howard: You think that network executives are not good at predicting the needs of the public?

Jerry: No, at seeing talent, and knowing what to do with it. That's their job.

Howard: It's a very difficult job. Sometimes they get it right, sometimes they get it wrong. And with you, they missed it, because nine years of killing on the Carson show should have triggered something in them.

Jerry: Something. Nothing.

Howard: Nothing.

Jerry: So he sends this letter: "Okay. Why don't you come in for a meeting?" Nine years later. I come in for the meeting. They go, "Do you have anything you would like to do if you ever did a show for us?" I said, "Not really."

Howard: Great meeting.

Jerry: Yeah. I said, "I just always wanted to have a meeting like this. This was my goal."

Howard: The meeting was the goal.

Jerry: The goal. So a week later—this is all true—I'm talking with Larry David at the Improv, telling him the story. We start talking, and then we go across the street to a Korean deli. We're making fun of everything in the deli. Larry goes, "This is what the show should be. Two comedians just making fun of stuff as they walk around during the day." And that was it.

Howard: Then did you go to a room somewhere and write together?

Jerry: Yeah.

Howard: And that's the process. So how many hours a day do you sit there and write?

Jerry: All day.

Howard: You always say the biggest regret you have about doing *Seinfeld* is that you didn't enjoy it more. And I totally get that. I'm never enjoying myself in the middle of a process. I didn't enjoy myself making my movie. Because it's so much angst.

Jerry: Well, I'm not big on enjoyment. I don't think it's that important. I think what's important is *they* enjoy it. That's what makes it work. I just think the Louis C.K. model should be the model for comedians. You know how Louis got

his show, the whole story? He said to them, "You want me to do a show, I'll do a show." I saw him on *Letterman* do this thing. It was so funny. They said, "Well, we want to know what you're going to do." He says, "I'm not telling you." They said, "Well, we can't do a show like that." He says, "You're right, we can't do a show like that. Let's not do this."

Howard: Louis described that on our show, and I was just like, "Yeah, right."

Jerry: It's great. Because here's what comedy is: we're going to blindfold you, we're going to give you a dart, and you try and hit the dartboard. That's comedy. Maybe you'll hit it, maybe you won't. Nobody really knows what they're doing here. It's not you steering me, coaching me. It's just, "Let me throw the dart. Either I hit it or I don't."

Howard: Are you particularly sensitive to that? Because when *Seinfeld* first came on, it wasn't doing that well.

Jerry: Didn't do well for four years. We had a very high-income demo. Horrible ratings but the people we got were high-income.

Howard: I think in this environment today, they wouldn't even keep *Seinfeld* on.

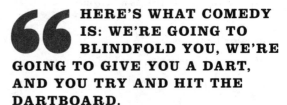

" HERE'S WHAT COMEDY IS: WE'RE GOING TO BLINDFOLD YOU, WE'RE GOING TO GIVE YOU A DART, AND YOU TRY AND HIT THE DARTBOARD.

Jerry: Yeah, they would. Same reason. You get rich people to watch your show, you're going to stay on.

Howard: Did [NBC executive] Warren Littlefield keep the show on the air?

Jerry: No, it was Brandon Tartikoff.

Howard: That was Brandon?

Jerry: Uh-huh.

Howard: Because now everybody sort of takes credit for *Seinfeld.*

Jerry: That's fine.

Howard: You don't care. Let them take credit.

Jerry: I don't care. Howard, I'm sixty. I don't care.

Howard: Wait, I'm going to pick one of your bits. I think you did it years ago. You go to a Chinese restaurant, and you're like, "I really admire Chinese people, because they're really sticking to this chopsticks thing."

Jerry: The line is, "I like how they're hanging in there with the chopsticks."

Howard: And you say "hanging," because they've seen the fork. Then you compare them to farmers trying to dig a hole with a broomstick. Like, why would you do that if you know the shovel has been invented?

Jerry: That's: "It's like a farmer taking a couple of pool cues to plow the field."

Howard: To me, this is a brilliant observation.

Jerry: Thank you.

Howard: Can you go to a Chinese restaurant and not sit there and work on material?

Jerry: I'm never not working on material. Ever.

Howard: So even when you're sitting with your wife, you're sitting with the kids, it's the material.

Jerry: Everything. Every second of my existence, I'm thinking, "Could I do something with that?"

Howard: Right. I imagine you like that, and that to me sounds torturous. You cannot let go. So if I came over to your house, and we were hanging out, you're kind of really looking for material.

Jerry: Not kind of. I'm looking for material all the time.

Howard: That's being at work twenty-four hours a day. It's neurotic.

Jerry: Making jokes is not work. It's a gift.

Howard: Have you ever been in therapy?

Jerry: No.

Howard: So when you're with your wife, are you authentically with your wife?

Jerry: No. I'm not authentically with her, nor am I authentically with you right now.

Howard: Right. You are somewhere else.

Jerry: Yeah. I'm looking for a joke right now. There's nothing here. Nothing!

Howard: I'm going to take one of the most brilliant observations you ever made, in my opinion. And I've actually heard this from other people who now seem to have incorporated it into their thought process like they thought it up. You did a bit early on about being in New York City with taxicab drivers, and you said, "Wow, who are these guys?"

Jerry: This is an old bit. "What does it take

to get a cab driver's license? I think all you need is a face—that seems to be their big qualification—and put it on the license. No blank heads are allowed to drive cabs. And the name was like eight consonants in a row. And I don't even know how I would report the guy. His name was Amal, and then the symbol for boron."

Howard: When I hear "the symbol for boron," I cannot help but think how brilliant that is.

Jerry: Thank you. And you like the choice of boron?

Howard: Boron is the right element.

Jerry: Yes, a lot of the other elements I could have picked.

Howard: Now, when you were writing that bit, did you worry that outside of New York, or big cities, that maybe people wouldn't get that joke? Do you worry about who it's going to appeal to?

Jerry: If it didn't work on the road, I would have not done it on the road. But it did. Because in the end, funny is funny.

Howard: So maybe a guy from Kansas understands that the symbol for boron is what we see on a cab?

Jerry: I watched Richard Pryor talk about how it feels to be hooked on heroin. And I get it. I've never done it. I don't even know what those drugs are.

Howard: Yeah. That is compelling.

Jerry: That the guy takes you there, that's the thing.

Howard: All right, so you're in a cab . . .

Jerry: Then I realized, "Why am

> ## I'M NEVER NOT WORKING ON MATERIAL. . . . EVERY SECOND OF MY EXISTENCE, I'M THINKING, "COULD I DO SOMETHING WITH THAT?"

I not scared, even though this is ridiculously dangerous? I would never drive like this, I have no seat belt on, and I'm not scared."

Howard: When that occurs to you, do you immediately write it down in a book?

Jerry: This question I get all the time. Why?

Howard: I'll tell you why. Because I have thoughts all the time. If I don't immediately write them down for my radio show, they're gone.

Jerry: I do write them down.

Howard: And did you write down the boron?

Jerry: No.

Howard: Where does that come from?

Jerry: Sitting with it.

Howard: What do you mean, "sitting with it"?

Jerry: I don't know. I think of the joke. It's like a symbol from the chart of the elements. So then I thought, "Okay, which element? I'm going to use an element as a reference here, and that will be funny."

Howard: Boron was your first choice?

Jerry: No, it was not.

Howard: What was your first choice?

Jerry: I can't remember. And then I looked

up the chart of the elements. And I saw it, "Oh, boron. That's the funny one."

Howard: You are naturally funny, and you do have that ability to figure that stuff out. But people don't realize the amount of work that goes into it.

Jerry: Nah, so what.

Howard: Okay, you've written it down. Now you've got to go perform it somewhere onstage. Before you go onstage, what do you do? Stand there in front of a mirror and memorize it? And also the delivery: you have this thing where you're getting worked up over something. And that's what sells the thing. It's more than just writing the material. You've got to be able to deliver it. And then you go up on a stage and deliver boron, and then fifty million other jokes. Who the hell remembers all of this?

Jerry: What else have I got to do?

Howard: That's your day? You memorize this material?

Jerry: How does Tiger Woods remember which club to use? What the hell else has this guy got to do?

Howard: Do you ever dream of the day where you could go with your wife to a Chinese restaurant and sit there and not think about the chopsticks?

Jerry: As long as I shoot myself in the mouth with a bullet. What fun is life if I'm not making jokes all the time? It's a torture I love.

Howard: Wow. You really know yourself.

Jerry: I guess I do. I guess I do.

Howard: Getting back to *Seinfeld*. Warren Littlefield wrote that if you would have given him another season of *Seinfeld*, he would have paid you $110 million for the year. A hundred ten million dollars.

Jerry: I could have got more than that.

Howard: You could have gotten more than that. And you said no?

Jerry: Right.

Howard: Is that the ultimate integrity? In other words, you said no because you felt you were done?

Jerry: *Integrity* is a nice word, and it's a flattering word. I appreciate that. But to be honest, the love affair between the people that were making the show and the audience was so intense. It was so white-hot, I had to respect that. And I could not go to that point where it starts to age and wither. And it doesn't take long. For example, you go see a comedian, and for an hour and ten minutes you'll love the guy. And at an hour and thirty, it's like, "I thought he was never going to finish." And you walk out with a whole different feeling. It's a small amount of too much—too much cake, too much anything. I wanted it to end with a fireworks burst.

Howard: And also that last season, you lost Larry David, so . . .

Jerry: Two seasons.

Howard: Right. Two seasons. Even harder.

Jerry: It wasn't really possible for a person to be the head writer and executive producer.

Howard: If he had stayed, do you think you might have done another season?

Jerry: Yes, possibly.

Howard: Why did he have to leave? What was his problem?

Jerry: It was hard, Howard. It's hard work. It's frustrating. And it wasn't his show, it was my show.

Howard: That's true. And I think at that point he got the bug to go do his own.

Jerry: Perhaps. And I think it worked out great for both of us.

Howard: Do you like his show?

Jerry: I love his show. I loved running the show on my own. That turned me into someone I never thought I could be. I never thought I could run the show on my own. It was great. So I'm grateful to him for that.

Howard: But when you think about $110 million—and I know you had a lot of money at that point—but $110 million. If I had said to young Jerry who was laboring away doing material, "There's going to be a $110 million payday the final season—"

Jerry: It's pretty crazy.

Howard: You would think you were nuts.

Jerry: Yeah. But if you're about the money, you're only going to go so far.

Howard: That's true. But maybe you overthought the situation. Maybe you did.

Jerry: Maybe.

Howard: Do you think the other cast members were upset?

Jerry: No, we sat and talked it over.

Howard: You did.

> ## I HAVE A SENSE OF TIMING. I HAVE IT IN JOKES, I HAVE IT IN MY SETS, I HAVE IT IN MY CAREER.

Jerry: We said, "How do we all feel?" But I have to say, I have a sense of timing. I have it in jokes, I have it in my sets, I have it in my career. I knew when to move to LA. I knew when I was ready for *The Tonight Show*. I knew when I was ready to do something bigger, like the sitcom.

Howard: Right.

Jerry: I just know. And I knew that was our moment.

Howard: So now here we are at your new show. Here you are on the Internet. I like it. I was surprised. You were driving Letterman's car. It was a car Paul Newman gave him. I'm not a car guy. I don't know anything about cars. If someone agrees to do your show, to talk to you in a car, do they have to give you their car to drive?

Jerry: No. In that case, he wanted to drive that car. Normally I would pick the car for the guest.

Howard: One of the interesting things you do is you go to a coffee shop, and you have a conversation with Letterman. But then you guys went walking into a hardware store just to smell the hardware store, because Letterman loves the smell of a hardware store.

Jerry: Yeah, me too.

Howard: You walked in there, and it appears to me people aren't really carrying on like lunatics. But there's David Letterman and Jerry Seinfeld in conversation. Do you guys clear out the place, or is that just reality?

Jerry: No, there was something happening on that street. But I want the show to have this comfortable hangout energy. The idea is, what if somebody had a talk show, and they only did it when they wanted to?

Howard: There's no schedule. You decide, "Hey, I want to talk to this guy." You call him up, and then you go out, and then you're talking in your car.

Jerry: Yeah. Then when we have six of them, we put them on. So you think you could do it? You think you're funny enough to do it?

Howard: Funny enough to what? To be interviewed by you? I do think I'm funny enough to be on your show in conversation.

Jerry: Okay. I'm just curious if you think that.

Howard: Have you ever heard me not be funny?

Jerry: No.

Howard: Or interesting?

Jerry: No.

Howard: Well, I'm probably too good for your show. Can I get to one question?

Jerry: What do you want to know from me, Howard?

Howard: Are you happily married?

Jerry: Extremely.

Howard: Are you?

Jerry: Oh God, yes. I love my wife.

Howard: I can't tell with you.

Jerry: You can't tell? How would you be able to tell?

Howard: I get the signal from you. I can tell.

Jerry: That was very Krameresque. "I have good signals, Jerry. Signals."

Howard: I spend time thinking about you. You don't remember that I had a conversation with you right before you really got serious with your wife. We had a conversation in the gym, and you said to me, because I was getting married, "Why would anyone get married? It boggles my mind."

Jerry: I was young, Howard. And also, I was trying to be funny.

Howard: Were you?

Jerry: Yes.

Howard: Are you really connected to your children and your wife? The reason I ask you that is because you are always thinking of material. I almost think that you wake up in the morning and go, "Okay, I'm having a fight with my wife, but I'm not authentically there with my wife in a fight. I'm thinking, 'Oh, this is funny. Everyone can relate to this fight. We're fighting over the waffles. Blah-blah-blah.'" There's no way you're there in the room. But you say you're happy.

Jerry: Why do I have to be in the room to be happy?

Howard: What do you do for fun with your wife?

Jerry: Just talk to her. She's, like, crazy. I could never be with a really normal person.

Howard: Does she feel pressured to be witty and funny around you?

Jerry: No.

Howard: Do you think she feels pressure sexually to get things exciting? Because you are Jerry Seinfeld and you could easily have a lot of women?

Jerry: No, you know what? Jewish men, and especially the Jewish male stand-up comedian, if I may, are known to be—in fact, there's no question about it—the longest-, most happily married segment of the show business population, by far.

Howard: Really? Because . . .

Jerry: Because they're smart, and they know it's a trick. And I've played the shell game before.

Howard: Isn't that part of being fifty-nine years old too? You kind of realize all of a sudden, all the bullshit.

Jerry: Yes, yes. Thank you, doctor.

Howard: Do you ever have to sit there and fake laugh for your wife? In other words, did your wife ever say to you, "I think I'm funny"?

Jerry: She is funny.

Howard: Is she funny?

Jerry: Funny enough.

Howard: Is she funny enough that she meets the Seinfeld criteria for intelligence and all that? I mean, you are evaluating her.

Jerry: Yes, that's why I married her. I'm evaluating you too, Howard.

Howard: Right. And?

Jerry: And I'm having a good time. And you're not that funny.

Howard: I thought I was.

Jerry: You're funny enough.

Howard: Funny enough.

Jerry: Yeah.

And Now a Word from Our President . . .

NOVEMBER 9, 1995

(20 years, 11 months, and 30 days until the election)

Howard: Remember when your first book came out? Everyone was saying you were going to run for president.

Donald: It's amazing.

Howard: It's all hype, right? You were never going to run for president.

Donald: I never even—I made a speech for a friend, and perhaps it was a decent speech 'cause everyone said I was a presidential candidate. Showed you how hard up they were. You make one good speech and you're president.

Howard: And of course, with your book coming out, it got you tons of national publicity and it helped sell the book.

Donald: But you look at what's happening now, it's so sad. You look at what Japan is doing, when you look at this whole fiasco with the cars.

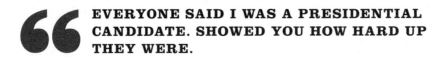

EVERYONE SAID I WAS A PRESIDENTIAL CANDIDATE. SHOWED YOU HOW HARD UP THEY WERE.

We had them. We had them, and we let them off the hook. There's so much to be done.

Howard: I'll vote for you. Donald, I don't know if you know this, but Ivana is running for Senate. She thinks it'll help her sell more of that jewelry.

Donald: How is your book doing?

Howard: It's doing very well. It is the fastest-selling book in the history of books.

Donald: How is it doing compared to your first book?

Howard: It's outselling my first book. Now look, the reason Donald Trump is calling in is not to congratulate me on my book, but he is the grand marshal of the Nation's Parade. It's the closing ceremony honoring the fiftieth anniversary of the ending of WWII.

Donald: During the Vietnam War, I got very lucky. I had a very high lottery number. So I've always felt a little bit guilty.

Ozzy Osbourne

JANUARY 29, 1996

Ozzy Osbourne has been on the show around twenty times. Usually he would come in with someone else, either his kids or his wife, Sharon. In fact, a lot of times Sharon, outspoken and brash and virtually unknown in those early appearances, was as good a guest as Ozzy. She would curse like a sailor and take crap from no one. Once she even had an on-air screamfest with the Insane Clown Posse. She came back at them so hard. (Sharon: "They called me a bitch, and I was just really upset because it's really demeaning for my reputation in this industry. Because I'm not a bitch. I'm a ballbuster. And I'm going to rip your balls off and shove 'em in your mouth—figuratively speaking of course, gentlemen.") I congratulated myself on discovering a gem. Sharon Osbourne: a radio gold mine.

At some point I said to Ozzy and Sharon, "You guys should do a show where they just follow you around with a camera. I would watch that because of the sheer craziness of you two." So their reality show was basically an idea introduced in one of my interviews. One time they asked me to testify to that in court. Someone was suing them, claiming that *The Osbournes* was really their idea. I never had to testify, but I handed over the transcripts of that show and it proved their case. I loved how they interacted, and was selfishly glad when *The Osbournes* premiered on MTV. I never missed an episode.

This interview is special because it's one of the only times Ozzy came in on his own. It was maybe the first time up until then that he came in sober. He'd been to rehab at the Betty Ford Center not long before, and it was sticking.

A lot of people have the wrong idea about Ozzy. They think of him as being out of it, a drugged-out zombie. As this interview shows, he's incredibly wise, thoughtful, and funny. Over the years listeners have complained about how hard it is to understand Ozzy with his thick British accent. That's a great advantage of this book: when that accent is stripped away, you realize his incredible wit and wisdom. Some of the greatest one-liners ever delivered on the show have come from Ozzy Osbourne.

Howard: Let me soak you in, man. Let me look at you.

Ozzy: Why, are you falling in love with me or something?

Howard: I'm not falling in love with you, take it easy. Look at how healthy you look! You know, now that I think about it, the first time I did interview you, your hands were shaking and everything. You were a mess. You were really messed up.

Ozzy: I was really on death's door, man. I was drinking four bottles of Hennessy a day, two cases of beer, about four grams of coke, all the rest of this garbage.

Howard: So, what are you drinking now?

Ozzy: I'm drinking coffee. I've got this new stuff. You've got to try it. It's called wheat, wheat—what is it called?

Howard: Oh, wheatgrass.

Ozzy: Wheatgrass. It's like horse piss.

Howard: You've done a complete turnaround in your life. I said the other day, "Ozzy looks about twenty years younger."

Ozzy: I've just quit smoking. Believe it or not, I'm a month without a cigarette. Out of all the things that I've put in my body, that—

Howard: It's the hardest.

Ozzy: Let me tell you something, I was watching the TV—CNN—the other day, and they had some of the guys from the tobacco company. And they all stood up there under oath and said, "Tobacco is a nonaddictive substance." Horseshit.

Howard: You can't use the s-word, Ozzy.

Ozzy: Oh, I'm sorry.

Howard: No, you're saying tobacco is an addictive substance.

Ozzy: It is the most addictive substance on the planet. Heroin, man. I was taking heroin and it was easier.

Howard: How long did it take you to kick heroin?

Ozzy: Well, I wasn't really into it. I wasn't shooting it. I would snort it from time to time. But I didn't like throwing up. I mean, I don't get that stuff, man. The first time I tried it was in Germany. I thought the guy gave me the wrong stuff, man. I was projectile—

Howard: You were vomiting.

Ozzy: *The Exorcist* pea soup was coming out of every orifice in my body for a month. I was going, "Man, the guy gave me some laxative or something." Tell you one thing, though, it cured my athlete's foot.

Howard: The first time you do it, you're throwing up and you're not enjoying it, so what makes you do it a second time?

Ozzy: Then I go to LA two years later and I'm staying at the Sunset Marquis, which at the time was the in place.

Howard: That's where we met up with you, but you didn't remember me.

Ozzy: Did we?

Howard: This is a really funny story. I've gotta take you back to this. I went to California. I had interviewed you a couple months before. Robin and I said, "Hey, let's stay at the Sunset Marquis because we hear Ozzy hangs out there, and maybe we'll run into him." So I was sitting by the pool five minutes, all of a sudden you came in with your wife and your daughters and everyone. And it looked a little weird, 'cause you know how you look. Your kids looked really conservative. They were all wearing nice white dresses. Your wife was beautifully dressed. And you, you know . . . The whole picture didn't fit. It looked bizarre.

Ozzy: You've gotta understand that the wife's the boss, man. I mean, I'm walking around Manhattan the other day, and she's like, "Ozzy, walk straight. Ozzy, don't look that way."

Howard: But you must like that.

Ozzy: No, it's like a pain up my rear end. "Ozzy, you've gone overtime in the bathroom." I'll wake up in the morning, and she's got her knees on my shoulders, squeezing my zits, going, "Just let me get it!"

Howard: In other words, Ozzy Osbourne has the same life that we all do.

Ozzy: We all do, man! Everybody's the same. Some days you get up and you look at your wife and you think why the hell did I ever—

Howard: So why do you stay married to her? Obviously, you could be living the life of a bachelor where you would be having sex constantly with different women.

Ozzy: I'm not interested. It's bad enough with the one. It's as good as it's going to get. It's as good and it's as bad. I mean, I could get the next Pamela Anderson with big knockers and all that, right? But you know it ain't going to last.

Howard: While you're doing that, it's kind of fun, though, isn't it?

Ozzy: It ain't worth a three-second leg shudder to worry "Is my dick going to fall off?" for the rest of my life.

Howard: That's true. You're worried about AIDS and all that other stuff that you could pick up.

Robin Quivers [co-host]: And not only that, but you get to keep all your money.

Ozzy: My first wife cleaned me out, man.

Howard: Oh, did she? Really?

Ozzy: A hundred shopping trolleys, she was gone, man.

Howard: I didn't realize you had a first wife.

Ozzy: She's now got a job swimming up and down Loch Ness while the monster takes a break.

Howard: Did you get married at a very young age to your first wife?

Ozzy: About three. I thought she was my mother for the first twenty-five years.

Howard: What happened? You were a young rock-and-roll guy—

Ozzy: I was just slamming every chick, smoking all the dope, doing all the drugs. You're young, you're successful, you've got a million dollars in the bank, and you think your dick's invincible. But then that big disease came: AIDS. And it was like [*screams*].

Howard: That slowed you down.

Ozzy: You go to the clap doctor now, and they all come out and go, "Yeah, I've got syphilis!"

Howard: Yeah, you're happy. So, you're very happily married. You're very happy to be married.

Ozzy: Yeah. Sharon, she's the other half of me.

Howard: So here's what happened in California. All of a sudden you walked by the pool. And I went, "Wow, there's Ozzy. He's probably going to come over and say hello to us because we just interviewed him." You blew right by us. I said, "Jesus Christ, this is really embarrassing. Maybe we should go over and say hello to him, but I don't want to go over and say hello to Ozzy Osbourne and bother the guy. Maybe he'll start yelling at us and punch me in the mouth. Who knows? Maybe he's not into it." I said to Robin, "I have a plan." Jessica Hahn had just got in the news. You know, it was big news that she was with Jim Bakker.

Ozzy: I remember that idiot.

Howard: So anyway, I turned to Robin and said, "I have a wonderful plan. Ozzy's not going to talk to us. I'll call up Jessica Hahn. I'll call her up, tell her to sit by the pool, tell her to wear next to nothing, and Ozzy will come over and talk to us." So I called up Jessica Hahn, and in five minutes, she got over to the Sunset Marquis. As soon as she walked in, you got up and walked right over to us. You sat with us, totally ignored me and Robin, and talked to Jessica Hahn for ten minutes.

Ozzy: Really? I must have been stoned.

> ## "YOU'RE YOUNG, YOU'RE SUCCESSFUL, YOU'VE GOT A MILLION DOLLARS IN THE BANK, AND YOU THINK YOUR DICK'S INVINCIBLE.

Howard: You were completely out of your mind.

Ozzy: People come up to me and go, "Hi, Oz!" And I go, "Hi . . ." And they're like, "Do you remember me? You spent four months in my house." And I go, "What?"

Howard: Did you black out all the time?

Ozzy: All the time. I've got kids that I don't even know, man.

Howard: You know what's weird? Because people will never understand this. Here you have a lot of money. You've got unbelievable success. I mean, what are the odds of anybody ever becoming a super rock star? You have everything in the world, and then you're on heroin and on coke. And people go: "How could he do this? How come he's not happy?"

Ozzy: But, you know, it's not unhappy. It's not being happy. It comes with the territory. You know: "Hey, man, would you like . . ." If you haven't tried it before, you want to try everything.

Howard: You get into it.

Ozzy: You just want to try it, you know?

Howard: How did you get off everything? Did you do it yourself or did you go to a rehab?

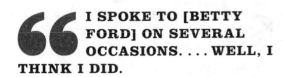

I SPOKE TO [BETTY FORD] ON SEVERAL OCCASIONS. . . . WELL, I THINK I DID.

Ozzy: I went to Betty Ford's and to the AA. And to be honest, I learned. I got a few basic things from it. But the bottom line is that if you want to do anything in this world, you've got to really want it.

Howard: You've got to do it yourself.

Ozzy: No, you need help. You know, my wife put me in Betty Ford—and this is the God's honest truth—hoping that they would teach me to drink like a gentleman. I go in there with a Giorgio Armani suit, I've got my tie, and I say, "Direct me to the cocktail bar." They all look at me as if I've just landed from Mars.

Howard: You go to Betty Ford and ask for the cocktail bar?

Ozzy: That's what I did, man! That's the only way she could get me in the goddamned place. So I walk in and I've got pocketfuls of Valium, quaaludes, coke. And they go, "Empty your pockets." And I go, "No, why?" "We've got to itemize it." Valium, quaaludes, cocaine, syringes, bottle openers.

Howard: They must have thought you were insane.

Ozzy: The only way my wife could get me

to go in was she said, "They'll teach you to do it properly." I thought I was doing it wrong because I kept waking up in weird and wild places.

Howard: Right. "Maybe I should drink like a gentleman. Just have a couple of beers."

Ozzy: That's what I went there for.

Howard: Take one or two ludes.

Ozzy: And then they go, "Uh-uh."

Howard: You can't have anything.

Ozzy: The doors are closed. And Betty Ford walks in and she's like, "Whoa."

Howard: Betty Ford actually showed up?

Ozzy: I spoke to her on several occasions.

Howard: Really?

Ozzy: Well, I think I did.✦

Howard: Did she start yelling at you?

Ozzy: No, no. She's very quiet. She would come and inspect the place like a queen. "There's a grain of coffee over there, a cigarette butt there. Give him fifty lashes."

Howard: Did you try to make out with her or anything?

Ozzy: Make out with Betty Ford? I don't even think Gerald Ford ever did.

Howard: Did you have a roommate?

Ozzy: I was sharing with a mortician.

Howard: A mortician?

Ozzy: This guy. And he was all nervous. You can't have a room of your own. And I'm with this guy and he's always crying. And I go, "Shut the f— up. Why are you crying?" I mean, this guy's older than my

✦ **For more on this from Sharon Osbourne, turn to page 531.**

dad, man. And my dad's been dead fifty years. He goes, "Oh, I'm so depressed." And I go, "Why are you depressed?" He says, "I work with dead bodies." I says, "You're in the right place, man."

Howard: Would they sit you in a group? And have you tell your problems?

Ozzy: Oh yeah. But you know what? I'm not dumb, you know. You soon get the gist of it.

Howard: Right, you play along.

Ozzy: You just go, "Oh yeah, oh yeah, oh yeah."

Howard: Anything to get out of there. Because you really didn't want to quit drugs at that point.

Ozzy: At the end of the day, I did want to quit. I just thought . . . I couldn't stand living, and I was afraid of dying. And that's, you know, you hear—like Kurt Cobain, who shot himself. That's just a long-term solution to a short-term problem. I've got too much to live for, you know? But when you're in that hole, when you're in that hole . . . it's a god-awful place.

Robin: How is it working sober?

Ozzy: To be honest with you, I do sometimes think, "Well, it would be a nice sunny day. I would sit there and have a beer." But I know me better than anybody.

Howard: You probably had a messed-up childhood, right? Did anyone beat you when you were a kid? Or did your dad yell at you or something?

Ozzy: It was the thing. "Hi, Dad." Smack.

> **I COULDN'T STAND LIVING, AND I WAS AFRAID OF DYING.**

Howard: See, that's why you need the beer.

Ozzy: When I was a kid, my father and mother would fight all the time. I used to say to my father, "Where you going?" He used to say, "Off my goddamned head." And I used to think there was a place called Off My Goddamned Head. I used to think to myself, "Wow, man, I can't wait to be old enough to go to this place called Off My Goddamned Head." Instead of rowing with my mom, he's going to this place called Off My Goddamned Head and is coming back singing.

Howard: Sounds like a great place.

Ozzy: When I'm old enough, I get there. I'm fourteen with a pair of stiletto boots. So I could look tall enough to get a beer. I find this place, get a beer, and I go, "No, that's not the stuff, man." I imagined it to taste like nectar. It tastes like horse urine. I says, "No, man, you've given me the wrong stuff, man. The stuff my dad drinks."

Howard: You know the reason you might have drank? When you're in your business, you go, "Where the hell's my next song gonna come from?" It's a nerve-racking business.

Ozzy: Joking aside, it really is.

Howard: I'm not joking.

Ozzy: There's only so many notes on a

> **" I LOOK AT THE OLD FOOTAGE AND SOME OF THE OLD PICTURES, AND I GO, "WHOA. IT'S LIKE JACK NICHOLSON IN *THE SHINING*."**

guitar, there's only so many chords. So you think, well—

Howard: Where's my next song gonna come from?

Ozzy: It's all been done before. Nothing's original.

Howard: I would drink. It makes me nuts, like even ratings and stuff. I have to sit here every day and I go, "Gee, I wonder if somebody's listening to this." I have no idea if they're listening. Maybe I'll smoke a doobie. It goes through my head. Mellow me out. You need to relax.

Ozzy: But then you end up in Betty Ford with all the Valiums, quaaludes, syringes. . . . See, everybody don't think it's for real, though, that I don't get stoned anymore.

Howard: I believe you.

Ozzy: I got no desire to. I mean, I'm on Prozac.

Howard: Prozac is different.

Ozzy: Yeah, I don't recommend that to anybody. Your wiener just goes up your—

Howard: You can't get aroused.

Ozzy: Oh, Miss World could walk through and it's like—

Howard: Really? No kidding.

Ozzy: No, it's dead.

Howard: You got to get something to get your wiener up.

Ozzy: Yeah, I've got an elastic bandage tied to the end of the bed.

Howard: Why the Prozac, though? Why don't you get completely drug-free?

Ozzy: Because I'm a psycho. If I wasn't on Prozac, this studio wouldn't be here, man. I would've come in with the flamethrowers. I'm nuts, man. I just go into this weird vibe, this weird thing. I look at the old footage and some of the old pictures, and I go, "Whoa. It's like Jack Nicholson in *The Shining*."

Howard: Apart from the Prozac, you are now drug-free.

Ozzy: Well, yeah. Coffee. But at the same time, I'm not one of those holier-than-thou people that say, "Because I done it, everybody else should do it." Hey, if you're out there and you're having a good time, you like getting stoned, just get on with it.

Howard: When you see these turds who maybe used to put you down, and now all of a sudden you're still lasting and everyone else—

Ozzy: That's what I was just saying the other day. In the eighties it was the Mötley Crües, the Poisons, and all this. I'm in the middle of this thing going, "Where do I fit, man?" And I'm still plugging along.

Stephen Colbert

AUGUST 18, 2015

Three weeks before Stephen Colbert was set to debut his new show replacing David Letterman, he came in for an interview. I had seen *The Colbert Report* a few times but was not a regular viewer. Nevertheless I was really excited. I was meeting the man who won the coveted late-night spot. I am fascinated by late-night television and the ratings wars. Anyone who has a late-night show, I have to have them on—especially someone who's taking over for a comedy giant like Letterman. Letterman was so inventive that replacing him is like climbing Mount Everest.

To me what was interesting was that Colbert had played a character on his Comedy Central show. Now he had to ditch that character and become himself for the CBS show. Up until then, no one knew who the real Stephen Colbert was. I think you really get an understanding of him from this interview. He's a very intelligent guy, very evolved and emotionally connected. He talked candidly about the tragic deaths of his father and his brothers in a horrific airplane crash. We spoke about his Catholic faith, which was a surprise, since I tend to find many in show business aren't quick to discuss religion. I think some are hesitant to admit a belief in God because they might be perceived as unhip or naïve. Stephen reflects on his faith and how it guides him.

After this conversation, there was no doubt in my mind that he would do well with the CBS show. His genuine wit, intelligence, and charm came through. I became a true fan that morning and went on to be a regular viewer of his program.

Howard: There he is, the famous Stephen Colbert. How great is this? Sit down. I can't wait to talk to you.

Stephen: Am I allowed to shake hands?

Howard: You have to put on the Purell. You're not afraid of shaking hands? You don't worry about germs or any of that stuff?

Stephen: No. I'm one of eleven children. The youngest of eleven. It was filth all the time.

Howard: You came from a very religious family. You're a devout Catholic, right?

Stephen: I'm a Catholic, yeah. *Devout* is a word I don't entirely understand anymore. I mean, the church is flawed. Boy, that's an understatement. The church is greatly flawed. But it was a beautiful gift to my family and my mother and me.

Howard: To have faith?

Stephen: Yes. We were daily communicants. We'd go to mass every day. We lived near a convent. My mom would go to mass every day and force me to go with her.

Howard: Don't you feel like comedians in a way laugh at people of faith? They're kind of like, "Oh, look at him, he believes in the Easter Bunny." You know what I mean? It's almost like you have to keep that quiet.

Stephen: We don't have to. I don't think that what I believe is prescriptive for everybody. It's just—it works for me. I don't mind being mocked about it. That's good. If you come up with a good joke about the Catholic Church, I might steal it.

Howard: You had a traumatic childhood. Let's be honest. That's a pretty heavy experience, what you went through.

Stephen: But when it happens to you at that age, everything is normal. You have no standard for what life is like, and so it just seemed normal to me.

Howard: Your father was a very accomplished guy. What was he, a doctor?

Stephen: An immunologist and then an academic. He was the youngest medical school dean ever. He was assistant dean at Yale Medical at twenty-nine. And

then he was a dean at St. Louis Medical. Remember Anthony Fauci when the whole Ebola thing happened—the guy who would come out and say, "You're not going to die"? He's the head of Allergy and Infectious Diseases. That was my dad's gig. When I was born, that was my dad's job.

Howard: Brilliant man. And you lost him when you were very young. How old?

Stephen: I was ten years old. Two of my brothers died at the same time. A plane crash.

Howard: The amazing thing about that accident is laws were actually changed as a result.

Stephen: After they listened to the cockpit recorder—which is something that I do not recommend anyone do—there was a rule created called the Sterile Cockpit Rule. Meaning below a certain height you cannot talk about anything other than the approach.

Howard: Did you listen to the tape?

Stephen: No, I read the transcript. I read it once a few years ago.

Howard: Why after all these years would you read the cockpit transcript?

Stephen: It happened by accident, actually. I wasn't looking for it. I was doing a little research on the accident itself. I had found out from somebody else that the Sterile Cockpit Rule had been instituted because of that crash, which I didn't know. So I looked it up, and the first thing that came up on the Google search was the transcript. I went, "I can't *not* read it now." So I read it, yeah. It doesn't end well.

Howard: How did it change your mother?

Was she able to have a strong face in front of you, or would she break down a lot?

Stephen: Both. There's no clean description of what life was like. She was there for me, and I sort of kept her going.

Howard: Which is a horrible responsibility for a little kid—to keep your mom going. You turn into a parent of sorts.

Stephen: Yeah. I used to joke that I raised my mom.

Howard: Is it difficult for you to be around a crying woman now because of your mother?

Stephen: Wow. That's deep, man.

Howard: Well, seriously.

Stephen: No, seriously, that's a very deep question, Howard. Not difficult. But I think there's no doubt that I do what I do because I wanted to make her happy. No doubt.

Howard: You're used to cheering up a woman.

Stephen: Yes. How do you know to ask that question?

Howard: Because I spent many years cheering up my mother as well. I didn't want to tell you this. No, what happened was my mother lost her mother when she was nine, and my mother became very depressed when her sister died, and I spent a lot of years trying to cheer up my mother. I became quite proficient at making her laugh and doing impressions of all the people in the neighborhood. Even to this day when I see a woman in distress, I feel like I have to jump in and solve her problems.

Stephen: That's not a bad impulse, though.

Howard: Well, it certainly makes for a career. So when you came home from your father's funeral, you decided then and there, "I want to be a comedian."

Stephen: Well, no. I think the story you're talking about is when we were coming back from the cemetery, my sister Mary made my sister Margo laugh so hard in the back of the limo. Those old limos that had the rumble seats that face back, like in *Mission: Impossible* when they're about to kill the ambassador. And my sister Margo laughed so hard that she fell on the floor of the limo and snorted and was laughing even in the midst of how we were feeling at that moment. And I remember thinking, "I want that. I want to be able to make that connection." That was important to me. It wasn't like I wanted to be a comedian or anything. That came later. I'd listen to comedy albums every night going to bed.

Howard: Bill Cosby, right?

Stephen: And David Frye.

Howard: No one ever talks about David Frye. They talked more about the guy who did the Kennedy impressions, Vaughn Meader.

Stephen: Yeah, I also had those albums. But I had inherited them from my brothers, and they were so old and so scratched that often I wouldn't know what the punch line was because it would skip. So I'd try to write Cosby's punch line in my head.

Howard: That's good comedy homework.

Stephen: That it was.

Howard: But you became a very bad student as a result of your father's death.

Stephen: I was a terrible student after Dad and the boys died because, you know, why would you study? What does anything matter? How could you possibly be threatened by a bad grade? "Oh, I might get a detention? You're kidding."

Howard: But you seem very well read?

Stephen: Oh, I read every day. I read almost a book a day. But I just read whatever I wanted to. We had a house full of books, and I read tons of science fiction and fantasy, but other things too. I remember saying, "Okay, I'm going to read the encyclopedia," and I read the whole thing.

Howard: So you go to some fucking college. I don't even know the name of it.

Stephen: A wonderful college called Hampden–Sydney College in Hampden Sydney, Virginia. Patrick Henry was one of the founders.

Howard: There was a point where you said you wanted to become a marine biologist, but you're deaf in one ear.

> **" I WAS A TERRIBLE STUDENT AFTER DAD AND THE BOYS DIED BECAUSE, YOU KNOW, WHY WOULD YOU STUDY? WHAT DOES ANYTHING MATTER?**

Stephen: I don't have an eardrum in my right ear.

Howard: Is that a birth defect, or did something happen?

Stephen: Since I was born. It's called a cholesteatoma. It's a benign sort of tumor. It's basically the skin on your ear is always growing to keep your eardrum soft. Mine grows in. It doesn't grow out.

Howard: So you can't hear out of that?

Stephen: Damn deaf in this ear.

Howard: And therefore you can't become a scuba diver.

Stephen: Well, I'm not waterproof.

Howard: So you go to this college for two years to become a good student.

Stephen: I become a *better* student, and I figure out what I want. I did some plays when I got to college, and I realized acting was the only thing that I would show up early, stay late, do any amount of work without anybody having to cajole me into doing it. And so I thought, "Well, this is a hint. I should probably be doing this. Where would I go if I wanted to stay in college and study theater?" I heard Northwestern had a good program, and I was very lucky to get in.

Howard: And then you join Second City. When you got there, you got free classes because you answered the telephones.

Stephen: Wow. That's a deep cut, man. You got good research.

Howard: You were there with Chris Farley.

Stephen: Yeah. We're hired the same day. We toured together around the country.

Howard: Was he right-out-of-the-box funny, or did he develop too?

Stephen: He was funny from the moment I knew him. When he came onstage, he could suck the energy right over to him. And yet he didn't believe he was funny. He was such a very sweet guy and really intelligent, which people don't give him credit for. He played an oaf. He played a buffoon. He was actually a smart, caring, sweet guy who was really loving. But maybe not of himself.

Howard: Sad to see what happened to him.

Stephen: Yeah, the day Farley died was the first night Craig Kilborn had been suspended from *The Daily Show* [for making derogatory comments about female colleagues]. I'd only worked there for like a week or something. And they said, "You. New Guy"—which was my credit in the show, New Guy—"New Guy, you're going to go on for Craig this week."

Howard: Oh my God.

Stephen: And I was about to go to makeup when they came in and they said Farley just died. I was just wrecked.

Howard: So wait, you did Second City, then pretty soon after you get *The Dana Carvey Show*, which was a big deal.

Stephen: Second City, then a small show called *Exit 57* for two seasons. That gets canceled in October. I had a baby in September. So I've got a baby for a month, no job, pulling my hair out, and I get the Carvey gig.

Howard: That's a big gig, by the way—a network show for Dana Carvey. And the guys working on that—

Stephen: A legendary group of people. Louis C.K. was head writer. Robert Smigel, who was Conan's first executive producer and an amazing guy. Comedy just leaks out of him. Charlie Kaufman, who wrote *Being John Malkovich*, among many other things. Rob Carlock, who ended up being Tina Fey's executive producer for all the stuff that she does. [Writer and actor] Dino Stamatopoulos. Steve Carell. God, so many other great people were on that show.

Howard: Were you destroyed when it didn't work out?

Stephen: Listen, the first show goes on the air right. And we're after *Home Improvement*, which at the time was the number-one show. Better ratings than *Seinfeld*. It was like twenty-five million people—numbers you never see anymore. Something crazy. I remember our first episode was like twenty-four million people.

Howard: Wow.

Stephen: And Dana is dressed up as Bill Clinton, and he's got working teats— like dog teats—on his chest and he's breastfeeding puppies and kittens, and something like ten million people shut off the TV immediately and they never came back. The next day Dana walked in—Steve Carell and I shared an office—and he goes, "Hey, guys, sorry I ruined your careers. You both should've been on *SNL*, and I've ruined that for you. I'd like to apologize, and I'll do my best to get you jobs after this." He knew we were canceled. We were on the air for six more episodes. And then dead nothing. For a year.

Howard: Nothing?

Stephen: No. No safety net. I got no community, because my community was Chicago, and I'd moved to New York. I'm tearing my hair out. Hiding from my wife so she won't see me tearing my hair out. Blowing through savings.

Howard: What do you do for the year? You're just sitting home?

Stephen: I wrote industrials. Novell Network Solutions, Devon Medical Supplies, stuff like that.

Howard: And that's why you took the job originally at Comedy Central working with Craig Kilborn? You didn't like the show that much, but you took the job because you were like, "Hey, I need a job," right?

Stephen: Well, they didn't use an audience at first. It was really crazy. They were doing setup–punch line jokes, and it would be dead. I was a temporary guy. My first six months, I think I did three pieces. The wolf was still at the door, without a doubt. And then—

Howard: And then Jon Stewart ends up taking over the show.

Stephen: I had left, actually, to do a show called *Strangers with Candy* for a few years. And then I came back and this new guy Jon Stewart was there.

Howard: He loved you?

Stephen: Yeah. I loved him, man. I loved

him. I remember I came back for the 2000 campaign, which was the greatest story of all time then. A tie for president. The greatest thing about a political campaign or a presidential campaign is, part of the job you're doing in political comedy is educating your audience to the thing that you're about to do a joke about. But the education is secondary. You want to get to the joke. Well, a presidential campaign is the only story to dominate the airwaves. And so you get to that moment—that moment of, like, climax, where you get to find out. And then, in 2000, it's like tantric sex. You get to the moment of climax, and it just suspends for thirty-two days. And you're right there, like—

Howard: I can't cum.

Stephen: Exactly. You just do it for thirty-two days. It's just the money shot for thirty-two days.

Howard: And we still don't even know that we got it right. Al Gore gave up too easy, didn't he? He should have kept going.

Stephen: My joke to Jon, the thing I pitched was, when the Supreme Court finally ruled and Al Gore conceded: "No, they're taking it to the Justice League. They're taking it to the Super Friends. But the Bush people are taking it to the Legion of Doom—Lex Luthor, chief justice."

Howard: You were not a political guy until you got working with Jon Stewart.

Stephen: No. He invited me to have an opinion.

Howard: You were on your own show already, about six months, and you host the Bush White House Correspondents' Dinner.

Stephen: My agent called me and goes, "Hey, they want to know if you'll do the Correspondents' Dinner." And I said, "To be, like, a guest?" And he said, "No, they want to know if you'll host it." And I said, "Have they ever seen my show?" And he goes, "I don't know. They want to know if you'll do it." And I said, "Hold on. Just tell them I'll call them back." So I called Stewart and said, "Hey, Jon, they asked me if I'll do the Correspondents' Dinner." And he said, "To be, like, a guest?" I said, "No, to host it." And he goes, "Have they ever seen your show?" I said, "I don't know, but I think I got to do it." And he goes, "Yeah, you got to do it." I assumed they knew what they were in for. It was all new material, but I just did what I did on the show.

Howard: A lot of people walked out during that.

Stephen: No, people didn't walk out. Some people in the room got upset, but they didn't walk out, that I know of. I did not see people walking out. I saw people doing this, with their hand on their mouth. And I remember people not talking to me afterward. No one on the dais made eye contact with me except [White House Press Secretary] Tony Snow. The late, great Tony Snow came over and he was really gracious. He was like, "Thanks, man. That was great." And

> **I CALLED STEWART AND SAID, "HEY, JON, THEY ASKED ME IF I'LL DO THE CORRESPONDENTS' DINNER." . . . AND HE GOES, "HAVE THEY EVER SEEN YOUR SHOW?"**

Antonin Scalia. Scalia comes over to me and he goes, "Really great stuff." And I'm thinking, "Don't you make me love you, old man." But I really didn't think that I was throwing Molotov cocktails. We were throwing a bottle of grape Nehi that admittedly had a burning rag in the neck of it. But we didn't know that the room was soaked with gasoline. That room was ready to be angry. Because there was a level of careful discourse at the time. It's hard to remember what it was like back in 2006, how you just could not say shit about the president because he was anointed with the war and that completely understandable fear and cautiousness in the country.

Howard: It was a different environment.

Stephen: A totally different environment. And we thought it was possible to do these jokes, and the room did not. But luckily, the audience watching at home *did* think it was possible to do those jokes.

Howard: Do you read what your Twitter followers say about your shows?

Stephen: Back on the old show, toward the end, I wouldn't watch the show at all. But if there was a special event, if we had a

> **CARSON SAID TO LENO WHO SAID TO CONAN WHO SAID TO ME WHO EVENTUALLY SAID TO FALLON, "YOU WILL USE EVERYTHING YOU KNOW HOW TO DO BECAUSE THE SHOW IS JUST TOO HUNGRY. YOU GOT TO FEED THE BEAST."**

surprise guest on, if somebody walked on you didn't expect, like if Kevin Spacey came on as his character from *House of Cards* or something like that, I knew that was about seven minutes into the first act. So that's about 11:38, and I'd go into Twitter to see what people's reactions were.

Howard: Would it deflate you if they weren't excited about it? If they said, "Oh, that sucked, it was hacky, it was blah-blah"—whatever it is they would be negative about?

Stephen: Howard, no one has said anything negative about me.

Howard: Letterman was legendary for beating the shit out of himself after a show because he felt he hit the wrong note. Are you one of those guys? Do you really just beat and tear yourself up when you feel like you fucked up a good opportunity?

Stephen: I started off as an improviser, and I still think of myself that way at my best. For written comedy, I feel like I've got a chance to shank that joke and really fuck it up because I've got the music in my head of how it's supposed to go perfectly. That's when I'm really going to hit a clam because I'm worried about hitting the music in my head.

Howard: How hard are you on yourself?

Stephen: I'm glad there's another show tomorrow, how about that? I'm glad there's another show tomorrow. It's tough if it's the last show of the week and—

Howard: And you've got to get through the weekend.

Stephen: And you shank it, and you go, "Goddamn it! I have to live with this feeling for three days."

Howard: One of the things you did on *The Colbert Report* that I loved was when you had a guest, the guest sat there and you ran around and you stole the moment from them. It was a brilliant thing.

Stephen: Because that character thought he was the most important person. The nice thing about your first late-night show is they're all cults of personality. I don't care what you say. That's why the show really is called *Letterman* or called *Fallon* or *Kimmel* or *Conan*. It was smart for Conan to call his *Conan*. Really, the name of the show doesn't matter. It's just the guy.

Howard: I love the late-night wars and all that kind of stuff.

Stephen: Really, you like the war part?

Howard: I love it all. When you got tapped to be the guy taking over for Letterman—

Stephen: I like that. "Tapped."

Howard: Did Les Moonves come to you? Were you the first guy he came to?

Stephen: I don't know. I'm the last guy he came to.

Howard: Does that bother you? Does that matter to you if you were the first choice of CBS to replace Letterman?

Stephen: If we were getting married, it would bother me. If this wasn't a business, it would bother me.

Howard: I've interviewed Neil Patrick Harris, and he said, "Yeah, they talked to me about it." They talked to this one. They talked to that one.

Stephen: I bet they talked to a lot of people over the years.

Howard: And it had to be a big decision for you, because you had such a great thing going at Comedy Central at that point.

Stephen: It was a big decision. I never thought that the next thing I would do would be something harder than the last thing I did.

Howard: This is harder?

Stephen: Well, I don't know. I haven't done it yet. It's certainly more material. I've gone from eighty hours a year to two hundred hours a year.

Howard: And it's a lot because I know—I don't want to say you're micromanaging, but I will.

Stephen: That's a very polite way of saying "control freak."

Howard: But I think you are a control freak in the best way.

Stephen: Aren't you?

Howard: I think that the rap with Letterman when he had that slot was, as he

got older, he became less and less interested in the daily running of the show.

Stephen: I don't know. I didn't work there.

Howard: That's what I heard. But the story I have is that you had a ninety-minute private meeting with Letterman.

Stephen: Before day one on the air, I wanted to go over there and really say thanks for the thirty years he was on the air. I started college in '82, which was the same year he started in late night. His late show on NBC was everything.

Howard: But when you were putting together this concept for—whatever your concept is going to be for taking over *Late Night*—did you sit and watch your competitors? You watched *Fallon*, I assume?

Stephen: Yeah. I've been on *Fallon* a bunch too.

Howard: But when you're putting together your ideas, do you sit there and go, "Okay, Fallon's got the impressions and the games. We can't touch that stuff"?

Stephen: No.

Howard: Everything is fair game?

Stephen: Sure. I think this is a true story that Carson said. I heard this from Conan. Carson said to Leno who said to Conan who said to me who eventually said to Fallon, "You will use everything you know how to do because the show is just too hungry. You got to feed the beast." And so anything I know how to do, I'll do on the show.

Howard: How important was it to get the right amount of money in your deal?

Stephen: I have a very good agent. You know James "Babydoll" Dixon? That's the real king of late night.

Howard: I know Babydoll. He's also Jimmy Kimmel's agent.

Stephen: And Jon Stewart's.

Howard: Isn't that a conflict? You're competing with Jimmy Kimmel.

Stephen: But I'm not. I'm not competing with Jimmy Kimmel.

Howard: But you are.

Stephen: I'm not. CBS is competing with NBC and ABC and TBS or whoever it is. Conan and Jimmy One and Jimmy Two, as I call them, we're friends.

Howard: Who's Jimmy One and Jimmy Two?

Stephen: They know. Both of them know who's number one and number two in my heart.

Howard: Did you in fact write an e-mail to Jimmy Fallon and say, "Hey, I'm not interested in the traditional feud between late-night shows"?

Stephen: No. We went out and had drinks.

Howard: Oh, you did?

Stephen: We're friends. I've known him for a long time.

Howard: In radio, my attitude was—and I'm not suggesting this—

Stephen: You're prescribing it.

Howard: Stephen, I swear to you, I wanted to tear the hair out of the fucking head of every competitor—anyone else on the radio. I felt I should be the only person on radio, and everyone should only listen to me.

Stephen: And did that make you happy, Howard?

Howard: No. I was miserable. But that's who I am. I'm wired that way.

Stephen: That's one of the things that I said to Jimmy when we went out and had cocktails that night. It was like, "Not many people know what this gig is like. And at the end of the day, wouldn't it be nice to, like, have a drink with each other so you can say, 'Can you fucking believe what this gig is like?'" That's what Jon and I were able to do once I was doing a gig like his. I didn't understand what this gig is like when you're the guy at the top and you have to keep your eye on everything in the show.

Howard: Yes, but the difference is that with Jon Stewart, you were following him. And with Jimmy Fallon, the two of you will be on at the same exact time.

Stephen: We were on at the same time for ten years, man.

Howard: Yes. But this is different.

Stephen: To you.

Howard: Yes, to you too.

Stephen: It's not different, no.

Howard: Really?

Stephen: It really isn't different. Why would it be different?

Howard: Because CBS and NBC are locked in a network battle.

Stephen: Well, then it's different for them.

Howard: Your career definitely depends on beating the shit out of Jimmy Fallon.

Stephen: I disagree.

Howard: I'll tell you what the difference is. In late-night television, the ratings come out every single day. It's relentless. Don't kid yourself.

Stephen: You're pouring poison!

Howard: I will guarantee you will end up resenting Jimmy Fallon. Because it's going to happen: his people are going to either steal a bit that you did or a guest that you had booked. It's going to fucking happen. It's going to go right out the window—all of that Catholicism. I will put money on it if you'll be honest with me and come back here in a year and tell me the truth.

Stephen: I will. I will tell you.

Howard: I've got to tell you the truth. I hate doing all these fucking shows. It's so much pressure for me. Because I always want to please the host.

Stephen: Not the audience?

Howard: It's the host. I want to make sure that everyone is like, "Oh, Howard is coming on. It's going to be crazy."

Stephen: I promise you, I have no expectations for you.

Howard: Really?

Stephen: Yeah. Whatever you want to do.

Howard: I have expectations for me. Do you know what I mean? I don't want to disappoint anybody.

Stephen: I know that feeling, because I was lucky enough to be on with Dave ten times, and I would go home after and watch frame by frame to see his face. Like, "I think that's a real laugh. I think I really made him laugh."

Howard: I'm the same way with all of these shows. I know how important these shows are. You put a lot of work in. And I've got to tell you something, I have done some late-night appearances on various shows that are ridiculous home runs. When I did Leno, it was, like, the highest ratings the guy ever got. And then I went on Dave, and I was dressed as a woman. I was great. You can't do better than that. And it's like, "Well, maybe I should—"

Stephen: You shouldn't do any of them then.

Howard: That's what I'm saying. I really don't even want to do any of them.

Stephen: Make yourself a rarity and your value goes up. And eventually, if you do it, you'll be like Lucille Ball on *Carson* where the curtain opens up and people stand up and applaud, and you don't have to do anything.

Howard: But don't be angry with me if I do Kimmel and Fallon and you.

Stephen: I promise you, I will not be mad. Unless you're right and I change completely when I go on the air. In which case, fuck you!

Howard: Right.

Stephen: It's preemptive. I don't mean it. But later, if I actually am mad at you, I'm not going to talk to you. So this is for later: Fuck you! Fuck you, old man!

Howard: All right. Let's end it on fuck me.

SEX & RELATIONSHIPS

I've never understood why people are so freaked out by talking about sex. We are animals. We procreate. We are no different from dogs or cats or anything else on this planet when it comes to sex. We have intercourse and then we have babies. That's what we're talking about. The whole notion that somehow this is disgusting is shameful and absurd. I think that's how you really get screwed up—by *not* talking about sex.

Much to my friends' delight, my mother got me a subscription to *Playboy* when I was thirteen. Our family was always making jokes about sex. They were very liberal about it. The family attitude was, "You want to make a joke about sex, then go ahead. What's the big deal?" So that's what I did when I started out in radio. Honest to God, I didn't do it to shock people. Not at first. But when I saw how outraged people were, and they started labeling me the devil and saying that I should be censored, then I absolutely had to run with it.

Many of those godly, upstanding people were the ones who really had issues. They were the real freaks. They were the politicians who would talk about the sanctity of marriage and how God intended it to be between a man and a woman, and then they'd end up getting busted trying to cop a blow job in an airport men's room. Meanwhile, I had been in a long-term marriage for twenty-five years, and after that ended I got involved in another long-term relationship and marriage that's still going strong twenty years later. Turns out I'm the boring monogamous guy.

What's interesting now is how society has changed since I started on radio—how talking about sex isn't as big of a deal anymore. Look at how widely accepted porn has become. I suppose I deserve some credit for making people comfortable about bodily functions. Sex is okay. It's nothing to be uptight about.

That's part of the reason that back in 1995 I brought on two lesbians to make out on *The Tonight Show with Jay Leno.* I thought it was ridiculous that anyone could be shocked by two women kissing. Leno actually cut the camera away when they locked lips. He wouldn't let viewers at home see it. Even so, it sure got people talking about lesbianism. Looking back now, it probably seems like a really crass stunt, but you had to shock people to get them to wake up.

Now they are awake. Maybe not everyone. There are still a lot of homophobes out there and people who are super-repressed. Overall, though, we are much more open to discussing our sex lives. That's been great for my interviews. Now I don't have to be so outrageous and provocative. I'm able to have very open and honest conversations about sex and how that factors into my guests' relationships. They are much more comfortable sharing that part of themselves. And when they don't want to go there, I'm way more understanding than I was in the past. I no longer get angry or feel bitter when a guest doesn't open up about their romantic life, because I understand wanting to guard a relationship. I feel similarly protective of my intimacy with Beth. That is sacred to me.

While psychotherapy has been a key part of my evolution, Beth has been just as essential. The biggest and most wonderful surprise in my life is the incredible love affair I have with her. Because this book is about opening up emotionally and having true, meaningful growth that leads to extraordinary conversation and interviews, it would be impossible to discount how important her friendship is. Words cannot describe the change in my attitude and spirit because of Beth. I am beyond lucky to have experienced her warmth and love. I have always felt safe when I am with her, and I am humbled by the charitable work she does. We've been together for nineteen years, and every day I thank God she wanted to be with me. You know I'm head over heels because I call her "Sweet Love." Yes, her name is "Sweet Love." Howard Stern, me—I call my wife "Sweet Love." She is a saint. Mother Teresa . . . well, like Mother Teresa in a bikini. Yes, a great beauty but so much more. Day in and day out she works tirelessly on behalf of animal charities. If she is sick or exhausted, she never complains about her daily routine of cleaning litter boxes and administering medication to the over nine hundred cats we've found loving homes for. I've seen her fearlessly reach into bushes to pluck out feral cats, swoop in and rescue distressed animals without regard for her personal safety. She works to raise funds to build animal shelters and is a tireless advocate for our four-legged friends. There isn't a day that goes by that she isn't on her Instagram account trying to match homeless animals with the best situation possible. (Check her out at @bethostern.)

Beth brought peace to my life. I remember the first time I saw her. It was a rainy, cold night in Manhattan. Friends had invited me to a dinner party, and she was there on a blind date, and we ended up talking. There was this light around her. She was just glowing. I was drawn to her. I guess that great philosopher Paula Abdul was right when she sang that opposites attract. She's blonde and I have dark hair. She loves to socialize and I'm a bit of a hermit. I'm sarcastic and can be an avalanche of negativity while she is so uplifting and positive. If I'm King Kong, she's Fay Wray. I'm the Beast to her Beauty, Belle. You get the idea. She balances me out. When I talk about being in a lighter place, that's the light she brought into my life.

Getting into a relationship where I was satisfied and feeling like there was all this love in my life opened me up in the same way psychotherapy did. I don't think I could have had one without the other. If I didn't have that component of a deep relationship, I'm not sure all of this other stuff would have kicked in. With Beth's encouragement, there was a general shift in my attitude.

She often gets invited to read her children's book at elementary schools. One day she was sitting and reading to a group of kids, and afterward this girl came up to Beth and started poking her and looked up and said, "Are you real? Are you *real*?" When you see Beth, you're not sure if she's Cinderella or Sleeping Beauty. I feel the same way as that kid. Sometimes I'll look at her and think, "Is this really happening? How could this person love me? How am I so lucky to be loved by someone who's so giving and warm, generous and kind? Is she real?" I guess that's the definition of a dream girl, and nineteen years in I still feel that way about her. The love that Beth gives me definitely leads to an empathy and generosity of spirit that carries over into my interviews.

JEFF BRIDGES

Howard: How do you decide what movies you're going to do now? How many do you do a year?

Jeff: I have a weird method.

Howard: What do you do?

Jeff: I resist working as much as I possibly can, because I'd love to do other things. I like my music, my family, hanging out with my wife.

Howard: Does it feel like a chore to have to go do a movie?

Jeff: No. Even before I was as successful as I am, I always had that thing. I resist. I resist just about doing everything. Getting married, any big decision in life, I resist.

Howard: How long did it take you to get married? How many years did you date your wife?

Jeff: About three years—living with my wife for about three years.

Howard: Why couldn't you commit? Because you're famous and with a lot of options?

Jeff: I have this theory. I don't know if this holds water, but it's just that if death is the end of the story, how the story ends, then marriage is a giant step in that direction. Actually, the fear of marriage is the fear of death.

....

HUGH HEFNER

Howard: You're not into guy-on-guy action, right?

Hugh: Listen, over the years, I've witnessed every variation on the theme. But no, definitely not.

Howard: Yeah, it's not like you and Bill Maher are getting into a swordfight.

Hugh: Back in the seventies, you know, when it was a more swinging time, there were more mixed doubles. But not in the last twenty years.

Howard: What men were lucky enough to be with you and all those babes? Jimmy Caan? Bill Cosby? Were those two in the corner with their pants down? What about Larry King, has he ever been up there?

Hugh: Where would I be without everyone else's fantasies?

Howard: And you don't wear a rubber?

Hugh: Only when it rains.

Howard: I heard you knocked up one of these babes, is that true?

Hugh: Never.

Howard: No?

Hugh: In my entire life, the only women to become pregnant were my wives.

Howard: Really? Now, how do you do that? The withdrawal method?

Hugh: Well, I know what I'm doing.

Howard: You must.

Hugh: Practice, practice, practice.

Howard: And how do you do divorce so well? I never hear them say a bad word about you.

Hugh: Well, my ex lives next door with the two kids. I see her every day.

Howard: Is that the move? Keep your enemies close.

Hugh: It certainly works better than when we were all together.

JENNY McCARTHY

Jenny: I'm very sexual, as you know. I'm a Scorpio. I love sex.

Howard: Were you always sexual? Or when you were younger, were you just the type of girl that would lay there, and then you realized that you could unleash your sexuality? Most girls who look like you don't put out that much.

Jenny: I didn't. I mean, I had a high school sweetheart for seven years. I was only with him. I masturbated on top of my teddy bear. He did all the dirty work, so to speak, until my mom sold it in a garage sale, which was really hard on me.

Howard: You would rub your clitoris into the teddy bear?

Jenny: Yes, I would just sit on it, so to speak.

Robin: Some kid got that teddy?

Jenny: Some guy bought the teddy bear for his kid, which is beyond embarrassing.

Howard: That was your move as a little kid? You would rub into your teddy bear.

Jenny: I didn't know about masturbation. The first time I had an orgasm, I didn't know what it was. I'm like, "Something just happened to my body." I tried to look it up in the dictionary because we didn't have Internet.

Howard: You looked up what? "Teddy bear rubbing my vagina"?

Jenny: No, "body-something." I just didn't know, and then one of my girlfriends was like, "That's an orgasm."

Howard: How old were you when you started rubbing your vagina into your teddy bear?

Jenny: I would say I was in eighth grade.

Howard: You were having orgasms in eighth grade.

Jenny: Yes.

Howard: But you didn't know what you were doing?

Jenny: I didn't know.

Howard: You just knew it felt good.

Jenny: I just know Tubby the bear was awesome.

ALANIS MORISSETTE

Robin: As a result of being in showbiz, did you start dating very young?

Alanis: I did. I started dating secretively when I was twelve.

Howard: At twelve you were having full sex?

Alanis: No. Dating and sex are not necessarily synonymous, Howard.

Howard: At twelve you had a boyfriend. What age were you when you lost your virginity?

Alanis: Well, I was the Catholic mind-set—can't lose your virginity or you're a whore kind of mind-set—for a really long time. I considered myself to be sexually active all through my teen years, starting at fourteen or fifteen.

Howard: But no intercourse?

Alanis: No intercourse until later.

Gary Dell'Abate [producer]: Was the first guy Dave Coulier?

Alanis: Yes.

Howard: Oh my God, you

poor woman. You're telling me your first was Dave Coulier from *Full House*?

Alanis: Yes.

Howard: You know, the woman who first had sex with me, the one I lost my virginity to, said, "I don't want to have sex with you. I don't want to be your first because you will always remember me as your first, and I don't want to be trapped in your head the rest of my life."

Alanis: No.

Howard: Write a song about that.

Alanis: How old were you?

Howard: I was a young sixteen. A very gawky and awkward sixteen. You decided to give your virginity to Dave. Why Dave?

Alanis: I was in love. And ready.

Robin: How old was he?

Alanis: I don't even remember. I always dated older men, though, that was the norm for me at the time.

Howard: You were nineteen?

Alanis: Yes.

Howard: He was, what, thirty-four?

Alanis: Something like that. Early thirties.

Howard: My God, that's scandalous.

Alanis: Is it?

Howard: Were your parents upset?

Alanis: No, I dated people with a bigger range between our ages than that.

Howard: Really? How big a range?

Alanis: I think the biggest gap between the ages would have been when I was about seventeen I dated someone around your age, Howard.

Howard: My age?

Alanis: Yes.

Howard: Who was that person? Was it Jack Nicholson? You're kidding me. Didn't your parents get alarmed?

Alanis: I think they were a little alarmed, but they also knew that I was this freak of nature in many ways.

Howard: You're very mature.

Alanis: At the time. Although emotionally, clearly immature as a young person.

GEORGE TAKEI

Howard: There's a lot of gay action in Central Park supposedly.

George: Oh there was, yes. The Ramble.

Howard: According to what I've been told, you go in there and there are guys with their dicks out and you can suck 'em off or beat 'em off. Is that true?

George: It's true.

Howard: You ever been?

George: I have. You do dangerous, sleazy things in your wild youth.

Howard: How old were you when you did that?

George: I was in my early twenties.

Robin: You didn't do it during your *Star Trek* years.

George: It was before *Star Trek*.

Howard: You went in there to the woods and—

George: And got a little relief.

Howard: What time of day?

George: Late at night.

Robin: Did you let people do things to you or did you do things to people?

George: Both. It's very shallow. You just go by how

he looks, and there are very little words exchanged.

Robin: You're not seeing this person ever again?

George: No, no. You're just going there to get relief.

Howard: Boy, it'd be great if they had parks like that for heterosexuals. I'm jealous. You mean, you just go into the Ramble and you see some dude and you think, "Oh, he's attractive," and then he just walks up to you and starts jerking you off or blowing you?

George: Yeah, exactly.

Howard: Whoa.

George: It's very impersonal.

Howard: But exciting.

George: Very exciting. The danger is part of it. The possibility that he could be a policeman, he could have a knife on him, he could be a lunatic, he could be diseased. Who knows? There's that tingle of excitement.

Howard: So if I'm a gay man I could go to the Ramble and stick my penis out and wait for someone to show up.

George: With you, I don't even think you'd have to have your penis out.

Robin: "Oh God, Howard Stern is here?"

Howard: Quite frankly, with my penis I don't even think it would hang out. My fly would be open and a little nub would be sticking out.

George: You have a pimple down there.

Howard: It ain't much. I mean, I would love to hang something out of my trousers.

George: You know, you're an amazing man to be talking about the size of your penis on radio.

Howard: Well, I'd do it on TV but they won't let me.

·····························

BRYAN CRANSTON

Howard: When you were having all this sex as an actor in the seventies, was it a wild scene? Were there two and three women at a time?

Bryan: I've been with a couple women before, yeah.

Howard: No kidding.

Robin: How'd you manage that?

Bryan: It was the seventies, Robin.

Howard: I was in the seventies. I couldn't get *one* woman. So you would go to an orgy and experience multiple women at once?

Bryan: No, I was at a party. This only happened once. It was almost by accident. I went into another room with a girl, and we were making out. And we flopped onto the bed. A girl walks out of the bathroom. And now I'm embarrassed—I didn't know if it was her house or where I was. And she came over and now was sitting down next to us. And she places a hand on the other girl's leg. You don't know if the other girl's gonna flinch from that. But she didn't flinch. It was almost like they were telepathically telling each other what they wanted to do, because not a word was spoken. It wasn't, "What are you guys doing? Can I join you?" It was something on some meta level that only women hear.

Howard: The seventies were great.

Bryan: The seventies were that. And it's pre-AIDS.

Howard: You didn't wear a rubber for that, right?

Bryan: No. Nuh-uh. Because every single girl was on the pill. And if you got the clap or crabs, it was like a badge of honor.

Howard: Did you ever get the clap?

Bryan: No. I did get crabs once. So I go to a free clinic in LA, 'cause I didn't have any money. And you sign up. And you have to state, "What is your complaint?" And I put, "Some itching." But I didn't want to say where. And then they go, "Bryan Cranston, come to the desk. You have itching. What area?" They're behind glass. And there's twenty-seven other people looking at you.

Howard: Why do think you chose to get married? You were on such a roll.

Bryan: Well, I got married young. I was twenty-three years old when I first got married. Lovely girl. She wanted to get married and have kids and things like that, and I was just starting my career. And it was just . . . cowardice, actually. I shouldn't have.

Howard: Did you know the day of your wedding you were making a mistake?

Bryan: No, but my brother did. My brother Kyle says to me, while we're getting dressed, he's putting on my bow tie, and he goes, "I can just walk out there and I'll tell everybody it's off. It's over. You don't have to go through with it." And I'm looking at him like, "What are you talking about?"

Howard: At the time, I can imagine you were mad at Kyle.

Bryan: A little bit, yeah. I was like, "Come on."

Howard: And then, years later when you're getting your divorce, you're like, "God, why didn't I listen to my brilliant brother?"

Bryan: He knew. He knew.

SARAH SILVERMAN

Sarah: I've had to switch over in my porn. I don't know how you can still watch all this babysitter porn. For me, my search words were always very *gang bang*. Very dominant. Stuff like that.

Howard: I don't like that.

Sarah: So I had to stop watching it because my nieces got into their early twenties, and it's so hypocritical 'cause that's when guys go, "I'm a feminist because I have a mother and daughter." And it's like, "Well, even if you didn't, women exist, you fuck." But now I'm the same way. It shouldn't have taken me my nieces getting into their twenties. Now I can't stomach watching a twenty-year-old get gangbanged. 'Cause I feel bad, you know?

JENNIFER LAWRENCE

Howard: Is it a mistake to fall in love with your costar? Whether it'd be someone as big as Bradley Cooper, a good-looking guy like that, or the director you were in a relationship with, Darren Aronofsky, is it a mistake ultimately to be in a relationship with somebody in the business?

Jennifer: I don't think so. I think, one, you don't really have a choice. If you're falling in love, you're falling in love. Just be a professional about it.

Howard: Will a camera guy approach you and ask you on a date?

Jennifer: No. I do the approaching.

Howard: You do that?

Robin: You don't mind? Just go on up and—

Jennifer: I'm always an aggressor. I make sure that they don't have a girlfriend or wife or something, or a boyfriend.

Howard: How many douchebags approach you on a daily basis with just the wrong approach?

Jennifer: I don't get hit on. My sex life is not lit.

Howard: Really? Are men afraid because you are a big earner and they think you're out of their league?

Jennifer: I don't know. The ones that do, I'm like, "Really?" I'm just kidding.

Howard: It's a little sad, right?

Jennifer: My life?

Howard: No, isn't it hard to know when someone really loves you at this level?

Jennifer: No, it's not really hard. Not at all. No. I can tell within five seconds of talking

to somebody. There's an excitement in someone's eyes that I have always been able to spot immediately. It's the excitement in the eyes. I don't know how to tell you. It's like a flicker, and I can spot it.

....

RUSSELL BRAND

Howard: You're smart enough to know that when you're going around fucking tons of women, you're hurting a lot of people.

Russell: I'm not! I'm being very nice to them.

Howard: Yes, you are.

Russell: What do you mean, Howard? I'm very loving, and I make it very clear—

Howard: Yeah, but you're a star, and they think they're gonna be the one, and that they're gonna convert you into being monogamous. And you know they get hurt.

Russell: Howard, I swear to you, I'm very, very loving.

Howard: So, what do you tell them to be loving?

Russell: Right, I'll tell you. Imagine it's you.

Howard: Okay.

Russell: I go, "Look, we're alive here for a short time.

I think you're beautiful. I think there's divinity within you. I think there's divinity within me. Let us connect this divinity."

Howard: I cannot believe you ever get laid with that line. You're lucky you're good-looking.

Robin: And famous and rich!

Howard: Can you imagine a guy coming up to you and saying, "Hey, there's divinity in you, and divinity in me"?

Russell: But it's the truth!

....

ANDY COHEN

Howard: People would be shocked to know this story from your new book. Which you have not revealed yet.

Andy: Right.

Howard: You met a heterosexual couple in Boston.

Andy: On my book tour for the last book. He said, "This is my cell phone number. Seriously. We want to party with you." And I said, "Oh okay. Interesting." I get home, and I'm a little soused up. It's around 1:30 in the morning.

Howard: You're in a hotel, I presume?

Andy: Yes. And I text the guy. I'm about to go to bed. I said to him, "I want you to be very direct with me and tell me exactly why you gave me your number tonight."

Howard: Good for you. I believe in that.

Andy: In the morning I wake up to a fantastic series of texts. They have explored recently with other women. They've never been with a guy. He's never been with a guy in his life.

Howard: Uh-oh. This is right up your alley.

Robin: Fantasy central.

Andy: And being a good boyfriend, he has said to her, "Is that something that's on your mind?" And she has said to him, "Listen, there are only two guys in the world I would ever be with. Paul Walker, who is dead, and Andy Cohen, who is gay." [He says,] "We would be willing to meet you, smoke it up and see where this goes."

Howard: Okay, now we're on.

Andy: One of the things that was on my turning-forty bucket list was, "How cool would it be to lose my virginity?" In my mind, if I ever did it I would want to do it with a straight couple.

Howard: You might fuck a woman.

Andy: That would be the goal. He sent me an *incredible* dick pic that *really* engaged me.

Howard: Whoa.

Andy: I start texting everyone I know. I text Kelly Ripa the dick pic. And I go, "Just FYI. Do you see this couple? Your boy is losing his virginity *tonight*." I said to them, "Find a cozy spot in the hotel lobby bar and I will meet you there after my signing." They almost faint when I walk in the door. And we wound up having a really great ninety-minute hangout.

Howard: When you're having this conversation with them, is there any physical flirtation?

Andy: He and I are playing footsie a little bit, on and off.

Howard: No shit.

Andy: Which was engaging me *intensely*. As it went on, it became clear to me that I wasn't going that night to lose my virginity. I don't think she, for her first time

with two guys, one of them being me, was ready for that intense of an experience.

Howard: Do you think she just wanted to watch her boyfriend fuck around with another guy?

Andy: Could be.

Howard: And what do you care?

Andy: Love it. Fantastic.

Howard: So what happens? You go upstairs.

Andy: We went upstairs.

Howard: What was she wearing, by the way?

Andy: She was wearing tight jeans, boots—

Howard: Compare her to a celebrity.

Andy: She looks a little Rebecca Romijn-y.

Howard: No kidding! That hot?

Andy: She's Jewish.

Howard: A Jewish Romijn?

Andy: Yeah.

Howard: Wow.

Andy: We wound up naked.

Howard: What happens?

Andy: What happens is a little bit of everything.

Howard: Did you touch her? Did you touch her va-jine?

Andy: Little bit.

Howard: Was it like, "Ew"?

Andy: No, it was nice. It was nice. She had great boobs.

Howard: Is he jerking you off while you're touching her?

Andy: He's slowly . . .

Howard: Touching?

Andy: Yeah, yeah.

Howard: So the involvement with the girl—I mean, wish she could just fucking jump out the window—but you're playing around with her. He's probably making out with her a little bit.

Andy: They really then went at it.

Howard: Did you have to watch them fuck?

Andy: Yes. And it was awesome.

Howard: You liked it?

Andy: *Loved* it.

Howard: Why? What did you love about it?

Andy: What's not to like? It was gorgeous.

Howard: And what do you do while they're fucking? Do you masturbate?

Andy: I look for openings that I can, you know, get in. He and I kind of then wound up . . . uh, you know . . . finishing up.

Howard: Doing what?

Andy: Just jerking off.

Howard: That's it.

Andy: Yeah.

Robin: So you're still a virgin.

Andy: Yes. But I'm starting a major book tour. Come to my event in Boston Friday night if you're a couple and then I'll start writing the sequel.

Howard: This story is in the new book.

Andy: I'm telling you much more than is in my book. Because it's you, and he's a huge fan of yours.

Howard: By the way, Stephen King is right now killing himself.

Robin: His book tours never turn out like this.

....

DAVE CHAPPELLE

Howard: You party a lot and everything? You one of those guys that has taken advantage of your newfound fame?

Dave: Nah, I can't. See, my girlfriend is pregnant.

Howard: What is with that? I mean—

Dave: Well . . . we had sex.

Howard: Where did you get this girlfriend?

Dave: In Brooklyn.

Howard: Brooklyn? Is that right? She's not a white chick, is she?

Dave: Noooo. She's Filipino. Which is, like, neutral.

Howard: Filipino? Well, that's almost a white woman.

Dave: Naw, that's neutral. They the black Asians.

Howard: Does she speak English?

Dave: Yeah. She don't speak Tagalog. She speaks only English.

Howard: That's not one of those girls you get sent over from the Philippines and pay her father.

Robin: You didn't buy her from a magazine?

Dave: No, no, I didn't order her out the mail.

Howard: Now, what are you going to do when this baby is born? Are you going to marry this Filipino gal?

Dave: See, there's a good question. Actually we got plans on getting married.

Howard: You're in love?

Dave: Yeah, man.

Howard: You don't look at other women?

Dave: I mean, I'm a man. I'm gonna look at other women sometimes.

Howard: But you're willing

to, for the rest of your life, not have sex—

Dave: See, I can't think about it like that. Let me ask you this: Do you think you would have made it being single? Now, think about this. For real. Do you think you would have made it being a single man?

Howard: Well, gee, I would like to think that I had some talent and that perhaps I would have made it.

Dave: But talent and focus are two different things.

Howard: I hear what you're saying. I don't think I would have been as focused. You're right.

Dave: Yeah, going out kills it, man.

Howard: It does. But I gotta tell you something: even though I'm single now, every night during the week I live like a monk. I'm focused. I don't go out.

Robin: That's not true. I hear that that's not true.

Howard: I do not go out. You can hear whatever you want.

Dave: You're single with married-man habits.

Howard: Yes, I am.

Dave: And you know what's out there.

Howard: I know. I know what's going on.

Dave: The booty's a booby trap.

Howard: It is.

Dave: It's not safe out there.

Howard: It can throw off your focus. So you're saying that you would just stay focused and get married to this Filipino girl?

Dave: Yes.

Howard: And that's gonna be your life?

Dave: That's gonna be my ticket out. You know, you got to think of these women like frequent flyer miles. I mean, if you doing nice things with this girl, and nice things with that girl, it never adds up. You got to get all your miles on one airline.

....

PAMELA ANDERSON

Howard: There was a guy in high school who gang-raped you.

Pamela: With his friends.

Howard: This is fucking crazy.

Pamela: I know. I wrote it all out the other day because I'm writing my new book. I was like, "Wow. I survived a lot." But everybody survives a lot. Everyone has gone through stuff. We're quick to judge people but they've probably had some craziness go on in their life.

Howard: You were a fourteen- or fifteen-year-old girl living in Canada, and you were gang-raped. Most people don't come back from that.

Pamela: And that was after the molestation when I was young. Then I had an older man try and teach me backgammon and raped me right after that. My first boyfriend kicked me out of moving cars. It was very violent. He tried to run me over all the time.

Robin: You're so beautiful. You'd think men would be so happy to be with you.

Pamela: I think I'm a button-pusher. I think I provoke people into craziness. Because it seems that even in my relationships I drive people completely insane. I don't know.

Howard: I think men want to own you. They want to take ownership of you. And they forget you're a human being and you might not want to go along with the program.

Pamela: I go along for a while. And when I don't want to do it anymore, I *really* don't want to do it. "I'm serious. I don't want to do this anymore. It's not a game. Bye!"

Howard: But men go, "Hey, wait a second, honey. You can't leave me." When you were gang-raped you couldn't tell your parents.

Pamela: I had hickeys all over my body because that's what they did to me. I went home and my dad grounded me until the hickeys were gone. So I didn't want to say anything. I was already in enough trouble.

Howard: Did you ever go into therapy for what's happened to you?

Pamela: I have been in therapy on and off for the last twenty years with this Jungian analyst who I love. We go into that. But I think I've done pretty good for myself. I think I'm a happy person. It probably has affected my choices. But I don't regret my choices.

Howard: Do you think you could ever really be in a good relationship and trust a man? Or have men broken the trust too many times for you to ever be in a loving relationship?

Pamela: I don't know. Because I'm not there yet.

Howard: When you first started to do *Playboy*, was there any fear? Did you say to yourself, "I've been getting all this horrible attention from men. If I put myself out there naked, more shit is going to go wrong."

Pamela: I thought I empowered myself. I felt like I turned it around. Like, "This is *my* choice." I took charge of it.

···

ROBERT PATTINSON

Howard: Relationships are complicated, you know? When you're as good-looking as you or me—and I relate to you in this respect—we could have anyone we want. It's always been that way for me.

Robert: People say that about being an actor or whatever, and I always think it actually kind of narrows things down. For one thing, you get all paranoid about everything. You have no idea why people like you or whatever. And then also, most people may think they want to have a relationship with you, but then they start a relationship with you and they actually realize, "This is not what I want at all." You get all the craziness. You can't do anything. There's basically a big imbalance in the relationship. It's tough.

Howard: I never looked at it that way. You're right. It does sort of narrow it down. You can't just go to a restaurant and pick up some girl. You could be looking at all kinds of legal problems. People are out to get you.

Robert: That's the other thing too, yeah.

Howard: The woman you're with is a really good singer.

Robert: FKA Twigs.

Howard: And there's a racial

element to that. I can't believe in this day and age that she gets shit from your fans because she's a black woman. People write her nasty things.

Robert: I think it's just professional trolls. They get so addicted to wanting to cause hurt and pain on someone. And it's one of the most difficult things to know how to confront, really. It's a faceless enemy. If someone came up in the street and said it, that's one thing. You'd know what to do. You'd know what to say. But when it's literally just a little random name on Instagram—

Howard: Some asshole in his basement.

Robert: And they're probably in a different country somewhere. It's just crazy. It might seem fake to them, but it's real in your life. And you think, "Oh, you can turn it off, whatever." Just to know it's there. It's like if you know there's one room in your house where, if you listen up against the wall, you can hear everyone talking shit about you. Even if you don't go to that room, whenever you feel bad about yourself

you're gonna go down there and start listening to the whispers.

Howard: I agree with you. I think it's the hardest thing. And as a guy, we try to fix things. I know if someone attacks my wife on Twitter—you get crazy. You want to go, "Fuck, I'm gonna go protect you." And you can't protect anyone from anything. You feel helpless.

Robert: I feel like you're feeding it. I feel like it makes me feel less powerful. You're trying to attack a reflection in the water; you just look crazy. The only way to show some kind of strength is to say, "None of this shit touches me."

....

GILBERT GOTTFRIED

Howard: In your book, you describe how you actually picked up a stripper and brought her home to your apartment.

Gilbert: Yes, yes, that was amazing. I somehow, miraculously, got a stripper up to my apartment. That's like one of those things if you're

writing a series they have certain rules with characters that you can't break. You know, like if Fonzie did a ballet. He would never do that. This is something that would never work.

Howard: Were you at the club when you picked her up?

Gilbert: It was at some event I got hired for.

Howard: Was she impressed you were the comic at the event? Therefore you were able to show her that you were famous.

Gilbert: I guess so.

Howard: Because that doesn't work for you, normally. Like, you're so gross fame doesn't even help you get laid.

Gilbert: Yes.

Howard: Somehow this stripper went for you.

Gilbert: Somehow we met for lunch, and I got her up to my apartment. And I'm on the couch with her and we start making out. I'm going out of my mind.

Howard: Are you the guy who slams his tongue down a girl's throat right away?

Gilbert: Yeah, not that light kissing stuff. It's like the Roto-Rooter man. We're on the couch and I'm thinking, "Oh my God, I can't believe I'm making out with this stripper." Then the clothes start coming off and she's wearing this Victoria's Secret–type underwear.

Howard: Wow. She was prepared.

Gilbert: Oh yeah.

Howard: Are you like, "I'll get as much as I can before she comes to her senses"?

Gilbert: Right. I get into bed with her. She's totally naked, and she's got one of these stripper asses that is rock hard. It looks like a cartoon in *Playboy*. I was getting ready to do her doggy-style. And there's her ass up in the air that's just perfection, as is the rest of her. I get my dick in. And if I say I lasted a full two and a half seconds I'd be lying. I don't even know if I moved it once. I just exploded.

Howard: I'd pay anything to see you fuck.

Gilbert: That would be a sex tape that would sell. I think my dick was inside her half a second and then boom. She looks over her shoulder, like, shocked and horrified.

Howard: She's like, "This guy doesn't look good but maybe he can fuck. . . . Oh, it's over."

Gilbert: Just this horrified look. Like she saw the Loch Ness monster. And she goes, "Did . . . did you . . . ?" And I'm there in total ecstasy, like [*panting*], "Yeah . . . yeah."

Howard: So did she get dressed and leave?

Gilbert: Oh yeah.

Howard: You talk about a walk of shame. *That's* the walk of shame: coming out of Gilbert Gottfried's apartment after he blew his load.

· ·

KATY PERRY

Howard: "I Kissed a Girl." What gives you an idea like this? You've never actually kissed a girl, right?

Katy: Yes I have.

Howard: You had lesbian sex?

Katy: No, that was incorrect, but thank you for asking.

Howard: You never tried it. You're twenty-three, right?

Katy: Yes.

Howard: You lost your virginity at how old?

Katy: We're getting into

that. Let's take it, then. It was out front of a construction site in Nashville, Tennessee, at seventeen. It didn't last long, and neither did the relationship.

Howard: You did kiss a girl and liked a girl, though? It's based on the truth.

Katy: It is based on the truth. I just want to make one thing really clear, because there's a lot of rumors going around: she's really hot.

Howard: Did she have cherry ChapStick? Was that really true?

Katy: She probably had some kind of vanilla bean Bath and Body Works concoction.

Howard: Where were you that you met this girl that inspired the song?

Katy: There was actually not one particular girl that inspired the song, but the girl that I did kiss I met through friends.

Howard: Okay, were you at a party?

Katy: No, we were just having cocktails at a bar with our other friends.

Howard: Does this girl know this song is about her?

Katy: No.

Howard: How did you end up kissing this girl at the bar? She just leaned in and started making out with you?

Katy: Yes.

Howard: Wow. You did kiss a girl, and you liked it.

Katy: I think that girls are beautiful creatures.

Howard: Would you like to make love to a girl?

Katy: I'm not so sure I would go necessarily all the way. I'm not sure I'm ready for that kind of commitment to another crazy personality as myself.

ADAM LEVINE

Howard: Congratulations. The "World's Sexiest Man" is getting married.

Adam: I'm getting married.

Howard: The woman you're marrying is probably in shock. Because you are a bit of a ladies' man.

Adam: Yeah, I have been.

Howard: What made you decide to stop the party?

Adam: It's so cheesy and stupid, but you know how everyone says, "When you know, you know"? It's kind of fucking true. Sometimes it clicks and you're there.

Howard: Sometimes the timing is right too, because you've got it out of your system.

Adam: I've gotten plenty out of my system. As far as I was concerned, I was cool with being single forever. I had just come out of a relationship.

Howard: I remember. I was admiring of you because you seemed to be handling single life very well.

Adam: I didn't have any plans to do anything. I was free. I thought I was going to be single for a while. That's when it gets you. I was like, "Oh my God, I just met this person at this point. This wasn't supposed to happen." But that's when you know.

AZIZ ANSARI

Howard: Arranged marriage for your parents?

Aziz: Arranged marriage, yeah.

Howard: Unbelievable. They knew each other for a couple of hours or something, then got married.

Aziz: Not even. My dad told his parents he was ready to get married.

Howard: How old was he?

Aziz: Maybe he was a little younger than I am now.

Howard: So in his thirties.

Aziz: Yeah. So what they do is the families—his parents found some parents of a daughter around my dad's age. And he said she was too tall. Then he met this other girl and said she was too short. Then he met my mom and was like, "Okay, she's the perfect height. Let's do this."

Robin: It's like Goldilocks!

Howard: Did you ever say to your dad, "You're entering this marriage, this social contract . . ." And it is a contract between two people. A couple hours, and then they got married!

Aziz: He said it was like thirty minutes! But you know, I've read a lot about arranged marriages, and they find that in the long term people in arranged marriages are really happy. 'Cause they really invest in the commitment to the relationship. So it starts off kind of cold, then builds to a boil. Whereas here I feel like everyone's looking for "boil" immediately. And after a while, you know . . .

Howard: Are they still married?

Aziz: Still married. Happier than any older white people that I know.

Howard: Unbelievable.

MEGYN KELLY

Howard: Would you ever get implants?

Megyn: No, I don't think so.

Howard: You're a C cup, aren't you?

Megyn: My husband calls 'em "Killer Bs." It's funny, we used to call 'em the "Killer Bs," and then when I got pregnant they became "Swimming Cs" and Doug [Brunt] was frolickin' in the ocean.

Howard: Really? So you and Doug still have a good sex life? Even after the baby? You know that that's a real issue.

Megyn: Well, there's a certain period of time where that's not possible. You know, after you have the baby that's off limits for a while.

Howard: You had sex during your pregnancy?

Megyn: There were no issues.

Howard: Even in the third trimester?

Megyn: Even in the third trimester. That's all I'm gonna say. Yeah, we never had any trouble in that department.

Howard: No kidding? Your husband's a real man.

Megyn: You know, I think it's Dr. Phil who says, "When the sex is bad it's 95% of a marriage. When it's good it's 5% of a marriage." And for us it's 5% of the marriage.

SETH MEYERS

Seth: In Chicago, I was taking classes at a place called ImprovOlympic. That's where I got to meet a lot of people. That's the first time I got to see Tina Fey and Amy Poehler perform was there.

Howard: But you weren't in Second City.

Seth: I wasn't in Second City. And then these guys from Chicago started an improv theater that was like Second City in Amsterdam, in Holland. And I auditioned for that, and moved to Amsterdam for two years.

Howard: So you did comedy in Amsterdam.

Seth: Did comedy in Amsterdam.

Robin: Were you doing comedy in English?

Seth: Yes. The Dutch, especially the Amsterdam Dutch, they speak English incredibly well.

Howard: That's crazy. I mean, that's unbelievable.

Seth: It was the best.

Howard: But at the time did you realize it was the best?

Seth: Yes.

Howard: It reminds me of when I was in college, I got out and I saw an ad for a radio station in Alaska looking for DJs and I was like, "Oh shit, I gotta move to fucking Alaska?" But if I had to move to Amsterdam, I'd be like, "Oh my god!"

Seth: Living in Amsterdam when you're twenty-three years old was not the worst thing in the world.

Howard: Are you a drug guy? Do you smoke a lot of weed?

Seth: I had smoked weed in college the way most people smoke weed in college. But living in Amsterdam is where I realized I don't really like smoking weed.

Howard: Yeah, me neither. And then the other thing that's legal there is prostitution. Did you try that?

Seth: No.

Howard: You never did it?

Seth: No, I never did.

Howard: Were you curious? Did you ever go see the windows?

Seth: I remember I had a friend—friends would visit me all the time, 'cause Amsterdam's such a fun place to visit. And I remember walking home one night fairly inebriated and my friend was like, "Hey, I'm just gonna say it: should we get a prostitute?" And I said no. And he said, "No 'no'? Or no 'convince me'?" So, no. But it's still a fascinating street to walk by. Like, when you walk in the red light district it's crazy.

Howard: I was reading your wife is a prosecutor or something?

Seth: Yeah, she works for the Brooklyn DA.

Howard: She works for the Brooklyn DA and she prosecutes like sex trafficking crimes.

Seth: Yeah, she's just starting there.

Howard: If you had a history of going to prostitutes, that would not have worked out.

Seth: No.

Howard: Do you ever feel like your job is completely ridiculous compared to hers? I mean, she's really doing something so fucking important.

Seth: The part that's even worse is my wife is very good at leaving it at the office. So I can't come home and be like, "Ugh, I had a really rough day at *SNL*. None of my jokes worked. You have no idea how bad that feels."

....

CHELSEA HANDLER

Howard: Are you dating someone now that is a romantic relationship, or is it just still this constant fucking?

Chelsea: Let me tell you something: I haven't had sex in a year. Not now. But I went one full year—not purposely—I went a full year after my show.

Howard: Not even fingered?

Chelsea: No, no. You think I'm gonna get fingerblasted and not fucked? What kind of operation do you think I'm running? So all of a sudden nine months had gone by, and I was talking to my girlfriend—we were in Spain or something—and I go, "Oh my God, it's been nine months since I've had sex." And she's like, "Oh my God, you can't do that." Like, I don't want that on my résumé. And it's not on purpose. It's one thing if you're going to try and be celibate, but I would never try and be celibate.

Howard: But how is that possible? You meet a hot guy—I know you—you walk right up to him and say, "I wanna fuck." You're that up-front.

Chelsea: No, I'm not like that. I'm a little shy when it comes to men I don't know. I can be forthright in this atmosphere or medium or whatever. But I'm not just, like, walking up to men.

Howard: So for a year, men didn't come up to you?

Chelsea: Yeah, some of them did. But nobody I was interested in. I could have sex with somebody. But I need to have sex with somebody I want to. But my other girlfriend said to me, "Don't you think it would be cooler to go the year? You're almost in the homestretch. Don't you think it'd be a cooler move to not fuck anybody for a year and say you did that?" And she was right. And I did it.

Howard: You waited. And what did you learn?

Chelsea: Nothing.

Howard: Nothing. When I was single, I was on a mad tear to get laid. 'Cause I

thought, "What if I die and I didn't have the sexual experiences I should've had?" And so it became like a thing against the clock. You know what I mean? It became very, very important to me. During that year, did you ever say, "Oh my God, what am I doing?"

Chelsea: It's like the opposite of your situation. Because I've had so much sex. So I didn't care about it in the way that you would. It was doing the reverse. I was like, "Well, you know what? Maybe I should

take a year off, obviously. Maybe it'll save my life or something."

....

JOHN F. KENNEDY JR.

Howard: So you're growing up in high school. At what point do you realize that not only are you good-looking, you got power over women and you're a Kennedy? At what point does it all kick in?

John: Well, the Kennedy part kicked in fairly early. The other part, I'm not sure it ever kicks in.

Bill Murray

OCTOBER 8, 2014

I remember the first time I saw Bill Murray, on *Saturday Night Live*. It was 1975, and I was a senior in college. He wasn't part of the original cast. He was stepping into Chevy Chase's role after he left the show. I had an irrational hostility to anyone new on that program. Like me, all of my friends were angry with the "new guy." But I quickly turned around and recognized that he was a master. He's one of the most incredibly talented human beings ever.

The idea of having him on the show was big to me. He had always been on my wish list of guests. He'd called in once, about three years before this, and had a good experience. When his movie *St. Vincent* came out, we thought we'd try to get him into the studio. As Gary can attest, booking Bill Murray is not an easy process. You can't get Bill on the phone. He doesn't have a manager or agent. Rob Burnett, who produced *Letterman*, told Gary that the only way he ever got hold of Bill was an 800 number. You leave a message, and maybe Bill calls you back or maybe he doesn't.

Fortunately, the movie studio that was releasing *St. Vincent* helped coordinate things. Even after he'd agreed to come on, we were all nervous. We thought there was maybe a fifty-fifty chance he'd show up. There's something pure and beautiful about how elusive Bill is, how reluctant he is to be in the public eye. You don't see that often in celebrities these days, when everyone is desperate for attention.

Bill talked about that in the interview. He's not trying to be difficult or create some mystique about himself. He just values his time and his privacy. He also talked about his divorce and all the work he'd been doing to understand himself better. We think of Bill Murray as a comedic genius, one of the funniest people who's ever lived. And he is. But he also has a philosophical side to him. He's a profound guy.

Howard: Who forced you into this room, Bill? Honestly. It's so rare to get you. Who put a gun to your head and got you here? Is there a story behind you coming here?

Bill: I was coerced.

Howard: You were?

Bill: It's like that.

Howard: Do you still like acting?

Bill: Yes, I do.

Howard: You wouldn't do it if you didn't like it. At this point you have enough money you don't have to do it.

Bill: It's a combination of things. I really enjoy doing it, and I may not have any other marketable skills.

Howard: You would rather be off playing golf somewhere.

Bill: Playing golf is fun. But, no, I'm not really that idle. I like to do things, and there is something that makes you want to express yourself, whatever it is.

Howard: Are you a good golfer?

Bill: I'm better than most people, it turns out. I'm a single-digit golfer.

Howard: Is this something that's important to you?

Bill: Well, I was a caddy, Howard, so that's how I came to golf. It's not that I want to dress any certain way or wear loafers without socks. I just really want to play golf. I was a caddy. I worked my way through school as a caddy. As a caddy, you could play on Mondays for free. Then all of a sudden I had some money so I didn't have to caddy anymore.

Howard: When I think of the life of a caddy, it's like, "Boy, go get me this. Give me that." Some guy is hiring you for the day to follow him around and do his bidding. Did you resent these rich guys who went golfing and you had to service them?

Bill: I can see how you could say, "Well, it's demeaning." But for me when I was ten, it was entry-level employment. You didn't have to have a license or Social Security number or proof of your residence or anything else. You just could do it. It was an extraordinary education for me because I learned a lot from men who had the wherewithal to be the members of a country club. You learned a lot about how you wanted to be treated, and you learned how to treat people by seeing how these people treated you. Show up, keep up, and shut up—that's what the caddy is supposed to do. I was capable of doing that. I could caddy for eighteen holes and say virtually nothing. I could also engage in a real conversation. I learned how to treat people. I learned a lot of that in golf.

Howard: Because no one gave you anything. You grew up in Chicago, right? Your family was poor. You guys weren't wealthy. You had, what, seven siblings?

Bill: Eight.

Howard: Eight siblings. Is that a nightmare for a kid growing up? You don't get the attention from your parents. You don't get maybe enough love. People overlook you. You think that's a bad thing, to grow up in a family of nine?

Bill: I was the forgotten middle child. But

in a family of nine there's, like, three or four that are forgotten.

Howard: Was that hard for you, being in this gang of kids where you really just can't get your mother's attention?

Bill: Well, it was my father, really. Because he would go to work and was usually back late at night. I only had so many hours to get him.

Howard: Was he mean to you?

Bill: No.

Howard: It was a tough life, right?

Bill: I wouldn't go so far as to call it a tough life. But it got hard when my father died. I was young. I was seventeen. So then it got hard. There was always financial pressure. We weren't wealthy. We lived in a nice town. I won't say we were poor. But we didn't take—our vacation took place in a car. We got in the car and we drove someplace. We didn't fly. I didn't fly until I was nineteen or something.

Howard: Was it a shock to your family when you decided to go into comedy?

Bill: No, it was a shock when my older brother Brian went in before I did. Because when my father died, he came back and got a real job. If he would have kept that, he'd be a very wealthy man today, and he gave it up to become an improvisational actor at Second City in Chicago and kind of blew everyone's minds.

Howard: When you win an award, do you put it somewhere? Do you have a trophy room? Or do you just kind of shove it away?

Bill: They're all just sort of up on a shelf.

Howard: That's what I would expect. I wouldn't expect walking into your home and seeing a little Murray trophy room.

Bill: I don't have the space.

Howard: You don't? Do you have a big home?

Bill: Yes. Bigger than the one I grew up in, I'll tell you.

Howard: You're a wealthy guy.

Bill: I save.

Howard: Are you frugal?

Bill: I don't know if I'm frugal, but I didn't blow a lot early on. If you don't immediately spend your first real paycheck, it adds up. I remember someone saying to me, "You did the right thing." I didn't buy a house for a long time.

Howard: You're not desperate.

Bill: Because I saved some money.

Howard: You see some actors who didn't save money. They lived this big lifestyle, and now they've got to grab movies that they don't necessarily want to do. And you are in that rare position where you don't have an agent, you don't have a manager. I mean, it's legendary: in order to get you to read a script, they have to somehow get it to you and you read it and then you may call.

Bill: I like it that way. I couldn't take the phone ringing and just juggling people trying to put you into their plan.

Howard: Do you have a cell phone?

Bill: I do.

Howard: Do you have one of these cell phones where you can e-mail and all that stuff?

Bill: Supposedly it gets e-mail, but I have no idea how to operate it.

Howard: It's not even that you're anti-technology. You just want to live your life and not be bothered by people.

Bill: I only got a phone to text with my sons. Because they will not answer a telephone, but they will answer a text. I'm not a very organized guy, Howard. I'm really not. I can't take on any more. I'm barely getting by. There's certain things I've got to take care of. I barely get those things done.

Howard: I love that. Yet I can't do it. I find that half my day is responding to everything.

Bill: I have a friend who's got a bicycle shop. He moved his bicycle shop because he was in, like, a little strip mall. He moved in the alley in back. He said, "I was working an eight-hour day to get four hours of work done. Because people just come in and interrupt or whatever. I don't have that much time to give away."

Howard: Were you always like that? Was there a time when you were a go-getter, like when you were like trying to get on *Saturday Night Live*? Was there a time where you had angst about all of this? Or were you always just not pressured by that?

Bill: I was really lucky. I followed in the wake of all these people. I was behind [John] Belushi and Harold [Ramis] and my brother Brian. I was, like, behind these icebreakers that were ahead of me. I got to learn what I did in Chicago at Second City, and then I came to New York.

Howard: Did you like living in New York?

> ❝ **SUPPOSEDLY [MY PHONE] GETS E-MAIL, BUT I HAVE NO IDEA HOW TO OPERATE IT.**

Bill: Yes. It was unbelievable. There was so much energy. If you were trying to write something and you got sort of like a writer's block, you just walked out on the street and the energy would just be like . . .

Howard: Is it better being famous than not famous? Isn't fame a wonderful thing? You can walk into a restaurant and everyone wants to be your friend. Isn't there some value in that?

Bill: I do not like people who complain about being famous. But I'd say to people, "You want to be rich and famous? Try being rich and see if that doesn't cover most of it for you."

Howard: I think about those early *Saturday Night Live* days, and you say, "Hey, it's great all these other guys broke ground for me, and I was able to walk right in." I don't see it that way with your career. When you walked into *Saturday Night Live* the second season, the world was against you. People loved that first cast so much. You replaced Chevy Chase. I remember the first time I saw you on TV, I was like, "Who the fuck is this guy?"

Bill: How dare you.

Howard: People didn't want to like you. You had to win them over, and I think the moment when you won everyone over

> ❝ **I'D SAY TO PEOPLE, "YOU WANT TO BE RICH AND FAMOUS? TRY BEING RICH AND SEE IF THAT DOESN'T COVER MOST OF IT FOR YOU."**

was when you did the lounge singer thing, where you just were singing "Star Wars." You did that, and I think the world just fell in love with you.

Bill: Well, that's when I felt like I'd done it. The first week I came, they just gave me a tryout and they gave me stuff to do. They gave me three great things to do, and I nailed them all. But then for the next few months I was the second cop, the second FBI agent.

Howard: Why? Because there were so many great players?

Bill: Great players, but mostly because the writers don't know who the hell you are, and they don't trust you. They don't know what you can do, so they don't trust you. They're not going to give you a good job. They're going to give it to Dan [Aykroyd] or Johnny or something. They don't want to take a chance on me. But when I wrote that sketch—and Tom Davis helped me write that—that was when I went, "Got it." That's when I really made my own mark there.

Howard: It was one of the funniest things, and you were always so fucking relaxed.

I had Robert Downey Jr. on yesterday, and I think the secret to him being such a great actor is that I've never seen a guy so relaxed on camera. You almost have to forget that you're in front of an audience. You've got to be completely loose, and yet you're nervous inside, right? You were nervous those first couple of times on *Saturday Night Live*, were you not? Were you intimidated at first? Because you walked into a weird situation. Chevy, for some reason, hated you.

Bill: No.

Howard: He didn't hate you?

Bill: He was really the breakout star, and he was spectacular. He really took the focus that first year. He was amazing. When he left, I think the original people felt like he had left them in the lurch. Like, "How could you do that? We're in this together." So there was that. And I was the avenging angel as the new guy too. But Chevy and I, we are fine. We have been fine a long time.✦

Howard: Did you have fun with him on *Caddyshack*?

Bill: There were some of the funniest people on the planet in that place at the time. Ted Knight was a really funny person.

Howard: Is it true that Ted Knight was fucking disgusted by you and Chevy because you guys clowned around and ad-libbed so much?

✦ **For more on this from Chevy Chase, turn to page 533.**

Bill: I don't know that to be a fact. I mean, that's after the fact you hear that sort of stuff. I like Ted. I got on great with Ted. Ted is a square.

Howard: He is the same in real life as he is on camera.

Bill: He really is that guy, but he's also really funny. Everyone worked differently. I mean, Ted was used to having his lines and his mark on *The Mary Tyler Moore Show*. There was Rodney [Dangerfield], who was a total madman. There was Chevy, who was his own kind of thing. Then there was myself, and there was Henry Wilcoxon. He was the guy who played the bishop. He was the biggest actor in the world in 1935. He came to America to star as Mark Antony in Cecil B. DeMille's *Cleopatra*.

Howard: Is it true that in *Caddyshack* you ad-libbed almost the entire movie? Everything we're watching there is you just sort of coming up with it off the top of your head?

Bill: There's one sketch that Brian wrote for someone else, which is the Dalai Lama thing. It didn't quite work, and he said, "Billy, would you try this?" So I did, and I added something to it.

Howard: Do you prefer a movie to a live situation like *Saturday Night Live*? Do you like that feedback of a live audience sitting there laughing and you know you're killing it?

Bill: It's apples and oranges. What it's really better than is taped television, because live television goes on at eleven-thirty at night and is over at one and you are done. Taped television, you start shooting and you shoot all night and then need to reshoot and there's no limit. And there's a live audience that has seen you do the same sketches, the same scenes sixteen times. And they're forced to stay there. They don't let them leave. It's like—I don't want to use the wrong term, but it's sort of like a holding pen for Guantánamo prisoners.

Howard: Were you one of those guys that wrote a lot of the sketches on *Saturday Night Live*, or did you depend on the writers?

Bill: I didn't write a lot of sketches. I wrote a couple. Lorne talked me out of being a writer, which I regret. I'd be rich too if I'd stayed a writer. Because the writers get paid forever. But I've got to live a life. If I had to write, I would have had no free time to live. As an actor, you could come in and rewrite and no one cares if you make it better. And because we were trained as improvisers, we were able to rewrite it on the fly, and writers would work with you.

Howard: Do you like Lorne Michaels? You've never done a movie for him, right? Once you left *Saturday Night Live*, your association with Lorne had ended.

Bill: I did one that Tommy Schiller wrote called *Nothing Lasts Forever*. That was Lorne's.

Howard: So you're still friends with him?

Bill: Yes, and I enjoy seeing him. He represents so much to so many different people.

Howard: I'm amazed he can keep finding so many great talents. But nothing resonated like that original crew that you were part of, right? It's never really been the same, has it?

Bill: Well, there's been extraordinary talent, let's get real. I don't want to start listing names because there's too many that I would forget. Let's just go, like, between Eddie Murphy and Carvey and Mike Myers and Will Ferrell and so forth.

Howard: Bill Hader—we had him yesterday.

Bill: I think Bill Hader probably did the best work anyone ever did on that show.

Howard: I said to him yesterday, "You're probably like in the top five or ten." I put him up there with you and Aykroyd.

Bill: It took them a little while to get going, but I think when he got rolling it was extraordinary. That group that he was in, with Kristen Wiig . . . I thought that group really had what that first group had, which was they had writing ability and they were more actors than stand-up comedians. The stand-up comedians all did what they did, and they became famous, and they're funny. But the actors seem to be able to make the material work on air, because the material is always being refined and rewritten. It's only written for a week. It could be done on Wednesday, and you've got to do it on Saturday. It's not like a film or a play, where you can rewrite it and rehearse it for weeks or months. You've got to just keep moving on it. Those actors in that group with Kristen and Bill, they

made stuff work that the other casts maybe didn't.

Howard: Talk about the first *Ghostbusters*. You love that movie. You're proud of that movie. It was a sensation. It was great.

Bill: It's great.

Howard: But that movie would not have been yours if Belushi didn't die. He was the original choice for that role, right? Did that bother you that they originally wanted to go with Belushi, or you just said, "Hey, it's a break."

Bill: It bothered me more that John died.

Howard: Right. It was tough. And yet you were getting something great out of it.

Bill: I don't think about that aspect of it much. The sad part is that John died. He was really an extraordinary human being. He was wonderful. He was more fun than a barrel of monkeys. He was really fun.

Howard: Off camera, you had a good time with him?

Bill: Oh God, he could make fun out of nothing. He didn't have to be drinking or on drugs or anything. He was still the best actor I've ever seen on a stage. He was extraordinary on the stage.

Howard: Was the partying legendary? In the sense that, you get off *Saturday Night Live* and then the real fun begins. Or were you one of those guys to say, "Fuck that. I'm going to go home. I've got to get my sleep. I'm an entertainer. I'm not going to partake in any of this."

Bill: I'm somewhere in the middle there.

Howard: Are you?

Bill: When you do that show, you're so jazzed. It's one o'clock in the morning and you've got sixty thousand volts' worth of adrenaline rolling through.

Howard: Are you still in touch with Dan Aykroyd? You guys are good buddies?

Bill: We are buddies for life. We have been through everything.

Howard: I love him. I always thought he's one of those guys you want on your team, if comedy was like a football team. You want that guy in a sketch because he could become any character.

Bill: He appreciated everyone's ability. He was very generous to me. We met when we were both, like, twenty.

Howard: I still think one of the greatest movies you did was *Groundhog Day*. I don't know if you enjoyed doing that, but I think it's one of the greatest.

Bill: It was a hard movie to make. But the script was an extraordinary thing. It was amazing.

Howard: When you say it was hard, is that because you were actually doing the same scene over and over again?

Bill: That's an acting challenge. Being put in a box, we call that. Like, "Put me in a box and I'll make it work." You make it really difficult for me and I will make it work, because that's where you have to be really creative.

Howard: Were you worried when you saw the script that it was going to be a shitty movie?

Bill: No.

Howard: You knew right away. You get a script, you can tell?

Bill: Yes.

Howard: One of the most amazing stories I've heard about you is the cartoon movie *Garfield*, where you do a voice. You read the script and you saw that it was a movie by Joel Coen, who is a great director. You wanted to work with him. You said, "I want to be in a Coen film. I'll do it." It turned out it was a different Joel Cohen.

Bill: Yes, there's two Joels. Some people spell it with an *h* and some people don't.

Howard: Literally, you showed up on set and had no idea you were doing *Garfield* the cartoon.

Bill: I show up in a recording studio like this, and started doing it, and it wasn't—I had to do a lot of work.

Howard: Was that hard for you? Did you say actually, "I got to get out of this thing. I thought it was with the Coen brothers."

Bill: Well, you put me in a box, I'll figure out how to make it work. They'd already shot the film. I was just this great mass of material in the corner of the scenes. So I had to figure out how to rewrite this thing so that would make sense, given what the scenes were. The humans were already in the scenes. I had to make up lines that went with what they did. I soaked through, like, four T-shirts a day working on this thing.

Howard: You must have liked it, because you agreed to do it a second time, right?

Bill: The first one made a couple hundred million bucks. Like maybe three hundred or four hundred. It was huge in South America, don't ask me why. I said, "Just don't ever do that again where you shoot the movie first." I'll be damned if they didn't do it again. I said, "What were you thinking?"

Howard: Roger Ebert gave *Garfield* a good review—your performance in particular. What do you think about reviewers? Did you know Roger?

Bill: Let's talk about Roger. Roger was something unusual, in that every reviewer claims to love movies—

Howard: He loved them.

Bill: He really did love movies. And he killed me early on. He knew I was a Chicago guy. He cut me absolutely no slack.

Howard: What did he say about you?

Bill: I got him at the Cannes Film Festival later. It took a long time, but I got him. He'd seen *Broken Flowers*, which was a movie that Jim Jarmusch was directing, which to me is like the best thing I ever did really. He said something in the midst of this giant press conference at Cannes. He said something really nice. I said, "Well, that's something coming out of you, pal. Because I was told when I was young that I should never be allowed to do anything but comedy." He bit and said, "Who said that?" I said, "You did, Roger, in the *Chicago Sun-Times*." He just went, "I was wrong."

Howard: Isn't there a lesson in that?

Bill: He was a good guy.

Howard: Here is the one that I'm most curious about: Tom Hanks's role in *Forrest Gump* was originally offered to you?

Bill: I did have a couple *Forrest Gump* conversations.

Howard: Didn't interest you?

Bill: No.

Howard: Do you think that was a mistake?

Bill: I've never seen *Forrest Gump*.

Howard: Get the hell out of here. Really? After you turn something down, I would think you'd be like, "Hey, let me see if I would like it." Just out of curiosity.

Bill: No, it's sort of the opposite. If I turn it down, I turn it down.

Howard: What a life you've had. Are you having fun? I don't mean now. Obviously, not now. This is torture. I get it.

Bill: This right here is rollicking.

Howard: But are you—I can't tell with you. Are you a happy man?

Bill: Right now, I'm kind of pleased.

Howard: Has the bane of your existence been relationships with women? Not that you didn't enjoy them. But for some reason marriage is just a fucking pain in the ass? Is there something that you question in your own life, like, "Why haven't I found that great love of my life?" Do you ever reflect on that?

Bill: Well, I think about that. I do think about that. I have kids who have children.

I enjoy that very much, and that wouldn't happen without women.

Howard: Are you lonely?

Bill: I don't think I'm lonely. It's nice to have someone to go to some of these things where you need a date, to have someone to bring along, but—

Howard: You went solo to Clooney's wedding?

Bill: Right. But, like, to go play golf in Scotland. That would have been fun to say, "We're going to walk around the most famous golf course in the world." That kind of thing. But there's a lot that I'm not doing that I need to do.

Howard: What?

Bill: Like working on yourself for self-development, or just becoming more of a person. Not more of a person, but more myself.

Howard: More connected to people.

Bill: More connected to myself. I don't have a problem connecting with people.

Howard: Are you impossible to live with?

Bill: I don't think so.

Howard: So where is the great love? You certainly can get women. You're very desirable, in my book. I would have random sex with you. But I'm saying—

Bill: I don't know. Maybe someday. But I have to do this other thing, and if I'm not really committing myself really well to that, it's better that I don't have another person. It's not to diminish the

relationship with a woman. I just can't take another relationship when I'm not taking care of the things I really need to take care of most.

Howard: Why are you not taking care of that?

Bill: What stops us from looking at ourselves and seeing ourselves is that we're kind of ugly if we look really hard. We're not who we think we are. We're not as wonderful.

Howard: I think you hit it on the head. I think the hardest thing in the world to do for anybody is to confront who you are and to sit there and work on it. Most of us want to run away from that. That's the way it is. Even if a lot of good stuff would come out of it. It's just too goddamn painful.

Bill: It's very subtle. It's kind of a human dilemma. It's original sin or something. It makes it very difficult to look at yourself.

Howard: Do any of these young guys on *Saturday Night Live* ever call you up and say, "Bill, I need your advice"?

Bill: Well, they don't have my phone number.

Harvey Weinstein

JANUARY 15, 2014

I went back and forth about whether or not I should include this interview. I really struggled with it, right up until the very last draft. I lost a lot of sleep over it. I would wake up in the middle of the night and lay in bed thinking about Harvey Weinstein—which, let me tell you, is a far cry from my usual midnight masturbatory fantasies of stepmom porn. I wanted the book to generally be very positive, and when I reread this interview, a heavy feeling came over me. The common thread between these conversations is honesty. Each person lets their guard down and is completely candid, whether it's Conan O'Brien talking about depression, or Jon Stewart discussing his complicated relationship with his father, or Sia describing her bipolar II diagnosis. It takes guts to be so forthcoming, and I'm in awe of how brave these guests are to get so personal. I have so much respect for them, and I'm honored that they choose to place their trust in me. That's not something I take lightly. So I wrestled with putting Harvey in the book, as well as the Bill O'Reilly interview that comes later, because they didn't show the same honesty and introspection as everyone else, and I didn't want to reward them for that. I didn't want to give them any further attention or recognition. More than anything, though, my reluctance to include Harvey's interview was because I didn't want to cause any more pain to the women who came forward. I didn't want to offend or upset them. I took the interview out and put it back in a few times, but ultimately I decided to keep it in—Bill's too—because, as I mentioned earlier in the introduction, I think it is an important reflection of our times.

Not only did I question Harvey about the highs of his career—his incredible films and the coveted place he held in show business—but I delved into the casting couch. We discussed sex and the power of the producer, and Harvey gave all of the appropriate answers. Like a good Boy Scout earning a merit badge, he said all the right things, and clearly understood the destructive nature of abusing that power and the devastation that would occur if he were out of control. Reliving the conversation only makes me angrier. When I asked him if he ever took advantage of his position, he laughed it off and told me, "It doesn't work that way . . . the movies are too expensive. The risks are too great. It doesn't happen that way." He treated my question as if it was ridiculous, not even in the realm of possibility for anything inappropriate to happen.

When I think about this, it all seems so tragic and sad. It reads like a story Harvey would make into a movie. A lonely boy who loved to read, made brilliant movies and careful choices, against all odds was embraced by the cool kids, threw the best Golden Globes after-party but, ultimately, tragically destroyed his life—and the lives of others, as we are learning. How could someone so brilliant not see what he was doing? In the end, I'm just pissed off for the women who were hurt.

Howard: What would you call your job? Are you a movie mogul?

Harvey: No.

Howard: You are.

Harvey: What I am is a guy who makes movies. I like to be called a filmmaker, if you will.

Howard: The thing that amazes me about you is how you pick these movies. From the earliest part of your career, you walk into a room, people hand you scripts, they pitch you ideas. You must get this all day.

Harvey: Yup.

Howard: Some movies might seem obvious to us. "Oh yeah. Of course, Harvey. Put money into these." But there are certain movies that you have made in your career that I would have said, "Are you out of your fucking mind?" The one where he's the stuttering king. What the hell is the name of that—?

Harvey: *The King's Speech.*

Howard: Who would put money into this thing? You think, "Yeah, it'll be a little art film." The film grossed $414 million. Even you had to be shocked.

Harvey: You know, Howard, when I was a boy, I got my eye poked out. Born in Brooklyn, grew up in Queens.

Howard: Do you have one eye?

Harvey: I have a bad eye. And I couldn't go to school. There was a librarian next door. I was bored to death. There was no three hundred channels. And radio wasn't cool. You hadn't arrived on the scene yet. So I asked Frances Goldstein, the seventy-two-year-old librarian—I said, "Help me do something." And then, at twelve, I fell in love with books. I fell in love with literature. I started with H. G. Wells's *Outline of History* through *War and Peace.* I'd read two or three books a week.

Howard: Is that the key? You've got to love to read.

Harvey: The key is, the scripts are in the words. When I read *The King's Speech,* you could even tell in the script, Howard, how moving it was. The story of this friendship, the story of this guy overcoming something—it moved me emotionally. And I felt if it moved me emotionally then it would move audiences. So this whole mogul thing is complete bullshit.

Howard: How many scripts do you read a week?

Harvey: I read probably five or six, and the company probably reads a hundred.

Howard: Most guys at your level don't read the scripts that much anymore, right? They

> " I SAY, "I THINK THE SCRIPT IS GREAT, BUT ON PAGE SIXTY THE GUY WHO ROBIN WILLIAMS PLAYED AND THE OTHER PROFESSOR, THEY GIVE EACH OTHER A BLOW JOB. I DON'T UNDERSTAND THAT BLOW-JOB SCENE." AND MATT AND BEN SAID TO ME, "WE WROTE THAT FOR STUDIO EXECUTIVES. YOU WERE THE ONLY ONE WHO EVER POINTED IT OUT. . . . WE JUST WANTED TO SEE WHO THE FUCK READ THIS GODDAMN THING."

just kind of check out and hire people to read for them.

Harvey: I'll give you the best Hollywood story that I've never been able to say on the air, and I'll tell it to you first. This is what I do. I'm not the mogul. But this is what I do. Years and years ago, John Gordon, a producer who used to work for me, and Kevin Smith, the guy who created *Clerks*, say, "Yeah, we just read a script by these two young actors. It's fantastic. It's called *Good Will Hunting*. We want you to read it. They need a million dollars. They just got their script out of Warner Brothers and they need one million dollars, otherwise Warner Brothers is going to make the movie with DiCaprio and Brad Pitt, and it's going to be directed by Michael Mann." I read the script. I have a meeting with these guys. Kevin Smith and John Gordon are there. They say, "What do you think of the script?" I say, "I think the script is great, but on page sixty the guy who Robin Williams played and the other professor, they give each other a blow job. I don't understand that blow-job scene." And Matt and Ben said to me, "We wrote that for

studio executives. You were the only one who ever pointed it out. We had meetings with Warner, MGM, Paramount. We just wanted to see who the fuck read this goddamn thing."

Howard: That is an *amazing* story.

Harvey: And that is how *Good Will Hunting* got made.

Howard: The movie business is so scary. It's like gambling, really, when you think about it. You could have the best script in the world, the best movie, and then it just all screws up. And when it doesn't go right, it has to be heartbreaking.

Harvey: It's human nature, unfortunately, that you have to deal with. You have a beautiful script, and if the director's drunk or, you know . . .

Howard: Here's what I think is brilliant. The movie *The Artist*. $15 million to make. I wouldn't have put a dime into this thing. If you told me, "Howard, I'm gonna give you a gift. If you put a million dollars into *The Artist*, I'm gonna give you part of the gross." I would have said to ya, "Fuck you. You're insane." It grosses $133 million. On paper, you think, "Well, it doesn't have a superhero. What am I gonna do with this movie?"

Harvey: Howard, I call my company. I go, "Guys, I wanna do a movie." They go, "Great." This is after *The King's Speech* wins an Oscar. "But I've got a few things I want to talk to you about. Black and white." And the guys go, "Black and white? You just won the Oscar. That's fine." I say, "It's gonna have French guys in the movie, but the subtitles will be in English." They go, "Okay, it's a foreign-language film. We've done that before with you." I say, "There's one other little caveat: it's silent." They go, "You're doing a silent movie?" They literally bring me to the board of directors, and the big thing for me—I'm so used to autonomy, Howard, I didn't even know we *had* a board of directors.

Howard: Like, who are these guys? Who is this board of directors?

Harvey: I mean, Goldman Sachs is on the board.

Howard: These are the guys who put up the money.

Harvey: [Advertising group] WPP. They're part of the financial structure of the company. We put in money, they put in money. And these guys are going, "You're sure? Black and white? Silent movie?"

Howard: People still challenge you, though?

Harvey: They challenged me on that one. And they're right to challenge me. But I just had an instinct.

Howard: Have you ever been stopped from doing a movie by your board of directors and regretted it?

Harvey: I developed a project called *Lord of the Rings*. Maybe you heard of it.

Howard: Now, this is an amazing story to me, the *Lord of the Rings* story.

Harvey: When I was in college, I had hair. I remember my hair. And I sat around and smoked cigarettes. Everybody was into *The Lord of the Rings*. And I loved it. It was action, heroic. You know, the subtext was World War II, and how do we deal with evil. So when the opportunity came to me to do this—'cause I had done Peter Jackson's *Heavenly Creatures* with Kate Winslet. First time she made a movie. First time Peter got nominated. So Universal and I were going to combine on *Lord of the Rings*. They said, "This is a daunting project." They drop out. Now it's just me.

Howard: Daunting because financially it's a lot. How much does it cost to make?

Harvey: At the time, it was going to cost $180 million to do the three. But more importantly, to develop the technique, the thing that you see, the thousands of armies, the amazing special effects, I had to write a check for $10 million to develop a company called Weta. And then we wrote the three scripts. I loved the scripts. And then we were able to show Disney what it looked like: ten thousand individual soldiers fighting. The battle scene was great.

Howard: Clear something up for me. You sell your film company, Miramax, to Disney.

You make a lot of dough on that. It seems like the right decision to make, but you were in the middle of trying to get *Lord of the Rings* done. Disney looks at *Lord of the Rings* and says, "Forget it. We don't want it."

Harvey: Michael Eisner in particular. I don't want to blame all of Disney. There were a lot of executives there who wanted to do it. But the boss of the studio said to me, famously, "I don't think anybody'll see this." And I go, "Michael, there are so many students and people around the world who've read these incredible books. And these three scripts are great." He goes, "I don't believe that. And these hobbits and elves and dwarfs and, you know, whatever—"

Howard: It's make-believe. We don't believe in Spider-Man either. But he still said no. Let's not be so arrogant to say Michael Eisner didn't get it. A lot of people would have balked at the price tag. You've got balls of steel and you've got some special vision.

Harvey: So what I said to him was, "Look, we executive-produce the thing individually, and we can get 5 percent of the gross if we do this." And Michael said, "All right, I'll split it with you. Nobody's going to see it. Your gross is not going to be worth anything." Well, the three movies grossed $2.3 billion. I actually said to Michael, "I want it for my kids, for their college education. And now I'm just shopping for which university to buy." Is Harvard for sale?

Howard: Yes, everything's for sale.

Harvey: Okay, I'm going there today.

Howard: So Disney did participate?

Harvey: They got half of the gross.

Howard: How much did the three movies gross altogether?

Harvey: $2.3 billion in the theaters and another probably $2 billion in the ancillaries—$4 billion.

Howard: Do the math for me. Five percent of $4 billion. I could never figure that out.

Harvey: But then some goes back to the theaters. It's about $100 million, $125 million. So they probably got sixty and we got sixty. But I have to split with my brother. My mom likes that.

Howard: Sixty million dollars is a lot of money. But doesn't it sort of freak you out that you had to give away half of that to Disney? Because you really were the guy who was behind pushing this thing through. Does that keep you up at night?

Harvey: No.

Howard: It doesn't?

Harvey: No. It bothered me at the time. Now we have *The Hobbit*, and Warner Brothers is saying to us we have the first *Hobbit*. The other two don't count. "You only get one *Hobbit*." I go, "But you need three movies to tell the story of *The Hobbit*." They go, "No, it's only one movie." I go, "Well, why do you keep calling the other two *The Hobbit*?" Anyhow, welcome to Hollywood.

Howard: Those Golden Globes look like fun, Harvey. It must be great to be the king. Who was at your table?

Harvey: First of all, there was a magnum of champagne at my table. Does that happen at the Academy Awards? We had a few drinks—

Howard: That makes it fun, doesn't it?

Harvey: Yeah. So Meryl Streep was at my table, Julia Roberts was at the table, Taylor Swift was at the table. These were all nominees from our company. Idris Elba was at the table, and there were guests, husbands, you know. And then U2 was at the other table with Chris Martin, with my brother.

Howard: That's fun. Then you threw a party afterward, right?

Harvey: Mm-hmm.

Howard: And the list of people at the party, I read in the paper, was like something fucking crazy. Everyone's gotta go to your party.

Harvey: They don't *have* to go. What they understand about our parties is we don't compete. So in the room, I'm making a movie with Amy Adams next year. I'm not mad that she won. I'm doing something with Bradley Cooper. I'm happy that he's nominated.

Howard: Why is it important to throw these parties? Does it make it so everyone wants to do business with you?

Harvey: First of all, it's cathartic. No matter what anybody says, nobody's that cool. You do get into it. You do want to win. I mean, in those hours that you're there. And you want to let off steam at the end of it. So it's just a fun way of getting people together.

Howard: *Silver Linings Playbook* was your movie, wasn't it?

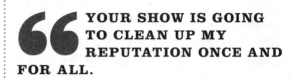

YOUR SHOW IS GOING TO CLEAN UP MY REPUTATION ONCE AND FOR ALL.

Harvey: Yeah.

Howard: What did that make, like $430-something million?

Harvey: It grossed $130 [million] in the US and about another $120 million—a quarter of a billion dollars. It was a $20 million movie.

Howard: Be honest with me: did you expect that movie to break that big?

Harvey: Again, I never expect anything to do anything. But I will tell you that David O. Russell is one of our premier directors. I mean, he will go down in history as great as great can be. He writes beautifully, and he directs even better.

Howard: So when he came to you with that, you were just like, "Okay, I read it. Boom, I'm giving you the money to make the movie."

Harvey: See, Howard, here's the difference. Your show is going to clean up my reputation once and for all. *Silver Linings*, a young woman in my office came to me when I first started the Weinstein Company—this is how long it takes to get your own production slate. Previous to that, I was doing old movies and Miramax things that I developed. She came to me and said, "Read this book. It's called *Silver Linings Playbook*." I said, "Is it a best-seller?" She said, "No, it's just great." I read the book. I bought the rights to the book.

Howard: How much did you pay?

Harvey: Fifty grand, against an option for another hundred or two hundred thousand if it gets made. And I hired David O. Russell to write the screenplay. I said, "David, here's a book. Read it. If you'd like to write this screenplay, I'd love you to write it, and then you can go on to direct it."

Howard: Wow. So really his project in every single way.

Harvey: It's his project, except we found the book. And so this is the thing that people go, "Oh, he's a mogul." The image of a mogul I have is a guy who smokes cigars, not a guy who reads three books a week and ten or twelve scripts.

Howard: At the end of the day, you're a guy who loves to read, and when you see a good story, you know it.

Harvey: Yeah, that's it. That's what I do.

Howard: But what about the accoutrements? I mean, your wife is gorgeous.

Harvey: Thank you.

Howard: By the way, how old are you now? Sixty-one?

Harvey: Yeah.

Howard: You got a one-year-old?

Harvey: I have an eight-month-old.

Howard: That couldn't have been your idea.

Harvey: [*laughs*]

Howard: The fuck is that? Are you home at all with this kid? I mean, good Lord.

Harvey: Of course.

Howard: Are you? No you're not.

Harvey: [*laughs*] Yes I am, Howard. By the way, that kid travels everywhere with us. Everywhere.

Howard: Why not stay single? I gotta figure every starlet in Hollywood wanted to at least blow you, you know what I'm saying?

Harvey: [*chuckles*]

Howard: Did you ever get to experience the . . . I'm gonna say the mogul aspect? Do a little coke, hang out with, you know, I don't know, Julia Roberts. Give you a hand job. Something. You never got any of that?

Harvey: Howard, as you know only too well, it doesn't work that way.

Howard: It doesn't really?

Harvey: No. I'll tell you who it works that way for. It works that way for the actors. You know producers are—

Howard: No, come on. Every girl knows that if she's a competent actress and she could get on your good side, you could make her a star over-fucking-night. Don't fucking tell me it doesn't work that way.✦

Harvey: Howard, I wish. The movies are too expensive. The risks are too great. It doesn't happen that way.

Howard: You can't walk into the room,

✦ **For more on this from Gwyneth Paltrow, turn to page 535.**

pull your pants off, and say, "Okay, honey, let's talk. . . ."

Harvey: John Frankenheimer, the great director, told us stories about his day in the movies. We were born way too late.

Howard: I've read about the great moguls, the Louis B. Mayers. They got blow jobs.

Harvey: [*laughs*] I assume. But these guys, this round, nothing.

Howard: Really?

Harvey: Really. I hate to disappoint you.

Robin: It's not even fun anymore.

Howard: I know a few famous directors. I've asked them the same question.

Harvey: Directors are different because directors can make the decisions on the casting.

Howard: I'll tell you, though, I know a couple of famous directors. I'm not going to embarrass them by telling, because I've talked to them off the air. They tell me they never really got laid that much.

Harvey: It's really nothing. Nope.

Howard: Well, maybe that's an honorable thing too. Because, really, to abuse your power—

Robin: Yeah, shouldn't women be able to get into the movie business without all that?

Howard: Hell, no.

Harvey: Of course. Not only that, but you have women like Meryl Streep and Julia Roberts who are deeply committed to excellent causes. And Charlize Theron—

Howard: She's a great beauty, Charlize Theron.

> **" HOWARD, I WISH. THE MOVIES ARE TOO EXPENSIVE. THE RISKS ARE TOO GREAT. IT DOESN'T HAPPEN THAT WAY.**

Harvey: Not only are they great beauties, but they're so bloody intelligent and brilliant. You sit down with a girl like that, you don't want to do stupid shit. You want to just talk to them and say, "Be in my movie, please." Because you know what they do? They enhance the material.

Howard: There are big fucking egos on these films. It's got to be kind of a weird thing. When you're partying with everybody at your big parties, you're trying to be loose. You're trying to be the fun guy, the guy everyone wants to do business with. But then when you're actually doing business with people, you've got to come off like a fucking executive who means business. It's almost like parenting, being in your role. Like, you've got to walk in and show everybody: enough with the bullshit.

Harvey: How come it doesn't work that way with my kids?

Howard: I know. Well, that's a whole different story.

Harvey: I mean, I have four daughters. I say, "Girls, let me tell ya. I'm Dad. This is how it is. This is what we're going to do." And they say, "Dad, please stop. You're annoying. Whatever. We've got more important things to do." They're all texting, you know, etcetera.

Howard: I can be so effective at work and so in control, and then when I'm around my kids I'm like, "I don't know what to do, because nobody's listening. Nobody cares."

Harvey: My kids say, "Dad, come on, you don't know what's going on. You don't know the music. You don't know this, you don't know that. Here are the books you should be doing. Here's the film you should be making." And when I get to the office and someone says, "Can I get you a coffee? Can I get you a water?" And I say, "Thank you, dear God." People asked me how I mellowed out: I have four daughters, one son. Those four daughters, I mean . . .

Howard: Do they want to be in the business?

Harvey: No. I mean, they all know the business.

Howard: Your wife, what a powerhouse. She's talented. She has the clothing line. And boy oh boy, sex with her must be through the roof.

Harvey: [*laughs*]

Howard: I see her as very sexual. Some women, you see them, you don't get too charged up. Do you worry about her running around behind your back at all?

Harvey: No.

Howard: How do you know?

Harvey: She's a great woman.

Howard: You know that she loves you and you love her.

Harvey: Yes, yes. It's the same thing you have with Beth.

Howard: It's a solid marriage.

Harvey: It's a solid marriage.

Howard: You're very happy.

Harvey: I love her. She's great.

Howard: And you don't dream about strange pussy or anything?

Harvey: [*laughs*] I dream about *Lord of the Rings*.

And Now a Word
from Our President . . .

FEBRUARY 5, 1997

(19 years, 9 months, and 3 days until the election)

Howard: You whipped [Miss Universe Alicia Machado] into shape. I don't know how you did it. I see all these diet plans. God bless you. Congratulations.

Donald: Well, that was an amazing one, Howard.

Howard: How did you do it?

Donald: She went from 118 to almost 170.

Howard: And you got her back to 118, didn't you?

Donald: Well, she's almost there. Probably 145 or something. [*laughs*]

Howard: Whoa. What did you do? How did you do it?

Robin: Did you make her walk from Venezuela?

Donald: Well, you know, it was an amazing phenomenon. She weighed 118 when she won. She was as beautiful a woman as I've ever seen. She gained 55 pounds in about nine months. She was an eating machine.

Howard: What did the girl eat?! To gain 55 pounds in less than a year!

Donald: I think she ate a lot of everything. Well, there was a lot of pressure to terminate her crown.

Howard: You were smart. You turned it into an event.

Donald: It has become a major event.

Robin: Everyone wants to see what she looks like on pageant night.

SHE WAS AN EATING MACHINE.

Rosie O'Donnell

NOVEMBER 6, 2017

One summer afternoon not long ago, I was sitting in my living room talking to my good friend Rosie O'Donnell, who had come to stay with Beth and me for the weekend. Yes, you heard me right: my good friend. Me putting those three words in front of Rosie's name would have been inconceivable back in the nineties, when I was constantly attacking her and saw her as my archenemy. Had you told me then that one day I'd not only make peace with her but consider her one of my closest confidants, I'd have said you were crazy, but that's exactly what happened—and it's all thanks to Rosie's kindness.

I was awful to her for no good reason. I was just at a time in my life where I was angry at and jealous of anyone who was having success. I'm reminded of that John Lennon song "Jealous Guy": "I didn't want to hurt you/I'm just a jealous guy." I lashed out at anyone and everyone whose career was prospering, because in some magical way, I thought I should be the center of the universe, and whenever it seemed like someone else was, I couldn't accept it. This was a case of sibling rivalry, as if the whole entertainment business was my evil, annoying brother stealing the spotlight. The only one who should have been flourishing was me. I wasn't willing to share the audience with anyone else. I wanted all of the marbles for myself.

That's a very hard way to live. You walk around in a constant state of anger, and that anger was directed at Rosie and about ten million other people too. It was my mission in life to ridicule and knock them all down. Rosie had done nothing wrong. She simply had a different broadcast style than my own, offered a different kind of entertainment. She wasn't out to swallow the entire world like I was, and for that I had put her on trial and convicted her in my stupid kangaroo court.

After I spent some time in therapy, I realized how childish this attitude was and how my sense of entitlement, and my inability to say no to myself, was the root of so many of my problems. As I started to think less about myself and more about others, I began to appreciate Rosie, especially when she announced she was gay. That really struck a chord with me. I had an older cousin, Stacy, who came out in the 1950s, when he was thirteen. This was in a tough neighborhood in Brooklyn, but my family was very accepting. My mother would set him up on dates, and even as a little kid I appreciated how courageous Stacy was. The same went for Rosie. I couldn't imagine how much guts it took for her to come out, especially considering the potential risk to her career, yet she did it.

That wasn't the only thing to admire about Rosie. As we discuss in this interview, she walked away from her own talk show—probably the biggest television show on the air at the time. She said no to more fame, more money, more of everything. Before therapy, I would have thought this was a ridiculous move. Give up a hit show—are you kidding? But therapy helped me see this wasn't silly, it was strong. It was Rosie being a badass, choosing to follow her own instincts and heart. She didn't suffer from the insatiable hunger that I did, and rather than hate her and ridicule her for it like I would have prior to therapy, I respected her decision and started talking on the air about how amazing I thought she was.

I can't remember which one of us was the first to reach out, but we began having a dialogue, and it was easy right from the start. There was no awkwardness. Rosie is so smart and mature that she recognized my issues for what they were. She didn't take it personally. She quickly became one of the most positive influences in my life. Probably the best example of how supportive Rosie has been to me is the way she encouraged me to pursue painting—one of several passions I developed as a result of therapy, which motivated me to engage with the world in ways I never had before.

Therapy made me realize how most of my life revolved around radio. It consumed me, placed me in a self-imposed quarantine. I didn't interact with many people outside of those I saw at work. So I decided to rediscover chess, which I had played as a child in Roosevelt, Long Island. Back then, the game helped me cope with the isolation I felt after all my friends and their families had left town as part of the white flight that was happening all across America in the 1960s. My parents refused to partake in this. In the same way they embraced my cousin Stacy's sexuality, they were adamant about not succumbing to racism. They put their money where their mouths were. While staying in Roosevelt taught me important lessons about tolerance and living by your convictions, it also left me with few friends, and so I spent much of my time outside of school in my bedroom moving pieces across a board against imaginary opponents and reading Bobby Fischer's regular column in *Boys' Life* magazine.

As an adult I hadn't played in probably thirty years, and so I began receiving lessons from a brilliant guy named Dan Heisman, who lived in Philadelphia and would instruct me over the computer. I got better and better, and eventually I reached a rating of 1800, which is fairly good for a guy who didn't really start until late in life. (To give you an idea of what that means, at his peak Fischer's rating hovered around 2800.) But then I would go play games in person at the legendary Marshall Chess Club in Greenwich Village, and I would get annihilated. Even twelve-year-olds were kicking my ass. I couldn't stop obsessing over what I did wrong. I would take a walk with Beth, and she'd say, "You're not paying attention to me. You're playing that game over and over in your head." She was right. Rather than enjoy the moment with her, I'd be thinking, "I can't believe I made such a dumb move. How did I lose?" I saw chess as the ultimate standard for intelligence, and when I got outplayed I felt diminished and stupid. This was not a game but a statement about my self-worth. I stuck with chess for three years, but finally I had to give it up because I went insane. Eventually my compulsion to be the greatest crept in and strangled the fun out of it.

So my passion shifted to photography. Once again, I studied with a veteran practitioner, an excellent photographer named Doug Gordon. I spent hours poring over books on lighting, learned Photoshop, invested thousands of dollars in equipment. I got good enough that I shot Beth for several magazine covers. Then suddenly after three years, it dawned on me: "Any idiot with an iPhone can take a beautiful picture." Just like with chess, I couldn't be leisurely about photography. I had to be the absolute best. Eventually my perfectionism crept in and strangled the fun out of it.

I gave up photography and decided to pursue painting. I had no idea where to start. I couldn't draw a straight line. And here's where Rosie came in: I knew she was into crafts, so I asked her if she had any advice. I was hoping for a tip or two, and I knew she was busy so I didn't expect to hear from her anytime soon. Right away she sent me a long, exhaustive email showing me all the materials and equipment I would need and where to find it—with links and everything. It was an amazing outpouring of information. She went above and beyond, and her generosity and encouragement meant everything me. It touches me so much when someone extends themselves like that, because I'm not used to that kind of love. I'm just not.

Once again, I bought all the supplies, read a small library's worth of books, studied under several fantastic teachers, including an exceptional watercolorist named Rick Brosen. It's been four years since I started doing watercolors, and I'm still painting like crazy. I'd be lying if I said those old demons don't creep in. I'll think, "Why can't I be as good as Caspar Friedrich or Eugène Boudin?" Never mind the fact that those guys didn't have to spend hours every day putting together a radio show. I have such high standards. I talk about it constantly with my therapist. I know I can't be great at everything, but damn if I don't try.

One thing I realized after reviewing this interview with Rosie is that it isn't necessarily chess or photography or painting that interests me; it's learning, being taught, getting that kind of devoted one-on-one attention. Rosie was a child when her mother died, and she describes here how she would break bones in her hands so that she could go to the doctor and get the kind of affection and doting from nurses that she was missing at home. While I didn't lose a parent, I still felt such tremendous loneliness growing up, and I suppose having a teacher gives me the attention I've always desired. I don't know if Rosie realized it when she sent me those e-mails about art, but that day she took on the role of a teacher, which has become so important to me.

It is that kind of honesty and wisdom I value so much in my friendship with Rosie. If the situation had been reversed all those years ago, and she had been the one trashing me, I don't know if I could have been as forgiving. When we were sitting in my living room that summer weekend, I remember thinking, "How stupid am I? How could I have missed out in my life on someone so special because of some dumb posturing on the radio?" I'm so grateful for her graciousness.

Howard: Rosie O'Donnell is here. She's in a [Showtime] project called *SMILF*.

Rosie: Turn on my mic, Howard.

Howard: So unprofessional. You look great, by the way.

Rosie: Thank you so much.

Howard: People don't realize, you were like the most popular girl in high school. Weren't you like prom queen or something?

Rosie: And homecoming queen. And senior class president.

Howard: You were the kid who lit the world on fire.

Rosie: Well, you know, when you have a hard life at home . . . I really loved the attention from the adults. I wanted the teachers to love me, and they did. They were these public school teachers who took an interest in our family with no mom and a dad that was not really qualified. They really raised us. So I was very interested in doing well.

Howard: I think it is so phenomenal and worth reminding people that at, like, sixteen you go and try stand-up comedy. All your friends from school and teachers are there, so you killed the first night.

Rosie: I was so good, Howard.

Howard: You were so good. And then the next time you went up, none of them were there and you tanked.

Rosie: Tanked beyond words. Like the worst of my career. Dead silence.

Howard: Then you said, "Oh I have an idea. I'll take Jerry Seinfeld's material and I'll perform that."

Rosie: It wasn't even that thought-through. The guy who owned the club, Richie Minervini, goes, "Don't worry that you bombed. Come back tomorrow." I'm like watching Merv Griffin, and there's Seinfeld, and I'm like, "All right, I'll just do that." I think that a joke is a joke, right? Streisand doesn't write any songs. Bette Midler doesn't write any songs. Why do I have to write a joke?

Howard: Right, why can't Jerry Seinfeld be my writer?

Rosie: Exactly. He was pretty good.

Howard: And then the other comedians were like, "Hey wait a second, you're stealing Jerry Seinfeld's act."

Rosie: I said, "Yeah, he was on *Merv Griffin* yesterday."

Howard: You weren't hiding anything.

Rosie: No, it wasn't a big secret.

Howard: In a sense, you're like an actress. You said, "Tonight, I will be doing Jerry Seinfeld's material and my interpretation of it."

Rosie: Yeah, exactly. "This is a scene from *Hello, Dolly!*" I didn't really get it. And so then I was so depressed. I thought, "Well, how the hell am I going to write material?" That same guy Richie Minervini, who owned the East Side Comedy Club in Huntington, he said to me, "Why don't you be the emcee? So you can go on every night and you just get used to talking to the crowd and used to doing it." I was doing that and Shirley Hemphill from *What's Happening!!* was the headliner that weekend. She was there a day early. She came to the club and she said to [Richie], "You're going to book her. She's opening for me." And he's like, "She's new. She's sixteen. She can't." Shirley said to him, "Little one is going on or the big one is not."

Howard: Wow, she loved your act, and you didn't even have an act.

Rosie: I didn't have an act. My act was Ms. Pac-Man. That was my act. [*makes Ms. Pac-Man sound*]

Howard: That was the act?

Rosie: Pretty much.

Howard: You did a Pac-Man routine.

Rosie: Well, when you're sixteen, you take from your own life.

Howard: Unbelievable. When you started to act, I think for three summers in a row you were in the three biggest movies of that year. I'm talking about *A League of Their Own*, *Sleepless in Seattle*, and then the *Flintstones* movie. Three in a row.

Rosie: I know, right? Crazy.

Howard: I just figured you'd work full-time as an actress.

Rosie: I wanted to. And then I had the baby—Parker—who is now twenty-two.

Howard: That was the reason you went to the talk-show business? Because you wanted to stay home?

Rosie: I wanted him to grow up with his cousins. I wanted him to be in his own bed. And I hadn't had a nanny until I did the movie *Harriet the Spy*.

Howard: Do these kids realize what you sacrificed for them?

Rosie: They do not, and I'm still pissed off about it, Howard.

Howard: Was your agent at the time really pissed off that you were not going to continue with movies, and do a talk show? Because talk shows are really tricky.

Rosie: At the time they said that they didn't think it was a good idea. But I knew three number-one movies in a row, three summers in a row—there wasn't a lot more places to go as the funny friend, right?

Howard: Man, did that thing take off or what?

Rosie: Yes, but it was also timing. It's like when you catch the wave, who else is on it? I was on ABC at a time when there were three channels, maybe five. There were not a lot of options. At that time, remember, somebody was killed [after appearing] on *Jenny Jones*, right before I went on. People were getting beat up every day. All of these horrible, negative shows every day. Here was a show with an entertainer who liked people and wanted all the guests to thrive and be good.

> **THREE NUMBER-ONE MOVIES IN A ROW, THREE SUMMERS IN A ROW— THERE WASN'T A LOT MORE PLACES TO GO AS THE FUNNY FRIEND, RIGHT?**

Howard: You're right, there wasn't much like that on the air.

Rosie: No controversy. If somebody said in the pre-interview with the producers, "I don't want to talk about my divorce. I don't want to talk about this," I would say, "Fine with me. I don't care what you want to talk about. Let's just have fun."

Howard: That was really a formula for success. In a way, I feel like what Ellen's doing now is a continuation of what you did, am I correct?

Rosie: Totally. It's the same exact producer. It's the same executive producer. It's the same staff. It's the same show. She doesn't owe that to me. I took from Merv Griffin. It's just a formula.

Howard: *SMILF* is "Moms I like to fuck" or something. What is it?

Rosie: Single mom I'd like to fuck. It's an acronym that the kids are talking about nowadays. I had not heard of it either. When I first heard it I was like, "Smurf? What is this?" Then I watched the short film that [series creator and star] Frankie Shaw did and it's—you would love her, Howard. Smart, sexy, funny.

Howard: What do you play?

> **I COULD NOT WORK. I COULDN'T STOP CRYING ON LIVE TV.... THE DOCTOR SAID, "YOU MUST GO ON MEDICATION."**

Rosie: I play her mother. She's mentally ill. She's, like, bipolar—untreated. Childhood trauma.

Howard: You love that shit, right?

Rosie: Are you kidding? This is mother's milk for me.

Robin: She can act this with her eyes closed.

Rosie: I know this role.

Howard: How do you prepare to be a mentally disturbed mom? What do you do?

Rosie: The first thing I did was I asked if we could shoot with no makeup for me. Self-care is one of the first things to go when you're suffering.

Howard: You don't care how you look.

Rosie: No, and it's been a challenge for me. Sometimes I go through Wikipedia images of me, and I go, "Wow, I was at an opening with my hair not even blow-dried and sweatpants?" I have major depressive disorder. Luckily, I'm medicated and—

Howard: What do you take?

Rosie: Effexor. It's a very hard one to get off of. I tried to get off it once, and I will never do it again.

Howard: What happened?

Rosie: Within a week and a half I was in the bed crying, couldn't get up.

Howard: You said, "Look, I've been on this stuff long enough. I want to get off this drug."

Rosie: I went on right after Columbine. The last week of April 1999. I could not work. I couldn't stop crying on live TV. I couldn't find the reason. The doctor said, "You must go on medication." I went on Prozac. I was on it for about four years, and then I had what's called the Prozac Poop, where it sort of stops working. They switch you. Since about 2003, I've been on Effexor. It's been really great for me. I know it's not for everyone, but for me, I knew I have to participate in my mental health.

Howard: Do you think your issues are a result of not having a mom—growing up, essentially, an orphan? Your father was not equipped to be a dad. Do you think that's where it's from? Or do you think it's a biological, chemical imbalance?

Rosie: I think it's both. Because there's a tremendous amount of people who suffer in the way that I do, in my father's family. I've met aunts who tried to kill themselves. One who did. Some who had ECT, Electric Convulsive Therapy, which Carrie Fisher had toward the end.

Howard: Like a shock therapy, right?

Rosie: If you're at a place where nothing else has worked, that's what they recommend. Thank God, I've never gotten to that place.

Howard: Was the impression of the doctor that while everyone was upset about Columbine, you were excessive? You were over the top and couldn't even recover from it because of your illness, right? In other words, yes, you were thinking about Columbine, but it's also you're thinking about your own children. It just puts you down so bad.

Rosie: I couldn't believe that I lived in a country where children were being shot in the high school. And then the constant viewing of that. It was bad after 9/11, but after Columbine, they showed over and over the bloody bodies jumping out the window. I couldn't get it out of my— I thought, "How can this be America? How can this be America?"

Howard: Did you become suicidal as a result? Have you ever been suicidal?

Rosie: I think I have suicidal ideation.

Howard: What does that mean?

Rosie: It means you think about it. You don't ever make the plan, necessarily, of how you're going to do it, but sometimes you think— there's a great lyric in *Hamilton*: "Sometimes it's easier to just swim down." When you feel like there's no chance you're going to get to the surface again. I've had that probably three times in my life, all as an adult.

Howard: All over big tragedies.

Rosie: Yes. All over world events. Columbine was the first one. 9/11 was the second one. Katrina was the third one. And Mr. Donald Trump has been the fourth one.

Howard: Yeah, talk to me about Trump. I haven't seen you on the show for a couple of years. A lot has happened since I last saw you, including the fact that there was a debate during the election. It was Hillary

Clinton, as we know, and Donald Trump. In the middle of that Megyn Kelly, if you remember—

Rosie: I remember.

Howard: Megyn Kelly asks a question and he really singles you out. "I don't make fun of women, just Rosie O'Donnell. She deserves it, and everyone hates her, and I'm the one who blah blah blah."

Rosie: Then the crowd laughs, and Megyn Kelly does not defend me. She says, "No, not only Rosie O'Donnell." As if there's anyone you could put in that equation who would deserve that kind of treatment.

Howard: Where were you during it?

Rosie: I was at opening night of *Hamilton*.

Howard: You're kidding.

Rosie: That was the opening night. When I walked out, there were a lot of press groups going, "What do you think?" I'm like, "This is the best musical I've ever seen in my life." They're like, "No, not about that."

Howard: At that point, I'm sure most Americans thought Trump didn't stand a chance of even winning.

Rosie: No. In fact, when he came down that escalator with all that paid crowd, I was laughing my ass off.

Howard: At what point did you start to get nervous about Trump's candidacy? Was it like by the time Jeb Bush gets out, and then Marco Rubio gets out, and he starts to narrow the field?

Rosie: When he got the nomination, I think that's when I was shocked. I went and met with the Hillary Clinton campaign and offered my services in any capacity. Because I knew what he was capable of. I also knew, from fighting him for a decade, how to fight him.

Howard: How did the fight start? What happened? You spoke about him on *The View*?

Rosie: Right. Because right before we went live, he did a press conference. Tara Conner [winner of the 2006 Miss USA pageant, then owned by Donald Trump] was down in the Village drinking, and she kissed a girl, and it was on the cover of the *Post*. He held a press conference where he announced that he had forgiven her. I was like, "This is like an orange Huggy Bear from *Starsky and Hutch*. He's like the pimp telling everybody, 'This girl misbehaved and you better watch it.'" I was saying how he's not the moral arbiter of twenty-year-old behavior. "Who does he think he is? He doesn't own this girl."

Howard: You were critical of him.

Rosie: Correct. Then I pulled up some facts, easily accessible on Wikipedia, and announced the truth. Which was that he'd been bankrupt four times, that his father gave him all his money, that he notoriously did not pay contractors, and that he's generally a sexual predator.

Howard: That set him off.

Rosie: Like you couldn't believe, Howard. He went on every show. Every show allowed him. He went on Matt Lauer and David Letterman.

Howard: Blasted you.

Rosie: Not only blasted me. Said, "She's a degenerate. I'm going to take her wife. She's a pig. She's horrible." Things that I thought the National Organization of Women would be like, "Hold it. Foul—that's a foul." Nobody did anything, really.

Howard: Now he could potentially be the president of the United States and be your number-one enemy. I'm sure there was a fear factor there for you.

Rosie: No, actually, there was none. That's the weird thing. Even before I went out that day on *The View* to talk about him—because we had a little morning meeting—Joy Behar said, "You're not really going to say that." I said, "Yes, yes." She goes, "Aren't you afraid?" I remember thinking, "Afraid of what?" I'm not going to be afraid of this schmucky guy.

Robin: He's a private citizen.

Rosie: A private citizen who's a phony. He's a phony. I wasn't afraid of him at all. I never even thought of it. Now people are saying, "Well, aren't you afraid because he's the President?" I'm like, "No." He doesn't have any kind of real power. Everybody with an IQ of over 100—he loves the IQs—can understand that he's an idiot.

Howard: On Twitter, when you had your heart attack, Trump did wish you well.

Rosie: I know. Which was crazy. "You must be trying to kill me, because I almost died of a heart attack reading you being nice to me."

Howard: I imagine you being in the

middle of this is a weird sort of fame that you're not looking for. You probably just want to extract yourself from the dialogue if you could.

Rosie: But I can't, because it's been over a decade at this point. I was target number one for him, and God knows there have been many—and many much worse than me that he's done it to. I do really feel like he is the clear and present danger to the world and to life itself.

Howard: Do you think that Trump is going to make it through his presidency?

Rosie: No way on God's green earth.

Howard: You think Bob Mueller—

Rosie: I don't think. I know it with every cell in my body. I know it.

Robin: But you don't know it for a fact.

Rosie: Robin, you might not know it, but I know it.

Howard: Rosie knows that. You would have sex with Bob Mueller, I believe.

Rosie: Listen, I would do whatever Bob Mueller needs. I would talk to his wife, make sure it was okay.

Howard: For the good of the country, if they said, "Listen, Bob Mueller is all backed up. Rosie, we need you."

Rosie: I would look at Bob and say, "I'm here to serve my country, as you are, sir. I'm sure there's somebody more attractive who could do it better, but if this is what you need, Bob, let me know."

Howard: Speaking of attractive . . . Since your heart attack—we haven't talked about this because you haven't been back in a

long time—you had the stomach stapling. What percentage of your stomach is out of commission?

Rosie: Yes, this is called the gastric sleeve, so probably they'd leave about a quarter of your stomach, the size of a banana.

Howard: You are now tiny.

Rosie: I'm fifty pounds less than I was.

Howard: I mean, this has got to be fantastic for you. Did you go out and shop? Did you get a new wardrobe when you lost the fifty? You don't give a shit about that stuff.

Rosie: No. And you know what else? I can't see the difference. I can in a photo. If I look at a photo, I go, "Oh, wow." But I can't look in the mirror and go, "Oh, I look different." I have that sort of body dysmorphia.

Robin: You can't appreciate it.

Rosie: I don't know. I can't see it almost.

Howard: I sense you got sad when you said that. Why? Because you can't see the beauty, or you can't see how attractive you are?

Rosie: I think it's just more of a disconnect. I think it's what your body does to protect you if you were a kid who was sexually abused, which I was.

Howard: Right.

Rosie: You disconnect from your body. You dissociate and you almost don't pay attention to it. You don't want to love it because it's kind of betrayed you in some way. I remember when I was very thin. My thinnest as an adult was probably like 160.

||||||||||||||||||||||||||||||||||||||||||||||||||||||||||||||||||||||||||||||||||||||||||||||||||||||||||||||||||||||||||||||||

" I SHOULD HAVE DIED. THE DOCTOR SAID, "THERE'S NO REASON YOU SURVIVED THIS HEART ATTACK. WE DON'T KNOW WHY YOU DID. WE DON'T KNOW HOW YOU DID. BUT YOU WILL NOT SURVIVE ANOTHER ONE."

||||||||||||||||||||||||||||||||||||||||||||||||||||||||||||||||||||||||||||||||||||||||||||||||||||||||||||||||||||||||||||||||

I was 160 at some point and I was going to work at the Improv in LA, and I stopped to get gas. And these two very handsome, nice guys in their twenties came out and helped me with the self-serve. On the way to the Improv, I stopped at Baskin Robbins. I didn't even notice it. I didn't even realize that's what I was doing. It was only in therapy six months later that I realized I felt scared by the attraction of these men, and I wanted to make my body something that would not get them out of the little area where they sell candy to help me.

Howard: Do you proselytize for this operation? Do you tell people who are overweight to get the operation, or did you have some negative effects from it?

Rosie: I had zero negative effects. I wish I had done it ten years before; however, it wasn't available ten years before. Now, listen, you only have this surgery when you're near death.

Howard: Which you were.

Rosie: I should have died. The doctor said, "There's no reason you survived this heart attack. We don't know why you did. We don't know how you did. But you will not survive another one."

Howard: You described when you were having the symptoms of a heart attack, you just looked it up online and you took some Bayer aspirin.

Rosie: Exactly. I thought it had to be worse. It hurt—my arms hurt—but you've seen people, mostly men, on TV get a heart attack, they grab their chest, they fall down, right? I thought to myself, "This can't be a heart attack." Because a heart attack would, like, knock me out. Yolanda King, Martin Luther King's daughter, had the same heart attack on her fiftieth birthday, which is when I had mine, and she was dead before she hit the floor. I'm very lucky. It's called the widow-maker. I had 100% blockage of my LAD. That's one of the three main arteries that carries most of the blood to all your body.

Howard: You tweeted the other day that we all knew about Kevin Spacey, meaning the Hollywood community. Did you really know about Kevin Spacey?

Rosie: Yes, because I'm a person in Broadway. He's been a Broadway guy for a long time, and he is notoriously handsy. Did I know he was trying to rape children? Of course I did not know that. I also didn't know that Harvey Weinstein was actually raping women.

Howard: Allegedly.

Rosie: Well, okay, allegedly. I knew that Harvey Weinstein was a guy who used the casting couch and was, like, a big bragger about everyone he took to bed. I knew that Harvey Weinstein was a horrible man when he called me a cunt to my face.

Howard: When was that?

Rosie: The first movie that Night Shyamalan—

Howard: M. Night Shyamalan?

Rosie: Right. The movie *Wide Awake* was his directorial debut. It was a Miramax film. I was in it with Dana Delany and Denis Leary. He finished the film, turned it in, and Harvey didn't like the cut. So Harvey recut his film. The kid was only twenty-six. He called me, crying, and said, "Could you go with me into the meeting?" I went with him to the meeting. He and I were in this meeting, and I said to Harvey, "You don't tell Picasso, 'More blue.' You're the guy who frames it and sells it. You're not the artist here." At that, he said, "You fucking cunt. You fucking talk-show-host wannabe piece of shit." I said, "Well, this will be our last conversation, sir."

Howard: Wow.

Rosie: So I knew he was a bully creep. But I never thought he was raping women. You know, being fifty-five, I grew up when the feminist movement was just beginning, and I really had this idea that we were going to continue to get power and equality. What Frankie Shaw—when I saw that she wrote,

> ## "I KNEW THAT HARVEY WEINSTEIN WAS A HORRIBLE MAN WHEN HE CALLED ME A CUNT TO MY FACE.

directed, stars in, produced [*SMILF*], I thought, "This is feminism come to birth in two generations later."

Howard: Being in movies, though, was that the highlight of your life? When you're hanging with Madonna in *A League of Their Own*, then you become friends, and the biggest star in the world is sort of like your buddy.

Rosie: Yes, it's weird. I remember she was friends with Sandra Bernhard and I was a veejay going, "How do you be friends with Madonna? How's that possible?" And then cut to, it's me.

Howard: Are you guys still close?

Rosie: Yes.

Howard: It would seem to me you would be, because you both have a bunch of kids. Are we done having children? I think it's enough.

Rosie: My therapist said to me recently, "You have overinvested in the mother narrative." I was like, "Correct."

Howard: Is that because you want to save every child out there? Do you think there's some of that?

Rosie: I think it's because I didn't have a mother. I really wanted to have a mother. Every child, I think, wants to have that one person who's going to be your forever person. I used to take my friends' moms and totally be the kiss-ass nice. My friends were like, "Will you stop talking to my mom." You're supposed to hate your mother when you're fourteen or fifteen, right?

Howard: Yeah, you didn't get to go through that.

Rosie: No. And so when my kids went through it—and some are still, I took Parker to therapy. I was sobbing in therapy for like forty-five minutes. He's just looking at me—he's fourteen—and the therapist says to him, "Is there anything that you want to say?" He goes, "Yeah, do you think you could adjust her medications?" I was like, "You bastard. You bastard."

Howard: I don't think we ever talked about this, but were things so bad as a kid that you would break your own bones?

Rosie: Yes.

Howard: Why, Rosie? What was going on there? How would you break your own bones?

Rosie: Usually with a very heavy wood hanger. Remember when we were kids, they had those very thick wood hangers?

Howard: My mom used to hit me with one of those.

Rosie: Correct. Those things. Or when it was bat day at the Mets stadium, they had these little wooden bats.

Howard: How old were you when you would hit yourself?

Rosie: It started right after my mother died when I was about eleven. I would repetitively hit something, usually on my hands, and it would get so numb. And then I would know when it was broken and then I would stop. I think what I liked—what I've learned through years of therapy, now as a fifty-five-year-old adult woman—similar to cutting, when the pain on the inside is so intense, you just want a way for it to stop. Your brain literally can't handle the physical pain and the emotional pain. One of the receptors turns off. So when you feel like you're drowning by all of the emotional stuff . . . And there was horrible stuff going on at my house at night. That's something that scars you in a way, that unless you've lived through it it's hard to articulate.

Howard: Do you think it was a cry for help? Because when you broke a bone, you got to be taken to a doctor, right? People knew you. At some point, did anyone think to say, "Gee, Rosie, why are you always coming in with broken bones?"

Rosie: No. That was not the time, in the seventies. They do that now. Today it would. But I liked going to the doctor because there were nurses who would put the warm cast on me and talk to me and—

Howard: Mothering.

Rosie: Correct. Then when you go to school, you're not the kid with the dead mother. You're the kid with the cast and everyone signing it. I don't know. It took me till I was about twenty-two to stop doing it.

Howard: How many bones do you think you've broken in your body?

Rosie: Boy, I don't know. It's mostly my hands, but I'd say at least a dozen times in my life.

Howard: If you saw Donald Trump drowning, if he fell off a boat, would you jump in and save him?

Rosie: That is a really interesting question. I don't know that I would jump in. I might throw him a floatie. If he was drowning, I have to say, I probably would. Which I hate about me. I'm such a bad hater. I don't want him to die. Do I want him to spend the rest of his life in jail? I certainly do.

Howard: By the way, earlier in this

> **❝ I'M SUCH A BAD HATER. I DON'T WANT [DONALD TRUMP] TO DIE. DO I WANT HIM TO SPEND THE REST OF HIS LIFE IN JAIL? I CERTAINLY DO.**

interview you said that you would service Bob Mueller.

Robin: Has he called in?

Howard: Robin, he's waiting outside to be serviced.

Rosie: Robin, come with me. I know you're much better at it.

Anderson Cooper

MARCH 31, 2014

Over the years I've received countless pitches and job offers. You'd be shocked by how many films and TV shows you could have seen me in had I not turned them down. One of the most interesting was in the early 2000s when Lloyd Braun, then the head of the ABC Entertainment Group, offered me the chance to come to the network and take on a role similar to Barbara Walters. This was back when most people considered me the love child of the Boston Strangler and Squeaky Fromme. Lloyd knew me better than that. He had been my attorney on the film *Private Parts* before joining ABC. He is a visionary. By the way, I consider anyone who offers me great jobs to be a visionary. Just pay me that small price and you earn the title. But Lloyd is especially deserving of it. The hit show *Lost* was his idea. He also helped develop *The Sopranos*. He appreciated my skills as an interviewer even back then, and he wanted me to join ABC and do a series of hour-long specials.

It was an intriguing offer, but I had an even bigger vision: I wanted to be a part of the ABC News division. How mind-blowing would it be to see that ABC News intro with the iconic theme music, and then my face pops up on the screen with the official title of ABC News correspondent. That would have been so offensive to so many people. I was always looking for the chance to thumb my nose at the establishment. I knew the idea of ABC News bestowing their gravitas on me would make people crazy, which I found hilarious. Me with my flowing Prince Valiant locks wearing one of those reporter's jackets with the ABC News logo stitched onto the chest—it would have caused such controversy.

However, I didn't see it as merely a goof. I truly believed I could add something to their journalistic endeavors. I had proven I had a unique talent for getting celebrities to open up to me. Imagine the kind of interviews I could land with ABC News credentials: presidents, dictators, dignitaries. "Colonel Gaddafi, I don't get it. You rape and pillage your own people but you only make yourself a colonel? Why the humility?" Or, "Mr. Gorbachev, if I was a world leader I would get rid of that wine stain on my head. There has to be something you can do. Dermabrasion maybe? Don't they have that in Russia, or is there a shortage of it like toilet paper?" I told Lloyd that if he could make me a part of the news division, I would seriously consider his offer, but it didn't pan out.

All these years later it feels vindicating seeing my interviews with Donald Trump reexamined with such seriousness by news outlets, including ABC News. I'm sure Peter Jennings is rolling in his grave. I've always been bothered by how snobby and clubby the media can be about who they consider a true journalist. Journalists can come in all different shapes, sizes, and costumes—even if the costume has a big "F" on the chest for Fartman. This is why I love Anderson Cooper so much. He has spent his entire career bucking the conventional notion of a journalist.

First, there is the fact that he is an openly gay news anchor. I know it's 2019, but I never underestimate what a struggle that remains. For him to have his face out there every day in front of a country that still has plenty of bigots takes courage. I'm suprised CNN has never gotten a pipe bomb delivered to their offices. Oh, that's right, they did.

Another thing that impresses me about him is that he comes from money and he manages to have a healthy work ethic. His mother is Gloria Vanderbilt. His family is basically American royalty. I've interviewed and been around plenty of rich and famous kids who wind up making nothing of their lives—or worse, losing them. Or they do make something of their lives but they end up being self-entitled jerks. Anderson has managed to have success of his own making and still be totally down-to-earth.

That's probably the thing that impresses me most about him. He does all this reporting from war-torn countries, risks his life to tell big stories and change people's lives for the better, and then he'll host *New Year's Eve Live* with Kathy Griffin. Walter Cronkite never would've been able to pull that off. He'd have lost all credibility. Somehow Anderson doesn't. By not pretending to be a self-important Journalist with a capital "J" and by letting his sense of humor come through, he shows you that he's just a normal human being like the rest of us, and you end up trusting him even more.

Howard: Before I get into your rich history—

Anderson: No pun intended.

Howard: I want to know: Why is it that Fox News is doing so well and CNN is not? Is it because the days of the advocate are really here and now? It's not enough to just be a news guy and have a news channel; you have to have a point of view now and almost give the audience your point of view.

Anderson: I do think in cable news that the networks that have strong opinions—whether you're a conservative network like Fox or a liberal network like MSNBC—when there's not a huge news story going on, they're entertaining, and those are what people tune in to. Throughout its history, CNN has done well when there's some big news event happening and people

are tuning in to see what's going on. It's a difficult position to be in when there's not a story that's captured people's attention, because people aren't tuning in.

Howard: Is CNN the *New York Times* compared to Fox being the *New York Post*? Is that a fair assumption to make?

Anderson: I don't know. It's hard to compare it like that. But I do think CNN is about reporting and sending people out reporting about what's happening.

Howard: I would always think a guy who grows up wealthy—your mom inherited the Vanderbilt fortune.

Anderson: She inherited a lot of money when she was ten years old, yes. She made a lot of money on her own. She did the whole designer jean thing. She was the first one doing that, and perfumes and stuff. She made more money in her own life than she ever inherited, certainly.

Howard: Right, she was a very successful woman. I'm saying, when you grow up around that kind of wealth, I'd think you don't worry. Yet you do, right? It's important for you to prove yourself, right?

Anderson: Yeah, I got a job when I was ten, because I was obsessed with the looming financial collapse, and I was convinced that everything was going to collapse, and I needed to start socking away money.

Howard: What was that job?

Anderson: It was embarrassing. I worked as a child model, because there's not much that you can do when you're ten.

Howard: You were a child model? No one ever offered me that position.

Anderson: Really?

Howard: Can you believe it? I mean, I'm perfectly structured. You modeled?

Anderson: Yes, it's embarrassing.

Howard: Why is that embarrassing?

Anderson: It's a weird kind of way for a ten-year-old kid to—a lot of the kids who did that were pushed by their parents. My mom was like, "Okay, if that's what you want to do, fine, go ahead." I was the only one who didn't have a parent who would bring me to the auditions. I would go by myself.

Howard: At ten years old, because you grew up in the city, you probably know how to take a subway.

Anderson: Yes, true.

Howard: On your own, you said, "Hey, I'm going to go down to a modeling agency"?

Anderson: Yes.

Howard: Your mom had to be involved in some of it.

Anderson: You know, she wasn't, actually. She thought it was a weird idea, and she was like, "Look, if you want to do it, go ahead and apply." Also, my mom made it very clear to me that she would pay for my college and stuff, and then that was it.

Howard: Would your mom reassure you and say, "Listen, Anderson, my son, we have so much money"?

Anderson: No.

Howard: No? She would not reassure you.

Anderson: No.

Robin: You stand to inherit a lot.

Anderson: No, there's no inheritance.

Howard: Hold it a second. Your mother inherited money. Why shouldn't you?

Anderson: I don't believe in inheriting money.

Howard: If your mother leaves you $10 million, what would you do?

Anderson: It's not going to happen.

Howard: What do you mean, it's not going to happen?

Anderson: My mom has made it clear to me that there's no trust fund. There's none of that.

Howard: But why? Why is that?

Anderson: I think it's a curse. An initiative sucker. Who has inherited a lot of money that has gone on to do things in their own life?

Howard: You are right.

Anderson: From the time I was growing up, if I felt that there was some pot of gold waiting for me, I don't know that I would have been so motivated.

Howard: Your mom is a classic example of somebody who inherited money and then did incredibly well.

Anderson: Yes. I think that's an anomaly.

Howard: Donald Trump inherited some money and then was able to do well.

Anderson: You can point to a few people. But the list of people who have—look, there's a bunch of people who I grew up with who probably inherited a lot of money, and I don't know what they are doing. Like, I've never heard of them.

Howard: But you grew up in the lap of luxury, and yet you had this incredible fear. Where did you get this Depression mentality?

Anderson: My dad was from Mississippi. We are from a really poor family. He died when I was ten. There's a saying that my mom actually used to say to me when I was a kid, which is, "A fatherless child thinks all things are possible and nothing is safe."

Howard: What were the ads that you did as a child model?

Anderson: I worked for Ralph Lauren a lot as a fittings model. I would go to his office and, like, stand with him, put the clothes on, and he and his brother, Jerry, would adjust the clothes. I did a lot of ads for Macy's. I did modeling for Calvin Klein also.

Howard: You probably were making a serious chunk of change?

Anderson: I was doing seventy-five dollars an hour, which for a kid—

Howard: A ten-year-old kid? That's amazing. And you were saving it. You were in modeling from ten to thirteen years old. Why would you leave at thirteen?

Anderson: I'll tell you: because I got propositioned by a photographer.

Howard: Male or female?

Anderson: A male. Somehow he got my number, called me up, and offered me money. It so freaked me out. I never told anybody. I just stopped. I was like, "Forget it."

Howard: Because that is a frightening thing to a thirteen-year-old.

Anderson: Yes. I wish I remembered his name because I would like to talk to him.

Howard: Did you tell your mom?

Anderson: I did not, no.

Howard: How much money did he offer you?

Anderson: Two thousand five hundred dollars. Which I thought that was a little low.

Robin: That's why you quit. Not enough money.

Anderson: I don't know. I don't know what the rate is.

Howard: At that point, you were obviously aware you were gay, but it wasn't like you wanted to be with an adult man.

Anderson: I was thirteen years old. I wasn't even thinking about sex with anybody. I think he saw that I was on my own, that I didn't have a parent or guardian there—

Robin: That's what they see: your vulnerability.

Anderson: I don't know. Maybe he saw my big worry line and he realized, "This is a kid who wants money."

Howard: How old were you when you knew you were gay?

Anderson: I knew it from the time I was five years old.

Howard: Did you go to your mother and say, "I like boys"?

Anderson: No. There were tons of gay people in our house. My mom and dad had tons of gay friends all the time.

Howard: Never a big issue?

Anderson: No, it wasn't. I came out in high school to my friends. I came out to my mom, I think, when I was in college.

Howard: It wasn't that traumatic for you?

Anderson: Obviously, there's a couple of years when you're twelve or thirteen that you think, "Oh, it would be better, it'd be easier . . ." But it just felt totally natural, totally right. And I was like, "Let's get started."

Howard: You were, I would imagine, a very bright student, because you went to Yale. When you go to Yale, the world is your oyster and—

Anderson: What does that mean? That's so ridiculous. People buy the hype. It's interesting: some of the smartest people I've ever met were there, and some of the dumbest in life. There are some people who are so brilliant academically, but when they get out of college, they're lost.

Howard: Your career is so unusual. You get out of college.

Anderson: I get out of college. I didn't know what I wanted to do. My brother committed suicide in my senior year of college. I was lost. I spent a year doing odd jobs, traveling around. I did carpentry work. I was all over the place.

Howard: You mentioned the suicide of your brother. That was plastered all over the newspapers. I remember it.

Anderson: Yeah.

Howard: Were you close to your brother?

Anderson: Yeah, yeah, very close. I mean, I say that . . . That's the thing about suicide. It starts to make you rethink everything about your relationship with the person. I didn't know he was that—

Howard: You didn't see any signs?

Anderson: No. I mean, I knew about a month before that he was having some issues. I knew he started to see a therapist and stuff, but I didn't know the details. And it so scared me—the idea that he would be in some way weakened or in trouble—that I totally didn't deal with it.

Howard: Was he older than you?

Anderson: He was two years older.

Howard: It's so sad too, because you say, "Why didn't I pick up the signs? How can I not know this about my own brother?" But at that age, we're all caught up in our own lives.

> **THERE'S NOT A DAY THAT GOES BY THAT YOU DON'T THINK ABOUT IT. THAT'S THE THING ABOUT SUICIDE. IT INJECTS A LANGUAGE AND VOCABULARY INTO YOUR LIFE THAT'S SUDDENLY THERE.**

Anderson: Yeah, and also he was so much smarter than me. He had gone to Princeton, and he was working at *American Heritage* as a book editor. And it was so inconceivable to me. It was inconceivable.

Howard: It's mind-blowing. Because with guys like you, because you're smart and you grow up in a wealthy family, you think that—it's like the Paul Simon song "Richard Cory." You think, "He's got everything. How could a person of privilege . . . ?" And yet, depression—go figure.

Anderson: It's interesting. The week after he killed himself, I went to his apartment. And I was driving in a cab back to my apartment—'cause I hadn't left the apartment; there were reporters camped outside trying to get pictures and stuff— and somebody on the radio said exactly that in the cab that I was listening to. And I'll never forget it, 'cause it struck me so weird, such an odd way to see it. And, of course, it makes sense that people see it that way. But to me—

Howard: Does this still shape your life at all?

Anderson: Absolutely. It informs everything.

Howard: Like, you wake up in the morning, the first thing you think about is, "My brother killed himself."

Anderson: It's not the first thing, but there's not a day that goes by that you don't think about it. That's the thing about suicide. It injects a language and vocabulary into your life that's suddenly there. And that's why [members of the same family] commit suicide. If your parent commits suicide, there's a much greater chance that you will commit suicide later in life.

Howard: Do you worry that you have that same tendency?

Anderson: I don't anymore. I certainly did at that time.

Howard: You did at that time?

Anderson: Yeah, sure.

Howard: I knew a guy who killed himself in front of his mother. And that's what your brother did?

Anderson: Right.

Howard: And I said to myself at that time when it happened, "What an angry thing to do." It's a punishment. It's like, "I'm going to show you."

Anderson: I think everybody is different. And I don't think my brother—my brother was not consciously thinking at the time. I think he had this impulse that he could not contain. And perhaps he'd had the impulse before that he had been able to contain.

Howard: Why kill yourself in front of your mother?

Anderson: I think it was just—she was just there. He'd woken up from a nap. He was disoriented, my mom said, and came into her room and said, "What's going on? What's going on?" And she was like, "Nothing's going on. Are you okay?" And he ran up to his room. It was on the second floor. It was a duplex and a penthouse. And she ran after him. And he went out onto the ledge.

Howard: And jumped.

Anderson: Yeah.

Howard: No hesitation.

Anderson: There was hesitation. He actually stayed on the ledge for a while, and then finally jumped.

Howard: The "What's going on? What's going on?" leads you to believe that maybe it wasn't an angry act to your mother, but that it was just a disoriented guy. Was he on drugs?

Anderson: No, no. He didn't do drugs at all. I don't know. To this day, we don't know. Look, he was certainly depressed. He was certainly—in retrospect, I realized he was depressed and scared about a lot of stuff.

Howard: But it sounds like a reaction to a medication or a drug.

Anderson: For a long time, my mom thought so. He was on asthma medication. I'm not sure.

Howard: Could be.

Anderson: Anything is possible. But with suicide we like to think it's this clear thing, one way or the other. And it's not. That's the horrible thing about suicide. The family members are left for their entire lives wondering why.

Howard: That's a very healthy attitude that you have, because I think most of us try to find a reason why.

Anderson: I did for a long time.

Howard: Because then we feel we have some control over the situation.

Anderson: Honestly, that's why I started going overseas to wars and traveling and putting myself in very extreme situations. And I gradually came to understand that sometimes there isn't any *why*.

Howard: You put yourself in *really* dangerous situations. You wanted to be a reporter. Somehow you figured that out. And you weren't working for anybody.

Anderson: It wasn't even so much that I wanted to be a reporter. I'd always been interested in wars and insurgencies, particularly obscure countries and insurgencies. But I was also, at that point, really interested in survival. Why some people survive and other people don't. Why two people growing up in a family, why one of them—why I survived and why my brother didn't.

Howard: Do you think this is a reaction like, "I don't care about my own life"?

Anderson: No, it wasn't a death wish. But, look, I was in a lot of pain. And I wanted to be around other people who were in pain as well. In America, people don't talk about grief. They don't talk about loss very much. It makes people very uncomfortable. And I wanted to be around other people who—where life and death was very much a real issue. And where it was something that people were dealing with every single day. Because I felt like I was dealing with this every single day.

Howard: And then dealing with a mother who's got to deal with that. That's another thing.

Anderson: Right. My mom was incredibly cool. I said to her, "Okay, I'm going off to wars now." She could have very easily said, "Please don't do this."

Howard: Was it ever an issue in your broadcast career that you were gay? "Oh, if it comes out that I'm gay—"

Anderson: Well, I'll tell you, there were a couple of issues. And I don't want to sound like I'm making excuses for not being more public. But it's a criticism I've gotten, and

I totally understand why I've received it. I was traveling to really dangerous places by myself. I had no security. Nothing. I'm going to a lot of Middle Eastern countries, where it's illegal to be gay. I'm wandering around Somalia by myself, in the early nineties. And so I didn't want to get killed. There was that issue. And I felt like I had enough baggage as it is, being my mom's son, that I didn't want to be known as the son of some famous guy trying to be a reporter, and then on top of it to be the gay guy who's trying to be a reporter. So I thought, "You know what? I just want the focus to be on the stories I'm telling, and completely on work."

Howard: What gave you the idea when you were over in these dangerous situations in these countries to start taping?

Anderson: I figured I have to have a reason to go. I can't just be, like, a war tourist. So I made a fake press pass and I borrowed a camera, and I snuck into Burma and hooked up with some students fighting the Burmese government.

Howard: That is crazy.

Anderson: Yeah, it was a little crazy.

Howard: Who do you send these tapes

> ❝ IN AMERICA, PEOPLE DON'T TALK ABOUT GRIEF. THEY DON'T TALK ABOUT LOSS VERY MUCH. IT MAKES PEOPLE VERY UNCOMFORTABLE. AND I WANTED TO BE AROUND OTHER PEOPLE WHO—WHERE LIFE AND DEATH WAS VERY MUCH A REAL ISSUE.

to that takes notice and starts using them?

Anderson: It was a scheme. I got a part-time job as a fact-checker at this thing called Channel One, which is a show seen in high schools throughout America—about half the schools in America at the time. I did that for, like, five months, and then I came up with this idea of "I'm gonna start going to wars. It's something I feel personally about. I feel depressed. I want to go to these places. I want to see things. I want an interesting life." Since I had a relationship with Channel One, I said to them, "I'm quitting. I'm going to wars. I'll show you the videos. If you like them, you can put them on and it will cost a thousand dollars per story." I just made up some figure, and they were like, "Well, okay." Because I knew if I said to them, "Will you send me?" they'd be like, "No, we're not going to send you. It's dangerous. You have no experience. We're not going to do it." I just made it impossible for them not to at least look at the tape.

Robin: How did you finance this?

Howard: Your mom wasn't going to pay for this.

Anderson: No. But I could live in Africa

> ❝ SOMETIMES I WOULD SAY TO THEM, "CAN YOU PUT THE AK DOWN AND JUST HOLD THE CAMERA SO I CAN DO A STAND-UP?"

for five dollars a day. I was living in Burma for nothing.

Howard: Were bullets whizzing by your head and the whole deal?

Anderson: In Burma, there were mortars going off, yeah.

Howard: And who tapes you?

Anderson: I would shoot myself. I would tape myself.

Howard: A selfie?

Anderson: I would turn the camera around, yeah. Sometimes, like in Somalia, it was so dangerous you had to hire armed kids. 'Cause there were so many gunmen walking around, you would hire your own gunmen. And then sometimes I would say to them, "Can you put the AK down and just hold the camera so I can do a stand-up?"

Howard: Do you miss the action at all?

Anderson: No, I still do it all the time. I still go for CNN.

Howard: But it's not the same when you go for CNN. It's a little less—

Anderson: It's different now because I'm more recognizable. So there's security involved. It's actually more dangerous now. It's far more dangerous than it was back then.

Howard: You will step in. If you're covering a story and you see some kid laying in the street with flies on his head or something, you will step in and give him a meal, right? It's not like you just don't associate with anybody.

Anderson: It depends on the situation, but

yes. Like in Haiti, there was a kid. After the earthquake, we were the first team on the ground. I spent a month there for CNN. We were in a riot, and somebody threw a stone, a cement brick onto a kid's head and it split open. And I went and helped the kid.

Howard: Why did they do that? They were attacking the kid?

Anderson: It's a long story. They were basically trying to disperse a crowd from stealing stuff. Some, like, bandit guy just took a cement block and threw it into the crowd, and it cracked open this kid's head.

Howard: And what did you do?

Anderson: Honestly, I started running toward it thinking I was going to take a picture. Because everyone ran away from this kid. And this kid had blood pouring out of his head, and his eyes were rolling back in his head. He was probably ten or eleven years old.

Howard: Oh my God.

Anderson: I took two steps, and I was like, "I'm not going to videotape this. This is horrible." So I grabbed the kid, and I just brought him back.

Howard: You're a hero.

Anderson: No.

Howard: That's a heroic thing. I gotta tell you, I'd be scared. I'd shit my pants if I was in a riot and people are starting to throw stones and cracking people's heads open. I probably would run the other way. But that's the kind of man I am.

Anderson: No, that's not true. You never know how you're going to react.

> **I DO BELIEVE THAT THERE'S SOMETHING IMPORTANT ABOUT BEARING WITNESS, AND THAT THERE'S NOTHING WORSE THAN SOMEBODY DYING IN SILENCE.**

Howard: Oh, I know how I'd react. I'm pretty sure I know.

Robin: We've seen him in a crisis.

Howard: Believe me, Robin would see me and go, "You should step in." And I'd go, "Feet, don't fail me now. I'm getting outta here." I can't believe you still want to do that. Are you married now?

Anderson: No.

Howard: You have a boyfriend.

Anderson: A partner, yes.

Howard: Same guy for a long time.

Anderson: Yeah.

Howard: Does he go with you to Burma and all these dangerous places?

Anderson: No.

Howard: He's like, "What are you, fucking high?" My point is, you've got this great life. Now you're a celebrity. You're on CNN. What are you running off to these crazy countries for? Don't you just want to be the anchor guy?

Robin: Yeah, what do you like about it?

Anderson: It's real life.

Howard: I hate real life.

Robin: Look, the Kardashians are real life too. Go cover them.

Anderson: No, that's not real life. You

know, to me, I never ask that question. To me the question is, why *wouldn't* you go?

Robin: Do you ever get frustrated? Because you're covering all these stories that really are important—you're going to Haiti, you're going to Somalia—and yet very little changes.

Anderson: Sometimes that's really frustrating. But if the mark was that something has to change, you would end up going insane. For me—this is gonna sound really clichéd and hokey—but I do believe that there's something important about bearing witness, and that there's nothing worse than somebody dying in silence. Horrible things happen to people all around the world all the time. But for somebody who's lived a good and decent life to starve to death in Baidoa, Somalia, and die on the side of the road with their child and nobody know of their passing, nobody even remember their name, is an added horror. And so I do believe that there is value in at least learning people's names and telling their stories.

And Now a Word from Our President . . .

NOVEMBER 4, 1997

(19 years and 4 days until the election)

Howard: Who's the new model you're dating? The dark-haired beauty?

Donald: They do say "dark-haired beauty." I've really been going out with a lot of people. I just love it.

Howard: How are you having sex with these women? You've got to be nervous about herpes, AIDS, warts, chlamydia. I talked to a very high-powered guy who recently became single. You know him. Everyone knows him. And he said to me, "It's really great. There's lots of really beautiful women. I'm scared out of my mind. I really don't want to die. I don't want to get AIDS."

Donald: It's frightening.

Howard: What do you do? Just wear a rubber and hope for the best?

Donald: Well, I wouldn't say I do this, but you could send a lot of people you really like to the doctor before you ever get to know them. Isn't that terrible?

Howard: That isn't so terrible. I

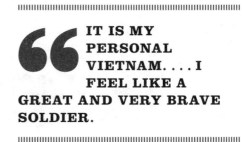

IT IS MY PERSONAL VIETNAM. . . . I FEEL LIKE A GREAT AND VERY BRAVE SOLDIER.

would do the same thing. When you have to say to a woman, "Listen, you have to go to my personal doctor, and I'm going to have you checked out," is that a tough thing to say or you just got the balls to say it?

Donald: I'll tell you, it's amazing. I can't even believe it. I've been so lucky in terms of that whole world.

Howard: You've never gotten a disease?

Donald: It is a dangerous world out there. It's sort of like Vietnam—the Vietnam era.

Howard: It is your personal Vietnam, isn't it?

Donald: It is my personal Vietnam.

Howard: You've said that many times.

Donald: I feel like a great and very brave soldier.

Howard: A lot of guys who went through Vietnam came out unscathed. A lot of guys who've gone through the eighties having sex with different women came out with AIDS and all kinds of things.

Donald: This is better than Vietnam.

Howard: A little better.

Donald: It's more fun.

Howard: But every vagina is a land mine. Haven't we both said that in private?

Robin: *Potential.*

Howard: A *potential* land mine. That's right.

Donald: There is some real danger there.

Howard: So when you go to a bar, do you ever go with a fleet of doctors and have them check all of the women and then party with the uninfected?

Donald: You mean the *few* uninfected. There aren't too many.

Howard: So you say to a woman—you're romantic with her, let's say you do some kissing—and you say, "Listen, I don't know about you but I really wanna go all the way with this thing. Would you go visit my doctor?"

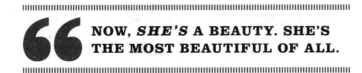

" NOW, *SHE'S* A BEAUTY. SHE'S THE MOST BEAUTIFUL OF ALL.

Donald: I'll tell you what, the whole romantic process is terrible. Because you meet somebody, and you start really liking that person, and you start getting warm toward that person. And then you're really going at it and you have to say, "Excuse me, we have to stop now." It's not like the seventies. The seventies were the best time. I'm old enough to have gone through the seventies.

Howard: Me too. I had one girl during the seventies . . . So, Donald, your daughter, Ivanka, is on the cover of the *Daily News* today.

Donald: Now, *she's* a beauty. She's the most beautiful of all.

Howard: You've got all this money. Why not put your foot down and say she can't do this [modeling]. She's fifteen years old. Be a kid and just stay home.

Donald: She wanted to do it. And she's very beautiful. She's fifteen now, just going on sixteen, and she's five foot eleven. And she's just great at it. She goes to school. That's the priority.

Howard: And what about guys? Is she dating?

Donald: She's surrounded. We had a rock star come up to her, and you wouldn't believe what this guy looked like.

Howard: What was his name?

Donald: I didn't even know his—

Howard: What band was it?

Donald: He had more tattoos on him than I've ever seen on a human being, and she thought he was absolutely awesome.

Howard: Oh, jeez. 'Cause you figure a guy thinks not only is she gorgeous, but he can back the Brinks truck up.

Donald: It wouldn't be that easy. But she's doing great. She's become a real top model. She's amazing.

Howard: Okay, so let's get into the book [*Trump: The Art of the Comeback*]. You wrote this book, and there's more revelations than I can handle. First of all, you write about how you hid Michael Jackson and Lisa Marie Presley at Mar-a-Lago.

Donald: That's actually where they fell in love.

Howard: You claim that you heard them having sexual intercourse.

Donald: I did? Did I say that in the book? Does that sound exciting to you, or not?

Howard: Yes, it does! And you say they were really doing it!

Donald: I think they were really doing it. They were in the tower. They were holding hands. They were kissing. And I say this in a positive way. I don't want to be ratting on anybody, I think they really were in love.

Howard: The worst day of your life was when you lost $900 million, or were down to $900 million?

Donald: No, I was down to a very low point. I had billions and billions in debt. I had $975 million personally guaranteed. It was around 1991. I think I was on the front page of the *Times* and the *Wall Street Journal*, saying how could he possibly come back from this disaster? Real estate was crashing, casinos were crashing, everything was crashing, and that was my low point. And I got a call, and the call was from Ivana, who I took very nice care of. I mean, she's very lucky to have been married to me. You say that better than anyone else.

Howard: Will you have sex with a woman when she's having her period? Go ahead.

Donald: Um, well, I've been there. I have. As we all have.

Howard: You have? But you don't like it?

Donald: Well, sometimes you get there by mistake.

Howard: Have you ever had a black woman in bed? Ever?

Donald: Well, it depends on what your definition of "black" is.

Howard: Interesting. His bed is like a rainbow.

Donald: Like the rainbow coalition. As Reverend Jesse [Jackson] would say.

Howard: So what is the perfect date?

Donald: The perfect date is you meet at seven for drinks.

Howard: Seven-thirty you're in bed. [*laughs*]

Donald: [*laughs*] Then you promise to take her out to dinner, but you never get there. And the amazing thing is, you can have a second date around eight-thirty.

Howard: What's the name of your favorite condom?

Donald: I don't know the name of it, but I'm using 'em, I'll tell you that.

Howard: What a life! I'm fascinated by this.

Donald: I hope they work. If they don't work, I'm in trouble.

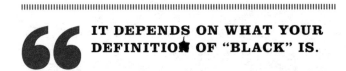

IT DEPENDS ON WHAT YOUR DEFINITION OF "BLACK" IS.

Paul McCartney

JANUARY 14, 2009

I've never been more excited for an interview than I was for Paul McCartney. As my listeners know, the Beatles were everything to me when I was growing up. It wasn't just the Beatles albums. I loved McCartney's solo stuff, his time with Wings. I'll never get the chance to interview John or George. I'd interviewed Ringo, and that was incredible. But this is Paul McCartney we're talking about, maybe the greatest songwriter who's ever lived.

With a guy like Paul, there's too much material, too much ground to cover. I'd need a hundred thousand hours to get through his whole life, and I've only got an hour or so. In a case like that, I can't have too much of an agenda. I can't be rigid in my questions. I have to just let the conversation flow naturally.

I've been asked, "Was it fun to interview Paul McCartney, your childhood hero?" No. There is no enjoyment in it whatsoever. The pressure is so intense, the sense of responsibility so enormous. I want to please the audience and I desperately want to please Paul. I'd love to please myself, but I know that's not going to happen. No matter what I ask him, no matter how well the interview goes, he's going to walk out of that studio and I'm going to obsess over all the questions I did not ask.

That's how I feel after every interview, no matter who it is. Honestly, it's never fun. But it's not about fun. It's about having a job to do, and trying to do it well. Reading this interview back over, I think I did that.

Just because it's not "fun" doesn't mean I'm not able to appreciate it. Are you kidding? It's mind-blowing. If someone had told me when I was a little boy that one day I'd get to sit in the same room with Paul McCartney and talk to him, I don't know what I would have said. It would have just seemed impossible.

Howard: You've got to answer some Beatle-type questions first.

Paul: That's okay. I like the Beatles. Very good band.

Howard: Just tell me something about *Abbey Road* for one second, because we were having a discussion and everyone was throwing out that question. I had heard that *Abbey Road* was not supposed to be called *Abbey Road*. You were going to call it something like *Mount Everest*.

Paul: Yes.

Howard: This is true? What is the story there?

Paul: Well, you know, you're making an album, and toward the end of the album you start thinking, "We need a title for this." So you're looking around, you're fishing around, and the engineer, Geoff Emerick, who was our Beatles engineer, did all the great sounds for us, was smoking cigarettes called Everests. So *Everest*.

Howard: It's a good name.

Paul: It's big. It's heroic. That could be good for the album. So that was the working title. But the more we thought about it, "No, this is not great." And just one day, we were in Abbey Road, working, and I just suddenly said, "Well, look, why not *Abbey Road*?" Because if we did that,

> **RINGO WAS ALWAYS LIKE THAT. HE WAS THE ONE, IF FANS CAME TO HIS DOOR, HE'D JUST SAY, "PISS OFF."**

we can just run outside, there's a level crossing as we call it, there's a crossing, and we could just stand there, we could get photographed, come back to work, it'll take two seconds, that's it, and it's not a bad title, *Abbey Road*.

Howard: Isn't it weird how just a simple thought like that becomes a legend? I mean, that's iconic now, *Abbey Road*.

Paul: Yes.

Howard: And yet it could have been called *Everest*, and that would require the Beatles to fly to Mount Everest for the whole photo shoot. So in a way, it was sort of a lazy approach.

Paul: It was a cheap approach.

Howard: What do you think of Ringo now coming up with a statement he will not sign anything. He's just peace and love.

Paul: I love him. I mean, you've got to love Ringo. The truth is, Ringo was always like that. He was the one, if fans came to his door, he'd just say, "Piss off." And he would not have any of it. You know, "This is my private life. Out there, I'm a Beatle. That's fine, and I'll do things. You know, when we go to shows. But I'm at home with babies and a wife. I don't want that."

Howard: He said, "I will not sign anything." Listen, Ringo's not that busy. What is he busy with?

Paul: I just signed outside.

Howard: Absolutely. It's not a big deal.

Paul: Listen, he has the right to do whatever he wants to do in life. And he doesn't want to do that, and I think it's very brave of him.

I like that about Ringo. I mean, he went up to Liverpool. Liverpool was just declared the capital of culture in Europe. And so it was a big year for our hometown. So Ringo goes up there, and he opens the ceremony. He plays. The whole city loves him. He's the favorite son. And he comes back down to London, he goes on a talk show, and the guy says, "Well, you must love Liverpool and miss it." And he goes, "Not really."

Howard: Wow.

Paul: You know how they make statues out of hedges? Well, there was one with the Beatles in Liverpool, and his head got cut off shortly after. You know, you got to love him.

Howard: How are you and Yoko doing?

Paul: Fine.

Howard: Wasn't there a thirteen-minute track you wanted to release that the Beatles had done and then Yoko said no?

Paul: It wasn't Yoko. George didn't like it. The thing is, I was asked to do something in the sixties. I got asked to do a piece of music for a thing called the Carnival of Light, just a real hippie thing. I just went into the studio before a Beatles session, and when the guys came in I said, "Can we just have fifteen minutes where I just organize a little bit of craziness? Is everyone up for it? Just wander around and hit anything you want, say anything you want, ping the piano or go on the drums." The guys said, "Yes, sure." I said, "We'll just do this for fifteen minutes, and then I'll give it to a guy to put a lot of echo on it." So we did that. It's fifteen minutes of avant-garde Beatles

music. And because the Beatles were such a big thing, it now is of interest.

Howard: You were willing to let it out there, but George was against it?

Paul: Yes, I thought it might be good on the anthology when we were putting everything out. That was every old bootleg we've ever done, and I thought it might be an interesting part of the sixties story. I thought that was a perfect place for it.

Howard: Is that good for Pete Best financially, because some of that stuff did include him? Did he get a cut of some of the dough?

Paul: Yes.

Howard: Did you ever say, "You know, I feel so bad for this son of a bitch. We threw him out of the band."

Paul: No. I know the family and stuff, and we chat.

Howard: Has he written you letters from time to time? "Come on, help me out. This is killing me."

Paul: He's got his pride, Howard.

Howard: Was he fired from the band because he was so good-looking?

Paul: No, you know what? The truth was we just kind of fell in love with Ringo's drumming. Ringo was in another band, and we had Pete. We're working. And we used to go see this other band, and think, "God, that drummer's good." And one night Pete couldn't do it, and Ringo sat in for him, and we all just went, "Oh my God, what is happening?" It was something funny going on.

> **❝ I LOST JOHN. STUART [SUTCLIFFE]. LOST LINDA. IT'S VERY TOUGH. YOU WANT THEM BACK. YOU WANT THEM BACK ALL THE TIME.**

Howard: Is the lesson learned from that never miss work? Just show up, and don't give anyone that opportunity?

Paul: Even if you're very ill, show up. Don't let Ringo sit in for you.✦

Howard: I haven't spoken to you since George Harrison died. How you doing with that? That's got to be major.

Paul: Well, you know, how you deal with everyone dying. I mean, I lost both my parents. I lost John. Stuart [Sutcliffe, original Beatles bassist]. Lost Linda. It's very tough. You want them back. You want them back all the time, you know? But I think in the end, you do what I do, I think what most people do, which is just remember the great stuff. You know you can't get them back.

Howard: Are you sad? Do you wake up every day feeling like there's an empty hole in your heart?

Paul: No, not every day. But, you know, my life now, if there's ever a reference or if ever I think of a story including George, obviously there's a sadness to it now that wasn't there before.

Howard: Is his son in touch with you at all?

Paul: Yes. He's great. Dhani's a lovely boy.

Howard: He's a musician?

Paul: He's a musician. He's really good.

Howard: Biggest mistake, though, for any kid of a Beatle is to go into music, right?

Paul: Well, what are you going to do? It's like children of famous actors, children of famous anything. They're born with the gene. And so you had Julian [Lennon], he's got John's genes. You got Sean [Lennon] and Dhani. My son, James, is a great musician. And Ringo's kids are all great drummers.

Howard: What's your philosophy? Does James have to go out and make a living, or do you say, "Look, I'm a wealthy man. I'll set you up. I will give you a couple million bucks. You got a trust fund. Go ahead, go live your life. Go be a musician and never get a job."

Paul: I think what you end up doing is kind of something in the middle, because I want any one of these kids, particularly my kids, and obviously all the other kids you're talking about, to have the hunger that we had.

Howard: How do they get that?

Paul: Well, I think you can't get it, is the answer. So you have to come in somewhere in the middle.

Howard: So if your son says to you, "I want to be a musician," you support that and you don't say to him, "Hey, go get a regular job at a florist's."

Paul: If he wanted to go and be a florist, he would have done that. But it's in his genes. Since he's nine, he's been playing guitar.

✦ **For more on this from Ringo Starr, turn to page 537.**

Howard: Are you depressed by the world's situation right now?

Paul: Yes, not exactly happy about it, but I'm an optimist. I've been around a little while. You've seen stuff. You've seen Vietnam, you've seen Nixon, you've seen 9/11. We're not in a very good place at the moment, especially the economy. But I am an optimist, you know? I sort of think it comes around.

Howard: Where are you living right now?

Paul: England.

Howard: You don't go out to the Hamptons anymore?

Paul: I do in the summer. I go out there to be photographed by paparazzi.

Howard: Absolutely. We'd love to see you date. I heard Christie Brinkley was very into you and was really on the hunt for you one night. That's what I heard.

Paul: Well, you know . . .

Howard: You should bang her. You should do it. Give it to her one time.

Paul: Howard, you are just so bad.

Howard: And how do you like being a father now with a young kid?

Paul: I love it.

Howard: You love it?

Paul: I really love it.

Howard: Are you hands-on?

Paul: Yes, man.

Howard: What do you mean?

Paul: Typical morning, Monday morning, I get up at six-thirty. I make breakfast. I get her up. I get her dressed. We watch the TV.

Howard: There's no nanny?

Paul: No nanny. I drive her to school. I talk to the moms, talk to the teacher, pick her up after school. I love it.

Howard: But you have to share custody. Isn't it hard to let go of her?

Paul: Well, you know what, in truth I don't really want to talk about that, because that's very private.

Howard: Very private, but you can talk about it with me. The other kids are jealous or resentful of your young child?

Paul: No, they've got all their own kids to deal with.

Howard: They don't feel like some kid's going to get more of their loot of McCartney fortune?

Paul: No.

Howard: All right, here's the first single from the new album ["Sing the Changes" from *Electric Arguments*, McCartney's third album under the name The Fireman]. I like it.

Paul: Made up in a day.

Howard: You're saying there's thirteen tracks on the record, and you did one in a day?

Paul: Yes.

Howard: Doesn't that lead to regrets, though? Don't you go, "Oh, maybe I should put more thought into it"?

Paul: It's like improvisational theater— improv—that I've heard about for years. You hear actors talking about it, and I always wondered, "What would that be like?" You know, just making it up as you go along. Once you do it, that's it. The whole idea is that you're going to dredge up something from your subconscious. And actually, a journalist the other day, from *Rolling Stone*, read me back the lyrics to this one, and it sounded like a poem. I go, "Wow," because I'd never heard them. I just made it up, we cut it and pasted it, and I just go, "Yeah, that sounds nice."

Howard: Let me ask you a question. Did you have to go to your daughter Stella—she was very vocal against you getting married to your previous wife—did you have to go to her and say, "Honey, you were right"?

Paul: No. You don't talk about stuff like that. You just get on with it. It's okay.

Howard: My daughter just graduated college. She had a college class on the Beatles, and it was, like, her favorite thing. It's insane.

Paul: Well, you should've let your kids grow up listening to it, Howard.

Howard: You struggled with cocaine for a good year, right?

Paul: True.

Howard: And when you were in the Beatles?

Paul: I didn't struggle. I was a young man, and that was part of the picture at that time. But I would advocate young people not to do it. It's no good, man.

Howard: But how did you get off of cocaine? You were addicted.

Paul: I was not addicted.

Howard: You were addicted. You were on it for a year. Everyone knows you were addicted.

Paul: No, I was actually very lucky. Because all of this stuff, as you know, kids particularly, it's a peer-group thing. Suddenly it appears and somebody's doing it, and you don't have the wisdom to say, "No, I can stand back from this."

Howard: You tried heroin too?

Paul: No, no, no. The same person I knew who introduced me to coke, he did heroin. And he said to me, "Do you want to try?" It's just the fear. I said no.

Howard: Oh, really? Because I wasn't making a joke. I've read that for a year you did cocaine, and you felt that you were addicted to it.

Paul: No, I wasn't addicted to it. I was very lucky because it was actually just before it broke mainstream. So for that year, I just sort of did it like, "You know what? This is a mug's game." And I stopped it. And then just about everyone I knew in the world—including lawyers, bankers, businessmen, everybody, the straight people—suddenly started getting heavy into it. So I was very lucky actually. So I'd say to kids . . . A lot of people knowing you, the good thing about this is that you can advise kids. I used to say to kids, "Look, I know it's a peer-pressure thing. So what I would advise you to do is, you can't say, 'Oh no, I've never tried it.' Because then the kids will say, 'Sucker.' So I said to say, 'Oh no, no, no. I've been through that. I gave it up.'"

Howard: And now they go, "Wow. Cool." Do you still smoke pot?

Paul: I don't know nothing about that.

Courtney Love

MAY 30, 2013

Courtney Love is the perfect guest. She is unfiltered. She'll say whatever comes to her mind. I earn my money on those days when I interview Courtney. I have to be very focused to keep up with all of her digressions and detours.

I think people underestimate her. Her music has gotten a bit overshadowed by her personality and all her antics. Go listen to her songs. They're incredible. That's what makes her so interesting. I've often wondered, "How the hell does she manage to get through each day, let alone create such powerful art?" This is a woman who lost her husband to suicide. I don't care who you are, that sort of thing could destroy anyone. It could make you turn away from life and stay in bed for the rest of your days. She hasn't done that. She's still out there engaging with the world. There's something courageous in that.

In this interview, when I asked Courtney why I hadn't seen her in three years, without missing a beat she said because her last record flopped. How many people can push aside their ego and point out a failure like that? I have a hard time admitting failure, but she just lays it out there. I love that.

Ultimately my feeling about Courtney is that she's a very intelligent woman. That comes through in this conversation. She might have issues, and all kinds of things in her life that I can't even begin to understand, but she really does have a unique perspective and some interesting things to say.

Howard: Hey, baby. What do you say? Looking good. Thin and trim. Looking hot.

Courtney: How you doing, baby?

Howard: Boy, it's been a long time.

Courtney: It's been three years.

Howard: Is that right?

Robin: That's a long time.

Courtney: Yes, for you and me and Robin, it's a long time. What am I now? This is my fourth [appearance]—not including the crazy call-ins.

Howard: Why have you taken a three-year hiatus from us?

Courtney: Because that record flopped.

Howard: Yeah, so what?

Courtney: I can always come on here and bitch, I know.

Howard: Yeah, you always loved to voice your opinion. In fact, I can't decide if the invention of Twitter has been good for you or bad for you.

Courtney: Bad, in the sense that—well, I learned my lesson. When I do my Twitter now, I'm always super happy, fake-friendly, nice. Initially, I didn't know what it was for, so I just called everyone a whore, and then I got two defamation suits that cost me, like, $780,000.

Howard: You're not kidding. One of those suits was against a fashion designer.

Courtney: It was my first day. I didn't know what it was. I was like, "You fucking—" Can I say that?

Howard: Yeah.

Courtney: Right, we're not on 92.3 anymore.

Howard: That's right.

Courtney: Then, "You fucking whore." I didn't know what it was.

Howard: You were critical of the fashion designer's clothing, is that what it was?

Courtney: I felt like she'd stolen from me. I have to say "I felt like" and "allegedly," which is just as bad as the FBC. Was it the FBC? FBA?

Howard: FCC.

Courtney: FCC, yeah. She "allegedly" stole from me. I have it on CCTV. Okay, she allegedly stole from me.

Howard: So she sued you, cost you a half million dollars to settle the thing out. Twitter got you in trouble that way.

Courtney: Yeah, then I got another one. It was like a pile-on. That was $600,000.

Howard: And what did you do there?

Courtney: It's so minor, and it's ongoing, so I can't really talk about it.

Howard: You know what it is about you? You love to speak out. You love to talk. You're unfiltered, and an invention like Twitter is dangerous.

Courtney: I should have your job.

Robin: You could get sued here too.

Howard: That's right.

Courtney: Do you say "allegedly"?

Howard: I don't go around disparaging someone unless I'm completely sure of my facts.

Courtney: You disparage people sometimes.

Howard: I wouldn't say something unless I knew that to be 100 percent true and that I could back it up and prove it. You like to lash out sometimes.

Courtney: The fact that in one case someone had told me they didn't engage in prostitution, you know—

Howard: See, that's what I'm saying. You throw things out there—like prostitution and a name. You can't just blurt things out.

Courtney: I've learned my lesson. It's a million-dollar lesson, Howard.

Howard: Do you have someone that reads your tweets before you put them out?

Courtney: No, I do myself. I'm actually very responsible about it. I haven't gotten into Twitter trouble in over two and a half, three years.

Robin: Why is it so important to you to be on Twitter?

Courtney: Because I make a lot of money sometimes. I was smoking these e-cigarettes, which I didn't bring, which sucks. You can smoke anywhere. It's just steam. I tweeted about them, and then all of a sudden I made a ton of money doing some viral thing for them.

Howard: Do you need money?

Courtney: Not really.

Howard: Exactly. You sold 25 percent of the Nirvana catalog for $50 million.

Courtney: Something like that.

Howard: And you're worth about $100 million.

Courtney: That's according to celebritynetworth.com.

Howard: Yes. Is that off?

Courtney: It's off. It's a little low.

Howard: It's a little low. So let's say you're worth $150 million. Why do you care about—

Courtney: I know that sounds so hubristic. I should be more, "I'm sorry it's so high! I need food stamps! I need FEMA housing!"

Howard: I like your honesty. So if you're worth $150 million, why do you care if you make money on a cigarette that you smoke?

Courtney: It's the Kurt money, the

> ## "IT'S THE KURT MONEY, THE NIRVANA MONEY. IT'S BEING MANAGED BY OTHER PEOPLE, AND I JUST CONSIDER IT CURSED.

Nirvana money. It's being managed by other people, and I just consider it cursed. So I prefer to make money that's the "Courtney money."

Howard: You've said that running the Nirvana business is cursed money. You've said that before.

Courtney: I said it to you probably first.

Howard: You did. And the reason it's cursed, you say, is that it's brought you tremendous wealth, but also aggravation. I can't even figure out what's going on with this Nirvana money now. Let me ask you a couple questions so I understand it. You and those two other guys, Dave Grohl and the other guy, the three of you own—

Courtney: They own one half. They own the Nirvana LLC, which is T-shirts.

Howard: Publishing is all Kurt's.

Courtney: He wrote everything.

Howard: So you own that. But then you gave over all of that to Frances Bean [Cobain], your daughter?

Courtney: No, no, no, that's a lie. Frances has what Frances has.

Howard: What does she have?

Courtney: About 40 percent.

Howard: Of the Nirvana money?

Courtney: Of the publishing money. But

then I sold 25 percent, and I had a really, really lousy lawyer.

Howard: How does that happen to you all the time?

Courtney: It happens to everybody all the time. It's just the music business. I've got a great agent now. His name is Jeff Franklin. He's like seventy years old. He like invented rock, right? I met him, told him the worst thing I ever did was go to Bellevue on a stretcher for crack. He goes, "Did you have fun?" Which made me love him immediately, right? And he said, "Listen, so-and-so"—Lady PooPoo, whatever, LaLa, whatever, some artist—"has $400 million."

Howard: Right.

Courtney: "She has *$100 million*. The guys take $300 million. That's just the business. Deal with it!"

Howard: Madonna too?

Courtney: No, she watches her pennies.

Howard: Well, shouldn't she?

Courtney: She's careful.

Howard: That's the smart way to be.

Courtney: Jay-Z, he's got a guy named John Maneely. They don't give awards out for honesty in the business. They really don't.

Howard: If you know Jay-Z's guy is honest, why not use him?

Courtney: 'Cause he works with Jay-Z. Jay-Z is a full-time job.

Howard: Do you think you're attracted to bad people because then the drama continues? Like, if you had a calm life, it wouldn't be as interesting?

Courtney: I think when it comes to men and lawyers, I have the worst taste. But when it comes to friends, I have the best taste ever.

Howard: Are you seeing anyone now? Do you have a man in your life?

Courtney: I don't talk about my personal life.

Howard: You say men, it's been a disaster.

Courtney: Not lovers.

Howard: Well, what are you referring to when you say "men"?

Courtney: Boyfriends.

Howard: Exactly. Lovers are boyfriends.

Courtney: Not really. Not fuck buddies.

Howard: Why has it gone bad?

Courtney: I have weird judgment calls, I guess. I don't know. I'm very passionate. I get really into it. And then I get really out of it.

Howard: You even say sexually you're fantastic, 'cause you try harder than these pretty girls, right?

Courtney: I think there was a quote somewhere.

Howard: Yeah, you said you'll blow a guy, you'll let him do anal, you'll let him do it all.

Courtney: Aw, Howard, not on the first date!

Howard: No, I'm saying you wait till the second date. Obviously. You're a lady. But there's a lot to be said for that in a way— that you try harder. You care in bed. You're into it. I don't know what goes wrong. You would like to be married again and in a deep relationship, right?

Courtney: I don't think I want to get married again, no.

Howard: Do you think a guy could put up with you? You're such a strong force, such a strong personality.

Courtney: I am such a pussy.

Howard: Are you a pussy?

Courtney: Kind of.

Howard: How did you end up doing LSD when you were three years old?

Courtney: Four.

Howard: How did that happen?

Courtney: My father gave it to me.

Howard: Do you think that you were parented so poorly that the hardest thing in life for you to do was to be a parent? Because you didn't have any good life lessons in that?

Courtney: Well, I'm really good with my daughter right now.

Howard: I heard.

Courtney: Really good.

Howard: But you won't see each other, you'll only tweet each other.

Courtney: No, we e-mail too. And phone-call.

Howard: How painful is that?

Courtney: What? It's not painful, it's great. It was painful when she was gone. That was like not having a limb.

Howard: Why do you think she doesn't want to see you, though?

Courtney: Well, I haven't been in LA.

Howard: You don't go to LA at all? When's the last time you saw her?

Courtney: I haven't seen her for three years.

Howard: Oh my God. That's got to kill you.

Courtney: It was so extreme. It was like a restraining order and da-da-da-da.

Howard: What the hell went down? I never even talked to you about it.

Courtney: *She* doesn't really know what went down. She was surrounded by—how does a twenty-year-old need three assistants and four law firms and two accountants?

Howard: She's got a lot of money.

Courtney: Yeah.

Howard: Have you met her fiancé?

Courtney: I talked to him on the phone. He's seems really, really nice. Did I just burp really loud? Yeah.

Howard: Courtney, you could send them a ticket and have them come to New York and see you, right?

Courtney: We just started talking on the phone about two months ago. I don't want to get too into her private stuff. She's really private.

Howard: She doesn't want to be a performer?

Courtney: No, she got offered this modeling job and—I mean, major prestige modeling stuff and major prestige movies. When she was thirteen, she got offered for *Twilight*. She was offered Bella in *Twilight*.

Howard: Is that right?

Courtney: That's a true story. Someone saw her picture in a magazine, and sent me the script. She was like, "That's a sexist Mormon piece of shit." She's an artist. She's drawing mostly. It's, like, graphic novels. That's what she wants to do. She doesn't want anything to do with being

Kurt Cobain's daughter or Courtney Love's daughter. She's really working on that.

Howard: What does she do when she meets other kids her age? Does she hide the fact that she's Kurt Cobain's daughter and Courtney Love's?

Courtney: She's really, really picky about who she lets into her life.

Howard: It's got to be difficult, right?

Courtney: I still don't think she needs four law firms, three assistants, and two accountants.

Howard: Aren't you impressed that Dave Grohl was able to make this music career outside of Nirvana and have this big band, Foo Fighters?

Courtney: Yeah, I didn't know how big they were. I was in Guitar Center. I was buying a Telecaster for my guitar player, and I look up and I thought I was watching the Super Bowl. It was fucking Foo Fighters. They're fucking huge.

Howard: Huge! How do you not know that? They're one of the only rock bands making a living.

Courtney: He was always an ambitious boy.✦

Howard: But you were critical—you didn't like when Nirvana supposedly had their reunion with Paul McCartney. That really bummed you out.

Courtney: No, I was given the incorrect information. Krist [Novoselic] and Dave can sing a song with Paul all they want. I don't give a shit. But I thought they were doing a Nirvana song with Paul McCartney, which I thought that was kind of cheeseball.

Howard: It rubbed you the wrong way.

Courtney: I loved Wings and, like, "Jet" and what's the song from the James Bond film? "Live and Let Die." It used to be my favorite song. "Helter Skelter," he wrote that song. There wouldn't be a Sonic Youth without him. I mean, I love Paul McCartney. But I thought it was a cheese thing if they were gonna do, like, "Teen Spirit."

Howard: Let me understand what's going on with the business of this Nirvana thing. I don't get the whole business. The Muppets—

Courtney: The Muppets thing brought me to my knees. I had no say in that.

Howard: Okay, so the Muppets recorded a Nirvana song.

Courtney: And made Kurt into a Muppet!

Howard: So how do you not have a say in that? You have 50 percent of the rights.

Courtney: They took the management away from me and Frances.

Howard: *Who* took the management away from you?

Courtney: A bunch of lawyers, man.

Howard: How can they do that?

Courtney: It was slick. It took them a few years. Slowly, by degrees.

✦ **For more on this from Dave Grohl, turn to page 538.**

Howard: So who made the decision to put the Muppets with Nirvana?

Courtney: I have no idea. A guy named David, who works for a guy named John. Esquire, esquire.

Howard: That's like saying they went into your bank account and took out money.

Courtney: Yeah. It brought me to my knees. To see Kurt as a Muppet, I just started sobbing.

Howard: You started sobbing?

Courtney: I fell on my knees and went like, "I give up. I'm jumping off a bridge."

Howard: That's when you usually call me! Is that a new tattoo on your arm? *Let It Bleed*, it says. Is that old or new?

Courtney: That one I got right with the whole Frances trauma.

Howard: "Let It Bleed" is the Rolling Stones song you're referring to.

Courtney: It's a bad Rolling Stones song, but it's a good title.

Howard: Why would you tattoo *Let It Bleed* on your own arm? What are you saying?

Courtney: I don't know. It was like in the middle of the night, the East Village. I got a tattoo the way you're supposed to. At least I didn't get it like a poseur. You know, like, plan it out and go over your drawings.

Robin: Think about it five months.

Courtney: Exactly, Robin.

Howard: You don't like that.

Courtney: No. It should be in the East Village. It should be by a sailor who doesn't know what the fuck he's doing. And then

" TO SEE KURT AS A MUPPET, I JUST STARTED SOBBING.

you get it cleaned up by one of those trendy guys later.

Howard: So you're telling me you walked into just a random tattoo place. That's the rock-and-roll way to do it.

Courtney: That's the proper way to do it.

Howard: And you said to him, "Put *Let It Bleed* on my arm."

Courtney: That's exactly what I fucking said.

Howard: Because, what, you felt you had been wronged by the world and you were bleeding?

Courtney: Yes. But I was also back then taking Adderall, which is amphetamine salts.

Howard: What are you taking now? Are you drug-free?

Courtney: I take Ambien to sleep.

Howard: Every night?

Courtney: No.

Howard: Why do you need to take Ambien?

Courtney: Don't you ever take Ambien on the plane?

Howard: No. Very rarely. I have a bottle that's lasted me seven years.

Courtney: Mine hasn't lasted seven years. It's lasted, like, six months, though.

Howard: So you're not taking Ambien all the time?

Courtney: No, because if you stay up, you get freaky.

Howard: Crack was the greatest drug you ever took?

Courtney: No! I hated it!

Howard: Did you? I know you said you—

Courtney: No, I know I called in a lot and was out of my mind. But back then, remember, you were still on 92.3 *and* they didn't have TMZ. So I didn't get in all that crazy Lohan trouble. I got taken to Bellevue, and that was the end of the crack.

Howard: Right. You went to Bellevue. They cured you of your crack problem.

Courtney: Well, going to Bellevue is a pretty easy way to get someone off crack, okay?

Howard: In other words, 'cause you see such horrible things that you realize—

Courtney: I saw hermaphrodites, you know? Black, white, with fecal matter, talking to Satan, manacled to the wall. I didn't need to see that shit.

Howard: That was your rock bottom?

Courtney: That was gross, man, yeah.

Howard: What about heroin? How'd you get off that?

Courtney: That was easier. On *Larry Flynt*, which was fourteen years ago, I gave [director] Miloš Forman my word that I wouldn't do it again. And I never did it again.

> ❝ **GOING TO BELLEVUE IS A PRETTY EASY WAY TO GET SOMEONE OFF CRACK.**

Howard: Did you go through a cold turkey experience?

Courtney: Yeah. I lost thirty pounds, and I stopped Valium and heroin in the same thirty days.

Howard: Why do you think you became a drug addict?

Courtney: Um, I don't really know.

Howard: Bad childhood?

Courtney: No, I'm too Jewish to really—

Howard: Are you Jewish?

Courtney: You know I'm Jewish.

Howard: I didn't know that.

Courtney: For God's sake.

Howard: "Courtney Love" is *Jewish*? Love-owitz?

Courtney: It's a fake name, Howard.

Howard: What is your real name?

Courtney: It was Harrison when I was born. My grandmother on my mother's side is Jewish.

Howard: Were they bad parents?

Courtney: I didn't really know them. 'Cause I was in boarding school at nine.

Howard: They had the money to send you to boarding school?

Courtney: Oh, my mother was *really* rich.

Howard: Is your mother still alive?

Courtney: Yeah. And writes books about me and shit.

Howard: Oh, so you're not talking to her.

Courtney: No, I don't talk to her.

Howard: Well, of course that's why you do fucking drugs. You don't know your mother, and she writes books about you.

Courtney: No. The first time I did heroin, I didn't like it.

Howard: Were you at Charlie Sheen's house the first time you did heroin?

Courtney: No, that's a myth.

Howard: Where were you?

Courtney: I was in Flea's apartment.

Howard: Were you shooting it?

Courtney: Excuse my burping. It's disgusting.

Howard: What's going on with the burping?

Courtney: I don't know, man.

Howard: What are you eating?

Courtney: I didn't eat anything this morning.

Howard: What were you doing? Were you shooting heroin?

Courtney: Back in the nineties, we all shot it.

Howard: Were you afraid of the needles? Did you share needles?

Courtney: Yeah. I didn't do it myself. I had someone else do it.

Howard: So weren't you afraid they would use a dirty needle or something?

Courtney: No, I'd always wash mine out.

Howard: You never prepared your own heroin?

Courtney: I didn't like the smell.

Howard: Were you doing it every day?

Courtney: No, no, no. That took a long time.

Howard: How hard is it to kick? The physical aspect.

Courtney: It's not bad.

Howard: Really? Why do we see movies where guys are shaking?

Courtney: I know. It's so lame. You know what's harder to kick? Xanax and Valium.

Howard: And those are so-called legal prescription drugs.

Courtney: And booze.

Howard: You don't drink at all now?

Courtney: I never did drink.

Howard: No kidding? Not at all?

Courtney: Never. I swear to God, I was never a drinker. If I do drink, once in a while I'll have a tequila shot.

Howard: Do you love rock and roll?

Courtney: I live for it.

Howard: So are you disappointed with what's going on with rock? 'Cause rock is dead, in a sense.

Courtney: It's kind of dead, isn't it?

Howard: It's dead. It died.

Courtney: I'm touring—I'm starting touring.

Howard: Is that a good idea for you to be touring if you think your health could be compromised? I'm talking about your mental health and also drugs.

Courtney: No, it makes me feel better.

Howard: When you tour.

Courtney: Yeah, I can't stand the whole socialite blah-blah-blah.

Howard: The series of pictures that I look at to this day, and not in a pervy way, but almost like I'm amazed. You were onstage, you had no panties on—

Courtney: I did wear panties. They were just very skimpy.

Howard: No, hold it. Look at this picture.

> **"** INSTEAD OF THEM GETTING ME A PSYCHIATRIST OR A BEREAVEMENT GROUP, THEY JUST PULLED A FUCKING TOUR BUS IN FRONT OF MY HOUSE.

Courtney: You always have accused me of not wearing them. You've shown me this before. You can't see my pussy 'cause I am wearing *panties.*

Howard: I'm going to show you your pussy. Here you are onstage.

Courtney: Let me see this. [*looks at photo*] That is not my pussy. That is a strip of fabric.

Howard: All right, when you were in the audience, though, the audience completely molested you. You stage-dove into the audience. Your titties are out—and they're nice, by the way. Look, look there. Exhibit A and B. What was that like, that experience?

Courtney: Well, what was it like for Eddie Vedder? What was it like for Kurt?

Howard: No, people were fingering you.

Courtney: They were fingering me. I was trying to prove a point. It was right after Kurt died, too, when I did it the most. I was in just so much weird psychic pain. And instead of them getting me a psychiatrist or a bereavement group, they just pulled a fucking tour bus in front of my house. "Get in."

Howard: And does that cure you?

Courtney: No, but the shows were apparently legendary. I can't remember most of them 'cause, uh, *wasted.*

Howard: Lana Del Rey, did she do a version of "Heart-Shaped Box"?

Courtney: Yes, she did. Isn't that cute?

Howard: And didn't you tweet her and say, "You know, that's about my pussy"?

Courtney: It's about my vagina, yeah.

Howard: That song is about your vagina?

Courtney: It actually is, yeah.

Howard: And what is Kurt saying about your vagina in that song?

Courtney: I don't know, let's figure it out. "She eyes me like a Pisces when I am weak/I've been stuck inside her heart-shaped box for weeks."

Howard: That's not a compliment. He was stuck inside your heart-shaped box.

Courtney: It's not a complimentary song.

Howard: So was Kurt angry about your pussy?

Courtney: No. I write love/hate songs. Kurt wrote love/hate songs. My best love songs were, like, "I fucking hate you."

Howard: Toward the end, were you and Kurt making love at all?

Courtney: The last few weeks, no.

Howard: Why? Were you fighting over his heroin use?

Courtney: No, he was weak. He was weak.

Howard: Does that bother you that you guys weren't on good terms when he died?

Courtney: We were on good terms. He was just really weak.

Howard: He couldn't fuck at that point or think about anything other than his own condition.

Courtney: He couldn't think of anything but drugs.

Howard: It is sad. So sad.

Courtney: It's really sad. You know, I wonder now if we'd be divorced, and it'd be amicable, and he'd maybe live on the Upper West Side, marry a model, have twins, you know? And how my alimony would have gone. I don't know that that marriage would've lasted twenty-two years. Maybe.

Howard: You'd probably be in a Twitter war with him today.

Courtney: [*laughs*]

Howard: You've said that if Kurt came back to life right now, you'd kill him. For leaving you alone. I get that.

Courtney: I said that once, yeah. But, you know, both me and Frances are really angry at him.

Howard: Of course.

Courtney: It wasn't the right thing to do. He was so young, Howard. He was twenty-seven. And you think you're ninety when you're twenty-seven, but you're not.

Howard: If he could've been saved, maybe he would be enjoying his life right now.

Courtney: Yeah. I mean, look, all he had to live through was, like, Eminem, which he would've probably liked.

> **I WONDER NOW IF WE'D BE DIVORCED, AND IT'D BE AMICABLE, AND HE'D MAYBE LIVE ON THE UPPER WEST SIDE, MARRY A MODEL, HAVE TWINS, YOU KNOW? AND HOW MY ALIMONY WOULD HAVE GONE.**

Howard: Do you think it would have disturbed him to live through Eminem?

Courtney: It would've disturbed him to live through Limp Bizkit. I can say that with authority.

Howard: Really? You think so?

Courtney: Yeah. Limp Bizkit was just sort of the end of it, man.

Howard: That was the moment when rock died, with Limp Bizkit?

Courtney: I feel that.

Howard: Look how together you are. You went to a doctor. A lot of people will say, "Courtney Love is crazy."

Courtney: I know, they do that. Why do they do that?

Howard: Because you're wild.

Courtney: If they could've proved I'm crazy, they would've been able to take the Nirvana stuff like *that*.

Howard: You went to a doctor, and the doctor pronounced you perfectly normal.

Courtney: I went to the psychiatrist that runs Bellevue.

Howard: And you said to him, "I want to know if I'm crazy."

Courtney: And I took these two tests called MMPI-2.

Howard: Were you scared shitless to take those tests?

Courtney: No.

Howard: What if they had said you *were* crazy?

Courtney: No, if I was bipolar or manic-depressive, I would've said, "Oh, okay."

Howard: "I'll deal with it."

Courtney: Yeah.

Howard: And you're telling me you're not bipolar. You're not manic-depressive.

Courtney: No.

Howard: You are a perfectly normal person.

Courtney: Well, I'm a drug addict.

Howard: But aside from that, there is nothing that would indicate mental illness.

Courtney: I'm eccentric. I'm eccentric, and I voice my opinions about shit.

Howard: But you're not mentally ill. You don't hallucinate. None of that.

Courtney: No, I don't have voices in my fucking head.

Howard: When you came on my show and said you sucked Ted Nugent's dick when you were twelve years old, was that—

Courtney: No, I was fourteen.

Howard: When you were fourteen. You still stand by that statement?

Courtney: It's in my book.

Howard: It is?

Courtney: Yeah.

Howard: It's documented.

Courtney: I said it on this show. It's true.

Robin: Did he know you were fourteen?

Courtney: Yeah, that was the whole point! Knowing there was a line of underage girls who had to go in there, and there was the first cock I had ever seen, and it was just like this giant, nasty, ugly, gnarly thing.

Howard: Was it a big cock?

Courtney: No, but I can't compare. You know how Disneyland looks really big when you're little?

Howard: Yeah.

Courtney: It could've been teeny, for all I know. All I know was I was in a little yellow tube top, with little rosebud boobies, and I should *not* have been in that room.

Howard: I feel sad.

Courtney: I feel sad about it too! I wish I could say to you, "I walked out."

Robin: Well, you're the fourteen-year-old. You're not the one who—

Howard: That's right. You were a kid.

Courtney: I know, but there was a line of us, and there were guys, and it was like this demand. Like *Howard Stern on Demand*? It was like Ted Nugent on Demand. And so when he was on here with his guns and his conspiracy theories, finally I was like, "You know what, I'm gonna tell my Ted Nugent secret on *Howard*."

Howard: I see sadness in your life. Such sadness. Your husband commits suicide. Your father gives you LSD when you're four.

Courtney: But I'm a pretty happy camper.

Howard: Are you?

Courtney: *Yeah.*

Howard: Why do I feel sad when I'm around you? I feel like there must be sadness here.

Courtney: Because you're an empathic man.

Howard: Yeah, I feel sadness here.

Courtney: You're an intelligent, empathic man.

Howard: So you're going on tour. Maybe on the tour you'll take your top off. Is it possible?

Courtney: I'm a little old for that shit these days.

Howard: No, you're not, honey. You look good. What are you doing? Are you doing any Botox? What are you doing to stay youthful-looking and young?

Courtney: No, I haven't had a fill-in for years. I did it, and I looked like a pillow.

Howard: So you're not doing anything?

Courtney: No. I mean, I had Botox six years ago, and it prevents the lines from coming.

Howard: You got a face-lift or anything like that? Look at you.

Courtney: I got my nose done.

Howard: That's it?

Courtney: Well, I had those crazy lips, and I had to get the lips fixed.

Howard: I don't get why women make their lips so fucking big.

Courtney: I was living in Beverly Hills, and I was all on pills, and I just got caught up in that shit. You know, just wanting to look like a trout.

Howard: That's a hot look.

Courtney: Yeah, koi fish.

Howard: You look good. You look really good.

Courtney: You look good too. And you look content. You look very thoughtful. You're like Rodin's *The Thinker*.

Howard: Really?

Courtney: Yeah, you're overthinking stuff. I don't know. I feel like I'm not going to get invited back for a while because we're not having, like, "Wowwww, party in my pants!"

Howard: No, I like the interview. I love you.

Courtney: I'm just being a little more ladylike than usual. I'm trying to be ladylike. I'm practicing my finishing-school skills.

Howard: Honey, you're doing great. You don't have to worry about me. I'm in your corner.

Courtney: I know you are.

Kim and Khloé Kardashian

DECEMBER 8, 2009

I have to be honest: I never got the Kardashians. Not in the way I don't get electronic dance music. I don't like EDM. It just sounds like thumping to me. But I know there's a skill to it. I know the way those DJs are arranging beats is a craft. It must be if they're selling millions of records. With the Kardashians, for the longest time I didn't understand what their particular talent was. I didn't know if they had one.

Then I had Kim and Khloé on the show, and I totally got it. You know what their skill is? Being honest. They are incredibly good at it. They don't give canned responses. In this interview, they talked about everything from dating black men, fame, their family life, and most importantly what it smells like when Kim takes a dump. It might sound juvenile, but it's the kind of conversation regular people have. They are genuinely hilarious.

I admire the closeness and family ties that truly led me to believe they enjoy each other's company. It seems that the sisters are there for one another in an authentic way. We all crave a family that has our back. Maybe that's why they've lasted for years and years, unlike so many in the reality TV world who fizzle out after two or three minutes.

In a lot of ways, what they do is similar to what I do. I go on the air and tell people about my life. That's in large part how I've made my living. They do the same thing on TV, though they take it to an even greater extreme. I may tell you something funny about myself on the air, but I'm not bringing you home with me the way they do. I couldn't take that kind of scrutiny and craziness.

I enjoyed having these two on the show, and was surprised by how natural they were in this interview. I loved their candor and sense of fun. Some in my audience criticized me for having them on. I don't care. I'd have them on anytime. They were great, and they were interesting. I'm rooting for them.

Howard: Hey, girls. Tell me what it's like to get on TV, be a reality star. What do you have to do? A lot of people want this. Don't you feel pressure that you always have to come up with something sort of odd and almost antisocial to be interesting on the show? You know what I mean?

Kim: Yeah, I know what you mean. It was so funny, 'cause after season three, we were like, "Okay, what are we gonna do now?" Like, "Season four is coming. We're so not that interesting." And then Kourt got knocked up and this one got married, so we had season four.

Khloé: Now season four is fascinating.

Howard: How did you get the reality show?

Kim: Well, I think there was the dynamic of having ten kids. My mom and Bruce, between the two of them, there's ten of us. We all were kind of hanging out in LA, Hollywood, you know, being seen, and my mom met up with Ryan Seacrest, and they came up with this idea.

Howard: Because Ryan Seacrest felt the family was interesting.

Kim: Yes.

Howard: And this was after they had the sex tape of you with that guy. What's his name? Ray J.

Khloé: "That guy." I like that name better.

Howard: Do you feel embarrassed by that tape, or are you happy about it? I heard Vivid paid you five million bucks for the tape? Is that true?

Kim: I don't think that anyone would ever be happy about something like that.

Howard: But it launches you in a way. I mean, the fame comes about because of the tape. Same thing with Paris Hilton. When she got the sex tape, everyone really got interested in her.

Kim: I can get definitely how you could say that and think that. I think when you're going through it . . . Like now, I'm just like, "Ugh, I wish no one would even bring that up. I wish no one would even talk about it."

Howard: But five mil is pretty good. I don't care what you tell me, at the end of the day that's decent money. Did you guys grow up with money? Your dad was a lawyer.

Kim: Yeah.

Howard: Robert Kardashian, who died of cancer, right?

Kim: Mm-hmm.

Howard: A very famous attorney. Represented O.J. and all that stuff.

Kim: Yeah. I mean, we grew up in Beverly Hills. We definitely had a really privileged life. But my dad was extremely strict. We all had to get jobs. We knew at eighteen we had to be out of the house. We had to pay for everything.

Howard: Let me take you back a bunch of years. When your dad was alive, your mom was good friends with Nicole, O.J.'s wife. The week before Nicole was murdered, you guys actually went away on a vacation with her, right?

Kim: Yeah, every spring break we would go to Cabo San Lucas, Mexico.

Howard: And Nicole was beautiful and a nice person, right?

Kim: Incredibly sweet.

Howard: I guess you knew O.J. killed her, and then your dad had to represent O.J.

Kim: I think at that time, I just believed—me and my sister Kourtney . . . Khloé was a little bit younger—but Kourtney and I just believed everything that my dad would do.

Howard: Right.

Kim: We were such daddy's girls. 'Cause we felt like, you know, my mom had remarried so fast, and it kind of broke my dad's heart. She moved on. So we just sided with my dad no matter what it was. So at the beginning my dad definitely did believe in O.J. He couldn't believe that his best friend would do that.

Howard: So you think he really believed that he was innocent?

Kim: Yeah, for a long time. We always were at my dad's house, and there was Bob Shapiro and Johnnie Cochran. They're having all these meetings, and we'd go there. Then we'd go to my mom's house, where Faye Resnick was living and she was really close to the Brown family. So we'd hear one thing, and then go to my dad's house and it was all pro-O.J. And we're like, "Wait, what do we believe?"

Howard: Right, 'cause your mom was probably sitting there going, "O.J. killed my best friend, and now my ex-husband's defending him." And you guys are caught in the middle of this whole thing saying, "Gee, who's right? Who's telling the truth?"

Kim: I know for us as kids, it was very hard. For me personally, I just felt like if I was at my mom's, I couldn't really talk about my dad. If I was at my dad's, I couldn't talk about my mom. Now, after the O.J. trial was done, they became best friends, and my mom and my dad and my stepdad played golf together and it was fun. But during the trial, it was awful for us kids.

Howard: After the trial, your dad and O.J. had a falling-out, right?

Kim: I think so. He kind of kept it away from us. I mean, that was, like, Uncle O.J. and we'd see him all the time. I remember the day he got out of jail, I went to his house with my dad and said hi to him. Then after that, I don't think we saw him again. I think they had a falling-out.

Howard: O.J. never hit on you guys?

Kim: No. [*laughs*]

Khloé: No.

Howard: Uncle O.J.?

Khloé: Uncle O.J., no. [*laughs*]

Howard: Now, your parents' divorce: Did your dad leave your mom or did your mom leave your dad?

Kim: I think, my mom was twelve years younger, and I feel like she just felt like she—

Khloé: My mom left my dad.

Robin [*to Kim*]: You're being a diplomat.

Khloé: Yeah. My mom left my dad.

Howard: And then your mom runs off with Bruce Jenner.

AT THE BEGINNING MY DAD DEFINITELY DID BELIEVE IN O.J. HE COULDN'T BELIEVE THAT HIS BEST FRIEND WOULD DO THAT.

Kim: Married five months after they divorced.

Howard: Wow. Do you think they were having an affair? Is that what was going on?

Khloé: No, they got introduced. They went on a blind date, after she got divorced.

Howard: When you first saw Bruce Jenner . . . I'm fascinated by his plastic surgery. He was one of the most handsome men in America. I mean, if I could've had a face like that—

Robin: You'd never touch it.

Howard: I would never touch it. Every guy wanted to look like Bruce Jenner. What do you think? Did he go psycho in some way or berserk? Like, have you ever spoken about it?

Khloé: How old was he when he got his face-lift?

Kim: He was in his, I think—

Khloé: Like, young.

Howard: He was young, right?

Kim: Everyone has their own issues, and I guess he wasn't comfortable with himself, and he wanted to fix his nose and the guy talked him into doing something else.

Howard: Do you like him?

Khloé: I love him.

Kim: We love him.

Howard: Why do you think you guys love him so much? And since your mom left your dad and all.

Khloé: I think why I personally love Bruce so much is because he's never tried to force himself on us as, "I'm your dad now." He's always been so accepting of knowing he's our stepdad.

Howard: Yeah, I noticed on the show he has a good way of just staying out of things. He steers clear. "I don't have control over these girls. I can only give them advice when they ask."

Khloé: He's really secure in himself in that respect. Also, I love that he lets us love my father still. He's not jealous of that.

Kim: There's pictures of my dad all around the house.

Howard: You ever see Bruce naked?

Khloé: Ew, no.

Kim: No.

Howard: You've never seen his penis?

Khloé: I would die.

Howard: You would kill yourself.

Khloé: I would kill myself if I saw his penis. Die, I would die.

Kim: I wonder if he has bikini waxes.

Howard: I wonder too, 'cause he seems a little, you know, feminine that way.

Khloé: He's very hairless, actually. I've seen his chest.

Kim: He's still ripped for being, like, sixty.

Howard: So let me understand something now. What's with you two? Only black guys, is that the thing?

Khloé: I'm only black guys.

Kim: She's only. I'm not.

Howard: What happened there?

Khloé: Once you go black, you just never go back.

Howard: Is that true?

Kim: Not true. I don't think it's true.

Khloé: Kim, when have you gone back from black?

Kim: I've had a boyfriend my whole life.

Khloé: Well, and he's been black. So what are you talking about?

Kim: I'm just saying I'm totally half and half.

Khloé: Where is the other half?

Kim: Like before.

Khloe: And then once you went black, you haven't gone back. So hello, it's a true statement.

Howard: What is it? How do you think this whole thing happened?

Kim: Maybe because we have such big asses, like the black guys like.

Howard: And so how old were you girls when you started having sex with black guys?

Kim: I had a boyfriend in high school.

Howard: Where did you meet a black guy in Beverly Hills?

> **" MAYBE BECAUSE WE HAVE SUCH BIG ASSES, LIKE THE BLACK GUYS LIKE.**

Kim: Well, I went to an all-girls Catholic private school.

Howard: That's how.

Khloé: That's what ruined us.

Howard: Right, that's what did it. Are black guys better in bed?

Khloé: I don't know.

Howard: You don't know because it's all you've ever slept with.

Khloé: Yeah.

Kim: I'd say it's just all about the chemistry between people. [*laughs*] I'm really, like, uncomfortable when I talk about, like—

Khloé: I'm not.

Howard: What? About sex?

Kim: Yeah. I don't know, I get really nervous.

Khloé: I think people perceive Kim as being so outgoing and very—

Kim: Like this sexual person and stuff.

Howard: You do seem sexual to me, though.

Khloé: She's not at all. And she's so shy.

Howard: But I always see pictures of you in bikinis and showing off your body.

Kim: 'Cause I like to go to the beach and stuff.

Howard: Are your boobs real?

Kim: They are. Mine are.

Howard: Both of you?

Kim: Yeah.

Howard: No kidding. Nice rack.

Kim: Kourtney's aren't.

Khloé: Mine aren't as big as hers, but she has a nice rack.

Howard: Kim's got huge boobs. What are you, a D?

Kim: I'm a 34 D.

Howard: Do you feel angry that your sister was born with a D and you were not?

Khloé: No, I actually like my boobs.

Kim: When I was, like, eleven, my boobs started to get really big. And Kourtney, who's my older sister, was so flat. And I would cry and she would make fun of me in front of all the guys. Not at school, but the guys outside of school. She would just be like, "Kim has the biggest boobs, the biggest nipples." And, like, make fun of me when I was eleven.

Howard: You were good friends with Paris Hilton. Both of you were, or just Kim?

Kim: She was friends with Nicky [Hilton].

Howard: Paris Hilton you would think would be happy for your success. She sort of came out of nowhere. Her family was interesting. Her background was interesting. She became a reality star. You could say the same for you guys.

Kim: Mm-hmm.

Howard: But Paris Hilton is jealous of you, isn't she?

Kim: You know what? I haven't talked to her in a few years.

Howard: Why? You were good friends.

Kim: We were good friends.

Howard: What happened? You got famous and she couldn't deal with it, right? Be honest.

Kim: If you say so. I don't know.

Howard: I'm asking you. What happened?

Kim: I don't know.

Howard: Why was there a falling-out? Did you ever say to her, "Paris, what's going on here?"

Kim: I never did.

Howard: Why? You know why you're not speaking. Let's be honest.

Kim: Well, I mean . . .

Howard: Why be afraid to say it?

Kim: I did speak to her once when she went on a radio station and said that my ass looks like cellulite, like in a trash bag or something. She did call me to apologize.

Khloé: Cottage cheese.

Kim: Cottage cheese. That's what she said it looked like.

Howard: She needed to put you down. So, what, does she feel you copied her success or—

Kim: I'm sure.

Howard: Somehow you take away from something that she has?

Kim: I'm sure. But we've never had a conversation about it. We just one day did not speak again.

Howard: Don't you guys compete for the same dollars? Part of the way you guys make a living is you can show up at a club and get paid $25,000 or something for just showing up, just to be at a party. Isn't it true now you can appear at a club somewhere and get more money than Paris Hilton herself, right?

Kim: I don't know. What's her going rate?

Howard: I heard yours is $25,000 to appear.

Khloé: Kim's is more.

Howard: I want you to come to a party, 'cause I'm opening a new club. What do I have to pay? Fifty?

Kim: If it's a birthday or a New Year's, then it would be a lot more. If it's just a regular Wednesday, say about forty.

Howard: Do you guys put all the money in the same pot?

Kim: That stuff that we do together, it goes—

Howard: That all goes in one.

Khloé: Yeah.

Howard: So you have to split that with your mom too?

Khloé: No.

Kim: She'll get, like, a manager percentage.

Khloé: She gets commission 'cause she's our management.

Howard: Commission? Commission shmission. Time to end that.

Kim: You tell her that. You should call her.

Khloé: Well, Kim and Kris are twins.

Kim: We're twins.

Khloé: They are obsessed with each other.

Kim: My mom came to me, she told me about the show idea. I said, "Oh my God, I'd love to do it. Do you need me to go into the meetings? Help you?" We've always from the start been on the same page.

Khloé: I just think my mom knows Kourtney and I aren't as into it. Kourtney is a lot more into art.

Kim: She couldn't care less.

Howard: Sometimes it seems on the show like Kim gets more attention than Khloé. And Khloé, you get jealous, so you'll get like, "Hey, we have a family business. Kim's

making all the decisions, she's calling all the shots. Who the fuck is she? She's just one of the sisters." Is Kim in a sense too full of herself?

Khloé: No, I don't get upset about Kim making decisions. Sometimes I feel like Kourtney and I and Kim, we work so hard, but then Kim's the one that gets all the credit for it.

Howard: All right, Khloé, let's get down to it. You got married. You married a rich guy. What is he? A basketball player?

Khloé: He plays for the Lakers.

Howard: Of course he's a black guy, which you love.

Khloé: Duh.

Howard: And this must be a big black guy. How tall a guy are we talking?

Khloé: Six-nine, six-ten.

Howard: I don't mean to be gross, but he must have a penis like a horse.

Khloé: It's amazing.

Howard: It's amazing, right?

Khloé: It's pretty fun.

Howard: And you're not tall. How tall are you?

Khloé: Five-nine.

Howard: You can handle something that big?

Khloé: Honey, yeah.

Howard: Is he the biggest penis you've ever had?

Khloé: Yeah.

Kim: Oh, I don't wanna know this.

Howard: Well, the public needs to know. Show me with your hands.

Kim: What?! That's like a horse.

Howard: Yes, that's exactly what I imagined. It's as big as your sister.

Khloé: Yeah, it's as big as Kim's leg.

Howard: And, Kim, you're banging Reggie Bush?

Kim: Mm-hmm.

Howard: That's a football player?

Kim: Mm-hmm.

Howard: He too has a big penis?

Kim: [*laughs*]

Howard: Yeah?

Kim: I don't like talking about stuff like that.

Khloé: His schlong.

Howard: Who has the bigger penis?

Kim: Well, Lamar does probably.

Khloé: Two of Reggie.

Howard: Reggie is banging you.

Kim: Yes, he is.

Howard: Can't be a white guy ever. It's always gotta be the black guys.

Kim: I guess so.

Khloé: Maybe Kim would bang you. Oh, you're married.

Howard: I'm married. I'm in a loving relationship. I hardly look like a black guy. So are you going to marry this guy Reggie?

Kim: You never know. We've been together going on three years.

Howard: You're in love?

Kim: Yeah, of course. We'd like to take our time, though, you know? I was married. I got married at nineteen for four years, so I think that now I definitely want to just take my time.

Howard: Don't be a two-time loser.

> ## SOMETIMES I FEEL LIKE KOURTNEY AND I AND KIM, WE WORK SO HARD, BUT THEN KIM'S THE ONE THAT GETS ALL THE CREDIT FOR IT.

Kim: Yeah, I won't be a two-time loser.

Howard: Kourtney got in trouble for what? Drinking and driving or something?

Khloé: That was me, honey.

Howard: That was you?

Khloé: Yeah.

Howard: What happened to you? You seem like a good girl.

Khloé: I'm now a good girl.

Howard: What happened? Tell me what went wrong.

Khloé: Um, I just had a couple too many drinks, and I thought I was a lot less drunk than I really was. I mean, honestly, when you're in the club and you're dancing, it's like you're kind of sweating it out and you're fine. And then when you get in the car, I think it kind of hits you. I was a point-oh-nine—limit's point-oh-eight.

Howard: They gave you the test?

Kim: Were you so nervous? Did you see the cop behind you?

Khloé: No, I didn't see the cop behind me. They gave me the test. I failed. They took me in to jail that night. I was in there for nineteen hours. Kimberly and my mom actually came as my visitors to jail.

Kim: There were hookers in there with her.

Khloé: Everyone else was in there for

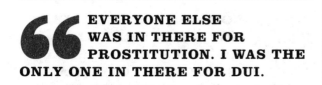

EVERYONE ELSE WAS IN THERE FOR PROSTITUTION. I WAS THE ONLY ONE IN THERE FOR DUI.

prostitution. I was the only one in there for DUI.

Howard: Either of you girls ever have lesbianism?

Kim: No.

Khloé: No.

Howard: I can see Kim doing it.

Kim: Really?

Howard: Yeah, I could see you definitely getting it on with another girl.

Kim: No.

Howard: You seem more like the party girl, though. Kim actually is kind of mellowed out, but you—

Khloé: Me?

Howard: You do a little coke? What are you up to?

Khloé: I don't do drugs. I am a drinker all the way.

Kim: All of us, we've never gotten into drugs.

Khloé: So many of my friends have done drugs, and I've seen such negative effects of it.

Howard: And Kim and Khloé's QuickTrim diet products are available at GNC stores nationwide. Now, you just lost a lot of weight, right, Kim?

Kim: Yeah, well, Khloé lost about how much? Twenty-five pounds?

Khloé: Twenty-seven.

Howard: Holy shit.

Kim: I've lost about a good solid ten pounds, but I'm only five-two so it just makes a big difference on me. I can't really control what I eat. I like to eat.

Howard: So what happened? You take this product and you slim down a little bit? Kills the appetite?

Kim: I have the biggest sweet tooth, so it just really curbs that and it, like, speeds up your metabolism and just makes you lose weight.

Khloé: Makes you regular.

Howard: Makes you regular? Do you doody a lot on this thing?

Khloé: A little.

Howard: How many times a day? How many times a day you doody?

Khloé: Just once.

Howard: What about you, Kim? You too?

Khloé: [*laughs*] Look, she's gonna die.

Howard: Kim, do you doody more than once a day? I could see you being pretty regular.

Khloé: She's so embarrassed.

Howard: I can see you two or three times a day making a doody.

Khloé: Kim, it's okay.

Howard: Don't be embarrassed.

Khloé: It's normal.

Kim: Not that much, no.

Howard: How do you girls clean up after you doody? Do you ever use baby wipes like I do?

Kim: Wet wipes. Wet wipes in every bathroom.

Khloé: All the time.

Howard: Who makes the bigger doody, you or your sister?

Khloé: Kim. Kim is a killer.

Kim: How do you know?

Khloé: The bathroom . . . like, the stench, Kim.

Kim: When do I ever go to the bathroom in front of you? We don't even live together.

Khloé: I can smell it from my house.

Howard: Wow. Does Reggie say anything about that?

Khloé: Reggie leaves.

Kim: She's making it up.

Howard: Do you ever doody in front of Reggie?

Kim: My brother and his ex-girlfriend, they were, like, so obsessed with each other they could never be apart. He would go to the bathroom and she would sit on his lap in there.

Khloé: You're lying.

Kim: I swear.

Howard: Do you think if you guys hadn't been successful in terms of becoming famous, it would have like wrecked your life?

Kim: Not at all.

Howard: Not at all? Was it not a burning passion for you to get famous?

Kim: No. We're having so much fun while this ride is lasting, but we all have really normal lives outside of this. We have our clothing store, Dash, and stuff that we did before what we're doing now.

Howard: Right, you were working before.

Kim: I was a stylist and had this closet organizing company, and we had our clothing stores. We would just continue to do that kind of stuff.

Howard: By the way, girls, when you're with your boyfriend or your husband, do you black it up at all? Do you have an ability to talk in—

Khloé: Not at all. No, I hate people like that.

Howard: You don't like when white people put on the—

Khloé: Yeah, like, you are who you are. I don't like people that try to . . . Like, you just accept who you are and . . . I just . . . I don't like people to talk differently about other people.

Kim: We sound like the biggest Valley girls.

Khloé: We *are* Valley girls.

Howard: Do you girls ever masturbate with a vibrator?

Khloé: Yeah.

Howard: You do. You like it?

Khloé: Kim, are you okay?

Kim: I'll let Khloé answer this one.

Howard: Kim, you don't? You never touch yourself?

Kim: I don't talk about stuff like that.

Howard: Would you use a vibrator or do you use your own fingers?

 WE'RE HAVING SO MUCH FUN WHILE THIS RIDE IS LASTING.

Kim: I don't know.

Howard: Be honest.

Kim: I don't know.

Howard: What do you use? What does she use? You know.

Khloé: I've never seen her do it.

Howard: You only think about black guys when you masturbate?

Khloé: I honestly just think about my husband right now.

Howard: Come on.

Khloé: He has eighty-two games a year and—

Howard: Do you trust him to go on the road by himself?

Khloé: One hundred percent.

Howard: You don't think he'll cheat?

Khloé: No.

Howard: Look what happened with Tiger Woods.

Khloé: Right, but I just don't.

Howard: Is he sort of your type, Tiger Woods?

Khloé: Not mine at all. I'm not really into golf.

Kim: Golf reminds me of, like, Bruce.

Khloé: Yeah, Bruce and golf.

Howard: This is more for Khloé than Kim: Would you ever date a guy as light as, let's say, President Obama? Or would they have to be darker?

Kim: I think he's too light for Khloé.

Howard: Too light, right? She goes super black. Wesley Snipes black.

Khloé: It's not about the color of skin.

It's about the chemistry. I think President Obama is so handsome.

Howard: You would have sex with Obama if he was single?

Khloé: I would do it for our country.

Howard: You would?

Khloé: Yeah.

Howard: You know what? You're a true patriot.

Khloé: I am.

Howard: What magazines do you look at when you want to pleasure yourself? Like *Jet* and stuff like that?

Khloé: We just open up a football magazine. Kim does.

Howard: When you were growing up, did you ever fantasize about O.J.?

Khloé: [*laughs*] No.

Howard: Anal sex? You girls down for that? Who likes it?

Khloé: Look, Kim's about to cry.

Howard: Kim, do you like anal? Yes or no?

Kim: I'm not answering it.

Howard: Exit or entrance? Come on, answer.

Khloé: That's why Kim shits so much. I'm just kidding.

Howard: Can a brother spank you girls?

Khloé: I love being spanked.

Kim: Yes. Yes, I'll answer that.

Howard: You both like being spanked? Like getting your hair pulled?

Kim: Yeah.

Khloé: I love it.

Howard: Do you like talking dirty in bed?

Kim: Yes.

Khloé: Love it.

Howard: You love all that?

Kim: Yes.

Howard: You like sixty-nine? Who doesn't like that?

Khloé: Yeah.

Howard: And anal, yes or no? Will you do it, Khloé?

Kim: I think Khloé will do anything for her man.

Khloé: For my husband, anything. I will do anything for my husband.

Howard: Fair enough. Kim, would you do it for your man?

Kim: I'll do anything for my husband.

Howard: For your husband?

Kim: I will do anything for my husband.

Howard: If only I was a black man.

Khloé: If only.

MONEY & FAME

I don't remember a time when I didn't want to be on the radio. Radio has been my life for so long that, like the Willie Nelson song, it's always on my mind. For most people, that song is about a woman. For me, it's about a microphone. There will be moments when I'll look at a clock, and if it reads 1:07 my first thought is, "Westchester 107 WRNW." If the clock reads 1:01, I think, "DC 101 'Kick-Ass Rock and Roll.'" It's in my DNA. I have dreams—actually, nightmares—about the music running out. There is dead air, and I can't recover or do a thing about it. I can't get it together to fill that space.

I didn't get into radio for money. I got into radio because I needed to be heard. I would have done it no matter what somebody paid me. I didn't have much of a choice—it was the only thing I could imagine wanting to do for a living. I didn't have anything to fall back on. Plus, I didn't really start making a lot of money until later in my career. So I always lived pretty modestly.

That's also just who I am. I'm not a materialistic guy. I have a couple of beautiful homes, but that's because I hate going out. I'm a homebody, a total recluse. Since I spend so much time at home, I want to be comfortable. But that's it. I'm not into cars and all of that. I remember when I was around forty my midlife crisis kicked in. I decided to buy a brand-new Corvette convertible. 'Cause that's what men do, right? I'm six foot five. My head stuck out of the car like I was a Big Bird float in the Macy's Thanksgiving Day Parade. People were recognizing me and waving to me. I even had one guy jump into the car. I was at a stop sign and he hopped right over the door and into the passenger seat. That was it for me and cars.

I think it's so interesting to talk to guests about their own experiences with money— whether it's Kid Rock talking about his private plane or Kendrick Lamar talking about taking care of people he came up with in Compton. I also love hearing about how they handle fame. While money has never been a big thing for me, fame is definitely something

I find gratifying. I remember as a teenager walking into parties and no one paying attention to me. I was so awkward. When I got famous, I could walk into any room and suddenly was the prom king. I'd be lying if I said I didn't enjoy that.

Not everybody does, and it's great to hear those other perspectives, especially that line of demarcation in people's lives—the very specific and finite moment when they went from being a nobody to a somebody, and how that changed everything forever.

STING

Howard: The first time you hear "Roxanne" on the radio, where are you?

Sting: Oh, man, I remember that. I was painting my kitchen. I had a basement flat in Bayswater, in London. My little son was on the floor. I was up some ladder painting some white emulsion on the ceiling, with the radio on. And that song came on. And I started singing. And I went, "Fuck, I'm on the radio!"

JONAH HILL

Jonah: So I lived in Seth's [Rogen] old apartment. He moves out, I move in. Michael Cera and I spend every day there. We walk around the neighborhood. It's right by Canter's Deli in the middle of the city [LA].

Howard: How did you have money? Did they pay you for *Superbad*?

Jonah: Enough to get this apartment after *Superbad*, but it hadn't come out. So Michael and I walk around every day, talking about bullshit that twenty-year-old guys talk about. I remember I bought a newspaper August 17, 2007. It was literally the craziest day. It was the day *Superbad* came out. And it started to get crazy when billboards were around, but people didn't know what it was. My friends were like, "I saw a fucking billboard of you on a whole building." They literally built a billboard above my shitty apartment. And it wasn't getting me laid. I'm like, "Look outside the fucking window!" So Mike and I go outside my apartment to get a bite to eat. And I'm not kidding you, it was like what you see with Beatlemania on TV.

Howard: It really clicked for the women. They understood who you were.

Jonah: It wasn't even women. It was just people would go fucking nuts when they saw us. And McLovin—I mean, Chris [Mintz-Plasse], forget about his life.

Howard: Does McLovin get laid a lot now?

Jonah: Yeah, I made sure to get him laid on that tour. That was my job. The *Superbad* tour was the fucking best thing ever.

Howard: Do you mean the promotional tour?

Jonah: The promotional tour. Because the movie fucking ruled. I don't want to sound like a douche, but it played great. It played like a rock concert. So we would go and do Q&As, and it was like after a rock concert. We'd just make them laugh for an hour and a half. So the movie comes out, we'd just become famous, and I'm like, "Yes!" And the next day they ship us to Europe, where we're not famous. The next day. I'm like, "Give me a week! Give me a fucking week!"

Howard: You want to use your superpowers.

Jonah: I'm like, "Shit, I just won the lottery, and you guys are making me move to a place where my currency has no value anymore!"

....

CARDI B

Howard: I think part of what charms people about you is that you were working in a strip club and then of all sudden you've got this huge career. Was the strip club a horrible existence? Did you hate it? Did you come to hate men? I mean, I've seen some weird shit go down in strip clubs.

Cardi B: You wanna know something? I feel like a lot of people want me to lie and be like, "I hated it. I went through so much. I don't recommend it." I don't tell girls to go do it. But I'm not even gonna front: it really saved me. Before I was

working in a strip club I was a cashier at Amish Market.

Howard: Didn't your boss say to you, "You'd be better off working at the strip club across the street."

Cardi B: He was like, "You have a nice body. I'm telling you, you should just work across the street. They make so much money. You look like one of those girls. I'm telling you." He was Turkish.

Howard: Were you nervous to go over there and audition?

Cardi B: I was really scared because I didn't know the type of things that go down in there. I was so young, and everybody shames stripping. I was ashamed that I was dancing naked.

Howard: Fully nude or with bottoms on?

Cardi B: With bottoms on. But I still felt so ashamed for the first couple of months. I used to cry after work. 'Cause all I used to think was I could only imagine how embarrassed my parents would be. The imagery of my mom and dad came into my head when I used to give lap dances. But then it's like, "I

made $500 today." And then, "I made $2,000."

Howard: Did you have to tell your parents you were working in a strip club? 'Cause at some point they're probably saying, "Where are you getting all this money from?"

Cardi B: I told my parents that I was babysitting some really rich white folks' kids.

....

INSANE CLOWN POSSE

Howard: Your kids who are growing up now, do they know how to fight? Do you toughen them up? You guys are multimillionaires, right?

Violent J: Our kids are learning in the streets.

Howard: What do you mean, "in the streets"?

Violent J: I mean our kids are coming up the way we came up.

Howard: No, they're not.

Shaggy 2 Dope: Mine are. I got half custody, but my kids stay with their mom and she don't live in a friendly neighborhood.

Howard: Really? Don't you support them?

Shaggy 2 Dope: I take care of them. I mean, they come out to my house and they're cool. But they go to public schools around there and everything. And they get into fights at school. I box with my kids and stuff. Teach them how to box.

Howard: Toughen them up. Great dad. I love it. Listen, you gotta teach the kids how to fight. They're going to need it. It's a skill they need.

Shaggy 2 Dope: Especially once they get to high school and everyone figures out who their dad is, everyone's going to want to fuck with 'em.

Howard: Doesn't the mom sue you for more money? A lot of these women will say, "Hey, the guy I had the kids with, he's got a great lifestyle and my kids come home to a shitty neighborhood." How do you get away with not giving her more money?

Violent J: First of all, he doesn't get away with it.

Shaggy 2 Dope: No, I don't.

Violent J: He gives her crazy bucketloads of money.

Shaggy 2 Dope: I get raped in my ass, yeah.

Howard: You're paying a lot of support.

Shaggy 2 Dope: Yes, sir.

Violent J: Insane fucking money. It's not even my business, but let me chime in. Fucking ridiculous, stupid, insane money.

WOODY HARRELSON

Howard: You say you bet with Willie Nelson when you guys are hanging out. Like, what are the stakes for a dominoes game?

Woody: I mean, it varies. It can be anywhere from $100 to $500.

Howard: That's it? You don't get crazy?

Woody: I mean, we're playing game after game after game, so it can add up a bit.

Howard: Right. Because you're both very wealthy men. You are worth $65 million.

Woody: Where did you come up with that?

Howard: I have it right here off the Internet, a very reliable source: $65 million.

Woody: I'm feeling a lot more secure than when I came in the door.

Howard: You didn't even know?

Woody: I had no idea.

Howard: Do you have any idea what your net worth is?

Woody: Um, no, I really don't. I try not to think about those things. Those things scare me.

Robin: Who handles the money?

Howard: Who's handling that?

Woody: That's all in the wifey's hands.

Howard: Really?

Woody: Everything's in the wifey's hands.

Howard: You're a brave man.

WILLIE NELSON

Howard: There were times you would have zero money. You would go to a pawnshop and hock your guitar, which is your most beloved possession, right?

Willie: Yes.

Howard: You would actually have to pawn your instruments.

Willie: I'd have to pawn in the middle of the week in order to get enough money to make it to the weekend.

And then I'd have to go get it out of the pawnshop to go play the gig.

....

DAVID SPADE

David: You go to these parties and you sort of feel dumb after a while. There's *too* many famous people there. And you feel sort of dumb. Like, "What am I doing here?" And all the girls have six-inch heels on. I couldn't be more of a pipsqueak. Even worse than normal. So I just walk around and say hi to the ones I know.

Howard: I know exactly what you mean. It seems like a good idea to go to these things and see famous people. And then I go, "Why is this enchanting? I don't get it."

David: By the way, you're always being career-checked. Just, like, *when* you go to that party is interesting. The *Vanity Fair* one's a really big one every year, 'cause they bring in people from all over the world that you never see in the same room. That's what is fun. And so you get your invite. And I never really paid attention in the

old days. But then one time things were slowing down. You know, the career comes and goes, Howard. It's not all a straight line. Little bit of a roller coaster. And my show wasn't on—something dumb—and they go, "I wouldn't go this year." That's how the PR people say it: "I don't think it's gonna be good this year." And you're like, "No, I'll go." And they're like, "No, you can't go." That was the first time I'm like, "I'm not invited?" And they're like, "It's just that there's *so* many people."

Howard: Oh, that hurts.

David: And then the next year, I guess things were doing better. I got invited. But no plus-one. That's how a lot of things go. No plus-one.

Howard: That's how it works?

David: This is the dirty, behind-the-curtain of these parties. And then they said, "You can go at midnight." It starts at eight-thirty or nine.

Howard: Are you fucking kidding me?

David: You go to the party like a salmon going upstream. Everyone's

pouring out and you're like, "I'm here! I'm here!"

Howard: David, you're blowing the lid off things. This is one of the reasons I'm glad I do not live in Los Angeles. There's so much of that culture out there— evaluating who is doing well in show business.

David: Yes. They decide for you. If you think you're doing well and everyone's kissing your ass, just call to get in parties.

Howard: David, is it worth it? What about if you took the attitude, "Fuck these parties. I'm never going to one again. Because I don't want to be evaluated." Who is doing the evaluating?

David: I'm doing it too.

Howard: Yeah?

David: Yeah, I'm like, "What the fuck is Snooki doing here?"

....

LOUIS C.K.

Howard: You said once that when you were a comic and you started making some money, you stashed $100,000 in cash somewhere. Because you needed to know, no matter what, even if you got ripped off—

Louis: I could put my hands on that money, yes.

Howard: You needed the $100,000 to be there. Have you now taken that $100,000 in cash and put it in a bank?

Louis: I did, because I can't have people robbing my house.

Howard: Right, but there was a period of time where you did that?

Louis: Yeah, because I grew up with nothing, and all the way until I was, like, forty, I never had money. When there's checks going around or people are paying your bills for you, I'm like, "I don't believe that money is really there."

Howard: It's probably not there. Those guys probably took it a long time ago, but they're paying your bills.

Louis: Also, you see the movies about the Depression, people jumping out the window because their money vanished in the click of a button. I even bought gold coins because I'm like, "Even this cash . . ." Once you get into that mind-set, you go crazy, because people tell you

rats could eat your money, bugs could eat your money.

Howard: You didn't keep it in a safe, right? You hid it in a shoebox.

Louis: That's right. For me, money is like oxygen. You breathe it in and out. You don't hold your breath. What are you going to do then? You just have to let it go.

....

GARY BUSEY

Howard: You must be worth a lot of money. You're constantly working. How much are you worth? Announce to my audience.

Gary: Priceless.

Howard: Seriously, are you a multimillionaire? You've got to be.

Gary: No, I'm not a multimillionaire.

Howard: You're not?

Gary: You must remember what Benjamin Franklin said: "The man who is rich rejoices with what he has."

....

ROBERT DOWNEY JR.

Howard: Did you have to audition for *Iron Man*?

Robert: I did. I screen-tested.

Howard: [Director] Jon Favreau, did he have to fight for you?

Robert: He fought for me. And I'll never forget it.

Howard: Do you know who they wanted to play Iron Man?

Robert: It was between me and another guy.

Howard: Who was the guy?

Robert: It wouldn't be fair to mention his name.

Howard: Of course it's fair.

Robert: Nah, it's not. He never had a chance.

Howard: You weren't gonna let that happen. You gotta be a gunslinger, right?

Robert: Absolutely.

Howard: You got to go in and be like, "I'm gonna get this fucking role."

Robert: Yeah, you don't have to do it all the time. You just have to do it at the crucial times. Otherwise you're some wackjob and everything is a firefight.

Howard: It's so funny, because now I look at you and go, "He's Tony Stark. There's no question about it." But before somebody gets the role, you don't know that.

Robert: Right.

Howard: But now nobody could take that role from you.

Robert: I got so lucky, too. When Stan Lee developed this character in that unpopular Vietnam era—it just became relevant again. And I had the perfect backstory to do it. I mean, I wouldn't wish my backstory on anyone else. But now I look back on it and I go, "Wow." You know?

Howard: That's probably why you had to audition. Because your backstory was you were out of control, you were this, you were that.

Robert: Absolutely. And I was in my early forties, and younger is better and all that stuff.

Howard: So you really had to fight for that role.

Robert: I did.

∙∙∙∙∙∙∙∙∙∙∙∙∙∙∙∙∙∙∙∙∙∙∙∙∙∙∙∙∙∙∙∙∙∙∙∙

DAVE GROHL

Howard: When you were in Nirvana, you got married, and probably everyone said to you, "What are you getting married for, man? There's tons of girls on the road to screw you," right?

Dave: No. See, it wasn't like that with Nirvana. We came from the punk rock scene and it's not really like that.

Howard: The punk rock scene is like, "Hey, man. Don't get caught up in it."

Dave: Right. No hang-ups.

Howard: Kurt was all about, like, "Hey, man. We're not in this for the money, man."

Dave: Yeah, none of us expected any of that stuff to happen.

Howard: But when it does, it's nice.

Dave: Hell yes.

Howard: Why deny it?

Dave: It's good.

Howard: They always made it seem like Nirvana was all upset about the commercial success.

Dave: I think most people thought we were just like these brooding, negative guys. I was psyched, man. I was.

∙∙∙∙∙∙∙∙∙∙∙∙∙∙∙∙∙∙∙∙∙∙∙∙∙∙∙∙∙∙∙∙∙∙∙∙

BARBARA WALTERS

Howard: Did you want everything for yourself? Do you think that you were so hungry for success that you would get insanely jealous if, say, Diane Sawyer got the interview instead of you? What was the obsession to get everything and do everything?

Barbara: I don't think it was as much an obsession as it was a need financially and otherwise. When I wrote my book, *Audition*, I talked very personally about my family, and my father who had been in show business.

Howard: Your father owned clubs.

Barbara: He owned great nightclubs called The Latin Quarter in New York and Boston and Florida. And we lived in penthouses, and he was an entrepreneur. Then he lost everything. Everything.

Howard: You went from great wealth to—

Barbara: Nothing. My friends didn't have to work. I did. So it began with that, with having to do it, from losing everything. And then also I think I've always had this need—and maybe you do too—I always felt I was on the outside looking in.

Howard: You never felt successful?

Barbara: Well, in the early days it was very hard for a woman. It was very hard to get a job or to be accepted. When I was first on the *Today* show, the host who came on the program after Hugh Downs would not let me do any of the serious hard news questions. That was a man named Frank McGee. It went all the way up to the president of NBC. And it was the one time I really fought the battle and—he could ask three questions and I could come in for the fourth. So it wasn't obsession so much as it was, "Hey, I want to work!"

STEVE MILLER

Steve: When *Fly Like an Eagle* came out, we started off with a theater tour of, like, twenty-six cities. And then we were in arenas. And then we were in football stadiums. Nobody had played football stadiums. So it was really tough. We were developing stages and PAs. I mean, you had the Grateful Dead going out and playing with 250 home-stereo amps. That was 400 degrees on the stage. They had, like, 200 McIntosh amps. People were just making shit up, trying to figure out how to do this. You remember the Beatles at Shea Stadium?

Howard: Yeah, and it was awful musically.

Steve: With the three bookend speakers—one in front of second base and one at third and one at first.

Howard: Anyone who was there couldn't hear a fucking thing.

Steve: You couldn't hear anything. So now we're playing football stadiums and we're making this stuff up. We're making up the light shows. We're fooling around with laser.

Howard: After you put out *Abracadabra*, I felt like the record business had changed a lot and you just kind of got sick of the whole fucking thing.

Steve: The *LA Times* put out an article saying Capitol Records should be embarrassed for releasing my music and that my latest record was "unmitigated slop." You know, Howard, I had just sold almost twenty million records in a few years. I had been working nonstop for, like, fifteen years. And I had *Abracadabra* and Capitol didn't believe in it and didn't want to release it in the States. Well, I had a different deal with Phonogram in Europe. I canceled my American tour and went to Europe, and it was number one everywhere in the world except the States. Then it became number one in the States, and I came back and I went, "Okay, I'm going to go buy a boat and I'm going to name it *Abracadabra* and I'm out of here." And that's what I did.

Howard: How long did you go on the boat for?

Steve: Six years.

Howard: And what did you do? You just went and saw the world?

Steve: No, no. I moved to Seattle. I lived in Seattle and I went boating from May to September every year, and I learned how to navigate and run a twin-engine diesel. That five to six years that I had off was good for me. I got healthier. I lived a normal life. I learned to do some other character-building things. Boating in the Pacific Northwest—I wasn't, like, riding around with a captain. I was running a twin-engine diesel fifty-five-foot boat.

....

TINA FEY

Howard: As a mom, now you're away from Hollywood, and your kids are in school, and there are other moms and other kids, and they want to have kids over to the house. Suddenly, you have to open your door to a lot of moms who are fucking excited that they're going to Tina Fey's house. Are you wary of that?

Tina: Not so much anymore. In New York, everybody's a big shot of some sort.

Howard: But not everyone's famous.

Tina: Right, but I don't think it's as prized a commodity here as it is in LA.

Howard: Can you become friends with the other moms?

Tina: For sure.

Howard: Oh, you can?

Tina: I think so. I hope so.

Howard: What happens when you catch them taking pictures in your house?

Tina: You have to find a school where people won't do that.

Howard: It's very, very hard.

Tina: Yeah.

Howard: And I'm sure it's a confusing thing as a parent, because you don't want to make it about you.

Tina: Yeah.

Howard: But the kids probably even think, "Well, gee, are they coming here to see my mom, or are they coming here to see me?"

Tina: We're not quite there. My kids are still pretty little. But, yeah, I always feel like, "That'll be kind of a bummer for them." But then I'm like, "But oh, I won't be famous by then."

Robin: You think it'll be over by then?

Tina: I'll be done. It'll be over.

Howard: Somebody told me a famous story about you. You were at a birthday party for your kids, and one of the children showed up to the party with a script pinned to their blouse and you were forced to read it. Is that a true story?

Tina: I read it, and it became *30 Rock*.

Howard: Is that right?

Tina: It was totally worth it.

Howard: *30 Rock* was an idea of one of the kids.

Tina: *30 Rock* was a child's idea.

....

JAMES CORDEN

Howard: Is it true that your wedding cost £250,000? Which is more than dollars. True or false?

James: It was around that, yeah.

Howard: No kidding. You really do love this woman. Why so much? Because you had so many guests?

James: Because I enjoy having a nice time.

Howard: This is crazy. £250,000. I could take that and put it in a money market or something, put it in T-bills, and live on that for the rest of my life.

James: I'll tell you why I don't put as much value on money. I genuinely believe I would rather waste money than time. Time is the only currency I think of that is actually worth anything with any real value. Time is the only thing that exists. You don't lie on your deathbed going, "I wish I just made a million more dollars." However, when I am on my deathbed, my wedding that weekend is something that I'm going to remember.

CLAIRE DANES

Howard: Four Golden Globes. Does this turn you on when you get these awards? Or you don't care?

Claire: You and arousal.

Howard: Are you aroused right now? That's what I want to know. No, seriously, what's going on with these awards? Does that matter to Claire Danes? You seem like you're above all this.

Claire: Well, the nice thing about winning awards is that you don't have to win them again. You've been validated. It's okay.

Howard: Is the cool thing to take the awards and put them in your bathroom? In other words, you don't want

to display them too proudly because then you're a tool. So what do we do?

Claire: I put them in the office.

Howard: And when you have me over for dinner, you'd say, "Oh, by the way . . ."

Robin: "Let's take a tour."

Howard: No, you wouldn't tell me that's your Emmy. You'd wait for me to notice it. Is that the move?

Claire: That's the move.

KENDRICK LAMAR

Howard: The influence this music has on a whole different culture—it's pretty mind-blowing when you have that kind of influence. When someone like Obama says, "Kendrick Lamar's song is my favorite song," it's pretty heady stuff.

Kendrick: That's a lot of pressure, right?

Howard: I think about guys in rock and roll. They start to get successful and they can go crazy—crazy with the fame, crazy with the money, the women, the whole thing. Because

when you grow up like you did, poor, and nobody's handing you anything, you can go nuts. What keeps you grounded? Or are you grounded?

Kendrick: You can go crazy, fast.

Howard: Are you going crazy?

Kendrick: Nah, I'm not going crazy. I'm all right. You gotta have grounded people around you, people that are going to tell you the truth.

Howard: How do you know who those people are?

Kendrick: Well, these the people that are honest with you since day one. They have to be honest with you. When you know that you're wrong—and everybody knows they're wrong in certain situations—no matter how much fame or fortune or what your status is, they're able to tell you you're wrong. And you have to respect that.

Howard: Your parents were living—where did they live before they moved to California?

Kendrick: Chicago. South Side Chicago.

Howard: Was your dad in a gang?

Kendrick: Yeah, he was affiliated.

Howard: So they decide to move to Compton, and all they have is like two garbage bags filled with clothing. These are poor people. And they move to Compton. Before you were born your dad worked at KFC and your mom worked at McDonald's. That ain't an easy life. There's no money around. How many kids were in your family?

Kendrick: My immediate family? Four of us.

Howard: And it's extreme poverty, right?

Kendrick: Definitely, definitely.

Howard: How do you avoid getting into the gang lifestyle in Compton, when your dad is not telling you it's a bad thing?

Kendrick: Well, he's actually telling me. You know the saying, "Do as I say, not as I do." He gave me the reality of it. But what he taught me to be as a man, you have to go through things, you have to

see for yourself. You can go through everything in the world, but I'm still gonna go out there and get my hands dirty. I think it was really the act of my mother being a dreamer. So they gave me that duality, they gave me that balance.

Howard: You never joined a gang?

Kendrick: Nah.

Howard: Don't you thank God for that? Because I've interviewed guys who were gang-affiliated, and then when they get this level of success like where you're at, the gang does come back and says, "Wait a second, you don't leave the gang now because you're successful. You're tied for the rest of your life." And so even if you want to get out, you can't. I mean, thank God you didn't.

Kendrick: Yeah, definitely. And it comes with a respect. I grew up in that culture my whole life, so I know it from my family, my relatives, my friends. It just comes from the respect they have for me. You know, to understand that this dude is talented. He can

potentially save our life from near and afar. And that's exactly what's going on. Because they have kids now, and now their kids want to do something else other than be in the streets the same way we was taught.

Howard: Do you feel responsibility that you have to provide money, financial care for people in your family? Is that on your back now 'cause you succeeded, or are you free of that obligation?

Kendrick: It's really not just a financial thing, is something I learned. It's more of an opportunity, an idea of doing something more than what we used to. Just having the idea and the inspiration of being more than you know. Setting small goals. Setting higher standards for yourself. That is the thing that I always preach to my family. You can do more. Look at what we doing. Look at what I'm doing. Look at where we come from. It don't just stop with me.

....

KID ROCK

Kid Rock: I don't even know what to do with all this

fucking money, to be honest with you.

Howard: You've been very philanthropic. People should know that about you. You give to a lot of charities. You raise a lot of money for charities, right?

Kid Rock: Ah, whatever.

Howard: No, you do. That's a good thing. But you really have that much money that you don't know what to do with it?

Kid Rock: Tons.

Howard: What does "tons" mean? A hundred million?

Kid Rock: How much do you have?

Howard: I'm not bragging here. You are. A hundred million dollars, do you have? Do you have a hundred million dollars? What is that wink? Are you coming on to me? Are you Harvey Weinstein now? Are you harassing me? No, seriously, are you worth a hundred million dollars? Look at that smile. Look at these stats. You've sold more than twenty-six million albums. By the way, are you in the Rock and Roll Hall of Fame?

Kid Rock: No.

Robin: Are you eligible?

Kid Rock: I'm eligible.

Howard: I saw that you inducted Cheap Trick.

Kid Rock: I did Cheap Trick, I did Bob Seger, Lynyrd Skynyrd, and ZZ Top. They keep calling me to induct people, but like, "Yeah, but you ain't gettin' in."

Howard: Isn't that weird? I think you deserve a place there, right? Don't you? You don't give a shit? You don't give a shit.

Kid Rock: I don't fucking care.

Howard: Why don't you give a shit? Is that just posturing?

Kid Rock: 'Cause I got a big new airplane, I got a beautiful granddaughter, I got a double-wide in fucking Nashville, a beautiful home in Michigan. I hunt in Alabama. I stay in Florida when it's fucking cold in Michigan.

Howard: What kind of plane do you own?

Kid Rock: A big Challenger Bombardier with western interior.

Howard: You own it? Look at you!

Kid Rock: Who would've thought? Actually, I was saying this last night. This is fucked up, by the way. I'm gonna get in tons of trouble for this. You're like, "Tell me."

Howard: Tell me. What? What would you get in trouble for?

Kid Rock: I had this house in Malibu for forever. This big, expensive house. This $12 million fucking house. I'm like, fuck, I hate this fucking house. Every time me and my fucking girl go out there, we're trying to find someone to fix this, fucking fix that. I sold it, bought this big-ass fucking airplane. People say there's nothing better than fucking good pussy. That fucking plane is fucking better than any fucking pussy you will ever put in front of—

Howard: Really?

Kid Rock: Oh! Do you fly commercial ever? No you don't. Fuck no you don't!

Howard: I don't fly anywhere.

Robin: By the way, now you say, "But I love my fiancée."

Howard: Why is a plane better than pussy? In the sense that it gives you the freedom to go anywhere you want?

Kid Rock: I will live in my fucking double-wide trailer in Alabama and sell everything. Not leave anything for my children or grandchildren. I'm not getting rid of that fucking plane.

Howard: What do you do with the plane?

Kid Rock: Whatever I fucking want.

Howard: When you came here to New York, did you take your private jet?

Kid Rock: Fuck, yeah.

Robin: Do you have a pilot on call?

Kid Rock: We got several of 'em.

Howard: So fame and money, the big thing is the private plane.

Kid Rock: Bingo. Abso-fucking-lutely. There's nothing fucking bigger than a plane. Nothing. These motherfuckers that live in LA—I feel bad for these motherfucking musicians who I *think* have fucking money. I'm like, "Oh you live in those fucking hills? You ain't got shit, motherfucker." It looks like Shamu. It's got gold flake in the fucking paint and western interior. I'm like, "Fuck it, I'm going wherever the fuck I want." I take my friends to dinner sometimes on the weekend. I go, "Hey, you guys wanna go to fucking Marquette, Michigan?" They're like, "For what?" And I'm like, "Just 'cause I got a big plane. We'll have dinner."

Howard: It must cost you a lot of money for fuel and maintenance and all that.

Kid Rock: I got a lot of problems. Money and pussy ain't one of 'em.

....

JON BON JOVI

Howard: "You Give Love a Bad Name" goes straight up to number one, right?

Jon: Number one.

Howard: Like a rocket ship. Where were you when you heard you had a number-one song? You got to remember that. Weren't you guys opening for 38 Special?

Jon: In Sioux Falls, South Dakota.

Howard: You get a phone call from who that tells you that this song has gone to number one?

Jon: It wasn't the song, it was the album. That *Slippery When Wet* was coming in at number one. Doc McGhee was trying to get to us.

Howard: Your manager.

Jon: He was our first manager. He had to charter a plane, which was big news to us. He charters a plane because you can't get there easy, you know?

Howard: Is this the last time you open up for a band? Once this thing hits, now you're on tour and you're going strong because it's one hit after another, right?

Jon: We never opened for anybody again. After Doc McGhee landed in that private plane, we never got on a bus again.

Howard: Wow.

Jon: Life changed.

Howard: Over and over again, every night, you're playing. I think you even described—did you have a nervous breakdown?

Jon: It was after the next record.

Howard: Really? Why? Because you were just touring too much?

Jon: We worked that record very hard. It's almost a cliché because it's happened to so many bands after us. You do 240 shows and the success, the skyrocket happens. But what you say to yourself is, "I gotta do it again."

Howard: That's the pressure.

Jon: I don't think it did that but what it did was, it really just pushed us. I just remember being really tired from the beginning. A guy in Dublin, Ireland, asked me a very profound question, now that I look back on it thirty years later. He said, "What are you doing here?" I thought to myself, "What an idiot. What a stupid question. We're playing tonight." Really, what he meant was, "Why did you rush to get back here? You should be home enjoying the success of *Slippery* and taking a nap for a while."

RACHEL MADDOW

Howard: Would you have ever considered working at Fox News if Roger Ailes said to you, "Look, I like you. I don't agree with you politically, but I think this will be a good mix, you being part of the Fox News team." Would you have taken that seriously?

Rachel: He once told me that he wanted to hire me at Fox. Actually, this is not that long ago. Within the last few years, he told me he wanted to hire me at Fox, and then he told me he'd never put me on the air. He would just hire me so nobody else can put me on air. I was like, "You'd pay me a full contract to not work?"

Howard: Would you consider that?

Rachel: Yeah. Who wouldn't consider that?

Howard: I used to say when the religious right was after me—they wanted to get me off the radio. I said, "Instead of raising money, saying, 'We've got to get Howard Stern off the air,' raise money and give me all the money and I'll stay off the air. I'm not looking to do this."

Rachel: Pay out my contract.

Howard: Yeah. Wouldn't that have been the deal of all time? Get paid not to work.

Rachel: I know.

Howard: What a dream come true.

CINDY CRAWFORD

Howard: Help me understand the modeling business, okay?

Cindy: Okay.

Howard: When you're a model, and you're just one of the girls working, before the *Vogue* cover, can you make a hundred or two hundred grand a year? Just being a hardworking model?

Cindy: Oh yeah. In Chicago, I could make that.

Howard: And so you're doing well. You're living on your own. You don't have to be talking to your parents about money.

Cindy: You're *sending* money to your parents.

Howard: Right. It's a great life. But then where you become a quote-unquote *supermodel* is this *Vogue* thing.

Robin: How do you get the *Vogue* cover?

Cindy: Now it's very different because you really have to be an actress. But then, you got a try. A cover try. I had done a shoot for American *Vogue*. And I guess they liked the pictures. So then you get this cover try. You would go, and they would do some pictures, and they would mock 'em up.

Howard: When the *Vogue* cover comes out, where were you at in your life?

Cindy: It was in '86. So I was twenty years old. I had just moved to New York.

Howard: Were you still with the high school boyfriend?

Cindy: Yeah.

Howard: Oh my God. This guy's like, "How in the hell am I gonna hold on to her?" Where were you when you saw the cover?

Cindy: I was coming back from a trip, and I was in an airport. I bought three. I was just dying for the lady to say, "Oh my gosh! That's you!" And she's like, "Honey, you have three of the same magazines." I was so deflated. She didn't even look up.

Howard: And you can only buy three. 'Cause if you buy, like, twenty, you look like a real asshole, right?

Cindy: Yeah, and I had to carry 'em back to Chicago. As if you can't get *Vogue* in Illinois.

··

ARNOLD SCHWARZENEGGER

Arnold: I was in such need to become somebody. I grew up in this little town in Austria, and it was after the Second World War. It was miserable. There was starvation. People were angry because they just lost the war. And there was frustration, alcoholism, all of those things. It was a tough life. And so I was determined. "I'm gonna get out of here, no matter what it takes."

Howard: When you would say to your father or mother, "I'm gonna get out of here. I'm gonna go to the United States. I'm gonna be the number-one bodybuilder in the world," did they think you were the biggest jerk on the planet?

Arnold: My parents really loved me, but they thought I was totally ill. Mentally ill. My mother went many times to our house doctor and complained to him: "There's something off with our son. Because he comes home for lunch and then he does 250 sit-ups instead of eating lunch. Then he comes home at ten o'clock at night. He works two hours down at the gym. Look at this wall here in his bedroom. Look at all these pictures of naked men hanging there. Should we be concerned about that? This kid is fifteen years old and there are all these naked men." They were all bodybuilding champions and boxers, but she called them "naked men."

Howard: Was it a lonely life? Going to the gym, constantly worrying about what you're eating, making sure that you figure out the right training. It seems so solitary.

Arnold: It was, in a way. But I had such joy and I was so happy when I went to the gym. You have to imagine, this is a boy that never got a compliment, really. Because it's not common in Austria for people to say, like in America, "Oh, you did really well in your soccer game, even though you tripped before you shot the goal. But you did your best, Arnold. Don't worry." In Austria, they say, "You idiot. You tripped over your own feet. You embarrassed me. You're an embarrassment." This is the kind of dialogue that's in Austria. So now here is this guy who gets always ridiculed like that and attacked by the parents and they are very critical—even though they loved me, like I said. But when I went to the gym, all of a sudden the guys were saying, "I can't believe this. You've been here for three months and you're bench-pressing already 185 pounds. You know something? You have unbelievable talent. We should put you in the weight-lifting club." Then all of a sudden by the age of sixteen they took me from village to village competing in weight lifting. And I got all the compliments. So this is what built my confidence.

Howard: But it teaches me something. It isn't necessarily that you were gifted physically. It was the hard work. It wasn't necessarily that you had some natural strength.

Arnold: You're absolutely right. The work itself and the belief in yourself is the most important thing. Because from the time you set the big goal, you will have the naysayers say, "This is stupid. You will never make it. This is ridiculous. Come on, no one has ever done this." But they totally forget that you *can* break new ground, and you *can* do things that no one else has ever done before.

Howard: To come to America and not know English and make it in the movies seems almost absurd and comical. And yet you've had one of the biggest careers. Have you ever computed all the money that you've generated in film? I think maybe you've had the highest box-office grosses of all time, am I correct?

Arnold: Yes, if you adjusted to today's money, without any doubt. But I tell you, you have done exactly the same thing. There is no difference. If you would have told somebody that you would be sitting here with such a successful radio show, they would have laughed. They *did* laugh at you.

Howard: Years of work. Years of work.

Arnold: "The kind of language you use, the way you do your interviews—we cannot have that on public radio." All this nonsense. And here you're the top in the world.

Howard: Nobody would've bet on me.

Arnold: But that is because you had a clear vision. You knew that someone shouldn't change your style or tone it down. No, you stayed true to yourself. And this is what you have to do.

Howard: Absolutely.

....

DAVE MATTHEWS

Howard: You like doing a cover of a song? 'Cause "All Along the Watchtower," you do that all the time in concert.

Dave: We haven't done it

in a little while but yeah. I actually learned that song because a long, long time ago I was living in Amsterdam and selling little bracelets I'd bought in Africa.

Howard: Yeah, there was a point in your career where you used to busk. That's what they call it, right? You would go out on the street and perform.

Dave: And then get shouted at by the buskers who had set up there. "This is my place!"

Howard: Could you make a decent living doing that?

Dave: I did okay. You know, I wasn't buying airline flights anywhere.

Howard: When you first walk out on the sidewalk— because I can't imagine this—is there just this pounding nervousness?

Dave: See, there was a pounding nervousness when I was nineteen. There was a debilitating fear. And then I'd just start doing it and no one would pay any attention. Maybe one person might stop. But the convenience with "All Along the Watchtower" was when it was a little bit chilly I could just

play the song and never stop playing it.

Howard: Yeah, it's a little monotonous, isn't it?

Dave: I would play it this way and that way. I could do it for an hour, swear to God. Until someone told me to stop and shut up. I did have one really humiliating experience. This guy came up and just put his hands on the strings and said, "Shhhhh." And then walked away with his pretty Dutch girlfriends. And they all went, "Ha ha ha." And I was just *crushed.*

··

ICE-T

Howard: Let me understand how you get this part in *New Jack City.*

Ice-T: Aight, I'm in the men's room in some club. I'm in the stall, right? And somebody's talking shit to me. And I'm just like, "Look, man, if they could put me under a microscope and find one molecule of me that gave a fuck then maybe they could angle me. But they can't. So they can't fuck with me."

Howard: You said that in the bathroom to your friend.

Ice-T: No, just to some random motherfucker talking to me over the toilet. And Mario Van Peebles, the director of the movie, was in there. And he said, "Whoever fucking said that is the star of my movie." So I come out after I wipe my ass. And now I'm in the club. And Mario walks up to me with that Hollywood bullshit.

Howard: What's Hollywood bullshit?

Ice-T: Hollywood bullshit is when people see you and they say, "We should work."

Howard: Right. And you know it's going nowhere.

Ice-T: Motherfucker, you could've called me. Just because we're in this party doesn't mean we gotta act like we're gonna be friends. Fuck you. So he says to me, "You should be in my movie." And I'm like, okay, you just wanna talk to these girls.

Howard: You're trying to impress everyone by telling 'em that you make movies.

Ice-T: Right. And her name is this, and her name is this, and her name is this, and I kept it moving. And he said, "Nah, call me tomorrow." So I called, and it was Warner Brothers. And they were like, "Yeah, we want you to come over here and read for this movie." And I was like, "For real?" So I went there and I looked at the script. They said, "You're gonna read for Scotty."

Howard: The cop.

Ice-T: I was like, "Yo, this is *all* the lines. This is the whole movie. I thought it was a part." Like, I'm not an actor. He's got dreads. I got a perm. He's the fucking police, man. I got an album called *O.G.* So I'm like, "Ah fuck, I'm scared."

Howard: You were scared.

Ice-T: I was scared. And I called my homies. "Yo, man, they want me to be a police." "Word? Can I be in the movie?"

Howard: [*laughs*] They want your part.

Ice-T: Even my boys in jail. I'm like, "Look, I know you stuck. But I just got offered to be in a movie playin' the police." "Word? If I was out could I be in the movie?" So finally, when I used to get my hair done, the ladies at my shop were like, "Motherfucker, if you don't

take this part you a sucker. And Ice, we know that you the kind of motherfucker that's gonna keep it real and stay true to the hood no matter how big you get. You gotta do this, Ice. You can act. You act for us *every day*, nigga. Stop playin'. Go in there and do the damn movie or don't come back to the shop."

RICHARD SIMMONS

Howard: Why do you think you always have to be the comedian? Why do you think you always have to be on?

Richard: That's how I've been since I was a kid. I think it's because I was obese as a kid. I didn't feel accepted. And I thought I had to have a bigger-than-life persona.

Howard: You were beaten with a bat when you were a kid, weren't you? Who beat you with a bat when you were a kid?

Richard: Just a guy in school who made fun of me every day and told me that I was a piece of garbage and that I was a fat pig. You don't forget those things, Howard.

Howard: Did you ever confront him as an adult and say, "Why did you do that to me?"

Richard: No, I confronted him when I was a kid. I took the baseball bat out of his hand, and I told him I didn't appreciate what he did. I didn't appreciate him making fun of me. And I have to tell you, thirty years later, Howard, I was in New Orleans. And I was at a department store shopping. And this man came up to me and he said, "Do you remember me?" And it was this boy with the bat.

Howard: Is that true?

Richard: True. And he said, "My wife is 250 pounds. And I'm wondering if you could call her for me."

Howard: What did you do?

Richard: I called her, and I sent her some videos.

Howard: That's big of you.

Richard: I'm forgiving.

WHITNEY CUMMINGS

Whitney: When you have success, everyone's like,

"Isn't it amazing!" But you have this whole new set of problems.

Howard: Your problem was you had so much success, I'm sure other comedians were jealous and it was driving you crazy.

Whitney: Maybe. My self-esteem is too low to say anyone is jealous of me. But family starts to get tricky. It was my first time giving money to family members, which very much complicates things. You're like, "Hey, can you pass the salt?" [And they're like,] "Okay, I'm gonna pay you back!"

JAMES CAAN

Howard: Do you have nightmares about turning down *One Flew Over the Cuckoo's Nest*?

James: No, I'm famous for [turning down roles].

Howard: You've been nominated for an Academy Award. You've never won an Academy Award. Which is a shame. *One Flew Over the Cuckoo's Nest* would've been your Academy Award, yeah?

James: Maybe. I don't

know. Jack [Nicholson] was wonderful.

Howard: Why did you turn it down?

James: Miloš Forman [the film's director] came to me four times, not once. I said, "It's not visual enough."

Howard: What does that mean?

James: It all takes place within four walls. It's a nice stage play.

Howard: You didn't think it was a movie.

James: Exactly. Which shows you—

Howard: Well, no one knows everything. No one has a crystal ball. When you saw the movie, were you like, "Oh fuck, I should've done this?"

James: No. Listen, I've picked a couple that I was right about and I've picked a lot that I was wrong about.

Howard: But you know when you see a great film—

James: No, no, you can't. It's too late. It's like looking up a dead horse's ass. It's dead. It does no good.

Howard: I would want to scream. It's so hard as an actor to know what movies to pick.

Did you know *The Godfather* was going to be great?

James: I knew that the company I was keeping was great. I didn't know the film would be.

Howard: How would you know? You don't know.

James: No one knows. As a matter of fact, I was gonna make a fortune without acting. I made a deal with the studios. This was my pro forma, as they say. They would send me the script. If I liked it, don't put a penny in it. If I turned it down, put everything you got into it. I would've made a fortune.

MARK CUBAN

Howard: Is it true the night your team won the NBA championship you went out and got a $90,000 bottle of champagne and drank it?

Mark: Yep.

Howard: What's it like drinking a $90,000 bottle of champagne? Could you tell the difference?

Mark: Absolutely not.

Howard: Is that something you do just because you have the money? "I've worked hard. I'm a charitable guy. But maybe I could blow ninety grand."

Mark: Because I can. Absolutely.

Howard: But you didn't grow up with a lot of money.

Mark: Oh no. My dad was an upholsterer.

Howard: I don't care how much money I'll ever have in life, I could not spend ninety grand on a bottle of champagne.

Mark: I had to. We had just won the NBA championship. And it was such a unique moment. And there's a backstory. We were in Miami. The night before I had taken some Mavs customers to this club, LIV. I'm nervous as hell. I've got these customers with me. I'm not drinking. The DJ spots me and he says, "You know what we do to Cubans in Miami? We smoke 'em. Let's go Heat!" This whole club is going, "Let's go Heat! Let's go Heat!" So the next night we win, in Miami. We're drinking champagne in the locker room. And one of the guys, Jason Terry, goes, "We gotta go out." I'm like, "I

got the spot." I wanted to walk into that club holding that $90,000 bottle of champagne and the championship trophy just to shove it up their ass. But it gets better. Two years ago I had my identity stolen by two Puerto Rican guys in Brooklyn. They somehow figured out my credit card and they ordered pizza. The pizza guy shows up and he goes, "You're not Mark Cuban." He busted 'em. But ever since then, every six months I roll over my credit cards. I switch 'em. So I go in, the guy sells me on the $90,000 bottle of champagne, I give him my black AmEx . . . and it gets declined. I hadn't called in to turn it on.

....

ADAM SANDLER

Howard: What did you do to get on *Saturday Night Live*?

Adam: Stand-up. Dennis Miller, he saw me at the Improv.

Howard: You must have been good.

Adam: I had some good jokes. I did all right.

Howard: First of all, that's what I have learned. I've interviewed a lot of people who did *Saturday Night Live*. I always thought in the comedy community everybody was a prick. But Miller saying, "I know this guy Adam Sandler. He is really funny. Lorne, why don't you have him come and audition?" That's very generous of a guy.

Adam: I love the man. They were looking for new guys and actually the night I got on Rock was on. Me and him auditioned in Chicago that night.

Howard: It was you and Chris Rock and Lorne showed up?

Adam: Lorne loved Rock and immediately put him in the cast. I had some interesting jokes that he liked and he thought maybe I could write for the show.

Howard: You were pissed, right? Because you didn't want to be a writer. You wanted to be a performer.

Adam: I didn't know anything about writing.

It was like, "This guy doesn't get it. I'm the next thing."

Howard: Wisely, Miller said to you, "Take the writing job. Get your foot in the door." Were you going to actually consider turning it down?

Adam: Yeah, for a minute. I was young and I just did exactly what my father told me to do or what my friends were saying, and some of them were like, "What's a writer? Don't do that." And I said, "Okay, I can't do it then." My father was the guy who used to say, "If you don't make it by twenty-three, I want you to work for me or sell insurance."

Howard: So you get the word that you were going to audition for *Saturday Night Live* and Lorne shows up— the big *macher*. Then the letdown. Rock gets to be on camera and you are going to be a writer.

Adam: It was a heartache. I was flying back and I called on the plane. Back then it was a big deal. Fifteen bucks to use the phone on the airplane. I couldn't believe I was actually doing it. But I called my agent and I said, "How did they like me?" "They liked you. They felt some of your jokes were good. They actually want you to be a writer." And I remember falling back into the seat like, "That's it. They don't get it."

Howard: But you were smart that you went on and got your foot in the door. What was your first skit you ever wrote for *Saturday Night Live*?

Adam: I don't remember a hundred percent, but I think this Kevin Nealon thing where it was a boyfriend meeting a family and every time someone asked a question they just took a bite. And so they would have to finish chewing and then they would swallow and then answer. It was, like, a timing thing. But I didn't get on the air for a while.

Howard: Was there ever a low point where you started to think, "This is not going to work out"?

Adam: No, I never even thought it could not work out because I told too many people that I was going to be huge.

....

JEWEL

Jewel: While I was homeless there were people who were obviously trying to prey on me. But at the same time there were people who were nice for no reason.

Howard: You said that when you were homeless it was so degrading you'd actually lose your self-esteem, right?

Jewel: Yeah. Not that I had much. I moved out when I was fifteen. My dad and I had a terrible relationship. My mom left us when I was eight.

Howard: When you got signed, were you down on your knees thanking God?

Jewel: It was a trip. It was completely unexpected. I was singing at a local place. I was raised bar singing and you did five-hour sets. So I started writing five hours' worth of material. I didn't know how to play cover songs. My audience grew, and people started bringing me food. It was really touching. Then a local DJ put a bootleg of mine on the radio and it ended up in the top-ten request line on a big station, 91X in San Diego. Labels started going, "Who the heck is this girl?" Limousines were pulling up, and they'd take me out to dinner, and I'd feel bad because they were paying.

Howard: But think about your training. Five hours of material a night and reading a crowd and learning what turns a crowd on. Of course you were destined for success. You had so much trial-and-error and so much practice. So many artists today want to take a shortcut to fame. It doesn't work like that.

Jewel: The best thing an artist ever told me when I was quite young was, "Hard wood grows slowly." That's really the truth.

Sia

JUNE 18, 2014

People often say I have a natural voice for radio. Nothing could be further from the truth.

Back in college, the only time my voice sounded good was when I had a cold or had just woken up. Most mornings I would get out of bed and have this rich, booming tone. By the time I got dressed and walked over to the college radio station it would disappear, replaced by a Kermit the Frog–type croak.

I remember early in my career in New York I sent my reel to a commercial agency to get some voiceover work. I only included the rare occasions when my voice was deep. Based on that tape, I booked a commercial for a pop group called Voyage (pronounced Voy-ahge). My big line in the commercial was: "Take a voyage to Voyage." The agency reps were imagining my beautiful baritone selling millions of albums. I stepped into the recording booth, put on the headphones, and said, "Take a voyage to Voy—" I cut myself off. My voice wasn't what they heard on that tape. Kermit was in the house. "Sorry," I told the engineer, "let me try that again." And again . . . and again and again. Every time was worse than the last. I couldn't give them what they wanted. Why couldn't I do this? "Take a voyage to Voyage." It was only seven syllables. I was too nervous. My voice was too stressed. The head of the agency wasn't pleased. "What was *that*?" he said. At one point, he even accused me of being an impostor, or of having somehow manipulated my voice electronically for my reel.

I was humiliated. I assumed they would toss my tapes in the trash and hire a replacement, so I was shocked when a few weeks later I heard my version of the commercial on WNEW, WBLS, and other big-time New York radio stations. As bad as I was, I guess the record company reasoned since they already invested money in the spot, they might as well use it. I want to publicly apologize to Voyage if I had anything to do with ruining their career. I can't find any trace of the group online. I'm sure they would have been as big as the Beatles if they just had the right announcer.

Today, whenever we play old segments from the show's terrestrial radio years, listeners will call up wondering what's wrong with the tape. They think it's been sped up. Back then I so desperately wanted my voice to sound relaxed and resonant like the radio men I grew up listening to, with that deep timbre that almost rattled the speakers. I tried so hard to channel radio greats, bring out my inner Harry Harrison, Herb Oscar Anderson, Ron Lundy, and Dan Ingram. I would have settled for

Alison Steele on WNEW-FM. She had a deeper voice than me. After thousands upon thousands of hours on the radio, I still wasn't any closer. Finally, I gave up. I thought, "Forget it. Your voice is never going to be like that. Who cares about voice? A lot of guys with deep voices don't have anything to say. You're not like them. You're not an announcer. You're a *personality*. Content is how you win. You don't want to play the Beatles. You want to *be* the Beatles. Just be funny and interesting and create your own work of art."

This was so liberating. I no longer had to stress myself out. I was able to put aside that tension and nervousness and insecurity. And guess what? As soon as I did that, the minute I relaxed and let go, my voice started to sound like I always hoped it would. It's the same principle Maharishi Mahesh Yogi espoused called "support of nature." When you surrender yourself to your true nature, that helps you reach your full potential and achieve what you desire. Now my voice sounds right to me. I have a speaker in my shower, and often I'll play back a show I just did. With the water running, I'll turn the volume just loud enough that I can hear the tone of my voice but not the words. It sounds like real radio. I've finally gotten to a point where I'm able to hear my show and not throw up.

Sia was the exact opposite of me. She *was* blessed with a beautiful voice, yet for a while she chose not to use it—instead giving the songs she wrote to other pop stars to perform. I had been following her career for some time and was absolutely fascinated by this. My ego is so big, I couldn't understand how someone could write such brilliant material only to let another artist record it. If you couldn't sing, I'd get it. Sia, though, is as good as any singer I've ever heard. I wanted to talk to her about this. I wanted to ask her, "How do you feel that Rihanna had a huge hit with the song you wrote?" I couldn't be happy for that person. I could never create something and let someone else perform it. Sia said she loved it. She wasn't just saying that. You could tell she really meant it, which is such a testament to the kind of beautiful soul this woman is.

She is one of the most sincere, vulnerable human beings I've ever encountered. When she performs live, she wears a huge wig that hides her face. She wasn't hiding anything in this interview. It got to the point where she was very emotional. She was talking about suicide and just broke down. That happens every now and then, and that makes me feel good—not that a guest gets upset, but that they feel comfortable enough with me to allow this to happen. It means they're not threatened by me. They know they're not going to be humiliated in some way.

As Sia was crying I quoted her own song and told her she was a "diamond in the sky." I was so moved by her tears. It proved that even with all the electronic equipment in the studio and the knowledge that there were millions of people listening, it was still possible to have a real moment.

I defy anyone to read this interview and not fall in love with Sia. She's really special.

Howard: You know why I was so interested in you? Because when I first heard the song "Diamonds"—you know I love that song.

Sia: That was great, hearing you liked it. People were telling me.

Howard: I love it. When I found out that you wrote it, and then I saw a tape of you on the Internet singing it at a school or—

Sia: It was a weird Norwegian benefit for commerce or something, because the dudes I wrote the song with are Norwegian and they were being honored.

Howard: I've always been interested in

people who write songs for other people. First of all, you have a beautiful singing voice. There's no reason why you would write these songs for other people. But then when I read your story, I was like, "Wow, I get it."

Sia: It's money.

Howard: No, it wasn't money, though. It was also anxiety, right?

Sia: It was a combination. It was that I didn't want to be famous but still I wanted to work out a way to make my gift work in my favor without having to sell a piece of my, like, serenity real estate.

Howard: When you were a little girl, it was apparent from a young age that you were a singer-songwriter. Did people know? They were like, "Sia is the real deal. She can sing, she can write music."

Sia: Not really. I think they thought I was an attention seeker. I was tap dancing for attention right out of the—can I say the v-word?

Howard: The vagina.

Sia: The vagina.

Howard: Right out of the vagina, you were doing your thing.

Sia: Right out, I was tap dancing.

Howard: Your mother says you were singing right away, and then you had a bad childhood. Your parents split up. You were, what, ten?

Sia: Ten, that's right.

Howard: Ten years old. Was that a trauma for you?

Sia: I really don't remember. I remember using it to manipulate. Like, "I want this because my dad left." That's what I remember. I remember that lots of things were bummers. That was just one of them.

Howard: Did your dad contact you, or was he one of those dads who split and you never saw him again?

Sia: No, no, he came around. I would go with him in the school holidays.

Howard: But a weird relationship with your dad, right?

Sia: Super weird.

Howard: You even said you felt your dad was jealous of your success and your career, right?

Sia: Actually, we talked about that recently because what happened is, there was an article and someone said, "Do you think your dad is jealous of you?" My uncle Collie [Colin Hay, of Men at Work] was sitting next to me, and he answered, "Yes." And then I actually started to cry. I was like, "That would be a real bummer if that were true." And maybe it is.

Howard: Parents are jealous sometimes. Your dad wanted to be a singer and a songwriter?

Sia: Yeah, he's an incredible guitarist. He's happy for me, but I think it's impossible not to see something you wanted happen to someone else and wish it for yourself. Maybe it's envy and not jealousy at all.

Howard: It's almost unimaginable that when you think of your parents and you go, "How could they be jealous of me? Wouldn't they just be happy that I'm successful?" But I guess if your dad is a great guitarist, and he had dreams of rock stardom and all that kind of stuff. At one point, your dad was putting together an album, and you said, "Dad, I'll perform on that album." Which would be great for him. And he said, "No, you're trying to hog my big chance."

Sia: This is exactly how it went down. We're in the car. He's talking about his album. He's like, "I'm making an album. I'd like to put out this." I was like, "Well, Dad, if you want me to sing harmonies or anything on it, just let me know." He turned around, he looked at me, and he said, "No, it's my album and you're not on it." [*laughs*]

Howard: Wow.

Sia: The reason I tell that story is because there's a part of it that's comedy to me.

Howard: You laugh when you tell that story, but don't you think that's hiding the pain of that story? I mean, really there's nothing funny about it, don't you think? Is it really funny?

Sia: I do find him amusing. I think it's the only way to function within the relationship.

Howard: To get through it.

Sia: Because growing up, he had, like, two very unique personalities: one was called Phil and one was called Stan.

Howard: He called his personalities Phil and Stan?

Sia: Yeah. Phil was, like, the best dad ever. He was so nice.

Howard: Fun dad.

Sia: He was fun, but he was eloquent and he was kind and he was present and interesting and interested. It was Stan that was—when Stan came around, stuff got scary.

Howard: By scary, was it physical?

Sia: No, it was just like it was—

Howard: Mental abuse? Anguish?

Sia: Yeah, it was anguish.

Howard: Did you start to feel bad about yourself because your father would be the Stan character and just belittle you?

Sia: He never belittled me. It was never about me. It was an energy that came in the room that was intimidating. But it was intimidating to every single person in the room.

Howard: How often was Stan around?

Sia: I don't know. I can't really remember.

Howard: You were probably on some level happy when the divorce went down because maybe it was a relief.

Sia: It's possible. Isn't it weird how—I just have no idea. The thing is now I have a good relationship with both my parents.

Howard: How is that possible?

Sia: It's weird, isn't it? I think probably through like—I'm in the program, so I'm in recovery. And I think a large part of working the steps and stuff is there's an element of . . . For me, what I've come to realize is that I am not my past. That in order to move forward in life in any way, that I just—I didn't know who I was until three and a half years ago.

Howard: Does Stan still come around or no?

Sia: No, I think he's fully integrated.

Howard: Was your father ever diagnosed as a schizophrenic?

Sia: No. For me it felt like DID, dissociative identity disorder. But he's never been diagnosed as anything.

Robin: Never medicated or anything?

Sia: No, but I'm fully medicated. I'm medicated for bipolar II to the hilt.

Howard: This is a question that even psychiatrists can't fully answer: Do you think bipolar is nurture or nature? Is it something you're born with, or is it something that happens as a result of having this fucked-up childhood?

Sia: I have a theory, but I don't—

Howard: What's your theory?

Sia: I don't think it's fucked-up childhood in my case. I refrain from blaming anything on my parents. I think that everyone does their best and that if they didn't do their best, they're just sick too. What I do think is that I smoked too much pot as a kid.

Howard: And you think it fucked you up?

Sia: Yeah, I think I fucked my brain up.

Robin: How old were you when you started smoking?

Sia: Thirteen.

Howard: I'm for the legalization of every drug. I don't care. I think criminalizing the thing is ridiculous. But I can't do drugs. I can't smoke weed.

Sia: Paranoia.

Howard: Paranoia, right? When you talk about mental illness, I suffer from OCD really bad, and I've gotten it somewhat under control. I remember it kicking in after I did acid. I

WHEN I GOT SOBER AND WAS DIAGNOSED BIPOLAR II, I WAS LIKE, "I HAVE TO CHANGE EVERYTHING."

think that these drugs do something to the brain. They do, even pot.

Sia: My brain wasn't fully formed.

Robin: They do say marijuana at a young age might retard or slow down or prevent the maturation process.

Howard: Could be. Probably the drinking or the drugs or whatever you did, it was probably you trying to self-medicate, right?

Sia: Yeah, definitely.

Howard: You were trying to straighten yourself out.

Sia: I was just so labile. I was constantly looking for something just to feel some sense of equilibrium.

Howard: Were you relieved when you found out you were bipolar? "Oh, so this is what's going on"?

Sia: No, I was relieved when I found out I was an alcoholic.

Howard: You didn't know?

Sia: I had no idea. I had absolutely no idea. [*laughs*]

Howard: What do you mean? You thought you had it under control?

Sia: I thought I was relaxing. Pill popping and drinking. I just think I'm relaxing watching *The Real Housewives* for six months without leaving the house. In one sofa chair. Ordering drugs in.

Howard: Is that why you became a songwriter for other people? Because you were bipolar and because you were so uncomfortable onstage?

Sia: No, I became a pop songwriter because I was uncomfortable touring, getting famous. I didn't like the things that were coming with singing, and I just wanted to sing.

Howard: You don't like the attention.

Sia: I like the attention from my friends. I'm an attention seeker around my life, my friendship circle. I find that validating and that nourishes me and it's good for my self-esteem. But I don't need it from anyone that isn't in my friendship circle. So the clapping and the people being interested in me was not feeding my soul. When I got sober and was diagnosed bipolar II, I was like, "I have to change everything. I need to have a serene life with a routine. I can't go traveling anymore. I need to be on the sofa with my dogs and have a structured life."

Howard: Let me understand your career: How old were you when you got your first record contract?

Sia: Like, twenty-two, maybe?

Howard: Twenty-two years old, you get a record contract. Phenomenal. The first record doesn't really go anywhere. It sort of didn't happen.

> **I BELIEVE IN A HIGHER POWER AND IT'S CALLED WHATEVER DUDE AND HE'S A QUEER, SURFING SANTA.**

Sia: It really didn't happen. [*laughs*]

Howard: I'm talking about your own career now as a performing artist. Your career started to take off with this song. [*"Breathe Me" plays.*] What TV show was this on?

Sia: *Six Feet Under.* It was the final song in the final episode of the series.

Howard: When they put this on, this song took off?

Sia: Yeah, it resuscitated my truly dying career. [*laughs*]

Howard: Then when this song becomes a hit, they send you out on tour, and that's where you freak. You hated it.

Sia: Well, there were parts that I loved.

Howard: What's the worst part of it? Is it just being in a hotel? Not being around your stuff?

Sia: It's lonely. You have this family with you, this traveling family of wolverines that you create, and that's not lonely. But if you've developed relationships outside of that, when you leave them it's really hard to nourish them. I couldn't ever maintain a love relationship. I don't know. The traveling, the air conditioning is so weird. You become like a lizard.

Howard: As uncomfortable as you were with this sudden fame of "Breathe Me," a friend of yours said, "If you don't like that part of fame, why don't you start writing songs for other people?"

Sia: Actually, it was me.

Howard: Were you the one who came up with that idea? It's a brilliant move, because you could still be in the music business.

You mentioned money. When you get a Rihanna to record this song or someone like that, it's pretty incredible because it's an instant hit. It breaks through everything. But don't you sit there and go, "Oh, shit. I should have sang that song. It could've been mine." You're not whining that way?

Sia: No, because I'm so productive.

Howard: It would kill me not to sing that song. And you do such a beautiful song with "Diamonds." You say you wrote that in how many minutes?

Sia: It was somewhere between seventeen and twenty-two minutes that I wrote it. Then another twenty minutes to record the vocal. I know that long because we had a car waiting downstairs to take me to the airport. I remember saying, "I have twenty minutes."

Howard: Why did you only have twenty minutes to write that song?

Sia: That was the end of the session. I'd already written two other songs probably, and I was on my way to the airport to go somewhere.

[*Howard plays an early version in which Sia's nonsensical scatting suddenly transforms into the words "diamonds in the sky."*]

Howard: Where did that come from?

Sia: I have no idea. It was just channeled. It just came out.

Howard: Are you a religious woman?

Sia: Yeah, I believe in a higher power and it's called Whatever Dude and he's a queer, surfing Santa that's a bit like my grandpa. So yes.

Howard: God is Whatever Dude, a queer, surfing Santa?

Sia: Yeah. I'm a feminist, but it's a dude. It turned out to be a dude.

Howard: Do you believe from this higher power the words "diamonds in the sky" just showed up? Because you don't know where that comes from. It must be maddening. You just don't know. But the song is written so fast. The best songs are always written so quickly, aren't they?

Sia: I like to think so. [*laughs*]

Howard: When you heard Rihanna's version of it, you were at first confused because you thought it was you.

Sia: I did. It was insane.

Howard: Most artists will take your track and then put their own spin on it.

Sia: Actually, most people do it exactly the way I do it now. Most people generally stick to the program, but there's a few that do it. Adam Levine is doing one that's going to come out soon. He took it to a different place. Beyoncé took "Pretty Hurts" to a different place. I know that sometimes people add their own flavor, but for the most part the songs that I can think of—like "Cannonball" with Lea Michele, "Perfume" with Britney Spears, and "Diamonds"—

Howard: They do it the way you record it. How long is the process? How long does it take from the inception of "Diamonds" to the point that Rihanna is selling millions of copies of that?

Sia: That one was pretty fast, because of the fact that I wrote another song that is now Beyoncé's single, which is "Pretty Hurts." I wrote that song two and a half years ago for Katy Perry. She never heard it. I sent it to some other people. Rihanna put it on hold. She had it on hold for eight months. Then Beyoncé somehow heard it, and Rihanna's management hadn't paid for the track—which means, you put it on hold securely so no one else can take it. Beyoncé slid in and paid for the track and took it out.

Howard: You have so much credibility. As soon as you write something, why don't these ladies just grab it up?

Sia: Well, at that point, I didn't have that much credibility. I was still pretty new.

Howard: Sia, do a little bit of "Diamonds," if you would, for me.

Sia: Oh, of course.

[*Sia performs "Diamonds."*]

Howard: It's a sad song, isn't it?

Sia: See, I don't even know.

Howard: It makes me sad.

Sia: I don't really analyze my own work.

Howard: Do you know what it's about? Or you don't even think about that?

Sia: I just wrote it and I sang it and was like, "This is great. It sounds like something people would vibe out on ecstasy"—I still call it ecstasy—"in the dance tent at Glastonbury." I saw kids with their hands in the air. Or like in Ibiza on the beach.

Howard: I think about your life. You were so low because of your illness that you almost killed yourself.

Sia: Yes.

Howard: And so I think of *you* as the diamond in the sky.

Sia: Oh.

Howard: And that you're shining bright now.

Sia: [*starts crying*] I'm going to cry.

Howard: Right? Isn't that it?

Sia: You're so nice.

Howard: But you're shining bright like a diamond now. And it's so beautiful.

Sia: You're so sweet. I'm crying.

Howard: But isn't that the beauty? That you didn't kill yourself. You almost took your own life. How we would've lost out on this diamond in the sky.

Sia: I can't talk because I'm crying.

Howard: That's good for ratings. That's the idea.

Sia: [*laughs*] Thanks for pulling me back there.

Howard: Yeah, of course. But it got really bad. I mean, you called a drug dealer and you said, "Listen, give me two of everything. This is it. I'm doing it."

Sia: That was six months *before* I hit bottom. That was when I was like, "Oh, this seems like a great idea. Two of everything. Try it." And of course the pharmaceutical heroin won. And so six months later, that's when I was so depressed, I wanted to die.

Howard: Well, thank God for the twelve-step program, right?

Sia: I agree.

Howard: It does work.

Sia: It works.

Howard: Out of all that misery comes a

song like "Diamonds." I don't think a happy person or a person who hasn't suffered could write a song like that, with that much emotion.

Sia: You're going to make me cry again.

Howard: I'm serious. It's terrible you have to go through that kind of pain to write a song. But I think it's very unique, that song. It's very special.

Sia: Thank you.

Howard: And *you're* very special. You really are.

Sia: Thank you.

Howard: All right, go ahead and cry.

Sia: [*crying*] You're so nice too. Do you have children?

Howard: I do.

Sia: You're a good dad.

Howard: I am? I mean, of course I am.

Robin: Could you tell them?

Howard: Would you mind writing them a note? Let them in on it. Oy vey.

Sia: You seem very nice.

Howard: Actually, my kids think I'm Stan. Are you in a committed relationship?

Sia: I am.

Howard: You're into chicks and guys?

Sia: Yeah, I'm back on the cock. Properly back on the cock.

Howard: You don't miss vagina?

Sia: No.

Howard: You love who you love?

Sia: I am happy with what I have.

Howard: You are?

Sia: Yeah.

Howard: You're extremely happy?

❝ I DON'T GO ON TOUR AND I DON'T FALSELY SELL MYSELF.

Sia: Yeah, I am really happy. Except when I'm crying, when you make me feel happy emotions.

Howard: When you're in a relationship with a woman, are they baffled that you could suddenly go with a guy? Don't they think, "Well, you loved *me*"?

Sia: Not really. Most of the women that I've dated knew that I was straight. [*chuckles*] The queer community is really interesting, because I dated two women in my life and they were both butch. They were always attracted to straight women.

Howard: Do you think you went to women because men are just too fucking much to handle?

Sia: No, this last relationship I had, I thought she was a boy. Because her gender expression is male, so I really thought she was a boy. I was like, "Cute boy," and then I was like, "Cute girl. Okay, whatever."

Howard: "Let's go with it." You're so open-minded. There was a point in your career when you would go onstage and you would always wear a mask because I guess you just didn't want the attention?

Sia: Yes, I put a black cardboard box behind me and I wore a backpack and I painted myself into it.

Howard: But you like your looks. Because you're a good-looking girl.

Sia: Thanks, babes.

Howard: I thought maybe it was like me: I don't like going onstage because of the way I look. I was thinking, "Maybe she doesn't like the way she looks." But for you, it's just you're hiding your face so you can have your anonymity.

Sia: Yeah.

Howard: If someone takes a picture with you, you'll even turn your back and just give them the back of your head. That's my best angle.

Sia: Well, only press. Only for people with a large Twitter following who are going to post it. For fans, I'll just take a picture with them.

Howard: Right now, seeing you sing "Diamonds"—I enjoyed watching you sing. That's part of the joy. Who are the artists you admire the most? Who do you love?

Sia: Well, Jeff Buckley, but obviously that's never going to happen.

Howard: Wouldn't you love to have been able to see him sing?

Sia: I did see him sing, and I did enjoy it.

Howard: It's great to see him play the guitar or whatever the hell he did. You know what I mean?

Sia: I'm selfish.

Howard: You are selfish. What if he had worn a bag? You'd have been pissed.

Sia: So cruel. But I don't go on tour and I don't falsely sell myself.

Robin: You are never going to go on tour? You are not going to do that?

Sia: Well, maybe. Who knows?

Howard: That's going to be the career, and whoever buys your music buys it and that's it.

Sia: That's the fantasy.

Howard: I still think that the record business is based on people going out and seeing you. I had Willie Nelson on the other day. I had never bought a Willie Nelson record in my life. He comes in here. He's singing. We're talking about his music. I went home and bought three of his albums. Because I just had to hear it and really be a part of it. I think touring is still an important part, and you do want a number-one single. I think that you need to tour.

Sia: I disagree.

Howard: You do?

Sia: Yeah.

Howard: They have you medicated. What do they have you on?

Sia: Neurontin and Lamictal. They're both antiseizure medications that are used to quiet the electricity in the brain. Isn't that great? It doesn't affect my creativity at all.

Howard: Were you worried about that when you went on Lamictal?

Sia: Actually, no. I just wanted to be sane. I did not care about anything else. I just wanted to survive.

Howard: This new album—the single is called "Chandelier." Are we allowed to ask why it is called "Chandelier," or you don't need to know?

Sia: It's part of a songwriting formula, I guess. I write down titles. Because what labels really want is, they want a strong title that they can google. And one of my jams is to find a strong title with metaphor. Because the melody is all channeling and then the lyrics usually just go, "Blop, blop, blop," and it's simple for me when I have that in mind. I was writing pop songs on this day, and I wrote this one, and I was like, "Oh, this would be good for Rihanna." And then I was like, "Oh, I don't think I can give it away. I think I might have just written up a pop song for myself." I did not think I was going to end up with a song called "Chandelier." But when it turned into, like, an alcoholism ballad . . .

Howard: This is about your hatred of alcohol or the fact that you—

Sia: No, I don't hate alcohol, I love alcohol. It's a song about, I guess, the demoralization of alcoholism.

Howard: When you say you couldn't give it away to Rihanna, it's because it's too personal?

Sia: Yeah, I was attached to it.

Howard: You get attached to songs.

Sia: Occasionally, but never to the ones I give away, which harks back to your question earlier: "Doesn't it feel bad to have someone else sing 'Diamonds'?" No, because that one didn't feel personal to me. I like it and I appreciate it. I really love it, actually.

Howard: But "Chandelier" is too personal.

Sia: It was too personal.

Howard: All right. Here's "Chandelier." Give it your best shot. I know you've been up singing all night.

[*Sia performs "Chandelier."*]

Howard: Baby, this sounds like a big fucking hit song. Maybe you don't need to tour.

Sia: [*laughs*]

Robin: I feel we're so lucky because we actually get to watch her perform.

Howard: Yes. We're one of the few chosen.

Sia: It does feel nice to do it. I'm just scared of fame.

Howard: Would you be more comfortable if I wore a mask while you sing?

Sia: Just put some fucking pants on.

Howard: You're not kidding. Believe me, I could've beaten off to that song. Beautiful, beautiful song.

Sia: Thanks, Howard Stern.

Howard: Shine bright like a diamond, don't hide away.

Steve Rannazzisi

OCTOBER 6, 2015

The *New York Times* uncovered the story of how comedian and actor Steve Rannazzisi lied about escaping from one of the Twin Towers during 9/11. His publicist called up Gary and said Steve only wanted to talk to one person: me. He felt our show was the place he would get a fair shake.

Frankly, it wasn't easy for me to do the interview. I remember 9/11 very vividly. We were on the air when it happened. We had listeners calling us from near Ground Zero and reporting what they were seeing. It was absolutely horrifying. All the first responders who lost their lives, both at the scene and years later due to the toxic stuff they inhaled down there—those guys are heroes, and a lot of them were regular listeners of mine. They were part of the *Stern Show* family. So I had pretty strong feelings about this guy who'd made up something about 9/11 and managed to get away with it for so long. It's just one of those lines that you should not cross, and he crossed it. I was very uncomfortable.

At the same time I felt tremendous compassion for him. I could see he was remorseful and in a lot of pain. Some might say, "The only reason he was apologetic was because he got caught." I didn't see him like that at all. He was really suffering. In fact, he'd been suffering *before* he lied. That's what caused him to lie in the first place. He'd felt so bad inside that he needed to make something up so that people would like and care about him. The conversation is a fascinating insight into how badly we need love and acceptance, and how far we'll go to get it.

A lot of listeners weren't as open-minded as me. I remember reading their e-mails. They didn't care how he presented himself. They couldn't forgive him, but I'm glad we had him on. It was a cautionary tale: in those moments where you feel the need to tell a lie, take a breath and say, "Wait a second . . . Steve Rannazzisi." Living with a lie, the fear of exposure, might be the most uncomfortable fate, and nothing is worth that kind of trouble.

Howard: Steve, you're a fan of the show. You've been on the wrap-up show a million times. I thank you for coming in because I know it ain't easy. I'm sure you're nervous. I want to understand this whole thing, because I can't wrap my head around it.

Did you out yourself, or did somebody bust you?

Steve: The *New York Times*.

Howard: The *New York Times* figured this out. How did they figure out that you were lying about your experience during 9/11? Did you ever figure out how they busted you?

Steve: No. I mean, there's videos out there, obviously, that are the sources they cited. But to be honest, it was a complete out-of-the-blue situation. I got a phone call on a Monday. It was a big week for me. I had a comedy special coming up, *The League* was back on—

Howard: Did you speak to the reporter?

Steve: I didn't speak to the reporter. He just called and left me a message on a Monday, and the article came out on a Wednesday.

Howard: What was the message? "Hey, please get back to me about this. Do you have a comment about what I'm about to write?"

Steve: No, it was: "Hey, I'm doing an article about your special and *The League* and 9/11. Just give me a call back." So I knew what the tone of it was. And I sent it to my publicist, and he just let me know, "This guy's got two different versions of your 9/11 story."

Howard: It had to be either a friend or a family member who knew you were making this story up about being in the Twin Towers when they came down. Because that's the only way a guy would even bother investigating this, don't you think?

Steve: Perhaps. I don't know. I mean, it's been fourteen years. In the beginning, it

was something that I said, and then I did some podcasts a couple years later. But since then, no one has ever talked about it. I was on the show *The League* for the last six years, and no one had ever asked me in an interview about it. No one ever asked, you know, if it was true.

Howard: Since this whole thing went down, do you ever say to yourself, "Why?" Are you aware why you lied about being in the Twin Towers?

Steve: Absolutely.

Howard: You are aware why?

Steve: Well, I'm becoming more aware as I speak to people.

Howard: Sometimes when you make up a story like this, the easy answer is to say, "I did it for some sort of attention." But I mean the real, deep *why* . . . There's gotta be something deeply psychological about this. You want people to love you or something like that.

Steve: To be honest, I think it's—when I moved to Los Angeles, it was about a month after 9/11. And, you know, I moved with my girlfriend, and she got a job right away and she started making new friends.

Howard: Was she in show business?

Steve: No. She got a job as a nanny and

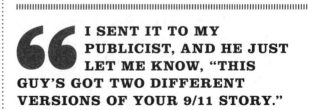

> **I SENT IT TO MY PUBLICIST, AND HE JUST LET ME KNOW, "THIS GUY'S GOT TWO DIFFERENT VERSIONS OF YOUR 9/11 STORY."**

started making friends, and she was making money. And I was hanging out at comedy clubs and—

Howard: Trying to make it.

Steve: Not even make it. "Make it" was not even a thought in my mind. Just fit in. Survive, make some friends, and just try to start living a life.

Howard: It's a hard life to break into, the life of a comedian, right?

Steve: It is.

Howard: Steve, do you think it's like— you know these women who will hurt their child? I forget what they're called. Munchausen by proxy or something. Is it kind of like, "If people feel bad for me, maybe they'll like me"? Is that it?

Steve: Maybe. Perhaps. But it's not like I moved to Los Angeles with this story, with the thought of "I'm going to go out there and trick everyone."

Howard: Was it calculated?

Steve: It wasn't calculated at all. It was as simple as sitting at the Comedy Store and everyone is like, "Hey, you're from New York?" "Yeah, yeah." "Were you just there? 9/11? You were around?" "Yeah, I was downtown. I was there." "You worked there?" "Yeah. Yeah, I did." And, and . . . you have, like, fifteen seconds to kind of go, "Wait, hold on. Stop. I'm sorry. That's not true." And if you pass that fifteen seconds, it's sort of like—

Howard: It becomes the story.

Steve: It becomes the thing where you're

like, "Now I have to be the guy who is very strange and weird and just said I lied about 9/11." And, Howard, I truly in all of my heart wish that I had that voice that I feel like I have now—that's like, "Hey, man, take a breath. Relax. People are going to like you. People are going to understand who you are when they get to know you. You don't need to lie about that. Take that back." And I didn't have it.

Howard: You know what's funny? When you see a guy who's as—you're successful. You're on a TV show. How many years has the TV show been on?

Steve: Seven.

Howard: Seven years. You see a guy who's successful, and you go, "Why did he need to?" But I guess, going back in time and saying, "I felt insecure and maybe people will somehow feel something for me." Do you think that's what was going on? In other words, "Hey, now I'm the guy from 9/11 and I got a little thing going here."

Steve: Well, I think it might have been like—you know, comedians are cruel people, especially in the beginning. And I kind of was like, "Maybe now people will not be as mean to me." You know, will not make as many jokes about me because they think . . . It's like, when you tell a couple of open-mic comedians, they talk to other people. And at the Comedy Store, you had open-mic comedians, successful comedians, and then you had stars come in. Like Pauly Shore was there all the time, and Dice

[Andrew Dice Clay]. And then those guys hear it, and then—

Howard: They notice you now.

Steve: Dice will be like, "Hey, how are ya?" And he started calling me Two. A nickname. And now I'm like, "I don't know how to ever tell anyone that this is not true."

Howard: The story was you were in the tower. You came out on the street and you just avoided being killed. You and your wife—your now wife—avoided being killed at the World Trade Center. And the fascinating thing to me about it is that your wife went along with it too, right?

Steve: Yes, she had to. She had no choice.

Howard: Did she ever say to you, "What are you doing? We weren't in the Twin Towers"? Or did you guys just ignore talking about it?

Steve: We talked about it, and she did say, "What's going on here?" I mean, I was there and I was downtown and I did walk across the Brooklyn Bridge and I did witness it, as many of us did.

Howard: As many of us did.

Steve: So to me, when I took her story in a way—she worked on the twenty-fourth floor in the financial center—I just sort of put myself in her position. When I told her that, she was like, "Why would you do that?" And I'm like, "It just slipped out. I don't know what to do now to fix it."

Howard: So early on you had that discussion?

Steve: We did. And we just kind of like— "We are two people who have no idea what to do. Let's just let it go away." And it did go away for a while.

Howard: Did it resurface because you went on Pauly Shore's podcast and a couple other places, and then it became a bigger thing again because now you were caught in a lie?

Steve: When I did the Pauly Shore stand-up special, he came to my house to interview me. And he was one of the people, like I said, who had heard the story. So I wasn't sure he was going to ask, but I had a feeling that he might. I had a thing in the pit of my stomach. And when he did, I just told the story the way that I thought he might have heard it. And then after, I was like, "I have to ask him not to put that in, and I don't know how to do that."

Howard: And Marc Maron had you on his podcast?

Steve: Six months later.

Howard: And then you were like, "I still have dreams of people falling out of the buildings," and all that stuff. The lie becomes more elaborate, right? Because you try to make it more real.

Steve: Well, to be honest with you, I did have horrible dreams. I did. And the only thing that I . . . When I read articles afterward, I knew that people had felt the shift in the building. So I knew that that was something that . . . You know, as Marc asked me questions, I knew that . . . I said, "You know what, this is something that . . ."

Howard: Did your parents—

Steve: My parents had no idea.

Howard: That you had made up this story?

Steve: No.

Howard: They had never heard about this.

Steve: No, because they don't listen to podcasts and they don't go on my Wikipedia page or any of that.

Howard: Did you have any relative or friend say to you, "Hey, wait a second, this doesn't add up"?

Steve: My brother was in college. He's a lot younger than me. This was 2003, and I told him when I went to visit him.

Howard: You told him you lied? What did he say?

Steve: You know, "What you did was terrible. You made a terrible mistake. But I know it's not who you are, and I know it's not indicative of you as a person and how we were raised." My brother's a priest now, and we've spoken a lot about this. And the hurt and the pain and the nervousness that you hear now comes from because I know what I did was terrible and I know that I hurt a lot of people.

Howard: Right.

Steve: People that lost people. People that

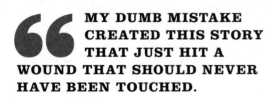

> **MY DUMB MISTAKE CREATED THIS STORY THAT JUST HIT A WOUND THAT SHOULD NEVER HAVE BEEN TOUCHED.**

helped people survive. Those people— those are the people that I truly am sorry. That's why I wanted to come on here, because I wanted to talk to you and your audience. Because you personify New York, and your audience—those are the people that truly in my heart I feel awful that my dumb mistake created this story that just hit a wound that should never have been touched.

Howard: I know that you had a big endorsement deal with Buffalo Wild Wings. They fired you right away, right?

Steve: Pretty much within a day or two, yes.

Howard: The TV show stuck with you, though. Were you in fear that they might just say, "We're not going to work with you anymore"?

Steve: We were shooting our last season. We only had a couple more episodes left to shoot.

Howard: After this all comes out, is it weird then going to the set and doing the show with these people that all assumed you're the Twin Towers guy? What is that like?

Steve: It was very nerve-racking.

Howard: Did anybody say anything to you?

Steve: To be honest, 95 percent of the people who know me now had never heard of this story. After 2009, anytime I was asked about it, I would sidestep and say, "I was downtown and it was an awful day in New York." I always tried to move on beyond that and step away from the awful lie that I told. The day that the story broke, I e-mailed my cast members and I told them what was going on, and some of them had no idea that this was even a thing.

Howard: What did they say to you?

Steve: All of them—and I can't thank them enough for the support—all of them said, "We know who you are. We know that this is not indicative of who you are."

Howard: But when you hang with people now, are you thinking, "They're looking at me differently"?

Steve: Sure.

Howard: It's hard, right?

Steve: Sure it is. But that's something I will have to live with and grow beyond.

Howard: Are you working with a psychiatrist now? To sort of help you unravel this whole mystery?

Steve: I am. I have been for the last couple years.

Howard: And is it helping you?

Steve: It is helping me. Because I didn't know what codependency was before a year ago. I didn't know what narcissism was all that well. I didn't know a lot about myself.

Howard: I'm sure there are moments when you go, "Today is going to be a really great day! Oh, that's right, I gotta go deal with this." I'm sure you're being punished enough with that. I'm sure that's a big punishment when you go, all of a sudden, "Today is a good day . . . but, oh fuck, I'm the guy who—"

Steve: Yeah. My family is wonderful.

My parents . . . I mean, when I told my mother—my publicist said, "You might want to call your parents and let them know. I don't know how big this is going to get."

Howard: That must have been an easy call, huh?

Steve: I was on my way to my son's school open house. And I had to call my parents on my way there, 'cause we were in LA and they were in New York and it was too late. And I immediately got emotional, and my mom just looked at me and said, "You are my son and I love you more than anything in this world. No matter what you've done, I will help you." My dad said, "I will help you." My dad's a volunteer fireman for over forty years. He goes, "I don't care if I have to walk you from firehouse to firehouse and you apologize to each one of them, we'll make it right."

Howard: The thing that I can't figure out is how your wife went along with it. Like, did she start to look at you in a strange way? "You started this thing; now I have to go along with it." Was this a rub in your marriage for a long time?

Steve: I think, um . . . I don't believe so, because my wife is—

Howard: She was loyal.

Steve: She is incredibly loyal to me and to my family and, you know, she's the light for me. So the situation that I put her in and then having her just go along with it . . . It was . . . I don't know. We're going to see someone together now.

Howard: Did you have to sit down with your kids and explain it to them?

Steve: My kids are six and three.

Howard: Too young for that.

Steve: Yeah, my kids don't know. They don't know why daddy's got to be in his office on the phone and why daddy's crying sometimes. They don't understand that. What was hurting me the most was like, "I hope that no one takes it out on them." You know, because they just started a new school. And you can yell at me, you can scream at me, you can berate me, and I will sit there and I will listen to it. But if anyone ever took something out on my kids—they don't deserve that.

Howard: Do you dread explaining that to them someday? You've got to. Because they'll read about it.

Steve: Maybe. I dread it, but I will use it to go, "Look, this is what can happen." The thing I want to explain to them is, you're going to have feelings of being less than and being not accepted. And your instinct is going to be, "I have to figure out a way to become accepted." Just take a second to have some sort of self-worth and go, "I'm better than this. I don't need to do that."

Howard: If I was your kid, I'd be, like— when you have to discipline one of your kids and you go, "Go clean your room," they're going to go, "Hey, you lied about 9/11. Go fuck yourself."

Steve: Yeah.

Howard: Have people confronted you about this? Have you had to go and speak to families and people who were actually hurt on 9/11 or killed on 9/11?

Steve: Pete Davidson, who's a comedian on *SNL*, his father died in the World Trade Center, and we spoke that day, and I apologized to him. And he was like, "Obviously people make mistakes. Because I'm twenty-one and I'm going to make a ton of mistakes. But the one thing I want to make sure is that *I'm* the 9/11 comedian. *You're* not the 9/11 comedian. I want to make sure you understand that."✦ But that's why I'm here today. The reason I came in here to speak to you is, like I said, I know how affected you were. I know you were on the air. I know that your audience are people that were truly affected. The guy in Iowa or somewhere behind the computer that writes how I should kill myself and I should get my kids and we should burn alive—I apologized. I said I was sorry. That guy I don't owe any more to. But to the people that I've hurt, to the people that were truly affected . . .

Howard: Yeah, look, I'll be honest with you. I'm looking at the phone, and people still want to fucking scream at you. People are angry, and I'm angry too. This is such a horrible thing that happened in our history, and to lie about it seems so fucking wrong. But at the same time, I know you're a human being. And I know that you probably did not want to hurt anyone. If anything, you were doing

✦ **For more on this from Pete Davidson, turn to page 540.**

this to be accepted. Does this feel like a big relief right now off your shoulders? As bad as this is, coming here on the show—I mean, this is not why you want to be on this show. You want to be on this show because you want to be funny and that's what you do for a career and you want to celebrate your success. But does this in some ways feel like a relief?

Steve: In a sense. Because it's out now, and I don't have to kind of wait and see what's going to happen and be very cautious anymore about things. The relief is that I don't have to live with a lie anymore. But it does come with a lot of baggage and feelings of embarrassment and being ashamed. My brother, the priest, explained this to me. He goes, "There's a difference between being ashamed of something and having shame." Shame means that you're a liar and you cannot break from that path. I'm ashamed of what I did. I'm ashamed of telling that lie—that horrible, immature lie. That's what I'm ashamed of. But I don't have shame on me, because I know who I am, and I know who my parents raised, and I know how I'm going to raise my kids.

Howard: You feel deep down inside you're a good guy?

Steve: I really do. I believe that. This is not going to make everybody happy. Nothing I say today is going to make everyone happy.

Howard: Nothing. There are some people who could never forgive.

Steve: Absolutely.

Howard: You know it's too painful for them, and they don't understand, and they don't

> **"THERE'S A DIFFERENCE BETWEEN BEING ASHAMED OF SOMETHING AND HAVING SHAME."**

want to understand. Steve, I don't know you, and I don't know the show or anything. But I tell you what, I think it takes balls to come in here and talk about this. And I think you are asking for people's forgiveness. And I think none of us are perfect. A lot of us have fucked up royally. Not all of us. There's degrees of fucking up. But, look, I don't think you were trying to hurt anybody. I don't think you were trying to profit off this thing. I think this was someone who felt real lonely and abandoned and wanted for some reason— this is my take on it. Who the hell knows? I'm no psychiatrist. But it seems to me that you needed this in order to feel better about yourself, and I think you are doing a good job of explaining yourself, if that helps you at all. I thank you for coming in and telling us your story, 'cause my inclination would be to just fucking hide in the house and never come out again.

Steve: I thought about that for a while. And to be honest with you, my wife's like, "I don't think you should go on *Howard*. I don't know if you should do that." A lot of people said that. And I said, "You know, I'm a true fan, and I've listened for many years, and I think that he will be able to listen to me. And I know that his audience are the people I want to say I'm sorry to."

And Now a Word
from Our President . . .

NOVEMBER 9, 1999

(16 years, 11 months, and 30 days until the election)

Howard: Let me talk to you about this president thing, 'cause this has gained some steam. The fact of the matter is, this third party, this Ross Perot party, is really considering you.

Donald: Well, they really like me, but they like me for one reason: the polls really like me.

Howard: Between you and me, you have a book coming out, right?

Donald: Right.

Howard: I think this is great advance publicity for the book.

Donald: Well, that's true, but I am really considering this. But it would be very, very important to have your endorsement.

Howard: You're not running, though, that would destroy—it's fun to get the publicity and hype—

> ❝ **THE POLLS REALLY LIKE ME.**

Robin: Donald doesn't do things by committee. He can't work with Congress.

Howard: Right. You wouldn't do that. And you're having too good of a life. To even consider that horrible job. And it is a horrible job.

Donald: Now, do you think Clinton is a happy man, Howard?

Howard: Yes. I think this has been his career.

Donald: Now, what do you think is going to happen to Clinton when he retires as a young man of fifty-three or fifty-four?

Howard: He's gonna run a company or something.

Donald: Well, do you think he'll stay married? [*laughs*]

Howard: I think he will, 'cause he's got the perfect marriage. He does whatever he wants.

Donald: I think she might even encourage him.

[*Collective laughter*]

Howard: I don't think she wants him on top of her, and that's the way it goes. It's unbelievable. Hey, let me get a glimpse of your life. Let me get a glimpse of your life.

Donald: Go ahead.

Howard: From what I read about this supermodel you're dating, who is a knockout—

Donald: Melania Knauss, from Austria.

Howard: So you're telling me you're in a monogamous relationship? You're not cheating on her?

Donald: That is correct.

Howard: You're completely satisfied by her?

Donald: She is very satisfying.

Howard: Are you living with her?

Donald: No.

Howard: She implies that you're very busy during the day, she's very busy during the day, and then you link up at night.

Donald: The perfect time to link up.

Howard: And does she leave after you have sex, or stay over?

Donald: No, generally she'll stay over.

Howard: Oh, too bad.

Donald: Generally.

Howard: So, you're there with her now?

Donald: Yes. In fact, she's listening right now to the radio.

Howard: And do you have to talk to her a lot? Or does she keep quiet?

Donald: She's quiet.

Howard: Good.

Donald: Quiet, beautiful, very nice. And very smart.

Howard: Boy, I can't think of anything more perfect. The only thing I think she can't do is turn into a pizza after you have sex with her.

Donald: That's about as good as it gets. I'm having a lot of fun, Howard. I'm having a lot of fun in business. My business has been great.

Howard: Right.

Donald: And the city is booming, as you know. You know, Rudy's done a very good job.

Howard: He has been great.

Donald: Whether people love him or don't love him, Rudy has been a great mayor, and the city's been booming. I'm the biggest developer in New York now, by far, and I'm having a lot of fun.

Howard: I tell ya, you're smelling more than roses, my friend. Who you gonna vote for, Rudy or Hillary?

Donald: I'm a Rudy man. Frankly, he's done such a good job, how can you not let him go on to the next stage? I wish he could be mayor for another four years.

Howard: You have to reward a guy who has done a good job.

Donald: Absolutely. And I think she's very nice. I've met her a bunch of times.

Howard: All right, so the point is you're banging this supermodel, and after you're done you'll have another supermodel. But it seems to me you're digging this one.

Donald: Well, she's very exceptional.

Howard: You would never marry again.

Donald: Well, I have to tell you this, Howard: marriage really is a great institution.

Howard: The fact of the matter is, your life is pretty much perfect. And you would never get married again, but this woman thinks you're going to marry her.

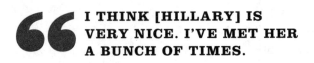

I THINK [HILLARY] IS VERY NICE. I'VE MET HER A BUNCH OF TIMES.

Donald: Well, this has been a good year.

Howard: Has she brought up marriage?

Donald: No, she has not.

But I do love the concept of marriage, if you have the right woman.

Howard: Does she dress up real hot? Like, miniskirts and stuff?

Donald: Well, she's a conservative person, but she will wear some wild stuff now and then.

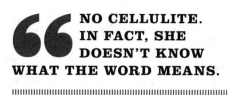

Howard: Do you go to regular restaurants with her and stuff? Like, you walk in, sit at a table, does she ever not wear panties—

Donald: Howard, you're talking about a potential first lady. This is not appropriate.

Howard: Forget that. Please, you gotta help me out with this, 'cause I have no life.

Donald: Well, I'll say this: we get along very well.

Howard: Where do you take her on a first date? How tall is she?

Donald: She's five-eleven, I guess.

Howard: Mmm. Not an ounce of cellulite, right?

Donald: No cellulite, no. In fact, she doesn't know what the word means. Howard, you should come out with me sometime. For a presidential candidate, I have the best time.

Howard: Well, Donald, seriously: good luck with the presidential run. I'll be following that closely.

Donald: You have to endorse me, Howard.

Howard: Sure, I'll endorse you. What else do I got to do?

Donald: I've made billions of dollars. Hey, look, I watched [George W.] Bush the other day on television.

Howard: Right.

Donald: And I'm not sure that's what you want.

Howard: I'm not sure that's what I want either. He knows less than I do about world politics.

Donald: And I watched the debate between [Bill] Bradley and [Al] Gore, and I don't think that's what you want either.

Howard: It'd be interesting, four years of you.

Donald: Take a good look at it. I'll tell you what, this country won't be ripped off anymore.

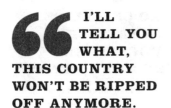

> I'LL TELL YOU WHAT, THIS COUNTRY WON'T BE RIPPED OFF ANYMORE.

Howard: The guy's a good businessman.

Donald: We'll get lots of good deals, and lots of lower taxes. But I'll make a decision over the next few months.

Howard: Let me talk to that broad in your bed.

Donald: Maybe I should get her in. Do you want me to get her in?

Howard: Yeah, let me talk to her. What's her name again, Melanie?

Melania: Hello?

Howard: Hey!

Melania: Hey, how are you?

Howard: You are so hot.

Melania: Oh, thank you.

Howard: I see pictures of you, and can't believe it. You're a dream.

Melania: So, are you coming out with us?

Howard: Yes I am, baby. Let me tell you something: I want you to put on your hottest outfit.

Melania: Okay. No problem.

Howard: What are you going to wear?

Melania: Oh, I don't tell you now. You will see.

Howard: Let me ask you this: What are you wearing right now?

Melania: Not much.

Howard: Are you naked? Are you nude?

Melania: Almost.

Howard: Ohhhh. I have my pants off already. So what are you, in love with Trump?

Melania: Sorry?

Howard: Are you in love with Trump?

Melania: Yeah, we have a great time.

Howard: Do you want to marry him?

Melania: I'm not answering that.

Howard: You don't even care. You're perfect. And what do you do, go over there every night and have sex?

Melania: That's true. We have a great, great time.

Howard: Every night you have sex?

Melania: Even more.

Howard: You ever steal money from his wallet?

Melania: No, I never do that.

Howard: You like to go to beaches?

Melania: I do.

Howard: What do you wear?

Melania: Actually, I like to take more private . . . bikini on the beach.

Howard: Bikini or thong?

Melania: Thong. When I say "bikini," I mean thong. I don't want to have a line. Lines on the body, not good.

Howard: And you have a big chest for a model.

Melania: Mm-hmm.

Howard: Do you like a man with soft, dimpled buttocks? 'Cause that's me. Let me tell you, you are perfect.

Melania: Oh, thank you. Do you want to speak with Donald?

Howard: She's tired of me.

Melania: Take care. Bye-bye.

Donald: So what do you think of that, Howard?

Howard: Jesus Christ.

Donald: How's that accent? How's that voice?

Howard: Boy, that chick is something. And she's not that chatty.

Donald: No, she's very smart. Maybe too smart.

Howard: All right, Donald, I don't want to keep you from having sex. Have you had sex today?

Donald: I can't answer that.

Howard: Is she naked?

Donald: She is naked, actually. It's a thing of beauty.

Howard: Ugh.

Robin: This is a [presidential] candidate we're talking about.

Donald: That's right. You're now dealing with a candidate, Howard! Is this your average interview with a presidential candidate, Robin?

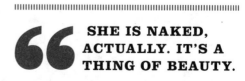

SHE IS NAKED, ACTUALLY. IT'S A THING OF BEAUTY.

Howard: You know what? This is why you'd be a great candidate, because you're refreshingly honest. Clinton's doing the same stuff, he just won't talk about it.

Donald: The level of quality is not there either, Howard.

Howard: Hey, Donald, listen: we're going to follow your candidacy. You have an open invitation on this show. Donald Trump is a great friend of this show, and "President Trump" will be a reality. Thank you.

Donald: Take care of yourself.

Conan O'Brien

FEBRUARY 25, 2015

This is possibly the best interview I've ever done.

We'd had Conan on years before, and again, same old story—I just clowned around. We harassed him with a ventriloquist dummy, something juvenile like that. This is another one of those second-chance interviews where I thanked God Conan was willing to come in and let me have a real conversation as opposed to me being an attacking maniac.

Late-night hosts are like parents. Their job is to tuck us into bed at night, make us smile, soothe us. What I do is different. I'm not going to put you to sleep. I'm going to blast you awake. There's a reason we drink coffee in the morning and not at night. I'm not warm milk. I'm caffeinated. I'm going to tell you everything is *not* all right. I'm not all right. You're not all right. The world is not all right. What I do is too hot for television. I mean "hot" in the way that Marshall McLuhan used the word. You've got to be "cool" on TV. You can't heat things up too much. People get uncomfortable. When you see a guy growling and gritting his teeth and baring his fangs, it looks ugly. When you eliminate the video and just go with the audio, it becomes wonderful. It becomes refreshingly honest.

Given its time constraints, the late-night talk show format can be limiting, whereas my audience gets a sense of who I am because I have four hours to stretch. Sometimes I'm sensitive, sometimes I'm harsh, sometimes I'm a total asshole. It's a full range of emotion. You get to see a complete person. I have an intimacy with my audience that very few entertainers experience. That's why I enjoy this interview with Conan so much. Sure, you watch him all the time. But who is he? What is his life like? What are his real feelings?

He talks openly about his longtime struggle with depression. I don't think he'd talked about it much before this. I'm not sure he planned to when he came into the studio that day. Conan said something in passing about getting down on himself. It was just a quick, fleeting thought. I got the sense that there was more there and that he was willing to talk about it. That's something

I always have to be prepared for when doing an interview. I have to be open to veering from my agenda and going to a new place.

I had no regrets afterward, no awkward moments of beating myself up for leaving something out of the interview. There was a deep satisfaction. If I had to pick out one interview for people to read, one that I think is the gold standard, this would probably be the one.

Howard: I don't know how many people know this about Conan. Not only did he go to Harvard, but he was the valedictorian of his high school in Brookline, Massachusetts, which is an upscale neighborhood. You've got to be pretty fucking smart to—

Conan: There were gangs there, but they were wearing Izod shirts.

Howard: Here you are, the most brilliant student—your father is a doctor?

Conan: Microbiologist.

Howard: A brilliant guy. Harvard guy himself, right?

Conan: Yeah, he went to med school there.

Howard: I mean, a family of geniuses. When you are sitting there, doing an interview with an actress or an actor who is a complete nitwit, people who are mind-numbingly dull and dumb, and you are intellectually superior—have you ever had your IQ measured?

Conan: I don't think I have, actually. Have you?

> **THE CLASS CLOWN IS THE GUY THAT GETS UP AND SETS THE CLOCK AHEAD TWENTY MINUTES. THAT GUY ALWAYS DIES IN A MOTEL SHOOTOUT.**

Howard: I don't want to know because I'm probably a lot stupider than I think.

Conan: You see, I think people give me credit for having this intelligence that . . . I think I have a lot of emotional intelligence. There are certain things I know a lot about, and there are areas where I am staggeringly stupid.

Howard: But in order to get into Harvard, don't you have to have huge SATs?

Conan: Mine were okay, but I don't remember them being great.

Howard: How did you get into Harvard?

Conan: I think I was interesting to them. First of all, I was a creative person. I was a good writer and I think I had won some national fiction-writing contest. I think that got their attention. I was interesting to them, and I have an interesting name. Believe me, it was not on SATs.

Howard: Were you considered a popular kid, or the nerdy, brainy kid?

Conan: I was a little bit of both, but I think over time I was the guy who—it's the same thing in my broadcasting career. I'm not one of those guys that blows people away when I come out of the gate. I was kind of a nerdy kid. It took me a long time to grow into my body—within the last several weeks. I was very skinny, and then I would say, by the time I was a junior in high school, people knew I was funny. But I was not the class clown. The class clown is the guy that gets up and sets the clock ahead twenty minutes. That guy always dies in a motel shootout. The guys who I admire, the guys who I really think are funny, are very quiet and they were sort of under the radar.

Howard: I subscribe to that as well. The class clown was sort of an idiot.

Conan: He had a lot of testosterone at an early age, but he is always the one who is in a prison right now somewhere. I had every intention of being a serious student and probably trying to go into government or trying to go into—I was really interested in being a serious writer. It was a complete accident. I had a roommate who said, "I am going to this thing called the *Lampoon* to try out," and I was oblivious.

Howard: The *Harvard Lampoon*.

Conan: So I said, "Well, I'll go with you." He gave up, I kept going, and I suddenly felt like a duck that had been put in water for the first time. It just felt great.

Howard: The stories I hear about when you were at the *Lampoon* are bordering on maybe the most brilliant bits I've ever heard. I say this with tremendous respect: the thing you pulled on Bill Cosby while you were in college is fucking genius. You wanted to meet Bill Cosby. After all, he was a very popular comedian, the rape aside. You decided you wanted to meet Bill Cosby, and you brilliantly created an award.

I SAID, "THAT'S JUST TRASH. YOU CAN THROW THAT IN THE BACK, MR. COSBY."

Conan: We invented an award that didn't exist. The thing I realized is that people will come and pick up an award, and you've already got the Harvard name. People will come. I swear to God this is a true story. We invented this award.

Howard: How old were you?

Conan: I think I was nineteen, and I knew nothing about show business. Bill Cosby's coming in with his entourage on Butler Aviation at Logan Airport. I remember it to this day. I wrote it down on a piece of paper: "I'm scared. I've got to go and get Bill Cosby." Now, you and I know the thing to do is you call a limo company, and they go and pick up Bill Cosby, who is the biggest comedy star in the world. I don't know that. What I do is I take the T—the subway—back home to Brookline, and I borrow my dad's station wagon. Let me tell you about the station wagon—and people think I'm making this up, but I swear to God this is true—my parents always bought cars used and old and junky to save money. My dad bought a Ford LTD with wood paneling. He got it from a motel in Maine. And on the side of it it said, "Spruce Point Inn." It had a tree on it. I borrowed that car. I drove to Butler Aviation.

Howard: You are out of your mind.

Conan: I'd never seen a private plane before. Bill Cosby gets out with these two guys. Wearing a tuxedo.

Howard: Was he wearing a tuxedo for his award?

Conan: He was wearing a tuxedo for his award. He gets off the plane in a tuxedo, ready to go right to the *Lampoon*. He walks out, I'm going, like, "Mr. Cosby, hey!" He's looking past me for the stretch limo. There's no stretch limo, so I open the door and go, "Come on in." I started driving him, and he's crunched up in the backseat of this really crappy car. I'm driving him over to Cambridge. It's about a twenty-minute drive. He leans over in the back and he picks up a Quarter Pounder with Cheese wrapper and he holds it up and does a, "What's this?" I said, "That's just trash. You can throw that in the back, Mr. Cosby."

Howard: "You can clean that up."

Conan: "Yeah, just throw it in the back, you'll be fine. We'll be there soon." I mean, I was a complete idiot. We went to the *Lampoon*, and then we had him come out to the front steps. We went and bought a bowling trophy, and we slightly altered it.

Howard: When you say "we," how many guys are in on this?

> **" I USED TO THINK I NEEDED TO BE INCREDIBLY UNHAPPY TO BE FUNNY.**

Conan: I don't remember. There's at least eight of us. We told everyone at the school that he's coming. He's a huge star, so a massive crowd blocks the street. He comes out, and that's when I saw what a master he is because he didn't even have—I saw this guy not really do material. He just went out, but in that Bill Cosby way. He's got the rhythm, and he's killing. And I was standing behind him saying, "If you look at a transcript of this, it doesn't read funny."

Howard: But it's funny. Do you think he still has that bowling trophy somewhere, thinking he won an award?

Conan: I think he cherishes it to this day. Actually, someone recently found pictures. It's the beauty of the Internet. Me looking like a nineteen-year-old woman wearing a tux, and he's smiling.

Howard: You go to Harvard, it's almost like a ticket to success everywhere. And you pick the one business where, like, the garbageman could walk in and probably get a writing job if he plays it the right way. You know what I mean? It's not necessarily based on Harvard or academics. It's being funny, and it's a bitch.

Conan: There is a lot of self-doubt, and I'm also someone that gets depressed and I get down on myself.

Howard: Do you suffer from depression? I mean, are you medicated?

Conan: I'm medicated.

Howard: You are?

Conan: Yes.

Howard: So you go to a psychiatrist and you—

Conan: I go to a psychiatrist and I'm somewhat medicated. Not crazy levels but . . . I used to think I needed to be incredibly unhappy to be funny. Then you get to a point where you think—and people tell you that's not true—you get to a point where you don't care if it's true or not. You just think, "You know what? I'd rather be happy."

Howard: It seems like that's the myth. You've got to be this miserable, depressed human being in order to be funny. When you went for the medication, you were so bad, in other words, you just said, "Fuck it. I don't care. I won't be funny, but I can't live my life being a depressed guy. I'm a father—"

Conan: Yeah, I've got two kids. I've got a wife. I just need help. Also, I realized I'm wasting time. I'm being so negative sometimes in rehearsal and being so negative about everything we're trying that it's actually a drag on us being able to do good work. It's getting in the way.

Howard: With the medication, are you happier now?

Conan: For the most part, yes. Someone explained it really well. It's like a lever, and it gives you a little bit of a push. It doesn't change your personality but enables you to keep going. I think that's what it does. It's almost like a little bit of oil on the gears.

Howard: Did you take it as a defeat when you finally gave in to the medication?

Conan: At first I did. I remember when the person told me. I went in for the test, and they said, "You're depressed." And I said, "I'm not depressed," and actually argued with them. Then she read me a sheet. She said, "I just asked you fifty questions, and you answered forty-eight that pointed to depression." But I was arguing with her.

Howard: Suicidal ever?

Conan: No. God, no.

Howard: Never that bad.

Conan: I like myself too much.

Howard: But you would wake up in the morning and sometimes you would go, "Fuck. I just can't stand what I'm doing. Nothing seems funny."

Conan: It's funny, because to come here to do this show we just walked near 30 Rock, which is where I did the NBC show for so many years, for sixteen years, and also *Saturday Night Live* for almost three, four years. Almost twenty years in that building. And I loved it. It was great. It was one of the best things that's ever happened to me. But just walking here to do this, walking near 30 Rock, and remembering every morning walking into that building and having this incredible anxiety and you feel like it's a low-ceiling cloud. I would take the elevator up and my heart's pounding and, "We've got to make this good," and there's pressure.

Howard: I can't think of a person who's been more through the mill than you when you started that talk show. [*Washington Post* TV critic] Tom Shales fucking eviscerated you.

Conan: Yeah, everybody did. At a certain

NOBODY IN SHOW BUSINESS SHOULD COMPLAIN. IT'S RULE NUMBER ONE. DON'T COMPLAIN. . . . WE MAKE CRAZY MONEY AND WE'RE GETTING TO LIVE OUT OUR DREAMS.

point, they wanted my contract to be week to week, which if you know anything about television is unheard-of.

Howard: That's ridiculous.

Conan: It's never happened in the history—I mean, I don't think you can get someone to work on your *house* week to week. I remember thinking I should just put an egg timer on my desk, and I'd be talking to a guest and it would ding, and I'll look at the door and someone would give me the thumbs-up and I'd crank it back up. The thing that kept me going during that period was I cared so much. I wasn't married. All I did was live, sleep, breathe comedy. And I had been doing that since I was eighteen. I remember thinking, "I am not going to be known as the loser who tried to replace Letterman for nine weeks and disappeared." I remember thinking, "That's not going to happen," and I have a strong will. It was like I got shot fifteen times, but I will not die because I'm not going out that way.

Howard: I'm telling you, I cannot think of a person who has a stronger will than you. Really. Because you went through so much stuff. And then if you're suffering from depression, forget about it.

Conan: This is an absolutely true story. It was the first couple of weeks of the *Late*

Night show and I was seeing a new therapist here because I had moved back to New York to do the show. I went in and I'm lying there and I said, "Man, I really think no one likes me. I think people hate me. I think people think I am not good at what I do. And I think people want me to go away." And my therapist said, "Listen, these are voices in your head, okay? We all have those negative feelings, but they are just feelings. They're not real." And I said, "Fuck you, it's the cover of *USA Today*." And I held [it] up. That's the greatest thing you can do with a therapist. I said, "Oh, no, no, no, it's right here." There's actually a pie chart.

Howard: Gary played me a piece of tape. I was on your TV show in 2006. They had just announced that you were going to be the *Tonight Show* replacement for Jay [Leno] when Jay retired. It was many years off. I turned to you on your show, and I said, "It's going to go horribly wrong. When your time comes, Jay will fucking not let you have that show." The audience was going wild and they were laughing, and you were like, "Hey, it's a hundred years from now." I said, "Wow, I sound like I knew what I was talking about."

Conan: You knew exactly what you were talking about. It's funny because I look back on that whole thing, which was craziness. I don't like to talk about it much. I really try to avoid talking about it. I'll tell you why.

Howard: Why?

Conan: Because for a long time, I decided first of all, nobody in show business should complain. It's rule number one. Don't complain.

Howard: You sound like a whiner, you make that kind of money.

Conan: We make crazy money and we're getting to live out our dreams. And then you're complaining, and anyone listening is rightfully thinking, "You're a jackass." The other point is, on my TBS show I made a point to be like, "I'm going to be positive, and I'm going to keep doing it." Because I would make jokes about it and gloss over it, and I would read the next day, "Conan can't get over it." I thought, "Let it go." If I talk about it for a second, someone is saying, like, "Oh my God, Conan, enough already. Shut up."

Howard: What people don't understand is that you beat the odds, and it's very rare to get a talk show and to be in this kind of thing. People don't understand another thing. I remember there was a point where you were hosting *Late Night with Conan O'Brien* and Fox came to you and said,

"We're going to give you twenty-something million dollars to jump over to Fox."

Conan: Yes.

Howard: NBC heard about it, and they said to you, "Well, we're going to give you eight million dollars, but we're going to give you *The Tonight Show* when Jay retires."

Conan: Yes.

Howard: You had such a fixation on *The Tonight Show*, as many performers do, because it's rare to get that offer. You said, "Fuck the twenty million dollars. Fuck you, Fox. I'll stay with NBC because I want that *Tonight Show*. I want my shot."

Conan: Here's the other thing that was really important to me that no one thinks about. I never made a decision in my career based on money. Not once. I'm not going to lie, it's nice to have money. But I've also not had money, and I'm okay with that. We wanted to keep my body of work. All I ever wanted was a body of work. That can sound pretentious to people, but next to my family, my wife and kids, my body of work is the most important thing to me.

Howard: It's your legacy.

Conan: It's my legacy. I put so much into it. I'm proud of the good stuff. I'm very proud of it. So the idea of leaving NBC on

> ❝ ALL I EVER WANTED WAS A BODY OF WORK. THAT CAN SOUND PRETENTIOUS TO PEOPLE, BUT NEXT TO MY FAMILY, MY WIFE AND KIDS, MY BODY OF WORK IS THE MOST IMPORTANT THING TO ME.

bad terms, or leaving and not having access to sixteen years of work that I'm incredibly proud of was crushing to me. That's something that never comes up.

Howard: That's interesting. I get what you're saying. Having that archive.

Conan: Having the archive. The irony of the whole thing is that I stick around and then I go through all this stuff, and then end up in a situation where I'm completely cut off from sixteen years of my work. That was the part that was most painful. Nothing else.

Howard: Because you weren't motivated by money, you don't regret turning down Fox for the twenty-something million dollars?

Conan: No, I don't. Because I stuck around, I did another five years on NBC. I worked hard. I thought I did some good work in that five years. I do not regret anything. I don't regret trying. I feel like a lot of, in your career and in your life, it's all how you play the cards that you're dealt. And I was dealt certain cards at certain times and I've been extremely fortunate. I am the poster boy for luck in show business. But I also think I've been dealt cards at times which aren't the best, and I'm proud of the way I've played them. I think that's all you can do.

Howard: Don't you think it's even harder to play the bad cards when you suffer from depression? Seriously, where some of us would get down, you're going to get *really* down.

Conan: Yes.

Howard: Were you ashamed during that, like, "Oh, I failed. How is the world looking at me?"

Conan: Yes. The number-one sign that someone's going through a rough time usually is that they grow a beard. I wasn't even thinking, but suddenly—I'm not a guy that has, like, tons of testosterone—I had a beard overnight. A beard invaded my face.

Howard: It's true. When they talk about prisoners of war, the guys who made it through the prison-of-war camps, every day they did their shaving routine. In other words, to hold on to their dignity and humanity. The ones that didn't survive, they let their appearance go. They fell apart physically.

Conan: It took me about three years to just figure out what the hell happened. It really did. It took me a while to get any distance on it and figure it out. It all went so crazily wrong so fast. You're looking at it from different angles, like, "Wait a minute. I pulled into the intersection.

> **"** THE NUMBER-ONE SIGN THAT SOMEONE'S GOING THROUGH A ROUGH TIME USUALLY IS THAT THEY GROW A BEARD. . . . SUDDENLY, I HAD A BEARD OVERNIGHT.

There was a motorcycle. I started to take a left. Suddenly there's a laundry truck and then I'm on my back and there's fire. What happened?" It took a couple years to process it.

Howard: I was a big supporter of yours during that time. I had offered to come on the last week of your *Tonight Show*. I don't know if you heard about that.

Conan: I didn't, no.

Howard: I wanted to come on and tell America what I thought of the situation. I had offered myself up over the air. Then I heard that NBC forbid me from the *Tonight Show* but—

Conan: I don't know if that's true.

Howard: It's probably not true.

Conan: But also it's me trying to remember. It was like the fall of Saigon. There was just so much chaos, and it literally felt like you could tell me a million things happened that week and I wouldn't know. What I do know is I was trying to get out in a gracious way. It meant a lot to me on the last show to be gracious.

Howard: You haven't run into Jay since, have you?

Conan: God, no.

Howard: You know you're going to run into each other someday.

Conan: I don't think we are. We don't travel in similar circles. My thing is I've always had a rule, which is I don't want to *not* run into somebody. I don't want to go into a restaurant and there'd be people that I can't run into. I've tried to live a life where I can pretty much run into anybody. I think life is short.

Howard: Being married, having a wife and kids, does that ground you? Was that the best thing for you when you were—

Conan: I don't know what would've happened to me if I didn't have my wife. I married the best person in the world for me. She's so great. What's great for me is I come home and my wife—she's proud of what I do in show business, and I make her laugh—but that is not what we talk about. It is not the focus of our lives.

Howard: You know what's amazing to me about the two of you? That you live in LA, and you see people who are constantly running from the paparazzi. I never see pictures of you and your wife and kids.

Conan: I've never taken my kids to a premiere.

Howard: Smart.

Conan: I really would like my kids to think I'm a Realtor. A very successful Realtor.

Vincent Gallo

AUGUST 26, 2004

If Conan O'Brien is the best interview I've ever done, then Vincent Gallo might be the craziest—one that longtime listeners often point to as an all-time favorite.

Vincent is an actor and director. He made his name with his film *Buffalo '66*. When he came on the show he'd just done a film called *The Brown Bunny* that caused a lot of controversy because the actress Chloë Sevigny gives him a blow job. Not simulated. A real one.

The film got panned by the famous critic Roger Ebert, and he and Vincent got in a big feud. So we surprised Vincent by having Roger call in. He also hated his hometown of Buffalo, and wasn't shy about saying it, so there was no shortage of people from Buffalo calling to get into it with him.

The scary thing is that I see so much of myself in Vincent. In this interview, he is pure, unadulterated id. The anger, the lashing out, the desire to burn it all down—I've known all too well what that feels like. It's as if a werewolf lives inside of you. That beast is one scary dude, ready to howl at the moon and rip the throats out of anyone he encounters.

This rage can be useful. When I'm writing for the radio show, I will force myself to tap into some of the ugliest things you could ever imagine. Absolutely heinous stuff. I encourage everyone who works on my show to do the same. I want them to excavate every dark and diseased thought they have. Then we take that raw material and we decide how to present it in a way that people can handle. Early in my career, I didn't do this editing process. I just spewed all my angst and bile into the microphone. I would let it all out. We're seeing that today in all corners of society. The more extreme you are, the more attention you get—the more likes and retweets and comments. I understood that formula long before the Internet existed.

What I didn't understand all those years ago was the damage that is caused by unleashing one's id. There is a price to pay. You hurt people. You damage relationships. No amount of ratings are worth that pain. Now there will be times when I'm interviewing a guest and they will say something totally uncensored and revealing, and part of me will be thrilled because I know it is radio gold. Yet another part of me will want to cut them off mid-sentence and redirect the conversation because I know later on they'll feel awful for having been so candid.

I was similarly torn when I reviewed this interview with Vincent. On the one hand, I recognize it is some of the greatest radio ever done—not merely the greatest radio *I've* ever done but the greatest radio in the history of the medium. On the other hand, I wish I would have given the guy a hug and said, "Are you okay?" At the end of the interview, he reached into his pocket and pulled out a list of people upon whom he wanted to place a death curse. Think about that: he had written down the names of all those he felt had wronged him, and he sincerely hoped that by some supernatural force he might end their lives. Many times on the radio I've wished death upon my enemies, even dropping to my knees beside my turntables and praying to Jesus, but I was just joking around. I wasn't serious. I was doing it to get laughs.

Or was I? Revisiting this interview really got me wondering about my motivations back then. Now I realize I was using humor to mask my own murderous rage. I was more like Vincent Gallo than I cared to admit.

Howard: Vincent Gallo is an actor.

Robin: An actor and model.

Howard: Started out his career as a painter. Evidently, according to the notes I have, made quite a living at it.

Robin: Look at him—a renaissance man.

Howard: Yes, and then decided to give it all up and go into film. Hey, man, how you doing? I read your little piece in the *New York Times* this Sunday.

Vincent: Yeah, and they fucked me.

Howard: Don't say the f-word. Don't say that. We don't have free speech. We live under the Taliban-like regime of the FCC. You can't say the f-word, my friend. The first words out of your mouth—

Vincent: All right, I'm sorry.

Howard: No s-word, f-word, t-word— for woman's breasts. Why did the *Times* f— you?

Vincent: They had this real phony-baloney call me up and brown-nose me. I kept saying to her, "Listen, I've been misquoted and chopped and edited a million times. I'd rather not talk to you unless you ask

a question, and I'll think it through very carefully and then I'll write down my answer, and when I feel it's perfect, I'll say it to you out loud." She said, "No, no, no. Just talk freely. As soon as we're done, I'll edit the whole piece and I'll call you back, and anything that you said that I shortened or changed in any way, unless you're satisfied, I'll take it out." I said, "Okay."

Howard: You fell for that?

Vincent: Yes, I fell for that. You think, you know, the *New York Times*. I forgot it was a memory from childhood where I thought they were a legitimate paper or something. I was in dementia. They also said that they would use the photo that I supplied. I give them the photo, I do this conversation with this witch—who, by the way, make a mental note that I've cursed you with cancer too.

Howard: It did work in the case of Roger Ebert. Are you glad you wished cancer on him?

Vincent: Roger is a nice guy.

Howard: But you gave him cancer.

Vincent: I gave it to him, but I put him

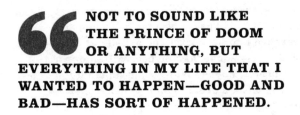

NOT TO SOUND LIKE THE PRINCE OF DOOM OR ANYTHING, BUT EVERYTHING IN MY LIFE THAT I WANTED TO HAPPEN—GOOD AND BAD—HAS SORT OF HAPPENED.

in remission. In the end, it was good for him, because the scare is good. He's eating better. He's changed his whole life. He's exercising.

Howard: I'm sure you did him a favor.

Vincent: In a sense, yes.

Howard: Tough love. He gave you a horrible review for one of your films.

Vincent: He gave me the worst, and that— can you say "prick"?

Howard: Yeah.

Vincent: The prick sidecar, Roeper—that half a man. You know what he said? At one point, Roger said that in the review—

Howard: I'll read it to you. "The film consists of an unendurable ninety minutes of uneventful banality. Imagine long shots through a windshield as he collects bug splats. Imagine not one, but two scenes in which he stops for gas. Imagine a film so unendurably boring that at one point, when he gets out of his van to change his shirt, there's applause." So you said, "Roger is a fat pig—"

Vincent: Yeah. All the fat bastards in the world, don't pick on me for that, because it would have nothing to do with fat people.

Robin: What did Roeper say?

Vincent: On his show, Roger says, "Vincent Gallo should bill this as the worst movie ever made, because people might want to go and see it as a curiosity piece." And then Roeper chimed in—that worm. I mean, he's a miserable little worm.

Howard: You don't like him?

Vincent: No, I don't like him. So he came in with, "I guess if somebody told me in the corner of the room there was a pile of steaming hot excrement, I'd go over and look. But I'd be happy I didn't make it." Roeper would be happy if he took a dump more than once a week.

Howard: Do you agree with this review of the film? Because I've read quotes from you.

Robin: Which film is this? Is this the new one that's coming out?

Vincent: Yeah. This is *The Brown Bunny*.

Howard: *You* even said that you don't like the film.

Vincent: That's another misquote. First of all, it came out of a British paper. They're animals.

Howard: Right. They just say whatever they want.

Vincent: They're pigs.

Howard: It says here, you say, "This is a disaster of a film and a waste of time. I apologize to the financial people on this film. I assure you it was never my intention to make a pretentious film, a self-indulgent film, a useless film, and an unengaging film."

Vincent: No. What I said was, "This was

my idea of a good film. I make a movie because I'm entertaining myself. I'm making what I think is a good film. If the people don't like it, I'm sorry for them."

Howard: So you do love the film?

Vincent: That film is the best thing I've ever done.

Howard: You got so angry with Roger Ebert that—by the way, I'm not putting you down for this. I have wished cancer on my enemies many times, Robin, as you know.

Robin: Yes.

Howard: It has worked for me as well. It's an effective policy.

Vincent: Not to sound like the Prince of Doom or anything, but everything in my life that I wanted to happen—good and bad—has sort of happened.

Robin: Wait a minute. Let me get this straight. You're saying, everything you've ever wished on anybody has come true?

Vincent: If I've had a focused long-term hate, yes, things happen.

Howard: Where do you think the anger comes from? Bad father? Mother? What happened to you?

Vincent: They were not the greatest.

Howard: Where did you grow up?

Vincent: In Buffalo.

Howard: There you go. Bingo.

Vincent: The whole city is bad. 'Cause they're the kind of—can I say "asshole"?

Howard: You used to be able to say that.

Vincent: "A-hole"?

Howard: A-hole, yes.

Vincent: They're the kind of a-holes in Buffalo, they hate their own. There's no homecoming there.

Howard: Nobody is proud of you.

Vincent: Proud of me? The worst reviews in my life.

Howard: If you could say to Roger Ebert, right now, anything you want to, would you—I see he's on the phone. Hold on. Roger?

Roger Ebert: Hi.

Vincent: Hey, Roger. How are you doing?

Roger: I'm okay, Vincent. How are you?

Vincent: I'm pretty good.

Howard: Vincent claims he did you a favor by giving you cancer because you are now a health fanatic. You've lost weight, and, in fact, it's probably the best thing that ever happened to you.

Roger: Without a doubt. But, unfortunately, Vincent's aim is very bad. The reports were that he hexed me with colon cancer. That was another example of the press being inaccurate.

Vincent: It's only because I'm suffering from prostatitis. It's because I came out of a prostate massage just before—I don't know if you've ever had a prostate massage.

Howard: I have. My doctor has given it to me.

Vincent: I was getting them once a week for a while there.

Robin: For what?

Vincent: Because I had an enlarged

prostate. I think because I held back once or twice or something.

Howard: You two have since made up?

Roger: Yes, I think so.

Vincent: We already made up. Roger is my idol.

Howard: Roger, you stand by your review?

Roger: I'm not saying if I do or not. It's going to be reviewed on *Ebert and Roeper* this weekend.

Howard: Now, Vincent does not like Roeper.

Vincent: That line—the "steaming pile of excrement."

Roger: Actually, Howard, what is worse: to say that he made the worst film in the history of the Cannes Film Festival, or to say it was a steaming pile of excrement? Which is the greater insult?

Howard: Well, Vincent stands by his film, says it's his best work ever.

Vincent: I think the excrement line was—

Robin: The excrement is really getting to him.

Howard: Roger, do you really feel this is the worst film ever made?

Roger: The film that played at Cannes in May of 2003 was the worst film I had ever seen there. However, I have seen the new version. It is twenty-six minutes shorter. Let me tell you that I did not miss one single second.

Vincent: I had to show the film to have an extension on my completion date, and that's why I showed in Cannes.

Howard: All right, so it was an unfinished film. Vincent, in your opinion, if your film is not the worst film ever made, what is the worst film ever made? You're very critical of your own industry. You've even called De Niro a hack, I think.

Vincent: Well, no. What I said about De Niro—he's never forgiven me. If you say my name around him, he makes that—

Howard: That face?

Vincent: Yes, that one face.

Howard: What did you say about him?

Vincent: I said that he's created, he's influenced a bunch of bad actors. He's had a negative impact. There's, like, a thousand people calling themselves actors doing De Niro.

Roger: Who are the De Niro clones? Would you include Sean Penn? I think he's a good actor.

Vincent: I like Sean. He flirted with the De Niro clone, but he is a good actor.

Robin: DiCaprio?

Vincent: No. Leonardo is a real movie star.

Howard: You said Leonardo is the best-looking girl you've ever seen, didn't you?

Vincent: That was a compliment.

Howard: He's a hot chick?

Vincent: I just meant that he was really handsome.

Roger: Talking about that, Howard, you know the most amazing thing that Vincent told me?

Robin: What?

Roger: He doesn't like the way he looks.

Howard: I know lots of chicks who want to do him.

Roger: When he was doing some modeling, people called him a model. It made him feel bad because he knew that he wasn't a model.

Vincent: That's right. There was a time when they were putting ugly people with pretty girls in fashion. Richard Avedon used me for Calvin Klein, and that was the point—

Roger: I think he's got a very striking presence.

Vincent: Thank you, Roger.

Howard: All right, Roger, so this is essentially patched up. It sounds like a lovefest to me.

Roger: Well, I didn't take it very personally in the first place. If you're a critic, you have to be able to take it as well as dish it out. If I'm going to call his film the worst film in the history of the festival, that to me is really more of an insult than wishing me colon cancer, pancreatic cancer, whatever kind of cancer you wished me. It didn't really bother me. Furthermore, I know that actors sometimes feel like that and very rarely do they say how they really feel. I once received a long letter from Sean Penn defending his performance in a movie. It was very thoughtful, and I was so grateful for it. I had criticized the performance. I was so grateful. It wasn't just like, "Up your ass." It was more like, "Here's what I tried to do, and here's why I think it worked."

Robin: Well, Roger, can he look forward to this week's show?

Roger: I'm not supposed to reveal anything, but let me put it this way: he doesn't get two thumbs down.

Howard: Interesting.

Vincent: See, didn't I tell you? Roeper. Didn't I tell you? Hey, Roger, say hello to your wife for me.

Roger: I will.

Howard: Thanks, Roger.

[*Roger hangs up.*]

Vincent: He has an incredible wife and they have a really nice relationship.

Howard: Yes, it's a black woman he's married to, you know that?

Vincent: Yes.

Howard: Were you shocked?

Vincent: No, no, no.

Howard: I was shocked a little bit. I didn't think he could get a black woman. I'll be honest with you, I didn't think he could get a *woman*.

Vincent: They really like each other a lot. It made me feel lonely.

Howard: You will never marry, you said, because you like feeling alone. You like feeling isolated.

Vincent: I'm used to it.

Howard: But I know you have sex with a lot of different chicks. You're not a fan of women, I don't think. I don't think you like women. You say horrible things about them.

Robin: What does he say?

Howard: Everything that guys say in private.

Robin: He says it in public?

Howard: He says it in public. The woman who gives you oral in your film—this film is controversial because there's—

Robin: Real sex?

Howard: The actress Chloë Sevigny. How was her oral technique? Was it good? That's the great thing about movies: you could get a hot actress to give you oral.

Vincent: Let me tell you something. When you're in LA, you could get head walking from one hotel to the one next door. You don't work four years on a film to get head.

Howard: Wait a second. Was it really necessary for Chloë Sevigny to give you oral for real? Couldn't it have been simulated?

Vincent: I was using pornography as things used to enhance sexual pleasure, sexual fantasy. I used icons of pornography and attached them to consequence, guilt, grief.

Howard: Was she good at it? Bottom line.

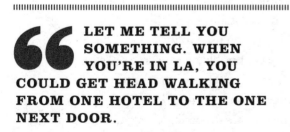

LET ME TELL YOU SOMETHING. WHEN YOU'RE IN LA, YOU COULD GET HEAD WALKING FROM ONE HOTEL TO THE ONE NEXT DOOR.

Vincent: When you do things in a film, I know this is hard to believe—

Howard: Come on, don't you tell me this.

Vincent: When you do things in a film, you remember it in the moment. Afterward you don't remember.

Howard: But you were able to get aroused in the film. A lot of guys can't perform.

Vincent: Not for nothing, there is the Porno Awards every year. I do a dramatic scene, open my pants, and have a full erection and cum within a certain period of time, and then go into an emotional breakdown. Now, come on. Come on.

Robin: Let me ask one thing, though. Did you have to do several—

Vincent: We did more than one take.

Robin: Uh-huh.

Howard: You bet you did. You once called director James Cameron a pig.

Vincent: If I called him a pig, then he's a pig.

Howard: You're mad because he put Leo DiCaprio in *Titanic* and not you?

Vincent: Listen, I would be the first one in any of those films. I'd be so happy. The only reason I did movies, I'm from Buffalo. There's no money there. There's nothing.

Howard: You haven't made a lot of money in movies. You're not in it for the money.

Vincent: I do it for the money.

Howard: You do?

Vincent: I do it for the money. You do it for the money, once you get there. When you first were in radio, you do it for things, pathological things, ego—

Howard: To get my father's attention.

Vincent: To get your father's attention. Once you're there, then you do the best job you can. But what gets you there maybe is simple things like survival and ego and revenge.

Howard: Quentin Tarantino is an a-hole, you say.

Vincent: He's a collage artist.

Howard: He's not a real director. Too much weed?

Vincent: I didn't say it, right?

Howard: You made a fingertip motion like you were smoking.

Vincent: Day and night.

Howard: Day and night. Your relationships with women—your girlfriend, Bethany.

Vincent: Bethany Ritz, yes.

Howard: You said you sold your house because you couldn't get rid of the smell of Bethany. You're a very passionate man, aren't you?

Vincent: You live with a girl. Do you want to live there after the girl's gone?

Howard: I'm emotionally detached, so don't ask me. I could.

Vincent: Not me. I've got to get rid of it. I burn everything. I erase everything. There's those guys in LA, they got their bachelor pads and there's ten different girls that go in and out of their lives in that same house. You've got to change the house.

Howard: Surely, you are a ladies' man. You've been seen hugging and kissing Daryl Hannah. You've made out with her, right?

Vincent: I made out with her one time.

Howard: How do you get to make out with a Daryl Hannah? Tell me the secret.

Vincent: You move right in. You put your head down a little, act like you're a sensitive little bunny, and then you move right in.

Howard: Right, the artist.

Vincent: Yes, the artist. I pretend that I'm an artist.

Howard: It didn't go any further than that? Why not?

Vincent: I'm very fickle.

Howard: Not your type?

Vincent: She's really pretty and everything. She's very tall.

Howard: Too tall for you?

Vincent: I think so, yes.

Howard: Felt intimidated?

Vincent: No, just there's a certain reach and range. I like things to be in a certain spot.

Howard: You dated Paris Hilton, even. How was that? What's it like to go out on a date with Paris Hilton?

Vincent: Fun.

Howard: Really?

Vincent: Paris is the greatest.

Howard: Sexual?

Vincent: Can I say? Yes, the greatest.

Howard: The greatest sex. I saw the video with her giving oral to that guy. It looked great.

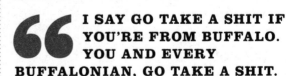

I SAY GO TAKE A SHIT IF YOU'RE FROM BUFFALO. YOU AND EVERY BUFFALONIAN, GO TAKE A SHIT.

Robin: She was trying out for your movie, probably.

Howard: She's very vapid, isn't she? You're a cerebral kind of guy.

Vincent: No, no, she has qualities and behaviors that are unusual and interesting.

Howard: Tell me what they are.

Vincent: She has an original point of view about everything. She's a bright person, very bright.

Howard: Why didn't you stay with her, then? You didn't want to be the laughingstock of Hollywood, is that it? What would be the reason that you wouldn't stay with her?

Vincent: I wasn't in love.

Howard: All right, let's take a few phone calls, Vincent. People seem to be anxious to speak to you. Go ahead, George.

George: What's up, man? I just wanted to say thank you so much for screwing over PJ Harvey, man. Her new album is unbelievable because of you.

Howard: You went out with PJ Harvey?

Vincent: No. I never went in there, touched it, sniffed it—nothing.

Howard: Nothing?

Vincent: Listen, believe me, I'd brag. I tell the truth. I'll tell you everyone whose ass I went up.

Howard: Tell us everyone you've had sex with.

Vincent: Not too many famous people. I go with broken-down, lost girls. That's my thing.

Howard: You like to save them.

Vincent: No, take advantage of them. I like to be the last straw.

Howard: You like to break them.

Vincent: Yeah.

Robin: Just before they're in the mental institution.

Vincent: Yeah. That's where I get them. No, I get them there too.

Howard: All right, let's go to your hometown of Buffalo. Allison from Buffalo. Go ahead, Allison.

Allison: Don't blame Buffalo for your failure—

Vincent: I say go take a shit if you're from Buffalo. You and every Buffalonian, go take a shit.

Howard: No, you don't want to say the s-word.

Allison: We will. We will take a big shit.

Howard: Hey, hey, hey—

Vincent: Go take a big shit.

Howard: Come on!

Robin: Enough, enough, enough.

Vincent: Can I say "crap"?

Howard: Yeah, crap, go ahead.

Vincent: Go take a crap if you're from Buffalo.

Allison: We will. We will take a big crap.

Vincent: You miserable bastards. You're all miserable there.

Howard: Why do you hate the Buffalonians so much?

Allison: Because he was very lonely in Buffalo, that's why.

Vincent: You're ten-cent nickel-and-dimers. Go to the Mighty Taco and have a meal.

Allison: I hope your next movie is as good as the last one you made.

Vincent: Thank you. Then it'll be another masterpiece, you moron.

Howard: All right, so obviously things went badly in Buffalo.

Vincent: I've taken the high road with Buffalo a million times, but those days are over.

Howard: Were you unpopular? Did you graduate high school from Buffalo?

Vincent: Let's say I had my ups and downs with school.

Robin: Is your family still there?

Vincent: Yes, my mother and father, and my sister.

Howard: You talk to them at all?

Vincent: Now and then I say hello. I'm a nice guy.

Howard: But you hate them?

Vincent: No. Yes.

Howard: Why do you hate your parents, seriously?

Vincent: I'm only kidding. My mother is really nice, and my father—I liked my father when he was more of an evil bastard, though. He had this stroke and he's not evil anymore, and I liked him better and now I don't.

Howard: It's like, "Dad, what good does it do me now if you're nice?"

Artie Lange (former *Stern Show* staff member): Can I ask you something?

Howard: What is it?

Artie: I don't know how much of the notes you saw, but it said there that Vincent when

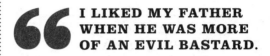

66 I LIKED MY FATHER WHEN HE WAS MORE OF AN EVIL BASTARD.

he was twelve was a chronic self-pleasurer. He did something that his father caught him doing, and I can't remember what it was, but he said his father beat him for nine days, then left for two weeks because he was so embarrassed about what he did, and then came back and beat him for six more.

Vincent: [Growing up] I got arrested for exposing myself and masturbating.

Howard: Really?

Vincent: Yes, I did. I was on a bicycle. I would go up to women in office buildings that were working late and show them my—

Howard: Really? Did you ever go to a psychiatrist to figure that whole thing out?

Vincent: I did. I went to a psychiatrist for eleven years.

Howard: Why expose yourself? What was the reason? Do you still get into it?

Vincent: No, not at all. That's the interesting thing: when you're masturbating like ten times a day, you start to look for anything else that could make you cum again. There was books. There was magazines. We broke into an adult bookstore, we took porn. We did everything we could.

Howard: You would pleasure yourself ten to fifteen times a day?

Vincent: I had Vaseline and plastic pouches

66 I HAD VASELINE AND PLASTIC POUCHES PLANTED ALL OVER BUFFALO WITH PORN.

planted all over Buffalo with porn. I swear. One day they bring me home. The cops come and they say, "Go in and call your family."

Howard: Because they had caught you in front of a woman?

Vincent: Yes, exposing myself.

Howard: A housewife? A woman with a family?

Robin: Office woman.

Vincent: And probably with a family, yes.

Howard: Of course, a MILF.

Vincent: That's what I liked.

Howard: You liked the MILFs. The cops catch you, they bring you to your father, and—

Vincent: No, I go upstairs in my room. I had a cross in my room. This was my last God moment. I looked at the cross and I begged God, "Please, make it yesterday. Turn the clock back an hour. Who's going to notice? An hour, and I won't get caught. I won't do it again." I hear the cops and then I hear the cop car. My father comes in, and it was a nine-day beating. He told me that I was never allowed to be happy again, that I ruined the family, that I should never be happy again. A year later a bra commercial came on, he smacked me in the head, choked me.

Howard: He tried to beat this out of you.

Vincent: Two years later he choked me. Until I was thirty years old, I would go visit Buffalo, and anytime something he didn't like, he would say, "And don't think we forgot what you did." Then one day, when I was thirty years old, I said, "Forgot what? I jerked off? So what?"

Howard: Wait a second. You did more than that. Did you ever expose yourself to people after your father whacked you around?

Vincent: No.

Howard: So it worked. The old man knew what he was doing.

Vincent: The old man was a genius.

Howard: You've had sex with men or no?

Vincent: No, no.

Howard: Have you ever been a male prostitute?

Vincent: No.

Howard: That was part of your legend.

Vincent: What I did was I danced once at a gay bar that's called Gaiety, as a punk rocker, because the punk scene and the fag scene was sort of intermingling at that time. I went up. I had a blue Mohawk. Somebody said, "Yeah, you just dance to a song." I put on a punk song and danced.

Howard: Who is the best sex of your life? A famous person?

Vincent: The famous girls don't—

Howard: They don't do it well?

Robin: They don't do it?

Artie: Anjelica Huston.

Vincent: I'd do bukkake with her. That's

all she gets. I'd have sex with somebody else and then do bukkake with Anjelica. She's a miserable, miserable thing.

Howard: Anjelica Houston is miserable? Really? Why is that?

Vincent: Just spoiled, nasty, selfish ego. I remember when we were doing *Buffalo '66*, I needed to change something—the time, fifteen minutes—and I asked Ben Gazzara first. I didn't ask Anjelica first. That cost me six hundred roses.

Howard: It's hard to be a director. You have to put up with egos. All right, let's go to Zolar. Zolar, you're on the air.

Phil: How come it says Zolar? I said I'm Phil the fag, and he isn't being very open about his experiences in the Gaiety, is what I'm calling about. Remember when you used to pleasure men back in the Gaiety?

Vincent: You keep jerking off to that. Whatever it takes for you.

Howard: Vincent says that didn't happen. Let's go to Anthony. Anthony, go ahead.

Anthony: Howard, this guy is such a poser. Come on. De Niro's derivative. Tarantino's a jerk. Is he serious?

Howard: Yes, he is serious.

Vincent: Yes, I'm serious.

Howard: He said people are derivative of De Niro. Yes, Garo. You're on the air.

Garo: You might want to ask him about how he was one of the people who helped recover bodies during 9/11.

Robin: Were you?

Vincent: I did some metal work there.

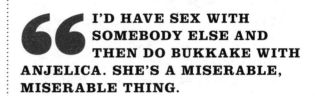

> **I'D HAVE SEX WITH SOMEBODY ELSE AND THEN DO BUKKAKE WITH ANJELICA. SHE'S A MISERABLE, MISERABLE THING.**

I didn't touch any of the bodies. I was a welder.

Howard: You used to be a welder?

Vincent: Yes.

Howard: So you went down there and volunteered your services?

Vincent: Yes. I had so many eye splints. It was so unhealthy down there that I wound up taking—I had a rental car, fortunately, right at that time. I had just been in the Toronto Film Festival, and I left New York immediately because it was so toxic at that time.

Howard: Who do you wish cancer on right now?

Robin: Yes, who's on your cancer list? [*Vincent pulls out a small piece of paper.*]

Howard: Oh, good, you do have a list.

Vincent: Donald Forst from the *Village Voice*. Deidre Williams, that pig from the *Buffalo Evening News*. Colin Brown, the editor of *Screen International*. Lisa Schwarzbaum, you piece of crap from *Entertainment Weekly*. Dick Peck, the queer who gave me the bad review in *Artforum*. Theresa Peters, Kirsten Dunst's agent who ball-busted me just before we were supposed to shoot with Kirsten.

Howard: That's it?

Vincent: You know who's the worst of them all?

Howard: Who?

Vincent: Do you know this girl Paula Froelich from Page Six and that guy Chris Williams?

Howard: Yes.

Vincent: Them.

Howard: You don't like them? Why?

Vincent: She's just a mean, nasty, smelly, scuzzy broad. Disgusting. Yeah, and Paula— go ahead, write whatever you want, because you're next in line for a curse.

Howard: Good for you.

Vincent: Yeah, I'll curse both those horrible boobs.

Robin: Oh dear, oh dear. Check every day, girl.

Vincent: Yeah, feel the lumps.

Howard: See what happens when your father beats you for fifteen straight days? See the anger? I know that anger, pal. You've got to do what you've got to do. Listen, it feels good, though, right?

Vincent: It feels great. I should get my own radio show. It's the greatest. Now I see how you wake up in the morning.

Howard: It's the only reason to wake up— to curse people out.

And Now a Word
from Our President . . .

Howard: Donald Trump's on the phone. He can't call in tomorrow due to a flight scheduling problem, so wanted to quickly call and get on the air. Donald?

Donald: Howard.

Howard: By the way, your archenemy, [former gossip columnist and television host] A.J. Benza, is here.

Donald: A.J.'s a nice guy. Even though I hear he said negative things about me in his book.

A.J.: Just one chapter's worth. That's all.

Donald: I can't believe it.

Robin: Did you know you went after his girlfriend?

Donald: I did more. I *stole* his girlfriend. But I didn't know I was stealing his girlfriend, Robin.

A.J.: He so knew. He knew.

Donald: Hey, A.J., nobody told me I was stealing your girlfriend.

A.J.: Well, you're such an honorable guy, I have to believe you.

Howard: Wait a second. Isn't it one of the greatest things in the world to be able to steal A.J.'s girlfriend?

Donald: I just didn't know it. You know, I've always liked A.J. A.J. can't rightfully stand me now, and I can understand that.

A.J.: No, I shouldn't—

Donald: At the time, I did something I didn't know I was doing. I had no idea it was A.J.'s girlfriend, and it's just one of those things.

A.J.: Okay, okay. Let me fast-forward. I'm dating Kara Young. I move to LA. So me and Kara break up. So she was a free agent. Even though we were still in love, she was a free—

Howard: So why are you faulting Donald Trump?

A.J.: Listen, I'm not mad he went after her when we were broken up. But then I got back to town, and I approached Donald at a party at Charles Evans's house and said, "Hey, this is not some arm piece for me. I love this girl. Now, stay away. I had naked pictures of your wife a long time ago, and I was a cool guy and gave you the shots." You said, "You're right. I'm sorry."

Howard: Wait a second. You had naked pictures of Donald Trump's wife?

A.J.: Chuck Jones had Xeroxes he was handing out, and I gave them to Donald. He said, "A.J., you're a stand-up guy." Then he forgets what I did for him. Now, if he was cool, he would've walked away. As a man's man, he should have said, "There's plenty of girls out there. I'm sorry."

Howard: I gotta say something here. I gotta take a little umbrage with you. You were broken up with the girl—

A.J.: But when I got back with her, he was still after her.

Howard: Wait a second. Trump starts going out with her, *he* starts developing feelings.

A.J.: Fine.

Howard: You broke up with her!

A.J.: We dissolved it.

Howard: It's her decision at that point. He didn't go after her when you were with her.

A.J.: Yes, he did. The second time we were together.

Howard: Because he already had feelings for her.

Donald: But I succeeded. Here's the problem. First of all, we have to say she's a wonderful girl. She's really a fantastic girl.

Howard: Must be, if you guys are fighting over her.

A.J.: We're not fighting over her.

Donald: Nobody's fighting. Nobody's fighting.

Robin: Donald, did you know? You knew A.J. wanted her.

A.J.: He knew. Second time, he knew.

Donald: Well, the second time, but by that time, I was there. What am I going to do? I was there. A.J., once you're there, you're there.

Howard: A.J., I'm being serious now. You're a little out of line with this.

A.J.: No, no, no, no.

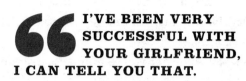

I'VE BEEN VERY SUCCESSFUL WITH YOUR GIRLFRIEND, I CAN TELL YOU THAT.

Howard: You guys broke up. He starts to develop a relationship with her, and feel for her. You suddenly march back in, and, "This is no arm candy. I want her. Be a stand-up guy and back off."

A.J.: Well, the night I approached him, he should've been a stand-up guy and—

Donald: I really don't remember that, A.J. Where did you approach me?

A.J.: I approached you at Charles Evans's party.

Donald: Yeah, I remember seeing you, but don't remember you saying that.

A.J.: I was with Kara. I was with Kara that night. I told him I had feelings for the girl.

Howard: Maybe *he* had feelings for her.

A.J.: He should've said that.

Howard: He's not going to tell you that.

A.J.: Why not?

Howard: 'Cause you're a gossip guy.

Donald: I've always liked A.J. Although again, I hear he treats me lousy in his book. But he should treat me lousy. I took his girlfriend. Hey, A.J., if someone took my girlfriend, I'd treat that person very badly.

A.J.: I've already done that to you, but you don't know about it.

Howard: What does that mean?

A.J.: I've been there. A few years ago.

Howard: Who did you take from Donald Trump?

A.J.: No names. No names. No.

Donald: I don't believe so, A.J.

A.J.: What do you think, you're the world's best lover?

Donald: I've been very successful with your girlfriend, I can tell you that.

A.J.: I got news for you—

Donald: It bothered you a lot, and it should bother you.

A.J.: She tells me how successful you are too, and you don't sound that great. She tells me you cut your own hair. Is that true?

Howard: But meanwhile, wait a second. Wait a second.

Donald: And she tells me you're losing your hair, A.J.

A.J.: I am.

Donald: And that you're going for transplants. Are you going for transplants, A.J.?

A.J.: I didn't go. I'm not going to go.

Donald: You're not going to go? 'Cause I had heard you're going. I think it's fine. I think it's okay to go.

A.J.: Oh, shut up. You got plugs. Does the world know that?

Donald: I don't.

A.J.: I know all the dirt on you, man. You want to start throwing rocks? Wanna throw rocks?

Howard: Wait a second.

Donald: Did you call me up?

Howard: Wait a second, wait a second. Donald, A.J.—

Donald: Do you call me up and beg me to leave your girlfriend alone?

A.J.: No. What, beg?

Donald: Hey, A.J., she was with me the day she convinced you to go to LA to get rid of you. C'mon, you know that.

Howard: But, Donald, how did you feel following A.J.? Seriously.

Donald: I didn't even think about it.

Howard: Really?

A.J.: He doesn't think of nothing but himself. Doesn't think of nobody but himself.

Donald: I assume A.J.'s clean. I hope he's clean.

A.J.: What do you mean, "clean"? Germ freak. Meanwhile, this guy doesn't shake hands, but he bangs Russian people.

Howard: Russian people?

Donald: Russian? Who are you talking about "Russian"? I don't know anything.

 HE USED TO CALL ME WHEN I WAS A COLUMNIST AND SAY, "HEY, I WAS JUST IN RUSSIA. THE GIRLS HAVE NO MORALS. YOU GOTTA GET OUT THERE."

A.J.: Listen to me. He used to call me when I was a columnist and say, "Hey, I was just in Russia. The girls have no morals. You gotta get out there." He's out of his mind, this guy.

Donald: Howard, when you win, you don't feel the way he feels.

A.J.: Why'd you win? You got stuck with a Stepford wife. Why'd you win? I'm best friends with Kara.

Donald: A.J., I won your girlfriend. I won your girlfriend, A.J. You know it, she knows it, and everyone knows it. A.J., I have undisputable proof, and you know it.

A.J.: Can you do me a favor? Can you call her cell phone four hundred times like you did last week? And keep hanging up on her?

Donald: Who does?

A.J.: You! We always know it's you.

Donald: Stop being ridiculous. Why don't you try going back to her, A.J.?

A.J.: We're best friends. She was with me two nights ago at my book party.

Howard: Why don't you go back with her?

A.J.: I'm not trying to do that. She's got a boyfriend. We're totally best friends.

Donald: You're not going to be able to go back to her. I've ruined that for you, whether you admit it or not.

Howard: Hey, Donald, I love it when you guys argue about poontang. Is there any girl worth two guys feuding over?

Donald: I'm not feuding. I'm happy where I am.

A.J.: There's no feuding over Kara.

Howard: You did her, and you're happy.

Donald: Right. I'm very happy where I am.

Howard: And, A.J., you did her and *you're* happy.

Donald: Hey, Howard, I just heard A.J. was very venomous in the book. I'm not going to read the book, but he was very venomous to me.

A.J.: He read the book. He read it immediately. He's the most vain man in the world. He read it instantly.

Donald: He's mad 'cause I stole his girlfriend.

A.J.: I hated you even before you had my girlfriend. You're the most pompous prick in New York City.

Howard: Wait a second. Now it's getting personal.

> ## "HE SENDS THINGS TO HER, NEWSPAPER CLIPPINGS WITH HIM MENTIONED, CIRCLES HIS NAME AND WRITES "BILLIONAIRE." YOU HAVE NO IDEA. HE'S OUT OF HIS MIND.

A.J.: Personal? What's more personal than a girlfriend? Jesus.

Howard: I see it this way. If I could be Solomon for a second, 'cause I love both you guys. Everyone can weigh in.

A.J.: And I don't hate Donald Trump. I don't. I don't. I don't hate him. I just hate the way he acts.

Howard: You been to Mar-a-Lago?

A.J.: I have. It's a fun place, but it's for blue-haired people.

Donald: But, A.J., I think you're a nice guy.

Howard: Thanks for taking the high road, Donald.

A.J.: High road? You have no idea. Does he want me to bring proof into this?

Howard: Proof of what?

A.J.: I'll bring proof of how low-down, how stupid this guy is.

Howard: Why are you saying that?

A.J.: He sends things to her, newspaper clippings with him mentioned, circles his name and writes "billionaire." You have no idea. He's out of his mind.

Donald: Total nonsense. A.J., a couple questions. First off, did you call my secretary and beg her, beg her with tears in your eyes, to have Donald leave her [Kara] alone?

Howard: Look, you're both making accusations.

Donald: You called my secretary, Norma, seven times, begging to get her back.

A.J.: I'm not trying to get her back. This was two years ago.

Howard: Well, it's a shame to see this.

Donald: I hope she has a new boyfriend. I think she has a new boyfriend.

A.J.: Think? You know, you know. You call her all the time.

Howard: Let's end this for a second.

A.J.: This will never end. With a lie like this? You can't beat a lie like this.

Howard: Let me give you my take. A.J.'s dating a girl, Kara Young. They go together. They break up.

Donald: They didn't break up, Howard. They were together when I went out with her. I didn't know that, but they didn't break up. He's saying that to put a positive spin.

A.J.: When you did *Playboy*, she was with me in LA.

Donald: I don't even know about that.

A.J.: Oh, bullshit. This guy is out of his mind.

Donald: Hey, A.J., let me tell you a little secret. Right now I have a great girlfriend. I'm as happy as hell. I don't know if you do.

A.J.: Stop making phone calls to Kara, then.

Donald: Oh, stop it. I didn't do that at all.

A.J.: If this guy wants to throw stones, I got a brick to throw, man.

Howard: Yeah, but he's throwing stones and you're throwing stones. Let me say what I think. A.J., if you're not with a girl anymore—

Donald: She dumped him.

Howard: Whoever dumped who. If Donald goes out with her, and then you try to go back with her, I'm telling you—

A.J.: We got back 'cause we love each other very much. I was still in California.

Howard: I gotta see a picture of this broad.

A.J.: I just thought when I told him I'm back, we're back, we're going to try to make a go of it—

Howard: Yeah, but he had feelings for her.

A.J.: Then he should've told me, "It's not going to happen that way. I've got a thing for this girl." He said, "You're right. I'll back off."

Donald: I don't even remember the conversation.

A.J.: He remembers nothing.

Donald: I remember seeing you at Charles Evans's party, but I don't remember a conversation like that.

A.J.: A very selective memory.

Donald: Why don't you try going back to her?

A.J.: Why do you keep saying this?

Donald: I'm going to call her and give you a reference. She calls *me* all the time.

A.J.: Here we go. Can I tell you something? When I'm at lunch with her, and she shows me her phone and I see it's you who's calling her *constantly*, what other proof do you want me to give you than that?

Donald: A.J., A.J., first of all that's false and it's bullshit. Here's what you do: try making a play for her, A.J. Maybe you can get her back.

A.J.: He'll never be happy until I say I'm going back for her. I make no bones about losing Kara.

> ❝ **I THINK IT'S SIMPLY A CASE OF THE AQUA NET FUMES GOING TO YOUR HEAD. YOU'RE A LITTLE LOOPY.**

Howard: So why don't you go back with Kara? Seriously.

A.J.: I've always said this, and it's the truth: when I'm back in New York, living here full-time, not coming back every two weeks, and if the timing's right, and we have the same kind of relationship—absolutely.

Donald: Well, then try getting her back, A.J. She left you once before. Try getting her back. Listen, she said you borrowed two thousand dollars from her and never paid her back. Pay her back. You make enough money.

Howard: Hey, can you guys go on tour together? This is better than—

Donald: Howard, look. A.J. is a nice guy who unfortunately doesn't like me because of what happened.

A.J.: I think it's simply a case of the Aqua Net fumes going to your head. You're a little loopy.

Howard: You're not going to steal *my* girlfriend, are you?

Donald: No, I promise.

Howard: You know what? If Donald Trump is after your girlfriend, and she goes out with him, he's doing you a favor.

A.J.: One hundred percent right. You're 100 percent right. I believe in that.

Donald: Hey, A.J., trust me, she didn't love you. I'm doing you a favor.

A.J.: Why don't you get her on the phone? Get her on the phone right now, big shot. See if she'll talk to you. Let her talk to us.

Donald: A.J., if she wasn't taken away from you, you wouldn't feel so bitter.

A.J.: He's such an ass. You know what? I can't wait for your daughter to get a little older for me. I can't wait.

Donald: Hey, A.J., believe me, you have zero chance.

A.J.: Oh yeah?

Donald: Any girl you have I can take from you. Any girl. You're full of shit.

A.J.: There's no one more full of shit in the world. You know what? Set up a boxing match. I'll swing a pillow.

Howard: He's a billionaire. He's not going to fight you.

Donald: The last boxing match I saw you in was Chuck Zito. He beat the crap out of you.

A.J.: It was one punch. It was honorable. I make no bones about that.

Donald: A friend of mine was there, Howard. He said he never saw someone so unconscious. They thought he was dead. Matt Calamari saw it, said it was three seconds.

A.J.: Hey, is Matt that big pussy bouncer you walk around with?

Donald: Yeah, why don't you say it to his face.

A.J.: I would love to. I'm scared of no man.

Howard: Don't you think this girl is playing you guys a little bit?

A.J.: She's playing nobody. She's got a guy.

Donald: Let me just put it to rest. Kara's a wonderful girl. I broke up with her a long time ago.

A.J.: Yeah, he broke up with her. Why does Marla Maples only take a million of your dollars and move across the continent? 'Cause nobody wants to be with you. You're out of your mind.

Howard: Well, I gotta tell ya—

Donald: You know, you're writing a book like you're a big shot. You're not a big shot. You're a loser.

A.J.: So why'd you always like me, then? I'm a loser, then why'd you always like me, you asshole.

Donald: You're a nice guy. I do think you're a loser, but you're a nice guy.

A.J.: Do me a favor. Travel with Calamari and a whole army, 'cause I'm going to take a fucking baseball bat to your fucking head.

Howard: Oh, wait a minute. Easy with the f-word.

Donald: Hey, how did you do against the cabdriver? And how much did that cost you? It practically ruined you.

A.J.: Forty thousand dollars.

Donald: Which is more than you had.

A.J.: Funny bastard. Listen, you funny bastard, come out of your ivory tower and I'll beat your ass in. I can't wait to beat your ass in.

Howard: Now, wait a second, wait a second, wait a second. Why do you guys have to fight over this woman?

A.J.: Last thing I'll say, last thing I'll say. I promise I'll shut up. Last thing I'll say. I don't care what he says to me. I'm going to kill you one day.

Howard: What was that? "Kill you"? Take that back.

Donald: Hey, A.J., you know what you should do? You—

A.J.: I called off so many dogs on you. So many guys were trying to bury you. I said, "No, he's too high of a figure." Now I'm going to call the dogs on you again.

Howard: No, you're not.

A.J.: You'll see.

Howard: Over a girl?

Gary: This is going to get really weird. Line seventeen. Kara's on the phone. I had to convince her to come on.

Howard: Let's clear this up. Donald, you want this?

Donald: No, let her speak with A.J.

A.J.: No, no. Leave him on, Howard. Leave him on.

Donald: Kara? Put her on.

Howard: Kara?

Kara Young: Hello.

Howard: How are you? By the way, I was just looking at pictures of you. You are beautiful.

Kara: Thank you.

Gary: She hasn't heard a thing.

Howard: Okay, Donald Trump and A.J. are having a terrible situation over you.

Kara: Right.

Howard: They're both much insistent. A.J. feels Donald backstabbed him, and stole you away from him.

A.J.: The second time around, not the first time.

Howard: Donald's saying, yes, in fact—

Robin: Donald's saying he stole her the first time.

Howard: Right.

A.J.: Donald's saying the first time I went to LA. He's just being insane.

Howard: So, what's the real story here? I'm trying to help Donald and A.J., bring these guys closer together.

> ❝ **I'M GOING TO TAKE A FUCKING BASEBALL BAT TO YOUR FUCKING HEAD.**

Kara: I think there's no danger of that happening.

Howard: Right. What happened, Kara? Did you love A.J.? Did you love Donald? What happened?

Kara: I have a completely different boyfriend right now.

A.J.: Right. I told them that.

Kara: This is all things that happened years ago, and I consider myself to be good friends with both of them.

Howard: Why should they fight, then?

Kara: They shouldn't fight, 'cause it's something so old. They both have very big egos.

Howard: Can I ask you a question? They're both very similar kinds of guys.

Kara: I don't think they're that different from each other.

Howard: Right. And there's the rub.

Kara: I think there's an age difference, and A.J.'s more of a wilder kind of guy. But they both have very big egos.

Howard: Who's better in bed? That's one of the questions.

Kara: I'm not going to talk about the guys I was with.

Howard: Donald feels he ruined you for A.J.

Kara: No, I think it was the luckiest day—or unluckiest day—of their lives that they met me. I was a complement to them, and they both know that.

A.J.: It was my luckiest day.

Robin: Did Donald steal you away from A.J.?

Kara: No, he didn't steal me from A.J.

A.J.: Thank you.

Kara: He was already moving to LA.

A.J.: Thank you.

Kara: I did meet Donald. He was an intriguing person. I met him—

Howard: Donald, you're still there, right?

Donald: Mm-hmm.

Howard: Go ahead.

Kara: I started seeing him, and it's not someone you could go out with a couple of times without it being pretty well-known.

A.J.: Yeah, 'cause he calls the papers himself. That's why.

Donald: Oh, that's nice, A.J. A.J., how come you sent me a letter last week asking me to be on your show?

A.J.: I didn't. My producer did. I was mortified. I was mortified.

Donald: Did your show send me a letter begging me to be on your show?

A.J.: Yes.

Donald: 'Cause I have it right in front of me.

A.J.: I had nothing to do with it. I was mortified.

Donald: Oh, you had nothing to do with it. I see. You don't run your own show?

A.J.: They wanted you in the audience, assface.

Kara: You know what? I can't believe you're still doing this, after all these years.

A.J.: Baby, he called in.

Kara: Donald feels like I came off like a whore in the book, like I cheated—

A.J.: He said he didn't read it.

Kara: Okay, well, I don't appreciate that. 'Cause that's how I came off and that's not what happened.

Robin: Did you read the book?

Kara: Yes, I did, and I loved it. It's like *The Kid Stays in the Picture*. It made me cry. It's not exactly factual. Some things didn't happen in order.

A.J.: She's right, she's right.

Howard: Kara, like Solomon, I'm trying to solve this.

Donald: Kara, you were going with A.J. when I met you, correct?

A.J.: Not when you started dating her.

Kara: I'm not going to tell lies here, so . . .

Donald: Is that a correct statement, Kara?

Kara: Yes.

Donald: And you left A.J. after you met me, is that correct?

Kara: Yes.

Donald: Okay. That's all I said, Howard.

Howard: This is crazy.

Donald: Excuse me, so far I've been borne out 100 percent.

Robin: I wouldn't say 100 percent, Donald.

Kara: We did not date at the same time.

A.J.: Thank you. Now, why can't this asshole hear that?

Kara: You both have very big mouths. Has anything ever happened that's improper? Has anyone tried to see me when they shouldn't have? Yes, they have.

A.J.: Of course.

Kara: And that's a fact, and everyone knows it.

Howard: Why argue with each other?

Donald: A.J., just view it very positively. You wrote a book—

A.J.: I can't take this guy.

Howard: All I know is I wanna f— Kara, read A.J.'s book, and watch Miss Universe. Man, that was something.

Joan Rivers

MARCH 24, 2014

Joan Rivers was one of the most frequent guests on the show. I had her on at least forty times. She was also one of the *first* guests. From the beginning of my career, she had my back. When she was the semiregular host of *The Tonight Show,* she appeared on my show. She was one of the most famous and successful women in America, and was willing to talk to me when no one else would.

She also used to invite me to her home. I was a pariah. People were afraid of me. She'd have me over for these fancy tea parties. It wasn't just to shock her friends. She genuinely liked me and my work. She was just lovely to me.

Whenever she wanted to come on, I said yes. Some of my audience would go, "Who cares about Joan Rivers?" I cared. She was relevant to me. Nobody had a quicker wit than her. As I'm writing about her now, I'm just picturing her walking into the studio with all of the junk she used to sell on QVC. She'd give it to us—give some jewelry to Robin and some to me for my mother.

I can still picture her sitting down on the couch and being ready to go and so prepared. I'd think, "How has this woman been in show business so long and stayed so youthful?" I just couldn't believe it. Every sixth or seventh visit she'd be embroiled in some controversy where she'd said something nasty about someone. And she never apologized. Never. She would always say, "These are jokes. Tell these people to fucking get over it." I'm telling you, I can close my eyes and see her walking into the studio.

I'm still angry about what happened to her. Yes, she was eighty-one, and who knows how many years she might have had if she hadn't gone in for that surgery, but I can't stand that the operation went wrong. I feel tremendously robbed.

I gave the eulogy at her funeral in Manhattan. It was dead silent as I walked up to the podium. I stood there for a moment and looked out at the hundreds of mourners. Then I said, "Joan Rivers had a dry vagina." For a second, no one knew what to do. Then there was this huge eruption of laughter. Of course, that's what Joan would have wanted.

Choking back tears, I went on. "Extremely dry. I know this because she told me so. Two months ago on the radio, in front of millions of people, she told me that when she took a bath, her vagina was like a sponge and that all the water in the tub would get sucked in. *Whoosh*. But she wasn't done. She explained that if Whitney Houston had a dry vagina like hers she would still be alive and never would have drowned."

Joan had been telling vagina jokes for years. Those and the rest of her jokes she had written on note cards and filed very methodically in a huge index, almost like an old library card catalog. Her daughter, Melissa, framed one and gave it to me. I have it on my desk to remember her by.

I also have this interview. It took place five months before Joan died and was one of the last times she appeared on the show. I miss you, Joan.

Howard: I was thinking about you. Hey, baby.

Joan: Yeah, sure.

Howard: Well, I had to. You were coming in. Boy, you look great.

Joan: Yeah, sure—for me.

Howard: For you, you look good.

Joan: At this age, as long as it's not a body bag.

Howard: How old are you?

Joan: A hundred ninety-two.

Howard: I thought it was so touching how you appeared on the *Jimmy Fallon* show, the debut. You hadn't appeared on *The Tonight Show* in how many years?

Joan: Twenty-six years. I was banned. Carson banned me, which was stupid. And that moron Leno kept the ban up.

Howard: Why?

Joan: 'Cause he's a moron.

Howard: Yeah he is. He's a dummy.

Joan: 'Cause he's a fucking asshole, that's why. And I'm glad he's gone. He never made me laugh.

Howard: But, you know, you're absolutely right. It's ridiculous. My criticism of Jay

is that he followed whatever Letterman did. In other words, Letterman always had me on. So Jay always had to have me on. And I used to say to myself, "It's only because I'm on *Letterman* that he wants me." But I would go on and do it, until I had a falling-out with him. But you're absolutely right. It's such a dumb thing. He gets *The Tonight Show*, invite Joan Rivers on!

Joan: He should have had me on the first night.

Howard: Absolutely.

Joan: Jimmy Fallon's people, so smart, called me and said, "How'd you like to be on the first night?"

Howard: And you graciously—

Joan: Graciously? I was there three days ahead. I was camped out!

Howard: And you got big applause, 'cause everyone's aware of your history. You say Johnny should have had you back on. Are you magnanimous in that way? When someone—

Joan: I cannot hold a grudge.

Howard: You can't? If someone calls you

up and says, "Let's get over this," you're okay with that?

Joan: Unless it's affected my child.

Howard: Then you become vicious.

Joan: Dead.

Howard: How many shows do you presently have on the air?

Joan: Three.

Howard: Let's think about it. QVC—

Joan: QVC isn't a show. I do the jewelry, the clothes, it's wonderful.

Howard: You've got a show where you're in bed interviewing celebrities.

Joan: It's on the Internet, called *In Bed with Joan*. It's going great.

Howard: Okay, so you've got that show going on. Then you've got—

Joan: *Joan and Melissa*. It's on Saturday nights on WE.

Howard: Is that the gay network?

Joan: No.

Howard: Which network is that? There's so many fucking networks, you can't keep it straight.

Joan: I don't care. I just have a good time.

Howard: Then you've got *Fashion Police*. The number-one show on E! Jennifer Lawrence criticized you. She said you

> " I FEEL LIKE I'M WORKING BETTER THAN EVER, 'CAUSE I DON'T GIVE A SHIT ABOUT ANYTHING WHEN I WALK ON THAT STAGE.

shouldn't be critiquing women, judging their outfits.

Joan: Right.

Howard: And you were in a war with Jennifer Lawrence.

Joan: Yes.

Howard: And what about her point there?

Joan: First of all, she's an amazing actress—move that aside. Whenever we said she looked good, she'd say, "I love *Fashion Police*. *Fashion Police* is so good." We didn't like one stupid dress, and she came down on us. "How dare you criticize women! Women should be left alone!" Meanwhile, she's in the Dior ads, you can't even see her face, she's so airbrushed. You see two nostrils, and you think they're her eyes. If she's so gorgeous, don't have yourself airbrushed. The hypocrisy is so annoying.

Howard: Speaking of airbrushing, I'm looking at you. Not a wrinkle.

Joan: This is Botox.

Howard: You're Botoxing still? Because you look wrinkle-free.

Joan: Of course!

Howard: You have the skin of a nineteen-year-old.

Joan: Yeah. Sure.

Howard: I'm serious. You don't have one wrinkle.

Joan: But it's Botox, Howard.

Howard: It doesn't hurt when they stick in the needle?

Joan: I wouldn't know 'cause I cover my face.

Howard: You're almost embalmed at this point.

Joan: Yes.

Howard: Is it true your new tour is called the One Foot in the Grave Tour?

Joan: Yes. Before they close the lid. All my tours are called that.

Howard: Do you think about death constantly?

Joan: I worry about how it's going to affect Melissa. I worry about that.

Howard: I started to do the math. Maybe I got like ten good years.

Joan: No, you've got more.

Howard: Well, look at you. You're eighty. Do you feel like you're running out of time? That's how I feel.

Joan: Yes. That's why I work so much. I *love* what I do. I want to get it all in.

Howard: I get it. Lately I've been wanting to learn how to play guitar.

Joan: Do it!

Howard: I am. Because I feel like I want to get these things in.

Joan: Do it while you can remember. That's what I worry about. That I'm going to get up onstage and tell the same joke three times.

Howard: And that happens. I won't name names, but I've seen a few.

Joan: I'll name a few.

Howard: No, don't. But they get onstage, and they fucking suck 'cause they're forgetting their jokes.

Joan: I know.

Howard: How do you know when it's time to get offstage? Do you feel like you've gone down in your comedy abilities?

> ## I SHOULD HAVE NEVER LET JUDI DENCH TALK ME INTO GETTING MATCHING VAGINA PIERCINGS.

Joan: Honest to God? I feel like I'm working better than ever, 'cause I don't give a shit about anything when I walk on that stage. I hate sitting down, Howard. I should have never let Judi Dench talk me into getting matching vagina piercings.

Howard: You don't take anything for granted.

Joan: No, no, no.

Howard: Is there a person who's going to have to tell you your comedy abilities have gone down?

Joan: I'll have to tell myself.

Howard: You're gonna know?

Joan: Don't you think you would feel it?

Howard: You would think so. But then again, some of the greats haven't known that they suck.

Joan: But maybe their egos are so big. I don't know. I'm terrified.

Howard: But then what are you going to do? Sit at home all day?

Joan: Gonna kill myself.

Howard: You're gonna kill yourself? Would you kill yourself?

Joan: Oh yeah.

Howard: You have the strength to kill yourself?

Joan: You don't know until you're there.

Howard: Have you thought about it?

Joan: Oh yes.

Howard: You never fucked Johnny Carson, did you?

Joan: No. I'm the only one. You wanna get depressed?

Howard: 'Cause Johnny fucked everything.

Joan: Everything. Nobody *ever* tried to make me. I must've been ugly.

Howard: No, you weren't ugly.

Joan: Never got grabbed in an elevator, nothing.

Howard: No one?

Joan: No one.

Howard: You haven't had sex in, what, how many years?

Joan: I would say a good seven years.

Howard: You're done. That's it.

Joan: Truly, I'm done.

Howard: Like, you have no feeling down there.

Joan: Oh, I call my vibrator Barbara Walters.

Howard: Wow, even in your eighties you masturbate?

Joan: People who are *dead* masturbate. My doctor told me a ninety-six-year-old woman died, and they found a saltshaker up there.

Howard: How about at those old-age homes where they're fucking like crazy?

Joan: Yeah.

Howard: They go senile, then fuck like crazy. Did you tell Melissa, "If I get

Alzheimer's, just fucking kill me"? 'Cause in those old-age homes, can you imagine? They'd all be fucking you.

Joan: Oh, that'd be great!

Howard: Alzheimer's freaks me out. All you have is your brain, your mind.

Joan: Especially comedians.

Howard: Do you sometimes forget a joke and are like, "I have Alzheimer's!"

Joan: All the time. I'll go to the doctors. I'll call Melinda—I mean, Melissa.

Howard: So let's go back to this. You walk out on *The Tonight Show with Jimmy Fallon*. It must have been a great moment for you.

Joan: How about this: The limo dropped me off at the exact spot where I first came forty-eight years ago. And then I'm backstage with J.Lo and this one and that one. And then in the car on the way back, I started to cry. I thought about that girl who walked in there forty-eight years ago.

Howard: With my own career, it's not like I can point to a moment and say I've made it, but with comedians, it's very different. You went on *Carson* and killed—*killed*—and you're a star overnight.

Joan: Yeah.

Howard: I wanna do "Brackets" with you. You probably don't know what it is, but these are guys all over eighty years old.

Joan: Hot.

Howard: When I tell you two names, you gotta figure out which one you would fuck.

Joan: All right.

Howard: All right. Then we'll get down to it, and we'll figure out who the top guy over eighty is for you to fuck. Okay, you ready? Don Rickles or Bob Newhart?

Joan: Probably Don. We'd have more in common. He's Jewish. And I've never seen a foreskin.

Howard: That's important to you? That he's Jewish?

Joan: No. I just don't want to see anyone with a foreskin.

Howard: Jerry Lewis or Jerry Stiller?

Joan: Oh, never Jerry Lewis. I despise Jerry Lewis.

Howard: Everybody hates Jerry Lewis, but why do *you* hate Jerry Lewis?

Joan: Because he's nasty. He didn't want me in Vegas. He'd never use me on the MS show.

Howard: The telethon? You? He's got fucking circus performers on there.

Joan: He's got Siegfried and Roy! *After* the accident!

> ❝ **IN THE CAR ON THE WAY BACK, I STARTED TO CRY.**

Howard: Okay, so it's Jerry Stiller, then. Jerry Stiller and Don Rickles you'll fuck. Tim Conway or Mel Brooks?

Joan: Oh. A trio. Ménage à trois.

Howard: You like both guys?

Joan: Mel Brooks, my friend goes out with him.

Howard: That's right, he's a widower. How old is she?

Joan: About sixty-five, and gorgeous.

Howard: You have to pick one to fuck.

Joan: Mel.

Howard: Okay. Final bracket: Shelley Berman vs. Shecky Greene.

Joan: [*laughing*] Jerry Lewis.

Howard: Let me tell you something, Joan. You are triumphant again. I love you.

Joan: I love you.

Jay-Z

NOVEMBER 15, 2010

People know me as a rock-and-roll guy, and sure, that's mostly what I listen to. But I've always loved having rappers on the show. Their stories are often so fascinating: their difficult upbringings, their brushes with the law, their overcoming enormous odds. Few rappers have had as improbable a story as Jay-Z—from selling drugs on a bench in a Brooklyn housing project to selling out Madison Square Garden.

There are times after a guest leaves the studio when I will sit there and think, "We'll probably get together and hang out soon." I'm under some delusion that we've built up this intense personal relationship. Jay-Z was like that for me. We were vibing on such a deep level that it felt like a genuine friendship. It was that intimate. By the way, I haven't heard from him since.

In this interview, the old temptation to outshine my guest resurfaced. I thought about telling Jay-Z how I had been raised in a black neighborhood. "You think you had it bad? You grew up a black guy in a black neighborhood. I grew up a *white* guy in a black neighborhood. Now that's *real* adversity." Listen to how combative that sounds. Had I said that, I would have been challenging him. That's narcissism—the inability to have anyone take my place in the spotlight. That's my inner child. Therapy has enabled me to understand this urge and resist it.

The screen saver on my computer is a simple quote. It came from my psychiatrist. I was telling him about a magazine photo shoot I had once done. They had painted an apple to look like Earth and I was pretending to take a bite out of it. That image always haunted me. It represented my desire to swallow the entire world—the childish, life-destroying hunger to have every woman, every dollar, every radio listener. I told all this to my therapist and he said, "Wanting everything makes life a nightmare." I said, "I have to stop you there. I need to write that down. That is very profound."

I felt like I needed to see that quote every day. A couple of years before, when I was pursuing photography as a hobby, I learned how to use Photoshop. I placed the quote in bold red letters on top of one of my favorite photos I've ever taken: a black-and-white shot of Beth and me pressed close together and staring into the camera. I used that photo instead of a blank background because I wanted to see Beth and remind myself of just how good I already have it. *Wanting everything makes life a nightmare.* It's the first thing I read in the morning. I wake up, turn on my computer, and there it is staring me in the face. It's a good reminder that wanting too much can destroy everything good. I think this feeling lives inside all of us to one degree or another. If you only take away one piece of advice from this book, let it be that. It is the best guidance I know for leading a happy life.

I have plenty of time to be in the spotlight. I'm on the radio for four or five hours a day. My audience has heard about me growing up in a black neighborhood over and over again. So I resisted mentioning this to Jay-Z. I quieted my inner child. I didn't gorge on planet Apple Earth and leave him with only a thin core to stand on. This enabled his story to come forward—and what a compelling story it is.

Jay-Z is a great example of why I love doing these interviews: how drastically they can change people's opinions and perspectives. Maybe there's a white guy out there who doesn't have an understanding of what it's like to grow up black in America. Hopefully by the end of this interview, he has gained some enlightenment. That's what these conversations can do. As Jay-Z says, "At the end of the day we're all the same. I really believe that."

So do I.

Howard: People recognized that you were a great rapper when you were a little kid. They didn't even call it rap at that time. They just understood your poems were strong. When you were a little boy, you would run around writing poems in this little chicken scrawl up the sides of pages. You would write these little notes to yourself, little poems, rhymes.

Jay-Z: People understood before I really understood. Like my cousins especially, you know. Me and my cousin didn't speak for three, four years 'cause he thought I was wasting my talent when I was on the street hustling and not pursuing my dreams every day actively. I was pursuing in my mind and I was still writing. But for me, life was happening now. I needed to move now and I couldn't wait for rap.

Howard: In your book, you start describing that you're a hustler. I didn't even know what that meant really. But a hustler means a guy who ends up—I don't want to say owning people, but can figure them out,

and he gets people to do what they want him to do.

Jay-Z: Well, that's part of it. A hustler is anybody that gets up every single day and figures out a way to make good for themselves in this society. It has multiple meanings. You know "all good"? You know how some people say "all good," sometimes it's all bad? Like, "My pops died, but it's all good, though." You know how you use "all good" in so many different ways? *Hustler* is another one of those words. A hustler is anybody who has the drive to make something happen for themselves. Being in the street meant that we had to find a different way because there were no jobs available. The school system was shot. So

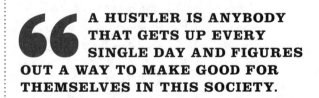

> A HUSTLER IS ANYBODY THAT GETS UP EVERY SINGLE DAY AND FIGURES OUT A WAY TO MAKE GOOD FOR THEMSELVES IN THIS SOCIETY.

we had to hustle to find a different way to make means for ourselves.

Howard: People might not understand you being a crack dealer, but it seems like in your neighborhood this was some kind of hustle.

Jay-Z: Well, anything without proper context . . . without the proper context, you can judge someone totally wrong. So, given the circumstances that we were in—I'm not saying we were good. We made horrible decisions. We were sixteen years old, fourteen years old. We're gonna make bad decisions. 'Cause our decisions were of life and death. So, given those proper contexts, you can see why a person can make such horrible decisions. I'm not saying to forgive us for our decisions. Just understand the circumstances and not dismiss us as being just crack dealers.

Howard: Were you a great crack dealer?

Jay-Z: Incredible.

Howard: You were the best?

Jay-Z: Not the best, but I was really good.

Howard: Here's why I think your life is weird. You're the type of guy who had this talent, but at the same point you were like a crack dealer. And a hustler. And the reason it's so weird is, when you're that artistic and you've got so many things going on inside yourself, you could have landed on a land mine in your life and just gone to jail for a really long time.

Jay-Z: Absolutely. Or got killed.

Howard: Or got killed. You shot your brother in the shoulder, I believe. Point-

blank, pretty much, didn't you? Because he was fucking around with you.

Jay-Z: Yeah.

Howard: You were an angry guy.

Jay-Z: Yeah.

Howard: Do you think your anger comes from your father leaving you?

Jay-Z: Of course.

Howard: It's gotta be, right?

Jay-Z: It was around that time, you know. I was around twelve, and my pop left about eleven. Those years are foggy. Anywhere between nine and eleven, my pop had left. I had a bunch of anger.

Howard: Did you have a close relationship with him up until that point?

Jay-Z: Yeah. The closest.

Howard: When you're growing up in your household, your mother and father seemed like they were getting along okay, or were they fighting all the time?

Jay-Z: They had little hints. Our house was the party house. So we had a huge record collection. Mom and Pop had their names on their own records. You know, they could share kids, but they didn't share records. Which is weird, looking back on it.

Howard: Was your dad a musician?

Jay-Z: No. He sang a little bit in church, but he was just into music really heavy. So to answer your question, our house was filled with joy. People would come over all the time. Our house was always crowded. We had the fun house. So you know, up until that point, I didn't really suspect anything. I thought it would be like that for the rest of my life.

Howard: Your dad was working. Your mom was working. Were people home with you during the day or were you pretty much on your own?

Jay-Z: Pretty much on my own.

Howard: You think you were angry about that?

Jay-Z: I didn't realize it, but looking back on it I probably was a little angry about it.

Howard: You had brothers and sisters. How many did you have?

Jay-Z: I'm the youngest. I have two sisters and one brother.

Howard: And even when you have that and your parents aren't home, there's gotta be some anger brewing. And even though it's the party house and it seems like it's filled with a lot of love, you gotta be saying to yourself, "Where the hell is the love for me? Where is everybody?"

Jay-Z: Right.

Howard: I mean, you understand now as an adult they had to work and do their thing, but it probably seemed to you like you were being ignored.

Jay-Z: Right.

Howard: And so then all of a sudden at twelve, your dad just comes out and says he's leaving?

Jay-Z: Well, he didn't announce it. I found out what really happened was his brother was killed and—

Howard: What were the circumstances of that?

Jay-Z: Life in an urban area.

Howard: You mean he was shot in a violent way?

Jay-Z: He got stabbed, actually.

Howard: Stabbed in a fight?

Jay-Z: Yeah. And it really sent [my father] into a spiral, and he would go out and look for the guys and—

Howard: Were you scared out of your mind?

Jay-Z: I didn't know. My mom would tell him, "You have a family here. You can't go out there and do something to somebody. What about your son?" And he couldn't deal with that sort of pain. It was like almost a split. It was between his brother and his family, which was his blood as well. So it was really traumatizing to him, and he never was the same after that. But I didn't notice growing up.

Howard: You just didn't know what was going on.

Jay-Z: I just knew he left.

Howard: Did your mother spend every day crying? Like, "My husband's gone—"

Jay-Z: Nah, my mother is super strong.

Howard: But she had to be.

Jay-Z: I'm sure she cried behind closed doors.

Howard: Was your dad still close by? Was he living in Brooklyn?

Jay-Z: He was about fifteen minutes away in some other projects.

Howard: I know you reconciled with your dad at some point. Just before his death, right?

Jay-Z: Yeah.

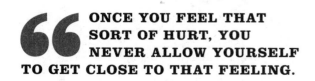

ONCE YOU FEEL THAT SORT OF HURT, YOU NEVER ALLOW YOURSELF TO GET CLOSE TO THAT FEELING.

Howard: When you reconcile with him, this is after you're famous and everything?

Jay-Z: Yeah.

Howard: Is that bittersweet? Because now you're this big, rich, successful guy.

Jay-Z: No, because it was, like, *Black Album* time. So I had dropped about seven albums. It wasn't like he saw me make a little bit of money and ran to the money. It wasn't that. He was still who he was.

Howard: He put it out there that he wanted to reconcile with you?

Jay-Z: My mom actually made it happen.

Howard: That's pretty big of your mother to make that happen.

Jay-Z: Yeah. I told you she's super strong.

Howard: What do you go into that meeting with? Do you go in, like, "I'm going to tell him off"? Or "I'm just going to try and understand"?

Jay-Z: I went in with a lot of anger, thinking, "Yeah, I'm going to tell him off." And it didn't happen like that.

Howard: What happened when you walked into the room? Did he look the way you thought he would look?

Jay-Z: Yeah, very.

Howard: Do you remember him being this big strong guy, and all of a sudden walks in a frail old man?

Jay-Z: No, he's actually a very tall, strong man. He looked healthy. I had no idea he would die the next month.

Howard: What did he die from?

Jay-Z: He had a bad liver from drinking and doing other things to his liver his whole entire life.

Howard: Did you know he was sick?

Jay-Z: Yeah.

Howard: Did he tell you he was sick, or he didn't even want to discuss it with you?

Jay-Z: We didn't discuss it. We had so much to discuss that day.

Howard: So when you finally get in the room with your dad . . . All these years of hurt, anger. I mean, look at how you acted out. You did a lot of things to hurt yourself. You were dealing crack. You could have ended up in jail your whole life. You were in a lot of dangerous situations. You've got all this anger. You sit down with him. You prepare to tell him off. In walks this guy. You don't even know he's going to die a month later, but you stand there. What do you say to this guy?

Jay-Z: Just my entire life of pain and the things I went through, you know, I got to express them to him. And express them in a way that was freeing to me.

Howard: What did he say to all this? Did he apologize?

Jay-Z: No, at first he tried to . . . you know, he was stubborn. He was a very stubborn man. He tried to hold on to it and say, "You knew where I was. I was right up the street." And I was like, "I was a child. I shouldn't have to find my father. I'm a child." And then after those words were said to him, then he dealt with it in a real way. And it allowed me to forgive him.

Howard: The man says to you, "Well, you could have come seen me. I was right up the block." Which is a ridiculous statement.

Jay-Z: Yeah, but it was a defense mechanism. It was his own stubbornness kicking in. He was fighting it. He didn't want to let the truth get all the way in because he knew it was painful.

Howard: Did you end up hugging him?

Jay-Z: Yeah.

Howard: Did you see him again after that? Or was that it?

Jay-Z: He passed a month later.

Howard: Did your father ever get the guy who killed his brother?

Jay-Z: No.

Howard: Never caught him?

Jay-Z: No. I wouldn't tell you that in this program. The honest truth is no.

Howard: You know, isn't it weird how you always still look for your father? It's like a hole in your heart, right? You can't even go on to be a good married man if you didn't fix the hole in your heart about your father, am I correct?

Jay-Z: Absolutely.

Howard: You couldn't stay in a marriage if you're sitting there thinking all the time, "My father left me. My wife is going to leave me."

Jay-Z: You don't even get to that point. Because you don't allow yourself. 'Cause once that's happened to you . . . Your father,

growing up he's like Superman to you. He's everything. So once you feel that sort of hurt, you never allow yourself to get close to that feeling. You don't even want to feel that good because you know the flip side of that. So you don't let anyone get that close so they won't hurt you.

Howard: Have you ever been to therapy?

Jay-Z: No.

Howard: You seem to be pretty self-realized. Reading your book, you seem to have a good understanding of the hurt and the pain and everything. You're able to feel it. But don't you think that's something you need to talk to someone about?

Jay-Z: I talked. I've spoken to the world about it.

Howard: But wait a second. Before you become a father yourself, before you even got married, didn't you want to sit down with someone and say, "Shit, how much of this is going to affect my relationships with everyone? How am I going to stay focused on one woman? How do I get over the fear that someone is going to leave me?"

Jay-Z: I've been dealing with that my entire life. And I've been dealing with that through my music. So, you know, I deal with that daily.

Howard: That's enough?

Jay-Z: Yeah. You know, I got a million therapists.

Howard: You think that's really therapy?

Jay-Z: Yes, of course. Of course. Listen to the albums. Read those songs. Read the level of self-realization and all the things

> ## I DON'T LET MY SUCCESS SEPARATE ME FROM WHO I AM.

that I've been through. All that therapy is in that music.

Howard: I find it very hard to self-analyze. There are a lot of things in my life I don't want to look at. I need somebody to sit there and push me. That's why I'm in analysis.

Jay-Z: You can make albums or go sit with a therapist.

Howard: But look at what I do for a living. I sit here every day, and I'm honest. I'm honest with my audience. I talk about it, but I make a joke about a lot of things that were serious.

Jay-Z: That's a form of therapy.

Howard: I was watching *The Real Housewives of Beverly Hills*, these five white ladies all pulled back with the plastic surgery, and they're going to the Jay-Z concert. I don't even think they knew what the fuck the Jay-Z concert was.

Jay-Z: I think at the end of the day we're all the same. I really believe that. We all have the same anxieties, fears, aspirations. My first album, I knew there was a generation of kids who went through the same thing that I went through that the record companies didn't even understand.

Howard: In other words, it goes beyond race. It's alienation, really, what you're talking about. Being lost. And lots of kids relate to being lost.

Jay-Z: Right, but on my first album, I was really just trying to talk to my friends. I was telling our stories. And when they heard them back, it was like, "Someone relates to my pain." My first album, it had emotions on it. "Gotta learn to live with regrets." That was the last song on that album. "My mama used to hold me, told me I was the best / Anything in this world I want I could possess." Those sort of things happened for all my friends. Their mothers had to hold them and tell them this thing and give them this self-esteem. So when these guys were hearing these words back . . . I would go to shows and big guys would have tears in their eyes talking to me, telling me, "Man, I feel like you looking in my window."

Howard: When you go back to the projects, do you run into guys that you knew back then who are even down on their luck now? Do you get self-conscious about your wealth and about your success?

Jay-Z: Sort of. Survivor's guilt with the world, with where I come from. That's why for me, I try to stay attached to the culture.

Howard: Can you, though? How do you stay attached to the culture? Seriously. Where do you go? You can't go to—I saw you at a hotel one time. I didn't bother you. I was there with my wife. We were staying at the same hotel. You and Beyoncé had, like, twenty security guards around you.

Jay-Z: Two.

Howard: But they look the size of twelve guys.

Jay-Z: I'm just really sensitive to that because I don't want people to think that we're traveling with a posse.

Howard: Sorry. But you know what I'm saying. I don't see how a guy as famous as you—

Jay-Z: I don't let my success separate me from who I am. You don't have to be sitting on a bench in Marcy Projects to represent the culture. Everywhere I am— right here, right now. Me telling our story is representing the culture. I'm pushing our culture forward. I'm bringing the light on a subject *again* that people wouldn't normally talk about. 'Cause it's going on right now.

Howard: But with the passage of years, don't you think you lose touch? You've got to. It's gonna happen. You're living a fairy-tale life.

Jay-Z: Of course. I don't sit on the bench in Marcy Projects. I've lost touch in *that* way. But who I am as a person, I'm still telling these stories as if they happened yesterday. I'm still in touch with those emotions and feelings of who I am—as if they were yesterday.

DRUGS & SOBRIETY

I'm not a drug guy. I tried them early in my life, but I realized pretty quickly they weren't for me. I think they mess up your entire outlook. I think they destroy your work ethic. I think a million different negative thoughts about drugs, but they sure are fascinating to talk about.

Sometimes the conversations can be funny, like Snoop Dogg and Seth Rogen talking about their love of weed. Sometimes it can get dark, like hearing about Anthony Kiedis and Drew Barrymore being exposed to drugs when they were just kids. There are Don Henley and James Taylor who got clean and stayed that way, and then there is Scott Weiland who, no matter how hard he tried, just couldn't.

That's another reason I like talking about drugs: because I know it's a subject all my listeners have some experience with, if not themselves then with family members or friends. It's something they can relate to. Yet there are few shows or other media outlets that actually talk about drugs in a way that doesn't vilify them or look down on people who use them.

There's such a stigma about drug users and addiction in this country. It's a shame. Especially the way it's criminalized. I may have a million negative thoughts about drugs, but I've always maintained that they should be legal. All of them. Locking someone up over a drug is absolutely absurd.

I think you'd see a lot less addiction if drugs were legalized. You'd see less demand. Because drugs are illegal, there is a mystique and a sexiness about them. Part of what draws people to drugs is that they're taboo. When you remove taboos, those things suddenly lose a lot of their appeal. It's just like when I came to Sirius. Their attitude was, "Oh, you want to talk about sex? Go ahead! Talk about anything!" I thought, "Wait a second. Don't do that. Tell me, 'No.'"

By talking about drugs in an honest way, I feel like I'm doing my part to take away that stigma. Maybe that means one of my listeners can have a similarly honest conversation about drugs with someone in their own life. Don't get me wrong. My show isn't a public service. I talk about drugs because the stories are endlessly entertaining. They make for great radio. If they also provide some real help to listeners struggling with addiction, so much the better.

Ultimately, I enjoy talking about drugs because I have a true fascination for all types of out-of-control behavior. I'm so restrained and well-behaved in my personal life. It's a bit like talking to people who jump out of airplanes. Don't they know the parachute might not open?

SNOOP DOGG

Howard: Snoop, can any man smoke weed with you, or is it a closed club?

Snoop Dogg: I feel like marijuana is a universal language for all people. That's one thing about the marijuana: when we do smoke, we don't go out and kill nobody. We don't get crazy. Everybody gets calm and it's a beautiful situation. I mean, it's beautiful. It's like everybody gets a chance to know each other. It's like a lot of people wouldn't even speak, but when they on that they real calm and cool and collected. They just need to legalize it. Alcohol is still one of the number-one killers in the world. Drunk driving and, "I killed him 'cause I was drunk. I raped her 'cause

I was drunk." You don't never hear nobody saying, "I killed them 'cause I was high on weed."

Howard: How much weed are you smoking a day now? Like, you smoke six, seven times a day?

Snoop Dogg: What?

Howard: More?

Snoop Dogg: What'd you say? Six, seven times a day? Six, seven times a *session*.

Howard: I'll tell you something. I went to LA, and I smoked weed. And it almost killed me. Why is it so much stronger now? Seriously, don't you get paranoid at all when you smoke this stuff?

Snoop Dogg: I get paranoid that they gonna stop making it.

Howard: I couldn't even talk. I kept thinking people

were out to get me and stuff.

Snoop Dogg: Hey, Howard, every time you see me, I'm on it.

Howard: Really?

Snoop Dogg: And we have beautiful conversations.

Howard: Yeah, and you're always in control.

Snoop Dogg: Exactly.

Howard: You gotta be the world's greatest weed smoker.

Snoop Dogg: Something like that. You know, I try.

CHRIS CORNELL

Howard: An OxyContin addict—you innovated that. You started that. A lot of people don't credit you with that.

Chris: Before they were writing about it, before anyone knew about it, yeah,

I was in trouble with that. I was doubling and tripling up on depressants. I was in rehab for a month and I actually re-upped for another month voluntarily. Which most people, you know, they can't wait to get out.

Howard: It's smart to stay in.

Chris: I didn't have anywhere to go, really. I couldn't go back around anyone that I knew. Everyone I knew had problems of one substance or another. All the relationships were awful. Honestly, I didn't know up from down for a while.

Howard: Was OxyContin great in terms of it just numbed everything out for you? They call it "hillbilly heroin."

Chris: Yeah, it's—you don't know what's going on. You don't feel anything. Kicking it is so hard because all of a sudden your whole body comes to life, and you'll have had all of these physical problems you didn't realize you had because you don't feel a damn thing. And so your knees will hurt. Your joints ache. Your brain hurts. It's very depressing. It's very hard to stay off. Getting off isn't as hard as staying off.

·····

QUENTIN TARANTINO

Howard: For *Inglourious Basterds*, you got Brad Pitt. To convince the guy—and I don't know if this is true—you go to the hospital right after his twins are born to Angelina Jolie?

Quentin: She was in the hospital when I went to visit, yeah.

Howard: She's in the hospital. Where do you go to visit him?

Quentin: I went to the house in France.

Howard: In France? Is that where she gave birth, in France?

Quentin: Uh-huh.

Howard: So you write this script, and the whole time you're writing it you're thinking of Brad Pitt for this role.

Quentin: Yeah, he likes the script and wants to discuss it. He lives on a vineyard so we're just like one bottle of rosé after another. We're down into bottle three of the rosé. I was there till like three in the morning. Actually, one of the things he did that was really cool—he had this big brick of hash, and he was gonna give me some for the night. So he takes this brick of hash and he whips out a knife and cuts me off this big sliver.

Howard: Was it the best hash you ever had?

Quentin: It was pretty good. But the thing about it that was really funny is I go, "Do you have a pipe to go with this?" And he just handed me a Coke can. He just reached into the refrigerator and gave me a Coke. And I was like, "Oh, I know how to do that. I know how to do the Coke can thing." I thought that was one of the coolest things. I thought that should be in a movie or something.

Howard: I've found with hash, you can't possibly have an intelligent conversation when you're smoking it.

Quentin: I disagree about that. Hash is different than pot. Because I don't get paranoid with hash.

Howard: Really? I find it

worse. If I'm sitting there with Brad Pitt, I know I gotta get him for my movie. Now we're smoking hash. We've been drinking wine all day. I'd be so fucking paranoid I'd have to run out of the room. Why do you think you don't get paranoid on hash?

Robin: It's a chemical reaction you have, Howard. He doesn't have that.

Quentin: But I'm not the only one in this. A lot of people will say pot gets them paranoid and hash just kind of chills them out. They're stoned but they're not afraid to leave the room.

Howard: You should've said to him, "Brad, that's very unprofessional of you to take out hash."

Robin: "I don't want to work with you now."

Quentin: Brad Pitt don't smoke shit hash. It's like [the saying], "Irish don't drink shit Guinness." Brad Pitt don't smoke shit hash.

MARILYN MANSON

Marilyn: I left rehab because I got bored talking about God and listening to people who could not succeed at a successful life of drinking and drugs and alcohol like a normal person does. When you're happy, drink and do drugs; when you're unhappy, don't.

Howard: You didn't like rehab because they give you the whole twelve-step and you've got to believe in a higher power?

Marilyn: No, I said quite simply—they would sit down in a circle—I said, "I know you're going to say I'm in denial. I know you're going to say this. I just want to ask a simple question: Does anybody know any artists that were great after they quit doing drugs versus when they were? I know you guys say they're all dead, but I'm just asking a question because I want to know if it's drugs or if it's depression that I am suffering from." They finally asked me to leave because—

Howard: You're undermining everyone's treatment.

Robin: Yeah, you're not supposed to sit there and ask questions.

Marilyn: You're not supposed to ask questions. You're supposed to listen. It seemed like Christian school again.

ALEX TREBEK

Alex: I went to this party at a home in Malibu, and I didn't know the people hosting the party, and they had hash brownies. And I love chocolate.

Howard: Right.

Alex: I ate about four or five hash brownies. The party was on a Friday night. I didn't leave their home until Monday morning.

Howard: Is that really true? No exaggeration?

Alex: Not an exaggeration. They put me to bed Friday night, almost comatose, and I did not wake up Saturday, started to wake up Sunday, and then I went home.

Howard: That is so unfair. I remember reading about parties where they'd spike the punch with acid and they wouldn't tell anybody. I mean, that's an awful thing to do to somebody.

Alex: To me, drugs are highly overrated.

ANTHONY KIEDIS

Howard: You left your mother and said, "I'm going to live with my dad." 'Cause your dad, in your mind, was way cool.

Anthony: And so was California.

Robin: Where was your mom?

Anthony: She was in Michigan. And I'd been going out to California for years to visit my dad, and I was like, "This is great."

Howard: And no restrictions at your dad's. You could do dope with him. You could hang with him. He'd bring you chicks. In fact, didn't you bang your father's girlfriend? That was the first sexual experience you had?

Anthony: It was. Girlfriend sort of. It was a girl he was seeing.

Howard: Right. And you said, "Dad, I would like to have sex with her."

Anthony: I asked him.

Howard: And he said, "Sure, son."

Anthony: He said, "I don't know. I'll have to talk to her."

Howard: He didn't think that was weird.

Anthony: He thought it was being generous. And sharing.

Howard: What do you think of that now?

Anthony: I wouldn't do that with my kid. It's kind of twisted.

Robin: You know that's wrong.

Anthony: I know that's wrong. But he didn't. And I understand that he didn't, and he thought he was being kind.

Howard: So you grew up with no boundaries whatsoever.

Robin: What were the drugs you were doing together?

Anthony: You want a laundry list?

Robin: Yeah, at what age and when are you doing drugs with your dad?

Anthony: Started smoking pot at eleven. Sniffing some cocaine by about twelve, thirteen. Taking Tuinals. Drinking champagne. Quaaludes.

Howard: It says in your book your dad would blow pot smoke in your face at age four to get you high.

Anthony: Yeah.

Howard: Is he still alive, your dad?

Anthony: Yeah. He's good.

Robin: I told you he runs the fan club.

Howard: You let him run the fan club?

Anthony: Yeah.

Howard: Why not? He got you laid and let you smoke weed with him. Damn right. He can run my fan club. He's a wild guy.

Anthony: Yeah, he's a good man.

Howard: But I think as a result of him never saying no to you, you must've grown up in a world where *no* was not an issue. And therefore there were no boundaries.

Anthony: I had to find my own *no*.

Howard: And that's hard when you're a drug addict.

Anthony: It took me a long time.

SLASH

Howard: Does rehab not work?

Slash: Just depends, you know? It's like anything else:

it depends on how committed you are when you go in.

Howard: Rehab worked for you, right?

Slash: Yeah, it worked for me. But I refused to go to rehab until I finally decided I wanted to get clean, and I needed a place to go where nobody was going to bug me so I could just get my shit together.

Howard: You stopped smoking cigarettes too, right?

Slash: Yeah.

Howard: What's more difficult to get off, heroin or cigarettes?

Slash: Cigarettes is an ongoing thing that never goes away. I have nicotine supplements.

Howard: When was the last time you physically smoked a cigarette?

Slash: It's been more than three years.

Howard: Wow, good for you.

Slash: I still have my moments, certain things trigger it.

Howard: That's a tough one to break. It is harder than heroin, right?

Slash: It's not physically as stressful as heroin is, or alcohol—which is the worst one, as far as I'm concerned.

Howard: Because cutting off alcohol, you get the DTs. Was that the tough part?

Slash: Yeah, fuck.

Howard: And you'd just rather take a drink than experience that?

Slash: That's why I used to drink 24/7. Because I learned way early on if you get up in the morning with a hangover, you can just drink it away. I did that for [*laughs*] twenty-five years.

....

LANCE ARMSTRONG

Howard: Do you think you really needed it? Do you think that you wouldn't have won as much as you had if you hadn't taken enhancements? Or maybe it was just psychological? Like, maybe you still would have even without it.

Lance: We don't need to get into the pharmacology, but EPO was so powerful.

Howard: You will be charged up.

Lance: It's a ten percenter,

Howard. That's what was crazy. We were all like, "Wow." We had a choice. You're right. Not everybody made the choices we made. Almost everybody did. But not everybody. I admire those people that said, "I'm not going to do that. I'm going to go home, or I'm going to be out of the sport."

Howard: In other words, if they could have cleaned up the sport enough where everyone was on an even playing field and you knew for a fact that no one was taking EPO, I'm sure you would have complied. The idea being that, if everyone's taking it, why am I not taking it?

Lance: Right, but there was no test. Who knows what would have happened? I like to think that the results would have been the same. There are other people that would have said, "No, it would have been different." I mean, again, the sport is not that simple. It's a complicated sport. There's a lot of work. A lot of tactics.

Howard: The amazing thing is, after testicular cancer, if you hadn't gone back into racing, you never would have been caught, because you never would have done another Tour de France. The guy who came forward because he was pressured into it, you would never have known him if you just retired after cancer. None of this would have happened.

Lance: I'll raise you one, because you're right. Then I had a career after cancer from '98 until 2005. And then I came back. Had I just stopped in 2005, it would have been over.

Howard: That's it?

Lance: Yeah. The comeback from '08, '09, and '10, and part of '11 was that bridge to the past. That's what made the story relevant. That's what made the authorities— that gave them the possibility. It was the bridge. Legally, it was the bridge. Publicly, it was the bridge.

Howard: Do you ever regret becoming a great cyclist? Do you ever regret it for a minute?

Lance: No. I regret a lot of other things, but I don't regret that. All in all, I'm still ahead.

BRADLEY COOPER

Howard: I didn't know this about you: you stopped doing all drugs, all drinking in your life, and you did it all on your own. You didn't need any help with that.

Bradley: No, I had friends, I had people helping me.

Howard: You had people help you.

Bradley: Yes, of course.

Howard: Do you miss it at all? Do you think you'd like having a glass of wine?

Bradley: No, I would be too scared.

Robin: Did you have a real problem?

Bradley: Yeah. Oh yeah.

Howard: What was the epiphany you had when you stopped doing all that stuff?

Bradley: I think it was, more than anything, you have one life and this is the road you're on, and you know what? You're not going to fulfill your potential.

....

DREW BARRYMORE

Howard: At fourteen you knew to get emancipated from your mother.

Drew: Yes, we hand-shook, and it was a very respectful court date.

Howard: Didn't you go to Crosby's house?

Drew: I had to live with David Crosby for two months.

Howard: What is it like living with David Crosby?

Drew: Pretty wild. I'd go on tour with them, and I would freak out over Neil Young.

Howard: Were you in love with Neil Young?

Drew: I was just like, "Okay, that's the coolest human being ever." I'm such a Valley girl, and he was probably like, "Oh, God."

Howard: I can't imagine what it's like at fourteen to be hanging out with Crosby, Stills, Nash, and Young, on tour with those guys who are fantastic artists, and then also working in a coffee shop. You probably, at that point, should have a nice little stash of money. But your mom was buying BMWs. She bought a new house. You were the wage earner. She quit to manage you full-time.

Drew: I was like, "Oh, this is not going to go well."

Howard: Did Crosby ever say to you, "Listen, Drew, it's bedtime. Time to go to sleep."

Drew: Yeah.

Howard: He did? He had rules?

Drew: I felt bad for them. They had to take in this kid. They were parents themselves. I had just come out of being in an institution for a year and a half, and it was a very severe lockdown. No Hollywood rehab, thirty-day Malibu beachside bullshit. This was school of hard knocks in the most severe way.

Howard: It's almost like joining the military for a thirteen- or fourteen-year-old.

Drew: It was boot camp. You would get the boot all the time. I hated it at first. I had nothing but freedom up until that point. Dancing on tables at Helena's and Studio 54 and Limelight and every club on the planet, and partying it up, doing whatever I wanted whenever I wanted. All of a sudden it was, "You have

no freedom. You will figure out your life. You have the best insurance policy ever. You're staying here until we tell you you've changed." It was so upsetting at first, but over the course of that year and a half, I left there the [*voice breaking*] most humble person you could ever imagine.

Howard: They saved your life, didn't they?

Drew: They saved my life.

······································

DON HENLEY

Howard: Did you start to believe that drugs were the secret to writing good songs? 'Cause that can start to fool you too. You think, "Whatever I'm doing, I've got to keep doing. 'Cause that opens up my creativity." Did you get tricked by that kind of thing?

Don: I think we bought into that for a while. We called it "instant courage." Writing songs is hard. You have to talk about your innermost feelings, things that are very personal, and we used alcohol and drugs, as did a lot of bands at the time, to

get the stuff out. And then after a while it backfires. It turns on you. It freezes you up.

Howard: Joe Walsh, who I know very well, credits you guys for getting him sober. You gave him the hard line. You said, "Joe, we're going back on tour, and if you want to be in the Eagles, you have to stop doing drugs." And you knew what you were talking about, how difficult it was. You guys saved his life, didn't you?

Don: Well, I don't know—

Howard: You did. He's a different man now. What got *you* off drugs? At one point, did you say to yourself, "I'm going to get the fuck off all this nonsense"?

Don: I did it myself. I always knew that I would stop. Finally, one day I said, "That's enough. I'm tired of feeling bad." I knew it was affecting me psychologically, beginning to stifle my creativity, and I knew I was going to get married and have kids.

Howard: How old were you at that point?

Don: I was, oh gosh, it was

in the mid- to late eighties.
So, forty.

Howard: I think by forty
you gotta figure that stuff
out. Or else you end up
dead.

Don: You do. And I
didn't—I'm not bragging,
but I didn't go to a
program. I just said
enough's enough.

CHARLIZE THERON

Charlize: I can't smoke weed
anymore.

Howard: Me neither. Too
paranoid?

Charlize: Not paranoid. I
just become so uninteresting.
I don't want to talk. I literally
just switch off. I have nothing
to say.

Howard: You live in
Hollywood. Do you have a
medical marijuana card?

Charlize: I do not, no. But
everybody around me does.

Howard: Everyone has
edibles. They're walking
around with all kinds of
weed.

Charlize: Yeah. In my
twenties, I was a wake-and-
baker. And then one day I

just couldn't do it anymore.
One day I just sat on the
couch and couldn't move.

Howard: You try anything
heavier? Did you ever do
coke or acid?

Charlize: I definitely
experimented, yeah.

Howard: X?

Charlize: Yeah.

Howard: Did it make you
crazy?

Charlize: No, I had a
fucking great time on it.

Howard: You liked it?

Charlize: Yeah.

Howard: Did you get
touchy-feely with people?

Charlize: Yeah.

Howard: Oh, Jesus. Where
the hell was I?

Charlize: [*laughs*] I didn't do
a lot of it. But definitely, in
my twenties, I would always
feel like maybe if I had kids
I would be missing out on
this life. And then I hit my
thirties and I was so fucking
done with it. I had the best
twenties ever because I did
everything I wanted to do.
And so there's not a part of
me now that goes, "God, I
so wish I . . ." I was done. I'm
done.

Howard: So when you have

kids now—you have two
kids—you're not sitting
there pining away for the
old life?

Charlize: I am asleep by
eight forty-five, and I fucking
love it.

JOHN STAMOS

Howard: Do you miss
getting high?

John: No, not at all.

Howard: You mean, if I go
out with you, I can't drink
now?

John: You can drink. I can
watch you.

Howard: You will not drink?

John: No.

Howard: Wow.

Robin: So that time you
were [visibly drunk] on that
Australian talk show—

John: Hammered!

Howard: Oh, were you?

John: Yeah.

Howard: Is that part of
rehab? You have to come
clean about—

John: Yeah, you do kind of
have to, the first step. You
speak to fifteen or sixteen of
these strangers, kind of lay
out your whole life.

Howard: But, John, don't you

get nervous when you do this rehab with a bunch of not-famous people, and you have to come clean about your life? Someone could go to the press and reveal your secrets. 'Cause people are dicks.

John: I trusted everybody. It was an anonymous-type situation. I really don't have anything to hide anymore.

Howard: That's good.

John: My father passed away, I got divorced, and it sort of sent me down the wrong path.

Howard: And then your mom died, which really sent you down the path. She wasn't that old either, right?

John: She was seventy-five.

Howard: Which isn't that old nowadays.

John: It was very hard.

Howard: I remember when you were working on [the Broadway play] *The Best Man*, you said you weren't drinking at all, and I believed you. And you could lay off the sauce.

John: I could, yeah.

Howard: So, what happened? You would go back to it when you stopped working?

John: The times I went back, I'd just start to deteriorate. I'd lost my morals, my discipline. I just lost myself. More and more, I was dipping into that dark place. It just happened more and more.

Howard: I've seen you in that dark place.

John: Right. Well, it stunted my growth emotionally. Maybe I *would* be married right now with kids.

Howard: No, you wouldn't.

John: And with my career . . . I've got a good career, but—

Howard: I know what you mean. You do get very dark sometimes.

John: Thank you, Howard.

Howard: No, I mean that. You get very introverted.

John: Well, those days are gone. I feel great. I feel very even now.

Howard: Were you in denial at first?

John: No. I walked through those doors and said, "Can you help me? I need someone to help me."

Robin: Did you have an intervention, or decide this on your own?

John: I had a horrific DUI I'm so embarrassed by.

Howard: Yeah, you wrote me and said you were upset about it.

John: Well, I could've hurt somebody.

Howard: You could have.

John: It was really stupid and ignorant of me. I hated myself, and said, "I have to stop this." And I walked through those doors, and said, "I'm going to apply myself 100 percent to it." Which I haven't in the past. I could get by with 30 or 40 percent, and do well. But that's bullshit. I could do better, and be present all the time.

Howard: How hard is it to give up all substances? How far can you go with it? Can you be around people who are partying?

John: One hundred percent. Because I stopped for a while, and it was fine. You know, the beauty of doing a lot of therapy like I did, which I know you're a proponent of, is that you have to look at *why* you're doing it.

Howard: Right. 'Cause you can't get better otherwise.

John: Right. And I was upset about losing my mom. 'Cause we kind of became codependent. For many years, it was my purpose to be there for her. Be a good son.

Howard: You lost your purpose.

....

SETH ROGEN

Howard: Have you ever analyzed why you smoke so much weed? Do you ever wonder? Because most people don't get as baked as you do.

Seth: No.

Howard: I mean, you really need to be high a lot. Like, you're probably high right now.

Seth: A little bit.

Robin: Do you wake and bake?

Seth: I do. I woke and boke.

Howard: I find it very refreshing that you're so open about it. Because the biggest taboo in Hollywood: drugs. They'll tolerate any kind of behavior. But drugs is kind of a touchy subject.

Seth: A lot of people ruin their lives with them, I think is part of the reason. [*laughs*]

Robin: Yeah, how *did* drugs get this bad rap?

Seth: Exactly. I don't know what it is!

Howard: They always say marijuana is the gateway drug to everything else.

Seth: I think that's bullshit. It's just the easiest drug to buy. And if you're gonna do heroin—who starts with heroin? No one starts with fucking heroin. You can't even *meet* a heroin dealer until you've known a bunch of weed dealers for a while. You gotta work your way up. So, yeah, I think it's bullshit. Heroin guys were gonna do heroin anyway. They just had to start somewhere.

....

SCOTT WEILAND

Howard: Have you ever calculated how much money you've spent on drugs?

Scott: It's not the drugs that costs the money. It's the rehabs.

Howard: What do they charge for rehab? A good rehab?

Scott: At the time when the economy was really rollin', it got up to $90,000 a month.

Howard: Jesus Christ. And you would go away for five months.

Scott: That was the time that I kicked heroin, yeah.

Howard: You say in your new book that you experimented with heroin because you thought it was opening up the creative process.

Scott: Well, you know, I looked at all the great writers from the Beat generation. The jazz players.

Howard: They all did it.

Scott: Yeah, they all did it. And it was starting to make its resurgence.

Howard: It's become romanticized with artists.

Scott: It was at the time. It all kind of ended when Kurt [Cobain] died.

Howard: Well, you are clean. Except you drink.

Scott: Yeah, it goes back and forth. It goes back and forth.

Howard: Between drinking and not drinking?

Scott: Yeah.

Howard: But you're not doing heroin anymore.

Scott: Nope.

Howard: You're not doing cocaine.

Scott: Nope.

Howard: You're not smoking weed.

Scott: Nope.

Howard: But this is what kills me about you. Why drink? Why not live the sober lifestyle once and for all?

Scott: Well, that's really what I wanna do.

Howard: You can't do it, though. You're not strong enough.

Scott: No, I am strong enough. I was sober for four years. Like, completely sober for four years.

Howard: Were you in hell?

Scott: No, it was the happiest time of my life.

Howard: Wouldn't giving up drinking make your voice stronger?

Scott: Yeah, I'm sure it would.

Howard: But it's your only joy.

Scott: No. It's not a joy. It's something that I really want to give up.

Robin: Do you smoke?

Scott: I've always smoked, yeah.

Howard: You gotta give that up. 'Cause your voice—that voice is your meal ticket.

Scott: David Bowie, Mick Jagger, they smoked.

Howard: So what. Why do you always compare? Why do you always look at everyone else? We're talking about you.

Scott: Because I look at the people that are the legends and set my parameters based on that.

Howard: Right. But I want to see you live.

JAMIE FOXX

Jamie: I'm having such a good time, and I'm not knowing I'm fucking up. Listen, you know me, I was going hard. I'm not playing, and I'm going way hard.

Howard: What were you doing? Weed? Drinking? Coke?

Jamie: I mean, I'm drinking, I'm doing every fucking thing you can possibly imagine. That's when ecstasy—

Howard: Ecstasy? That will fuck you up.

Jamie: I was fucked-up when we went to the Golden Globes. I don't tell a lot of people this story. Went to the Golden Globes, we got active before the Golden Globes, and we kept saying, "Three." I said, "Man, I'm nominated in three motherfucking categories [for *Ray*]. Crazy, huh?" We get out and we walk the red carpet and we're so gone, we're going, "Three, three, three."

Howard: You're high as a kite.

Jamie: All that's missing is a string.

Howard: Oh my God.

Jamie: And then I get a call, and on the other end of the phone it says, "Hi, Jamie Foxx." I say, "Who's this?" "This is Oprah."

Howard: Uh-oh.

Jamie: "You're blowing it, Jamie Foxx. You're blowing it." I said, "What do you mean?" She said, "All of this gallivantin' and all this kind of shit, that's not what you want to do." She said, "I want to take you somewhere that'll make you understand the significance of what you're doing." We go to Quincy Jones's house. He says, "Hey, we just don't want you to blow it, baby." So we go in the house and there's all these old actors, black actors from the sixties and the seventies, who look like they just . . . they just want to say, "Good luck." They want to say, "Don't blow it."

Howard: Wow. It's almost like an intervention.

Jamie: Yeah. All these actors. They are saying, "Get it together." And then Oprah says, "Okay, you want to meet who you're supposed to meet here?" I said, "Yeah." "He's right there." And it was Sidney Poitier.

Howard: I was going to say it: "I bet you they brought out Sidney Poitier."

Jamie: Standing in a tuxedo.

Howard: The classiest guy ever.

Jamie: Yeah, and he says, "I want to give you one thing. I want to give you responsibility. When I saw your performance, it made me grow two inches." So I break down. Everybody sits me down. It was actually Sidney Poitier's birthday. They made me understand the significance of it.

Howard: The history of it.

Jamie: They said, "Sidney

did it, and it was a character that we could all embrace. Ray Charles is also a character that we can embrace."

Howard: This is bigger than you.

Jamie: Yeah, it's way bigger.

....

JAMES TAYLOR

James: Fortunately, the past thirty years I've been clean and sober.

Howard: Do you go to meetings and stuff?

James: I still do, yeah. It's sort of an ongoing treatment, not a cure.

Howard: Do you go to a party sometimes and feel like, "Oh, man, I wish I could have a drink"? Do you still have the urge?

James: You know what? I miss beer, but I don't crave a drink.

Howard: Right.

James: And it took me such a long time to get my nervous system back after methadone. I think that as dangerous as it was for me to be an opiate addict, and the five times that I should've OD'd have given me real caution and respect for it.

But I do think that, in a way, I wasn't seeking—I wasn't partying, I wasn't seeking oblivion, I was basically self-medicating.

Howard: You were trying to just somehow feel normal, right?

James: That's right.

Howard: Were you worried about your children, when they were born, that they would somehow inherit the addiction thing?

James: I do worry about 'em, and I've got four kids and thankfully they have minimal memory of me as an active addict.

Howard: Do you tell them about it, or do you just not?

James: I tell them that it's a family disease, and the chances are good that if they mess around with it, they won't be able to—

Howard: Control it.

James: Yeah. So easy to get into that, yeah.

Howard: We think because someone is so talented, and they have music in them, that would satisfy them, and they wouldn't want to go near a drug or drink?

James: Well, you know,

it did satisfy me, and it has been the main thing—

Howard: The main focus of your life.

James: The main positive thing, yeah. It's been a life in music, and I do think that it, in a very real way, saved my life as something positive that kept me going.

....

WHOOPI GOLDBERG

Howard: How do you become a drug addict? 'Cause it seems you were in a tremendously sad place to become a heroin addict.

Whoopi: For me, you know, it was the times. It seemed like a good idea at the time. Everybody looked really cool.

Howard: How bad was your habit?

Whoopi: Kinda bad.

Howard: And you didn't have the money. You weren't a rich person.

Whoopi: No, I wasn't rich. But I could make money happen. It was kind of a skill.

Howard: How did you make money happen? You took a lot of shit jobs?

Whoopi: A lot of shit jobs.

Howard: What was the shittiest job you had at that time?

Whoopi: Probably cleaning toilets.

....

MARK WAHLBERG

Howard: You stopped smoking weed, right?

Mark: Absolutely.

Howard: And you stopped because of your kids. It's because your daughter said to you she smelled weed somewhere—

Mark: No, no. She smelled a skunk. We were driving and she smelled a skunk, right? And she said, "Mommy, what's that smell?" [My wife] said, "It's a skunk." And my daughter said, "Oh, Daddy smells like that sometimes."

Howard: And that registered for you.

Mark: Absolutely.

Howard: And you stopped smoking weed altogether.

Mark: Completely.

Howard: And you like weed.

Mark: I *liked* it.

ROGER WATERS

Howard: You drink?

Roger: Yeah, of course.

Howard: [*laughs*] Of course. You don't do drugs though?

Roger: No.

Howard: Did you ever? Did you go through a period where you were just wasted?

Roger: Yes. It was short, like only four or five years.

Howard: But it must've been intense.

Roger: I'll tell you what it was. From the age of fourteen I was addicted to nicotine.

Howard: Right.

Roger: And I became a nicotine addict. As a consequence of that, I spent a lot of years in the early seventies completely out of my brain on hashish. Because you—those of you who know—can mix hashish with tobacco.

Howard: But that's still pretty intense—hash.

Roger: It flips you out. It's bad for you. Makes it hard to concentrate on anything.

Howard: Did you do acid?

Roger: How I wrote *Dark Side of the Moon*, I'll never know.

Howard: [*laughs*]

Roger: Very rarely. Twice.

Howard: Did it open you up creatively?

Roger: It maybe—I dunno.

Howard: So when you write *Dark Side*, it doesn't really influence you, right?

Roger: No.

....

JIM CARREY

Howard: Were you doing a ton of drugs in the seventies when you were coming up?

Jim: I experimented. Pot was kind of a compulsive thing for me. I tended to go away, just me and my apple bong.

Howard: Would you go onstage high?

Jim: I only went up maybe twice after smoking a joint. And I slaughtered. I mean, I slaughtered the house. I annihilated everybody. At one point [Sam] Kinison was at the back of the room, and just for fun he was heckling me. And I was killing him. I was killing everybody. And I walked off stage and they said, "Wow. What the hell was that?" And I said, "I'm high."

Howard: Isn't that dangerous in a way?

Jim: I actually called my dad after that. Because I had that kind of confusing moment of, "Should I or shouldn't I?" And I called my dad who was a jazz musician. I said, "Dad, you must've dealt with other musicians who were getting high to play." And he said, "I did, but I always figured if I made it that way I wouldn't be able to own it."

Howard: So you resisted the temptation to get high on-stage more.

Jim: Yeah.

....

MILEY CYRUS

Howard: I know a lot of lead singers, and it's a horrible life in a sense. When their band is out having fun, they're locked in a room with vaporizers having their day of silence and all that stuff because you worry about your voice.

Miley: Yeah, I've got the vaporizers.

Howard: You don't smoke cigarettes or anything like that. You protect your voice that way.

Miley: No, I don't smoke cigs. I used to but I don't smoke cigarettes. I miss weed, but I don't smoke weed. It's the longest I've gone without smoking weed. I haven't smoked weed in, like, eight months.

Howard: Did you do that 'cause of your voice?

Miley: I did that because this fucking project, this record [*Younger Now*] means more to me than—I say this about all of 'em, because they all mean something at the time—but this record means so much to me, and I wanted to be able to just tell people what I feel about the record in a non-stoned way. In a real way.

Howard: You wanted to be present.

Miley: I wanted to be present.

Howard: You won't do edibles or anything like that?

Miley: Not now. My mom's back there giggling like a motherfucker 'cause she's on some. All the ones I didn't take, she does.

Howard: I'm bad with weed. You don't get paranoid?

Miley: I think it set some paranoia into me. Then it started going into my real life when I wasn't stoned. I think I had so much built up from the last five years. It was when Snoop said, "You smoke more than anyone that I know." And I was like, "All right, I'm done."

Howard: You would wake and bake and then smoke throughout the whole day?

Miley: Yeah. I mean, I *love* that stuff. What I don't do is I don't drink coffee. 'Cause I think that's just one of the craziest drugs. I've done all the things. Coffee fucks me up more than any of it. I've done ayahuasca. Coffee's worse.

Robin: You've done ayahuasca?

Howard: Did you vomit and shit your brains out?

Miley: I didn't shit my pants. But I did puke a lot.

Howard: Did you learn anything from ayahuasca?

Miley: I did. You know what was crazy? I'm a vegan. And so when I was puking, I was puking up all the animals I had ever killed in the time I had eaten meat. I was envisioning *all* the animals. It wasn't just cows and pigs and things like that. It was, like, whales and zebras and all those things. And so it really hurt. Like, you were having to throw up a full zebra. And then Mama Ayahuasca comes in. That's the plant. The plant is female. And she said, "This is why you're a good person. Not only do you care about people, but you care about what people think are below them." People think they're above animals, right?

Howard: Yeah, that drives me nuts. Who decided that we're number one?

Miley: 'Cause we can speak. That's it. That's all we've got.

Howard: That's right. And barely.

Miley: And we sit on a toilet. So Mama Aya was like, "Because you care about the things that are so 'lesser than' for other people, that's how you know you're a good person—that you treat everything with respect."

Howard: Where'd you do it?

Miley: I did it in my house.

Howard: Oh, you didn't have a shaman.

Miley: I had a shaman. A shaman came to my house.

Howard: That's when you know you're famous: when the shaman comes to your house. Usually you have to go to Brazil.

Miley: The last thing I want to do is be throwing up in the middle of the jungle.

Lena Dunham

OCTOBER 1, 2014

I was a big fan of Lena Dunham's HBO show *Girls*. Here was a woman who didn't look like a conventional cookie-cutter Hollywood starlet, yet was completely uninhibited in showing her body. I know something about this having flaunted my gorgeous butt cheeks as Fartman a thousand years ago. Lena's fearlessness didn't stop there. She bared more than her skin; she bared her full self. This is also something I'm familiar with: being honest to a fault, addressing topics that can open yourself up to ridicule, exposing your darkest thoughts. To do that publicly can set off land mines in your life. I admired how brave she was as an artist, and how committed she was to the integrity of her show. Though part of me also wanted to caution her, "In about ten years you'll wonder, 'Why the hell did I want to reveal this or that?'"

Interviewing her was a little eerie. She was so in tune with my thought process—on obsessive-compulsive disorder, sexual assault, fear, self-esteem—it was like she was reading my mind. She was verbalizing things that I had always thought but didn't know how to articulate.

I was struck by the fact she was only twenty-eight. When I was twenty-eight I was working in Detroit, and I certainly was not operating on Lena's level. Far from it. It wasn't until I was in my thirties that I began to realize the level of commitment necessary to do well in radio. In Detroit, I wasn't successful because I hadn't opened myself up to the audience. I didn't have a handle on that. As a result, I wasn't relatable. If the masses were going to trust me, I had to trust *them*. I had to show faith that they would accept me for who I was, flaws and all. The more I opened up my life to them, the more they were willing to let me into their lives.

It wasn't until I got to Washington, DC, in 1981 that I had that epiphany: I had to reveal my true self if this was going to work. It took me ten years of just figuring out the basics of my craft before I could get there. Reading commercials, working the equipment, making a good segue with a record. While most audiences don't care how smooth the transition is between Steely Dan's "Reelin' In the Years" and the Young Rascals's "Groovin'," those kinds of fundamentals needed to be practiced until they became effortless. Only then could I get down to what really mattered to the audience and begin the process of developing something unique. It's the same for most creatives, whether you're a piano player or furniture maker or radio personality. You have to study and master technique before you can become an original. For Lena to demonstrate that kind of understanding and maturity at twenty-eight is very rare.

She possesses so much wisdom and clarity. I was writing this book while the Supreme Court confirmation hearings for Judge Brett Kavanaugh were taking place, and as I watched Dr. Christine Blasey Ford give her testimony I kept thinking of the powerful words Lena said about her own sexual assault and how difficult it is for victims to come forward.

I know I told you Conan O'Brien might be the best interview I've ever done, but Lena's candor makes this a very close second.

Howard: Hi, Lena. Good to see you.

Lena: It's so good to see you. Hi, Robin!

Robin: Good morning.

Lena: Oh, if anyone doesn't know, Robin lives in a box [referring to the glassed-in booth where Robin sits].

Howard: She sure does. And she better stay in there. But you know why she's in that box? Because I'm gross. Lena, explain your life to me. Because it seems to me very busy. You're on fire right now. You're hot. Everybody's wanting you. They want you to write a project or they want you to act in something. Your new book is getting rave reviews.

Lena: It's a lot. You know, I remember the moment when I realized there was never going to be a time that I had completed everything I needed to do. Like, I was never again going to go to sleep feeling like, "Well, I did everything I needed to do today, and now I can get a great night's sleep."

Howard: I like the book because you don't hold back. You tell people the truth. And of course, like me, you'll probably regret it—like, in twenty years. But you do. You feel compelled to tell the truth, you know?

And you talk about your OCD, which I like, 'cause I talked about it in my book, and I was glad I came clean. 'Cause a lot of people suffer from that. I used to be in denial about it. I used to just be in the bathroom doing rituals for an hour to get out, but I never acknowledged that I had it.

Lena: My parents realized something funky was going on pretty early, so I think I can give them credit for bringing the whole thing to light.

Howard: How old were you when you remember it hitting you?

Lena: I don't ever remember not having it. When did you start?

Howard: With me, I don't think I ever had it until after I did acid in college. I think it's a chemical thing that happened with me. But I don't know if that's real or not. I don't remember ever having any signs of it until I took an overdose of LSD, and it was awful. Like, my whole reality was rocked.

Lena: Oh my God, I'm so sorry that happened.

Howard: I think it fucked my brain up. I really do. How bad is your OCD?

Lena: I have had moments in my life when it was crippling. I've had moments in my life where it prevented me from going to school, from interacting with people. It turned me into this little ritual-doing, tic-having monster.

Howard: What type of rituals did you have?

Lena: Oh my God, everything from the standard flicking of the light switch to the less standard—I remember we had guests at my parents' house once, and I decided that I had to go into the room and stare at each of their toothbrushes until I remembered exactly what both of them looked like. And then if I didn't remember what the toothbrushes looked like, I had to go back in, because what if later there was a situation where I needed to remember what their toothbrushes looked like? The thing that's interesting about OCD that can sometimes distinguish it from other forms of mental illness is that you are completely aware of how absurd you're being in the moment.

Howard: Yes. *Yes.*

Lena: There's none of the comforts of psychosis. Of not knowing what you're doing.

Howard: You're sitting there and going, "This is *ridiculous*. I should stop doing this. But I can't stop it. I'll just—I'll give in to it."

Lena: Totally. And especially as a kid. I think kids always ascribe themselves a certain kind of power to control the universe that they don't necessarily have.

Howard: It's a control issue.

Lena: Yeah. My psychiatrist says to me that I don't have OCD, I have control issues, but I don't know. I think I have it under control. Somewhat. Do you take medication?

Howard: No, do you?

Lena: I do. I took something called Luvox for many years, a.k.a. fluvoxamine maleate, which I took until I was twenty-two. And then I took a break from taking medication. And once my sort of, uh, career started up more intensely—you know, OCD is often exacerbated by stress. And so I felt it coming back. So now I take a small dose of Lexapro, which I find really takes the edge off the situation.

Howard: Do you ever worry that the Lexapro could affect your writing, your edge, or anything like that?

Lena: No, I think that's one of the myths that actually keeps people from getting help that they need. I talk to so many people who go, "But what if my torture is a part of my creativity?" And it's like, since when does feeling a little more comfortable make it impossible for you to create? If anything,

 THE THING THAT'S INTERESTING ABOUT OCD THAT CAN SOMETIMES DISTINGUISH IT FROM OTHER FORMS OF MENTAL ILLNESS IS THAT YOU ARE COMPLETELY AWARE OF HOW ABSURD YOU'RE BEING IN THE MOMENT.

it creates all these hours in the day for productivity that were previously being devoted to, you know—the minutes that I was photographing people's toothbrushes with my mind are minutes that I will never get back. I don't know if you feel that way about your ritualistic stuff.

Howard: I don't feel that way so much, but I know it started to interfere with my work. When I was on the radio, it never interfered. Then all of a sudden, it became, "Oh, I can't play that record, 'cause that's bad luck." Or, "I have to put my finger over the record." Or sometimes when I was reading copy, I would have to say a word twice, and I would have to figure out a creative way to do that. When that started creeping in, that's when I knew I was really screwed. So I said, "That's it, I'm stopping the rituals." And I've been able to control it. I was surprised to read in the book that you slept in your parents' bed way too long, right?

Lena: So long.

Howard: You were afraid to sleep because you thought sleep and death were the same thing.

Lena: Yeah, I was like, "What's the difference?"

Robin: That's kind of a scary thought.

Howard: I think it's kind of a funny thought.

Lena: I mean, there is a clear difference between when you're alive and when you're dead. But—

Howard: No one could calm you down.

Your mom couldn't say to you in some rational way, "Sleep is different than death."

Lena: No, my parents would try to explain it to me. They'd be like, "You sleep so you *don't* die. It's good for you. It keeps you alive." But somehow being in their bed was the only thing that comforted me. So I feel terrible because there's no way they had sex between the years of 1986 and 1998.

Howard: Where do you think you got all these fears from? Even the OCD, it's all based on fear. Bad things are gonna happen.

Lena: Well, it's interesting. By the way, guys, I just noticed that Howard's been eating a delicious snack of grapefruit. What a virtuous man.

Howard: Yeah, but it's not good grapefruit. It's terrible. I'm not gonna finish it.

Lena: Like, mealy deli grapefruit?

Howard: No, I wish it was mealy. It is super hard. I've never had hard grapefruit before. It's like a fucking rock. I'm sitting here—I'm ready to hang myself from this.

Lena: This terrible grapefruit!

Howard: Why are you so afraid, you think?

Lena: I think it's a mix of sort of genetic factors. I am not the only person in my family with obsessive-compulsive disorder, and I'm not the only person in my family with an anxiety disorder. And then I also think being a kid is way harder than we give it credit for.

Howard: Yeah. Scary.

Lena: It's scary! I like being an adult way better. I talk to these people who are like, "I miss the carefree nature of being a child." And I'm like, "Being a child wasn't carefree."

Howard: No fun about it.

Lena: *No!* I'm more carefree than I've ever been because I can actually control my environment and make choices for myself rather than just being, you know, a player in someone else's movie.

Howard: But what's crazy is when you were a kid, you slept with your parents. Then you have a sister, right? And your sister, you had to sleep in bed with her 'cause—

Lena: Then *she* got scared. She inherited my scaredness and started sleeping in *my* bed.

Howard: And you start jerking off in the same bed with your sister.

Lena: I didn't call it "jerking off" in the book, Howard.

Robin: Yeah, there's nothing to jerk.

Howard: What did you call it?

Lena: I think I said "masturbate." Like an adult woman.

Howard: Want some advice? Not that you need any.

Lena: What?

Howard: "Jerking off" is funnier.

Lena: [*laughs*] Okay.

Howard: So yeah, your early masturbation was with your sister—well, not *with* your sister, but your sister would lay there next to you. That, to me, is a real buzzkill.

Lena: You may not know this, but I'm actually a very modest and anxious person, and even writing "masturbation" in the book was stressful to me.

Howard: Was it?

Lena: Yes.

Howard: I feel you're so open about everything.

Lena: I will randomly be a prude for no reason.

Howard: But you wrote about it in your book.

Lena: I know, but then now we have to *say* it and then I have to know that you *know* it. It's easy in my room, when I'm writing the book, to pretend.

Howard: How'd that work, though? I mean, what, you'd have to wait for her to go to sleep? My masturbation was the worst in my house. I was alone, but I was afraid my parents would hear.

Lena: Where did you do it? I want to talk about your masturbation, not my masturbation.

Howard: Yeah, okay. And then we'll get to your masturbation. We lived in a tiny little home in Roosevelt. And so when my masturbation would occur, I would do it quietly. And like a jackrabbit. I'd have tissues balled up in one hand. I'd masturbate really quickly, with the tissues, and then I'd do a sneaky operation into the bathroom to flush them down the toilet so my mother wouldn't hear it.

Lena: So cute and sad.

Howard: Very sad.

Lena: I would say it wasn't like full-scale masturbation episodes. It was more like I was young and trying to figure things out and had read, you know, *Our Bodies, Ourselves* and it was like, "What you're supposed to do when you're a woman is put your hand in your pants and move it around."

Howard: Did you ever say to your sister, "Listen, I need a night to myself"?

Lena: No.

Howard: Did your sister ever come to you later in life and say, "You were very noisy. I knew exactly what you were doing"?

Lena: No. You're making it sound like I was a chronic, every-night-in-bed-with-my-sister masturbator.

Howard: Six times a night, I heard.

Lena: I was referring to, like, one to two incidents of putting my hand down my pants in an experimental way.

Howard: I have a way of blowing things up, don't I?

Lena: I know you do. I'm not gonna be a part of your circus. No, I will. I will be a part of your circus.

Howard: I take this seriously: in the book, you say you were raped by a guy.

Lena: Yeah.

Howard: How did that happen? Was this someone you knew and took advantage of you?

Lena: Yeah. Yeah, I mean—it's complicated. This was an essay I was very anxious and self-conscious about putting in the book, because we are in a current culture where everything is turned into a game of telephone and it turns into a headline and, you know, a pull quote and not a fully formed story. But we're living in a moment where campus assault is an

epidemic. And the amount of young women who don't feel safe on their own college campuses and are violated by people that they know and then blame themselves because they're indulging in typical college behaviors, like drinking—so many of these young women are speaking out, and it gave me the strength to talk about something that I've been through that had been very challenging to make peace with.

Howard: Had you never talked about that publicly?

Lena: No, and I was very scared to. 'Cause it's felt like such a huge but private part of my identity. And I think I had a real fear of sort of becoming forever labeled as a victim. I've long known how empowering it is to talk about your experiences, but this is one that I was very afraid to touch.

Howard: Yeah, you know, I see these guys—even since when I went to college— they claim they love their mothers, and they're all wrapped up in their mothers, and then in the same breath if a chick says, "No," they're out on a date, they think "No" means "Yes." They still do to this day. If you hear "No," you just go, "Okay, that's it. It's over."

Lena: I mean, you have the correct attitude. I think so many people don't understand what the meaning of consent is. It's not like you start kissing and suddenly you've signed an implicit agreement to do everything in the world. If you're in the middle of having sex and someone suddenly becomes forceful with you and makes you do things that you don't want to do, that is an act of sexual assault—whether you started having intercourse with them or not. And I think so many women go, "But I put myself in this situation, but I opened myself to this person, and everything that happened is something I asked for." And that is a very dangerous mythology that we *have* to break down.

Howard: When this happened to you, did you go to any authorities? Did you tell anybody? Did you turn to a parent?

Lena: No.

Howard: Why not?

Lena: And I'm really close with my parents, and I didn't even give them the full story. I was hurt—I was physically hurt—so my mom made an appointment for me to go to the doctor, but—

Howard: What did you tell her happened?

Lena: I told her that I had gotten drunk and gotten into, you know, a rough situation that had left me uncomfortable, and I said, "Oh, you know, I don't really know if we used a condom. I feel like I should go to the doctor." And my mom—being a great liberal mom who does not want to shame anyone sexually—went, "Great. I'll make you an appointment with my doctor." And then I remember implying to the doctor what had happened, and her being very sympathetic, but also not trying to force me to talk. My best friend, Audrey, knew. She's the only person who knew.

Howard: Why do you think you didn't? The reason I ask is, I was talking to a

> **I THINK SO MANY PEOPLE DON'T UNDERSTAND WHAT THE MEANING OF CONSENT IS.**

woman I know very well that had a similar situation, and she said, "Oh no, I didn't tell anybody." She was afraid that her family would kill the guy. What was your fear in telling people? Were you ashamed? Or were you afraid that they'd blame you or something?

Lena: I think there's a big part of me that thought people would say, "You're lying. You exaggerated. He's more attractive than you are. Why would he want to do that to *you*?" You know, all the kind of self-hatred that we carry around on a daily basis.

Robin: Right, because it becomes an intense scrutiny of *you*.

Lena: Yeah.

Howard: So when you were writing the book, did you tell your mom you were going to write about this? And did you come clean to her and say, "Listen, remember that time you took me to the doctor? This was a rape."

Lena: Something I try to do in the essay is really capture the complexity of memory and the way that we really grapple with these experiences and try to classify them for ourselves and try to move on. When we've experienced a trauma, our relationship to it shifts every day. And so I just shared the essay with my mother, because I knew she's a very smart, thoughtful woman, and I knew that she would understand what it was.

Howard: Was she upset?

Lena: I think she was upset that she hadn't figured it out, because she's so intuitive and she thought, like, "How did I not . . . ?" It really shook her up. I think it was very hard for my father to read. I think it was very hard for my boyfriend to read. It's not an easy thing. And I'm sure it gave them anxiety that, you know, I had been drunk and taken a Xanax in that situation to begin with. Everything about it is uncomfortable, and it makes us examine—'cause the fact is, every guy who crosses a consent line isn't a straightforward villain. That's what's missing from this conversation, is women need to learn to speak out, and men need to talk to each other about consent. Everybody needs to take responsibility on their side of the equation.

Robin: Well, yeah, 'cause most of these guys don't even think they did anything wrong.

Lena: If you said to one of these guys, "You raped someone," they'd go, "What are you *talking* about? I love my mom. I love women. I'm a liberal person."

> **" I'VE BEEN RUBBING CERTAIN PEOPLE THE WRONG WAY FOR QUITE SOME TIME NOW. AND IF THAT'S MY LOT IN LIFE, I'M OKAY WITH IT.**

Howard: He knows. Trust me, he knows. He would know he did it. Maybe he won't acknowledge it because he doesn't want to think of himself that way. But he knows what he did. On a lighter topic, though . . .

Lena: Yeah. Off rape.

Howard: Off rape for a second. We'll get back to rape later. You say in terms of lovemaking, the first time you actually consented to having sex with a guy, that it was a disaster.

Lena: It was the worst. I mean, he was a lovely person, but it was just a goddamn disaster. I didn't tell him I was a virgin. The whole thing was just . . .

Howard: And you were not attracted to him. You kinda describe him as—

Lena: I said he looked like a middle-aged lesbian.

Howard: That's not a good thing to look like.

Lena: But I didn't mind it.

Howard: You didn't, but he might have. And you said that neither one of you came, because the chemistry just wasn't there.

Lena: I remember being like, "If this is what this is, I should just end it right now."

Howard: There's no point.

Robin: What's the big deal?

Lena: I've been waiting for *this*?

Howard: You know, right now people evaluate you extra-special because you've got a hit show. They're looking to take you down. You know that.

Lena: Yeah.

> **66 THE CONVERSATION AROUND MY BOOK ADVANCE AND AROUND MY SALARY HAS BEEN SO GENDERED AND SO MISOGYNISTIC. HOW OFTEN DO YOU HEAR AN ANALYSIS OF WHETHER A MAN DESERVES HIS MONEY?**

Howard: The book's out, getting good reviews, and all of a sudden you're getting *too much* success. Someone's gonna want to knock you down.

Lena: I've been rubbing certain people the wrong way for quite some time now. And if that's my lot in life, I'm okay with it.

Howard: Are you?

Lena: Yeah. I'm like, "There were some boys who were mean to me in high school, and there's some people who are mean to me on the Internet."

Howard: I think the rub is because you get nude on the show. Women freak out over that. Men freak out over it. They're *freaked out* by it.

Lena: Not in France.

Howard: Not in France. France, everybody's naked.

Lena: Yeah. All day.

Howard: That's right.

Lena: Every day. Everywhere. Naked and walking on the Seine.

Howard: No, but I also think people are jealous. I think especially some girls get jealous because they go, "Hey, she's not the traditional beauty like we are, and blah-blah-blah-blah," and they get fucking angry for some reason.

Robin: I think people see a juggernaut, and

it's like, "Wow, we watched her shoot to the top. Now let's wait."

Howard: Yeah, "I'm not gonna kiss *her* ass."

Lena: Last night I did a signing at Barnes and Noble Union Square, and it was the first time—you know, when you're on a TV show, you sometimes see some fans of the show in the street. But I haven't had the experience I'm sure you've had of really sitting and meeting people. And not to sound like a total love-in hippie, but I was so *moved*. I was like, "The fact that these people I get to connect with because of what I do"—rad girls, cool gay boys, supersmart people, genderqueer people. Just a really amazing assortment of people where I was like, "Oh, this would make a great dinner party." We're connecting over a shared worldview, 'cause they've seen the show, they've read my work, they understand what I'm about, and they accept it. What a beautiful feeling.

Howard: Don't you enjoy being recognized and having all that kind of fan craziness?

Lena: Not all the time. I'm appreciative that people watch the show, but that's not what keeps me going. It's not my motor.

Howard: You don't have that deep, dark,

empty hole inside of you that needs to be filled constantly with—

Lena: I mean, I'll find out when everybody forgets who I am. And then I walk around crying all day. Do you like it when people recognize you?

Howard: There's a certain joy in it for me. But also a certain nightmare.

Lena: I mean, you're not an easy person to hide.

Howard: I'm so tall that people look at me. They looked at me my whole life because I was so tall.

Lena: So it's not like you can walk into Zabar's and have a chill time.

Howard: No, and I was self-conscious *before* I got famous.

Lena: Yeah.

Howard: But are you embarrassed when— like, I know you got a lot of money for the book advance. Even the last time I spoke to you, I said, "Wow, you got three-million-something," and you didn't even want to *talk* about what you got.

Lena: No.

Howard: Are you afraid to be successful? Are you afraid people will be jealous of you?

Lena: Well, it's a few things. One is that I was raised that it was impolite to talk about money. That was a big thing with my parents. You don't ask people what they make. You don't ask people how much things cost. To me, what's way more uncouth than talking about masturbation is talking about money. And also the other

thing that's been really challenging is the conversation around my book advance and around my salary has been so gendered and so misogynistic. How often do you hear an analysis of whether a man deserves his money?

Howard: Oh, I get it every day.

Robin: Well, yeah, Howard does. He's like a woman.

Howard: Lena, I'm like a woman. You know that. I look like a lesbian.

Lena: You have that beautiful hair.

Howard: But you gotta think that through, that statement. Because football players get that a lot, and they're in show business, whether you like it or not.

Lena: I guess.

Robin: Football players, baseball players. A lot of people, yeah.

Howard: Everyone is sort of evaluated. "Hey, he doesn't deserve this or deserve that."

Lena: Actually, Howard, no—I really do think it's misogynistic.

Howard: You do?

Lena: Yeah, I really, really do. Women are taken to task for their success, and in an entirely different way. Female CEOs—Sheryl Sandberg has been beaten into the ground for not being *relatable enough* as a woman. It's like, what do you want from her? She's a female billionaire. That's fucking rad.

Howard: Yeah, and I know in show business a lot of women who are tough, they're called "bitches" and all that shit. And the guy is considered "strong." Yeah.

Lena: And the football player thing is more like, "They throw a ball. Shouldn't teachers get more money?" The thing about women is, "What have they done to deserve it?"

Howard: Yeah, I guess you're right. I don't think that way.

Lena: And it's assumed that when women get paid, they're, like, spending all their money on shoes and weaves and assistants.

Robin: That they don't have anything to spend it on, while the man has a family.

Lena: Yeah.

Howard: That's a good point. Any pictures in the book?

Lena: Yeah, one of my best friends, Joana Avillez, drew illustrations. I like pictures. I think they break up the monotony of reading.

Howard: No, I'm a big fan of pictures.

Lena: And there's boobs in the book. They're just illustrated boobs.

Howard: I could beat off to that. I used to beat off to cartoons. I remember *Fritz the Cat*. That was a big hit. That was a big day for me.

Lena: Live the dream, Howard.

Jimmy Kimmel

MAY 16, 2011

Jimmy Kimmel has a unique status on my show. He's been on more than thirty times—sometimes to be interviewed but mostly to just hang out. I would feel funny letting anyone else do this besides Jimmy. He's been listening to the show for so long that he understands how we work. "I've heard Howard's voice more than that of any human being, including my mother," he once wrote in a piece for the *Hollywood Reporter*. He knows how to fit into our dynamic. He can just sit there and be a part of whatever we're talking about, whether it's current events or the latest exploits of Tan Mom and other members of the *Stern Show* Wack Pack. He's okay with being quiet, allowing things to unfold, and then chiming in with whatever he thinks.

When he does interject, his timing is perfect. He's always so funny. Give him three seconds and he can come up with a joke about anything. So many times he'll say something and I'll think, "I wish I'd thought of that."

His career has been a lot like my own. He came up through broadcasting, not stand-up comedy. That's one of the things we discuss in this interview—which is the closest thing to a long-form conversation I've ever done with him. We talk about his unconventional path to becoming a late-night host and how he fits into that world. It doesn't surprise me one bit that ABC gave him his own late-night show. Not only is he funny, but there's a generosity and sweetness about him that makes him a terrific host. We've developed a wonderful friendship over the years, and I feel very lucky to have him in my life.

I'll give you one specific example of the kind of guy Jimmy Kimmel is. He'll often send me an e-mail: "Show was so funny this week. Loved the bit about Ronnie the Limo Driver's animal clinic." Or, "When you got on the megaphone and did that impression of your father saying 'halibut'—just unbelievably funny." He has no idea what despair and doubt I feel all the time. Despite my years of therapy, I still haven't mastered owning my own feelings about the show. I sneak on Twitter to check listener reactions. I hate that I do that. I truly do. It embarrasses me that after all these years I can still be so insecure—that I rely so much on the opinions of others. When Jimmy's e-mails come in, they feel like a lifeline. Once I sent him an e-mail that said, "Sometimes I feel like I'm just spinning my wheels." A few days later I got an embroidered pillow in the mail that read: NOT SPINNING WHEELS BUT SPINNING GOLD SINCE 1979. This is a guy who's busy twenty-four seven, yet he took the time to find someplace that made custom pillows. It's one of the most thoughtful gifts I've ever received. I put it on a shelf in my room where I can see it every day. It helps. I love him.

Howard: Hey, Jimmy Kimmel is here. He's only here till eight o'clock, but you know I like when Jimmy hangs out on the show. Bring him in. Skinny Jimmy. How much weight have you lost?

Jimmy: About twenty pounds.

Howard: What's going on with you? You look good.

Jimmy: You know, moderation.

Howard: You're kind of handsome.

Robin: You finally realized you're in show business?

Howard: Do you sense you're more handsome? Don't you think you are more handsome?

Jimmy: I wouldn't say that I think that. But I do now look back at pictures of myself, and I'd make fat jokes about myself, but I didn't really think I was fat. Now I realize that, yes, I was. And I still am probably.

Howard: Tell people why you're in town this week. You're in town for something called the Upfronts. Explain what they are.

Jimmy: It's a very confusing event that goes on in television every year. All the advertisers gather and then the networks tell the advertisers about the new shows that they have coming up. They're very excited about the new shows. They show clips of them and everybody sits there enthralled. And then, theoretically, advertisers buy

time on these shows. Then we cancel all of those shows in the next twelve months. Every one of them gets canceled.

Howard: I always thought it was weird because it's the only business where an advertiser commits money to a TV show that they don't even know how it's going to do.

Jimmy: It's not a gamble at all because if the TV show doesn't deliver that minimum rating that they've been promised, then we give them commercials on other TV shows. We're like the stupidest bookies in the world. If the Jets don't cover, we'll give you a few extra points until they do.

Howard: Is this a mandatory thing for you in your job, or do you just do it because you want to be in good graces with ABC?

Jimmy: There are certain areas of the network that are very supportive around me and one of them is the sales department. If it weren't for their support, I don't know if I'd still be on the air. I just feel like as a good guy I should go and do this for them because I know it means something to them. The worst-case scenario for them is their clients come out of that Upfront and they're like, "Oh my God, that was terrible. That was boring." This is my ninth year in a row doing it. The first year I just went on and made fun of everyone, and I said

I'D MAKE FAT JOKES ABOUT MYSELF, BUT I DIDN'T REALLY THINK I WAS FAT. NOW I REALIZE THAT, YES, I WAS. AND I STILL AM PROBABLY.

good-bye to the people that I was working for because I figured they'd be fired as a result of hiring me. And sure enough they got fired.

Howard: You're the Johnny Carson, so to speak, of ABC. You are their one late-night guy.

Jimmy: Sadly, yes.

Howard: What's amazing to me is you're very versatile. You were a radio guy. You worked at KROQ in Los Angeles and other radio stations, and then you got a job doing *The Man Show*. You were never a stand-up comedian and somehow you have this ability to go up onstage and deliver stand-up comedy. I would imagine that that made you a wreck when you first had to do these live appearances like the Upfronts where you had to tell jokes.

Jimmy: The first year I look like I'm on a ship because I'm rocking back and forth. I mean, just clearly terrified. I think it happened to work for some reason. People were charmed by my ineptness.

Howard: You were learning in front of a huge audience.

Jimmy: Yeah, on television. I really learned to do stand-up on television. Because I

started on a game show, *Win Ben Stein's Money*. I was the host some of the game and the rest of the game Ben Stein was the host. And then on *The Man Show*, Adam [Carolla] and I did stand-up together—which is in a way harder but also easier in another way.✦

Howard: Because you have someone there to comfort you?

Jimmy: Exactly. Then I got to my show, and the first year and a half I sat behind the desk. I didn't do a stand-up thing.

Howard: You evolved into that as you got more comfortable. You do that off a teleprompter?

Jimmy: Cue cards.

Howard: Have you ever done stand-up where you go to a club and actually have a memorized act?

Jimmy: Not really. I do charity events and stuff, but I can't memorize. I can't remember anything.

Howard: Me too. When you go to a charity event, you've got a cue card guy with you?

Jimmy: No, no, no.

Howard: What do you do?

Jimmy: I just stumble through the whole thing. I'll bring a little index card. I figure if I do too well with these charity events,

✦ **For more on this from Adam Carolla, turn to page 542.**

> 66 **I RECENTLY LOOKED BACK ON ONE OF OUR FIRST SHOWS. IT'S ONE OF THE WORST THINGS I'VE EVER SEEN. IF SOME OTHER GUY WAS STARTING A LATE-NIGHT SHOW AND I SAW THAT, I'D BE LIKE, "UGH BOY. MAN, TOUGH NIGHT FOR JIMMY. THAT'S NOT GOING TO WORK."**

they'll ask me to do more of them. So I go in, and I'm happy if I get like a five or a six. And then I go home.

Howard: I love all that late-night war stuff. Do you ever pinch yourself and say, "I can't believe I'm part of this"?

Jimmy: It is one of the strangest things. It really is. I mean, one of the weirdest things is flipping through the channels at that time and flipping past *yourself* standing like they do in front of a background like they have.

Howard: When you first started *Jimmy Kimmel Live!*, you didn't anticipate looking like them. You wore a T-shirt under your jacket.

Jimmy: I'd always have a single ball poking through my fly.

Howard: No, but you wanted to do it in a different sort of format.

Jimmy: Yeah, it's always stupid to do something different. People don't want to see different.

Howard: That's true. Even Merv Griffin—I go back to his day—he always came out, he did a little song, he did something to bond with the audience one-on-one. Jack Paar did it.

Jimmy: It's like the law. You have to do a monologue. People tune out after the monologue for the most part. You lose a lot of people when the monologue's over.

Howard: So you tried to do it without a monologue. You did it behind a desk.

Jimmy: Yeah, I did more like what Regis does. That type of thing, where I come out and BS. The first show I did I had no plan. I had a couple of taped bits that I was going to roll, but they were like twenty seconds long. I went out and really just kind of talked about what had happened. And I remember afterward we thought, "That went really well. That was really great." I recently looked back on one of our first shows. It's one of the worst things I've ever seen. If some other guy was starting a late-night show and I saw that, I'd be like, "Ugh boy. Man, tough night for Jimmy. That's not going to work."

Howard: The only thing I remember about your first show is that the plan was to allow the audience to drink and to have a bar. And ABC did away with that in two seconds because people were vomiting, right?

Jimmy: That's never happened since but somebody did vomit during the first show.

Howard: Well, it hasn't happened since because you stopped. They said it's a liability, right? If someone legally drank themselves into a coma, ABC might be liable.

Jimmy: That's what I was hoping for. To bring the network down.

Howard: The drinking stopped, but the guests are allowed to drink.

Jimmy: The guests are allowed to drink, yeah.

Howard: You have a whole bar set up back there. I've been backstage at your show, and it is packed with celebrities.

Jimmy: Only when you're there.

Howard: Who decides who can get into that bar? What is the process? If I'm a guy who appeared on a sitcom and I was only on for, like, three weeks—

Jimmy: If you've been on our show, in general, you'd be welcome to come back.

Howard: Can someone become loser-ish if they show up too often? It would be a big deal maybe if I showed up to the bar one time. But if I started showing up every week, then you guys would start to really think I was odd, right?

Jimmy: Well, yeah, because there have to be better things to do than that. And people forget: we're trying to work.

Howard: Talk to me about when Charlie Sheen kissed you on the lips. I'm a friend of yours, and I watched that show. I was skeeved out of my mind. And I knew you didn't know that was coming. Because, listen, Charlie Sheen has a reputation for eating out tons of fucking hookers and all this kind of shit. When a guy like that kisses you, do you worry?

Jimmy: No. I will eat gum off the floor. That sort of thing doesn't bother me.

Howard: Oh my God. My immediate thought would be, "Oh shit, I'm going to have a fucking problem with my lips."

Jimmy: Not me.

Robin: Howard would have to go to the hospital.

Howard: Yeah, I would have to be boraxed. They'd have to take borax and wash down my lips. Were you taken aback when he did that? Or did you say, "Hey, great showbiz moment. This is good for my show."

Jimmy: Well, both probably. I mean, it was kind of surprising the way it happened.

Howard: Were you incredibly frustrated that he wouldn't sit there and be interviewed? Because he was hot as a pistol at that point. Everyone was talking about him. There he was on your show. He was handing out T-shirts. He wanted to announce his tour or something. But he sort of had it set up that he was just going to drop in and then leave.

Jimmy: He came in in another guest's segment—in Mark Cuban's segment.

Howard: Charlie Sheen walks in. So you know it's gold. But he won't answer any questions. Does that tick you off?

Jimmy: Not really because I didn't think I would get any answers out of him anyway.

He's too smart, he's too fast, he's saying nonsense. Really, I didn't care. It was enough to have him walk on and do that thing.

Howard: You let him go with the moment. How does that work when a guy like Charlie Sheen drops by? Who makes the decision to let him in in the first place?

Jimmy: That was Mark Cuban. The guest had him come and do that.

Howard: Do you see a ratings spike as soon as you get a Charlie Sheen?

Jimmy: It doesn't really work like that, where we can analyze it like that. But it was all over the news the next day.

Howard: Has there ever been a guest that has driven up the ratings to an incredible amount? I know that Hugh Grant did that for Jay Leno back in the day.

Jimmy: When you're on, we always get a noticeably good number. But there aren't too many people. You'd be surprised at who the people are that actually have a noticeable increase. The Kardashians, for instance, get big ratings. People want to see what's going on with them.

Howard: Even though they see the reality show, they want to see them. They can't get enough.

Jimmy: They can't get enough of them. They have to have every bit of them.

Howard: Conan O'Brien. Is his show getting any ratings?

Jimmy: They do well in their target audience, I think. It's hard for me to say because I'm so absorbed in that world. I do hear things and kind of follow what everybody's doing.

Howard: When's the last time Letterman had you on?

Jimmy: I was on last year when I was here.

Howard: Were you kept in a dressing room like everyone else? Or because you are a fellow late-night talk show host were you brought into Dave's inner sanctum?

Jimmy: I did say hello to all of them after the show.

Howard: After the show? Did you request that or Letterman asked that you stop by?

Jimmy: Letterman asked that I stop by.

Howard: Wow, I've never been asked that. I have never been asked to stop by afterward. You're telling me the last time you were on they got word to you? They said, "Hey, hang out. Dave needs to see you after the show."

Jimmy: Well, he didn't *need* to see me. He just wanted to say hello. Our executive producer Jill Leiderman, she used to work at his show, and she was there with me. She was saying hello to him also.

Howard: Now you've been summoned.

Jimmy: Yes.

Howard: You would have rather have left, I'm sure.

Jimmy: No, no, no.

Howard: You were happy to be there?

Jimmy: I was delighted. Growing up, you and David Letterman—that was it for me.

Howard: Did he go, "Jimmy, hello." Like you're meeting Nixon.

> **[LETTERMAN AND LENO] DON'T NEED ME AND CONAN AND JIMMY FALLON AND CRAIG FERGUSON. THEY DON'T NEED US. THERE'S BATMAN AND SUPERMAN. THEY DON'T NEED AQUAMAN AND THESE OTHER ASSHOLES RUNNING AROUND.**

Jimmy: [*laughs*] More or less.

Howard: It was a very stiff conversation?

Jimmy: I wouldn't say it was stiff. It was funny. We talked, I don't know, maybe it was a minute long or something like that.

Howard: During the whole [Leno-Conan] controversy, weren't you upset that Letterman invited Leno to do a TV commercial during the Super Bowl?

Jimmy: Yes, I was very upset.

Howard: Thank you. That is *bullshit*!

Jimmy: I talked to him about it on his show also. I said, "He was drowning and you saved him."

Howard: He saved him. Why?

Jimmy: I have a theory about it.

Howard: Go ahead. Excellent. I love theories.

Jimmy: All right. My theory is that there's Dave and Jay. And they're the guys. They compete.

Howard: Head-to-head.

Jimmy: And Jay wins, obviously. Jay wins the ratings. But everybody thinks Dave is better.

Howard: Right.

Jimmy: And Dave *is* better. They don't need me and Conan and Jimmy Fallon and Craig Ferguson. They don't need us. There's Batman and Superman. They don't need Aquaman and these other assholes running around. And I think by consolidating that, the focus once again went directly on [Dave and Jay] instead of on Jay and Conan. And I think ultimately he probably just thought, "This is really funny. I should do this."

Howard: I think you're right. I think he thought it was funny. But you have a good point. I never considered that. Maybe in a weird way, he was sick and tired of everyone being mentioned with Jay, and this put the focus back on him.

Jimmy: "Jay's *my* archenemy."

Howard: Right. He's not Aquaman's enemy.

Jimmy: That's right.

Howard: "He's mine. He might be an asshole but he's *my* asshole."

Jimmy: "He's *my* asshole." That's just my theory on it.

And Now a Word from Our President . . .

SEPTEMBER 11, 2002

(14 years, 1 month, and 28 days until the election)

Howard: Donald Trump has agreed to call in and share his thoughts on 9/11. Hello, Donald.

Donald: Hello, Howard.

Howard: It's a sad day. But you're one of those guys who said to keep investing in New York, and people are doing it, right?

Donald: They are. I don't think it's ever been better. I guess it has a lot to do with interest rates being so low. But it also has to do with the fact that people want to buy a piece of the Big Apple. They really do. I've never seen it like this.

Howard: We haven't come back fully yet, have we? The tourism is off. A lot of businesses are struggling.

Donald: Well, the hotel market is terrible in New York. The office market is pretty average at best. The condominium market is extraordinary. It's the best I've ever seen it.

Howard: Because of low interest rates?

Donald: Well, I think it's that. But I also think it's the Enrons, where they don't want to invest in that garbage anymore. They want to get something where they can feel it and touch it, so they buy an apartment.

> ## MELANIA IS NOW IN BED, AND I'M IN MY OFFICE. AS TO WHETHER SHE'S NAKED, I'M NOT 100 PERCENT SURE.

Howard: Probably the most important question I can ask you on a day like this is, "Where is Melania, and is she naked?"

Donald: Well, Melania is now in bed, and I'm in my office. As to whether she's naked, I'm not 100 percent sure.

Howard: Take me back a year ago. Tell me where you were when you heard the horrible news.

Donald: Well, normally I'm in my office, but I was watching television. I wanted to see Jack Welch, who was being interviewed on a business channel, and I wanted to see it. He had a book coming out, and he just left General Electric, and it was interesting. He was just about to be announced when the planes hit. And I'll never forget, the announcer was just—it was amazing. He couldn't believe it. And interestingly, they never announced Jack would not be on.

Howard: Right.

Donald: It was just an amazing thing. And you know, I have two windows, windows where I live, that specifically look at the World Trade Center. You can't believe after looking at them for twenty years . . .

Howard: So you could look out your window and see the whole thing go down?

Donald: I saw the whole thing. I mean, specifically, I have two windows that are focused on the buildings. It's just unbelievable.

Howard: Wow. It's tough.

Donald: And it's a little like you were saying earlier. Things sound a lot tougher, but I'm not sure they're any tougher, in terms of security. It's also nice to know your enemies. You and I have plenty of enemies. It's nice to know who they are. Here, we don't really know the enemy.

Howard: I know. They're skulking around somewhere, and you just feel like you're a sitting duck.

Donald: But we have an idea of who the enemy is, and a lot of times the politicians don't want to tell you that.

Howard: Are you for invading Iraq?

Donald: Yeah, I guess so. I wish the first time it was done correctly.

Howard: Are you still against rebuilding the World Trade Center?

Donald: I'm not against rebuilding it. I guess the height thing—unless you're going to build things bigger and better. I looked at the proposals. I don't know if you saw them. They came out two weeks ago. They were terrible. They were fifty-story buildings. They were crummy-looking shapes. Now, the city's not going for it. I don't know how they did this, but they got it down to one firm and said, "You come up with an idea." They should get the top fifteen architectural firms in the world and come up with something spectacular. But unless you're going to come up with something spectacular, it'll never be the same.

Howard: A statue of your girlfriend would be perfect right there.

Donald: Well, that would be an idea.

Robin: No one's going to fly into that.

Howard: No one. No one.

Donald: But you know, the concept of the memorial is very important. But so is the concept of commerce. You know, if we don't rebuild something pretty substantial, and create lots of jobs in addition to a great memorial, then they've won. At least, they've won that part of the battle.

Howard: Yeah. It's an awful day today, and I want to thank you for calling in, Donald Trump.

Donald: Absolutely, Howard.

Lady Gaga

JULY 18, 2011

Lady Gaga is one of those guests who perhaps some of my audience didn't truly understand. There is a core group who rejects the notion of any pop star having value. They categorically throw them in the "no talent with meaningless songs" bin. Lady Gaga changed that perception. She walked in and gave the most raw interview. She left it all out there. She sat down at the piano, sang those songs in a whole different way—an acoustic performance—and blew the doors off my studio.

We got so many calls and e-mails, and they all went the same way: "Hey, man, I thought Lady Gaga was bullshit. She's now my favorite artist. I'm going out and I'm buying that CD." We didn't get a single negative comment. She's the real deal.

An interesting behind-the-scenes about this interview. I was telling Gary how badly I wanted her to play a few songs when she came in. We weren't sure she would, and we didn't want to ask her in case it turned her off from doing the show. So we conspired. "Let's just bring a piano into the studio and hope she'll do it." We ordered a piano. Then, a night or two before she was scheduled, her manager called and said, "I know this is short notice, but Gaga wants to play a few songs. Think you can get a piano?" Gary said, "Yeah . . . I think I can work on that."

Howard: You know, I was thinking about you. I was excited you were coming in, and I was reading the statistics: that you made $90 million, that you are more successful than Oprah Winfrey herself this year, that you're the number-one-earning artist this year. I was thinking, you know how much more money you would've made if it was like the old days in the record business? Don't you get freaked out that when you put a record on sale now, most people get it for free? Doesn't that freak you out at all?

Lady Gaga: I actually love it because I just really don't give a fuck about money at all.

Howard: Is that true? Or is that a thing you have to say so people will relate to you?

Lady Gaga: No, absolutely not. I just came

from my apartment in Brooklyn that's smaller than this studio.

Howard: You mean to tell me with all the money you've made, you haven't bought anything? I mean, aside from clothes.

Lady Gaga: I bought my dad a Rolls-Royce, and I paid for his heart surgery. That's it.

Howard: You paid for his heart surgery? Your father had heart surgery?

Lady Gaga: Yeah.

Howard: Was there a couple of years where you and your dad didn't talk because he was so negative about your career?

Lady Gaga: I don't know if *negative* is the word. It's more, "Hell, fuck it. I can't believe you're doing that."

Howard: He was upset that you would go to burlesque clubs and get naked and stuff like that.

Lady Gaga: I was doing a show, and my father was so sweet. He was like, "Oh, baby, I'm going to come see you live." And he'd show up and I'd be dancing to Judas Priest in a thong on a stage, and he'd have a freaking heart attack. And I'm like, "But, Daddy, it's art! It's performance art! It's the performance art of the future!"

Howard: He just didn't have your vision to see that maybe dancing burlesque was a good thing, right?

Lady Gaga: Honestly, I think my dad sees and saw a lot of himself in me. My dad was, you know—

Howard: A musician?

Lady Gaga: He was having sex with girls

 I JUST REALLY DON'T GIVE A FUCK ABOUT MONEY AT ALL.

under the boardwalk in New Jersey, going to see Bruce play. So I think he saw himself in me and got scared.

Howard: Was your dad your major influence, in that he'd play you records? Would your dad sit there and play classic rock for you all the time?

Lady Gaga: All the time. Every single night, it was sort of a ritual before and after dinner. He'd play Pink Floyd, Led Zeppelin, Bruce Springsteen, Billy Joel. I used to go, "Daddy, why is there money sounds in that song?" And he'd say, "Well, Pink Floyd wrote a song called 'Money.'" And then he'd explain it to me.

Howard: How long before you start to play the piano yourself?

Lady Gaga: I was four.

Howard: Did you take piano lessons?

Lady Gaga: No, not in the beginning.

Howard: And did you beg your parents for lessons?

Lady Gaga: I didn't. At first my mom just got me lessons, and actually my first piano teacher was a stripper at Scores.

Howard: Do you know how to read music?

Lady Gaga: Yeah, I can read music.

Howard: So when you compose a song, do you write it out with musical notes?

Lady Gaga: I can. It depends on what

we're working on. If I'm arranging violin or string orchestrations that need to be transposed, I'll do that, yeah.

Howard: And so your father must feel somewhat responsible for your career because he sat there with you and played you Queen, which was where you got the name Gaga. But then when you get into going out and being outrageous yourself and taking your clothes off, he freaks out and says, "I want nothing to do with this."

Lady Gaga: Not anymore.

Howard: Well, yeah, now he knows. So, what are you doing with all this money you're making if you don't care about money?

Lady Gaga: The Monster Ball [Tour] was really expensive, and the next show will be expensive, and I will pay for it.

Howard: Okay, the Monster Ball brought in about $116 million, do I have that right?

Lady Gaga: I actually have no clue how much money I make.

Howard: My point is, Joe Cocker went bankrupt from touring live.

Lady Gaga: I did too. Actually, the first time around, the first Monster Ball in America, that show was a theater tour, and I wanted to go all the way to Australia and bring everything with me. I actually was $3 million in debt.

Howard: Did your manager sit you down and say, "Look, Gaga . . ."

Lady Gaga: Yes, he's in the back room. He's probably laughing right now watching this.

Howard: He isn't laughing.

Lady Gaga: Oh, he is laughing. He said, "You will have no money." And I said, "Just keep me on the road and it'll come back."

Howard: Does he call you Gaga or does he call you Stefani [her given name]?

Lady Gaga: Everybody calls me Gaga.

Howard: Really?

Lady Gaga: Everybody.

Howard: You know what, I'm obsessing on whether or not I got a lap dance from your piano teacher. I used to go to Scores all the time.

Lady Gaga: She was fabulous. I used to say, "Why do you have such long nails? Because you play piano, and then you're telling me that when I play piano, my nails should be very short so I can have the proper position." And she'd say, "Someday you'll understand why my nails are long. Now, do that Debussy again."

Howard: When you were four years old, did you start writing music right away? Did you have songs in your head?

Lady Gaga: Yeah, actually I tried to copy Pink Floyd. I wrote a song called "Money." My mother had bought me Mickey Mouse staff paper, so I notated it with real notes. It was so cute. It was in the key of G. There was an F-sharp. It was really sweet.

Howard: At four years old, what did you think about money? Was money bad?

Lady Gaga: No, I just was confused as to why a rock-and-roll band would put the sound of a cash register in a song. I was like, "That's not rock and roll, Daddy. Billy Joel would never do that." And then he explained to me that Pink Floyd changed the way that rock and roll was forever.

Howard: Was it hard for you to decide in your career what type of music you'd play if you were kind of raised on hard rock and roll?

Lady Gaga: No, because I think that all those influences gave birth to me, in a way, and the artist that I've become is just who I was always destined to be. I moved downtown when I was nineteen, and there was a huge singer-songwriter scene. And, to be honest, I didn't want to be another one of the chicks in the pack. I wanted to revolutionize underground music in New York, so I made pop music.

Howard: Were you depressed earlier on? You were signed to a record label for, like, three or four months. I don't know who the hell it was.

Lady Gaga: Def Jam.

Howard: Def Jam. When you signed with them, you probably said to yourself, "Oh my God, it's finally coming true. This is my big break. I'm on Def Jam." And then is it mind-blowing to you when the record doesn't hit? Did you think it was over when that whole deal didn't work out?

Lady Gaga: Oh yeah. I was going to keep going anyway, but the concern is: How do you make your daddy proud? How do you make an honest woman of yourself for your family? I was more concerned with my parents not feeling like I was leaving a legacy for our family. My parents didn't come from money. They are both really hard workers, both in the Internet business

> ## I DIDN'T WANT TO BE ANOTHER ONE OF THE CHICKS IN THE PACK.

and communications. They both were the first to go to college.

Howard: Were you the embarrassment of the family? "Oh my God, she's pursuing this dream. It's never going to happen." I'm sure your parents were worried out of their minds.

Lady Gaga: No, not an embarrassment at all. I think it was just confusing because I was really, really smart in school, and I think that academia, in the theater sense, was what they saw for my future. And I just started doing a lot of drugs and moved downtown and started burlesque dancing.

Howard: But if you hadn't made it, it would have been the worst thing in the world, because you probably felt such pressure from your parents. Not that they were pressuring you. It's just an internal thing you were going through.

Lady Gaga: See, that's the thing: I already felt like I had made it. Me living in New York in an $1,100-a-month apartment, paying my own rent, doing my own shows, dressing how I liked, singing how I liked, doing my hair how I liked—I already felt like I had made it. So when I say, "I don't care about money," I only and always have just wanted to make music and do it my way. I can't explain my nerve. I don't know where it comes from. The "Edge of Glory" video, me dancing on the fire escape—I used to get high and dance on the fire escape and imagine that I was a star.

Howard: When you talk about getting high, you were doing some hard-core drugs. You were into coke and you loved ecstasy so much.

Lady Gaga: No, not then. I did later.

Howard: You did. So you still get high?

Lady Gaga: No.

Howard: No?

Lady Gaga: No way.

Howard: Still smoke weed?

Lady Gaga: Well, come on, that's not—

Howard: Weed doesn't make you paranoid?

Lady Gaga: You know, I really don't do it very often, and I'm really honest about it only because—

Howard: I like that you're honest about it.

Lady Gaga: I don't really like or respect artists that lie about what they do recreationally because it builds this separation between you and your fans.

Howard: But when is the last time you did coke?

Lady Gaga: Gosh, I don't even remember.

Howard: Did you think you had a habit? Were you addicted?

Lady Gaga: I was for sure addicted.

Howard: How did you get off it?

Lady Gaga: My father kicked my ass. Not really, but he called me out. And I love my dad. So when your dad calls you out—

Howard: Is that why you bought him the car?

Lady Gaga: Absolutely not. The reason I gave my dad the car and the reason that I am who I am is because of the way that they raised me. My past—using any drugs or dressing any certain way—was never a rebellion. It was never meant to be "Fuck you."

Howard: But don't you think you were unhappy? I had a period of time where I did a tremendous amount of drugs, and I look back on it now—and now I don't do anything—but I sense that I was lost. I was unhappy.

Lady Gaga: I was so unhappy.

Howard: And what was the source of your unhappiness?

Lady Gaga: I think that I was lonely and there was something about the drug that made me feel like I had a friend.

Howard: See, I think that of myself. I think that's what I was doing. I was very confused and feeling very insecure.

Lady Gaga: I didn't do it with other people. I did it all alone in my apartment, and I wrote music. And you know what? I regret every line I ever did. So to any of the little sweethearts that are listening, don't touch it. It's the devil.

Howard: There was a period of time where you were a songwriter for other people. And the famous story is that Britney Spears— which song did you write that she turned down?

Lady Gaga: A couple. I did one for her that she used called "Quicksand." And then I wrote "Telephone" for her.

Howard: Right, and she didn't record it.

Lady Gaga: Oh, she did record it.

Howard: But she didn't put it out on an album?

Lady Gaga: No.

Howard: And so when you are writing for other people, did it kill you inside because you probably said, "These are really good songs. I should be doing it"?

Lady Gaga: Hell no. Freaking Britney Spears singing my record, are you kidding? I was doing backflips and ordering drinks.

Howard: Do you ever feel almost, I'm gonna say the word *idiotic*, when you write a song, because of some of the thoughts that you might have? You go, "How could I write a song about a telephone?" or "How could I write a song about paparazzi?" Do you ever sit down and wonder, "Is this cool or not?"

Lady Gaga: I learn a lot about myself through my music. Sometimes I write shit and I'm like, "What the hell was I going through *that* day?"

Howard: What is the first song you ever wrote? I know I asked you about when you were four years old, but I'm talking about the first song you wrote?

Lady Gaga: That's called "To Love Again." I was thirteen.

Howard: Thirteen, and you're writing about love.

Lady Gaga: What the hell did I know?

Howard: Maybe you did know something. Did you have a boyfriend at thirteen?

Lady Gaga: No, I think I had a crush on a camp counselor.

> 66 **YOU SHOULD WAIT AS LONG AS YOU CAN TO HAVE SEX, BECAUSE AS A WOMAN YOU DON'T EVEN BEGIN TO ENJOY IT UNTIL YOUR MIDTWENTIES. WHEN YOU'RE SEVENTEEN, YOU DON'T EVEN KNOW HOW TO OPERATE WHAT'S GOING ON DOWN THERE.**

Howard: What age were you when you started having sex?

Lady Gaga: Actually, it wasn't until I was seventeen.

Howard: Was it a bad experience, your first sexual experience?

Lady Gaga: Well, it wasn't great. I mean, you know, in hindsight things get a lot better. I will say that, you know I got a lot of young fans. So I love you and I respect the show and I know you want to talk about sex and cocaine and all that, but the truth is I don't want anyone doing drugs, (a). And (b), honestly, you should wait as long as you can to have sex, because as a woman you don't even begin to enjoy it until your midtwenties. When you're seventeen, you don't even know how to operate what's going on down there, and you shouldn't try.

Howard: I admire what you're saying and I happen to agree with that. I have three daughters, so I really hope that they don't become promiscuous, because you can really get your heart broken.

Lady Gaga: But even if you're not being

promiscuous and you're just a kid with a boyfriend, I still think it's way too young. There's no way to possibly understand what it means to be fully intimate with someone at that age.

Howard: But you experimented with women, didn't you?

Lady Gaga: Yeah, that was college—which was brief.

Howard: You went to Tisch [School of the Arts], right?

Lady Gaga: Yeah.

Howard: NYU. And you dropped out after a semester?

Lady Gaga: I want to say I made it through the whole year, but I don't think so.

Howard: And that was because you said, "This is a waste of time. I'm more talented than most of the people here."

Lady Gaga: I was kind of an asshole in school. I was the girl in class who, you know, the middle-aged, white male teacher was giving us a list of books that we were to read, and I would raise my hand and be like, "How come there's no African-American writers? Why isn't there anything by anyone here who's gay?" I was kind of that annoying, pain-in-the-ass girl in class with her hand up who is trying to answer every single question and was trying to make the teacher look bad. It made me upset when I felt there was a biased approach to the way I was being educated.

Howard: Your parents must have been beside themselves when you dropped out of Tisch.

Lady Gaga: When they took me out to dinner on my nineteenth birthday, I'll never forget it, my mother was like, "Happy Birthday . . . and leaving school, what's wrong with you?!"

Howard: What gave you the strength to rebel against your parents? I'm a mama's boy. If my mother started yelling at me and telling me I had to stay in college, I would've just shit my pants.

Lady Gaga: I never saw it as rebellion. I just was like, "Mom, I don't like school." My dad said, "You've got one year to make something happen, and I'm not paying for shit." And I said, "Great, I don't want anything. One year. Got it." And I swear, this sounds crazy: exactly one year later, I got a production deal from a producer.

Howard: But did it pay you? How did you pay your bills?

Lady Gaga: I waitressed. I worked at a music publishing company for nothing, but I would run around in my outfits and leave my demos under people's doors.

Howard: I bet you met a lot of people who are still in that same position, waiting to make it. How do you know when you really have it?

Lady Gaga: You know you really have it when you've got the nerve. The worst thing that can happen is, I used to hang out with buddies in the bar, and I'd say, "How's everything going?" And they'd say, "Oh, I'm in a band." And I'd say, "Oh, when is your next show?" And they'd say, "We haven't played yet." Or, "You got any songs?" "Oh, we're still working on them." That fear of rejection—you never really go anywhere. And I was never afraid of being rejected. I sort of got off on it, like, "Oh yeah, you think I can't do it? I'll fucking show you. Me and my high heels are going to walk all over this stage and bring in people."

Howard: Well, you're right, you can't be sort of theoretically thinking about this career. You've got to go tackle it. But what I'm saying is, it's so sad that there are so many people—I'm sure you met a million of them—who have absolutely no talent and yet they're living the lifestyle and they're waiting for this big break. And you know it's never going to come.

Lady Gaga: I don't necessarily agree with that. I think talent is subjective. I think that once you harness what you're good at, you can create yourself. But also, you don't know how many times I have seen as a songwriter such talented singers get the biggest heads in the world after recording in one studio session with one big producer, and they go nowhere because they think that they deserve or are entitled to a certain lifestyle because they have a record deal. You know Jimmy Iovine, who I love more than anything, he's my boss. And Vince Herbert, who's my other boss—their favorite and least favorite thing about me is I ask them to pick me up, and they're like, "I don't even want to go to your neighborhood."

Howard: Do they get any input when you decide you're going to come out with a record?

Lady Gaga: Of course. It's Jimmy Iovine!

Howard: So?

Lady Gaga: He produced Fleetwood Mac.

Howard: But he also produced bombs too.

Lady Gaga: Well, at the end of the day, I wrote all the music myself. Always. I coproduce everything I do. I make it. I am constantly researching what's happening in the dance community.

Howard: How do you research that? Do you go to clubs like constantly and see what kids are doing?

Lady Gaga: I got a lot of friends that are DJs, and we just talk and I listen to music. And it's also working with different technology. There's lots of new things that are coming out.

Howard: Do you feel competitive, though? Do you hear certain records and then go, "Oh, man, I should've made that record. I can't stand this. Why didn't I think of that?" Can music become such a job that it fills you with dread?

Lady Gaga: No, it's more dreadful when people rip you apart. But at the end of the day, there's a really very big difference: what people say about you and what people actually do about you.

Howard: Does it rip you apart because you're saying, "I'm not even into the money in this thing. I genuinely want to make people feel good"?

Lady Gaga: Hell fucking yeah. My favorite is when people go, "Oh, it's not

> ## "IT IS LIKE SPREADING MY LEGS AND TAKING A PHOTOGRAPH OF MY VAGINA AND PUTTING IT ON THE INTERNET AND ASKING PEOPLE WHAT THEY THINK. THAT IS WHAT PUTTING OUT A RECORD IS LIKE.

personal." And I'm like, "How the hell is it not personal? I spent two years of my life putting everything into this."

Howard: Is putting out a new record like putting out a movie in that you sit there and wait for the box-office returns?

Lady Gaga: It is like spreading my legs and taking a photograph of my vagina and putting it on the Internet and asking people what they think. That is what putting out a record is like.

Howard: Will Lady Gaga go away?

Lady Gaga: No, I'm always going to be Gaga.

Howard: Gaga might become Stefani.

Lady Gaga: Well, I am Stefani.

Howard: Your mother won't call you Gaga, or your father, right?

Lady Gaga: Yes, they do. They call me both. Well, Gaga is also when they're mad at me. "Okay, Gaga," you know?

Howard: When did that transition occur, that your parents bought into Gaga as opposed to Stefani?

Lady Gaga: It wasn't a buy-in as much as they were so happy that I had finally found a happy place in my life. Because I was so depressed. And now my mother calls me Gaga. It's funny, when my dad had his heart surgery, that was one of the first times that I hadn't really cared about how I looked. And I remember I just wore his sweater for two weeks. I wore his sweater and some jeans and some sneakers. I was crying, no makeup, and everyone in the hospital knew it was me. Everybody. And I just remember my dad, the first fucking thing he said to me. He opened his eyes, and he was trying to get the tube out. They took the tube out, and the *first* thing he said to me is, "You look like fucking hell. What is wrong with you? Go home and put a wig on and some makeup and come back when you look like yourself."

Howard: It almost sounds like you're describing a transgender person when they finally figure out that they're a man trapped in a woman's body or something. You're saying you realized, "The only way I'm going to be happy is to become this person that I really want to be."

Lady Gaga: That I've always wanted to be.

Michael J. Fox

SEPTEMBER 25, 2013

When I was growing up, I assumed there was order to existence and that life wasn't purely random. I thought if I did everything right—if I was a good boy, listened to my parents, ate my vegetables, prayed to the Lord above—things were guaranteed to turn out well. I carried this magical thinking into adulthood. Sadly, this type of outlook left me unprepared with how to deal with adversity. When bad things happened to me, it didn't compute. When life kicked me in the teeth, I didn't know how to cope.

Probably that's why I developed such intense obsessive-compulsive disorder. I couldn't accept the chaos of life. I needed to feel like I had some measure of control. If I only touched a doorknob so many times then things would be okay. So often I'd think, "This isn't the way my life is supposed to go." What I learned after years of therapy is that there is no such thing as "supposed to" in life. We are not entitled to a pain-free existence.

Michael J. Fox's story is proof that it doesn't matter who you are, life can go haywire. He has one of the most remarkable success stories in the entertainment business: a Canadian kid who drops out of school, heads to LA to become an actor, and winds up one of the biggest stars of his generation. He effortlessly moved between television and film three decades before it was an acceptable trend in Hollywood. He racked up all kinds of awards. He was on top of the world. Then *wham*—he got diagnosed with Parkinson's disease.

Before Michael came into the studio that day, I assumed that he had it all together—that he was this poster boy for positivity, this relentless optimist who had quickly accepted his fate and chose to make lemonade out of lemons. The reality, as Michael explains here, is much more complicated. He doesn't sugarcoat things. He initially struggled to deal with his diagnosis, turning to alcohol and as a result nearly losing his wife, Tracy. In describing the terror of his illness, he uses the analogy of being stuck in the middle of the road with cement feet as a speeding bus approaches.

But he persevered. That's the lesson here. No matter what happens to you in life, the important thing is that you find a way to move forward. It may not be a straight path. Like Michael, you might make some mistakes. That's okay. You keep trying. Michael makes it clear that's not always easy. Having a glass-half-full outlook doesn't come naturally. He works hard at it. It's a choice he makes every day. He's even managed to keep a dark sense of humor as he talks about the benefits of masturbating with Parkinson's.

This interview shows Michael J. Fox in a way I had never seen him before. Our society has propped him up as this beacon of inspiration. He's become a kind of superhero. Really, though, he's just a regular guy doing his best to get through each day. He is so relatable, which makes him even more inspiring.

I've wondered: If the same thing happened to me, could I be as graceful and accepting? I don't think so. Whenever you're feeling like life is too much to handle, just open up this book and turn to this interview.

Howard: I would imagine most people don't even know how to react when they're in the room with you. Do people start acting like, "I'm so sorry. I'm so sad"?

Michael: People who don't know me do. But people that know me know I'm pathetic for a million other reasons.

Howard: People should've been sorry before you got Parkinson's.

Michael: Yeah, they really should have been.

Howard: You dropped out of school when you were in the eleventh grade. That's sort of badass to do something like that.

Michael: My father was really cool. He was a military guy and he was in the police department for a while. He was a no-nonsense guy. He was a no-BS guy. He thought acting in show business was really for weirdos and fairies. When I went to him and I said, "I want to drop out of school, and move to the States, and be an actor," he really surprised me. He just looked at me and said, "Well, if you want to be a lumberjack, go to the goddamn forest." He drove me down.

Howard: I thought you were from a showbiz family, because it seemed to me you came on the scene really young.

Michael: When we started *Family Ties*, I was twenty, but I'd moved down to the States [from Canada] at eighteen and I'd gone through three years of the kind of requisite eating plain macaroni and ducking the landlord and all that stuff.

Howard: When you got the job on *Family Ties*, it was nothing short of a miracle, right? Because Brandon Tartikoff, who was the head of NBC, said he didn't want you. You were too short. You didn't look right. This is what I heard—that you didn't look right with the cast.

Michael: His line was to Gary Goldberg, who produced it. Gary was defending me after hating me. Gary hated me at first. Then I got back in with him, and he became my champion. He wanted Matthew Broderick, and Matthew wasn't available. That was the story of my life back then. I found out about things after Matthew turned them down.

Howard: Is that debilitating as an actor,

when you find out the role you got was just turned down by a bunch of other people? Don't you want to feel special, like you were the only guy who could play that role? Or you didn't care?

Michael: As long as the checks clear.

Howard: Really?

Michael: Yeah, it didn't bother me too much because I was just a punk up-and-coming kid. When Gary was fighting for me with Brandon, Brandon didn't want to hire me. He wanted to fire me after the pilot, and he said, "I can't see this kid on a lunch box." Then later on, after *Back to the Future* hit, I had a lunch box made with my picture on it.

Howard: You sent him one?

Michael: I wrote, "Here's for you to put your crow in." He was really sweet. He kept it on his desk for the rest of his life.

Howard: After a success like *Back to the Future*—it's a franchise picture, and at that point in your life when that movie comes out and it's huge, everyone in Hollywood probably wanted you for films. Most people would've done a really scummy thing and split the TV show.

Michael: It never occurred to me because Gary was just so good to me.

Howard: I remember even thinking like, "What the hell's he still doing on that show? He could be in any movie he wants."

Michael: I had to delay running my film career into the ground.

Howard: What do you mean? Did you run

your film career into the ground? Do you think you played it wrong?

Michael: What happened was, it got all muddied by my diagnosis. I panicked and signed a three-picture deal and then didn't have a choice of movies I wanted to do.

Howard: Were you angry when you first got your diagnosis? Like, I would be, "This is not supposed to happen to me. I'm on a major roll in my career. I've got a great wife. I've got a family. This just doesn't happen to me."

Michael: I had that reaction. I had that, like, "Let me come back in the room and deal with the fact that I'm Michael Fox and this isn't happening to me—that I'm not an eighty-five-year-old man." The way [the doctor] put it too when I was diagnosed—he told me I had Parkinson's. I'm dealing with that. And then he said, "But don't worry, you have another ten good years left to work." I was twenty-nine years old. That was twentysomething years ago.

Howard: You mean you got the diagnosis of Parkinson's, you're told you have ten good years, and so you said to yourself, "Shit, I better do as many movies as I can right now and pack it in."

Michael: Yeah. And then I realized that that wasn't the best strategy. But I was never one of those guys that, like, people talk about their career. I was an actor. I was a schmuck. It was like, if I was smart, I wouldn't be telling Mallory [in *Family Ties*] to get off the phone.

Howard: In a way, look, we all don't know

〃〃〃

❝ HE SAID, "BUT DON'T WORRY, YOU HAVE ANOTHER TEN GOOD YEARS LEFT TO WORK." I WAS TWENTY-NINE YEARS OLD.

〃〃〃

how much time we're going to have with anything, so the Parkinson's forced you to make a bunch of quick decisions. "I'll grab everything I can" at that point, because of the position you were in. You probably could've taken your time and picked shows and a bunch of different things. I remember a couple of really good movies after *Back to the Future*.

Michael: Yeah, there were some good movies. It was a strange time because, like I said, the guy told me I had ten years left to work, and I didn't know—

Howard: What a terrible thing to go through.

Michael: An analogy I always make is it's like being stuck in the middle of the road with cement feet and a bus is coming. You don't know when it's coming. You can hear it but you don't know when it'll be there and you don't know how hard it will hit. Eventually, over time, I realized it's stupid to be waiting for that—that I should just go on with my life.

Howard: Did you go into therapy right away? I'm talking about psychotherapy.

Michael: A couple years later.

Howard: You waited a couple of years.

Michael: Yeah, my first reaction to it was to start drinking heavily.

Howard: Did you? What's heavily?

Michael: I used to drink to party, but now I was drinking alone and just drinking to just not—

Howard: Every day?

Michael: Every day.

Howard: You were self-medicating?

Michael: Yeah. Then I quit that and—

Howard: How did you quit? Did you go to AA?

Michael: Yeah.

Howard: Someone said to you, "Look, it's getting out of control."

Michael: Yeah.

Howard: You probably were like, "Well, who the fuck cares? I've got Parkinson's and my career is—"

Michael: Well, no. I had a young son and I was married and I didn't want to screw that up. Then once I did that, it was about a year of a knife fight in the closet, where I just didn't have my tools to deal with it. Then after that, I went to therapy, and it all started to get really clear to me.

Howard: What did you learn in therapy? How did it get clear? Like, "Hey, this isn't a death sentence and I can have a life"?

Michael: Just take one day at a time—just, whatever happens, don't project. The other [thing] is—when you said, do people get all . . . they don't know how to act. After a while, I figured that it doesn't matter. I'm just who I am.

Howard: Were you embarrassed at first? Like, when you couldn't control your body—when you couldn't control, let's say, your hand shaking or something. Were you embarrassed or ashamed?

Michael: No, I was just frustrated.

Howard: So you decide, "That's it, I can't act anymore." You walked away from show business. Was that torture for you? Because you love acting.

Michael: I just felt helpless. It just felt unfair in a way. I don't know. It's hard to explain.

Howard: Helplessness is the worst feeling ever.

Michael: Yeah.

Howard: We're under some sort of magical illusion that we're not helpless. Then it happens, and you go, "I'm in a situation where I'm useless. I can't do anything about it."

Michael: That's when it happens. That's when it gets better, because then you realize, "I don't have any control over this, and so fuck it—just be happy for what's going on." Then things started to really turn the other way. My marriage got great, and I started to—

Howard: Why did your marriage get great? Because all of a sudden you realized, "Wow, this person really has my back. She's with me"? Like, "I really appreciate her for maybe the first time."

Michael: Yeah, exactly.

Robin: Did you expect that she was

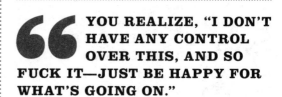

going to take off the moment there was trouble?

Michael: I didn't know, but she said she was in. Then I didn't believe that she was in, and then it became clear to me that she was definitely in. People have this image of her that she's like this rock. She's not this stoic champion. She's like this cool chick who could've bolted, but she didn't.

Howard: I think that's what people don't get about relationships, especially guys in Hollywood. "Oh yeah, there's tons of women out there. I'm trading in," and all this. If you have a woman who really cares about you and loves you, there's nothing better than that.

Michael: Laughs at your jokes the nineteenth time around. I'd make the same joke, and Tracy says I'm on a loop and it's getting shorter.

Howard: How's this affected your kids, when they saw you going through this? Because you're sitting at home going, "Shit, I'm a major fucking actor, and now I'm like in self-retirement and I'm a young guy."

Michael: My son was really young when I was diagnosed. My twin daughters, who

> **IF YOU ASKED MY KIDS TO DESCRIBE ME, I THINK ONE OF THE LAST THINGS THEY'D SAY WAS I HAD PARKINSON'S.**

are now eighteen, when they were born that was when I was on the upswing, when I was feeling good. It was so cool, because that was one of the big decisions with Tracy and I was whether to have more kids. Then we had more kids and it turned out to be twins, and it was just like this great affirmation. They've grown up with it their whole lives. I have an eleven-year-old, and so I'm just shaky Dad.

Howard: They just know you that way.

Michael: If you asked my kids to describe me, I think one of the last things they'd say was I had Parkinson's.

Howard: Is it physically painful, or is it just like—I don't know much about the disease, honestly.

Michael: It's not physically painful itself. If I have a rough day and I'm contorting into strange positions, after a while my muscles kind of complain.

Howard: Does Parkinson's make reading really difficult when you have to read your script every week?

Michael: It makes reading the newspaper hard in the morning. It's, like, rattling, but you get used to it.

Howard: Sex still good?

Michael: Sex is great.

Howard: That doesn't ever get affected?

Michael: No. I would say the only thing about sex is deciding who's going to be the agent of motion.

Howard: Yeah, who's moving faster. But you get some new moves, I guess.

Michael: She's like, "Do that again." I'm like, "I *can't* do it again."

Howard: That was spontaneous.

Michael: That just happened.

Howard: A couple of people want to talk to you real quick. Scott, go ahead.

Scott: [*on the phone*] Hey, Howard, I was recently diagnosed with Parkinson's, and I tell everybody the best part about Parkinson's is you ain't gotta try to whack off. It just does it for you.

Howard: Is that true, when you beat off—

Michael: You just gotta stand, and forget it.

Howard: It's probably like being with a woman. It's like you can't control your own masturbation.

Michael: It's like a bad hand job.

Howard: Is that really true?

Michael: Yeah.

Howard: When you masturbate, what, your hand just goes out of control?

Michael: Well, I don't do it with the frequency I did as a younger man. But, yeah, it just goes. It's like brushing your teeth. You just kind of lock into position, then it goes.

Howard: I heard a beautiful story that Muhammad Ali called you personally.

Michael: It was about ten, fifteen years ago. He said, "Now that you're in the fight, we'll win." It was just an amazing moment.

Howard: I would cry. That story gives me the chills.

Michael: I did cry. He is amazing. I have met him and been with him many times since. He's really in rough shape, man, but—

Howard: He is. Don't you think he got his Parkinson's from the fight game?

Michael: I'm sure that getting punched in the head by Joe Frazier can't be good for you.

Howard: No.

Michael: That's the thing. I personally don't wonder what caused that. It doesn't serve me. I got other stuff to do.

Howard: I get into the blame game with all my stuff. All my personal shit that doesn't go right in my life, I have to find something to blame because I think it gives me control.

Michael: Yeah, and it's a big lesson for you—like I said before, realizing I'm along for the ride. The thing is to make the best out of it.

And Now a Word from Our President . . .

JANUARY 7, 2004

(12 years, 10 months, and 1 day until the election)

Howard: You don't drink?

Donald: No.

Robin: Not at all?

Donald: No. Never had a drink. That's one of my good things. Never had a drink, and I never had a cigarette. Other than that, I'm a disaster.

Howard: No glass of alcohol? Never? Wine?

Donald: Never had a drink or glass of alcohol.

Artie: No weed or anything like that? No dope?

Donald: I never had any of that.

" I'VE BEEN VERY FAITHFUL.

Howard: No hillbilly heroin?

Donald: It was always women, Howard. For me, it was always women. . . .

Howard: So you're telling me, you haven't banged any other chicks since taking up with Melania?

Donald: No. I've been very faithful.

Howard: Really?

Donald: Yes.

Howard: I know you're lying. . . . How much money do you make a day?

Donald: Hey, look, I'm the biggest developer in New York by far.

Howard: You think you're worth two billion right now, right? Or more?

Donald: Honestly?

Howard: Honestly.

Donald: Much more. Honestly, much more.

Larry David

JANUARY 7, 2015

I never watched *Curb Your Enthusiasm*. I don't know why. I just never got around to it. But everyone kept telling me, "You have to watch it. This is you. You guys have a lot in common. You and Larry David are basically the same guy." People kept telling me that if we met each other, we'd be best friends.

What interested me most about him was the same thing that intrigued me about Sia: How could Larry be so much a part of *Seinfeld* and not be one of the actors, not get that ego-boosting, black hole–filling dose of fame? He didn't want to be a performer. He wasn't ready at that point. He felt more comfortable behind the scenes. Then finally, with *Curb,* he stepped in front of the camera.

With all the advance buildup from everyone in my world, there was pressure to form this intense bond between the two of us, to make some magical connection. Earlier in my career, I would have let that get to me. I would have been sucked into what everyone was saying and been preoccupied with meeting their expectations. They had such high hopes for this great meeting of similar minds. What if they were wrong? What if Larry hated me? As I've gotten older, I've learned to ignore this type of noise. I'm able to identify that external pressure and let go of it. As a result, Larry and I had a really good conversation.

Howard: Everyone has said to me for years, "How could you not have Larry David on?" Well, it's not up to me. It's up to Larry David. Let me look at you. Wow. Look at that. You look good. Sit on the couch. You know how many strippers have sat on that couch? This means you've arrived when you sit on that couch.

Larry: I can't even believe I'm here.

Howard: People always say to me, "You and Larry should be friends. You and Larry are the same guy."

Larry: I get the same thing.

Howard: But, Larry, argue why we shouldn't be friends. I am sure there are reasons.

Larry: Well, because we're both deep down despicable people.

Howard: Are you? You're a legendarily miserable guy.

Larry: By the way, that's really not true.

Howard: It's not? You're happy?

Larry: I have a very good disposition, I think.

Howard: So why do you get that reputation? I think I know what it is. The story goes, third season of *Seinfeld*—you're, of course, the co-creator of *Seinfeld*. Every reason in the world to be happy. The show is now successful. It's getting more and more notoriety. And they come to you and they say, "Larry, the show has been renewed for a third season." And you were in tears. It was too much pressure for you, right?

Larry: It's like a relationship. I just didn't think I could keep it up. Not in the erectile sense, but—

Howard: What was the pressure? Was it an internal thing where you said, "The show is so important to people. I don't want to disappoint them." Was that the pressure?

Larry: I always felt that, well, last year was so good, how am I going to top it?

Howard: But when you achieve a certain amount of fame and money and all of this stuff, isn't the pressure removed? Or it doesn't matter how much money or success you have? In other words, that pressure is coming from where? You're trying to prove yourself to your parents?

Larry: I'm trying to impress myself, I think.

Howard: And do you think that these ideas that you have, that everyone seems to respond to, that are so universal, do you worry they're just going to run out? Is that it?

Larry: You know, Howard, it's like when I drove a cab. I'd drop off a fare. I'd start driving around. "Where's the next one? There's nobody on the street!" And I'd be racing five other cabs down Second Avenue, and then somebody would raise their arm and eight guys would cut me off.

Howard: Wouldn't show business be the worst kind of career for a guy like you? That kind of lifestyle, where you don't know where your next job is coming from, you don't know where your next idea is coming from—you needed something more steady.

Larry: That's what my mother said many times. I remember when I was a chauffeur. I was working for a car service. This guy I knew from college was walking down the street, and I'm leaning against my limo with my hat on. I had the hat on. It's four years out of college now, and I'm driving a fucking limousine. And I see this guy, and I go, "Oh God."

Howard: And he probably has a good job.

Larry: Oh, he was in the nattiest-looking suit, beautiful briefcase, coiffed hair.

Howard: That killed me in the early days of radio. All my friends had great jobs, and I'd be making $96 a week. I was sitting there like, "Oh you're such a fucking loser." Let's call that guy now, let him look at your bank account. When you take a car service today, are you very sympatico with the driver?

Larry: I always say, "You know, I used to drive."

Howard: And they like that.

Larry: Oh God, they love that.

Howard: Because it's like, "Wow, okay, maybe there's hope for me."

Larry: And then I can tell him how to go and he doesn't get offended.

Howard: Were you particularly good at driving?

Larry: Driving a cab and a limo in New York made me a fantastic driver. It's the only thing in life I really have any confidence in, my ability in driving.

Howard: And you have a great sense of direction.

Larry: No, I don't have a good sense of direction.

Howard: So when someone would get in your cab, would you drive them around till you found something?

Larry: It was trial and error.

Howard: Would people yell at you?

Larry: Yes, yes, yes.

Howard: And does all of this become fodder as a writer? Are all of these experiences almost necessary to become a great comedy writer?

Larry: I don't know if they're necessary, but they're helpful.

Howard: Right, because as we look at *Seinfeld* or *Curb Your Enthusiasm*, most of the episodes are really from your everyday life. When we look at *Seinfeld* and we see the episode where you—there was one episode where George has mouthed off to his boss, and Kramer says to him, "Go back to work. Act like it never happened." Now, when you were a writer at *Saturday Night Live*, you mouthed off to Dick Ebersol, didn't you?

Larry: Yes.

Howard: He was the guy in charge. It wasn't Lorne Michaels. You were hired as a writer. You were very discouraged. It's hard to believe, but none of your scripts were ever chosen. You were a failure at *Saturday Night Live*.

Larry: Total, total failure.

Howard: And you were there during that legendary season where it was Billy Crystal and Martin Short. I mean, what a great season. I thought it was one of their best seasons. Christopher Guest, Julia Louis-Dreyfus. All-star cast. You're hired as a writer. Big money. You hadn't been making a lot of money. All of a sudden, you get in there, within five weeks you're completely irritated and disgusted with the job, right?

Larry: Yes.

Howard: Because they didn't recognize your genius. Am I correct?

Larry: My sketches would do very well at the read-through, and then they would invariably get cut, week after week after week. I thought they were funny. They got good laughs from everybody, and the writers really liked them.

Howard: It's embarrassing.

Larry: Yeah. And then one night,

> **"I SAID, "THIS FUCKING SHOW STINKS! IT STINKS! IT'S SHIT! I'M DONE! I'M GONE! FUCK THIS, I'M OUT!"**

before the show, another sketch of mine was cut, at 11:25, five minutes before the show was to start. I'd had enough. So Dick was sitting in the chair—you know, that director's chair—and he had headphones on, and I marched over to him. I said, "This fucking show stinks! It stinks! It's shit! I'm done! I'm gone! Fuck this, I'm out!"

Howard: Was this because you wanted the whole cast to hear? Because you were kind of embarrassed your stuff was getting cut? You wanted to really make a statement.

Larry: I was going with how I was feeling.

Howard: He must have been furious. It's five minutes before showtime. It's probably the worst time you could have picked to do this.

Larry: Honestly, he didn't pay much attention to it at all. He just looked at me and he nodded.

Howard: And that was it. You stormed out.

Larry: I stormed out.

Howard: So you go home.

Larry: I'm walking home in the freezing cold. Couldn't get a cab, walking home. And I'm starting to compute how much money I just cost myself.

Howard: Because you had a year contract.

Larry: Yeah.

Howard: And so the real Kramer—

Larry: My next-door neighbor, yeah.

Howard: Kenny Kramer. He said this to you: "Hey, Larry, what are you worried about? Go back on Monday, and pretend like it didn't happen."

Larry: Exactly.

Howard: And you did that.

Larry: I did. There's a writers' meeting every Monday morning, and I walk into the meeting. The writers had heard the outburst. They didn't know what was going on. And I sat down. [Dick] would go around, and he would ask everyone what they were working on for the week. I was about the fifth one on the couch. And then he got to me, and I said, "Well, I'm thinking about doing a circus sketch." And nothing!

Howard: And you had the job.

Larry: I had the job.

Howard: And that was such a profound experience that when you were writing *Seinfeld*, that stayed with you and you said that would make an excellent episode.

Larry: Oh, for sure, yeah. Now, "The Contest," that was in my notebook for three years.

Howard: You're referring, of course, to the masturbation contest on *Seinfeld*. That was something you jotted down, and said, "One day I'm going to make an episode of this." That happened in your real life.

Larry: Yes, but I wouldn't have even mentioned it to Jerry, because I thought it was so out of the question that he would ever want to do that show. I never even brought it up.

Howard: When you brought the script to the network, did they read this thing and go, "Fuck you, there's no way we're putting this on the air"?

Larry: Well, here's the thing. We had a board with all the upcoming shows on it, and the network after read-throughs would come in and go, "What's that one? What's that one?" And so this one, I said, "I'm not even putting it on the board." I don't want them to ask about it, because I knew that it was something pretty special. And then I had worked myself up into another lather, where I'm saying, "Okay, if they don't do the show, I'm quitting."

Howard: You were always quitting.

Larry: Yes, always quitting.

Howard: You're always sabotaging. Here's the greatest gig of all time, and you're going to sabotage it. When you would threaten to quit, would Jerry look at you and say, "Larry, I'm in love with you. I need you. The two of us together are an unbelievable team. Please stop."

Larry: He would say, "Don't worry. We'll work it out."

Howard: He was a calming influence.

Larry: Yeah.

Howard: Do you love Jerry?

Larry: Yes.

Howard: Whose idea was Jason Alexander, by the way? Was it yours?

Larry: He auditioned in New York, on tape, with a casting director.

Howard: Did you know right away when you saw the tape that it was him, or did you need more?

Larry: I knew in ten seconds.

Howard: Even though physically he doesn't look like you.

Larry: No, I just knew. I said to Jerry, "There he is." ✦

Howard: The first big job for you—and this was a show I really liked—was the show *Fridays*, which was ABC's answer to *Saturday Night Live*. You got a job as a writer on that, right? Before the *Saturday Night Live* job.

Larry: Writer and performer.

Howard: So you're on *Fridays*, and that's where you meet Michael Richards.

Larry: Yes.

Howard: Your career almost seems like *The Wizard of Oz*. Like you're Dorothy. You go to *Fridays*, you meet Michael Richards. You go to *Saturday Night Live*, you meet Julia Louis-Dreyfus. You were a stand-up comic, you meet Jerry Seinfeld. It doesn't seem like a master plan, but when you look back on it, you met all the right people. And when you finally hook up with Jerry and you get this *Jerry Seinfeld Chronicles* to do, is that when you say, "Oh, Julia Louis-Dreyfus would be good for this. Michael Richards would be good for this." Were those your casting ideas?

✦ **For more on this from Jason Alexander, turn to page 544.**

Larry: Yeah. Jerry was a huge Michael Richards fan. So he was talked about immediately. Julia, I remember, we were casting for Elaine, and I watched a few women, and then all of a sudden I thought, "Julia!" I mentioned it to Jerry, and she came in and just had a meeting with Jerry, and then she had the part.

Howard: They hit it off.

Larry: Yeah.

Howard: Did you think it was kismet right away when you started writing with Jerry? When you started working on this TV show, did you say to yourself, "We're onto something great," or did you just think, "Mmm, I don't know"?

Larry: I remember going out to dinner with him after maybe three shows had aired, and I remember saying to him, "I can't believe they're letting us do this. How are they letting us do this?" It seemed crazy.

Howard: Right. And Jerry was the calming influence out of the two, because you're like the guy who is saying, "This is going to end any time," or "I've got to end this, there's too much pressure."

Larry: I wanted it to end.

> ❝ I REMEMBER SAYING TO HIM, "I CAN'T BELIEVE THEY'RE LETTING US DO THIS. HOW ARE THEY LETTING US DO THIS?"

Howard: When you look back on it now, do you say to yourself, "Why did I go through so much angst? Couldn't I have treated this an entirely different way and enjoyed it somehow?"

Larry: If only. If only I could be that person.

Howard: 'Cause I always go through a lot of angst, and then after I leave something, or I get fired, I go, "I could have been so much calmer. Why did I fucking work myself up so much?" It's weird.

Larry: Yeah, I know. Same thing with this interview today. I was anxious about coming in. I had never been here before. For what? Nothing.

Howard: It's legendary how much you and Jerry have made. You've made a fortune. And you get embarrassed by that. You don't like to talk money.

Larry: Howard, honest to God, first of all, the reports about how much money I have are so insane.

Howard: But it's hundreds of millions of dollars.

Larry: No, Howard, it's ridiculous.

Howard: Really?

Larry: Yes.

Howard: Clear this up for me.

Larry: Okay, I'm going to, okay? I'm not going to give you specific numbers—

Howard: You're going to have to bring your accountant in.

Larry: But, Howard, it's ridiculous. And it's embarrassing because it's so untrue. First of all, when I was married, half of it went in the divorce.

Howard: Did that kill you to write that check?

Larry: No.

Howard: Why not, though? Because that money represented the culmination of driving a limo, driving a car, fucking *Saturday Night Live*, *Fridays* . . . I mean, you beat the odds. It's a billion to one to have success like that on network TV. Then you gotta write a check for half your money.

Larry: Well, first of all, because it didn't affect my life in any way. There's nothing I'm going to do differently if I had that money or if I didn't have the money. And whatever will be left goes to my kids. She'll have that to leave them as well. What's the difference?

Howard: So you were okay with it.

Larry: And she had to put up with me. Let her enjoy herself.

Howard: Anybody who's put up with you, they deserve a lot of money. Are you a good husband or a bad husband? Are you husband material?

Larry: No.

Howard: You are not.

Larry: No. I'm not husband material. I'm not boyfriend material.

Howard: Is it because to be a comic you have to be so self-consumed, you need so much time to yourself that how could you even devote attention to people?

" I'M NOT HUSBAND MATERIAL. I'M NOT BOYFRIEND MATERIAL.

Larry: I'd like to think that it's the work. That's a good thing to say, but . . .

Howard: Right, but it's just who you are. Were you able to be a good father, or was it tough for you?

Larry: I'm much better at being a father since they became teenagers. When they were very little, I had trouble getting on the floor.

Howard: Did you go into therapy at all to be a better parent?

Larry: No. But I think I was a good dad. I wasn't a great dad. The great dad . . . I can't stand the great dad.

Howard: Oh, they're horrible.

Larry: They're not even friends with you anymore. They're so busy they don't have time to get a cup of coffee. I can't stand them. Go. Go be with your kid. Who gives a shit. So the great dads, they renounce their lives.

Howard: They become like different people. Aliens.

Larry: They bother me, the great dads.

Howard: Do you socialize with Jerry, or is that over? Why do I feel like you guys are at odds maybe?

Larry: No, we're not at odds at all. I'm seeing him on Sunday.

Howard: What are you going to be doing? Are you just going to, like, go to lunch?

Larry: Yeah, we'll go to lunch.

Howard: You're gonna go to lunch. You gonna go to a diner?

Larry: I don't know where we'll go.

Howard: You're going to meet him somewhere and have lunch. And you'll sit there and talk. Who will pay? It will probably be you, won't it?

Larry: I will definitely try.

Howard: Who is your hero? In terms of writing. You've been in two Woody Allen movies. I think of you sometimes like Woody Allen. He'll write characters, but you know they're basically Woody. Is he one of the heroes?

Larry: Certainly, yes.

Howard: Who is the biggest influence in your life?

Larry: Probably Woody Allen. But I love Mel Brooks. He was definitely an influence.

Howard: Have you hung out with him?

Larry: Yeah, when he was on the show.

Howard: Do you pinch yourself when you think about your humble beginnings and how difficult it was in the beginning? Do you say, "Oh my God, I can't believe how far I came." I'm sure you never expected to be the performer on HBO. It's pretty mind-blowing, right?

Larry: Yeah, look, it's all very nice. But in terms of the pinching, nothing seems to penetrate me.

Howard: After an incredible run on *Seinfeld*, you don't say to yourself, "Hey, that was great." In other words, you start to feel like, "What am I going to do next? How am I going to top this?" You don't revel in anything.

Larry: I don't, no. I don't bask.

Robin: Has your mother seen your success, if she is still around?

Larry: No, she's not.

Howard: Did she see your *Seinfeld* success, at least?

Larry: She did. She couldn't quite believe that it was happening, and would call me up and say—this was when the show was number one in the country—"Do they like you, Larry? Do they think you're doing a good job?"

Howard: And your dad, did he get to see your success?

Larry: He did.

Howard: And was he proud of you?

Larry: Yeah, he was.

Howard: Was that a great feeling inside, to say to your parents, "Look, I did make something of myself"?

Larry: Um, yeah, it was okay. It was better than being a failure.

Howard: One last question: When you were in the real-life masturbation contest, it seems crazy to put yourself through that. Were you a big masturbator? Was that why this occurred?

Larry: I knew I wasn't going to get out of here unscathed.

Howard: Were you at the time a big masturbator?

Larry: Let's just say I was a young man and leave it at that.

Howard: So in other words, you would masturbate. And you're sitting and talking with your friends. By the way, this is a discussion that's hard to have with your friends because that's something you don't talk about that much, even with guys.

Larry: No, but let's talk about it on the radio.

Howard: What were you masturbating to, is what I want to know. What type of porn were you into? So wait, you were with a group of guys, and you turn to each other and you say, "Hey, do you think you could stop masturbating?" And you guys make a bet.

Larry: There were only two of us.

Howard: It was you and another guy. It's word of honor. Because you really can't sit there and monitor his masturbation. Or can you? Was he your roommate? How long in real life did you go without masturbating?

Larry: He was done in two days.

Gwyneth Paltrow

There was a time when I was a celebrity publicist's worst nightmare. I saw them as the enemy. Their job was to avoid controversy. My job was to create it.

In 1996, I had John F. Kennedy Jr. on the show. He came to promote his magazine, *George*. I had just appeared on the cover. He didn't stay more than twenty-five minutes. Gary kept interrupting the interview, saying his publicist was insisting John had to leave. Eventually, she came into the studio to pull him out. "Don't give me the evil eye, publicist!" I said to her. "How often do I get a Kennedy in here?" They claimed he had to get back to his office to finish the next issue of the magazine, but I know it was my fault. If the interview had been going well, he would have stuck around. I spent the whole time badgering him about his sex life: How old was he when he lost his virginity? Did he use condoms? Was the rumor that he dated Madonna true? I even had some of the show's female staff rate him on a scale of one to ten. (He scored all tens.) Looking back, I don't blame his publicist for wanting to get him out of there. I think about that interview now and I want to jump out of a window. I could've gotten into his real psyche. I could've let him be heard. I totally blew it.

That old attack-dog mentality earned me a lot of fans. They'd say, "Howard's the man! He's such a rebel! Did you hear what he said to JFK Jr.? The guy is crazy!" Some of these same fans are now angry that I've changed my interview style. They complain that the show isn't like it used to be and that I'm just sucking up to celebrities. Clearly, they aren't really listening. If they were, they'd realize that the show is just as shocking and provocative as it's always been. The difference is in how I get there.

On terrestrial radio, my interviewing technique was like bashing someone in the face with a sledgehammer. I treated my guests as props. I was like the Joker. All I wanted to do was cause chaos. Now I take what I call the "dinner party approach." When a guest comes into the studio, I imagine they are sitting down to dinner with Beth and me, and we are going to have a casual conversation. I try to be polite and warm them up with some small talk before delving deeper and asking them more probing questions. The result is that the guest becomes so comfortable that they speak without self-censorship. I don't have to harass or interrogate them. They wind up saying outrageous things voluntarily.

This interview with Gwyneth Paltrow is a perfect example. At first glance, Gwyneth might not seem to offer much that my listeners can relate to. She grew up privileged and went to private school. Her mother was a famous actor and her father was an accomplished producer. But this interview revealed her to be incredibly down-to-earth. She shared her grief over her father's death and delved into her "conscious uncoupling" from musician Chris Martin. By the end of our talk, she was advocating for the importance of blow jobs in a marriage. If I had taken my trusty sledgehammer and right at the top of the interview said, "Tell me about your blow job technique," that would have satisfied the small faction of my audience that doesn't want me to change, but it would have sent Gwyneth running out of the studio. The dinner party approach accomplishes all of the same things while treating guests with dignity and respect.

Afterward, the reaction from the audience was immediate. The e-mails poured in. They were raving about her. Her humanity came through loud and clear. That's what I always hope to accomplish with these conversations—especially with female guests. I always want more women to do the show. That's a priority for me. A large part of my audience is male, and I'd like to try to change how some view the opposite sex. I'd like them to see a woman like Gwyneth as a human being and not just as some hot chick they watch in movies.

This interview was a major turning point for the show. Gary has said it was probably the most important milestone for his job as a booker. The walls that publicists had put up were beginning to crumble, and many were no longer reluctant to offer us their A-list clients. I don't see publicists as foes anymore. They're just trying to do a job. Some have said to me after an interview, "Wow, I've never heard my client talk like that. They mentioned details of their life I never knew." My new approach satisfies everyone. The guest feels heard, the publicist feels safe, and the audience doesn't feel cheated. They still get their fix of blow job talk.

Howard: When you walk in a room—you're stunning—do people say to you . . . are they up-front about it, or do they try to act like you're not hot? Do they get cuckoo? Like, I get cuckoo. I'm honest. I go, "Wow, you're really hot." But is that inappropriate to say to someone like you?

Gwyneth: No, I love that. Are you kidding?

Howard: You like that?

Gwyneth: Yeah, of course.

Howard: Listen, looks are important. You are a leading lady. Do you worry about that? About getting older?

Gwyneth: You know what? I really feel appreciative that I've managed to keep working, and I have an interesting life, and I don't mind my wrinkles and stuff.

Howard: But I would think, as an actress, it would make you neurotic, because your whole life you're evaluated on your looks. Especially with these magazines—"Who Wore It Better?" Do you pay attention to that stuff?

Gwyneth: I basically don't read anything.

Howard: You don't?

Gwyneth: No. I live in a media vacuum. I just feel like, in a way, a lot of the stuff is projection, and it's not really about me. I feel like the *me* in my life, with the people that I love and my kids, is one thing; and I feel like I'm sort of this cartoon character out in the world that people say things about. That way, I'm able to make the separation.

Howard: It's like living a split life.

Gwyneth: Sort of, right.

Robin: So you don't take it personally when you see these attacks or insults or—

Gwyneth: Well, I try not to see them. And to be in denial is always a good tactic. I

> **SHE HAD TO TAPE HER LINES ON THE THIGH OF THE GIRL WHOSE VAGINA SHE WAS LOOKING AT.**

don't know, it just doesn't hit me the way it used to when I was younger.

Howard: The first movie role ever offered to you was Vanilla Ice's—what was the name of the movie?

Gwyneth: *Cool as Ice.*

Howard: *Cool as Ice.* That was the first major film that you were—well, you had done TV.

Gwyneth: I had done TV. That's right.

Howard: But Vanilla Ice came to you—

Gwyneth: Well, not him personally.

Howard: Right, but the director or whoever that was. And your father said to you, "I'll never forbid you from doing something, but this I'm forbidding you from doing."

Gwyneth: Yeah. I said, "You know, Dad, I don't know what to do. I got offered the lead in a movie." I must have been nineteen years old. I was so thrilled. It was, like, $50,000, and I couldn't believe it. He read [the script], and on the first page the guy asks for my phone number. And the phone number ends in "6969." And my dad—he closed the script.

Howard: You mean that's not funny?

Gwyneth: He's like, "I forbid it."

Howard: Did you go and see *Cool as Ice* afterward, to see who took the part?

Gwyneth: I actually missed that one.

Howard: Is it true that's the biggest regret of your life? That you didn't take it?

Gwyneth: Absolutely.

Howard: Meryl Streep took the role from you. Isn't it funny? Your dad and mom did not want you to be an actress. They did everything to discourage you, right?

Gwyneth: They did.

Howard: I guess when you grow up with . . . Your mother, by the way—I confessed this earlier in the morning—I can remember masturbating to her.

Gwyneth: That's good. I hope she's listening.

Howard: She's a very attractive woman.

Gwyneth: I agree. I hope you still do. Don't stop now.

Howard: Oh, I still masturbate to her. It's just not something I want to admit.

Gwyneth: That's fine.

Howard: But seriously, Gwyneth, when you grow up around a mother who is a successful actress, it is the most intoxicating thing, isn't it? To see her up on a stage, acting—how could you not want to be an actress at that point?

Gwyneth: And she was so powerful when she was onstage. She was so, you know, kind of an extra-extra version of herself, and so beautiful and funny and creative. And she had all these costumes. And I just—

Howard: It's exciting.

Gwyneth: It was unbelievable.

Howard: My father was a radio engineer, and I saw the way he had such reverence for these announcers. How could I not want to be an announcer and get his attention?

Gwyneth: Isn't that funny?

Howard: And then your father, being a director and all of that. I mean, you always want to be Daddy's little girl, so to speak.

Gwyneth: Yeah.

Howard: How could you not want to please him? So how do they come to you and say, "Don't be an actor"?

Gwyneth: I had always said, "I wanna do it, I wanna do it." And they said, "No you don't, no you don't." My dad, he wasn't as vocal about discouraging me. He was like, "Let's see if you really want to do it, or if you're any good."

Howard: Did you do the school plays and all that stuff?

Gwyneth: I did the school plays.

Howard: But you had natural ability. When your mom would be in a play, you would memorize the lines quicker than she could.

Gwyneth: Yes. When I was, like, three years old, I could recite Chekhov and all this stuff. My mother, she really had such a hard time with lines. I remember when she was doing this TV show and she was playing a doctor. A gynecologist. And she had to tape her lines on the thigh of the girl whose vagina she was looking at.

Howard: So she's pretending to look at a girl's vagina and she has all of her lines taped down? That's what I masturbated to! Now I remember! You're bringing it all back to me. *Boogie Nights* you turned down, right?

Gwyneth: How do you know that?

Howard: I know it.

Gwyneth: What the heck?

Howard: I investigated.

Gwyneth: That was my dad, again! And my grandfather. I really wanted to do it. But I was very, very close to my grandfather, and he was pretty conservative. I just thought, "I can't be totally naked and, like, giving a b.j. on-screen. I'll kill my grandfather."

Howard: The role that you turned down in *Titanic*, the Kate Winslet role—

Gwyneth: Howard . . .

Howard: Now, that—come on—that would drive me crazy.

Gwyneth: My mother will kill me to talk about turning down movie roles.

Howard: Why will she kill you?

Gwyneth: Because she says it's not ladylike.

Howard: "Not ladylike"? But it's part of the business. And it's very hard, especially for actresses. You only get to pick certain movies, and when you're offered a movie like that—*Titanic*, James Cameron, one of the biggest movies of all time—I don't know how psychologically . . . I would be throwing a fit that I turned that down.

Gwyneth: But then you do other stuff, and—

Howard: Why did you turn that down?

Gwyneth: I'm not even sure I officially—I know the story is that I turned it down, but I think I was really in contention for it. I was maybe one of the last two.

Howard: And then you just say no? That's it? "I have a vibe that this is not gonna be . . ."

Gwyneth: I don't know. You know, I look back at some of the choices that I made, and I think like, "Why the *hell* did I say yes to that? And no to that?" But then you look at the big picture, and you think, "There's a universal lesson here." You know, you can't hold on. What good is it gonna do me?

Howard: Well, if Martin Scorsese called me to do anything, I'd say, "Hey, he's a great director, I'm doing it." And yet the Cameron Diaz role in *Gangs of New York*—

Gwyneth: I didn't turn that down!

Howard: Ah, yes you did.

Gwyneth: I did?

Howard: Yes. Yes you did. Think back.

Gwyneth: Really?

Howard: She blocked it out. Gwyneth blocked it out.

Gwyneth: I don't think that's even true, is it?

Howard: Uh, yeah. It's true.

Gwyneth: You seem to know everything.

Howard: But you did not turn down *Shallow Hal*.

Gwyneth: [*laughs*] Oh my God.

Howard: I love this film. Do you love this film?

Gwyneth: I do. I think it's very funny.

Howard: That's a tricky movie to make. Someone says, "We're gonna put you in a fat suit." But I love that theme. I love fat people getting thin. I tell ya, I'm obsessed with it. Like *The Biggest Loser*. All that stuff.

> ❝ I DEFINITELY FELL IN LOVE WITH HIM. HE WAS SO GORGEOUS AND SWEET. AND I MEAN, HE WAS BRAD PITT!

Gwyneth: [*laughs*]

Howard: Were boys hitting on you at a very young age? Were you always this hot?

Gwyneth: No, God.

Howard: When did you start getting this hot?

Gwyneth: I was definitely not hot when I was little.

Howard: Why? Were you too thin or something?

Gwyneth: I was too thin. I had braces. And in the eighties, I thought it would be great to shave the back of my head, in that sort of eighties way.

Howard: Oh, that's not a good look.

Gwyneth: It was so bad. And I was really late developing. I didn't get boobs till I was fifteen.

Howard: And then those boobs came in, and wow.

Gwyneth: [*laughs*]

Howard: So at fifteen, you start getting hot. And you had some acting roles when you were a little kid. Your dad would put you in a little something here and there.

Gwyneth: Yeah, like a walk-on type of thing.

Howard: But then your godfather, Steven Spielberg—which is not a bad deal—Steven Spielberg puts you in *Hook*.

Gwyneth: Yes.

Howard: And so, you get to be in that movie. But the first big movie you get is *Seven*, right?

Gwyneth: No, the first big movie that I got was—it didn't make a lot of money, so it wasn't a big movie in that sense—but for me at the time, it was a movie called *Flesh and Bone*. It was with Meg Ryan and Dennis Quaid. I played this Texan grifter kind of girl. And it was the best. I mean, I was dying. I worshipped Meg Ryan. I was so nervous around her. I couldn't breathe and, like, have a normal personality at all. *When Harry Met Sally* was my favorite movie of all time. *Seven* came after that movie.

Howard: That's with Brad Pitt. That's when you started dating him.

Gwyneth: That's right.

Howard: That dude . . . you were probably the best-looking couple on the planet at that point, right? You and Brad Pitt?

Gwyneth: Really?

Howard: Don't you think?

Gwyneth: I don't know.

Robin: That's when you became a paparazzi target.

Gwyneth: Right.

Howard: Isn't that a good thing? You're dating Brad Pitt, paparazzi come, that propels your career and puts you in the limelight.

Gwyneth: I suppose it does, yeah.

Howard: It's not all that bad, is it?

Gwyneth: No, no. God, no.

Howard: From a career standpoint.

Gwyneth: I mean, I didn't think about it at the time, but I'm sure it was a good thing for my career.

Howard: So you're in a movie with Brad Pitt. You're young. Both of you are beautiful. You both can act. It's almost impossible not to fall in love.

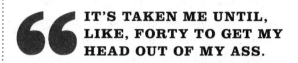

IT'S TAKEN ME UNTIL, LIKE, FORTY TO GET MY HEAD OUT OF MY ASS.

Gwyneth: Yeah, I definitely fell in love with him. He was so gorgeous and sweet. And I mean, he was Brad Pitt! You know?

Howard: Are you still friends with him?

Gwyneth: If I see him, we're friendly. I don't, like, hang out with him.

Howard: You were the love of his life.

Gwyneth: [*laughs*]

Howard: You were. You ended that relationship. That's pretty cool, when you fucking break up with Brad Pitt.

Gwyneth: That's not true. That's totally not true.

Howard: Now, this I know. This I know from people. It's not true?

Gwyneth: *Howard* . . .

Howard: Gwyneth, is it true or not?

Gwyneth: It's not, you know—no. It is not true.

Howard: Did your parents like him?

Gwyneth: *Loved*.

Howard: They loved him.

Gwyneth: My father was so devastated when we broke up. My father loved him like a son.

Howard: Is that hard? Do you almost feel like, when everything is right—(a) He's good-looking. (b) Successful actor. Your parents love him. Everyone loves him. Doesn't that make you go, "You know what?

I should just marry this guy." 'Cause you guys were engaged. "I should just marry this guy, because maybe my judgment's wrong"? How do you find that you're not right for each other? How do you know?

Gwyneth: I was such a kid. I was twenty-two when we met. And, it's taken me until, like, forty to get my head out of my ass. You can't make that decision when you're twenty-two years old, you know what I mean?

Howard: But thank God you knew that. Most of us don't understand. Most people get married in that situation. The fact that you felt good enough about yourself to even break it up—

Gwyneth: I don't think that was the case.

Howard: What do you think it is?

Gwyneth: I think I was a kid, and I wasn't ready, and, you know, he was too good for me.

Howard: Was he? No, he wasn't. No, that's not the case.

Gwyneth: Well, I honestly do think I was just too young, and I didn't know what I was doing.

Howard: You leave him, and then *Shakespeare in Love* happens.

Gwyneth: Right.

Howard: That's the defining movie, right?

Gwyneth: Yes.

Howard: Do you have an idea you're gonna win an Oscar for that? Do you go, "Man, I am killing this. I am nailing this role." Like a football player knows when they might win the Super Bowl.

Gwyneth: Definitely not. I had done a

bunch of small movies in England. I just thought I was doing another period piece in England.

Howard: The story that I hear is that you're over at Winona Ryder's house—

Gwyneth: Oh God.

Howard: Tell me if this is true, 'cause I love this.

Gwyneth: This is hilarious. Okay, go ahead.

Howard: You see the script for *Shakespeare in Love*.

Gwyneth: This is not true. At all.

Howard: It's not at all.

Gwyneth: No, no.

Howard: The story I heard is that Winona Ryder was considered—not that she had the role, but that she was reading this thing—and you read it, and said, "Hey, I'll go in on this too."

Gwyneth: No, that's not what happened.

Howard: And then she got pissed off because you got the role.

Gwyneth: Um, that's not what happened.

Howard: Too bad, it's a good story.

Gwyneth: I'm so sorry.

Howard: But clear this up for me.

Gwyneth: Basically, I was doing a lot of Miramax movies at the time. They asked me to do *Shakespeare in Love*. And I said no. Because I had been doing all these other things—

Howard: And also you love to say no to great movies.

Gwyneth: We've established this.

Howard: Right.

Gwyneth: And then I think in the interim

they were talking to other women. And then I ran into a guy called Paul Webster, who used to run a bit of Miramax, and he said to me, "What are you doing? Why did you turn this down? You *have* to do this movie." Oh, I know why! It's because I was in the breakup with Brad Pitt and I was very sad and "I'm not gonna work" and all that nonsense.

Howard: But you were falling in love with Ben Affleck at that point too, right?

Gwyneth: Was I?

Howard: Yes.

Robin: Wait a minute! She wasn't even broken up with—

Howard: No, she had broken up with Brad.

Robin: She was devastated.

Gwyneth: Yes.

Howard: Yeah, yeah, not *that* devastated.

Gwyneth: I was!

Howard: Although I can't imagine the lovemaking that went on. I mean, I would love a glimpse of that. Is there a film of that? Did you make a sex video?

Gwyneth: Do you know what's so sad is that it's before the days of videos on your phones. So we had nothing.

Howard: Oh my God. It would've been great. You don't have any pictures of the two of you together?

Gwyneth: God, I don't think . . . a couple, yes. There's a couple.

Howard: When you break up, do you rip up pictures, or—

Gwyneth: No.

Howard: You still have them somewhere?

Gwyneth: I have a couple pictures, yeah.

Howard: But when you get married, in the future, you gotta rip up those pictures then.

Gwyneth: Why? Every piece of your life is an important piece of your life.

Howard: Yeah, but if your husband finds out that you're saving these pictures of Brad Pitt . . . Let's say you even have them locked up in a drawer—your special little drawer that you think your husband doesn't know about, but he's already seen it—don't you think that those pictures should be destroyed?

Gwyneth: No. I think that your husband—whoever you marry—should accept you 100 percent, and accept your past and your exes.

Howard: "Why are you holding on to your Brad Pitt pictures?" I would say to you, since I'm your husband. I'd say, "Honey, I love you, but it bothers me that you're holding on to—"

Gwyneth: Would it bother you? No, it wouldn't bother you.

Howard: No, actually, I'm not the jealous type. A little bit jealous, but not that much.

Robin: Well, it *is* Brad Pitt, now.

Howard: Right. If it's Brad Pitt, I say, "Rip up the fucking pictures. Edit Brad Pitt out and put me in." But I'm saying, you were at the point in your life when you had broken up with Brad Pitt, and you go to the *Good Will Hunting* premiere, and you meet Ben Affleck there.

Gwyneth: No. I met him before that premiere. The movie hadn't come out yet. I met him at a Miramax dinner.

OF COURSE YOU WANT TO WIN AN OSCAR. IT'S ONLY ONCE YOU HAVE ONE THAT YOU'RE LIKE, "OKAY, WELL, I'M STILL JUST AS CONFUSED AND UNHAPPY AS I WAS YESTERDAY."

Howard: I'll tell you how I knew you were dating him. Because when you decide to do *Shakespeare in Love*, Ben Affleck goes to get the role in the movie because he wants to be with you, because he's been dating you. Am I right or am I wrong?

Gwyneth: Your sleuthing is—

Howard: Am I right or am I wrong? He's probably like, "I'm gonna lose this girl if—"

Gwyneth: No. I think Harvey Weinstein at the time was trying to put all of his people in all of the movies.

Howard: So, you get this role. You do it. And you win the Oscar. And so, Winona Ryder, you didn't take the script off her?

Gwyneth: No, I didn't.

Howard: Are you guys friendly, you and Winona Ryder? Or is she angry with you because she *thinks* you took her role?

Gwyneth: I don't know. I haven't seen her in years.

Howard: I think she thinks you took her role.

Gwyneth: I swear to God I did not.

Howard: You're raising your right hand on a Bible.

Gwyneth: I'm raising my right hand on a Bible. I swear to God.

Howard: And then you win the Academy Award. And you beat out Meryl Streep, right?

Gwyneth: I know.

Howard: She can't really act that well, right?

Gwyneth: Nah, not *that* well.

Howard: You're a better actress than her! You beat her!

Gwyneth: Definitely.

Howard: You beat her.

Robin: It's a sin to say that!

Howard: You beat her. Did you just say you're better than Meryl Streep? That's right. Go ahead, brag about it.

Gwyneth: No. Please, she's the greatest ever. That was crazy. I think it's only because she gets nominated every single time, they eventually have to give it to other people, right?

Howard: Was it important to you to win an Oscar? Was it a defining moment in your life? Or were you from the Marlon Brando school. Like, "Oh, this is bullshit. I don't care about awards."

Gwyneth: Of course you see that as the ultimate validation and affirmation that you're good. So I was thrilled to win. And of course you want to win an Oscar. It's only once you have one that you're like, "Okay, well, I'm still just as confused and unhappy as I was yesterday." You're like, "Huh."

Howard: So now, at this point in your life,

you're on top of the world. Not only have you dumped Brad Pitt—

Gwyneth: I did not!

Howard:—which is *so* cool. Let's go with that, okay?

Gwyneth: Fine.

Howard: Now you're with Ben Affleck. Holy Moses! I mean, could a guy who looks like me *ever* date a girl like you? It's impossible, right? You've been ruined.

Gwyneth: What do you mean?!

Howard: Because you're used to seeing a guy with an eight-pack, you know what I mean?

Gwyneth: Eight-pack.

Howard: Not even a six-pack. Even if I worked out and got to a six-pack, you still— no, seriously! You couldn't.

Gwyneth: You're taken anyway.

Howard: Well, of course. I'm not saying me. I'm saying a guy *like* me. I mean, you dated physically perfect people. Is it hard to figure out a guy's personality when they're as good-looking as Ben Affleck and Brad Pitt? It can get tricky. 'Cause when I meet a beautiful woman, I don't even know if she even has a good personality.

Gwyneth: I think that when you're in your twenties, you can get swept up in that kind of thing without knowing.

Howard: It's tricky, isn't it?

Gwyneth: When you're a kid you tend to be more shallow, and you're also immature, so you think that being with a good-looking person validates you in some kind of way. It's not true. It's ego.

Howard: Have you ever dated an ugly person?

Gwyneth: [*laughs*]

Howard: I don't think so, right? You should go ugly. They're way more attentive.

Gwyneth: Okay. I'm gonna go on Tinder when I leave.

Howard: But Ben didn't work out, right?

Gwyneth: No.

Howard: It was a couple years. You're not someone who changes partners easily. You get attached to people.

Gwyneth: I do.

Howard: Do your girlfriends say to you, "Are you *crazy*? This is *Ben Affleck*. You've got to stop this." Do they get ahold of you and try to knock some sense into you?

Gwyneth: Mmm, no. Not in that case.

Howard: And what about your parents in this case?

Gwyneth: Um . . .

Howard: Not so much.

Gwyneth: I think they appreciated how— you know, he's *super* intelligent, and he's really, really talented, and he's funny, but he wasn't in a good place in his life to have a girlfriend, so they were okay with us not being . . .

Howard: Not like with Brad, where they *loved* him.

Gwyneth: No. Brad was—my father, honestly, was . . .

Howard: Smitten.

Gwyneth: He was devastated.

Robin: He was more broken up than you, apparently.

Gwyneth: He was so sad.

Howard: So then, you meet Chris [Martin].

Gwyneth: Yes.

Howard: Your husband for a while, right?

Gwyneth: Right.

Howard: The amazing thing about that is when you said, "We're 'consciously uncoupling.'" This has become the biggest term. When you issued that press release, did you know that those words—"conscious uncoupling"—would become so big?

Gwyneth: Okay, no. First of all, when I sent out the thing, I made a mistake in that I didn't give it context. I didn't say, "This is a philosophy from this woman—this is not my term—and we're following this thing."

Howard: So when you had gone to her for couples therapy, and she said, "Look, let's think of it this way—"

Gwyneth: No, I didn't go to her, but I was with somebody who studied what she—I've never met her, actually. But it's a really very noble idea. And it's a great thing, I think, to try to do for your kids.

Howard: And it's working.

Gwyneth: It's working. But it is kind of a goofy term. And I didn't know it was gonna cause such a big thing.

Robin: I still don't know what that means.

Howard: It means they chose not to be enemies, right?

Gwyneth: Yeah. The idea is that you try to do it with minimal acrimony. You say, "Look, we're a family. We have kids. We're always going to be a family. Let's try to find all of the positives in our relationship, all the things that brought us together, the friendship." And we actually have a really

strong friendship, and we laugh and we have fun. But there are times when it's really difficult, and things happen, and you're like, "I'm sure he doesn't wanna hang out with me, and I don't wanna hang out with him." But for the sake of the kids . . .

Howard: You do it.

Gwyneth: You do it. And you know what else, honestly? When I was talking to friends of mine who had grown up and their parents were divorced, there was a common theme, which was, "Oh yeah, now my parents are great, and they were both at my wedding, but there was, like, five years where they didn't talk." Or, "There was seven years where they wouldn't be in the same room." And I was like, "Can we just skip to *that*?" Because I don't wanna do that to my kids. And we're lucky in that our parenting styles and philosophies overlap a lot. We see eye to eye on how to do it.

Howard: I've had Chris on this show, and I even said to him, "When you write a song"—he's written songs *about* you.

Gwyneth: Right.

Howard: When a guy writes a song about you, that's even more intoxicating than a movie set, right? Is that what did it for you? A rock star is probably the ultimate in terms of a romantic fantasy for a woman. True or false?

Gwyneth: I don't know, I really loved his music before I met him. And when my dad was sick and dying, his second album I had on repeat all the time.

Howard: Your dad died very young. Fifty-eight. I think about that, where I'm at in life, it's like, "Oh my God, that's *really young*."

Gwyneth: Really young, yeah.

Howard: He had cancer?

Gwyneth: He had throat cancer, and had the operation and radiation and everything, and then he was okay for four years. But then on my thirtieth birthday, we went to Italy. I went with some friends, my old friends, and my dad. My mom was doing the TV show in California with the lines taped on the vagina. [*laughs*] She wasn't able to be there. But he got double pneumonia and he died.

Howard: And you loved him.

Gwyneth: Yeah.

Howard: I mean, not everyone has a great relationship with their father, believe me.

Gwyneth: No.

Howard: But you actually did.

Gwyneth: He was actually kinda the love of my life.

Howard: Yeah. It's hard. It doesn't get any easier, right?

Gwyneth: No. I'll never forget when he died. Everybody was so nice. And anyone who knew him loved him and knew our relationship. And I remember somebody wrote me an e-mail saying, "Everybody has a father, but not everybody has a daddy." That's what he was. He was the best.

Howard: There was speculation that you breaking up with Brad killed him, actually.

Gwyneth: [*laughs*]

Howard: You did it.

> **I WOULD WAKE UP WITH MY RIBS IN A SPASM. I COULDN'T COPE WITH THE GRIEF. IT WAS REALLY OVERWHELMING.**

Gwyneth: It's true, actually.

Howard: It's true. I think that threw him right over the edge.

Gwyneth: That was the last straw.

Howard: So three weeks after your dad dies, you meet Chris. At a Coldplay concert. You went to see him because you loved his music.

Gwyneth: That's right. I was about to start filming this movie in London about Sylvia Plath. And Mary Wigmore, my best friend—I was like, "I can't get out. I don't know what to do."

Howard: You couldn't get out of your horror.

Gwyneth: I would wake up with my ribs in a spasm. I couldn't cope with the grief. It was really overwhelming. So I had these tickets to go see Coldplay from before my father died, and I said, "I can't go, I can't leave the house." And Mary said, "We can't just sit here and smoke cigarettes. We don't have to stay for the whole thing, but let's just go." Like, "Let's get you out of the house." So we went, and I cried the whole concert, and then we met afterward backstage. And he was very sweet to me.

> ## 66 I WAS LIKE, "THIS IS CRAZY. I CAN'T FALL IN LOVE WITH A TWENTY-FIVE-YEAR-OLD ROCK STAR."

Howard: Were you like, "Oh my God, this is almost a cliché because I'm falling in love with the lead singer of a band"?

Gwyneth: [*laughs*]

Howard: Was it something you wanted to resist? Or you just threw yourself—

Gwyneth: Yeah, he was twenty-five. I was thirty. So I was like, "This is crazy. I can't fall in love with a twenty-five-year-old rock star."

Howard: Yeah, because it's almost impossible for a rock star to stay in a relationship. They're on the road all the time. I don't care what anyone says, when you're separated more than two weeks, the heart just . . . it doesn't grow fonder, it goes colder. It does, right?

Gwyneth: It's very hard. There was one time when the babies were really little and he was going to New Zealand, Australia, and I think there was, like, five weeks where I didn't see him once.

Howard: Does Apple like her name?

Gwyneth: She loves it.

Howard: Because I remember when you named your kid Apple, that was another thing, like—

Gwyneth: I know.

Howard: "Conscious uncoupling."

Gwyneth: Just get me to shut the fuck up!

Howard: Yeah, shut the fuck up, you'll be fine! You gave a bit of advice to women that I think is fantastic, and I always wanted to tell you this. You were talking to the wonderful Chelsea Handler—

Gwyneth: Oh God.

Howard: You know what I'm talking about?

Gwyneth: I can't believe she told this story on her show.

Howard: It's so great. And I want the confirmation on this. I want to know if you really practice this in your real life. You said, "Look, there are times you argue with your boyfriend or your husband, and it gets heated." And you said to her, "You want my advice? Just blow your husband." You'll skip all the nonsense, because it'll just deflate the whole argument.

Gwyneth: Am I right?

Howard: You are a hundred percent right. But is this something you truly practice?

Gwyneth: First of all, I'd like to thank Chelsea Handler for telling this story publicly.

Howard: If I was married to you, I'd constantly pick arguments. "Okay, might as well blow me." Seriously, is that something that has worked for you?

Gwyneth: My point to her, when I was originally having this discussion with her, was, "Look, you're a very powerful woman. You're all over the place. You make all this money. . . . Sometimes you don't have to always fight. Like, be a girl and show him that he's a man."

Howard: It would be hard for a man

to date you who makes less money than you do and who is less powerful than you, right? I mean, you are limited in that sense.

Gwyneth: I think it depends on the guy.

Howard: Yeah, but a lot of guys aren't that secure. They get real insecure right away.

Gwyneth: It depends how many blow jobs you give them.

Howard: That's true. Why did you choose [the film] *Mortdecai*?

Gwyneth: Well, I had never done a movie with Johnny Depp. And I *love* him.

Howard: What do you mean, you *love* him? You're not gonna get carried away.

Gwyneth: No, no, no, no.

Howard: This is strictly professional.

Gwyneth: No actors for me.

Howard: And Johnny, when you meet him, you're not nervous at this point in your career to act with someone. I mean, you've acted with everyone.

Gwyneth: No, but I was a little . . . I mean, he's such an icon and you go into the room to rehearse and he's, like, rolling his cigarettes and he's so cool.

Howard: Do you feel like he's *too* cool? Like, "I'm not cool enough"?

Gwyneth: Definitely. He's got all his tattoos and his cool clothes and—

Robin: What is his way of working? Does he stick to the script, or is he doing—

Gwyneth: He sticks to the script. And he listens to music while he acts.

Howard: What do you mean?

Gwyneth: Oh, I hope I'm not telling tales

IT DEPENDS HOW MANY BLOW JOBS YOU GIVE THEM.

out of school, but he has a little thing in his ear and he listens to music.

Howard: Wait a second. You're telling me—

Gwyneth: It's the coolest thing ever.

Howard: You're doing a scene with this guy, he's talking to you, you're having dialogue, and in one ear he's listening to music?

Gwyneth: Yeah.

Howard: That sounds crazy to me.

Gwyneth: He's creating the whole world in his head.

Howard: What is he listening to?

Gwyneth: I asked him, and he said, "The movie evokes a kind of jazz/big-band feeling," so I think he was listening to that type of music.

Howard: Do you subscribe to any one technique of acting? When you see these guys, the guy who played Lincoln—

Robin: Daniel Day-Lewis.

Howard: Right. He had you address him as Mr. Lincoln. I'm talking about at the craft services table, you had to address this guy. Do you think this is crazy acting stuff, or do you just go with it?

Gwyneth: I think that it's a crazy job, and whatever people need to do to do it, more power to them.

Howard: I didn't have to address you as

Sylvia Plath when you were doing the role, right?

Gwyneth: No, but you need to address me as my character in *Shallow Hal*. Otherwise I won't speak to you.

Howard: Okay, I'm getting the wrap-up sign. I had about seventeen more hours' worth of questions, but this was fun.

Gwyneth: Thank you. I avoided you for twenty years, Howard.

Howard: Why did you avoid me?

Gwyneth: I was scared of you!

Howard: Were you?

Gwyneth: Well, I started listening to you when I was in eighth grade. When I moved to New York, I started listening to you guys—all the boys at Saint David's were obsessed, and they all turned us on. And so I listened to you for years when I was a kid.

Howard: I wonder how your dad would have felt if you had married *me*.

Gwyneth: He would have been so happy.

Howard: Oh, no, no, no, he wouldn't.

RELIGION & SPIRITUALITY

Tell me not to say something, and I'll say it. It's my compulsion. I was always taught that religion is one of those topics you should stay away from in conversation. Of course, that makes me want to talk about it even more. I love talking to my guests about religion. I love asking them about their beliefs.

Religion and spirituality are two very different things. Man tends to pervert religion. That's how you end up with priests sexually abusing altar boys and hucksters swindling little old ladies out of their life savings. That type of hypocrisy fascinates me. I'm always interested in exploring it.

The main reason I like discussing religion and spirituality on the show is a selfish one: I'm looking to get some clarity about my own beliefs. Maybe one day one of my guests will say something so profound that I'll finally figure out where I stand. I'm caught in a weird in-between zone. I had so much religious training growing up. All the time I spent learning about those bubbe-meises like Sarah and Abraham. Why go to all the trouble of having a kid in your nineties if you're just going to murder the miracle baby? What exactly was the lesson I was supposed to take away from that? Getting to sleep at night was hard enough without worrying about my father in an Abraham-like frenzy creeping into my room and slitting my throat because of his covenant with God. If only I'd spent those hours taking guitar lessons instead of studying scripture, maybe I would have ended up Howard Van Halen.

I love what Rodney Dangerfield says in the following pages about how he doesn't believe in God, he believes in logic. A big part of me agrees with him. I have often said, "There's no God. There's no way." Then I'll quickly think better of it. "I better not say that." I'm so paranoid. What if there is a God, and I get punished for not believing? "Well, there *might* be one," I blurt out. "Yes, there definitely is a God!" Like I said, I'm in a weird in-between zone—my personal purgatory. This indecisiveness is even more agonizing and confounding because it violates the single most important rule of being successful in radio, which I mentioned earlier in this book's introduction: you must have a definite opinion. I've defined my entire career by this principle. Yet when it comes to religion, I'm unable to follow it. Telling people, "There is no God," is good radio. Telling people, "There is a God"—also good radio. Telling people, "There is no God . . . but wait, maybe there is one," that's bad radio. I know it, but I still can't help myself. I'm afraid to offend the Almighty.

I so desperately want to believe. I don't want the party to end when I die. I can't grasp that the world is going to go on without me and not miss a beat. Really, at the end of the day, I'm hoping for the movie *Ghost*: I drop dead, wrap my arms around Demi Moore, and we make pottery for eternity.

....

STEVEN TYLER

Howard: Did you ever almost die? Did you have one of those near-death experiences?

Steven: Three or four times.

Howard: Really? They had to resuscitate you, or—

Steven: No, my friends put me in a tub in cold water.

Howard: Because you'd stopped breathing?

Steven: Yeah, and turned blue.

Howard: You think that would have scared the shit out of you. It doesn't.

Steven: No, man, it doesn't. Life is too good. You just keep snorting and drinking and taking pills and never knew it was too much. But you know what? Thank you, Lord Jesus, for me not dying.

Howard: Do you believe in God?

Steven: Yes.

Howard: You're a religious guy?

Steven: Yes.

Howard: You think you go to heaven when you die? Do you think about any of that?

Steven: Well, you got to think about this. If you're on a table—they've done this thousands of times now— and you're getting ready to die: the second you die, you can see the weight go down. It's tangible.

Howard: You think that's your soul going somewhere?

Steven: It's your soul going somewhere, and we're electricity, and it goes somewhere. All that you are goes somewhere.

LEAH REMINI

Leah: My mother joined Scientology because what it promotes is: "What are you doing? We're saving the planet. We're doing good things. What better place for your daughters to be but part of something so big?" In my mother's defense, she really did believe she was giving us a better life. She really did.

Howard: You go into Scientology and, as you described, you are indoctrinated. I look at my own experience with religion. I wasn't a Scientologist, but my parents put me into deep religious training two, three times a week for hours— sitting there, learning all kinds of scripture and stuff— and it made me fucking crazy. What a waste. Imagine if you would put all that time into guitar. I'd have been in a band right now.

Leah: But why? They put you there because they thought it would give you some basis for your life and some spirituality.

Howard: What's great about your mother, at least she was living a spiritual life. My parents weren't. They just put me into it. At least your mother was walking the walk. I'm like, "Why am I involved in this?"

Leah: Look, you are who you are, good and bad. Everything led you to this moment.

Howard: Absolutely. I think the thing that burns me the most is that even before you had your huge financial success with *King of Queens*, you were struggling financially and the church required you to pay, as you calculate, millions by the end of this thing, to get this quote-unquote *education*. Does that sicken you that you gave so much money to the church?

Leah: No, because I gave it

for the right reasons at that time.

Howard: Do you ever put yourself down? Do you ever feel duped so badly that you blame yourself? Like, "I should have been more intelligent. I should have known not to give them the money."

Leah: Yeah, at certain points I look back on my life. But at the same time, if I start regretting it . . . Howard, there's no in-between here. There's not like, "I don't feel like going to church." It's an extremist organization. So at any point, if I had a disagreement, it was, "Are you ready to walk away?" Because there's no other middle ground.

Howard: That's the weird thing with Scientology. Most religions, you can walk away—"Okay, fuck you." You can walk away, and then if you feel like coming back, come on back. Why is there such shunning? I don't get that. Why don't they want you to come back? Maybe you would grow out of this phase.

Leah: The policy is basically

that if you are attacking somebody . . . Here's Robin. She's going to courses and getting the counseling. And I'm saying, "Why are you going there? It's horrible. Don't you know? Go on the Internet." Eventually she'd say, "Listen, if this is something that I believe helps me, I don't need you putting in negative crap. Wish me the best." The policy is that putting that on her plate is a suppressive thing to do. You're considered a suppressive person.

Howard: That's the fucked-up thing. I know a lot of people who've studied to be rabbis, and then they've questioned it. They're [told], "Okay, leave. What are you going to do? I can't force you to be into this thing."

Leah: Here's the difference, honey. I could leave. They were like, "Fine, go." But the fact that I spoke publicly, that's the difference.

Howard: I don't know. I've come to the conclusion in my life that all religions are sort of nutty. I just don't get it sometimes. I almost don't even single Scientology out any different than Christianity.

Leah: But you should, because—the financial requirement, the time requirement, not acknowledging the fact that policies exist that break up families, that break up friendships. These things are there. Howard, my grandmother lived on Elizabeth Street in Little Italy. She used to go to church every day. It was all about the church. She goes in, she lights the candle. As a child, it was comforting to me. She'd go pray and she'd do the sign of the cross on my forehead and pray to this one and pray to that one if you lost your keys. It's always very comforting to me to have faith in something. For me, it wasn't pushed on me like it was pushed on you. But at the same time, now that I'm older and I'm out of the church, I'm reconnecting to a faith that I can go in, light a candle—

Howard: You've gone to a Catholic church and you're finding comfort there?

Leah: Amazing.

Howard: Because you want spirituality in your life?

Leah: I've always been spiritual. I was baptized as a Catholic and so was my sister, something my father was very insistent on. My mother's Jewish. But my mother, she didn't have religion in her life at all. Her parents died when she was very young. She didn't have that as part of her life. Scientology was more about helping people. They did really believe that.

....

ALEC BALDWIN

Howard: I thought at one point Tom Cruise had done himself in with his image and the Scientology.

Robin: Well, it was the jumping up and down on Oprah's couch that really was a problem.

Alec: Yeah, but that doesn't bother me. I'll tell you something: this podcast that I do for NPR and for WNYC—Lawrence Wright, who wrote *Going Clear*, that was made into

Alex Gibney's documentary about Scientology. It's a weird predicament. I'm a fan of Gibney. I'm a fan of Wright's writing. He's a great writer. And these guys do this movie. And in it, they say some very, very damning things. But in the end, people can say things about you and have opinions and however they color it, that it's negative and ugly toward you. But to imply criminal charges against someone . . . And I'm not saying that it's true. I'm not saying that they got it wrong, that they lied. I'm just saying: you gotta prove someone did something. We live in a world now where people think it's enough to just throw the mud on you and say it and not prove it. So when I look at Tom—that movie says some ugly things about Scientology, and by implication about him. But I sit there and I go, "I don't really care about that. 'Cause you gotta prove things that people have done." I really mean this. I have worked in this business, and I have worked with some people who—I could cry, literally cry, remembering what it was like to work with Tony Hopkins, and how much that meant to me. And Meryl. And Julie Harris, who played my mother on a TV show years ago. All the things I've done. And I enjoyed working with Tom, and I had more fun, and I was more thrilled to work with Tom—he was right up there with anybody I've ever worked with. And the rest of the guys my age, I couldn't give a shit about working with them.

Howard: I look at it sort of philosophically. Every religion to me is extraordinarily bizarre. There's weirdos in every religion, and there's all kinds of crazy shit that goes on in the name of religion. Who the hell would make fun of Scientology when your own religion is just as wacky, isn't it? I mean, all these are just stories.

Alec: Well, the question also becomes—and I don't spend a lot of time thinking about this—but who's been shot out of a cannon and shot into the stratosphere more than Tom? From

when he was very young, he became a big movie star. *Risky Business*—he was a kid. And he wasn't born on a soundstage in Hollywood. He was an ordinary kid from New Jersey. And he becomes this phenomenon. And it just keeps going. It doesn't stop. It just keeps going and going and going. Now he's been one of the biggest movie stars in the world for twenty-five years. I mean, that's a lot. And I say to myself, "Maybe there's a religion or maybe there's a philosophy that helped him negotiate that space." 'Cause you're gettin' the bends, man. You're like, "Who do I trust? What's real?" And I say to myself, "I don't care what you do. Whatever you need to do, whatever pill you need to take, whatever diet you need to go on, whatever type of pillow you need to sleep on, who gives a shit?"

Howard: It's none of your business.

Alec: It's none of your business. If you're not hurting anybody—and I don't know that they're hurting anybody. I don't

know that. People say things, and I go, "Okay, that's cool. I understand that there's some extreme situations there." But I go to work with Tom, we have a ball. It's, like, the height of moviemaking. You have a great time. And I really don't care.

WOODY HARRELSON

Howard: Were you a staunch Republican? Were you, like, against gay rights? One of these religious right types?

Woody: I was very Christian. But it was a little more compassionate form of Christianity than you sometimes get.

Howard: And so, what was the switch? Was it just being part of Hollywood that suddenly opened your eyes to different types of politics?

Woody: No, it was actually in college I started to shift. I was studying theology with the thought of possibly becoming a minister.

Howard: No kidding?

Woody: Yeah, yeah.

Howard: That makes sense,

now, for an actor to want to be on a stage being a minister. It kind of does.

Woody: Oh yeah. Certainly you're performing in a way. I really was interested in that. But I started to look at the Bible differently when it all got kind of broken down and I realized it was formulated by the Nicene Council of the early church, and they started making these little modifications according to what all the people in the room thought needed to be done, you know? And I started to see the man-made quality of the Bible. And I just started to shift off. It wasn't just that, but there were a lot of reasons why I started to shift from being religious.

WILLIE NELSON

Howard: Are you a religious man?

Willie: I don't know. Probably.

Howard: Because I would think, when these songs come from nowhere, you might say, "Maybe it's a gift from God," you know?

Willie: That's for sure.

Howard: What was the first song you ever learned as a kid? What was the first song that had an impact on you?

Willie: "Amazing Grace." I sang it in church every Sunday.

Howard: You got up in front of a congregation and sang?

Willie: Yeah, we all did. The choir.

Howard: That was the big moment?

Willie: What was funny, I'd play a place called the Night Owl the night before, and I was singing to the same people that night as I sung to the next morning.

BILLY CORGAN

Billy: I have had paranormal experiences in my life.

Howard: What happened to you?

Billy: I can't.

Howard: Were you abducted? What happened? I wanna know.

Billy: I'm turning red. I'm so embarrassed.

Howard: Don't be embarrassed. Share.

Billy: Let's just say I was

with somebody once and I saw a transformation that I can't explain.

Howard: The person transformed into something other than human.

Billy: Yes. I saw it.

Robin: Were you on drugs?

Billy: I was not. I was totally sober.

Howard: You were talking to someone. You were having a conversation like we are now. And the person said to you, "Look, something's gonna happen here. I'm gonna morph into something else." And you're like, "This is ridiculous."

Billy: That's not how it happened. Imagine you're doing something and you turn around and there's somebody else standing there.

Howard: A different human.

Billy: Sort of. It's hard to explain without going into detail. I'd rather not go into detail.

Howard: Okay, but did you say to the person, "What'd you just do here?"

Billy: Yes. And they acknowledged it.

Howard: And what did they

say they were? From another planet?

Billy: They wouldn't explain.

Howard: Billy, I've had that happen with a woman once. She took her makeup off and I didn't know who the fuck she was. She really tricked me. Wow—

Billy: Yeah, it's up there as one of the most intense things I've ever been through.

Howard: I think that's great. This conversation gives me hope. Because I want to know that there's an afterlife. And you're telling me there are supernatural things—

Billy: I'll tell you one quick thing that I can talk about that's kinda cool. Similar but less dark. I was working on my book, which I've sort of stalled on at the moment. But I was working on the book and I was being lazy about saving the book, and I hit some weird key and the thing blanked. I lost eight days' worth of work. And I lost my mind. At that exact moment in the other room, my girlfriend was cooking dinner, and she turned and saw a woman walking through

the kitchen. And it was my mother, who she's only seen in pictures—my mother at twenty-five years old walking fast with her head down through the kitchen. My girlfriend was like, "What the heck just happened?" So she followed the spirit, and there was nothing. She came in to tell me, and it had happened at the exact moment I blanked my book. So she was coming in one direction to tell me, "I just saw your mother as a ghost in the house." I'm coming to tell her, "Oh my God I just lost this eight days' worth of work." It was like this weird ripple in time thing.

Howard: And did your mother help you get your book back at least?

Billy: [*laughs*] I wish.

Howard: The woman could've done *something* nice for you. I like that she shows up now as a ghost— was never around when you needed her. A thought just popped into my head, though: Are you afraid to tell what you saw that day with this person who transformed because you're

afraid of their power and that they would hurt you?

Billy: No, not at all. I'd just rather tell the full story in a book or something.

Howard: My show's not good enough is what you're saying.

Billy: No, it's contextual. In this context it's hard to tell the story the way it happened.

Howard: Do you still know this person?

Billy: No.

Howard: I would. I would stay in touch.

Billy: No, not a good person.

Howard: Oh really?

Robin: See, that's what I'm saying—he saw somebody evil.

Billy: We're talking more on the demonic side here.

Howard: Oh my God. Ugh, that's depressing.

Billy: I think people kind of treat the Bible like it's a toilet paper fairy tale. And I've had enough experiences to think that a lot of stuff that's in there is based on things that happened in times where people probably had access to less knowledge, if that makes any sense. It's like in a world that has less access to information, the paranormal stuff could've gone on.

Howard: Have you ever told a psychiatrist these stories and they think you're crazy?

Billy: No, but I have talked to people who've had similar experiences.

Robin: Who are these people?

Howard: Keep 'em away from me.

Billy: I'll send you an e-mail if they're coming on your show.

····················

RODNEY DANGERFIELD

Howard: You still doing gigs?

Rodney: Yeah, I still work. Not too much recently, because I had so much to do with doctors and things that I couldn't work.

Howard: When is the next surgery?

Rodney: The next surgery should be months from now, I guess.

Howard: Your heart, right?

Rodney: Yeah, there's a flap in my heart that doesn't

function properly and the blood don't go through it the way it should. So I have to have an operation to remove that valve. With a pig's valve. And that will last longer.

Howard: Does this stuff scare the crap out of you?

Rodney: Here's what I say, man. It's the truth: "If I don't make it"—I tell every doctor this—"If I don't make it, I'll never know it." That's it. Then I'm going out in style. No suffering. No pain. Nothing. Just dead.

Howard: Dead.

Rodney: Dead.

Howard: Do you think there's an afterlife?

Rodney: I don't think so.

Howard: You don't.

Rodney: We're gorillas.

Howard: On the whole, and be honest with me, has life been just a big pain in the ass? I mean, did you ever enjoy yourself?

Rodney: No. I very, very seldom enjoy myself. The only time I enjoy myself is when I'm being creative and I write something that they appreciate.

Howard: It's hard to be joyful for you.

Rodney: Never joyful.

Howard: No matter at that height of success, when *Caddyshack* hits it, can you ever truly sit back and go, "Man, this is great"? Or do you always feel like a failure?

Rodney: Not a failure. But always I gotta do the job right. I gotta do it right. I'm a perfectionist. Suffer greatly for being a perfectionist.

Howard: Does it make you sad that you can't enjoy anything?

Rodney: No, 'cause I'm used to that.

Howard: I wrote a book and twenty-five thousand people were waiting for me to sign my book, and I couldn't enjoy it. For some reason, there's nothing joyous inside of me that allows me to enjoy anything. And I don't understand why. I figured maybe you figured it out.

Rodney: I guess it goes back to childhood. I could never enjoy anything.

Howard: Because you feel so crappy inside about the way you were treated?

Rodney: My mother never hugged me, kissed me, nothing, okay? Other kids go to sleep listening to a fairy tale. I went to sleep with a fight downstairs, listening to a guy yelling, "Enough! I've had enough!"

Howard: Did you think it was your fault?

Rodney: [*laughs*] I don't think so. I was four.

Howard: So there's no heaven, and mortality's gotta freak you out. I mean, there's no more. That's it. It's gone. I agree with you. I don't think there is. But a lot of people when they're faced with death, gotta go under the blade, they find God.

Rodney: That's it. They find him.

Howard: Judaism for you never mattered?

Rodney: No, never mattered. All religion never mattered. Atheist all the way. That's it.

Howard: That's it. No God.

Rodney: No.

Howard: You're a man of science.

Rodney: Well, I don't know about a man of science. But I'm logical.

··

KEVIN HART

Howard: I do admire your mom. When you started going up onstage, she never even came to see you, but she helped you out financially for a year.

Kevin: Yes, my mom was an overly religious woman, and when she decided to devote her life to God and really take that lifestyle and embrace it, she didn't put herself in a position where anything could alter that. Drinks, alcohol, smoking—she didn't want to be around anything. She knew that comedy was in that environment, so she never came. But when I made the decision to be a comedian, I was like, "This is what I want to do," and she said, "I will support you."

Howard: She was so supportive.

Kevin: She said, "I'll support you. You've got a year. You've got a year

to figure it out, and if you do, then you not only have my blessing, but my support. I just want the best for you."

··

SARAH JESSICA PARKER

Howard: You're raising the kids with religion or you're keeping that out?

Sarah: They'll make those choices for themselves.

Howard: Really, no religion?

Sarah: I didn't have any religious education and neither did Matthew [Broderick]. Neither one of us are in a position to do that.

Howard: There's no Christmas at your house?

Sarah: We celebrate Christmas, but not in a religious—

Howard: Just for the gifts.

Sarah: Just for the gifts. We love the tree, we love the tradition and the lights, and we decorate.

··

DANA CARVEY

Howard: I know you've said that the Church Lady

character was based on a woman you knew in church. It was that simple for you.

Dana: Yeah, and also just the condescension. Just that rhythm—I don't know where it came from, but it's every schoolteacher you ever had. I would tell a story about us missing church as a family. We were Lutherans, and then we come in three weeks later and the Church Lady would look at us and say, "Well, *apparently* someone just comes to church when it's convenient." And those rhythms were getting laughs in the clubs.

MARTIN SHORT

Martin: I was in this bar and Nancy Dolman, who would become my wife, walked in. She was, like, ridiculously beautiful.

Howard: Hot?

Martin: Insane.

Howard: So how did you get her?

Martin: She liked clown boys.

Howard: So what's your story now? I mean, you've lost your wife, which is awful.

Martin: Nancy and I were together for thirty-eight years.

Howard: Amazingly successful relationship.

Martin: Insane. Never a moment of packing a bag. Never. It was crazy. When someone dies, there's a tendency where people don't talk about them anymore.

Howard: Well, you don't know what to say.

Martin: But it's also people are afraid they're going to die someday so they don't even want to bring up the subject.

Howard: Right. It's like everyone's nervous about it. I would think that you go into such a depression that for a while you can't even act anymore and you can't do anything funny anymore. Because you watched the one you love leave. And you get angry, right?

Martin: But I had been through that when I was young. We were an Irish-Catholic family of five kids. I was the youngest. Then, within six years, three of those people died.

Howard: Your mother died, your father died, and you had a brother that died.

Martin: Brother David died in a car accident.

Howard: Oldest brother?

Martin: Yeah. And it's Hamilton, Ontario, Canada, 1970. So it's not like, "Bring in the nine shrinks." You have to get on your bike and ride around and figure it out. And you do.

Howard: Isn't that the worst, though? That there's no one to talk to you about death? We all hide from it. Here your older brother dies, your parents die, all within this short period of time, and you're walking around—psychologically, whatever's going on inside of you, you're probably even hiding from yourself because there's no one to talk to. You don't have a psychiatrist.

Martin: But I did have and do have amazing older siblings.

Howard: And were you able to talk to them about what was going on?

Martin: Absolutely.

Howard: Did you get to

say good-bye to your wife? Did you get to say, "This has been great"?

Martin: Here's what's interesting. I think about anyone who's sick—she had ovarian cancer—there are two groups of people. One is, they write letters to be read at [someone's] wedding in ten years. And the other person says, "I'm going to lick this. I am fine. This is not a problem." And that's where Nancy was.

Howard: Nancy was, like, up until the end, "I'm going to beat this thing."

Martin: Yeah, absolutely.

Howard: I think I prefer to be that person.

Martin: I don't know. I don't think we know.

Howard: Did it start to freak you out about your own demise, when you have to watch the one you love die? Do you stop to think about that?

Martin: I think at a certain point in an unbelievably soulful relationship, the people at some point merge and become one person.

Howard: You think you could ever be in another relationship?

Martin: I think I could. I think that would be a bit tricky.

Howard: And I think Nancy would want that.

Martin: Absolutely she would.

Howard: She'd want you to be happy. Did you become religious after that? Are you a guy that believes in God?

Martin: Yeah, I believe in God. I'm not, like, saying that I'm in organized religion. But I do believe. I used to think that it was like the Peter Pan principle. If you believed in it, then it would happen.

Howard: Then I'll switch my belief.

....

BONO

Bono: My father was Catholic and my mother was Protestant. And they both agreed that religion was a bit tricky and they should avoid it in its troublesome sense. And so we had a healthy disrespect for what you might call formal religion. But somehow I found a way to still have a faith. Because

you know that old thing: you get just enough religion to inoculate you against it? I never had that.

Howard: You had faith.

Bono: Yeah.

Howard: Do you need faith to be successful? Because at points—like, before your first album comes out, everyone's telling you you suck, right?

Bono: When did that stop?

Howard: No, come on. You've somehow approached every record company there is and they say no, right? What keeps you going? I mean, how do you know? You just believed that it would work?

Bono: Songwriting is faith. Like Edge: if he's moving from one note to another and that note didn't exist before he did, it's a leap of faith to the next chord. You speak to most musicians, they have some kind of faith. In that otherness. That thing, you know? And we've gotta be careful of doing [what] you see on the Grammys: "I want to thank God for giving me this song." And you think, "Well, that's really shite, that song. Don't blame that on God."

Howard: [*laughs*] Thank God? God had nothing to do with it.

....

PAUL McCARTNEY

Howard: When John made that statement, "We're bigger than Jesus." In a way, I get it. When you write that many hit songs, it's almost like every song is a hit. It's godlike. Back then it was unheard of. It's still unheard of. It's like a Bible.

Paul: Yeah, and also he didn't mean it how it came out. It sounded very arrogant. What he meant was, those days the church was in a bit of a state. No one was going to church. Nobody was bothering to.

Howard: Nobody had a religious feeling.

Paul: Congregations were low. He was sort of saying really, "Get your act together, because we are bigger than Jesus at the moment." Which infuriated—I still got a picture burnt into my memory of some young blond white kid when we were down in Lord knows where, Alabama or somewhere, hammering on the window of our tour bus looking like he was going to try and kill us. It was like, "Slow down, kid."

Howard: People with their Jesus, they don't want to hear any nonsense.

Paul: Better believe it.

Howard: It was such a point for me because I never had a religious feeling. And the Beatles actually meant more to me than any religion because I learned from the Beatles. It changed my attitude.

Paul: I think that's what John was pointing out. It wasn't that he was anti-Christianity or anti any religion. He was just pointing out that they didn't have their act together as much as we did at that point.

Steve Martin

MAY 16, 2016

The first time I heard of Steve Martin was when I was at WRNW in Westchester, a lowly disc jockey doing fill-in shifts, just working my way up. A copywriter for our sales department walked in one day and said, "Excuuuuuse me." I found that hilarious and thought, "Wow, this guy is really funny." Then I heard another guy at the station say, "Excuuuuuse me," and I thought, "Oh, the copywriter ripped this guy off." Eventually I figured out they were both doing a bit from Steve Martin's debut comedy album, *Let's Get Small*, which won a Grammy in 1978.

I followed Steve's career with fascination. After walking away from stand-up in 1981, he starred in movies, wrote screenplays and books, hosted *Saturday Night Live*, became a celebrated banjo player. That willingness to branch out made him one of the entertainers I looked up to most and tried to model my own career after. You would think most of my influences would come from radio, and while I found some inspiration there, most radio personalities when I was coming up tended to think narrowly. Radio was the bastard child of show business. It wasn't treated with the same respect as film or music or television, wasn't considered an art form like those other mediums. In fact, many disc jockeys themselves shared this disregard for the profession. They approached the job as if they were washing dishes in a restaurant. They clocked in, spun some records, read some commercials, clocked out, went home, and didn't think about it until the next day's shift. I believed radio could be bigger than that, and I was convinced the radio personality could be a much more prominent fixture in people's lives. I envisioned workers going into their jobs and parroting lines I had said on the air in the same way my colleagues at WRNW had swapped Steve's jokes. One of the things I take pride in is that I've always considered myself a radio guy. No matter what else I've done—books, movies, TV—radio has always been my mainstay. Yet the way I welcome new challenges and opportunities, my refusal to be content staying in my lane, is something I learned from watching performers like Steve.

We tried to get him on the show for years. Back in 1985, Gary wrote a letter to Steve's publicist inviting him on. We didn't even have a typewriter in our office, so Gary had to dictate the letter to one of the secretaries. He had it typed up on official NBC stationery and walked it over to the publicist's office. He literally hand-delivered this letter. He never heard back, so he followed up with a phone call. The publicist said we would never get Steve on the show. Ever. She told Gary he was out of his mind.

Many years later, I became friendly with Steve. He'd invite me to dinner at his home. He's every bit as witty in person as he is in his movies and books. We'd be sitting there at dinner, and throughout the conversation I'd be thinking, "I must be the biggest bore on the planet." When you're listening to Steve talk, everything just sounds so brilliant.

Even as I got to know him on a personal level, I would never say, "How about coming on the show?" I just won't do that with my friends. I can't. I'm too self-conscious. I'm not willing to put someone on the spot. I don't want a friend to make an appearance out of obligation.

The day finally came when Steve mentioned coming on, and naturally I jumped on it. It turned out to be a fantastic conversation—although it can definitely be tricky interviewing a friend. I think of things they've told me in our regular conversations. Did they tell me that in confidence? Am I allowed to bring it up? Will it offend them?

I seem to have avoided any of that awkwardness with Steve, because he's still talking to me.

Howard: Do you feel like you're a genius, or do you always feel like you have to be the guy working the hardest in the room?

Steve: What is a genius in comedy? That means you never fail, you never say a bad joke. I don't know what that is. You're just a working guy who's successful sometimes and other times not.

Howard: In your stand-up career, which was huge, you said it was never enjoyable, it was a real job, and in fact, even to sit there, and reflect, and act like it was enjoyable would be a distraction from the actual comedy.

Steve: I'll clarify that. It was absolutely enjoyable. But while you're doing it, you can't enjoy it. Because you're always thinking. As I said in my book, it's like your mind is three seconds ahead of itself. You're thinking, "What's next? What's happening? How did that go?"

Howard: Are you always thinking about what's going to be funny? Because it seems like everything out of your mouth is very witty, very well structured in terms of being funny. And it seems to come to you very naturally. Yet you describe in your book that it's the hardest thing in the world, comedy. You have to work at it. You spent ten years perfecting your act.

Steve: Well, in real life, I really enjoy being funny. In real life, with friends, sitting around, I really enjoy the banter back and forth. I do like being funny, but I've also had many friends who are so funny that you just kind of sit back and listen.

Howard: But some guys can't translate that to a stand-up career. There are some guys who are funny in the room with their friends and they cannot get on a stage and do it.

Steve: Well, that I don't know. It's a discipline, obviously. And the more you do it, the better. You just have to do it.

Howard: I would think with a family background like yours—

Steve: Here we go. Here we go. Robin, help me! Howard, I'm crying already!

Howard: No, Steve, honestly. I never bring this up when I've seen you personally, because I feel it's painful. You're born in Texas. Your family moves to Los Angeles when you're young. Your father wanted to be an actor?

Steve: I found that out later.

Howard: He never said that to you?

Steve: No, he didn't. First of all, my view of my childhood always was that I was very happy. Well, I was happy internally as a kid with friends and school, but maybe not so happy at home. I didn't understand that there was an alternative lifestyle, that other people were raised in a very happy home. But it wasn't awful at all. It was just—I had a complicated relationship with my father.

Howard: Your father was one of those guys who was just not communicative, right? He was a guy who was very isolated.

Steve: The strange thing was, after he died all these people came to me and said, "Your father was so much fun." Who are they talking about? By the way, later in life we reconciled. He would answer fan mail for me.

Howard: I happen to believe *The Jerk* is one of the greatest comedies ever made. And your father was critical of it.

Steve: It was the big premiere of *The Jerk* in Hollywood. Four of us go out for dinner, a friend of mine and my father and somebody else—I can't remember who. And my father said nothing about the movie.

Nothing. Finally my friend said, "Well, Glenn . . ." That was my father's name, and that's what I called him.

Howard: You never called him Dad?

Steve: No. In fact, I remember asking my mother, "What do I call him?"

Howard: Steve, clearly that's unusual, right? That you wouldn't call your father Dad?

Steve: Well, later I found out it was unusual.

Howard: So you were at dinner. *The Jerk* has come out.

Steve: And my friend says, "Glenn, what do you think of Steve and the movie?" And he said, "Well, he's no Charlie Chaplin." I didn't even regard it as an insult, because I thought, "Obviously, I'm no Charlie Chaplin. That's fine." But later, you know, I realized I was not getting feedback. If I said something— "I'm going to do the so-and-so show," or "I did the so-and-so show"—he'd have a critical response to it. So I just stopped telling him what I did.

Howard: Do you think he was jealous of you, because he probably had an ambition of being an actor? Do you think that as he saw you climb, it was too painful for him?

Steve: It was hard to interpret what he was thinking. I believe that my father had ambitions, and children came into his life and those ambitions stopped, and he had to go to work as a Realtor and wasn't able to pursue his dream. So I don't know. Maybe he was angry.

Howard: Seemed like he was resentful. Did he ever say why he had kids? Like, why bother if he doesn't like them?

Steve: Well, that's what you did. That's what you did.

Howard: Did your father ever hit you up for an acting part? Did he ever say, "Hey, why don't you put me in?"

Steve: No. I actually did ask him. He did a small part. Not a part, really—sort of a walk-on in the movie I did called *All of Me*.

Howard: Do you think you gave him that because you were subconsciously aware of his jealousy and maybe you could appease him by giving him a part in the movie and then he would be complimentary?

Steve: Wow! You are good! No, no, I don't. Because it wasn't like he was acting. He was doing it for fun.

Howard: The other thing I heard about your dad, which really blows my mind: you hosted *Saturday Night Live*, and your dad wrote a newspaper article in the local newspaper about how bad it was.

Steve: No, I'll explain that. He was the head of the Newport Board of Realtors and there was a local newsletter. It wasn't a newspaper. And he wrote a critical article about how it didn't help my career, which the opposite is true.

Howard: You would think a father would be so proud of his son. You're on *Saturday Night Live*. You're killing it. I mean, *Saturday Night Live* was just an amazing part of your career.

Steve: It absolutely was. But before we leave my father, I just want to repeat that later in life we became good friends.

Howard: How long a period of time did you not speak to him? Was it for many, many years?

Steve: It wasn't that I didn't speak to him. We spoke. But when I left the house at eighteen, I did not understand as I was going to college that you were supposed to call your parents and check in. I had no idea of that. I had no role model that said that you stayed in communication with your parents.

Howard: Was getting out of the house liberating for you?

Steve: Absolutely. I couldn't wait.

Howard: You went to work very young. Like, when I think about how brave you were—and I really do mean this. I'm not saying it sarcastically. At five you moved to California with your family, and at ten you decided to go out and get a job at Disneyland, right? Ten years old?

Steve: I was living in Garden Grove, California, and Disneyland had just been built. A friend of mine who lived two houses from me said, "Disneyland is hiring kids." And I couldn't think of anything more exciting than to work at Disneyland. So I picked up my bicycle—these were days when you could just leave the house on the bicycle and come home at five o'clock.

Howard: Getting a job at ten is probably indicative of how things were at home. Disneyland is the ultimate escape.

Steve: As I said, I didn't think of my childhood as ugly. I just didn't.

Howard: So you would go to school, and then Disneyland afterward and on weekends?

Steve: On weekends I would go to Disneyland and sell guidebooks out front. You'd make three dollars.

Howard: What would you do with that money? Would you just save it up?

Steve: Oh, boy. One time I went and bought a pair of shorts. They were four dollars and fifty cents, and my father flipped out.

Howard: Because it was extravagant.

Steve: It was extravagant.

Howard: So Glenn wasn't even proud of that? He wasn't proud of the fact that you would earn four dollars and had the wherewithal to buy your own shorts?

Steve: Well, I guess I never thought of it that way. But thank you for phrasing it like that.

Howard: No, I'm down on Glenn. I really am.

Steve: I just want to defend him a bit, because it's a complicated life in the thirties and forties and fifties, with these prototypes of what a man and a wife were, and how the father treated the children. There was discipline. It was just a very different time.

Howard: Toward the end of his life, you were able to sit down and have a real conversation with him for once and say, "Dad, you hurt me"?

Steve: No, I didn't do that. But he was very kind to me toward the end.

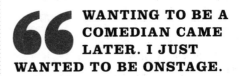

WANTING TO BE A COMEDIAN CAME LATER. I JUST WANTED TO BE ONSTAGE.

Howard: There was a rumor that you actually killed your father—murdered him with a pillow.

Steve: I think after this he is going to come back from the dead.

Howard: So you were working at Disneyland and you got exposed to entertainers. You think about it, a guy with your background, a kid, suddenly says, "I've got the bug. I want to be an entertainer."

Steve: Well, I didn't know what it meant to be an entertainer. I knew early that I loved comedy. I've never phrased it like I'm phrasing it now. I just loved comedy.

Howard: You never said, "I want to be a comedian"?

Steve: No, I didn't even know what that was. Wanting to be a comedian came later. I just wanted to be onstage, and that was a way to be onstage. I didn't sing or dance or act or do anything. All I had was a magic act. I would go see this comedian named Wally Boag at the Golden Horseshoe Revue. It was a free show and it was fantastic.

Howard: What did Wally do?

Steve: He did balloon animals.

Howard: There you go.

Steve: And he was just funny. He did corny jokes. I saw his show hundreds of times, and he was always fresh. He never did the same show.

Howard: Like an old show-business thing. You never know who's in the audience. Just go out and give them your best show.

Steve: He was so funny. So genuinely funny. My fantasy was, I'm sitting there in the audience watching—I would be twelve or thirteen or fourteen—and he would get sick and somebody would say, "Does anybody know this show in the audience?"

Howard: And you knew it?

Steve: I would be ready to go on.

Howard: Did you have his jokes memorized?

Steve: Oh, completely.

Howard: You knew the whole thing?

Steve: Yeah.

Howard: And you would go home and practice magic. Now, what does that mean, to practice magic, sleight of hand?

Steve: You practice in front of the mirror and you try to see if you can see anything that's going on.

Howard: Were you good at it?

Steve: I was good enough that when I was fifteen I worked at the Magic Shop [in Fantasyland at Disneyland], and I would be demonstrating card tricks with trick decks. And one time I just thought, "I don't need these trick decks. I can just do it with regular cards."

Howard: Don't you think if you're not sure how to be a performer, magic is a way?

Steve: Absolutely.

Howard: Because Johnny Carson used to do that too. He was consumed with magic, because he wasn't sure what the hell he was going to do.

Steve: When you're fifteen and you're trying to figure out a way to perform, a magic act is perfect. Because you buy a trick and then it's got patter written in the instructions. You know, "Good evening, ladies and gentlemen . . ." You memorize that and you've got a show. And I would do my show for my parents' bridge parties.

Howard: Did you have a special name?

Steve: No, I didn't think that far ahead.

Howard: And magic does not help with girls, right? It's not something that they respond to?

Steve: I don't know. I wasn't thinking about girls.

Howard: You were just thinking about a career.

Steve: I didn't have an idea for a career. I just liked being onstage, and only later did I think about a career.

Howard: You've got to skip ahead for one second here. I don't understand how you get out of college and then get a job writing for the Smothers Brothers. The Smothers Brothers were the biggest act on television.

Steve: I'll tell you how that happened. I was in college and I was working at a place called Ledbetter's doing my little shows, ten or fifteen minutes. I had written some stories, which later became the book *Cruel Shoes*, and I had met at my college—Long Beach State College—a dancer. I don't know what name she goes by now, but

Nina Goldblatt was her name at that time. She was so cute and she was a dancer on television, on the Smothers Brothers show. I started talking to her. It's the one time in my life where I actually had the courage to go up to somebody that I thought was adorable and start talking to her, and she was friendly. She was dating—not dating, had seen Mason Williams, who was the head writer of *The Smothers Brothers Comedy Hour*. She heard that they were looking for younger writers, because the mantra of the late 1960s was "Never trust anyone over thirty." The luckiest thing that ever happened to me. Because I was under thirty. I submitted my material and Mason Williams liked it, and they brought me in.

Howard: Was your mind blown that you got a job on this Smothers Brothers show out of college?

Steve: I did become very anxious about it and very nervous, and essentially I had a little bit of a breakdown. But I persevered in that discipline of learning how to write comedy.

Howard: You got nervous because you're working with probably some of the best television writers in the history of television, who are groundbreaking. You weren't insecure that you'd lose your job? You were excited?

Steve: I did worry about losing my job. But this moment happened. I'm sitting there and I'm watching them rehearse, and I knew I hadn't really come up with a lot of stuff. I'd written a good piece for the Smothers

Brothers at first and hadn't written much since. But one night—this is in my book, I'm not confessing it for the first time— I was sitting there watching the show rehearse, and Tommy Smothers came up to me and said, "We need an intro for this bit. Can you go write it?" I'm like, "Sure."

Howard: "Yeah, I can do anything."

Steve: Yeah. And I went up to my little room and I had nothing in my brain. Not a thing. Then I called my friend Gary Mule Deer. You know who he is?

Howard: No.

Steve: Oh, he's a great comedian. We were roommates for a while. I said, "Gary, I'm on the line here, and you have a great joke. Can I use it?" And he said absolutely. And the joke was this. It was Tommy's line. He said, "It has been proven that more people watch television than any other appliance." You know what? It freed me. And I was able to then just start writing and start thinking. You had to learn how to think in a certain way.

Howard: You mean it freed you because, "Hey, maybe I could write some absurd thing and it will—"

Steve: No, I felt I was over the hump of proving myself, even though I proved myself with somebody else's material.

Howard: See, I would have felt dejected that I had to go get this other material from this guy. And yet it kind of showed you the way.

Steve: You know, my will was so strong.

Howard: Meaning that you just had to succeed.

Steve: I had to.

Howard: You've said that about comedy. You've said that you didn't think you were the most talented guy in the room or the funniest guy in the room, but you worked harder than anybody. You put in ten years of developing your stand-up act, four years of going out and performing and kind of refining it.

Steve: Yeah.

Howard: And then four years of actually performing it and getting all those successes. And the strangest thing about all that is I figured you were a guy on top of the world, when you're on tour and you're already playing in Madison Square Garden. I figured this was the greatest time in your life. And when I read about it, you say it was the worst part of your life. People were laughing at just about anything you said, and it was the loneliest part of your life.

Steve: Very lonely.

Howard: Because you were one of the most famous guys in the world at that point, and it was isolating.

Steve: Yeah, it was isolating. I hated every moment. Because there was a moment right before [I had that] success where I felt so funny. I would go out and play to people who had only heard of me, they hadn't seen anything, and it was fantastic. It was just thrilling to be onstage and to know what you're doing. The moments early on when you get some fame and you're onstage and you're the conductor of laughs, that was thrilling too. Watching the audience grow, from clubs to suddenly—

Howard: What was the biggest crowd you ever played to?

Steve: I think it was twenty-five thousand.

Howard: I don't think anybody had ever done that before. I think you were the first.

Steve: People say that. I don't know if Richard Pryor had done it.

Howard: I don't think to that size.

Steve: Yeah, maybe.

Howard: I do think there's a very brave decision in there, leaving the world of television where you're successful. Because certainly writing for Sonny and Cher, writing for the Smothers Brothers, walking away from it and saying, "Now I'm going to go be a performer," your income gets completely shot, right?

Steve: Yeah, wiped out. But you know what I had? Residuals. I had residuals from writing, and that kept me going for a while. I remember one time I called David Brenner, who was very successful. And I said, "David, you know I get paid $300 for a show and it costs me $250 to get there. What do you do?" This was the best advice I ever got. It changed my career. He said, "What I do is I take the door and let the club take the bar. And I have a friend standing there with a clicker." I had decided at that time to be an opening act no longer. I said, "People do not attend or perceive the opening act. They're there for the headliner." I decided to only headline. So I went to a little club called Bubba's, I think, in Coconut Grove [Miami], and this

||||||||||||||||||||||||||||||||||||||||||||||||||||||||||||||||||||||||||||||||||||||||||||||||||||||||||||||||||||||||||||||||||||||||||

" I THOUGHT, "BUT THERE'S ANOTHER KIND OF LAUGHTER. WHEN YOU'RE AT HOME WITH YOUR FRIENDS AND YOU'RE LAUGHING SO HARD AND YOU'RE CRYING. YOU CAN'T STOP LAUGHING. . . ." AND I THOUGHT, "WHAT IF I COULD GO FOR *THAT*?"

||||||||||||||||||||||||||||||||||||||||||||||||||||||||||||||||||||||||||||||||||||||||||||||||||||||||||||||||||||||||||||||||||||||||||

was to be the first time I was going to only headline.

Howard: Ballsy move, right? Because who the hell knew you? No one.

Steve: So my income just really, really dropped. But that changed my life, because when I started headlining, people started paying attention a little bit.

Howard: Where do you think you get the guts to do that? Honestly.

Steve: Well, I think it's inevitable. I don't think it's guts.

Howard: You just had to do it?

Steve: Yeah, I had to do it.

Howard: When you started headlining, nobody is coming to these shows, right? I mean, it's very small.

Steve: I would be playing places that seated eighty people.

Howard: And there's some point where you're using other people's material, comedians you've heard.

Steve: That was early on.

Howard: And then you come to the conclusion, "I've got to do my own thing, but I don't want punch-line jokes." I don't understand that. What do you mean by "punch-line jokes"?

Steve: I'll explain it. I'm in college, and I'm studying philosophy, and I'm examining everything. That's the premise of studying philosophy in college is to examine everything that's going on here.

Howard: Existence.

Steve: And I started to really examine comedy, and I noticed there's two kinds of laughter. One is when you're watching the comedian and he says a joke and then you laugh at it, because you heard the punch line. And sometimes it's really funny and you're laughing. And other times it's okay, but you still laugh because you're laughing on the rhythm. And I thought, "But there's another kind of laughter. When you're at home with your friends and you're laughing so hard and you're crying. You can't stop laughing. And when you think about it, you don't know why you're laughing, you're just laughing." And I thought, "What if I could go for *that*? Go for trying to actually be funny, where people are really laughing? And you say, 'What are you laughing at?' And they go, 'I don't know.'" I realized that when I was doing jokes, there would be this laughter. But if I just tried slightly different material and the audience didn't have these punch lines to laugh at, they would pick their own place to laugh. They would determine when to laugh. I wouldn't be telling them.

Howard: It was that theory you had to test out.

Steve: Yeah, then I had to test it out. Maybe I'm twenty-one at this time or twenty. I dropped all the material that I had gotten out of joke books, and I said, "I have to write it all, otherwise it's not going to have a stamp of authorship on it."

Howard: Is it fun for you to speak about your life, or do you resent it? Do you not like reflecting?

Steve: It depends on the circumstance. Here, I'm having a great time. But I don't want to go do an interview with a website where I'm promoting a specific thing and then delve back into my past.

Howard: Because sometimes reflection can kind of be sad, right? It's just like, "Oh my God, I look back on all of this and it's just too much."

Steve: A lot of people think you look back and you say, "Wow, what a successful career. It's just amazing. It's fantastic." But I remember the flops too. Those flops don't go away. I remember Michael Caine told me once, "Steve"—I can do his voice—"I used to do any movie that came along. Anything. It didn't matter, because they disappear. They were terrible. Then this thing came out called VHS."

Howard: You've had so many home runs. But you'll look at it and go, "Oh yeah, some of those things just didn't work out." But you were trying to be creative. That's the problem with the film industry. There is so much riding on it now that you can't even risk a flop.

Steve: The film industry is two worlds. It's these blockbusters and the independent, low-budget film world.

Howard: Did you hate hosting the Oscars? Because when you wrote that open letter to Eddie Murphy when he was going to host, it was really funny. You said, "Be prepared for a bunch of assholes telling you how horrible you did." It seemed to me that you were trying to warn him, "Don't host the Oscars. It's a pain in the ass."

Steve: No, I wasn't. I've hosted it three times, and the first time I said, "I'll host under this condition: if I'm the first thing out there." Because those moments are so valuable. That's when the audience is hot and when the comedy is right. You don't want to follow a big dance number.

Howard: You want to go out and do your monologue.

Steve: Yeah, that's what I wanted. And I said no interviews. I just wanted to concentrate on what I was going to do. So the first time I was in a state of cold fear.

Howard: Really?

Steve: Yeah. Then the curtain goes up and you're fine, because you've done it a million times.

Howard: But there are millions of people watching that thing.

Steve: Yeah, but you don't think about that. I always worked to the crowd in that room. And I love the crowd. I found them very ripe for comedy.

Howard: But it's a crowd that wants to be

rewarded and praised. They are actors, and it's their big night.

Steve: I think you're overstating it. Everybody is a person. Of course they are nervous, but they are watching a comedian do comedy and they are fine. I like the audience.

Howard: And then you walked out and you felt in command?

Steve: Yes. But then the second time was the night the Iraq invasion started. That's too long a story to tell you all my thoughts I went through. But that was tough.

Howard: Were you thinking, "How can I make jokes if we've just invaded Iraq?"

Steve: Yes, but I had some experience with that. I was working at the Birdcage Theater [at Knott's Berry Farm in Buena Park, California], 1963, and Kennedy was shot. I'm thinking, "Well, they can't possibly be doing a show." And we got there and they said the show was going to go on. I thought, "This is going to be awful." And we went out and the audience was really hot for some reason. And I thought, "It must be true about some kind of escape." So I have this understanding from twenty years ago, thirty years ago, of an audience's reaction in times of stress. So I decided to acknowledge what was going on and then just go ahead. And it was successful.

Howard: You went on the Letterman show the night he had come back from that scandal. You were the first guest booked. That was a smart decision on Letterman's part, because you would know how to handle something like that. If you remember, Letterman was all over the tabloid press—his personal life. He was being ripped apart.

Steve: I can't remember what I did, but there were two segments. I sat down, and however I addressed it, it all seemed funny and fine. But in the second segment Marty Short came out.

Howard: Which made things a lot looser, and you would probably really welcome that, because there was tension, right? You were aware of it. It was his first show back.

Steve: I can't remember what my jokes were. But I went over them with their staff, and they said, "No, I think that's a little too much. But this seems fine."

Howard: Steve, is there anything you want to say that you have not said? Is there anything that I missed?

Steve: I will just say, I will be a little corny and say I really have enjoyed the show, and I've really enjoyed your personal change over the years. Did I tell you about the first time I realized you were funny?

Howard: No.

Steve: This would be in the—I can't remember, the eighties or nineties or something. One time I tune in and you are doing the pope. And I think you are doing a deathbed scene with another cardinal or something. And you said, "You want to know what I have under my hat? It's a bottle of ketchup."

Howard: You liked that?

Steve: The image of the pope's hat with a bottle of ketchup.

Howard: Thank God I said that.

Amy Poehler

OCTOBER 27, 2014

In the beginning of my career, I would visualize my ideal listener. He was a middle-aged man driving to his job. Picturing a man and not a woman wasn't a sexist thing. It was my daddy issues. I documented that in my last two books—how badly I wanted my father's respect, admiration, and love. He was a radio engineer and co-owned a recording studio. He worshipped the announcers and voice-over actors he worked with. How else could I get him to listen to me?

I don't need that imagery anymore. I've let go of it. These days it's not a man or a woman who I visualize. It's not a person at all. Now the process is what elite athletes often describe as "being in the zone." It's a hypnotic trance, a self-induced coma that begins at 7 a.m. When I emerge four hours later, I don't remember much of what I've done.

However, the idea that my show is only for men has persisted. The general perception is that my audience is comprised mostly of sex-obsessed drooling morons who only want to talk porn and . . . well, porn. It bums me out. Because it simply isn't true. Women have always been an important part of my audience. When I was working in Detroit, one of my program directors chastised me for taking too many female callers. He said it made me sound "wimpy." That just didn't compute with me. Some of my most loyal listeners have been women, like Mariann from Brooklyn who's been calling in for nearly three decades. The four years I was on *AGT* seemed to make me even more popular among women. I suppose they saw I had a kinder, more vulnerable side. I've heard from a few women that it wasn't until they saw me on *AGT* that they decided to give my radio show a try. According to stats provided by SiriusXM, women now make up about 40 percent of my listeners. Shocking, right?

I was thrilled to find out Amy Poehler is among them. As she makes it clear in this interview, she isn't just a casual listener—she is a die-hard fan. That a strong, talented, intelligent, sophisticated performer/writer like Amy knows who Tan Mom is and what Baba Booey means and is well-versed in "Hit 'em with the Hein" is extremely important to me. She is the kind of woman who so many critics and focus groups said wouldn't get my humor and viewed me as a Cro-Magnon. Amy's fandom serves as a middle finger to anyone who said I would never capture a female audience.

Howard: It's good to finally talk to you, because I see you all the time at Jimmy Kimmel's parties, and we never talk. I don't know what it is, I'm not good at parties.

Amy: We met very briefly, and you told me I smelled good, and I was like, "I'm . . . I'm winning." And I just left, like, forty-five minutes later.

Howard: It's a strange thing because I would always love to talk to you, and then afterward, I'd go, "Hey, Amy Poehler was there, but I didn't get to talk to her." And I always felt weird about that, you know?

Amy: I have a little anxiety, a little social anxiety, when it comes to parties. I kind of like to go in and then leave fast.

Howard: What is that? Because I'm in the same boat. I get there and I just get nervous.

Amy: Yeah.

Howard: But we're both reasonably intelligent. We should be able to carry on a conversation. And yet we freeze up.

Amy: Yeah, as soon as I walk into a party, I just want to leave. I just want to go home. I think as I get older, I've just gotten more anxiety around other people. I don't know, I just feel less interested in a lot of people's energy.

Howard: Me too.

Amy: Like, the same thing with concerts and stuff.

Howard: It's just too draining.

Amy: I don't want to go to rock shows anymore. It's too much.

Howard: What about even going to a movie?

Amy: I barely go to the movies.

Howard: Me too.

Robin: Broadway shows?

Amy: Yeah, no.

Howard: Oh, fuck that. But writing comedy . . . Do you write the majority of *Parks and Recreation*?

Amy: No, we have a cast of writers, and I write an episode a year.

Howard: Were you scared when you started *Parks and Recreation*?

Amy: Yeah.

Howard: 'Cause you'd never carried a show. And also everyone looks at you after *Saturday Night Live*—like, if that tanks, then your career is over and all that. Was all that pressure getting to you?

Amy: I knew working with Mike [Schur, the series creator], it would be really fun, and funny. We did kind of get hammered in the beginning because we were compared to *The Office*.

Howard: But when you go into a show like *Parks and Recreation*, you can't go into it in a cavalier manner, right? You've gotta go, "Shit, okay, I got an opportunity here. I'm coming off *Saturday Night Live*. I probably could pick a lot of different shows." It's not like you just go, "Oh, I'll go try this."

Amy: Well, you have to go where the writing is, right? That's where you get protected in television, 'cause writing is the king. So Mike Schur—I knew he would grab so many good people. And I was excited about playing one character for a while, because with *SNL* you play so many different people, all the time. And I felt like I could do it. I felt like, "Oh, I think this character's somewhat written for me."

Howard: Is it weird for you that you're always nominated for an Emmy, and Julia Louis-Dreyfus wins every year for *Veep*?

Amy: Bitch.

Howard: Yeah, that bitch. I mean, fuck her.

Amy: That bitch.

Howard: I mean, she's got serious money.

Amy: Bullshit. How many more does she need?

Howard: She's worth, like, billions of dollars. You could use that.

Robin: And she's got other Emmys. She doesn't need another one.

Amy: Yeah, she has so many Emmys from other shows.

Howard: But everyone I know who's a devout fan of *Parks and Recreation* says you so deserve it. I don't know how you feel about awards, but—

Amy: Well, it's more fun to lose than to win, in a way.

Howard: Why?

Amy: Because when you win, you have that adrenaline rush, you've got to give a speech, and then you have to go backstage, and all of a sudden everyone's like, "Well, she shouldn't have won." But if you lose, the whole night everyone's like, "You should've won."

Howard: How many times have you been nominated?

Amy: I don't know. Many times. I think for *Parks*, like, four or five times.

Howard: So this is the seventh season coming up.

Amy: Yeah, and every time they're about to say who wins, you think it's gonna be you. Like, every time.

Howard: Do you prepare a speech ahead of time?

Amy: Yeah, I do. I mean, isn't it annoying when people pretend like they're not prepared? They have a one-in-five chance of winning.

Howard: Yeah, and it's a very actress and actor thing to get up there and then act unprepared.

Amy: It stresses me out when people don't know how much real estate they're supposed to take up, and they just start, like, really sitting into it, and you're like, "You have forty-five seconds, dude. Get to the point."

Howard: What is the speech like? Do you thank me or—

Amy: I thank you. Baba Booey all the way.

Howard: You say Baba Booey.

Amy: Yeah.

Howard: Amy, you've said you've listened to this show.

Amy: Yeah, I'm a huge fan, and I'm freaking out right now. I love Tan Mom. She's my favorite.

Howard: And you said—this is a quote from you, tell me if I'm right—"The great thing about Tan Mom is that the least interesting thing about her is her tanning now."

Amy: You would think that would be the thing you want to talk to her about. But there's so much more.

Howard: Do you do a Tan Mom impression?

Amy: I'm not very good at impressions, but what I like about Tan Mom is her attitude.

Howard: Right.

Amy: So she's very like, "Oh, get over yourself. You're not even pretty." She's always telling people they're not pretty. She's really confident.

Howard: So, why write a book? You're so busy. How many kids you got, two?

Amy: Two kids.

Howard: You've got the TV show. This is gonna be the seventh and last season.

Amy: Yes.

Howard: How are we feeling about the last season?

Amy: Super sad. Great job. I love the people.

Howard: Why is it the last season?

Amy: Because we've done 125, and everybody's contracts are up. We've had this great run, but not huge ratings, so we're always kind of on the bubble every year. And we wanted to be in control of the ending, which is so rare in television.

Howard: Right, because you're saying, "If we're not this huge ratings success, they could cancel at any season." Then you never have the finale episode.

Amy: Yeah, we never have that last show.

Howard: This book—I didn't know you were such a sexual person.

Amy: [*laughs*] I do give sex tips in the book. I mean, they're jokes, but they're true.

Howard: But they're kind of not jokes.

Amy: No. I believe it.

Robin: What kind of tips?

Howard: I'm gonna go through them.

Amy: Oh, Robin, listen up.

Howard: Believe me, Robin needs to know this. She's always open to new things, that's why I love Robin.

Amy: I know. Me too.

Howard: Is it almost mandatory that you write something outrageous about sex in a book? Because you know sex sells, and you have to sell books.

Amy: It's funny, when this book came out, some stupid website pulls out two or three sentences, and says I'm talking about my drug use and divorce. Which I don't really. I kind of joke about those things, but . . . To answer your question, no, I didn't have to write about it. But I did think it was a funny bit.

Howard: You can joke about your divorce? You're not bitter about it?

Amy: No. Will and I are very, very good friends.

Howard: Will Arnett?

Amy: Yes. He's been here.

Howard: Yes.

Amy: And we are doing a really good job, I think, of—

Howard: Are you?

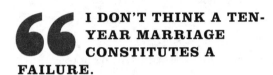

I DON'T THINK A TEN-YEAR MARRIAGE CONSTITUTES A FAILURE.

Amy: Yeah.

Howard: There's no bitterness?

Amy: [*laughs*] Well, you know, I don't think a ten-year marriage constitutes a failure. I think relationships are really tough.

Howard: So were you the one who ended it, or he ended it, or was it both?

Amy: It was kind of like—I don't know if I want to get into that. But I do think that it's interesting when you go through a divorce how everybody—divorce is, like, not that special. So people are kind of interested, and then they're just not anymore. It's kind of like you get all the pain, but really none of the sympathy. You know, 'cause it's so common.

Howard: You're right.

Robin: There's no ceremony. There's no funeral. There's no essential thing.

Amy: Yeah, yeah.

Howard: You're right. It's not that special.

Amy: It's not that special. And the pain that you're in is very specific to you, and special. And everybody reacts very differently. Your married friends get a little nervous that it's contagious. And your single friends—

Howard: Did you lose friends when you got divorced? In other words, because you're an attractive woman—

Amy: Oh, thank you, Howard.

Howard: You're successful. I would see why you'd be a threat to some women, once you're single. You know what I mean?

Amy: Well, it was weird to be single for the first time. I remember I went to a wedding, and I was single. It was, like, a drunken night, and then somebody I knew came up and was kind of drunkenly joking that I was hitting on her husband.

Howard: Oh, man.

Amy: Yeah. Which I wasn't.

Howard: But you did fuck the groom? Wasn't that true?

Amy: I did, yeah. But that's what we do. I mean, that makes sense.

Howard: No, but in other words, your whole world changes. And some of that is exciting, right?

Amy: Right, sure.

Howard: Was dating a cool thing for you?

Amy: It was new and weird. I hadn't dated when there was texting. I got married in 2003, and then all of a sudden I'm like, "Oh, right. Now you *text* somebody." There were times when I was out with guys, and I was like, "Oh, I think I might be on a date, but I don't know." It was a lot of that.

Howard: What do you mean? It was like, "Hey, let's go hang out"?

Amy: Okay, I'll tell you this story. I was at dinner with, um, John Stamos.

Howard: Yeah, I think I've been on a date with him. I'm not sure.

Robin: Yeah, I think John dates everyone.

Howard: He's very sexual.

Amy: Well, handsome men are really something else. First of all, they're so handsome, and John is—

Howard: Ridiculously handsome.

Amy: Yes. And you know, whoever was really the thing when you were a teenager—not to make him feel old, but same with Rob Lowe. I worked with Rob Lowe. When Rob Lowe came out of the shower in *The Outsiders*, I was, like, fourteen. And I was like, "Oh my God." And I tell Rob Lowe that all the time.

Howard: So where were you with Stamos? You're at a restaurant?

Amy: I was at a restaurant. We were having dinner and I was like, "Oh, maybe this is a date." But I didn't know.

Howard: How did you end up there with him?

Amy: He asked me to the restaurant.

Howard: That was a date.

Amy: I guess, I guess.

Howard: Yeah.

Amy: But I kind of, like, blew it.

Howard: Were you like, "There's no way John Stamos wants me"?

Amy: Yeah.

Howard: You were saying, "Oh, I'm not in his league." That kind of thing?

Amy: Yeah. But also it was—I don't know.

Howard: This was after your divorce. He called you up and said, "Hey, let's get together"?

> ## " I CAN'T BELIEVE I'M TELLING THIS STORY, BUT IT'S HOWARD STERN, SO THERE YOU GO.

Amy: No. We worked, um . . . I can't believe I'm telling this story, but it's Howard Stern, so there you go. We worked on a movie together—he did a little bit in a movie I did. And a bunch of us hung out. And then later on he was like, "Let's go get dinner."

Howard: And you were single?

Amy: I was separated.

Howard: And so, you're there, you're talking, blah-blah-blah. Does he say to you, "Hey, let's go to my place"?

Amy: No, he doesn't.

Howard: No?

Amy: No, no. And I remember thinking, like, "Oh, shit." Like, halfway through. Like, "If this is really a date . . ." I think I was wearing a Leslie Knope shirt [her character on *Parks and Recreation*]. I think I was wearing a shirt from work.

Howard: You weren't all hot stuff?

Amy: Yeah, I wasn't hot stuff.

Robin: You didn't really try.

Amy: It sometimes can be appealing, Robin.

Howard: Are you disappointed that you didn't, uh—

Amy: That I didn't fuck John Stamos?

Howard: Yeah.

Amy: Well, I think everything ended up the way it was supposed to end up.✦

Howard: Right. Not to dwell on this, but I'm fascinated.

Amy: I knew you would be.

Howard: Do you get paranoid that guys want to date you because you're the famous Amy Poehler?

Amy: No, you kind of weed that out pretty fast. But I haven't really had that experience. I've usually dated people that I've been friends with. And, um, I'm dating someone now. I have a boyfriend now, who I've known for a very long time, before we started dating.

Howard: The comedy guy, right?

Amy: Yeah. Nick Kroll. And so I don't really date people I don't know, if that makes any sense.

Howard: How you gonna work this with kids? Is Nick gonna move in with you? How are you gonna work all this out?

Amy: Slow down, Howard.

Howard: What are you gonna do?

Amy: Slow down. Why do you gotta—

Howard: That's tough. I've been through this.

Amy: I know. Well, your kids are older.

Howard: My kids are old. But listen, when I got divorced, I had a six-year-old. I mean, these are tricky waters.

Amy: Yeah, yeah. You just have to take it, you know, one day at a time.

Howard: Yeah. So, getting back to the sex tips in the book . . .

Amy: Okay, please. I can't believe that getting back to sex makes me feel better than—yeah, let's do it. Now I'm relieved that we're going back into the sex tips.

Howard: I never thought of—like, I never thought of—like, I think you're so funny and intelligent—

Amy: But you never found me sexy.

Howard: No, I never thought about you in terms of, like, what you would do in bed. And there you put it all out for us to read.

Amy: Okay, you know what, for your listeners, yes, I want them to think that.

Howard: Amy says she loves sex and that she's great at it, which is really setting yourself up.

Amy: Yeah. I dare anyone to prove me wrong.

Robin: Sexually confident. Love it.

Amy: Thanks, Robin.

Howard: How do you know you're great at it? What does that mean, you're great at it?

Amy: Well, that is a joke that I put in the book.

Howard: But no, it isn't.

Amy: No, it isn't. You're right. Well, I'm forty-three. I think women get really in their zone, and get really good at knowing what they like.

Howard: Why do you think you're good at it, though? Guys can beat off to a piece

✦ **For more on this from John Stamos, turn to page 546.**

of meat. So how does a woman know when she's good at it?

Amy: I think you enjoy it. I think you enjoy it, and you have fun. You're open-minded, and you feel good about yourself.

Howard: And what does "open-minded" mean? Do you put on outfits?

Amy: No. I mean, it's just like—

Howard: You agree to be tied up?

Amy: It's just like there's not a lot of shame or judgment in any of it.

Howard: If I say to you, "Amy, I'm your boyfriend. I'm in love with you."

Amy: Oh, Howard, this is a dream come true.

Howard: I'm sure it's a nightmare. If I say to you, "Would you please dress up as a cat?" would you do that?

Amy: I would say, "All right, it's a little corny, but—"

Howard: But let's try.

Amy: Sure, let's try it.

Howard: If I said to you I wanted to tie you up and do shit to you—and let's say you trusted me enough. Would you go for that?

Amy: Sure.

Howard: You would?

Amy: Yeah.

Howard: What if I left you in the bed spread-eagle naked, tied up to the bed, and I left you alone for a half hour. Would you be excited by it?

Amy: I would be worried about when I was gonna eat next. Yeah, I would be concerned about what my dinner was gonna be.

> **" I'M FORTY-THREE. I THINK WOMEN GET REALLY IN THEIR ZONE, AND GET REALLY GOOD AT KNOWING WHAT THEY LIKE.**

Howard: If I left the room and then showed back up in blackface, would that offend you?

Amy: I would find that hacky. No. In general, anyone with a bad sense of humor is a real turnoff.

Howard: If I put you in the bed, and I had you tied up, and I came back and I put ice cream on your vagina and licked it off, would that be a cool thing to do?

Amy: It would be fine. It would feel like a little much. Like it would be a whole *thing*.

Howard: Trying too hard?

Amy: Trying too hard.

Howard: A little too *Fifty Shades of Grey*?

Amy: *Yes.* That book, by the way, I read and was like, "Eh."

Howard: You weren't turned on?

Amy: No, I thought it was kind of—

Howard: You don't want to be dominated by some guy?

Amy: No, I *do*.

Howard: You do?

Amy: Sure.

Howard: So then why wouldn't that turn you on?

Amy: This is gonna be such a dumb reason, but I was like, "I don't believe

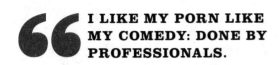

I LIKE MY PORN LIKE MY COMEDY: DONE BY PROFESSIONALS.

these characters." A twenty-five-year-old millionaire? Like, whatever.

Howard: The backstory has to be believable. It's like porn.

Amy: Yeah. Sure. Well, I know what kind of porn you like, which is your babysitter stuff.

Howard: Babysitter, massage room—

Amy: Yeah, massage room. Yup, that's nice. 'Cause it also involves a massage, which I always think is nice.

Howard: Always nice. I watched two girls give each other a shower last night. One was a reluctant lesbian, and the other one was full-blown lesbian.

Amy: I feel like the reluctant one maybe was on board from the beginning.

Howard: Yeah, it wasn't that convincing. I wanted her to struggle with her lesbian tendencies.

Amy: Sure.

Howard: I really did. You do say in the book men should stay away from porn. Because too much porn will desensitize you. And you're right.

Amy: Well, I like porn, and I think that people should do whatever they want. But the point being that this generation is so—porn is so accessible that sometimes guys don't actually connect to the person that's in front of them.

Howard: It's true. If I watch too much porn, then I'm not in my relationship.

Amy: Right?

Howard: But you say you do watch porn. What type of porn do you watch?

Amy: I do. [*laughs*] Oh my God.

Howard: What are you watching?

Amy: We got to that.

Howard: Yeah.

Amy: It's not too crazy. I like my porn like my comedy: done by professionals.

Howard: Right.

Amy: Women who are at the top of their game. I like professional ladies who are enjoying themselves. I'm not an amateur person.

Howard: Right. I'm with you on that.

Amy: Yeah, I want everybody to look good, and be good at their jobs.

Howard: Shit. I didn't know any of this about you.

Amy: Well, you know, we're just meeting for the first time.

Hillary Clinton

THE INTERVIEW THAT NEVER HAPPENED

I don't think I've ever tried harder to get a guest than I did with Hillary Clinton in the run-up to the 2016 election.

As you know by now from reading this book, Donald Trump and I go way back, and had I endorsed him for president, publically hitched myself to his candidacy and gone all in, who knows what might have come from it. Instead of writing this book, I might have been sitting on the Supreme Court. Chief Justice Stern. Imagine me in my custom John Varvatos robe, banging my gavel and picking the pubic hairs out of Clarence Thomas's Coke can. Maybe I'd be chairman of the FCC, in charge of the government branch that tried to put me out of business. Think of the cosmic irony in that. Perhaps a cushy ambassadorship

someplace warm, or at the very least I might have wrangled an invitation to Camp David.

But I'm no sellout. I have been a fan of Hillary for nearly as long as I've known Donald. This woman has dedicated her life to public service, and that's what I look for in a candidate. She was a first lady, senator, secretary of state. Her entire life has been in the service of our country. People would say to me, "You're just voting for her because she's the lesser of two evils." I'd say, "No, I wanted her as president before I wanted Barack Obama." I love Barack Obama, but I was a Hillary Clinton supporter going all the way back to 2008. I think she would have been a great president.

I saw long before anyone else that it wasn't going to be easy for her to beat Donald. I

> "MY AUDIENCE SPANS THE ENTIRE COUNTRY, INCLUDING THE SWING STATES. I KNOW THESE PEOPLE. THEY'VE BEEN LISTENING TO ME MY ENTIRE CAREER. I COULD TELL THAT THEY WERE JUST NOT FEELING HILLARY."

didn't see her connecting. My audience spans the entire country, including the swing states. I know these people. They've been listening to me my entire career. I could tell that they were just not feeling Hillary and that they were really embracing Donald. As I said in this book's introduction, I consider Donald Trump one of the best radio guests ever. He just knows how to connect with an audience. Hillary does not.

I was talking to my agent, Don Buchwald, about this. I said, "If Hillary did the show, my listeners might appreciate her commitment to public service and her decency and humanity."

Don immediately became obsessed with this idea. We both did. We wanted to do whatever we could to make it happen.

This wasn't the first time we set our sights on a Moby Dick–type interview subject. In the early nineties, we tried to arrange an interview with Michael Jackson. He was looking to rehabilitate his image after the child molestation allegations, and his team reached out to us. They had the idea of me organizing some kind of rally in his honor in New York. I thought that was stupid and had my own idea of doing a TV

sit-down with him at halftime during the Super Bowl. Don and I got as far as meeting Michael at his manager's Central Park apartment. Michael walked in dressed in his full military getup and the tape on his nose. We talked for about ten minutes. I couldn't stop staring at all the makeup on his face, which was practically dripping off. He was like the Elephant Man. After the meeting, we never heard from him again.

I knew I probably shouldn't get my hopes up about Hillary. I couldn't help it. I really believed that by coming on my show she would win over the type of voters she so desperately needed. I also thought my time on *AGT* might have made me more palatable in her eyes. I had been so astonished and humbled by how the American public had come to embrace me, thanks to that show. Often before we taped an episode, I would go out in front of the crowd and warm them up. I would tell the story of how in 1985 the chairman of NBC, Grant Tinker, had fired me from my radio show on WNBC and then said over his dead body would I ever be allowed back at the network. "Well," I'd tell the crowd, "now Grant Tinker is dead, and guess what? Here I am at NBC."

They would laugh and applaud, and it felt like a victory lap—like Rocky running up the steps in Philadelphia. Sure, a less fit and muscular Rocky. I punch my own meat but not in a fridge. Still, I was on top of my game. Even if Hillary wasn't a regular viewer of the show, maybe word would get back to her that it might be time to reconsider her opinion of me.

Thinking about the Michael Jackson Super Bowl idea and *AGT*, Don and I wondered if TV was the answer. Maybe Hillary would be more willing to do an interview on camera than on the radio. As fervently as I've championed the radio format throughout my career, I know there are still plenty of people who see TV as more desirable. There were a few big TV networks that had been after me to host an interview show. It wouldn't be a regular thing, just a few specials. SiriusXM was cool with it, since it didn't conflict with my radio show. But I'm very loyal to Sirius, and I wouldn't consider doing one of these TV specials unless it was for a really big guest.

The head of one of these networks was a huge financial backer of Hillary. Don went to him and said, "You get Hillary, and we'll get equal time with Trump. Then you'll get two specials."

It would've been easy to get Trump for an interview. All throughout the campaign he had been reaching out to me. He even asked me to speak at the Republican National Convention. In my calculation, all I'd have to do is ask and he'd do it.

So this network honcho presents the idea to Hillary. And she says no.

This only makes Don more determined. He's got a lot of connections of his own in the Democratic Party. Don went to them. He told them that we would even be willing to do a rehearsal before the show, so Hillary could see the line of questioning ahead of time. I wasn't going to bring up Monica Lewinsky. The old me would have tried that. That would have been the first thing I said. Now I see how that could only be viewed as an attack. I wasn't interested in that anyway. The interview would have been, "Who are you as a person? What makes you tick? Talk to me about your life as a young girl. What were your dreams? When did you first realize you wanted to be in politics?" I could have talked about her childhood for an hour. I wanted to get to know her as a human being. That Lewinsky stuff is pointless unless you get to know her first. Hearing her talk about the disappointments in her life? The audience would've fallen in love with her.

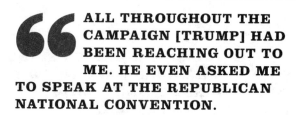

> **ALL THROUGHOUT THE CAMPAIGN [TRUMP] HAD BEEN REACHING OUT TO ME. HE EVEN ASKED ME TO SPEAK AT THE REPUBLICAN NATIONAL CONVENTION.**

I'm telling you, I was obsessed with this. I was Captain Ahab. I wanted it more than anything. I did all this research on her and discovered she liked gardening. I ordered a huge gift basket of gardening supplies, thinking I'd send it to her to break the ice. The basket was enormous. There was all sorts of gardening crap in there, like packets of seeds.

Then I reconsidered. I thought that might be coming on a little strong. That's not me. I don't beg. What I did instead was agree to give an interview to the *New York Times*. They had contacted me a while before about doing a profile. I said no. I hate doing interviews. I hate being on the other side of the microphone. I told Don to tell them yes.

In July 2016, the *Times* ran a huge story in the Sunday paper about how my style had changed over the years. The headline couldn't have been more perfect: "Confessor. Feminist. Adult. What the Hell Happened to Howard Stern?" Several celebrities were quoted saying what a great interviewer I was. Surely this would reassure Hillary about talking to me. I figured she reads the *New York Times*. Of course she does.

The article came out, and we heard nothing from her campaign. Then Don remembered this writer at the *Washington Post* who had been after him for a while about interviewing me. A few days after the *Times* story, another one dropped in the *Post*. This headline was even more direct: "Howard Stern Makes His Pitch: Why Hillary Clinton Should Do My Show." If you look at that interview and the *Times* story, I'm basically telling her the plan. I don't do that with guests, but I wanted her to know that she didn't have to worry. She'd be in good hands. She could trust me.

The *Post* story came out. Again, we heard nothing from her.

Then I saw her in the debates. Donald was shredding her. He knew how to do this. He was talking like a dude. He was saying things in a clear and definite way. People were digging it.

I don't want to sound arrogant. I don't want to say that I could've tipped the election. But how many votes did she actually lose by? In Michigan, Pennsylvania, Ohio, Florida—a couple thousand votes here, a couple thousand votes there. SiriusXM has thirty-three

 I WASN'T GOING TO BRING UP MONICA LEWINSKY. THE OLD ME WOULD HAVE TRIED THAT. THAT WOULD HAVE BEEN THE FIRST THING I SAID. NOW I SEE HOW THAT COULD ONLY BE VIEWED AS AN ATTACK.

million subscribers in America. We consider each of these to represent at least two people, since households often share a subscription. Do the math. Because I can't—multiplication isn't my strong suit. I'm not saying all SiriusXM subscribers are Howard Stern listeners. But let's just say that half are. Would that not have done something?

All it would have taken is for some guy to go, "You know, I work hard for a living. I drive a truck. I'm a contractor. I'm a store owner. I heard Hillary Clinton on the *Howard Stern Show* talking about her passion for people, and I was damn impressed." Who knows what would have come out of our conversation. Some little story that people could identify with. I can't tell you how many times I've done an interview where someone in my audience writes me and says, "I never cared about Lady Gaga." Or, "I never listened to Sia."

Or, "I always hated Rosie O'Donnell." And then they go, "But damn I love her now!"

To some people it wouldn't have mattered *what* we talked about. Just the fact that she had the guts to show up might've done the trick.

So why didn't she? I'll tell you why. She was afraid. She got tight. She thought it was in the bag, and she thought, "I could go talk to Howard and really screw things up." She thought it was a gamble. In my mind, the gamble was *not* coming on the show.

I was right. Had she done the show, it might've changed the election.

Becoming the first female president wasn't the only thing Hillary missed out on. She also missed out on one badass gardening basket. I never sent it to her. For me to go to all that trouble, submit to those newspaper interviews—no way was I going to waste those seed packets on her. I divvied it up among my staff instead.

And Now a Word
from Our President . . .

APRIL 16, 2004

(12 years, 6 months, and 23 days until the election)

Howard: So, are you going to stick with Melania? 'Cause the fame with this [*The Apprentice*] is way over the top.

Donald: Well, this has been crazy. You know, it was supposed to be a one-shot thing. We were going to do a deal with Mark Burnett, who's terrific. And he came in and saw me, and over the years—you know this, Howard—I've had a lot of networks want me to do reality. Watch me comb my hair in the morning. And I didn't want anyone to watch me comb my hair.

Howard: Who was saying that you dye your hair?

Donald: Well, Howard, I try to keep the white out, but there was one shot where it looked pretty damn dark.

Howard: I know that's your real hair. When I was on his helicopter, I saw him walk up to the helicopter. And you know how the wind blows? It was attached to his head.

> **OH, IT'S MY
> REAL HAIR.**

Donald: Oh, it's my real hair. In fact, I've gone on some shows recently where the announcers jump and touch it and say it's real. And I say, "I know, it's real. It's just the way I've combed it over the years, and I guess I shouldn't change."

Howard: Where's Melania right now?

Donald: She's right here. She's sleeping.

Howard: You gonna stick with her?

Donald: Well, I've had a great relationship with her. She's a good person.

Howard: So are a lot more chicks hitting on you now, 'cause of the show?

Donald: Honestly? Yes.

Howard: Wow.

Donald: It's crazy. I thought I was a well-known guy before, but this is crazy.

Howard: It's a whole new level for you.

Donald: I have friends in show business who can't understand it. They can't work, and I do this thing where I'm only supposed to be on for sixteen episodes, then head back into the wild blue yonder. And now I have Jeff Zucker of NBC calling me every morning to see how I'm feeling.

Howard: You're not giving your whole salary to charity, are you?

Donald: No. But I give much more than my salary to charity over the course of a year.

Robin: I was on the Internet. I thought it was *Fortune*—well, I forget what magazine it was, but they were saying, was it really true that he has all this money? 'Cause they talked about all these deals you did with Japanese companies—

Donald: Yeah, and they've all worked out great. I'll have to find out where this story came from and sue their ass off.

Robin: Well, they said you would put up $11 million to their billion.

Donald: Oh yeah, that makes me really stupid.

Robin: No, but then they're saying those guys don't get a return, and you always make out.

Donald: I know, and that makes me a bad person, right?

Howard: Hey, let me ask you something. I'm going to ask you the toughest question an interviewer's ever asked.

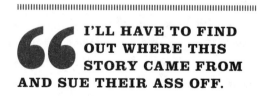

I'LL HAVE TO FIND OUT WHERE THIS STORY CAME FROM AND SUE THEIR ASS OFF.

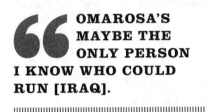

> **OMAROSA'S MAYBE THE ONLY PERSON I KNOW WHO COULD RUN [IRAQ].**

Donald: Go ahead.

Howard: 'Cause you're an honest guy.

Donald: I am an honest guy.

Howard: Okay, here we go: In November, who gets your vote?

Donald: I was never a fan of going into Iraq, 'cause this guy used to keep the terrorists out. He'd kill the terrorists.

Howard: Right. In fact, they should put him back in!

Donald: Look at that country. Do you think a regular guy—do you think Jimmy Carter's going to run Iraq?

Howard: No, there's nobody going to run Iraq better than Saddam Hussein.

Donald: I think Iraq is a terrible mistake. To think when we leave, it's going to be this nice democratic country. Give me a break.

Howard: Hey, Omarosa's [Manigault Newman, *Apprentice* contestant] crazy enough to run Iraq.

Donald: Omarosa's maybe the only person I know who could run it.

Howard: So, give the answer in one word: Kerry or Bush?

Donald: Look, let me just say, I haven't made up my mind.

Howard: Oh, that's not true. I know you have.

Donald: Look, Kerry's a friend of mine. He's a very good guy. He's a very tough guy. And I think he's going to put up a good fight. Bush—this is a terrible mistake, what's gone on in Iraq. Terrible mistake.

Howard: So who are you going to vote for?

Donald: I'll let you know when I make a decision.

Howard: Ugh.

Donald: I'll tell you what. I'm very disappointed this country's bogged down in Iraq, and North Korea is making nuclear missiles. And they tell people, "We're making missiles."

Howard: So based on what you're saying, why would you vote for Bush?

Donald: I might not. I haven't made up my mind 100 percent. He has been good from the standpoint of guys like me that pay taxes.

Howard: But when Bill Clinton was in office, did you suffer economically? No, you had boom years.

Donald: No, it was good years.

Howard: So the point is—

Donald: Well, this year I've had my best year. And you know why? It's called "interest rates." People are buying housing like never before. But if interest rates go up, it's all off.

Howard: Interest rates will go up after the election. Trust me.

Donald: I think they will. You can see the signs of it now. I think after the election when they go up, housing, everything is going to come to a halt.

Howard: So, is Melania getting insecure with how famous you're getting?

Donald: No, she's the most secure person I know.

Howard: Man, can you believe you're a television success?

Donald: No, I can't. It's unbelievable. Of all the—let's call this a business deal, 'cause with me everything's sort of a business deal—of all the deals I've ever made, this is the craziest.

Caller: [*on the phone*] Hey, Mr. Trump, it is an honor to speak to you, sir. The show is an ultimate success. I watched every one of them.

Donald: Thank you. That's nice.

Caller: In a hypothetical situation—I mean, saying you're not involved with Melania and there was no ethical backgrounds for business and whatnot— how many of those bitches do you think you could've banged?

Howard: Good question.

Donald: Boy, I'll tell ya. I love the thought, I'll tell you that. 'Cause they were attractive. Do you agree with that?

Howard: I mean, some of the bodies on them while they were sitting there . . .

Donald: They were amazing.

Howard: Which is more important: talent or looking great?

Donald: Looking great.

Howard: I agree.

Donald: I've had both, and I'll take looking great.

Ellen DeGeneres

SEPTEMBER 8, 2015

It was a miracle that we got Ellen DeGeneres to do the show. She is one of the busiest and most successful people in entertainment. If anyone knows the tremendous pressures and time commitments it takes to put on a daily program, it's me. I ran into her at a wedding and we got to talking. She must have enjoyed our conversation. She decided she wanted to do the show next time she was in New York. She had no agenda, nothing to promote. She just wanted to come in and talk. How refreshing.

When you hear her story and all the tragedy she's experienced, it's absolutely astounding to think she's achieved so much. Ellen is such a trailblazer. She was the first openly gay lead character in television history and her talk show has further moved the needle for the acceptance of gay Americans.

This is one of the most emotional interviews I've ever done. There's a moment when Ellen's talking about writing the bit that earned her a spot on *Johnny Carson*, and the awful trauma that inspired it. When I'm doing these interviews, I'm so caught up in my own process of leading the conversation that there's not a whole lot of time for me to sit and ruminate on what someone has said. This was a rare instance when a guest said something that just stopped me cold. It made me pause and reflect in the middle of the chaos of trying to hold an interview together.

Howard: I went back and watched you the first time on *Johnny Carson*. He called you over—the famous thing where he called you over.

Ellen: Anointed, yes.

Howard: You were anointed. Becoming a successful stand-up comic, people think, "Well, you're born funny." That was not the case with you. You grew up in Louisiana?

Ellen: Yes, New Orleans.

Howard: Were you like Bob Dylan? In the sense that he hated Minnesota. He just felt like he was completely in the wrong family and the wrong place.

Ellen: I wouldn't say that. New Orleans is a very special place, but I didn't know anything other than New Orleans until when my mother remarried, we went to a really small town in Texas.

Howard: Your mother remarried the evil stepfather?

Ellen: Yes.

Howard: Bad guy.

Ellen: Yes, bad guy. I lived there for a couple of years and then I moved back to New Orleans. All I knew was humidity and the South and hot and flat. That's all I knew, because that's the only place I'd been.

Howard: Your parents divorced when you were thirteen?

Ellen: Yes.

Howard: Now, that's traumatic. Because your dad moves out, you're with your mother, and your mother goes into a depression. I relate to this more than anything about you. When you have a depressed mother—my mother was severely depressed—you spend your lifetime trying to cheer that sad woman up. It becomes your burden because you don't want to see your mother sad. Maybe that's where you get the comedy chops. You do whatever you can to make her happy.

Ellen: Yes, I think for a thirteen-year-old girl, it just—and she was my best friend also. She and I got even closer when we lived alone, because my brother went off and joined a band and it was just my mother and myself. She wasn't depressed at first because it was her idea.

Howard: To leave your father?

Ellen: Yes. But then she just changed. I think she got lonesome and she started dating some really bad guys that would come home, and I'd have to save her from some bad situations.

Howard: You became the parent in a sense.

Ellen: Yes, and she became the teenager. Because she all of a sudden started, like, smoking and drinking. I was like, "Wow, I didn't know you." She became free all of a sudden and started having a dating life and being somebody that I didn't know that she was.

Howard: Was that scary to you, when you saw your mother out of control?

Ellen: She wasn't really out of control, but she was like a different person. It was a whole different side to her.

Howard: When you came out, your mother was good about it. She understood, yes?

Ellen: She was okay. She went to the library to try to learn about it, and all the books were in the abnormal psychology section.

Howard: Which is the worst place to learn about homosexuality, because every book is about how you're a deviant.

Ellen: Right. I think it surprised her because I had boyfriends. She hadn't seen me for a while because I had gone back to New Orleans. So the next time she sees me, I tell her I'm gay, and she was confused. She kept thinking it was going to change.

Howard: But your father threw you out?

Ellen: He didn't. The woman that he was married to, she had two daughters

> ❝ **THE NEXT TIME SHE SEES ME, I TELL HER I'M GAY, AND SHE WAS CONFUSED. SHE KEPT THINKING IT WAS GOING TO CHANGE.**

and she was concerned about the young daughters—

Howard: That you were going to seduce them.

Ellen: I don't know what she thought.

Howard: But when your father doesn't stand up for you, that's the most painful?

Ellen: Yes, he's not as—he's a really sweet guy, but he doesn't have that strength to say, "No, that's not okay."

Howard: That's heartbreaking, though, isn't it?

Ellen: Yes.

Howard: It really is.

Ellen: But you know what, all this stuff made me a very strong person. And I was a very weak person growing up. I was very sweet. That was the most important thing for my parents, especially for my father— that I was a sweet girl. It was always that, but I was small. I was very small.

Howard: Is that woman still in your father's life? The woman who said to you, "Ellen, get out."

Ellen: Yes.

Howard: Can you be around your dad and her and forgive them, or do you just say, "Fuck you, I'm done."

Ellen: No, I've forgiven them. She doesn't bring it up. I think she wants to think that didn't happen.

Howard: But is there something in your mind—and maybe you're not like this— but there's something disingenuous on her part, because now you're the famous Ellen DeGeneres. Now you're okay. Everybody loves you. But you needed her to be there for you when you *weren't* the famous Ellen DeGeneres.

Ellen: Look, a lot of people made mistakes. My mother made a mistake when she married that man and didn't really—

Howard: She didn't stick up for you.

Ellen: Yes.

Howard: He molested you—this man she married. You went to her and you said, "Mom, this guy's doing something terrible to me," and she didn't believe you.

Ellen: Well, I waited awhile because she had had breast cancer, and I knew that that would have destroyed her on top of what she was going through with breast cancer—to say, "The man you married is . . ." I waited because I thought I wanted to protect her. When I finally did tell her, it was years later, and she at first believed me. But then he told her I was lying, and then finally she stayed with him for, like, eighteen years, and during all that time the story changed every time she brought it up. Finally, eighteen years later, she was like, "The story changed too many times."

Howard: You can't go home when your

mother's with a guy who's going to sit there and fondle you. It's like you're homeless.

Ellen: I left.

Howard: Yes, you left. You never went to college?

Ellen: I went for, like, a half of a semester. Maybe a quarter of a semester. I don't like school. I'm not good in school. I never was. We moved every two years. I started a new school every two years. I never really got the hang of it. I'm a smart person street-wise, not book-wise.

Howard: When you were in high school, was that torture for you?

Ellen: Yes.

Howard: You said in high school you were in love with some guys. You dated some boys. In a way, it was a shock to you that you were gay, right?

Ellen: I'm still shocked by myself. I still shock myself to this day.

Howard: Why? But seriously.

Ellen: No, I'm kidding. I think I always knew that I felt like—and I did like guys. But I also hadn't slept with a guy. It was all innocent.

Howard: You've never experienced the joy of sleeping with a man?

Ellen: I have. Finally I did.

Howard: Ellen, we should absolutely discuss this. I don't know why any woman sleeps with a guy. I don't even get it. If I was a woman, I would not be with guys. They're gross. But you did experience the joy of a man? Was it a joy at all?

Ellen: Joy? Let me think about that. . . . I

> ## I DON'T THINK THAT I EVER SAID THAT I WANT TO BE A STAND-UP COMIC. I THINK IT'S THE PATH THAT WAS JUST BROUGHT TO ME, AND I FOLLOWED IT.

had a sweet boyfriend. He was sweet. But, look, it just wasn't for me.

Howard: How old were you when you said, "I want to be a stand-up comic"?

Ellen: I don't think that I ever said that I want to be a stand-up comic. I think it's the path that was just brought to me, and I followed it.

Howard: When you say it was brought to you—you were working a bunch of shitty jobs.

Ellen: For me they were shitty, but most people out there have those jobs and they're not shitty. I sold vacuum cleaners. I was a bartender. I was a waitress. I was a hostess. I painted houses. I mowed lawns.

Howard: Somebody came up to you at some point and said, "Hey, why don't you get up and talk?" Was it a luncheon or something?

Ellen: How do you know so much about me, Howard?

Howard: I know everything about you.

Ellen: Yes, it was a bunch of people trying to raise money for some legal—I don't even remember what it was. They had to raise money for something. They said, "We just need people to be onstage."

Howard: They say to you, "Go up and talk or do something funny."

Ellen: I had no material because I had never done anything. The reason I was funny, I guess, to friends is I would always be observational about situations. One thing I always observed is that people [when they're eating] would start a sentence and then take a bite. So I started the sentence. I said, "This is my first time onstage, and I'm so nervous I didn't even eat all day. So if you don't mind—" And then I took a bite, and then I ate and waited to chew and swallow. Then I'd start the sentence over, "Anyway, when you're walking—" And then I take another bite. I never finished the sentence. I ate the entire hamburger, fries, and then I said my time was up and I got offstage.

Howard: Now, that takes a lot of balls to do that routine.

Ellen: I had no bar. I had nothing that I had to beat. I didn't know if it would bomb or not because I had never done anything. And it actually—

Howard: And it killed.

Ellen: It worked.

Howard: You know what's amazing? I talk to so many comics about this. The first time a lot of people go onstage, they have tremendous success. Then the hard part begins because they say, "Maybe I could do this for a living." Then they go and they tank, and they tank, and they tank a million times. Did that happen to you?

Ellen: No. The next time, somebody told me about a coffeehouse at the University of New Orleans. Most people were, like, singing and doing different things. One person did comedy. I went and I played piano—which I don't play, but I know a few chords. I said, "This is a song I wrote when I was in the hospital." It was just chords and me screaming. That's all I did.

Howard: It was almost like you were acting. You were doing routines like sketches, in a sense.

Ellen: Well, I was a huge fan of Steve Martin and Woody Allen.

Howard: And Carol Burnett, right?

Ellen: And Carol Burnett. I liked silly. I'd just go up onstage and I'd hold different fabrics up. I'd hold a piece of cotton and I'd hold velvet, and after a while I'd say, "I'm just trying out new material." It was really corny stuff. Then I finally started writing, and really one of the first things I wrote was "A Phone Call to God."

Howard: Which you did on the Johnny Carson show the first time you went on. That has an interesting origin. It came out of a lot of sadness. Your stepfather, as you mentioned, was abusing you. He was bad. You would go to your room and have a conversation with God. But it wasn't a funny conversation, it was—

Ellen: Actually the "Phone Call to God" came from my girlfriend at the time who was killed in a car accident.

Howard: Cat was her name, right?

Ellen: Yes. And I passed the accident on the way home.

Howard: You and Cat—she was your first serious girlfriend, right?

Ellen: Yes.

Howard: You broke up and then she tried to sort of make up with you, and you looked away from her and ignored her because you were angry with her.

Ellen: We were at a club, my brother's band was playing, and she was there and she was cheating on me, which she did a lot.

Howard: You had no idea she was cheating on you?

Ellen: Yes, but I tried to ignore it for a little while because I liked her and so I wanted to be with her.

Howard: You were in love with her?

Ellen: Yes. She was at the club with some girl, and she kept saying, "When are you coming back home?" I had just moved out to try to teach her a lesson so that she would beg me to come back. I'd planned on going back. She kept saying, "When are you coming?" I kept acting like the music was too loud and I couldn't hear. I was really just playing a game. She left, and then I left after that and we passed an accident. It had just happened, and it was a car that was split in two. We slowed down, but everyone was just getting there—the fire trucks and everybody. We just kept going. We're like, "Jesus, look at that." The next morning I found out it was her in the car.

Howard: Did you feel a sense of guilt?

Ellen: Oh God, yes. I felt like I could

have stopped it. They didn't know for three hours who she was. I could have been there. I could have—

Howard: Did you play the what-if game? Like, "If I had just been nicer to her, maybe she wouldn't have been upset."

Ellen: She wouldn't have left.

Howard: That's when you started talking to God?

Ellen: Yes. I had moved into this basement apartment. It was one room. I couldn't even stand up, the ceilings were so low. It was, like, a basement of someone's house. I had a mattress on the floor and I was laying there. I had sort of started doing comedy then. I was writing. There were fleas everywhere. The whole place was infested with fleas. I thought, "Why is this beautiful young girl gone and fleas are here? I don't understand how something is here and something is not." I just started imagining how great [it would be] if we could just pick up the phone and call God and ask questions and get answers. I just started writing. And I didn't stop. I didn't take the pen off the paper for a second. It was nonstop writing. I couldn't stop it.

Howard: This became a signature bit

 WE PASSED AN ACCIDENT. IT HAD JUST HAPPENED, AND IT WAS A CAR THAT WAS SPLIT IN TWO. . . . THE NEXT MORNING I FOUND OUT IT WAS HER IN THE CAR.

of yours. Is that why Carson put you on, because his scouts saw you do that bit?

Ellen: Yes. I knew when I finished writing it. I literally was on that mattress on the floor in that apartment with no money and had just lost my girlfriend, and I thought, "I'm going to do this on *Johnny Carson*, and he's going to call me over to sit down on that couch."

Howard: You visualized that.

Ellen: Yes. I saw it. I saw it happening.

Robin: How long from there until it actually happened?

Ellen: I think it was . . . [*chuckles*] You probably know this better than me, Howard. Was it five years?

Howard: It was a while.

Ellen: But don't you believe that you visualized exactly where you are? Don't you? I truly believe that we create our lives.

Howard: I think you're right. I was dating a girl when I was sixteen and [years later] she brought the love letters in here on the show. I wrote, "How can you not be with me? I'm going to be the greatest radio performer that ever was." Or something arrogant like that. Meanwhile, I was nothing. I was horrible. But there was something in me that felt like maybe I could do this. It comes from nowhere. You have no right to even say it. It sounds stupid.

Ellen: But it comes from someplace that

knows who you are. I think that we can decide if we can be great or not.

Howard: Then the sitcom comes along, right? And that's a big deal for you. I feel like that's every comic's dream—getting a sitcom.

Ellen: Yes, you want the theme song.

Howard: That's what brings us to this decision to come out of the closet. Because the general thinking at that time is, "You're doing a show, you're dating guys." That's sort of the theme of the show: everyone likes Ellen dating guys. Then all of a sudden you come out and—

Ellen: It didn't make sense. They didn't know what to do with the show, because at some point, you've got to date guys, you've got to get married. It was on for five years. It wasn't even that. The writers didn't have a problem. It was me that came to the writers. It was me that said, "I need to do this." Because I had this dream that made me realize that I was—did I tell you the dream?

Howard: No.

Ellen: This is an amazing dream, and I don't remember my dreams ever.

Howard: Have you ever been in analysis?

Ellen: No.

Howard: Never?

Ellen: You don't need to analyze this dream. I have this little tiny bird. This finch. This beautiful little finch. And I love it so much. And I put it in this beautiful bamboo—one of those tiered bamboo birdcages. As I put it in the cage, the bird becomes me. And I'm still me. And the bird is me in the cage.

Howard: Right.

Ellen: As I put it in, I realize that the bars that are against the window—because I had it against the window to see fresh air—were wide enough for it to go out. And it had been like that all along.

Howard: But you never would leave?

Ellen: The bird was looking at me like, "Wait a minute." And I'm looking at the bird like, "Wait a minute, don't go. This is where you belong, and it's a beautiful cage." The bird who was me says, "I don't belong here," and flies out. I was like, "No matter how pretty this cage is, I'm not going to live in it." I was doing well financially. I was doing well professionally. But I felt I was not free.

Howard: Everything felt like a lie?

Ellen: Yes. I was scared of you outing me. I was scared of anybody. Because I was lying. I had so much shame attached to it too. You don't realize how much shame there is because society makes you feel like anytime you can't say it. When people would say, "Who cares? You don't have to tell everybody. It's nobody's business." When people use that as an excuse to not say it, when they say, "My personal life is my"—no straight person says that. No straight person says, "My private life is my own business." Only people who are ashamed or have to hide something.

I thought, "I'm not going to carry that shame anymore."

Robin: Did you talk to people about the decision?

Ellen: Everyone said no. My publicist—everyone said no. Well, the writers were thrilled. They were like, "Oh my God, this is going to be amazing to write for. It is going to be history-making."

Howard: Were you prepared for the shitstorm that went down once you came out? Did you think it mattered that much?

Ellen: No, I thought, "Is it going to be that much of a shock?"

Howard: That scumbag Jerry Falwell comes out, starts screaming about Ellen DeGeneres. All hell breaks loose. Even Elton John went as far as to publicly say, "Shut up already about your lesbianism," which is crazy.

Ellen: I really wasn't talking about my lesbianism. It was the press talking about my lesbianism.

Howard: Did you have a nervous breakdown at all? Did you just go berserk?

Ellen: No. I was on such a high of doing the right thing for me that I didn't care. But then when the show got canceled, when I lost everything, that's when I was like, "What am I going to do?"

Howard: Things career-wise seemed bleak because for three years you went into a terrible depression. Did you ever doubt yourself? Did you say to yourself, "I made a mistake coming out"?

I KNEW I DIDN'T MAKE A MISTAKE COMING OUT BECAUSE IT WAS THE RIGHT THING TO DO. I JUST WANTED TO BE TRUTHFUL.

Ellen: No. I knew I didn't make a mistake coming out because it was the right thing to do. I just wanted to be truthful.

Howard: Did your agents start abandoning you?

Ellen: Yes. I didn't have agents. I didn't have anybody.

Howard: You mean, they wouldn't touch you anymore?

Ellen: Yes.

Howard: Do you ever look toward those particular people and go, "Fuck you! Ha-ha-ha!" Do you ever do that? God, I would.

Ellen: No, I think in the beginning of coming back, I felt like that. But now I feel complete understanding that business is business, you know? We know that. We know that we are only as popular as the money we make for them.

Howard: Did you have a master plan in mind? Did you map out in your mind how the hell you were going to win over America when you started the talk show?

Ellen: I just wanted to be myself. I didn't want to be anything but myself.

Howard: When you look at the landscape when you started your show, Oprah was there, and Rosie was there. Did you really think it would succeed and last for thirteen seasons?

Ellen: Well, no, I didn't think that far ahead. We couldn't even sell the show. I had to go around and do stand-up. Station managers would come look at me and try to figure out if women at home with kids would watch a lesbian on TV. That was the big concern.

Howard: When I watch the show, it seems to me like a lot of these straight women who are in the audience really want to please you. It seems like they kind of are living, they think, the wild life dancing with Ellen. Do you sense the flirtation that they're having with you on TV?

Ellen: No, it's not flirtation.

Howard: There's something up there. They want to prove how cool they are. They're dancing with a gay person. There's something going on there that I have built up in my head, maybe.

Ellen: Yes, I think that's you.

Howard: I think there's something going on there. There's more to it. They want to get your approval and they want you to be attracted to them. That's what I think is going on.

Ellen: Maybe you're right on 1 percent of those women. I think the majority of the women are there because, especially if they are a mom, if they are married, if they're working—people wait for a long time, because it's hard to get a ticket. It's not a giant audience, and so people wait a long time. When they're there, they want to dance. They don't get to dance anymore, unless you go to a wedding. No one goes to clubs anymore when you're married and have kids. Then all of a sudden they're in a club atmosphere. Because that's what it feels like in there. That room is filled with just so much love and so much positive energy.

Howard: Someone told me—and I don't know who told me this—that you hate dancing at this point. It's almost as if the audience demands it. You want to stop dancing but you can't. What's the truth there?

Ellen: It's somewhere in between. I don't like when I'm out in public and people start yelling at me to dance. Like I'm a monkey.

Howard: Like you're Fred Astaire.

Ellen: Literally, there's no music and I'm just in a doctor's office. "Dance!" That's what I hear all the time.

Howard: You're saying to yourself, "Dance, monkey! Make me dance!"

> **"I'VE NEVER TAKEN DANCE LESSONS, BUT IT'S A FREEDOM AND A JOY WHAT HAPPENS WHEN YOU DANCE.**

Ellen: Yes, exactly. I answer them sometimes. I say, "There's no music." I do love music, and it did happen organically because I love music and I love to dance. I'm not a dancer. I've never taken dance lessons, but it's a freedom and a joy what happens when you dance. I started doing that just as a joke. And then the audience loved it. And then the audience started dancing with me. Then it became a thing. And now if I don't—if my back is out or if my knee is tweaked or for whatever reason I don't feel well and I don't dance—they leave angry.

Howard: And so you're trapped. You have to keep the dance going.

Ellen: I have to. At some point I'm not going to retire because I want to—it's because I can't dance anymore, because I have a broken hip or something.

Henry Hill

MAY 3, 2002

This is one of the first interviews where after all my work in therapy I was beginning to develop a more probing style. Henry Hill was the former Mafia hit man whose life inspired the movie *Goodfellas*. We first had him on the show back in the mid-nineties, and he'd been on three or four times since then. In those appearances, because Henry was an alcoholic and would come in drunk, we would just screw around with him and never get to any deep conversation.

  This time he was drunk again. I'd been thinking more and more about Henry. How much of his substance abuse had been self-medicating, trying to drown the guilt of having done the unforgivable? How did he feel about killing people? Did he carry that around with him? Was there remorse? He might not be in a physical prison, but he was clearly in a mental one. He was in hell. I wanted to understand what he was feeling. I thought, "Let's see if I can get him to be real with me. Let me see if I can get him to go there." And he did—as much as he was able to. He would say something introspective, then make a crass comment or a joke. I don't think he could fully allow himself to feel the pain he had inflicted on other people, and on himself.

Howard: All right, sit down. Oy vey. What's in the can? Heineken? What happened? You were doing so good. Did anyone tell you the prank we were going to play on you? Gary was going to tell you he was having trouble with one of his neighbors.

Henry: We'll burn the house down.

Howard: Let me ask you something, you were doing so—

Henry: We'll torch the joint, you know?

Howard: Henry, do me a favor and put the microphone in front of your face. Put the Heineken down.

Henry: Can I have a drink?

Gary: He wants a martini. We don't have that.

Howard: We can get that. You're telling me you can't get through an interview without drinking? What happened this time?

Henry: I slipped.

Gary: How long were you sober?

Henry: Almost ten months.

Robin: Have they caught you, now that you're off the wagon?

Howard: Oh, is that part of your—

Henry: They care in California.

Howard: But not in New York?

Henry: It's the five-hundred-mile deal, know what I mean? If you're five hundred miles outside of California, you can drink.

Robin: That's according to Henry.

Howard: Why'd you slip?

Henry: I'm an alcoholic, Howard.

Howard: I know, but you were doing good. Something must have happened.

Henry: It was so boring. No shit.

Howard: No s-word. You can't use the s-word.

Henry: Can I say "scumbag"?

Howard: "Scumbag" you can say. Just talk clean. That's your safest bet. You want a coffee? How long you been drinking? Since last night?

Henry: Couple days now.

Howard: A couple days ago you started drinking and haven't stopped? Did you fall asleep for a while?

Henry: Yeah, I slept.

Robin: Have you been alone?

Henry: I was with the cops last night.

Howard: The cops?

Henry: Yeah, the feds. They got me loaded.

Howard: Oh, jeez. Is that true? Is it because you're nervous coming here that you started drinking?

> ## ❝ I WAS WITH THE COPS LAST NIGHT. . . . YEAH, THE FEDS. THEY GOT ME LOADED.

Henry: I come here to dig up a shoebox.

Howard: What's in the shoebox?

Henry: Shhhh.

Howard: Money? Is it money? Okay, here's Paulie, who's in the mob. Go ahead, Paulie.

Paulie [*on the phone*]: Stool pigeon.

Henry: Stool pigeon, yeah. I'm a rat bastard.

Paulie: Stool pigeon.

Henry: I got the money, honey.

Paulie: You're so lucky you're still walking around.

Henry: You wanna know something? Come and see me. Yeah, I'm over here. How much cojones you got?

Paulie: Come and see you?

Henry: Yeah, I'm over here.

Paulie: One of these days . . . You know, you walk around with your head up in the air—

Henry: You're fucking right.

Howard: Hey, no f-words.

Paulie: You walk around with your head up in the air. We're gonna cut your prick off, stick it in your mouth. Believe me.

Howard: Paulie, are you in the mob currently?

Paulie: Many moons have passed. Many moons have passed since Lefferts Boulevard.

Henry: You sound like you got no cojones.

Howard: What group are you with?

66 LET ME TELL YOU SOMETHING. THAT LIFE, THAT *GOODFELLAS* LIFE— IT'S BULLSHIT.

Paulie: He who laughs first, laughs last, stool pigeon.

Henry: Yeah, I am a stool pigeon. I'm a proud stool pigeon.

Paulie: You're proud 'cause Tommy's not around. You're proud 'cause Jimmy's not around. You're proud 'cause Anthony Stabile's not around.

Henry: They're all dead. I'm alive.

Paulie: You're a big man.

Henry: I'm alive.

Paulie: You're alive. You're alive, walking around, disgraced. Disgraced.

Henry: [*laughs*]

Paulie: Yeah, you laugh. You drunken prick stool pigeon rat bastard.

Henry: You got balls? Come over here.

Paulie: Just remember, you still gotta walk out of that studio. You better have a hundred eyes around your head.

Henry: I don't need a hundred eyes.

Paulie: One of these days . . .

Howard: Henry, do you drink because you think the mob's going to get you?

Paulie: Sure, he's afraid.

Henry: Howard, I've lived in fear all my life. I've lived in fear when I was in that life with my friends.

Howard: In other words, they could've hit you at any time.

Henry: Let me tell you something. That life, that *Goodfellas* life—it's bullshit.

Howard: Don't use the s-word! You've got good things to say, but you can't keep cursing.

Paulie: He's got no respect. He doesn't even have respect for you, even after you ask him not to curse on the air.

Henry: Come on, you're a punk. You're a punk. You're on the phone. You're a punk.

Paulie: What? Am I supposed to be there in your face in the studio?

Henry: I'm telling you where I'm at.

Paulie: We know where you're at, believe me.

Henry: I'm a rat. I'm a happy rat. You're goddamn right. You know what? I did the right thing. I changed my life.

Paulie: You changed your life? You're a drunken prick disgraced rat bastard.

Henry: [*raises Heineken*] Salud.

Paulie: You believe all the shit he says?

Howard: Don't say the s-word!

Paulie: Excuse me. Do you believe all the crap that he says?

Howard: I'm just listening.

Paulie: You think that whole movie's true?

Howard: I don't know. You tell me.

Paulie: This guy's nothing. He was nothing. He was a piece of garbage.

Howard: You're saying Henry built himself up in the movie?

Paulie: He's a glorified rat bastard. That's all he is.

Howard: All right. Well, thank you for calling in, Paulie.

Henry: Thank you, Paulie.

Howard: Okay, we're with Henry Hill, who's drunk out of his mind.

Gary: You know who brought him to New York?

Howard: Who?

Gary: Martin Scorsese. He's in town to do voice tracks for the tenth-anniversary DVD of *Goodfellas* that'll be coming out.

Howard: Oh, that'll be great. He's loaded out of his mind.

Henry: I already did it.

Howard: You look a little like Joe Pesci now, as you get older.

Henry: Joe's a scumbag.

Howard: Why?

Henry: He thinks he's a wiseguy.

Howard: He does?

Henry: He's a waiter. He's a douchebag.

Howard: He hangs around with the tough guys?

Henry: He goes up to Pleasant Avenue. Fuck him.

Howard: Listen to me, no more cursing!

Henry: Okay.

Howard: Where's your bagel? Eat it.

Henry: I got my teeth. They aren't in.

Howard: Let me see your teeth. Put them in. Oh, man, they fell on the floor. Just put them in. I want to do a serious interview.

Henry: I'll put them in.

Howard: Okay. Who's going to win the Kentucky Derby?

Henry: I told you, [George] Steinbrenner's horse.

Howard: Are you saying that 'cause you *know* he's going to win? Do you know something?

Henry: It's fixed.

Howard: It is?

Henry: Yes.

Howard: Henry's just being a big shot. He doesn't know.

Gary: You know Henry's going to the Kentucky Derby, right?

Howard: Oh, you're going? Where are you getting the money to go to the Kentucky Derby?

Henry: The shoebox, the shoebox.

Howard: He's sitting here complaining to me that the old hundreds might not be able to be cashed in. What is the money from? From your old mob days?

Henry: Rockville Centre [Long Island].

Howard: You're telling me there's a shoebox full of hundreds in Rockville Centre? Is it from the Lufthansa flight?

Henry: *Capisce*. About $2 million.

Howard: Two million. You're being a wise guy yourself, now. You're lying.

Gary: The whole heist wasn't two million, was it?

Henry: Eight.

Howard: Eight million. And your share was two million?

Henry: Shhhhh.

Howard: What do you mean, "shhhh"? You just said it. So you're a wealthy man?

Henry: No. I'm broke.

Howard: You're broke? Don't drink. Put that down. Oy vey. It doesn't even matter. Listen, we're running out of time. Talk to me about disposing of someone.

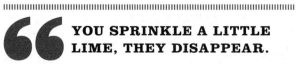

YOU SPRINKLE A LITTLE LIME, THEY DISAPPEAR.

Henry: You sprinkle a little lime, they disappear.

Howard: How long does it take a body to decompose from lime?

Henry: Three months.

Howard: Three months and they disappear from the earth.

Henry: You're laughing.

Howard: I'm not laughing. I'm laughing at you. You're ready to fall off the couch. What happened in your personal life that caused you to start drinking again? You said to me, "I'm fifty-nine years old. I can't live without drinking." Listen, I'm a little upset with you that you're drinking again. You were doing so well.

Henry: Get the hell out of here.

Howard: Is life so boring without alcohol?

Henry: Yeah, it sucks.

Howard: Do you drink because you want to forget about all the people you've killed?

Henry: Howard, you're the only person I've ever admitted I've killed people [to].

Howard: You did.

Henry: Yeah. Yeah, I whacked a couple. I whacked three. I'm not proud, know what I mean?

Howard: So is that why you're drinking?

Henry: You know.

Howard: To drown out the voices of the dead. What were their offenses? What did they do?

Henry: They were rats.

Howard: These are mob guys?

Henry: I ain't proud of it.

Howard: What did they do?

Henry: They were stool pigeons.

Howard: But you yourself ended up ratting.

Henry: Well, that . . .

Howard: I think the drinking is to drown out the voices of the dead. Do they haunt you?

Henry: What do you mean?

Howard: Do they haunt you?

Henry: No. They were scumbags.

Howard: The first time you killed one of these rats, how'd you do it?

Henry: I was sixteen when I did it.

Howard: The first one? You were sixteen? That must've been a hundred years ago. Tell everyone how you did it.

Henry: With a bullet.

Howard: To the head?

Henry: Yeah.

Howard: One bullet?

Henry: Yeah.

Howard: He didn't see it coming? Where was he, in the car?

Henry: Yeah.

Howard: Back of the head?

Henry: Why you guys kidding around?

Howard: Who's kidding? I want to know.

Henry: It sucks, Howard. It sucks.

Howard: Makes you feel bad.

Henry: Yeah. Then I went into the army, was a paratrooper and shit.

Howard: Don't say the s-word. Then when did you kill the second guy?

Henry: I was twenty-two. Another stool pigeon. They say whack him, so I whacked him.

Howard: How'd you do that one?

Henry: Behind the head.

Howard: Bullet? Ice pick?

Henry: Stabbed him in the woods. He knew he was going to die.

Howard: He took it like a man?

Henry: He cried.

Howard: He cried. Well, who wouldn't cry? I'd cry. Were you laughing at him when he cried?

Henry: No. No.

Howard: You understood.

Henry: I had to do what I had to do.

Howard: Wow. So you gotta lot to drink about.

Henry: Howard, I am so miserable.

Howard: Really? There's no joy in your life?

Henry: No joy in my life.

Howard: Listen to me, you're in a lot of pain.

Henry: I'm a scumbag.

Howard: Everyone knows that. You have a good side to you, and a bad side to you. Just like the movie. Henry, look at me. Talk to me about your misery.

Henry: I gotta go dig up the money.

Howard: Did you ever cry about it? Like

STABBED HIM IN THE WOODS. HE KNEW HE WAS GOING TO DIE.

the guy in the woods? Look at me. You can't look at me.

Henry: I'm looking. You're my psychiatrist. I listen to you every day.

Howard: The voices of the dead haunt you, right? You want forgiveness, right?

Henry: I do schuva.

Howard: Shiva?

Henry: I'm a Jew.

Howard: I thought you were Irish? What's a schuva?

Henry: I have a plan.

Howard: Henry's going to get elected prime minister of Israel, that's the plan. Henry, stop drinking.

Henry: I figured it out. I gotta do what I gotta do. I'm helping the kids.

Howard: Are you afraid of going to hell?

Henry: Fuck hell.

Howard: C'mon, not the f-word, Henry.

Henry: There's no hell.

Howard: [*laughs*] You better hope not. It's a sad life, Henry.

Henry: No. Fuck you.

Howard: Stop it, Henry! Henry, look at me. Who understands you better than me? You killed three people?

Henry: Yeah. So fucking what. Kentucky Derby tomorrow!

And Now a Word from Our President . . .

Howard: Donald Trump is here. Old friend of the show. Big star. Big TV star.

Donald: How are you?

Howard: I'm well, thank you.

Donald: Very good.

Howard: Mr. Trump, I was very proud of you. I saw you on a lot of shows talking about the fact that the war in Iraq is going horribly wrong. A lot of people in your position, a wealthy guy, could do very well with the Bush administration. You're speaking out 'cause you care. A lot of people are dying over there, young people, and perhaps for nothing.

Donald: Well, it's a horror. The war is a total disaster. It seems to me to be almost worse than Vietnam. I really like the Bush policies on taxation. I really believe in them. It's good. It puts people to work. But the war is a total catastrophe. And if anything is going to bring him down, that's it. And perhaps you and the FCC.

Robin: This is a war George Bush wouldn't have fought in himself.

Howard: That's the other thing.

Donald: Well, one of the greatest spin jobs I've ever seen—and I've seen a lot of spin—was what they did with Kerry. They made Kerry, whether he was a great war hero or modest hero, or at least went and got shot at—

Howard: He was a brave guy.

Donald: They made him into a guy who was a total war failure, and Bush is this great war hero. It's sort of amazing. The swift boat.

Howard: Yeah.

Donald: I thought it was one of the greatest jobs I've ever seen. He went into this whole thing as a war hero and came out damaged goods. It's really amazing. And Bush, who obviously wasn't a war hero, looking very good.

Howard: He's looking like a war hero.

Donald: It's amazing.

Howard: Bush, Ashcroft, Cheney. Seven deferments for Cheney. Five for Ashcroft. Bush clearly got privilege from his father. Fine. If I had a father who could get me some privilege, I'd admit it. I'd say, "Hey, I was lucky. I got out of this horrible war." The Vietnam War. He hasn't learned from history, though. He supports the Vietnam War. He says in theory it was a good war.

Donald: Well, that's not so good. You have to have a pretty hard line to still support that war.

Howard: Would you fire Bush?

Donald: Well, I love his tax policy and hate his war. So I guess we'll have to see what happens.

Howard: Stem cell research?

Donald: Totally in favor of it. I know people that are dying. With proper stem cell research, they could live. It just doesn't make sense, what they're doing.

Howard: It's saying, "To hell with science. Jesus first, science later." And it's scary.

Donald: It's a problem. It's a problem.

Howard: Everyone said under Clinton, a guy like you, a wealthy man, would do badly. Did you do poorly under Clinton?

Donald: It's a funny thing: the Republicans are known for business, and yet the economy always seems to tank under the Republicans.

Howard: Right.

> **IT'S A FUNNY THING: THE REPUBLICANS ARE KNOWN FOR BUSINESS, AND YET THE ECONOMY ALWAYS SEEMS TO TANK UNDER THE REPUBLICANS.**

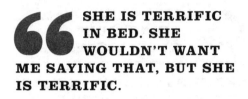

SHE IS TERRIFIC IN BED. SHE WOULDN'T WANT ME SAYING THAT, BUT SHE IS TERRIFIC.

Donald: So Clinton, who's a member of one of my golf clubs, and who happens to be a really good guy— but you don't think of him as a business guy. The economy was never stronger.

Howard: He was a strong president.

Donald: Now, the thing I like about this economy is low interest rates. But if interest rates go up, the entire real estate market collapses, the world collapses, and, you know, we go to hell.

Howard: Isn't it true that after the election, interest rates will go up?

Donald: I think probably so. As you know, real estate in New York is going through the roof. I refuse to tell you how long I've been doing this, 'cause if I said the years, my girlfriend would leave me. But I've been doing this a long time. And it's the single best market I've ever seen. And that, to a large extent, is the city is perceived to be doing well. I think Bloomberg is doing a very good job—

Howard: He's a great mayor.

Donald: I think he's doing a great job. I was with him last night.

Howard: What were you guys doing last night?

Donald: We went to Barbara Walters's semiretirement party.

Howard: Hot chicks there? Or is that kind of not the place for that?

Donald: No, and it didn't matter, 'cause I was with Melania. She's my hot chick.

Howard: This fiancée of yours, Melania, she must be terrific in bed. 'Cause for her to hold on to you all these years, she's gotta be doing something special. What's her secret?

Donald: Well, she is terrific in bed. She wouldn't want me saying that, but she is terrific.

Howard: Amount of positions she knows? Is it the oral?

Donald: Well, you know, she's overall terrific.

Robin: When are you getting married?

Donald: Sometime early next year, probably.

Howard: Prenup?

Donald: We'll have a prenup. You have to have a prenup. I have friends that have been destroyed. Men that are killers, tough to deal with, and yet a wife, five foot two, one hundred pounds, destroys them.

> " [MY FATHER] HAD A WONDERFUL SIXTY-THREE-YEAR MARRIAGE TO A WOMAN, MY MOTHER. . . . I HEARD HE ASKED HER FOR A PRENUP. . . . THIS WAS, LIKE, SEVENTY YEARS AGO! THE GUY WAS GREAT. HE WAS AHEAD OF HIS TIME.

Howard: Me too. I know guys who I've known for years, and they get married and are afraid to ask their wife for a prenup. You're a good judge of human character. Explain to me why a man is afraid to ask for a prenup. How do you do it?

Donald: Well, it's a very tough thing. Actually, doing business deals is easy. It's natural. Doing a prenup is a different deal.

Howard: 'Cause it's emotional.

Donald: You go up to someone, tell them you love them. In my case, you know, "Melania, I love you very much. You're the most beautiful woman I've ever seen."

Howard: Gorgeous.

Donald: "We're going to be together forever. But just in case, would you please immediately sign this?" Look, it's an unattractive instrument.

Howard: If Melania says to you, "What do you propose?" You'll say, "Talk to my accountant for a proposal." You're not going to get into the nitty-gritty with her, are you?

Donald: No, I'm not going to get into the nitty-gritty with her. You know, my father many, many years ago—he was ninety-three when he passed away. Many years ago. He had a wonderful sixty-three-year marriage to a woman, my mother.

Howard: Right.

Donald: Okay. I heard he asked her for a prenup. Can you believe this?

Howard: Ahead of his time.

Donald: This was, like, seventy years ago! The guy was great. He was ahead of his time. He asked for a prenup, and she threw him out of the house. She had good intentions.

Howard: So you haven't begun the negotiations with Melania yet?

Donald: I haven't actually begun that negotiation yet.

Howard: But she's picked out a lawyer?

Donald: She hasn't even picked out a lawyer yet.

Howard: I admire this. Quite frankly, the marriage laws are a bit archaic. A guy like you, you've built up wealth, you've worked hard. I see you hustle every day. No reason if you fall in and out of love you should have to give up all your money.

Donald: I have a friend who's a total, brutal killer. He just kills everyone. And he's had a couple of horrible marriages. Now he has a new girlfriend, and he tells me, "Donald, this is the one." His last wife ripped him off for about $50 million. She was with him for two years, made him dinner every now and then. She didn't make dinner that often, 'cause she was out screwing around. So now he calls me and tells me, "I've met the one."

Howard: How stupid.

Donald: I say, "Okay, that's great. Where does she come from?" She's a Las Vegas showgirl.

Howard: Oh boy.

Donald: Bad sign. So I said, "You're going to get a prenup, right?" He says, "Don, honestly, I don't need it." Now, here's a guy who's a genius businessman, but a schmuck.

Howard: So what happened?

Donald: He married her two years ago. About a week and a half ago, I asked, "How is she doing?" He says, "That son of a bitch, I'll get her. It's over." And I said, "Please tell me you had a prenup." He says, "I don't. I have to go through it again."

Howard: Oh my God.

Donald: Something happens to men. Hey, look, I love Jack Welch. Great businessman. He had a very unusual prenup. He was married for ten years. The prenup expires in ten years, and he leaves her in the eleventh year. And she sues him for $500 million. You would have thought he'd leave after nine and a half, right?

Howard: Right. Talk to me now about what's going on with *The Apprentice.* You were the original, but you have two other guys who are attempting to steal your thunder. One of them came in here the other day. Mark Cuban. Billionaire. He's got a show on now that's very similar to *The Apprentice.*

Donald: Right. With no ratings.

Howard: With no ratings.

Donald: Doing very badly.

Howard: Then you've got this other guy coming out, Richard Branson.

Donald: Who's actually a good guy. I think that show has a shot. You see the ratings this week?

Howard: Yeah.

Donald: What were they?

Howard: Number one.

Donald: We were the number-one-rated show. In fact, the *New York Times* did a front-page story this Sunday, saying we were the number-one show since May.

Howard: With that kind of clout, you pressured NBC into paying you more money, did you not?

Donald: I did.

Howard: So now, what, you're getting $1 million an episode?

Donald: Much more than that.

Howard: More than a million an episode! Is that true?

Donald: Yes. Jeff Zucker is so smart, so tough, that it's hard to get that kind of money.

Howard: It's not a lot of money considering what they'll get in advertising.

Donald: They'll make a billion dollars off of *The Apprentice.*

Howard: Now, Mark Cuban is the guy from this other show. I don't even know—

Robin: *The Benefactor.*

Howard: *The Benefactor.* Okay, did you see Page Six today? He came out and blasted you. He says you need the money.

Donald: Okay, let me tell you about Mark Cuban. I think he needs the money 'cause this guy—just so you understand, according to *Forbes* I'm a much richer man than Mark Cuban.

Howard: He claims that you lie about your wealth. He says you claim you're worth $1.3 billion, you're not even worth that.

Donald: No, no, I claim I'm worth $6 billion. *Forbes* claims I'm worth $2.5 billion. But let me tell you about Mark Cuban. Mark Cuban is trying to get publicity 'cause his show is failing so badly.

Howard: So he's using you.

Donald: Everybody uses me. Women use me, you use me—

Howard: I use you?

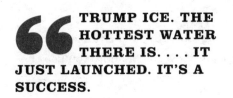

> **TRUMP ICE. THE HOTTEST WATER THERE IS. . . . IT JUST LAUNCHED. IT'S A SUCCESS.**

Donald: Well, you don't. But I'm a ratings machine. I don't know why he's doing it.

Howard: But why disparage you? He claims that—

Donald: Howard, Howard, excuse me. Before you say it—

Howard: Go ahead.

Donald: He said that Donald Trump isn't as good a businessman as you think. He mentioned four deals. One of them is Trump Ice. The hottest water there is. It's water.

Howard: I drink Trump Water.

Donald: It just launched. It's a success. He says it's a failure. The other is online Trump University. Last week I filed to maybe do an online university. I haven't done it yet, but he says it's a failure. The other thing was a failure was *Trump World* magazine. It launches tonight. We haven't even gone out yet. And by the way, it's going to be a success. So he mentions all this stuff. He doesn't mention my real estate, which is through the roof, which is the biggest stuff.

Howard: But he said you don't own those buildings, you just stick your name on them. This is what he said to me. I was shocked.

Robin: Do you own all of the buildings?

Donald: No, I own large percentages of the buildings.

Howard: Bottom line, you are worth minimally $2.3 billion, maybe as high as $6 billion.

Donald: Well, *Forbes* says $2.5 billion, but I've always disputed *Forbes*.

Howard: All right. That's all I needed to know.

Robin: We pointed this out the last time you were here: whatever you do, you say, "It's the most fantastic. It's the greatest thing."

Donald: That's not true. I don't say that. When do I say that? Excuse me, I say it when it's true. Hey, Robin, I have the hottest show on TV. She's a very negative person, Robin.

Howard: She is very negative.

Robin: I heard they were going Chapter 11.

Donald: That's minimizing debt. That's called intelligent business.

Robin: Hold on. They say Trump has to file bankruptcy on his casinos in Atlantic City, and Trump said this is the greatest thing.

Donald: It's true.

Robin: [*laughs*]

Donald: I only say it's good if it's good. That's true. Let me say one thing. The casinos are only one small part, 1 percent of my net worth, 'cause they're important to me 'cause I've been there so long.

Robin: Uh-huh.

Donald: I've made a lot of money with casinos over a fifteen-, sixteen-year period. I've made a lot of money. Now what I'm doing is making the casinos great. It's less than 1 percent of my net worth. I'd bet in the years to come, it'll be a big portion of my net worth.

Howard: All right, listen. Donald Trump. Continued success to you.

Donald: Thank you, Howard.

> **" EVERYBODY USES ME. . . . I'M A RATINGS MACHINE.**

Amy Schumer

AUGUST 23, 2016

We were one of the early supporters of Amy Schumer. Robin used to host a weekly interview show heavy on current events and political discussion. She would book many unknown comedians who were smart and could hold their own. Amy had been on a bunch of times, and we knew she was funny. I always wanted to promote female comics. Those were the years when Jerry Lewis was saying women weren't funny. That was such a turn-off. I thought, "If I ever run into this guy, I'm going to say something to him." Then when I started on *America's Got Talent* I received the following letter from him:

> Dear Howard,
> I've watched *America's Got Talent* since its beginning and felt compelled to write you and tell you how marvelous you are on the show. You bring energy, rhythm, information, and a wonderful way of getting your point across.
> I wish you continued success and know you've got a fan here.
> Regards Always,
> Jerry

All of my feelings about Jerry instantly melted away. I thought, "I'm not saying anything to him other than, 'I love you, Jerry.' That guy really knows what he's talking about! What a legend. All those great movies." It's amazing what one little letter can do. Despite Jerry's rapid seduction of me, I couldn't agree with him about female comics, so we booked Amy as a guest on the main show. She was fabulous. In fact, that's how Judd Apatow got turned on to her. He heard her interview and was so impressed that he reached out to see if she had any ideas for a movie, which led to *Trainwreck*.

She's been on the show a bunch of times since then. The reason I chose this interview is that it's not all for laughs. We delved a little deeper. We talked about her dad's multiple sclerosis and the subject of sexual assault. It felt good to have a conversation where heart and substance came first and punch lines second.

Howard: I feel you're doing too much.

Amy: You're right.

Howard: And you got sick.

Amy: Yeah.

Howard: And it got worse and worse and worse.

Amy: Yeah.

Howard: You burn the candle at both ends. Here's what's going on: the career is going great.

Amy: Right.

Howard: Got a young boyfriend.

Amy: Very young.

Howard: He's fourteen years old.

Amy: Sixteen in November.

Howard: But you got that new boyfriend, and you're trying to please him. You're trying to please everyone in showbiz. I even read you went to see the play *Hamilton*, and you gave the guy a $1,000 tip. I guess they served food there.

Amy: The fact that this is news—a couple tips that I've given have made news. People should be spreading their money around a little bit more. Well, I waited tables and bartended, so . . . And it's a little selfish because it feels so good to be able to do that and know that you made their night.

Howard: A $1,000 tip on a $77 bill. That's awesome.

Amy: Was it? It was $77?

Howard: Yeah. I track all this stuff. It was a $77 bar bill and you left $1,000.

Amy: Well, I drank a lot at *Hamilton*. I had to go to see that show three times, just so I could remember all of it.

Howard: Does it freak you out now in your life that when you do something generous like that it ends up in the newspaper?

Amy: Yeah. Now when I tip a lot, I say, "Please don't tell the press."

Howard: Oh, you do say that?

Amy: Yeah.

Howard: You know, to someone who wasn't thinking of telling the press, you must sound really idiotic.

Amy: Like, "Who are you?" Right. I know.

Howard: "I didn't know you were anybody."

Amy: I know. But then also that's a lot of pressure, because they're like, "Schumer's coming in. Get your money bags ready."

Howard: You played Madison Square Garden. Is that the biggest crowd you've ever performed in front of?

Amy: Maybe. I did that Oddball tour. I think there might have been like twenty thousand people at some shows. But that's a bigger lineup of comedians. It's not just me.

Howard: Is that a horror scene for you to do Madison Square Garden? If I was a stand-up comic, I would think I'd have trouble relating to an audience that vast, you know?

Amy: It was the best night of my life.

Howard: Really?

Amy: Yes. It's a really amazing room. And actually, no bullshit, it feels intimate. It was so cool.

Howard: Do you work the same way you would at a small club, like when you were starting out?

Amy: Well, a little bit. Probably a little bit too much. My stand-up, I think, feels pretty conversational and intimate. But I'm not going from clubs to that. I've been working up to that.

Howard: I don't think any female comic has ever played Madison Square Garden. That's true, right?

Amy: Yeah.

Howard: That's meaningful.

Amy: It is. It felt very meaningful to me.

Howard: Do you feel like some other comics start to turn on you? I noticed that. I've seen it in radio. Isn't there a jealousy that kind of consumes other comics when someone breaks out this big? Where it's like, "Everyone was rooting for me, and now they're not so much."

Amy: Of course. But it's not personal. It's not about me.

Howard: Have you lost friends? I'm talking about comics you choose to hang out with.

Amy: People that I was friends with in the very beginning, not a lot of them are left in my life. Some of them said to me, "I kind of can't deal with it." But I've been doing stand-up for thirteen years or fourteen years. So I've been friends with the same comics for about ten years.

Howard: That's sad, though. It's like, you can't hang out sometimes with your high school friends because they say fucked-up things.

Amy: Right. But I'm still really close with my high school friends. We did have a couple of years where it was tough, and then we found our way back to each other. Everybody kind of chilled out. And they're very much a part of my life.

Howard: Do you ever go out to dinner and does anyone ever pick up the bill besides you?

Amy: I wouldn't let that happen.

Howard: You don't let that happen?

Amy: No.

Howard: That's fucking awesome. All right, the book. Let me tell you what I think. First of all, I noticed the theme here.

Amy: What's the theme? I didn't know there was a theme. I didn't know you read it.

Howard: Well, your father. You're really hung up on your dad. I mean, you're, like, in love with your dad.

Amy: Oh, no, I'm not. That's very gross.

Howard: I don't mean in love sexually. I'm talking about you're in love in a sense that you spend a lot of time writing about your father, but there's not much about your mother. I didn't know your mother had an affair. Is that true?

Amy: Yeah.

Howard: Did your mother get upset that you wrote that?

Amy: Oh, I cleared everything with everybody. I wouldn't put a word in the book that wasn't okay. I told her I would leave the whole chapter out if she wanted. Or she could write a response. Or if there was anything in there that bugged her, I would've taken it out.

Howard: Did you think that maybe you were too young to write a memoir? Did that ever occur to you?

Amy: That's why I don't want to think of it as a memoir. Because it's like, yes, I am too young, and I don't know anything. But when somebody hands you a check for $8 billion . . .

Howard: Oh, it was *billion*.

Amy: It was *billion*. That's where you're wrong.

Howard: Wow. You're, like, the richest woman in the world now.

Amy: But I do feel like I have something to say, and so I was just like, "Here's what's going on up till now." And, you know, Lena [Dunham] is really young and I loved her book and I appreciated it. But when you hear this young asshole is writing a book, "What the fuck do you know?" I understand that.

Howard: But you got a lot of fans and they want to know what's going on with you. Now, the thing that struck me about this is that your mom had an affair. This is heavy.

Amy: It's heavy.

Howard: With your best friend's father.

Amy: Right.

Howard: That's like lighting a nuclear bomb in your life. That's why I think you're a little bit angry with your mom.

Amy: Yeah. But I was at a good age for that to happen.

Howard: Thirteen. Just when you're becoming a woman.

Amy: I was at a cool, stable place.

> ## PEOPLE THAT I WAS FRIENDS WITH IN THE VERY BEGINNING, NOT A LOT OF THEM ARE LEFT IN MY LIFE.

Howard: You were so together at thirteen. Yeah.

Amy: I feel like we're all in this quest to be like, "They did the best they could. They're human beings." You know? So that you can forgive them as much as you can. It's really hard. I go back and forth. I do have a little bit of anger for my mom.

Howard: Right.

Amy: But more than that, it's just pain. And the guilt. It's this cycle.

Howard: Is she in your life a lot now?

Amy: Not a lot. But, yes, she's in my life.

Howard: Because that's the feeling I got from the book—that you're angry with her. How could you not be, in all seriousness?

Amy: Well, you know, the anger is not as much . . . I was really upset about that. But more than that happening, it was reading back my journals, and I just felt brainwashed that she made me her support system during that. That's what hurt.

Howard: In other words, your mom has an affair, and she spent a lot of time convincing you that, like, "I'm not the guilty one here. I have my reasons for doing this." And so you get brainwashed into thinking, "Maybe Dad is the bad guy. Maybe he let her down or something."

Amy: Yeah.

Howard: And that's not fair to do to a kid, right?

Amy: Right.

Howard: So you went back and you included the journals of when you were a young girl. And then you comment on them as an adult. I think the whole book of that would've been cool, too. I would read that.

Amy: My journals are funny. From age thirteen to twenty-three, every day is documented.

Howard: I find guys don't journal a lot. Women journal more than guys, and women tend to save their journals somewhere. That's why I picked up this thing with your dad. You describe your dad as an alcoholic, right?

Amy: Oh yeah.

Howard: Do you drink a lot?

Amy: I drink every night.

Howard: You do? How many drinks would you have a night?

Amy: A glass or two of wine.

Howard: That's it?

Amy: If I have more than that, I'm not good. Then something's wrong.

Howard: So you're not an alcoholic.

Amy: No.

Howard: Your dad drinks a lot.

Amy: Well, now he can't. You know, he's like Stephen Hawking. But he sneaks wine every day. I don't know how he's getting it. Like, I pay for his home [aide]. And I'm like, "Stop giving him wine." I'll catch him. I just put it on Instagram. It's a video of me walking in and he's just sitting there drinking red wine at 4 p.m. I'm like, "Who's giving this to you?"

Howard: He's ill, right? He's got MS.

Amy: Yes. He's getting ready to get stem cells.

Howard: You even described in the book that your dad was shitting twice in public.

Amy: Yeah.

Howard: He gave the okay for that?

Amy: Yeah.

Howard: The first time he shit in public what happened?

Amy: The first time was we were at Adventureland. Ever been?

Howard: No. What were you doing there?

Amy: Actually, a water park would've been convenient. It's an amusement park [on Long Island]. My sister and I, we kept going on the roller coaster. And then one time, we got down and he wasn't there. I was maybe eleven or twelve. My sister was eight or nine. He wasn't there. We just kept riding the roller coaster. And then finally he came back and he was wearing no pants. Just had a long shirt. I swear to God. His shirt was long and the bottom was all wet. And he was like, "We have to go." I was like, "Okay." Like, he was never serious. And he always drove a convertible and I would always sit in the front because

I THINK IT'S IMPORTANT TO TALK ABOUT BECAUSE IT'S MADE ME FEEL LESS ALONE WHEN OTHER WOMEN HAVE COME FORWARD ABOUT BEING SEXUALLY ASSAULTED.

the back is too windy. And I kind of got a whiff. And so I was like, "Kim, you get to sit in the front today." She was like, "I do?"

Howard: Wow.

Amy: And then she just slowly leaned out the window as we're driving, like a golden retriever. And then we got back home, and before I got out of the car he said, "Please don't tell your mom."

Howard: And that freaked you out because you don't want to keep a secret from your mom, right?

Amy: Yeah. But it was more I just felt awful for him.

Howard: You felt sad for him.

Amy: I just thought that it was . . . this man, he's just been completely stripped of . . . I'll take a beat.

Howard: Yeah. See, that's what I mean. You feel sad for your dad.

Amy: I do feel sad for my dad. He has MS.

Howard: I know, but also I think because of the affair.

Amy: Yeah. I mean, look, he was no angel. I would bet all $100 billion I made on the book that he cheated on her. I'm sure.

Howard: And there was some sort of bankruptcy too, right?

Amy: Oh yeah.

Howard: Like, everything was bad.

Amy: It was all bad.

Howard: It wasn't a great childhood, right? It was shitty.

Amy: Yeah. I didn't have anyone I could get $100 from and everybody was shitting themselves. We were rich until I was, like, nine, and then we had nothing.

Howard: You say in the book you've fucked—how many guys was it?

Amy: Twenty-eight.

Howard: Yeah, that was even sad.

Amy: Why?

Howard: Because the first guy you banged kind of raped you.

Amy: Yeah.

Howard: I mean, not kind of. He did. You said you were sleeping and you woke up and the guy was on top of you doing it. That's pretty heavy stuff to put in a book.

Amy: Well, it's important, I think, to write about that, you know?

Howard: Yes, I agree.

Amy: I was in an abusive relationship, and I think it's good for men to read too. To be like, "Oh, that's not cool if I do that." I was in and out of sleep. We're just kind of lazily watching TV. We'd never had sex. And I could feel that he was touching me, and I thought he fingered me, and then it started to hurt. When I looked down, I was like, "What are you doing?"

Howard: Wow.

Amy: He was like, "I thought you knew."

Howard: And that was the end of the relationship, or you stayed in it?

Amy: No, we stayed together. I was worried about him. He felt really bad about it and was like, "I'm going to kill myself. I'm so sorry." And I'm like, "It's okay, it's okay." I'm comforting him because he was my boyfriend. I loved him, you know?

Howard: Yeah.

Amy: And then I got angry after. He messed me up. My trust issues are terrible.

Howard: Is that why you wrote about it? Because you're trying to warn women about how fucked up guys are?

Amy: I'm trying to, first of all, just speak out. So that, you know—I think it's important to talk about because it's made me feel less alone when other women have come forward about being sexually assaulted. And also, because it's not this perfect rape like people want. They want you to be raped perfectly. They want you to be a perfect victim. We're so critical, and it makes victims really not want to speak up. So I think it's me saying, "Look, I didn't have a perfect rape, but the way my virginity was taken from me, it was not in a cool way." It's also this situation of I didn't want to press charges against him. I used to talk about it in stand-up. It's like this gray area, the rape.

Howard: You want to know something? That isn't gray to me. I think that's just rape. I mean, I knew enough even when I was a horny teenage boy. When I was with a girl and I knew if she was sleeping, I wasn't putting my penis inside of her.

Amy: Well, unfortunately, you're in the minority.

Howard: Yeah.

Amy: And some women are like, "Oh yeah, it was my boyfriend. I was sleeping when he . . ." To me, that's really alarming. And I don't mean a gray area if it were rape or not. I mean of what to do. Like, how to handle it. It's not like, "Well, I'm going to the precinct and you're going to be serving time." It's more complicated than that, unfortunately.

Howard: I applaud you for writing that because I think I still to this day know a lot of women who will not speak out against their oppressor. They will not report it. In the book, you talk about how much of an introvert you are. Is it really as bad as you say it is? Even going to the gym or something, you worried about running into anyone you might know, right?

Amy: Yeah.

Howard: So all of this fame that you're having now, are you not taking advantage of going to parties and networking and meeting people? That's not fun for you?

Amy: No. That is my worst nightmare.

Howard: Going to a party where there are these wonderful celebrity types—

Amy: That's disgusting. That is my worst nightmare.

Howard: What, you think it's shallow?

Amy: Because it's so fake. It's just like people doing an impression of having a conversation. And you have to wear things that are uncomfortable. I like talking to people one-on-one. Two-on-one is fine. And where you can be comfortable and really have a conversation. I don't like the farce of it.

Howard: I read in the paper you went to the Met Gala. Was that a miserable night for you? You're dressed up and you've got to sit there and be "on" and talk to everyone?

Amy: I left not the second I could but earlier than I should've. But, it's exciting. You know, I got to meet Beyoncé. And she was like, "Is this your first Met Gala?" And

> **❝ I GOT TO MEET BEYONCÉ. AND SHE WAS LIKE, "IS THIS YOUR FIRST MET GALA?" AND I WAS LIKE, "IT'S MY LAST." AND SHE WAS LIKE, "UH-HUH."**

I was like, "It's my last." And she was like, "Uh-huh."

Howard: I'm sorry your mom fucked this guy. I'm sorry.

Amy: Thank you.

Howard: I really am. Fuck it.

Amy: Thank you.

Howard: You know what I'm saying?

Amy: Yes.

Howard: I'm being serious.

Amy: I know.

Howard: And I'm sorry about everything else.

Amy: Thank you.

Howard: Amy Schumer, I want to apologize for all men.

Amy: He's sorry about my whole life.

Billy Joel

APRIL 28, 2014

When I was a child, my parents gave me a choice: Boy Scouts or piano lessons. Don't ask me why I had to pick between those two. I have no idea. If I became a Boy Scout, my mother said she would be the den mother. I quickly chose the piano. The thought of Ray Stern lecturing a bunch of my peers about manhood made me break out into a cold sweat. I could only imagine her calling the local scout meeting to order, dressed in sandals with white socks, a whistle around her neck. Drained and exhausted at the shenanigans of young boys, she would scream and complain that they were not being raised properly, that all of their mothers were failing, and that they should read Haim Ginott on child rearing. The piano was the only choice. (If you're impressed by the fact I know this early pioneer in child psychology, it's only because I remember watching him as a guest on *The Mike Douglas Show*. I'm not that well read. Who could forget the name Haim Ginott? It stuck with me all these years later.)

From the very start, the instrument represented failure to me. Reading music, practicing scales, holding my hands properly—I was terrible at all of it. The constant words of my father telling me I was lucky to have lessons when he had nothing as a boy only made me feel worse. I never practiced. The teacher would come to our house and beg my parents to stop this absurdity. My father insisted I stay with it. Every time the teacher would arrive my mother would hide in her room. After years of practice, the only songs I could play were sloppy renditions of "Hang On Sloopy" and "Louie, Louie." (No wonder, because they both employed the same chords: C, F, and G.) Then one day my mother broke the news that the piano teacher had killed himself. He hung himself. She didn't say much more than that. For a while I assumed it was my fault. "Wow," I thought, "I must have been a real pain in the ass." Whatever guilt I felt was outweighed by my joy at getting to stop those lessons.

Not knowing how to play the piano didn't keep me from wanting to be a rock star. I played keyboard in a few bands with ridiculous names, like the Plumbers Union and Electric Comic Book. I remember once writing a letter to *Seventeen* inviting them to come photograph the Electric Comic Book. I wanted all the fame without doing any of the work. I just wanted girls to worship me. The magazine wasn't interested in my fantasy. I never heard back. The songs I wrote didn't go any better than my publicity efforts. "Silver Nickels and Golden Dimes" was about a prostitute so blinded by her greed that she couldn't find love. I wrote it in sixth grade. "Silver nickels and golden dimes / All you're hearing is the devil's chimes." What did I know about prostitutes? I'd certainly never seen one walking the leafy avenues of Roosevelt, Long Island—although I once found a few used condoms and nudist magazines buried in the bushes along Hausch Boulevard. Who among my neighbors was depraved enough to partake in such wild fornication and masturbation in public? My adolescent mind was filled with wonder. I'd like to interview *them* for this book. Jewel performed the song at my Birthday Bash in 2014. Maybe if I had a voice like hers my musical career would have gone somewhere.

By college I'd stopped playing. Yet my love for the piano was kept alive by performers like Billy Joel. Back in the mid-seventies at Boston University, while other students were out partying, I would stay in my dorm room listening to Billy Joel albums. Those records were so important to me.

Fast-forward thirty years. Beth and I were dating, and I parked my car in front of a restaurant we went to regularly. Much to my surprise, parking right behind us was Billy Joel. That began a friendship. Which is all the evidence you need that the universe is a crazy, magical place.

So many times you're disappointed by meeting your heroes, but not in this case. When I would sit and talk to Billy, I was dazzled by his intellect and fascinated by the way he explains the process of songwriting. To say that he is a genius is no exaggeration. He's also very funny. It was my perception that no one had ever seen the many sides of Billy Joel in an interview. I remember watching him on *The Oprah Winfrey Show* and thinking Oprah totally squandered the opportunity. I felt she didn't really appreciate who he was and that his contribution to American culture had been so vast. Despite whatever I've said on the air about Oprah, I think she's a great interviewer, but in this case it just wasn't the right fit. When Billy agreed to do my show, I was excited to finally give him an interview where he felt respected and appreciated.

This appearance was a rare three-hour event in front of a live in-studio crowd. All of my interviews are usually quiet affairs—no audience—and I prefer it that way. I was up for trying something new, and it worked. I wanted this to be special, so I invited a few artists to perform Billy's songs, including Pink, Melissa Etheridge, Boyz II Men, Idina Menzel, and Tony Bennett. It was a fitting tribute, and the three hours flew by. Billy went deep into explaining his craft, and broke it up with some great jokes. His wit and charm came through. This interview shows the Billy Joel I know and love.

Howard: I'm very excited. I've been waiting a long time for this. Of course, Billy Joel really doesn't need any sort of intro, but I'll give him one anyway. Billy has sold more than 150 million albums. Which is pretty incredible. And if you count that up, that's a lot of money. He's had thirty-three Top 40 hits, which, when you think about it, nowadays is insane, right? And six Grammy Awards, and he had the Kennedy Center Honors just in 2013.

Robin: And now us.

Howard: He's reduced himself to us. It's the low point in his career.

Billy: How ya doin'?

Howard: Billy, this is a lot of pressure for me, not for you. You wrote the song "Pressure," but this is what it's all about. Because, Billy, I feel like when we do these shows, there are questions that everyone wants to ask, and if I miss one, then I get yelled at. So I'm going to try and do my best. Are you nervous at all about this?

Billy: No.

Howard: No. You don't care. In fact, I called you and I said, "Do you want to know the questions in advance?" and you said, "No."

Billy: No. Because then I'll be rehearsing what the answer's gonna be. I hate rehearsals.

Howard: You're turning sixty-five.

Billy: Sixty-five.

Howard: Are you thinking about your age? And what does that do to you psychologically? Do you think about death? Because I am. I'm thinking about mine.

Billy: No, I'm thinking about life.

Howard: Are you?

Billy: Pretty much. You know, this is the senior citizen time of life. Which I hate: *senior citizen*. I'm an *old guy*.

Howard: But you don't feel old, do you?

Billy: In some ways. But there's a lot of benefits to this age too.

Howard: What are the benefits? Because I'm up peeing every fifteen minutes now.

Billy: You don't nickel-and-dime a lot of stupid stuff you used to. Your priorities are pretty well-balanced at this point. You know what's important.

Howard: But do you feel like you wasted time when you were young? Are there any regrets?

Billy: Sure, I've got regrets. Anyone who's really lived has regrets. If you have no regrets, what kind of life did you have?

Howard: And keeping with this theme of aging, are you a religious man? Are you thinking about "Is there a heaven or a hell?"

Billy: No.

Howard: There is no heaven or hell? Or you're not thinking about it?

Billy: I'm not going to say there is or there isn't. I just don't believe there is.

Howard: So you never go to a temple or a church, and you never sit there and pray?

Billy: I used to go to church. When I was a little kid, I mean. My family was Jewish, but I never had any Jewish upbringing.

Howard: Why were you at a church if you were Jewish?

Billy: Well, let me explain. I grew up in a neighborhood and it was mostly Irish and Italian and Polish. So everybody went to mass. I was in a Jewish family, but we never had any religious upbringing. The closest I got to Jewish was, you know, they clipped the tip. That was it. I had no say about that at all.

Howard: You were circumcised.

Billy: Yeah. And all my friends went to mass on Sunday, so I would just go with my friends to mass. I thought this was what you did. So I did the Catholic thing for a while, and then I tried to go to confession and they chased me out of the booth and everything. So I guess I'm not Catholic. And my mom decided we're gonna get religion when I was eleven, and she took me to a Protestant church, the Church of Christ, in Hicksville. And then I got baptized.

Howard: You did?

Billy: Yeah. I was baptized in a Christian church.

Howard: How many Jews can claim they were baptized in a Christian church?

Billy: All the Jews in Spain during the reign of Ferdinand and Isabella.

Howard: When you're a musician like yourself, you wake up every morning with a song in your head, right? It doesn't mean you're going to write the song, but you do come up with a song in your head every morning, right?

Billy: Yeah, I have a theme that I wake up with, then sometimes I try to shake it off.

Howard: You won't write any new songs.

Billy: I won't say "I never" or "I won't." I just don't.

Howard: But you won't record any new music. That's it. That phase of your life is over.

Billy: I have no plans to. I'm not going to shut the door on anything. If I come up with some great songs that I want to write, yeah, I would do that.

Howard: When is the last time you wrote a new song?

Billy: I haven't written songs. I've written instrumental pieces, music pieces.

Howard: Is that because it's sort of like a legacy thing? The older you get, and the more success you have, do you become more and more cautious? Like, "I don't want to have a flop album. I don't want to have an album that doesn't sell."

Billy: Nobody sells albums anymore.

Howard: No, that's what I'm saying.

McCartney put out a new album, and he didn't sell a lot of albums. So do you as an artist say to yourself, "Why would I make a new album? I don't want to be embarrassed. I don't want to have people not buy my album."

Billy: No, that's not it at all.

Howard: Then what is the reason?

Billy: I just don't want to. Everybody has a hard time understanding that. "Why don't you write new songs?" Well, you have to want to write new songs. I don't want to. Elton would say that to me. "Why don't you make another album?" I used to say to him, "Why don't you make less albums?" Sometimes when I used to write songs, it was a struggle. I didn't like writing, I liked having written. And sometimes it was a battle with the thing. I see this gigantic black beast with eighty-eight teeth trying to bite my hands off. That was what the struggle was, in writing.

Howard: Did you ever consider performing in a duck costume like Elton John? Was there a time?

Billy: No, no. But I would like to come up with a costume. I thought I might have a cape with a big P on my chest. You know, "It's Piano Man!"

Howard: I have to ask you about that song. You say whenever you go to a party,

EVERYBODY HAS A HARD TIME UNDERSTANDING THAT. "WHY DON'T YOU WRITE NEW SONGS?" WELL, YOU HAVE TO WANT TO WRITE NEW SONGS. I DON'T WANT TO.

> ## " I DIDN'T EXPECT TO BE A ROCK STAR. MY GOAL IN LIFE WAS ACTUALLY TO HAVE OTHER PEOPLE DO MY SONGS.

inevitably a piano player will try to impress you by playing "Piano Man."

Billy: Yes. Or "Just the Way You Are."

Howard: Does that annoy you?

Billy: No, no, not at all. I take it as a compliment. That's what I really wanted to do, is be a songwriter. I didn't expect to be a rock star. My goal in life was actually to have other people do my songs. I started out as a songwriter. Actually, I was in rock-and-roll bands all during my teenage years, and then when I got to my early twenties I said, "Okay, I'm not gonna be a rock-and-roll star. I want to be a songwriter." And I wrote songs, and the advice I got from the music business was, "Make an album, so they can hear your songs." Okay, made the album. Then, "Okay, you made the album. Go out on the road and promote the album." Okay. And I'm out on the road and I'm starting to become "Billy Joel," you know? And I thought, "This is a weird way to be a songwriter." It just happened to coincide with what they now call the singer-songwriter era—James Taylor, Carole King, Harry Chapin, Richie Havens, Cat Stevens. Just a whole bunch of singer-songwriters. And so I became Billy Joel, which to me is very kind of funny. I'm this rock star

and it's like, "Wait a minute, this is a big accident. You guys don't understand. I shouldn't be here." But my main thing is wanting the songs to be covered by other people, because you go through a gestation period when you're writing something and it's almost . . . the only thing I can compare it to is a pregnancy. You can't wait to get this song out, and then you go through the birthing process, which is very painful. I don't know what it's like to have a baby come out of me, but I know what it's like to have a kidney stone, and I heard it was pretty close.

Howard: Didn't the record company make you cut "Piano Man" down to three minutes and five seconds?

Billy: We had to edit it, yeah. It was originally five minutes and something.

Howard: Why did you have to edit it? Because they wanted a hit song?

Billy: To make it a single, to get played on Top 40 radio, they had time limits on what they liked to play.

Howard: And you were surprised that this song was a hit, right? It took you by surprise. You didn't know that this would be a hit song.

Billy: It's a waltz. Oom-pah-pah, oom-pah-pah, oom-pah-pah. And it's, you know, about a guy in a piano bar. It's not even a lyric, it's a limerick. "John at the bar is a friend of mine / He gets me my drinks for free / And he's quick with a joke or to light up your smoke / But there's someplace that he'd rather be." "There once was a girl from Nantucket . . ." It's a limerick.

Howard: You're not a man of a lot of hobbies, right? I know you love boating.

Billy: Yeah.

Howard: But piano's the thing that takes you out of this world.

Billy: Yeah. Piano can take me to another place. And I have hobbies—motorcycles and boats. And I love my dogs.

Howard: You've got a good life, right? You're happy.

Billy: Yes.

Howard: "Summer, Highland Falls"—I want to talk about that for a second, from the *Turnstiles* album. To me, that was you writing about depression. Terrible highs and lows. Like, the highs were too high and the lows were too low. Now I feel like your life is in place. But back then, when you were writing that song, maybe that was the worst time in your life?

Billy: No, that was—let's see, I wrote that in 1975–'76. I was moving back from California to New York. It was a transitional time. It's more about manic depression than depression. I keep reading things about me. "He was a depressed guy—"

Howard: No, but I had always heard that at some point in your life, like when you were a kid, you tried to commit suicide. I never knew the depths of your depression. But if that's true, it would seem to me that you were at a pretty low point.

Billy: Yeah, that's when I was twenty-one. I think a lot of people go through that when they go out of adolescence into young adulthood. It's a difficult transition

to make. But that song was . . . There was a relationship that wasn't really working out, and it was very disappointing, and you want everything to work out and when it doesn't, how do you deal with that?

Howard: But you said musically, when you wrote the song, you wanted it to reflect the highs and lows of manic depression.

Billy: Yes. The song has a musical theme. The left hand goes down, up, down, up, down, up, down. And the right hand is the manic *boop-da-boop-do.* So it actually kind of describes manic depression in the music.

Howard: Does superstardom free you of that depression?

Billy: I don't think so. It's a job. I don't walk around thinking, "Hey, I'm a superstar," and everything's great. You know, it's a job. I take off the hat when I go home. I take out the garbage, I cook food, I feed the dogs, I clean up the poop.

Howard: There are a couple songs I want to ask you about. "Captain Jack" is about a heroin dealer, do I have that right?

Billy: A drug dealer.

Howard: Why did you write that song? Because you were saying, "Gee, kids are ruining their lives with heroin"? Is that the message?

Billy: I was kind of puzzled as to why young, affluent suburban kids would go and score smack or whatever drugs they were scoring from a guy in an alley behind a housing project. Like, how bad can life be when you've gotta get that junked out? A little preachy, you

> ❝ **IT GOT ME SO HIGH I DIDN'T KNOW HOW TO DEAL WITH IT. I SAID, "OH MY GOD, I CAN SEE HOW PEOPLE CAN GET ADDICTED TO THIS."**

know—"your mother still makes your bed"—it's a little preachy, that song.

Howard: And you never tried heroin?

Billy: Oh yeah.

Howard: So you did try it. Here you're singing about "Why would someone try heroin?" But you had tried it.

Billy: I just tried it once, and there's a song I wrote about it. It's called "Scandinavian Skies." It goes into these weird, weird chords. It was a heroin trip.

Howard: Why did you do it? Was it because everyone at the time was doing heroin, and all the rock stars were trying it to see what the hell was going on? I mean, so many guys were doing it.

Billy: This was back in the early seventies—no, late seventies, I think. We were in Holland. I wanted to try it. You're in Amsterdam, and there was all this stuff going on, and I just said, "Lemme just try. Lemme see what this is like."

Howard: Did you shoot it, or did you just snort it?

Billy: I had it given to me.

Howard: With a needle.

Billy: Yeah.

Howard: And the effect was not pleasing to you. That's what scared you?

Billy: No, it got me so high I didn't know how to deal with it. I said, "Oh my God, I can see how people can get addicted to this." Because I was way out, and you just go to another place. You start drooling. And you get sick. I threw up.

Howard: This doesn't sound like a pleasant experience for you.

Billy: No, it scared me.

Howard: But at least you got a song out of it, right?

Billy: Yes.

Howard: "It's Still Rock and Roll to Me." The reason I like that song so much is 'cause you kind of comment on what it is to be a rock star. You have to be so cool, and everybody has to wear the right kind of clothes and this and that. And none of that was important to you, right? I mean, that was the annoying part of being a rock star, I think.

Billy: I was just kind of making a comment on style. Sometimes the press gave me a hard time, and I liked giving them a hard time back. My neighborhood, it's not "turn the other cheek." Someone hits you, you hit 'em right back. So I said, "It doesn't matter what they say in the papers, 'cause it's always been the same old scene."

Howard: "Still Rock and Roll to Me"—I'm talking about image now. When you're a rock star and you start to lose your hair, is that a traumatic thing?

Billy: [*laughs*] Yeah.

Howard: It is, right?

Billy: It sucks.

Howard: How old were you when you started to lose your hair?

Billy: I started losing my hair when I was in my fifties. Early fifties, yeah. My dad was completely bald, and his father was bald, and I said, "Oh no, no, no, no, I don't wanna go there. Please. I'm in rock and roll and I need my hair." I always had crappy hair anyway. I would torture it with a hair dryer and put all kinds of stuff in it. And it left me because I treated it badly. It deserved to go.

Howard: And it was a major trauma, right? Because when you're onstage, you're worried about your look. Did you ever consider a toupee?

Billy: Nah, I saw too many bad rugs in my life. If you're gonna go bald, embrace it, make it your own. Go real.

Howard: You ever have a rock critic write something or somebody walk up to you and say something horrible?

Billy: Yeah. I had a lot of hit records that I had almost nothing to do with except writing them. I didn't promote them or pick them to be singles. I didn't market them. The record company did that. But there was an assumption—and I would keep seeing this happen over and over again by certain people in the media—that I'm writing the song to be a hit like I'm cranking out cheese. Like, I'm just writing this stuff because I want to make money. Which is ridiculous because, sure, we all want to make money, but that's how I made a living. I just wanted to make a living. If the song

turned out to be a hit? Hey, other people liked it, okay. But I didn't write the song thinking, "I'm gonna sit down today and I'm gonna snap out another one of them hit records."

Howard: And that really hurts, right? Because you do have your integrity, and you made these songs because they've meant something to you. You can get a chip on your shoulder, right?

Billy: Yeah, I mean, there was an assumption that I was doing this for money. "He's sold out. He's doing it to make money." If I was really so worried about my money, I should've looked after my money—my real money—a lot better. I got ripped off twice really bad.

Howard: Yeah, anybody who was in it for the money might have had a better accountant or really watched everything.

Billy: Or just go to the bank once in a while and check that it's there.

Howard: "Movin' Out"—that was about the dumb things people save up for. They work hard, and you couldn't believe that they'd spend money on dumb stuff, right? Was that the essence of the song?

Billy: I'm trying to remember when I

> **I SHOULD'VE LOOKED AFTER MY MONEY—MY REAL MONEY—A LOT BETTER. I GOT RIPPED OFF TWICE REALLY BAD.**

wrote it. "Anthony works in the grocery store, savin' his pennies for someday." I've seen people, and friends of mine too, who are kind of pressured into taking a job just to make a living, take care of the family, and then they never really fulfill themselves. They're doing it because that's the cookie cutter—that's where you're supposed to go.

Howard: And that's sad to you? A guy who doesn't realize his full potential?

Billy: Yeah. Everybody's got something they love to do and they should be doing and they have a talent at or a propensity for, and I see people kind of wasting their lives sometimes, just not really putting their talent to that purpose.

Howard: Yeah.

Billy: For stuff. You know, you get a Cadillac, and okay, now you're fine.

Howard: That was your whole life. You're sitting there and getting a Cadillac. What was it all for?

Billy: Yeah. You end up with some stuff.

Howard: "Goodnight Saigon"—you have always said that you hate political songs, and you didn't like antiwar songs specifically, right? You hated Country Joe and the Fish—

Billy: I didn't like that stuff, nah. I don't like somebody telling me how to think.

Howard: Yet this song is about Vietnam and the war. You're not a guy who served in the army. You weren't a soldier. You've said many times you would've gone to Canada, as I would have. And yet you wrote this beautiful song from a soldier's point of view. Now, is that something hard to do? Do you have to go do research about being a soldier?

Billy: I wanted to do that for my friends who did go to 'Nam. A lot of them came back from that country and really had a hard time getting over it. And still, to this day, I think a lot of them are having a hard time. They were never really welcomed back. Whether you agreed with the war or not, these guys really took it on the chin. They went over there, and they served, and they never really got their due. And they sat me down and said, "We want you to write a song." I said, "Well, I wasn't there. I don't know what to write." And they said, "We'll tell you what to write." And they kind of went through it. It was really all about them depending on each other. They weren't thinking about Mom, apple pie, and the flag. They were doing it for each other, to try and help and save each other and protect each other. That really hit me. And I realized there's a great book about the Civil War called *The Red Badge of Courage* written by a guy named Stephen Crane. He wasn't in that war, but when you read that book you go, "How could that guy not have been in this war? It's so real and so authentic." He was just told. He talked to soldiers and found out what went on and wrote the book. I said, "Okay, I'll give it a shot."

Howard: Do Vietnam vets come to you after a show and say, "Thank you for writing that"? Or do they think you served in Vietnam because it seems like you really know what you're talking about there?

Billy: No, no. That was never brought up to me. But we bring them onstage and we have them sing with us.

Howard: That's a great moment in your live show.

Billy: It's finally, like, bringing them home and giving them a little bit of a parade and a welcome back. I like to do that for them.

Howard: Was the specific song you were referring to that you didn't like by Country Joe and the Fish—[*plays recording of "I-Feel-Like-I'm-Fixin'-to-Die Rag*]

Billy: Yeah. I was at Woodstock, and this hippie comes onstage and starts playing [*imitates vocals*]: "One, two, three / what are we fightin' for?" And I'm thinking, "This song sucks." But it wasn't even about the lyrics. It sucked as a song. And there's hippies up there [*imitates vocals*]: "Come on, everybody, smoke pot! Dah-dah-dah, do this, do that. . . ."

Howard: Were you at Woodstock?

Billy: I was at Woodstock.

Howard: Now, why are you not in the Woodstock movie?

Billy: I wasn't playing there. I was in the audience.

Howard: You were in the audience?

Billy: Yeah.

Howard: How old were you at the time Woodstock happened?

Billy: I was twenty.

Howard: So you weren't a superstar. You weren't known at that point. You actually went to Woodstock to hang out.

Billy: Yeah. I went on a motorcycle, on an old BSA. Which I'm glad I did, because the traffic was so bad you couldn't get beyond a certain part of the thruway.

Howard: How long did you stay for?

Billy: I stayed for about a day and a half. I wanted to see Hendrix. But then I had to use the bathroom facilities. And I'm not a bear, you know? The port-a-sans were pretty primitive, and there was a lot of mud. I think you had to do acid to stay there for three days.

Howard: Was there free love involved when you were there?

Billy: I was hoping.

Howard: You were hoping. But nothing happened?

Billy: No, I didn't get lucky.

Howard: The general perception is that everybody was getting laid at Woodstock, but there were a lot of guys hanging out who weren't getting laid.

Billy: Yeah, most of us, I think.

Howard: That's the real truth.

Billy: That's not why I went. I went to see all these bands, these great bands—Ten Years After and the Who and Hendrix.

Robin: So you never got to see Hendrix?

Billy: I didn't get to see Jimi. The last act I saw, I think, was Santana, who were great at that thing. But everybody was smoking pot, and I didn't do anything in those days. I didn't drink. I didn't smoke pot. I didn't do anything. And everybody was stoned all over the place. I was looking at people being like, "Wow, look at these people, they're messed up!"

Howard: Did you have a ticket to Woodstock, or did you just drive up?

Billy: Nah, you just walked in. The fence was down when I got there.

Howard: I did want to bring up one thing. I want Billy to stop riding a motorcycle. I don't like that he rides a motorcycle. He was in an accident years ago, and his thumb got all screwed up and it's like rubber, right? You told me the story once, when you had the accident.

Billy: This was in Huntington, Long Island. Somebody ran a red light. She ran a red light and she was in the intersection. I'm going through the intersection, and I ran into her and flipped over the car. I was wearing a helmet and boots, and I sat down on the corner. I was a little bit in shock. My hands were starting to swell up like watermelons. And somebody was asking me for an autograph. And I was like, "Whaa—"

Howard: Isn't that mind-blowing? That someone would ask you for an autograph as you're laying there and your hands are exploding?

Billy: I said, "How am I gonna sign it? With blood?" Then the policeman comes over and he needs my ID. You know,

"license and registration." I can't get my hand into my back pocket. I couldn't get my wallet out. The cop takes my wallet and he looks at my license and he goes, "Joel, William. William Joel. Hey, lady, you hit Billy Joel!"

Howard: You don't panic when you see your hands swelling up like that, living as a piano player?

Billy: Nah. They weren't that good to begin with. This is rock and roll. You play with your elbows if you have to.

Howard: Oh, come on.

Billy: No, piano is a percussion instrument. People think it's a string instrument, but piano you play like a drum.

Howard: And you hit the keys very hard, don't you?

Billy: Yeah, I used to break bass strings all the time. It's a percussion instrument. Play it like a drum. You *strike* the piano.

Howard: When you're in the studio and you're making a record, how long do you labor over that record?

Billy: They're all different.

Howard: Really?

Billy: Yeah. Like, *The Nylon Curtain* took me a year to make. And *An Innocent Man* took about two months.

Howard: And why do you think that is?

Billy: Sometimes you're on a roll, and you just go with it.

Howard: Do you ever get obsessive with a song? You hear it played back and you go, "No, I can still make it better"? How do you know when to put a song down and say, "That's it, I'm done"?

Billy: That's an art to learn. You have to know when to walk away. Sometimes it is what it is. Leave it alone. Move on. Next. Because if I spend too long working on something, I start to hate the thing.

Howard: Are the ones that come out faster usually the better songs?

Billy: Yeah. Better songs come quick. "New York State of Mind" took, like, ten minutes. "Just the Way You Are" was around in my head, musically, but the lyric came in about fifteen minutes. "Vienna" was one of those quickly written songs. It just kind of popped out when I was doing *The Stranger* album— which became a very successful album. I really don't remember where it came from or why it came out the way it did, but it was kind of a Promethean moment. It just kind of—*boing!*—sprang out of my head and there it was.

Howard: The story went that with "Vienna," you were in Vienna visiting your father.

Billy: Yeah.

Howard: You saw an old, old woman on the street. She was sweeping up or something. You felt bad for her. And your father said, "Don't feel bad for her. She has work. We honor these professions in Vienna." And you felt, "Hey, no matter how old I get, Vienna will wait for me." Right? "Because I

> **A LOT OF PEOPLE IN THEIR TWENTIES THINK THEY'VE GOT TO GET IT ALL TOGETHER BY THE TIME THEY'RE THIRTY.**

can be an old man and still people will treat me with respect."

Billy: Well, it was sort of just an observation that you have your whole life to live. A lot of people in their twenties think they've got to get it all together by the time they're thirty. And they kill themselves trying to get the golden ring by the time they're thirty. You have an entire life to live. So the lyric "Slow down, you crazy child"—you've got a whole life. We tend to put older people away, and by the time you're middle-aged, you're over the hill, and it's all about young people. So I said, "Wait a minute. Why do I have this whole life span? What's the point of it?"

Howard: So the message is, "Don't treat your life like it's gonna be over in five minutes."

Billy: Right.

Howard: Treat your life like you're in it for a marathon.

Billy: Some people will get there sooner, and some people will get there later. It's like, "Slow down. You're gonna be fine." Whenever you get there, you get there.

Jimmy Fallon

JUNE 14, 2017

In 1993, I had the opportunity to become a late-night host once. In the late eighties, Rupert Murdoch tried to recruit me to come to Fox and fill the slot previously held by Joan Rivers. I met with the Australian mogul in the inner sanctum of his Manhattan office, where he had four TVs—tuned to NBC, ABC, CBS, and Fox. There was another Australian guy there who would be my producer. With their thick accents, I couldn't understand what the hell they were saying. The offer was intoxicating. My own hour-long show on national television. I would be Fox's new savior, going head-to-head against Johnny Carson.

I took a couple days to think about it. Ultimately, Rupert and I mutually decided it wasn't the right fit, and we parted amicably. I was very busy with other projects: the daily radio show, working on my first book, and putting together a New Year's Eve pay-per-view special. I believe that special still holds the record for the highest-grossing pay-per-view outside of sporting events. I'm sure when Rupert saw it he was convinced we made the right choice to go our separate ways. I entered the special with my pants around my ankles sitting on a toilet that rose up through the stage floor—not exactly Carson's golf swing. My main reason for not doing the deal was that I could not live within the confines of a late-night show, having a guest on for six or seven minutes at the most. When I'm rolling and doing a good interview, I don't have to stop. I have no restrictions. I don't want to feel like I'm a passenger in a cab with the meter running. If I want to talk to a guest for three hours, I can do it. I like the lane I'm in.

I love having late-night guys on the show and hearing about their day-to-day grind, the agonies and ecstasies of how they prepare week after week. When Jimmy Fallon was named host of *The Tonight Show* in 2014, I thought he was the perfect choice. Since his days on *Saturday Night Live* when I became aware of him, I viewed him as a versatile comedian who could do it all—impressions, characters, even play the guitar. If you built your own talk show host, he would look like Jimmy Fallon.

This interview took place not long after he got criticized for having Donald Trump on and playing with his hair. I thought it was ridiculous how outraged people became. They were saying it humanized

Trump and turned the election in his favor. Come on, really? A guy rubbing Trump's head is going to change the way someone votes? I don't think so. People were just looking for a scapegoat. I thought it was bold of Jimmy to do that. Jimmy's job is to provide entertaining television, and it was just that: entertaining. I watched the clip several hundred times. I *still* can't figure out how that hair stayed on.

In this interview, he discussed what happened that night. You could tell he was still wrestling with it. Some have said his style of comedy should change for the times we live in, that his approach ought to be more political. That's one of the reasons I turned down Rupert Murdoch. In the world of television, in order to please the ratings beast, there are so many voices vying for control. I even experienced this a bit on *AGT*.

There were times during the pre-taped performances when I'd be brutally honest with contestants. I wouldn't be mean. I would just offer them a candid appraisal of their performance. I felt that if they were serious about pursuing their passions as entertainers, they would welcome constructive criticism from someone who has been in the business as long as I had. If they didn't advance in the competition, at least they could take away something concrete from the experience that would help them improve. I thought this tactic made for interesting television. Yet when I watched the show each week, I found that these sorts of interactions were occasionally trimmed down or edited out altogether.

The producers never gave me any criticism. They said they loved what I was doing. In fact, because of my radio experience, they tasked me with an important responsibility. During the live portion of the show, they had me wear an earpiece. Whenever we were running a bit ahead of schedule, they would ask me to fill the time. "Howard," I'd hear in my earpiece, "we need you to stretch for thirty-five seconds." I would subtly nod to let them know I'd received the message, then I would riff until the red light on top of the cameras flashed, indicating it was time to wrap it up. I took pride in having this duty.

However, just from observing what made it into the finished episodes, I began to adjust my performance. I respected the producers' expertise. They knew what they were doing. The show wasn't a hit by accident, but by trying to give them the type of material they seemed to favor, my approach got softer. Why bother putting out my true feelings if they only ended up on the editing floor? It got to the point where I felt I was compromising a little too much. Viewers weren't getting the real me. So I decided it was probably time to leave.

Overall, the experience was great. I departed on good terms with everyone. I absolutely loved being on that show. Still, it reinforced what I'd always known about working in TV. It is a gigantic machine. There is so much riding on every second of airtime, with the armies of executives and all of their changing opinions, the countless research conducted to pinpoint what is working and what isn't. The fine-tuning and second-guessing is unending. This can lead to well-meaning but preposterous suggestions—like Jimmy Fallon changing who he is.

Jimmy is the show business equivalent of Halley's Comet. A performer like that comes around infrequently. How many people could go from stand-up to *SNL* to starring in movies to hosting a late-night show? He plays music. He does spot-on impressions. Sometimes he does both. Not long ago, Beth and I ran a charity event for the North Shore Animal League America. Beth is their national spokesperson. Into the room walked Jon Bon Jovi. Jimmy was already there, and when he spotted Jon he jumped onstage and started singing a pitch-perfect rendition of "Livin' On a Prayer." Everybody in the room broke up laughing—even Jon. The guy can do it all. He is an extraordinary talent.

You wouldn't suggest Halley's Comet alter its direction. The same goes for Jimmy. Just shut up, sit back, and enjoy the show.

Howard: How many years now have you been hosting *The Tonight Show*?

Jimmy: Three years.

Howard: Isn't that something?

Jimmy: It's crazy. I don't even understand it. It's crazy.

Howard: You've said it's better to host *The Tonight Show*, because when you do *Saturday Night Live*, you have to wait all week. If you think you fucked up at *Saturday Night Live*, you wait all week and criticize yourself.

Jimmy: It was the worst.

Howard: But *The Tonight Show*, you always know you have the next night.

Jimmy: Yeah, exactly. So if you go, "Ugh, I was a little off on that, I had no funny jokes in the monologue," it's like, "Doesn't matter, dude. Get your stuff together, 'cause you gotta make people laugh tomorrow night."

Howard: Right.

Jimmy: It's like, "Who cares? Stop crying about yourself."

Howard: How were you balancing all this? I mean, you've got two kids.

Jimmy: Yeah.

Howard: You got a wife.

Jimmy: Yeah.

Howard: Got the fucking *Tonight Show*, where they're scrutinizing the ratings like crazy right now. And you know Colbert's having a pizza party if he beats you. I mean, I would lose my goddamn mind. Seriously, there's only so much energy that you can put into all this. Are you in therapy at all?

Jimmy: I now and then do it. But I don't

even have time to go to it. Can they come to you?

Howard: I don't think it works that way.

Jimmy: I'm trying not to read anything, you know?

Howard: You're afraid something will be written about you. Why can't your wife just cut out holes in the paper where there's stuff about you? Like if you were in prison.

Jimmy: My horoscope is missing, and you go, "Why is Virgo not here?"

Howard: I know what you mean, though. It's a lot of pressure on you.

Jimmy: It's weird, yeah. I'd heard that there was gonna be a Page Six thing or something about me being, you know . . .

Howard: An alcoholic.

Jimmy: An alcoholic. And it ended up being the cover.

Howard: Before you go to the bar, do you say to yourself, "I better skip it," because the *New York Post* could find out about it?

Jimmy: Yeah.

Howard: You do.

Jimmy: I wouldn't go to a bar.

Howard: No, right? Now you have to go drink at home. Alone. There's a little-known fact about you, actually, concerning drinking, which is so interesting. When you were a kid, you used to like to watch *Saturday Night Live*, which was your dream, to be on it. But your parents would allow you to drink beer while you watched *Saturday Night Live*.

Jimmy: They would buy me beer, yeah.

Howard: How old were you?

Jimmy: I was probably fifteen.

Howard: Wow, what nice parents.

Jimmy: They'd rather me drink at home. This is their logic. I don't know if I'm gonna do it with my kids. I'm gonna give them tequila. Get 'em started on tequila. It's better for you.

Howard: Right. Just shots.

Jimmy: Yeah, they would rather me be at home and safe and not drinking and driving. So I would have one friend over—or usually by myself, 'cause I was that much of a nerd. I didn't want anyone bothering me during *Saturday Night Live*. I really loved the show. I would pay attention to every single thing. I would see what cast members weren't mentioned in the opening [credits], 'cause they would do that now and then. They wouldn't put your face in the [credits] if you weren't in the show. So I'd be like, "*What?!* Dana Carvey is not in this episode?! You gotta be kidding me!" I would really geek out.

Howard: And your parents were kind of liberal. They'd be like, "Have a couple of beers here rather than run out."

Jimmy: They're crazy people. They really are. They belong in a mental institution. My mom was a nun at one point.

Howard: No kidding.

Jimmy: Yeah.

Howard: That's so fucking crazy.

Jimmy: Isn't that bizarre?

Howard: Was your dad a priest?

Jimmy: No.

Howard: No? Did you ever ask your dad how he seduced a nun? 'Cause that's gotta be hot.

Jimmy: I don't know that he had that much game.

Howard: In other words, he had the foresight. He saw her in that fucking outfit and the whole thing and he was like, "You know what? I wanna fuck her."

Jimmy: I don't think he was peeping in a convent or something.

Howard: How did he meet her?

Jimmy: Brooklyn. They just grew up together, went to high school in Brooklyn.

Howard: Oh, and then she goes off and becomes a nun.

Jimmy: For like a week. But technically, it counts. She had the habit.

Howard: She married Jesus. Jesus is her first husband.

Robin: And then she cheated on him.

Howard: Wait a minute, this is an amazing story of seduction. Your father was quite the player. He knew her in high school. But he didn't date her in high school?

Jimmy: No, they didn't date. They just knew each other—neighborhoods and stuff.

Howard: And he thought she was kinda hot.

Jimmy: Yeah.

Howard: But then he finds out she becomes a nun. And then does she *leave* the nunnery?

Robin: The convent.

Howard: The *convent*.

Jimmy: I think *nunnery* is a word.

Howard: Is it a word? I don't know.

Robin: It is a word.

Howard: But did she leave the convent? I like *convent* better. Did she leave the convent because of your dad?

Jimmy: I don't think so, no. I think she couldn't take it.

Howard: Is this one of those things that's uncomfortable to talk about with your parents? Like, you don't want to know too many details?

Jimmy: No, I want to. I asked them.

Howard: Bring your mom on this show. I'll get everything out of her.

Jimmy: They are insane people.

Robin: She went from being a nun to buying him beer for *Saturday Night Live* when he was fifteen.

Howard: Yeah, what a mom. I still think about that great story you did on *The Tonight Show* when Nicole Kidman was a guest. She wanted to fuck you. Fuck your brains out. She comes over to your apartment before you were married. I still don't understand how you didn't bang her. How did you not pick up on this?

Jimmy: Here's what happened. My friend Rick calls me and he goes, "Dude, I'm with Nicole Kidman. She wants to come to your apartment. She wants to meet with you

> ❝ **MY FRIEND RICK CALLS ME AND HE GOES, "DUDE, I'M WITH NICOLE KIDMAN. SHE WANTS TO COME TO YOUR APARTMENT."**

about . . ." A project. Nora Ephron redid it. *Bewitched*. So I go, "Wow. Cool." It ended up going to Will Ferrell.

Howard: They were thinking of you being Darren.

Jimmy: Darren, yeah.

Howard: I could see that.

Jimmy: It'd be fun. So I go, "Great. Fantastic. But my place is a mess." I don't know what's going on. "Nicole Kidman? Let's meet somewhere else." He goes, "No, Nicole wants to go to the apartment. Just get some cheese and crackers." I go, "Cheese and crackers? What cheese?" And he goes, "Just get Brie and crackers." And I go, "Okay." I don't even know what Brie is.

Howard: Right.

Jimmy: So I go into the deli by my house. I go, "Do you have any Brie?" The guy's like, "What?" So I grab Brie, which I don't know what it is, and I bought saltines.

Howard: Saltines.

Jimmy: So embarrassing. And I put it on a plate, and I opened the plastic wrap of the saltines and I kind of fanned it out a little bit, to make it look fancy.

Howard: Nice.

Jimmy: I don't have a cheese knife. I have a butter knife. And this thing of Brie. I go, "Do I take this thing off?" The plastic. The rind. I don't even know it's called the rind at the time.

Howard: Who knows that?

Jimmy: I don't even know what to do with this. Do I scoop out the middle? This whole thing's a nightmare.

Howard: See, I would've opened a can of nuts. Then there's no qualm about—

Jimmy: Unless you have a peanut allergy.

Howard: Oh, shit, yeah. All right.

Jimmy: Can't win anymore.

Howard: So she walks in.

Jimmy: She walks in, and I go, "Wow." I was nervous.

Howard: And did you think she was hot?

Jimmy: Gorgeous.

Howard: Gorgeous, right?

Jimmy: Gorgeous.

Howard: I mean, it's a no-brainer.

Jimmy: By far the most beautiful person who ever walked in my apartment.

Howard: But you thought it was like, "Oh, she's discussing the movie."

Jimmy: I'm trying to be a professional. I mean, I want to be someone you want to work with in a movie for three months.

Howard: Not just some guy who's gonna jump on top of me.

Jimmy: Yeah. Plus, I wouldn't even consider that I would have a chance in my life with Nicole Kidman. So she sits down and she goes [*mimics Australian accent*], "Now, what are all these wires?" Or something like that.

Howard [*mimics Australian accent*]: "What are all these wires?"

Jimmy: Yeah. I can't do Australian, but—

Howard: Me neither, obviously.

Jimmy: And I go, "That's a Nintendo game. I have a Nintendo game." And she goes, "What games are you playing?" Now she's British.

Howard: Close enough.

Jimmy: Now she sounds like Ricky Gervais.

Howard: Now she's David Bowie.

Jimmy: I'm about to have an affair with David Bowie. So I go, "It's *Mario Kart*." I teach her. I say, "Do you wanna see how to play?" I don't even know what I was doing. I taught her how to play the video game.

Howard: My God.

Jimmy: *Mario Kart*. It was so lame.

Howard: And you didn't get the part.

Jimmy: I didn't get the part.

Robin: I wonder what Will Ferrell did.

Howard: He probably banged the shit out of her. He knows what to do.

Jimmy: But I never heard this story until *The Tonight Show*. She came on the show and she goes, "I have a story. Do you remember meeting me?" And I hate those things, because I don't remember meeting anyone. So I go, "Uh, gosh, I don't even know what this story is." And she told the story on *The Tonight Show*.

Howard: Except she said she was interested in you sexually.

Jimmy: Yeah.

Howard: And you're like, "Wow, really?"

Jimmy: I go, "So what did you think?" She goes, "Well, I thought maybe you were gay." I go, "Let's not be ridiculous. It's not *that* crazy."

Howard: "Well, fuck you."

Jimmy: Yeah. Let's not go to *that* extreme. I was just playing video games.

Howard: When you were on *Saturday*

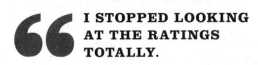

I STOPPED LOOKING AT THE RATINGS TOTALLY.

Night Live, and your fame first starts coming, did you have crazy sexual experiences? Did you bang tons of women and stuff?

Jimmy: No.

Howard: I see you being respectful.

Jimmy: No, yeah, I am.

Howard: You kind of are.

Jimmy: I just kind of go and have fun, and I just don't get in anyone's way.

Howard: I wonder who else you could have gotten.

Jimmy: I know! It might come out on the show.

Howard: Do you hate any of these late-night guys? Remember how I always interview you and you're like, "I don't hate any of the late-night guys"? You've got to hate some of them now.

Robin: Now that they're coming after you so heavily.

Howard: They are really coming. Even Colbert. Every minute he's having pizza parties when he wins in the ratings. It has to piss you off.

Jimmy: No, no, no. We have a pizza party every Friday losing, so . . . We don't care. I don't care.

Howard: Don't you hate the ratings? Aren't they so much goddamn pressure?

Jimmy: But we've had this conversation. *You* love watching the ratings and looking at them.

Howard: I was obsessed. I had to be number one.

Jimmy: Yeah, I thought that too. But then I stopped looking at the ratings totally.

Howard: Can I tell you something? Here's the deal. Right now, it's all 'cause of Trump.

Jimmy: Yeah.

Howard: Everyone is obsessed. *The Tonight Show,* to me, with Jimmy Fallon, it would be disingenuous of you to change *The Tonight Show.* You are not a political guy. I mean, you'll comment on politics. You were one of the first to do Trump. You did the impression, and you had him on, but right now everyone is obsessed. People who don't like Trump just want to fucking hear somebody bashing Trump. But you're in this weird fucking zone.

Jimmy: Yeah.

Howard: Because you know how everyone says, "Oh, Jimmy rubbed Trump's head." Bullshit. Nobody cares about that. I don't think people give a shit about that. Where are you at with that?

Jimmy: Well, that was just—God, we've had him on forever, you know? On the show.

Howard: Yeah.

Jimmy: And I didn't even think he'd get remotely this far.

Robin: Nobody thought.

Howard: No.

Jimmy: Hillary Clinton had this in the bag.

Howard: Yeah.

Jimmy: So he came on, and we always ask everyone to do bits. We asked Hillary to do a bit, and she said no. 'Cause she's like—

Howard: "Fuck you."

Jimmy: "Please. I got this."

Howard: "I'm gonna win. Why do I need one of your bits? If I do a bit, I can only screw up."

Jimmy: Exactly. But then he came on, and two seconds before he came on, they said, "You can mess up his hair." We've been asking him to do this. 'Cause he has the most famous hair in the world.

Howard: Right.

Jimmy: So to see if it's real, or a toupee, or whatever—

Howard: Yeah, I thought for sure something weird would happen.

Jimmy: I thought people might be like, "You did it!" But no one did. And then I just . . . People were so upset. And I was like, "Oh, man." I just read the room wrong, yeah.

Howard: You can never win with politics.

Jimmy: You can't.

Howard: No.

Jimmy: I didn't know. I never thought it would be a thing of like, "Wow, I'm making him look cool."

Howard: I don't know that you did. I just think with everyone so political right now—

Robin: Well, some people actually went so far as to accuse Jimmy of getting Trump

elected, by running his hands through his hair.

Howard: You did that?

Jimmy: Yeah, that was me.

Howard: Well, hey, that's pretty fucking powerful. Did you get upset with all the scrutiny on you? Lots of people have interviewed Trump. Lots of people. You just—it's like you're a lightning rod when you're number one.

Jimmy: It hurts. I'm a people pleaser. I think that's one of my traits, and I really just want to—maybe that's why I'm the guy at the party where I'll get up and I'll do something. I want to make people happy.

Howard: Did you go into a depression when people started criticizing you?

Jimmy: Not that long of it, but, yeah, for a little bit. Just a couple of nights. Tossing and turning. I didn't know where to look and what to read. Here's what happened. Here's where I made a big mistake, is that I didn't talk about it the next night. I thought—

Howard: Bullshit.

Jimmy: I thought it was gonna blow over.

Howard: You think you shoulda come out with some kind of statement?

Jimmy: I don't know.

Howard: Fuck that. Your strategy going into *The Tonight Show*, if I have it right, was: "I'm the guy who's just the life of the party. I have fun. I can dance. I can sing. I can fucking do impressions. I'm there to have a good

" I'M DEFINITELY NOT A POLITICAL COMEDIAN. I DON'T KNOW HOW TO DO THAT.

time." I don't think you should change that strategy.

Jimmy: Yeah, I don't . . . I can't. But also I don't know what's gonna happen. I've had Obama as president for my whole career as a talk show host. I don't know what this world is yet. I'm still figuring it out. I didn't plan the future. I'm definitely not a political comedian. I don't know how to do that.

Robin: So when you read in the paper that you're now gonna get more political because of all of this, that's just somebody making all that up?

Jimmy: Yeah.

Howard: You know what else is weird? If you are political—because sometimes you will be political—then they'll say, "Oh, he's trying to be political."

Jimmy: Yeah. "Look at him, he's trying—"

Robin: "Moving in on Colbert's territory."

Howard: I tell ya, man, they're gonna beat the fun outta you. I'm telling you.

Jimmy: You think so?

Howard: I'm telling you. You gotta stick with your game plan.

Jimmy: Yeah. I can't do it. I don't do that stuff.

Howard: Don't react to this bullshit.

Jimmy: Yeah.

Howard: You wanna say "Fuck you" to any of the other late-night guys?

Jimmy: Let me think about it.

Howard: Think about it? What about it? Say "Fuck you" to Colbert. Just for once.

Jimmy: Nah, I can't do it.

Howard: You can't do it?

Jimmy: I can't do it. No, he's good, and I like him.

Howard: Tell him, "You know what? Don't get all fucking full of yourself. We're in this for the long run."

Jimmy: For the long haul.

Howard: Tell him.

Jimmy: I can't do it. This is what therapy is?

Howard: Jimmy, yes. They'll get you going.

Jimmy: They'll ride on me until I break open?

Howard: You're better than all of 'em.

Jimmy: I like all those dudes.

Howard: Call James Corden a chubby British shithead. Go ahead. Do it. Right now.

Jimmy: You want me to do it *now*?

Howard: Do it now. Go to war with somebody. It's time. It's time to go to war with James Corden. You can't lose that battle.

Jimmy: I can't.

Howard: Pick on somebody. Start.

Jimmy: I can't.

Howard: Conan, you can go after.

Jimmy: I can't go after anybody.

Howard: Go after Andy Cohen.

Jimmy: I can't go after Andy.

Howard: Call John Oliver a nerd. Somebody. Go to war with somebody.

Jimmy: "Go to war with somebody." This is getting silly.

Howard: Listen, man, you're super talented. You're the fucking guy. You'll just do it, and that's it.

Jimmy: It's all fun.

Howard: As long as it's fun.

And Now a Word
from Our President . . .

FEBRUARY 27, 2006

(10 years, 8 months, and 12 days until the election)

Howard: How are you, Donald?

Donald: I'm fine. This is my daughter Ivanka. This is my son Don.

Howard: Hi, Ivanka. Nice to meet you.

Ivanka: How are you? Nice to meet you as well.

Howard: And Don is here as well. All three of you are on the show [*The Apprentice*] this year.

Don: Yes.

Howard: Is there a lot of pressure to come in big with this? Everyone always looks at you and expects you to be number one.

Donald: I don't know. You know, the finale, as you see—I just gave you the ratings—was number two. That was last month. Number two for the week in television. The show's been number one for a lot of the time. It's always tough, Howard. You know. Your show, if you drop 1 percent, there's a headline: "Howard Stern Ratings Drop."

Howard: Right.

Donald: Then you read the story, and it's like, "Holy Christmas! The show's doing well."

Howard: Can I say something to you?

Donald: Yes.

Howard: You're like me. I get crazy about everything. I'm telling you, I'm nuts. I sat down and started to analyze what Martha Stewart said. [Stewart hosted a spinoff of *The Apprentice* that lasted one season.] In a way, she was saying there was too much *Apprentice* on the air. Which is something you were saying as well. Then she said, "This guy Burnett came to me and said, 'Donald doesn't want to do this forever.' They said to me, 'The plan is to fire Donald in a cute way,' then I would take over. That was my goal. And when that didn't happen, both of us are stuck on the air. It's too much *Apprentice* on the air. It should've been one *Apprentice* moving into the other *Apprentice*." And I'm thinking, I don't think she really criticized you.

Donald: You see, I viewed it as negative. I viewed it as negative. Because I don't want to be fired when I have the number-one show on television, okay?

Howard: Right.

Donald: That's number one. Number two: Do you fire Jennifer Aniston three years ago when *Friends* was blazing?

Howard: No, no.

Donald: You wanna fire her and put someone else in? It doesn't make sense.

Howard: I am the same way. I was at war with, who was it—oh, right, Jack Black. I listened to a piece of tape where he went on another radio show and criticized me. I heard the tape and blew my stack. I said, "That Jack Black," and I went into a thing with him for about a month. Jack Black comes into my studio and goes, "I don't know what I did wrong. I want to apologize, but I don't think I said anything wrong." I said, "I'm going to play the clip to your face." I play him the clip, and I'm listening to it, and I think I must be going insane. The guy's not saying a word about me. I must be mentally ill.

Robin: Well, it's one thing for Donald to say, "Oh, that's my friend Martha. I don't know what she's saying." But you go into attack mode. All they have to say is "Donald Trump" and you go into attack mode.

Howard: You're like me.

Robin: And you slay people. You don't just knock them a little bit, punch them once. You just destroy. She felt destroyed by you.

Donald: Well, I never really thought of that, but Howard is that way. As a longtime listener and friend, Howard is that way. When I called up innocently—A.J. Benza, he didn't say anything so bad, and I went crazy.

Robin: You had actually taken *his* girlfriend.

Donald: I did, I did.

Howard: You took his girlfriend and killed him on the air.

Donald: I'm proud of that. You know what? She's a wonderful person too. I'll tell you, I'm very proud of it. And he didn't even say anything that bad. And the thing I'm most proud about? Howard once said that was in the top five of *The Howard Stern Show*.

Howard: It was. I love arguing. Did you and Martha really have a friendship? Or was it just one of those things where you'd see each other casually?

Donald: It was more casual, but we had a friendship. We liked each other. And the one thing you have to understand: I had nothing to do with the show. I owned the show with Mark Burnett. Martha just got paid a fee. I had nothing to do with the show.

Howard: I think in time—I'm just guessing—I think in time [you'll realize] Martha Stewart did not say anything bad about you.

Donald: Okay. I mean, that could be. You know what? I'll forget when you forget all your little disputes.

Howard: I can't forget my little disputes.

Donald: It's a personality sickness.

Howard: Do you ever forgive anyone? Have you ever been in a feud?

Donald: The answer is, rarely.

Howard: Right.

Donald: Rarely. I'll tell you, Don sort of said something to me today. Don said—go ahead and say it, Don.

Don: Basically, he's too nice to people he doesn't know that well. But people who he starts to dislike, with merit or not, he just takes it way too far.

Howard: He just takes it too far. Have you ever been in therapy for this? You do have anger issues.

Donald: No, I haven't. I haven't.

Howard: Why?

Donald: 'Cause I'm too busy to be in therapy. That's the good news. I'm so busy, I don't have time.

Howard: Isn't it hard, though—and I'm going to ask the kids this question—isn't it hard being Donald Trump's kid? 'Cause you know if you screw up with him, he will not be forgiving.

Donald: [*laughs*]

Don: Definitely. He wouldn't treat us differently than anyone else.

Howard: In other words, if you don't buy into Donald Trump's world, even as his children, you're out. So it doesn't allow you to rebel. You've never had the chance to say, "Hey, Dad, screw you! You're wrong!" Am I right or am I wrong?

Don: There's definitely truth to what you're saying.

Howard: I would think it'd be very difficult to be Donald Trump's kid.

Ivanka: There are some advantages as well.

Howard: I understand. I'm not saying he's a bad dad or anything like that.

Ivanka: It's a part of what's great about him, though. Because you understand things. He's so blunt, there's no ambiguity about how he feels, and you can go to him and say, "How do you feel about this?" and know you're getting an honest answer.

Don: It's black or white.

Howard: So if you went up to your father, and you said, "You know what, Dad? You're an f-ing a-hole—"

Ivanka: We would never say that.

Howard: Well, hold on a second. Let's say you screwed up, or got angry with him. Would your father be able to come to you afterward and hug you and say, "I'm proud of you for speaking up"?

Ivanka: I think he likes it when we speak up. We don't always agree with him, and don't have to always agree with him.

Howard: Right.

Ivanka: We now work with him, and have to bring something to the table— our own viewpoints. But that being said, there's a way to disagree with someone while being respectful and not insulting.

Howard: And also, you always have to keep in mind your father's a very wealthy man. It's a nice security blanket. If you go outside the line, he could cut you off. Because he is that kind of guy. Be honest, be honest.

Donald: I will call in those will lawyers. I will cut them out of that will so fast. Those kids will have nothing.

Don: He says that with a smile, but he's not kidding.

Ivanka: With a twinkle in his eye.

Howard: Have you guys ever said, "Dad, how much is in the will, and how much am I getting?" Have you ever discussed it?

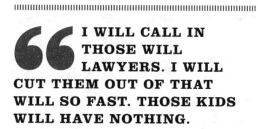

> ❝ **I WILL CALL IN THOSE WILL LAWYERS. I WILL CUT THEM OUT OF THAT WILL SO FAST. THOSE KIDS WILL HAVE NOTHING.**

> ❝ IVANKA AND DON AND SOON ERIC WILL BE WORKING WITH ME, AND SO I'LL BE DOING THINGS FOR THEM. THEY'LL BE WORKING ON DEALS, SO THEY'LL GET A PIECE OF A DEAL. CERTAIN ADVANTAGES.

Don: Not really.

Howard: You want to discuss it now? You want me to broker this whole thing?

Don: I think Howard will do a better job than we will, so maybe.

Donald: You know, it's a funny thing about wills. Wills are very hard to talk about with parents. And you know, the kids, they're very good businesspeople. They went to Wharton. They got all As. They were great students—great everything. We talk about deals. The big deal is, how much am I going to leave them? How much taxes are going to be paid? How much this, how much that. They find that hard to bring up. And the reason they don't is because of respect, in all fairness.

Howard: Aren't you annoyed by this new baby coming on the scene?

Donald: Here we go.

Don: Dilution. Dilution.

Howard: Let's be honest. Couldn't he stop with these children?

Ivanka: I think it would be much more difficult if we were around thirteen or fourteen. In a lot of ways, it was more difficult when Tiffany came around, 'cause we were still in the nest. Now we've grown up. We're working for him. It's sort of a separate thing. The age gap is such that—

Don: Yeah, it's probably worse for her.

Howard: Yeah, we gotta cut Tiffany out. Tiffany doesn't deserve a dime. How about it, Donald? Is it fair in a will to say certain children get more and certain children get less?

Donald: I think it is fair, but what happens is Ivanka and Don and soon Eric will be working with me, and so I'll be doing things for them. They'll be working on deals, so they'll get a piece of a deal. Certain advantages. It depends on—I love all the kids. You have to. I know parents who have bad kids, truly bad kids. Never talk to them. I have really good kids. Tiffany's a great kid also.

Howard: I'm very impressed that you went to the Wharton School of Business, 'cause that's one of the hardest schools to get into.

Robin: One of the best.

Don: The best.

Howard: Do people think your dad bought—did you put a wing on Wharton?

Don: Not at all, actually.

Donald: The fact is that it's a great school. To me, it's the best school in the world probably for business. To get in, you have to be very smart. You have to have great boards. You have to have great marks, or you don't get in. I don't care who your father is.

Howard: All right, Ivanka, what kind of SATs do you have to have to get in?

Ivanka: Oh, I don't know. Very high. It's not just about one component there. You have to have the grades, you have to have the SATs, you have to have the extracurricular activities—

Howard: So you guys are really smart. What kind of SATs did you have?

Don: We all did very well.

Howard: Over 1500? 1600?

Donald: Yes.

Howard: Over 1500?

Donald: Way over.

Howard: No kidding?

Donald: I produce intelligent children.

Ivanka: I actually think SATs mean nothing.

Howard: Did you get 800 in math?

Donald: Yes.

Howard: They got 800s on math? Did you guys get 800s in math?

Don: Close.

Ivanka: Close, yeah.

Howard: Really? Look at Donald smiling.

Donald: I produce smart people.

Robin: You're taking full credit, Donald.

Donald: Only the good things I take credit.

Don: The thing about Wharton is, we grew up with those people whose parents did donate the wings, and they didn't get in. So he couldn't buy our way in even if he wanted to, really.

I PRODUCE INTELLIGENT CHILDREN.

Howard: All right, let me ask you a tough question. Wharton School of Business. What's 17 times 6? Go!

Don: Uh, 96?

Howard: Wrong!

Don: . . . 94?

Howard: Wrong!

Ivanka: See, I don't think this is a practical application.

Donald: It's 112.

Howard: Wrong! 102.

Donald: . . . 112. It's 112?

Howard: Is it 112? Look at you, you genius. Your kids didn't know.

Donald: That's why I'm the dad.

Don: No, no, it's 108! 'Cause—

Robin: It's 102.

Howard: It's 102? It's 102! I'm right! Donald, Don, Ivanka, you're all wrong! Give me a job! So, Ivanka, you are obviously a very attractive woman.

Ivanka: Thank you, Howard.

Howard: There's no question about it. Your father says you're one of the most attractive women on the planet. I don't disagree. What's going on with you? You're quite the package: you're wealthy, you're bright, you graduated Wharton. Hey, Donald, do you ever discuss sex with your daughter?

Donald: No.

Howard: You do not?

Donald: No.

Howard: Donald, seriously. You know about sexual predators and things like that.

Robin: You are one!

[*Collective laughter*]

Howard: I wasn't gonna say that, but it's true. Seriously, that's an uncomfortable topic for you as a father.

Donald: Yeah, I think so. I mean, the kids probably know more about it than I do, when you get right down to it.

Howard: Let me ask you a question, kids. And this is gonna matter a lot. I know Donald, and I respect the man, and I've always loved him. Your parents are on a boat. The boat begins to sink. You only have room to save one of them, one parent: Donald Trump or your mom. Who do you save? Ivanka, you go first.

Ivanka: I think in that scenario, I'd probably just drown myself. It's a decision I don't feel comfortable making.

Howard: Ivanka, you mean to tell me there's no one on the horizon for you to date?

Ivanka: There are a few people on the horizon but no one specifically.

Howard: Would you ever date a black guy? That would not go over at Mar-a-Lago.

Ivanka: [*laughs*]

Donald: Yes, she would.

Howard: She would?

Donald: Absolutely.

Ivanka: I have no problem with that. I have not dated a black guy.

Donald: I would have no problem with that.

Howard: You would have no problem with that?

Donald: I would have no problem. I would love that. That would be wonderful.

Robin: [*laughs*] He would love that.

Howard: I'm talking about a very black guy.

Robin: "A very black guy"? What does that mean?

Howard: Very dark-skinned. Wesley Snipes.

Donald: Like Seal.

Howard: Darker than Seal.

Ivanka: No, I would have no problem with that.

Howard: And you have a couple of prospects—

Ivanka: You know, I'm just having fun. I was in a three-and-a-half-year relationship. I'm not really focused on guys right now. I'm hanging out with my girlfriends, just having a good time.

Robin: Donald, when should she get married? When have you decided she will get married?

Donald: She should get married prior to twenty-eight or thirty, I think. And it should probably take place at the new ballroom at Mar-a-Lago, right?

Howard: Is that the answer, really? That's what you want for her?

Donald: I think it would be nice sometime prior to thirty.

Ivanka: I agree with that.

Donald: *If* you meet the right guy. If she doesn't meet the right guy, she doesn't have to get married ever. Forget it.

Gary: Howard, we have one minute left with them.

Howard: I want to thank all three of you, and wish you the best of luck with *Apprentice 5,* which is an amazing accomplishment, when you think about it. Who would've thought Donald Trump would be one of the biggest television stars? And here you've done it again.

Donald: Thank you, Howard.

Bill O'Reilly

OCTOBER 1, 2003

When I got into the radio business, broadcasters who specialized in politics usually just mediated discussions with their listeners. "Give me a call," they'd say, "and tell me what you think." There were a few exceptions—notably conservative radio pioneer Bob Grant, who wasn't afraid to mix it up with his audience—but for the most part it was all very civil and nonpartisan. Now it's the complete opposite: political radio—and TV, for that matter—is nothing but left- and right-wing pundits telling you what *they* think, and if you don't agree with them then you're quickly dismissed as some kook or member of a deep-state conspiracy.

I admit I am to blame for a lot of this. As Bill O'Reilly said in this interview, "I couldn't do what I do if you hadn't come first." O'Reilly, Rush Limbaugh, Sean Hannity—they essentially took the shock jock model I made famous, shifting the focus from sex and bathroom habits to government. The difference is how predictable these guys are. I've always wanted to surprise my audience, keep them guessing about what they could expect from me. Today's political radio personalities rarely say anything unexpected. You always know exactly what you're getting. It's so redundant and boring, which I suppose is what their listeners are looking for. They want their beliefs to be affirmed, not challenged.

That said, I respect Bill O'Reilly as a broadcaster. I don't have to agree with someone politically in order to hold their skills in high regard. I watched his show. I enjoyed it. I respect that he became a number-one cable guy.

What I don't respect, however, is Bill's hypocrisy. When he interviewed me on his show, he tried to corner me. He said something like, "You go to Nobu and you live in the Hamptons, but you try to present yourself as one of the people. You're not one of us." Look, I get it. Bill was trying to provoke me and get me to react and create an interesting show. I know how it works. I know better than anybody. Which is also how I know Bill was taking it further. He was genuinely trying to embarrass me and ridicule my success. He knew nothing about my struggle, about my journey. I'm someone who made it against all odds. I wasn't handed anything. I wasn't a trust fund kid. I came from a rough neighborhood. Yet here I was being shamed for working hard and becoming successful. Isn't that what the Fox News crew is always yapping about? How we're supposed to work hard and pull ourselves up by our bootstraps and make the American dream happen? Rather than celebrating me as a prime example of that, Bill was trying to paint me as some out-of-touch rich prick.

His hypocrisy was laughable. "One of us"? Yeah, right. I've seen Bill O'Reilly at Nobu. I've seen him at parties in the Hamptons. Shortly after I moved to Sirius, we were at the same party, and he came up to me and said, "Howard, I'm thinking of giving you a five-minute spot on my show once a week. You could use the publicity." All I could think was, "Are you kidding me, dude? *You* are giving *me* a spot? You don't have the career I have. Don't try to bully me."

What's even more hypocritical than his workingman shtick is his holier-than-thou attitude when it comes to sex. In this interview, he railed against gangsta rap and how rappers call women "bitches" and "hos." Yet look what he was accused of doing behind the scenes at Fox News.

There's a certain arrogance that comes with success. It's unavoidable. I have it. I won't lie. But you have to maintain a level of self-awareness and humility. You can't completely buy into your own fame.

Howard: Let's meet Bill O'Reilly. He's never been to the studio. From Fox News. He's tall. Like, six foot five, I think. Let's see. Wow, you are a tall guy. What are you, six five?

Bill: You're taller than me—six four.

Howard: You a Boston University grad, or Harvard?

Bill: Both.

Howard: Wow, look at you. Harvard. Like, what year? Were you a master's?

Bill: Yeah, I got a master's at the Kennedy School in '95. I was at BU when you were there, and I knew you, and—

Howard: Are we the same age?

> **I COULDN'T GET A DATE. I'D SHUFFLE AROUND AND ASK, "IS ANYBODY AVAILABLE?" AND THEY'D ALL FLEE.**

Bill: I was in the master's program. And you were flunking out of the regular program. But I saw you, 'cause you were walking around the hall, and I knew you were from Long Island—you just had Long Island written all over you—and so am I. And you were the only guy taller than me.

Howard: Is it true you do remember me?

Bill: I do. 'Cause you shuffle. You just shuffled down the hall.

Howard: I do have an odd walk. So things are going well for you. I was just saying on the air that before you became a whole *macher* on everything, that you were an anchor guy, the *Current Affair* guy.

Bill: *Inside Edition.*

Howard: *Inside Edition.* You can't get paid a lot of money for that.

Bill: Oh yeah. I was making good money there. We had an enormous following.

Howard: Over a million a year?

Bill: Yeah.

Howard: Really?

Bill: Mm-hmm.

Howard: So you were already wealthy from that.

Bill: Well, I spent a lot of time as a reporter, working my way up. But *Inside Edition* was a big cannon.

Howard: And when did you realize to let it all loose and let your opinions out?

Bill: Well, I did that for six years. And how many Madonna stories can you do?

Howard: Right. It gets boring. It got old.

Bill: Yes. It was a decent show. We did investigative work. I just decided I needed to go back to school, needed a breather. That's when I got the Harvard master's.

Howard: So why all this school? What were you planning to do?

Bill: I was basically planning on being a news analyst, getting back to the news business. But I wanted that credential: Kennedy School of Government. You can get a lot of pinheads up there. Looks good on the résumé. Goes well with Nassau Community College.

Howard: And it says here in my notes that you were a ladies' man.

Bill: Um, that's a myth. I was like you. I couldn't get a date. I'd shuffle around and ask, "Is anybody available?" and they'd all flee.

Howard: So you were *not* a ladies' man. You didn't bang a lot of chicks.

Bill: What does that mean? I don't understand.

Howard: Let me ask you about your sexuality.

Bill: I knew you were going to do this.

Howard: Even I didn't know I was going to do this.

Bill: Before you do it—

Howard: When did you become gay?

Bill: Before you do that, you got me here under false pretenses. 'Cause you told me there'd be lesbians here. I've combed the building. There's not one.

Howard: What is your story with porn, by the way? You're against it?

Bill: For kids, yeah. Adults, I don't care.

Howard: You didn't watch porn as a kid?

Bill: Interestingly enough, on *The Factor* last night, the ACLU now says it should be legal for adults to have sex with children.

Howard: That's ridiculous.

Bill: Okay, but listen to me now. This is a logical progression of the "progressive, secular society." You start out with "anything goes" for the adults, then whip down to the kids. So I draw the line. If you're eighteen and wanna lock yourself in the basement and—

Howard: You don't watch porn?

Bill: I really don't have time to watch. I did when I was a kid.

Howard: So you watched porno as a teenager?

Bill: Yes.

Howard: And you pleasured yourself?

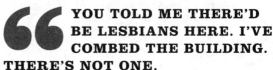

YOU TOLD ME THERE'D BE LESBIANS HERE. I'VE COMBED THE BUILDING. THERE'S NOT ONE.

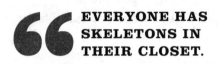

" EVERYONE HAS SKELETONS IN THEIR CLOSET.

Bill: Well, look, Howard—

Howard: What are you, running for office?

Bill: When I was eighteen, nineteen—

Howard: No, when you were fourteen.

Bill: When I was that age, they didn't have videotapes.

Howard: What did we have? We had stag films.

Bill: Yeah. When I was up in Marist College, they'd bring one in every month, and everyone was like, "Oh yeah!"

Howard: You went to Marist College?

Bill: I did. I have three degrees.

Howard: I would think that guys who went to Marist College aren't that bright, but you—

Bill: Well, I wasn't. I evolved. I was like you at the time.

Howard: You were at Marist, then able to get into Harvard. That's quite the accomplishment.

Bill: It was.

Howard: I went to Hamburger U. So, you're telling me you didn't start pleasuring yourself to porno until you were eighteen to twenty years old?

Bill: Yeah, in my college years, that sort of kicked in. I came from an Irish Catholic home, all right? So running a porno movie inside the house would not have worked, if you get my drift.

Howard: My father would've killed me, and I still took the chance.

Bill: Is this of interest to anybody, by the way?

Howard: Yes.

Bill: Oh? This is huge, huh?

Howard: What do you want to talk about? You want to talk about Al Franken? Mix it up?

Bill: No, I—

Howard: Why are you so angry with him? I think he's a bright guy.

Bill: Yeah, well, my next book—did you plug my book, by the way?

Howard: Yeah. The book is called *Who's Looking Out for You?*

Bill: It's going to debut at number one on the *New York Times* list.

Howard: And Bill hosts *The O'Reilly Factor* on Fox News.

Bill: Good. That's all I need.

Howard: How much money you making now?

Bill: A lot. Not nearly as much as you, though.

Howard: Where are you living now, on Long Island?

Bill: Yes, on Long Island.

Howard: Married guy?

Bill: Mm-hmm.

Howard: Kids?

Bill: Mm-hmm.

Howard: We're never going to find out you were having an affair?

Bill: I hope not. I'd like to find out first.

Robin: No skeletons in the closet?

Bill: Oh, sure. Everyone has skeletons in their closet.

Howard: Let them out!

Bill: They're boring. I threw snowballs at school buses when I was twelve.

Howard: Hot wife?

Bill: I never talk about my personal life. For security reasons.

Howard: Who's attacking you?

Bill: Just like you.

Howard: What are you talking about? I talk about my personal life.

Bill: But you have security concerns.

Howard: Well, yeah, on occasion I have people who are cuckoo, but I don't have any real problems.

Bill: Okay. Well, I do. We're dealing at the highest levels here, and people are trying to hurt me.

Howard: Are you serious?

Bill: I am.

Howard: People who don't like your opinions?

Bill: Exactly. People who are outraged that I have the power I do. People who don't like what I say on the air. Um, foreign people.

Howard: You're a conservative.

Bill: I'm not a conservative. I'm an independent.

Howard: You don't think you're leaning more toward the president, and toward the conservative agenda, even on social issues? You don't like rap music.

Bill: Well, let me define this. I'm against gay marriage, but I'm for gay unions. But I don't want any sexuality defined. If you have a union and designate someone, if you go to the hospital, your overseer, that's fine with me. Gay marriage I don't think is necessary because, under the law, if you legalize gay marriage, those guys who want to marry six babes—I know you know who they are—they'd have to get legal too under equal protection. As for rap, only gangsta rap. I think it's a corrupting, corroding influence for children. Every teacher I've talked to from a poor neighborhood, they've said these kids have adopted the f-word. They're calling fifth-grade girls "hos" and "bitches." And don't give me this argument about parents, 'cause a lot of these poor kids don't have parents who care about them. I'm conservative on some issues. I'm liberal on some issues. But I'm a common-sense kinda guy.

Howard: What did Al Franken say about you?

Bill: Look, I'm not going to sell any books for him. I'm just happy my book knocked him out, and we're going to be number one.

Howard: Right. But what did he say about you?

THIS IS EXACTLY WHAT I SAID: "WHAT ARE THEY CALLED, 'COYOTES' OR 'WETBACKS'? WHAT'S THE SLANG TERM THAT BORDER PATROL USES?"

Bill: He was basically saying I was a liar. And I haven't lied about anything. I've been on the air seven years at *The Factor*, and I'm on the radio two hours a day. And if you can't pull any inconsistencies out of that, then c'mon. He's making money off of smearing people. He did it to [Rush] Limbaugh. He's doing it to me.

Howard: But you do that too.

Bill: No I don't. I never do ad hominem attacks.

Howard: You got in trouble for referring to Mexicans as "wetbacks," did you not?

Bill: Yeah, but I didn't do that.

Howard: You didn't?

Bill: We were having a discussion in the context of who the people are that are smuggling people in. This is exactly what I said: "What are they called, 'coyotes' or 'wetbacks'? What's the slang term the border patrol uses?"

Howard: Oh, I see.

Bill: That's it.

Howard: Let's get back to the threats against your life. This is serious stuff.

Bill: Yes it is.

Howard: You have security people? Who do you think is after you? Jesse Jackson or something?

Bill: Look, it's not any kind of organized

thing. The rap thing, when I was doing that, that got real intense.

Howard: That got people pissed off.

Bill: But I do what I do.

Howard: Have you ever been directly threatened?

Bill: Yes.

Howard: By somebody you directly criticized on the air?

Bill: No. But we have plenty of people, every day, doing this stuff.

Howard: Have you ever backed off a position because you've been directly threatened?

Bill: No. Look, I'm one of these crazy guys that's on a mission here to try to at least provide a workingman's perspective. One of the reasons I came on this program is because most of your audience are working people. And they're getting hosed. They're getting hosed. It's not for the fat cats. It's not for rich people. They're getting screwed.

Howard: By who? The US government?

Bill: No. It's elements of the whole society stacked up against the working people. Because, if you don't know how it works—see, you got lucky 'cause you're talented.

Howard: Well, thanks for saying that.

Bill: I've said this before: I couldn't do what I do if you hadn't come first.

Howard: Thank you for saying that as well.

Bill: But if your audience doesn't figure out who's looking out for them, they're going to be in divorce court. They're not going to have a good job. They're going to get kicked in the mouth, every step of the way. I learned that the hard way. The fun of this book, *Who's Looking Out for You?*, is I say, "Here's the stuff that *I* did. The stupid stuff that *I* did. Don't you do it."

Howard: What is something stupid that you did?

Bill: Oh, I trusted the wrong people.

Howard: Who did you trust?

Bill: When I was in the business, working my way up—you know when you're in these little stations, they're giving you a hard time. It's legion.

Howard: Right. And you point out in your book you got hosed.

Bill: I got hosed. You bet. Look, I'm from Levittown, you're from Roosevelt. It's the same place. All of my friends are still back there. Some of them have good lives, and some of them don't. The ones that figured it out have okay lives. And the other ones are wreckage.

Howard: So you give people examples of how to improve their lives.

Bill: Not improve their lives. How to read people. You gotta know how to read people. Who's looking out for you, and who isn't. Gangsta rappers are not looking out for you. They're not looking out for the poor kids in the ghetto.

Howard: What about if they're just expressing themselves?

Bill: Express themselves another way, then.

Robin: More than the rappers, the people that put [their music] out.

Bill: Oh, they oughta be hung. They oughta be hung. These fat, rich white guys who live up in Greenwich, Connecticut, making millions of dollars, corrupting these children, telling them to go out and peddle crack. Where's that going to get you?

Howard: You really think people are going to listen to that and think it's okay? You think that's the real problem? Do you think violent movies cause violence?

Bill: No. But I think a steady diet of it does.

Howard: No.

Bill: If that's all you do.

Howard: Let me tell you something. That's all I do. And look at me. Let me just say one thing about your personal life. You got a hot wife? When did you get married?

Bill: I got married seven years ago. I was a bachelor for a long time.

Howard: Had a little bachelor pad?

Bill: Uh, yeah. I had a little bachelor pad.

Howard: Ever bang two girls at the same time?

Bill: I don't know what that means.

Howard: You know exactly what that means.

Bill: No, I can't. I can't define these terms.

Howard: Why are you uptight about sex?

Bill: I'm just a puritan.

Howard: No, you're not. No, you're not.

Bill: I am.

Howard: I think you've had sex with more than one person at a time.

Bill: Is that right?

Howard: Yes. Yes I do.

Bill: Are you Carnac, or what?

Howard: I'm asking you. I'm asking you point-blank.

Bill: I'm telling you, the nuns told me not to answer.

Howard: So that's a yes.

Bill: I'm not answering these questions.

Howard: Ever score with a black chick? Because you're starting to turn into the pope. You can still be a fun guy.

Bill: I'm the pope now?

Howard: Yeah, all of a sudden you're turning into—

Robin: My problem is people who "uh-uh-uh-uh-uhhh," you find out that they're beating women.

Howard: Have you beaten a woman?

Bill: No. Let me save you all this inquisition. If I had done anything, *anything*, Al Franken would've had it in his book. He had every creep in the world trying to find dirt on me. Didn't find anything. So if it was there, they would have gotten it.

Howard: Why did you get married?

Bill: Why did *you* get married?

Howard: I'm divorced. But because I was in love.

Bill: Okay. There you go. Everyone gets married for that reason, don't they?

Howard: I'm asking *you*, though. You're an uptight guy.

Bill: I don't talk about my personal life.

Howard: Yes you do. You sign a prenup?

Bill: I'm never gonna talk about that.

Howard: Well, you're talking about looking out for the small guy, even if he doesn't sign a prenup?

Bill: I say in the book, "You better get a good lawyer."

Howard: Before you get married?

Bill: Anytime. For everything.

Howard: Have you ever made love to a black woman? What do you got, two kids?

Bill: I just don't talk about those things. I know what you're trying to do. I listen to the program.

Howard: You want to take some calls?

Bill: Can you screen them?

Howard: Hopefully not. Chauncey, you're on the air. Go ahead, Chauncey.

Chauncey: Yeah, Bill isn't that much of a puritan, because I saw him at a *Playboy* magazine party about seven years ago.

Bill: That's correct. I got an invitation to the Playboy Mansion.

Howard: How is that for you?

Bill: A riot. I love to go to those places and just watch.

Howard: You didn't partake?

Bill: Partake in what?

Howard: You didn't pick up a chick that night?

Bill: There's not enough chlorine to get me in that grotto.

Howard: I'm with you. I hear that. Have you ever had sex with a *Playboy* Playmate?

Bill: No. I have not.

Howard: You for the legalization of marijuana?

Bill: No.

Howard: Really? I'm shocked. You've smoked marijuana for sure, right?

Bill: I have not.

Howard: I don't believe that.

Bill: Never done it.

Howard: Who cares if someone smokes weed?

Bill: I don't care. I just don't want it available where it gets down to the children.

Howard: The children have it anyway.

Bill: I would decriminalize marijuana. I wouldn't legalize it.

Howard: Oh, okay. I'm fine with that. Could you have imagined that Fox News would become so successful?

Bill: I'm stunned. I'm stunned. It's been seven years.

Howard: Isn't it amazing CNN didn't react to you guys faster?

Bill: Well, you know, they're just too politically correct. You cut through. Nobody thought you could, but you did, 'cause you're bold. I am too. And that's the key ingredient.

Howard: That's what people like to hear.

Robin: Do you take a drink every now and then?

Bill: I don't drink.

Howard: Wow, you are boring.

Bill: I'm boring. I'm the most boring guy in the world.

Howard: Your wife is thirty years old.

Bill: Is she that old? Time to get rid of her.

Howard: No, seriously. That's a smart move for guys, right? You attracted to any of the anchors on Fox? Like Laurie Dhue?

Bill: They're all beautiful ladies, absolutely.

Howard: Ever date any of them?

Bill: How could I date any of them?

Ed Sheeran

MARCH 7, 2017

One of the things about aging that bothers me most—along with waking up five hundred times a night to pee—is how it gets more and more difficult to stay in touch with new music.

In the summer of 1967, I was thirteen, and I had just finished a few weeks at Wel-met Camps in Narrowsburg, New York. I had been going there since I was eight or nine. It had no amenities, horrible food, a man-made lake with some sort of weird fungus growing in it—yet it was heaven to me. Those six weeks were the only time each year when I was ecstatically happy. If I ever got in trouble at school or misbehaved at home, all my mother had to say was, "Okay, you're not going away this summer," and I would snap to. Summer camp was total freedom from the conformity of everyday life that I hated. We would hike into the woods, build a lean-to, dig a hole and lash logs together for a latrine, collect rocks for a fire pit (careful not to use shale that could explode in a fire), lay a tarp on the ground and sleep in sleeping bags. I was a regular Howard Bunyan. At the end of those six weeks when my parents came to pick me up and drive me home, I'd be miserable and on the verge of tears. One time I was so angry that I just sat in the backseat cursing out loud. Every word out of my mouth was "fuck" or "shit." Finally, my parents said that if I didn't stop they were going to pull over to the side of the road and make me walk home.

Unlike at school, I was popular at summer camp. I had my first girlfriend there. It's also where, that summer of '67, I heard *Sergeant Pepper's Lonely Hearts Club Band* for the first time. One of the counselors had the album. I was like Christopher Columbus just discovering America. It was a game-changer for me. It was so unique and original. It was probably the same feeling you had when you first heard the Craptacular on my radio show—my own personal *Sergeant Pepper's*.

As soon as I got home, I ran out and bought my own copy of the album. I had a record player in my room, and I called to my mother: "Mom, come in here! You gotta hear this!" She sat on my bed next to me and we listened to the entire album. The song lyrics were printed on the back—it was one of the first times a band had done that, maybe even the first. As the music played, my mother and I read along. I have vivid memories of a scholarly moment when, like two rabbinical students, we poured over the lyrics to "Being for the Benefit of Mr. Kite." The experience was more personal and profound than any religious training I'd received up until then. It might be the closest I have ever felt to my mother. To my astonishment, she actually enjoyed the music. It made me so proud that as an older woman she could get into the Beatles, especially because all of her friends hated them. I was so happy to share that with her.

That day made a huge impression on me. I never wanted to be one of those old fogies who say, "Back in my day was when music was *really* great." Being aware of new music has also been a prerequisite for my job, so that I can comment on contemporary culture. In the nineties, when I was in my forties working at K-Rock, I was very much up on alternative rock: Soundgarden, Stone Temple Pilots, Nirvana. I loved all that stuff. I never thought I would be in danger of being out of touch.

Then recently I was looking at a list of the top five songs in the country and it happened. "Oh my God," I thought. "I don't know any of them. I'm officially that guy. Who's this Lil Xan, and why is he getting all these face tattoos? Wait, he once dated Miley Cyrus's little sister? Miley Cyrus has a little sister? When did that happen? And who's this Mac Miller that Ariana Grande is grieving over? A Jewish rapper? How the hell did I miss that?"

The good news is I'm not completely hopeless. One young artist I love is Ed Sheeran. He is such an incredible songwriter and singer, yet he is not at all impressed by his own fame. He'll play in front of fifty thousand people at Wembley Stadium, then he'll come on my show and—as he does here— talk about getting hammered with his mates at a local bar.

There is a lot to be learned from Ed about being grounded, fearless, and hardworking. People criticize millennials for being unmotivated and entitled. Ed defies those stereotypes.

Howard: I feel like you went through a lot. Your second album exploded and you had an incredible year. I'm talking, like, billions of streams of your songs. Your concert tour makes tons of money. Everything is going great. Then all of a sudden you say, "Fuck it, I'm getting off social media. I'm gonna take time off. I'm gonna travel the world." You went off with your girlfriend and traveled the world.

Ed: I think the reason I took a break and got rid of social media—life is all about balance, and my life was very, very, very imbalanced midtour 2015. I was kind of like, "I haven't really got any stable mates around me. I haven't got a stable girl in my life. I wake up every day,

do a show. I'll be in the most amazing places in the world. I'll be in, like—the Philippines—and all I'll see is a bar. 'Cause I'll finish a show, go straight to the bar and get hammered, and fall asleep and fly elsewhere." I just needed to find the balance for it. And the balance in my mind was taking myself out of it for a year and figuring some stuff out.

Howard: Social media got to you, right? The people saying shit about you. Some people, it can bounce right off their back, but you were like, "There are people criticizing me, telling me I'm losing my hair, I look too heavy, I'm this, I'm that, I'm the other thing."

Ed: Yeah, I think social media is a really,

really, really weird place. I'm not an insecure person at all, and you make yourself insecure 'cause as a musician you're constantly compared to people like Justin Bieber or One Direction or Justin Timberlake—people that are very, very good-looking human beings. People are like, "Well, he doesn't look that way. Does he deserve that success?" And you kind of create a complex in your mind. I have a lyric where I'm like, "I constantly compare myself to men I don't even know." You're constantly looking at people, being like, "I should look like that." And I think stepping away from that, you get back to your—'cause I am quite a confident person. I don't really have that many insecurities, and I kind of created them by just reading online.

Howard: Isn't it funny that people will resent you for not looking like Justin Bieber or Justin Timberlake? You think they'd worship you and say, "My God, more people look normal than look like some pretty boy."

Ed: I'd like to think that if I haven't got a ripped six-pack and I am a bit chunky, it's nice for a regular joe. Like, "He can do it, I can do it."

> 66 **I'D LIKE TO THINK THAT IF I HAVEN'T GOT A RIPPED SIX-PACK AND I AM A BIT CHUNKY, IT'S NICE FOR A REGULAR JOE. LIKE, "HE CAN DO IT, I CAN DO IT."**

Howard: What I think is refreshing about you—because to me, looking at music and having seen it evolve, rock and all that—there's so many people that are so image-conscious. When you go and shoot a cover of *Rolling Stone*, are you thinking, "I wanna look really good and have my hair just the right way and put some makeup on"? Or do you just go in there and shoot the fucking cover?

Ed: I always feel really awkward at photo shoots. I'm not a massive fan of the way I look on camera. I play music. I don't really like being the cover boy.

Howard: When you shoot a video, is it like, "I want to make that as simple as possible"? You'd really probably prefer to be an artist in the sixties and seventies, before videos and before MTV, right?

Ed: I didn't appear in, like, my first six or seven music videos. I kind of made cameos in them. And then when [my] song "Thinking Out Loud" was coming out, I wanted it to have the biggest reach possible. In my mind, I was thinking, "It needs a video that will go viral. What will go viral? What is the least-expected thing of me?" And I was like, "Ballroom dancing." So that was, like, the first time I properly appeared in a video.

Howard: The only videos I truly love is when it's just a guy sitting there, playing his guitar and singing—the performance. All this nonsense of there's gotta be a story and it's a little movie, it sometimes drives me fucking crazy. Because here you are thinking about the music, and then you have to go collaborate with a guy who has a visual sense of this thing, and suddenly you're jumping around a treadmill. As innovative as that is, it has nothing to do with the song you wrote.

Ed: That's when music turns into marketing.

Howard: For sure. I think it's refreshing you're not one of these guys that appears to be marketing constantly. We were just talking this morning about how Jimmy Buffett is building a retirement home called Margaritaville.

Ed: If I was to do anything, there's a local brewery near me, and I'd love them to make me a beer. That's the one thing I would endorse. [Or] ketchup—if there was a bottle of ketchup.

Howard: You have the worst diet and the worst drinking. I was reading a story about you. You wrote arguably Justin Bieber's biggest hit song, and I guess you get to be friendly with him. You guys had a drunken night together. You go to a miniature golf course or something. He lays down on the ground and puts a golf ball—I guess it was your idea?

Ed: No, no, it was his idea. And he didn't have a tee in his mouth so it was literally just resting on his mouth.

Howard: And you whacked the ball, except you hit him in the jaw. Because you guys were loaded, right?

Ed: No, I was loaded. He's completely sober now. He just drinks water and eats salmon.

Howard: Who would say to a drunken man, "Hey, try to hit this ball out of my mouth"?

Ed: He's pretty fun, man. Hanging out with him, there's never a dull moment, never a dull moment.

Howard: Doesn't drink at all now?

Ed: No. I've known him six years now, through the kind of, like, time where he was addicted, and he's a completely different person.

Howard: Would that be torture for you to have to give up drinking completely? Is that something you could never imagine?

Ed: I have this conversation with Americans all the time. There's a different culture in England. People go to bars here to get drunk. People go to pubs in England to hang out and socialize. The drinking culture in England is a social thing. So I never ever rely on drinking. I can go months without it. I just enjoy hanging out with my mates and having a pint.

Howard: Okay, you got rid of the phone, you got rid of social media, and you traveled the world. I bet you more ideas came to you for songs.

Ed: Oh, 100 percent. And when the ideas come in—the worst thing in the world is being in the studio and you're, like, midflow, *bang bang bang*, and you get a text and you go into your phone and that's an hour of your time gone. If you don't have any distractions—I was literally writing four or five songs a day 'cause there was nothing else to do.

Howard: Talk about these world travels. I worry about you. You go to Iceland and you are visiting an active volcano and your foot slips into this hot volcano, to the point that they even said, "Don't take off your sock because you've bruised your foot and you've burned the flesh." And you said, "No, it hurts." You take off your sock and your skin comes right off. What the fuck are you doing?

Ed: I kind of have this attitude to life where I'm like, "Eh, fuck it." I was told not to walk off the track, and then I saw this little bubbling puddle, and I was like, "That looks really interesting." I walk right up to it, and they're like, "Don't walk over there!" And literally the ground I was standing on collapsed. I've never in my life felt like I was gonna die, but it was like one of those—you know when people are like, "Your life flashes before your eyes"? It doesn't. It just goes really, really, really, really slowly. And I just felt myself falling in. Third-degree burn. The worst thing about it is we had gone over there just to see the northern lights. I had this burn, went to the hospital, got them to put on the fake skin and everything, got back. I was kind of, like, shaking from the pain. Passed out from the pain. Woke up at the hotel to, "Well, there

you have it, folks. That's the best sighting of the northern lights in the past twenty years. Hope you caught it."

Howard: You missed the whole thing. Didn't you have something with your hand? What did you do to your hand?

Ed: I was playing drums with two beer bottles outside a bar in Nashville—and for, like, a while . . . for at least half an hour—with the singer Gavin DeGraw. He was kind of singing over it while I was drumming. It was, like, four o' clock in the morning, and the last thing it went *doosh*, and the bottom of the beer bottle had this kind of jagged bit and it went right up into my hand. And this was the day before my last show with Taylor. I had, like, twelve stitches, and then went onstage the next day and split my hand onstage and had to go get it stitched.

Howard: Before you settle down with your girlfriend and everything, you're hanging with Taylor Swift. She's got that whole fucking posse of hot chicks that hang out, and you are in the middle of all that, right? You're the songwriter, you're the singer, you're the performer. Why did romance never happen between you and Taylor? You spent a lot of time with her.

Ed: When I first met Taylor, I was in a relationship and she was in a relationship

YOU KNOW WHEN PEOPLE ARE LIKE, "YOUR LIFE FLASHES BEFORE YOUR EYES"? IT DOESN'T. IT JUST GOES REALLY, REALLY, REALLY, REALLY SLOWLY.

and we just formed a friendship through that. Then both our relationships ended and we just carried on being friends.

Howard: Was she angry with you that you dated all of her friends?

Ed: No, she encouraged it. She's the world's best wingman.

Howard: You said in *Rolling Stone* you went through quite a few of Taylor's friends. Dating. Whatever that means. Hooking up, I guess, is the proper term.

Ed: Not "quite a few."

Howard: A couple.

Ed: A couple.

Howard: You talk about, "Hey, it shows growth"—the fact that you're not still doing that and you can stick to one woman.

Ed: I've been in that world, and for me, having home mates and having a girl properly grounds me.

Howard: Is that why you continue to live in England, 'cause those are real friends?

Ed: Yeah, and you know what? They don't ever ask me for anything. Anytime I hang out with them, they never ask me, "How's your music going?" They'll just, like, tell me something weird that happened to their mate. You kind of get your veil ripped off and you're back to being normal.

Howard: If figures are true, they say in 2016 you made $33 million, which is a lot of money from where you grew up. I thought that part of the reason you went and traveled the world and got away from social media and phones is that people were hitting you up for money.

> ## SHE'S [TAYLOR SWIFT] THE WORLD'S BEST WINGMAN.

Ed: I honestly don't mind helping out friends and family. I honestly don't mind at all. But it was like, you'd help out someone and never hear from them again. I thought the reason I was helping you out is 'cause we were mates. And they'd just kind of fall off the face of the earth.

Howard: Why does that happen?

Ed: I think there's an element of people are embarrassed about doing it. But I don't really care. I'd rather help someone out than carry on being friends.

Howard: When you help someone out, though, don't you expect them to pay you back?

Ed: It's nice to have the promise in there, but I don't expect that. I don't expect that at all. For me, I've always been someone who, if I have ten dollars, it goes that day. I survived and was really happy without any [money], and I've survived and was happy with it. I don't mind when it comes in or when it goes out.

Howard: Your story is not unlike so many other artists. You were sleeping on people's couches at the beginning of your career and sort of relying on the good graces of friends.

Ed: Music's a weird thing because literally

> ❝ **MUSIC'S A WEIRD THING BECAUSE LITERALLY IT'S ZERO OR ONE HUNDRED. YOU MAKE NOTHING, AND THEN YOU MAKE A LOT.**

it's zero or one hundred. You make nothing, and then you make a lot. So to be a successful musician, you have to be broke. You have to spend three or four years living on couches and relying on strangers being kind to you.

Howard: How many guys do you know who do the whole living on couches and everything and then don't make it? It's crazy sad.

Ed: The only ones that I know that don't are the ones that had a plan B. So the moment you go, "Ah, I don't want to sleep on this couch anymore. I have this really good job I can go to"—that's the moment that it doesn't happen. I actually haven't met anyone who has set their mind on something and not achieved it, eventually. There are actors that make it when they're fifty, and they become the biggest actor in the world when they're fifty, and that's because they haven't had a plan B and they've just been like, "Nah, fuck it, I'm gonna do it."

Howard: Wasn't Jamie Foxx, early on in your career before you became famous— didn't you live at his house for a while? You were a struggling artist. You hadn't been signed yet. Every record company had passed on you. And I guess Jamie Foxx's manager or somebody had heard you in a club and said, "Come on, hang out with Jamie"? And you hung out with Jamie, and then Jamie put you up in his house.

Ed: The thing that that did for me—the amount of confidence I'd lost being in England and doing the same rounds over and over again. Going into record labels and them being like, "It's not gonna happen. It's just not gonna happen." And then me being like, "Fuck it, if I can make a sort of living doing gigs in London, I'm sure I can go over to LA and do it." And so there was this guy called John who ran a night called Flypoet in Inglewood. I flew over and I did that night, and I said to John, "Do you know any other shows that you can book me in for?" So he booked me in for a bunch over the month, and I ended up playing the Foxxhole [a night hosted by Jamie Foxx at the LA club the Conga Room]. And then Jamie's manager said, "Come on the radio show," which I think is a Sirius show as well. I played on that, and Jamie said, "I've got a studio at my house. Do you want to just use it for free?" So then [after that] I flew home, and within a month of going there with, like, zero confidence, being able to fly to LA with nothing, and end up at one of the biggest movie stars in the world's house recording—in my mind, I was like, "Well, I must have *something*." And so going back to England, I sort of had, like, this charged battery.

Howard: When you live at Jamie Foxx's house, do you buy your own food? Do you offer to go out and do some grocery shopping or some chores?

Ed: When I first got to Inglewood, I did this gig and I made $700 from selling my CDs. And then when Jamie invited me out to his house, I was like, "Right, I'll get a yellow cab." Assuming he lived in Beverly Hills or something like that. And he lived, like, two and a half hours outside Los Angeles. My bill ended up being about $800, so they had to lend me $100. So when it came to me offering to buy food, I was like, "Yeah, I haven't got anything, sorry."

Howard: Is fame getting so weird? I read some story where some guy scammed the Super Bowl to get four tickets—

Ed: And I got blamed for it!

Howard: Yeah, some guy called up and said, "I'm with Ed Sheeran's team and I want Super Bowl tickets." And I saw today, there was a guy here who said he was part of your team. He was trying to get into the building. Guy had nothing to do with you. Is this shit going on constantly?

Ed: Constantly. We had a thing yesterday. Thankfully, it was shut down. It was from a newspaper in England, and it was like, "We have it on good authority that Ed is having an affair with three different girls while he's been with Cherry. It's been in this Kensington apartment. This is the address and this is his mobile number. These are the texts." Bear in mind I don't have a phone or live in Kensington. "Good authority." And the time they said I'd done it, I was in Ghana.

Howard: But that can destroy a relationship. As much as Cherry might love you and trust you, when that gets in the paper, it sucks for her and you.

Ed: I have a really good relationship with her family, and even though it isn't true, the seed of doubt, the tiny, tiny seed of doubt it plants . . . But thankfully, I was so confident that it didn't happen I was like, "Fuck it, print it. I'll sue you and I'll win." And they were like, "Okay cool, you win." I would have fucking taken a lot of money from them.

Howard: I'll tell you a crazy story. When I first started dating my wife, they put in the paper that I was at dinner with a blonde. She was the blonde! She knew it, and she was even a bit pissed. She said, "I don't know why I'm upset. It was me!"

Ed: I heard a great story about Elton John. There was a newspaper in England that outed him. They said, "Elton John is gay." And he said, "No I'm not," sued them, got a million dollars, and *then* came out. Amazing.

Howard: I was watching you on the Grammys. I'm talking about when you won— Song of the Year or Album of the Year?

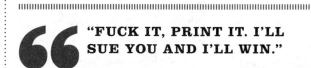

"FUCK IT, PRINT IT. I'LL SUE YOU AND I'LL WIN."

Ed: Song of the Year.

Howard: Song of the Year. And you looked like you were having so much fun that night. I don't know if awards mean anything to you or not. I'm sure that's not why you got into music.

Ed: I had been nominated for thirteen Grammys over four years and lost all those and flown my parents out every single year. And every year they're like, "This year's the year." And every year would be like, "Maybe next year." And for me, I was kind of on cloud nine because, for one, I won, and Stevie Wonder was presenting it to me.

Howard: Read your name in braille.

Ed: You know what's weird about that? He had invited me to play the *Songs in the Key of Life* Tour in New York the year before, and he said to me, "You're going to win Song of the Year at the Grammys next year." Like a year before. And then he was the one that presented it.

Howard: That's sort of weird.

Ed: I think he can see the future.

Howard: I love that you do cover songs in your concerts. You cover Stevie Wonder at all?

Ed: Yeah, I used to put in elements of "Superstition."

Howard: Yeah, when you were performing, there was a tribute. First Beyoncé went, then you come out on guitar and do a Stevie Wonder thing, and then she joined you, kind of duetting and all that. Boy, I really loved her performance with you, and you looked like it was just another day. You don't seem to get nervous.

Ed: I was quite nervous. It's a weird thing, rehearsing that. You don't realize how talented someone like Beyoncé is until you're right next to her and you're like, "Wow." You've never seen anything like it. Just vocally, and the singing is so on point. That's a Stevie Wonder song, and he's quite complicated with the riffs he does. I was making mistakes left, right, and center. And she was just like *bam bam bam*.

Howard: So you're there in front of Stevie Wonder. I remember watching. Stevie Wonder was digging it. Stevie was really digging it. And then they cut to a shot of the audience, and Jamie Foxx was sitting in the audience and he was really digging it too.

Ed: Yeah. It was a really, really cool reunion.

Howard: You hadn't seen him in a long time, right?

Ed: Because I had this charged battery in my back, I just started smashing out independent EPs in England, and doing tours all over. So by the time I got back and broke the US, I'd spent, like, four years touring the UK. I hadn't had the opportunity to see him. So he had literally seen me one day living in his spare room and then one day at the Stevie thing.

Howard: Do you still have keys to Jamie Foxx's house? We should go over and take a look.

Ed: I'd love to go back there and say hi.

GONE TOO SOON

I once read somewhere that no one can sit and contemplate their own death for very long. It's just too painful and overwhelming. You can't stay focused on it for more than a few moments.

I bring up death often in my interviews, especially when it involves artists who died before I got the chance to talk to them. Prince. Kurt Cobain. Chris Farley. Whitney Houston. John Lennon. Since I never had the opportunity to know them, I like to hear from people who did.

Several died by either suicide or overdose. I always want to figure out why. Why were they in so much pain? Why did they feel like death was their only option? Were there signs? Could they have been helped?

Take Chris Cornell. When he killed himself, that just rocked me. He had such a beautiful spirit. He'd been on the show a few times over the years, and I got a great vibe from him. Granted, it was only in that artificial studio setting, but I really felt like we had developed a friendship. Chris was so smart and self-aware. As he says in this section, he had seen what happened to Kurt Cobain and the pain it caused his family. In my mind, if anyone would have avoided that same ending, it was Chris.

While there is sadness over the next few pages, there is also joy. It is an opportunity to celebrate these creative geniuses. What a privilege that they walked the earth for as long as they did. What an honor we got to experience their brilliance at all.

JAMIE FOXX ON PRINCE

Howard: Prince's death must have hit you pretty hard because you knew the guy, right?

Jamie: It hit me really hard because not only did I know him, but I musically worshipped him. When I was a kid I would listen to his music. My grandmother didn't understand. "What's this devil man? He's singing about pussy." He had a song called "Pussy Control." "He's singing about pussy." I met him for the first time December 31, 1998. It was about to be 1999. It was the MGM in Las Vegas. And I look and I say, "Man, I know that ain't Prince over there, dawg. Goddamn." And I ran up. "Man, you know who you is?" I started kinda cryin'.

Howard: That's the problem. It's hard to have a real conversation like that 'cause you kind of want to be cool.

Jamie: Aw, man, all my cool went out the window. I started naming the albums. I'm fucking up the titles and shit. And he was so cool. He knew I was shook. "Thank you so much. I appreciate it. Thank you." And I was like, "Damn, the motherfucker is so cool." And I asked him for a picture. I fucked up. He says, "I don't do that." I was like, "Fuck!"

Howard: I love your whole rap about what Prince would wear and he's the only guy who could get away with wearing that shit.

Jamie: We did a show in Minneapolis, and we walked outside and it was sort of snowing. And there was this big shadowy figure in the alley. "He wants to see you." I said, "Who?" He said, "The kid wants to see you." I said, "Who's the kid?" "Prince." So we go to Paisley Park, and they had us waiting. They had me in this white room. It was like four in the morning. I had all my comedian friends with us. And that motherfucker came out, dawg, and he had a one-piece on. Like Dorothy Hamill. A bodysuit with the boots sewn in it. And he had his hair done. The most beautiful man I'd ever seen in my life. Me and my homies were like, "This nigga is *pretty*." I mean, he looked better than Halle Berry. Man, it was mind-blowing. He talked about music. He talked about what he wanted to do with music, and where he came from. That's why when he passed away there were so many tears.

Howard: Where were you when you heard?

Jamie: In LA. I was just at the crib. We couldn't believe it.

Howard: It was one of those moments where you're just like, "I don't believe Prince has died."

Jamie: You can't believe that, man. When he passed, I couldn't understand. You blame. I'm like, "Who the fuck was around him? How you let this happen?"

MARTIN SHORT ON GILDA RADNER

Howard: Was Gilda a great love of your life?

Martin: Yes.

Howard: And the

relationship went on for how long?

Martin: We went out for about two years. But we'd break up for a month or something.

Howard: What went wrong? Was there a time you were considering maybe proposing?

Martin: Gilda was four years older than I was. And everyone—I'm telling you, Howard, if you were at a party and Gilda walked in, every guy wanted to go out with her, and every woman wanted to have her as a best friend. She just had an amazing, amazing power.

Howard: She had that quality.

Martin: Yeah. I didn't understand how if you had all these gifts, how you couldn't always be happy. And she wasn't always happy. So that caused a lot of stuff. And honestly, my parents had just died from illness, so I had just been through this stuff where I had seen, like, my mother, this happy woman, struggling to be happy and live. And I thought, "Gee, she didn't

get the break that, Gilda, you have." But it was because I didn't understand that you could have all these things and still not be happy.

Howard: So would you say, "Gilda, how can you be depressed today?" Because I'm assuming you're saying you'd wake up in the morning and she'd be bummed out about life and complain.

Martin: It was just she would go through stuff. She wasn't always depressed.

Howard: Would you lecture her and say, "Gilda, my mother's ill. She wants to live but she's ill. It is a terrible thing. And look at you. You've got everything in life."

Martin: Yeah.

Howard: So she'd probably get pissed off at you for not understanding her. And you're pissed off because, like, "You have everything and you're pissing it away."

Martin: But I'm telling you it's because she was twenty-six and I was twenty-two. That's a big thing at that age. At twenty-six, I might have understood women a little more.

Howard: Was she a star already at twenty-six?

Martin: No. This is before *Saturday Night Live*.

Howard: So you were in a sense both struggling.

Martin: Yeah.

Howard: Who ended up breaking up with whom? Is it Gilda says to you one day, "Martin, I love you, but I just can't live with you"?

Martin: I don't know. We'd break up and then we'd get back together. And we broke up, and I think we assumed we'd get back together.

ROBERT PLANT ON JOHN BONHAM

Howard: You and Bonzo were the first two to hook up? You were in a band together?

Robert: Oh, yes, two or three.

Howard: And what a drummer he was.

Robert: Stunning, yes.

Howard: Maybe the best rock drummer that ever lived, let's be honest. Because he wasn't doing what the other drummers were doing. He was more like a jazz drummer.

Robert: He was really into Elvin Jones and he was into—what's the name of the guy who used to play with Little Richard? Earl Palmer. Yes, he had just great chops. He came up to me one night—I was playing a gig in the Black Country [the English Midlands]—and he said, "You know, you're all right. You're not too bad. You'd be a lot better if you had the best drummer in the world." I said, "Well, everybody would, yes." I said, "Where is he to be found?" He said, "You're looking at him."

Howard: I was watching the Kennedy Center Honors, when Heart is singing "Stairway to Heaven," and you're sitting next to Jimmy [Page]. I could tell you guys were into it, and you even shed a tear. I've watched that clip fifty times. What are you thinking about? Are you reflecting that Heart sounds good? Are you reflecting about Bonzo Bonham and saying, "God, I wish he was here with us"? There was something that moved you, and I'm dying to know.

Robert: What it was was his boy playing drums—Jason. You see, when I just recounted that story of me playing in the dance hall and him standing and telling me what he could do for me, I thought all those years later that it was just one ridiculous loss.

Howard: I guess it hit you like a ton of bricks. "I miss my friend. His son is here. I wish he could see this."

Robert: Yes, I wished a lot of things like that, all the way along the line. The thing is, music is a spectacular healer. It's a stimulus for all. It's the alternative to a lot of the intensity that's around us. That's what it is. It's a panacea.

....

NORM MACDONALD ON CHRIS FARLEY

Howard: Farley was out of his mind even off camera, right?

Norm: Yes, he was.

Howard: They send you to the Catskills for some bonding retreat when you first were hired, and he runs into your room naked, right?

Norm: Yes, sir. Naked.

Howard: And he had a tomato shoved up his ass?

Norm: He said, "Would you like to see my impression of a salad?" Then he poured salad dressing all over his head, and started shoving baby tomatoes up his ass.

Howard: Did you think, "This guy is the greatest," or "What the fuck is this guy doing?"

Norm: I thought it was the greatest thing I ever saw. Then he said, "I have to tell you a secret." And I was like, "Oh God, the great Chris Farley has to tell me a secret! Something about *Saturday Night Live* I should know." It was a big, big resort, and he kept purposely looking back, making sure no one's around, taking all this time to find a room. We finally find it, he locks the room, and says, "This goes nowhere. This stays between you and I. 'Pat' is a woman!" [The androgynous *SNL* character played by Julia Sweeney.]

Howard: That's awesome. I love hearing that.

Norm: That's what I loved about him, that he would do this for some stranger. I'm telling you, *everyone* loved Chris Farley. The young, the old, the smart, the stupid. I wish so much he could've done this show.

Howard: Me too. I never met him.

Norm: I kept telling him, "You have to do it." He said he was afraid. He was one of those guys that couldn't understand. He kept saying, "If only I could be funnier than John Belushi." And I said, "You're way funnier than John Belushi." I don't even think John Belushi is funny; I think he's a serious actor that was kind of tortured. It always stunned me that someone could be walking through life, and all he hears is laughter but for some reason doesn't think he's funny.

Howard: [Chris] just felt like an unfunny guy.

Norm: I do remember him telling me when he was a boy, his father was, like, six hundred pounds.

Howard: I didn't know that.

Norm: And I remember him telling me as a boy he'd walk with his father, and all he would hear is people talking.

Howard: People goofing on the dad?

Norm: Yeah.

Howard: That was his sadness.

Norm: I don't think that ever left him.

······················

JENNIFER HUDSON ON WHITNEY HOUSTON

Howard: It's very difficult to figure out the right song for you because your voice is so big, so powerful, that when you make a pop record or a record for the masses, they have to figure out how to, like, tone you down in a way, right?

Jennifer: No matter what I sing—I don't care what I'm singing—it's considered spiritual, inspirational, or something like that. And it's like, "I'm glad you feel that, but that's not the nature of the song." It's a blessing and a curse.

Howard: Because some people's voices are so big they sound almost like church singers. And you're like,

"Wait a second, I want to be a little more mainstream."

Robin: One of the people who did manage to do that was Whitney Houston.

Jennifer: She did. Like nobody else. Yes, she did.

Howard: After her death, where did you sing "I Will Always Love You"?

Jennifer: At the Grammys. It was, whew, such a trying time. I didn't think I was gonna be able to get through it. Had Whitney not passed me the torch herself, I would not have done it. Because I have that much respect for her. But when I did a tribute to her at the BET Awards, she came backstage and she did her famous bow and she was like, "I turn my torch to you." So that's why I was like, "Okay, I'll do it. But I just don't know if I'm going to be able to get through it."

Howard: Why'd you think you couldn't get through it? Were you afraid that you wouldn't be able to deliver the goods that night when you sang this?

Jennifer: I hadn't sung this song since high school. And

I barely had the news that she passed. We were getting ready for the pre-Grammys and my assistant flew in the room and was like, "You heard?" And I'm like, "Heard what?" And he's like, "Whitney Houston passed." It wasn't even minutes, and the phone rang and it was like, "They want you to sing." So it was just a lot. And it hit so close to home in so many different ways. I used to sing this song in my mother's house in the hallway, in harmony with Whitney on the record. So I really got emotional on the stage. It was like, "I'm singing this song on this stage in honor of Whitney Houston because she's not here to sing it for herself." And right now I could cry just thinking about it. And I don't feel like it's any closure with her being gone. It's just like: "What happened? How? Why?"

....

PAUL McCARTNEY ON JOHN LENNON

Howard: I never understood the democracy of the Beatles. When you go to John, primarily your writing buddy, and you say, "Okay, I have written this song," does he get it right away, or does he sometimes say, "I don't get it. We're not doing this."

Paul: No, he'd get it.

Howard: He'd get it?

Paul: Yeah. You got to remember, we grew up and we were kids together.

Howard: Your father, by the way, did not want you hanging around with John Lennon.

Paul: He didn't mind. He didn't mind John.

Howard: Didn't he say that John was a bad influence, and you almost had to sneak out and meet with John when you guys were young kids?

Paul: Well, almost. By the time I met John, I had a little say in the matter.

Howard: The song "Get Back"—when you were recording it, Yoko was in the studio, and every time you sang "get back" John accused you of staring at Yoko. He took it as an insult because you were telling her to "get back to where you once belonged."

Paul: No, that's not true. No. Those were very paranoid times. Let's face it: we didn't welcome Yoko in the studio because we thought it was a guy thing. The guys' wives and the girlfriends weren't really welcomed in the studio. They could come into the control room for a quick visit, but to actually sit in the studio with us, it was like, "No, excuse me, we are working."

Howard: Did you have the guts to say that to John?

Paul: No. It was kind of obvious, though.

Howard: Weren't you acting out passive-aggressively in the sense that you're sitting in the studio, you're just steaming, rather than saying, "John"—in a kind of loving way—"this is hurting me. I can't work this way if I have someone observing." But everyone was just kind of sniping.

Paul: I don't even think we were sniping. I think we were just fuming and sulking.

Robin: Did John ever say, "Look, I'm bringing . . ." He didn't ask permission to do that?

Paul: No, he didn't. The thing is, it was really just the initial shock of Yoko sitting on one of the amps. "Excuse me, that's my amp." She couldn't use a stool?

Howard: I think that would be mind-blowing, Paul.

Paul: It was mind-blowing. But later on, we suddenly sort of thought, "You know what? John's in love with this girl. If he wants to bring her in the studio, we've got to cope with that." We learned to cope with it. I now feel that he had the right to do that. It might have been better if he'd been a little bit more diplomatic and said, "Hey, guys, I really love her and I just want to be near her all the time." But we had to figure that out, and we did eventually.

DENIS LEARY ON DAVID BOWIE

Howard: You got to know Bowie?

Denis: No, here's what happened. I was co-hosting a comedy show over in London. But it also ran on the Comedy Channel, which turned into Comedy Central here. It was called *London Underground*. I was the American host. There were two guys who were the British hosts. I would bring over comedian friends of mine as the American comics, and they would usually have a British musical act as well. Some great acts. Sinéad O'Connor was there. Elvis Costello was there. And usually what happened with the musical acts is they didn't really hang around with the comedians. None of the comedians were famous yet, you know what I mean? So they just came and did a sound check, and when it was time for them to go on camera they sang their song and then they split. Bowie was the fourth week. And I'm a Bowie freak. So I was like, "You know what? I don't give a fuck what happens. I gotta meet Bowie. Even if they tell me not to go in an area, and he's in there—"

Howard: It's almost like you're pursuing a woman.

Denis: I was gay for Dave, I'll be honest with you. I was gay for Bowie.

Howard: Hey, we all were.

Denis: And I think my wife would've understood. It was an old West End theater. You had to go outside to smoke, in an alley. So I go outside to smoke a cigarette. And I'm still in the process of trying to figure out, "When am I gonna meet him? How am I gonna do it?" And I looked up, and he was literally right here.

Howard: Right in front of your face.

Denis: He's like, "Hey, man, you got a light?" Howard, I swear to God. I panicked, but I was also like, "I gotta say my stuff 'cause it's not gonna last long." So I lit his cigarette, and before the cigarette came out of his mouth, before I could say anything, he went, "You're friends with Steven Wright." Steven Wright and [Bobcat] Goldthwait had already made it. He's like, "You know, I met him, but I don't know what he's really like. What's he really like?" So I'm like, "I'm in with Bowie! I'm so fucking in!" And I'm like, "Steven, Steven, blah-blah-blah." He was like, "Interesting. Now, what about Bobcat Goldthwait?

I had him flown in for one of my gigs." And I'm like, "Bobcat? I know Bobcat. Blah-blah-blah." And as soon as I finish telling him the Bobcat thing, somebody goes, "All right, we're all set for you, Mr. Bowie." And he goes, "All right, mate, see you later." Puts his cigarette out and walks away. I see him onstage that night. Never see the man again.

Howard: What was your agenda, though?

Denis: I wanted to say, "Dude. Your music. Stones. You. Beatles. I mean, that's how I survived till fucking punk rock and the Clash and the Ramones came in. That's how I got through." I hated prog rock and all those fucking seventies fucking cocksucker fucking singer-songwriter motherfuckers.

Howard: So you wanted the opportunity to say to Bowie, "You meant everything to me."

Denis: Right. By the way, the most boring fucking thing you could say to David Bowie—what everybody else says. "Oh my God, you're my hero." "Great. Fuck you."

Howard: "Yeah, I wrote a song about that."

··

KEVIN NEALON ON GARRY SHANDLING

Kevin: Have you ever done a sitcom?

Howard: The only sitcom I was ever on was *The Larry Sanders Show.* The late, great Garry Shandling. I know he was a friend of yours. I never wanted to be on a sitcom, but because I loved that show so much and I loved Garry, I figured I'd do this walk-on. . . . You were very close. I don't mean in a bullshit show business way. How did you meet the great Garry Shandling?

Kevin: I don't remember specifically when I met him. Maybe at a comedy club. But we just kind of melded. Our lives melded together. We became really good friends.

Howard: And eerily, which is not a word I've ever used—

Kevin: Lake Eerily.

Howard: Yeah, Lake Eerily. Eerily, he said to you right before he died, "You know what? Before I die, you and I

gotta go back out on the road and do stand-up together."

Kevin: That's right. He sent me an e-mail. I was in Phoenix doing a gig, and I would check in with him every once in a while. We'd talk about material on the phone.

Howard: What do you mean you'd talk about material?

Kevin: If I had a gig or something for a corporation, I would call him. He loved working on jokes. He was a real craftsman when it came to jokes and writing. He had some of the greatest jokes. Two of them I can think of right now. He goes, "Sometimes when I'm lonely I'll shave one leg so it feels like I'm sleeping with a woman." [*Howard and Robin laugh.*] Or he'll say, "You know, I can't afford my own private jet, but I can afford to pay other people to get off my commercial flight."

Howard: He was a genius.

Kevin: He was a genius. So funny.

Howard: When he would do *The Tonight Show* back with Johnny Carson and he would do stand-up, he would kill it every time. You looked forward to his appearances.

Kevin: I would look forward to it, and I would see what he was wearing. He had these nice Armani suits on that just hung, and his material was great, and his timing—I thought, "This is the guy, man. This is the guy I'm going to learn from." And you know what? I never met anybody before who meditated. He was into meditation. . . . I never saw anybody French-kiss a dog before.

Howard: He did?

Kevin: He did.

Howard: Why would he do that?

Kevin: Because he loved this dog I brought back from Hawaii. I was in Hawaii with my wife a couple weeks after he was in Hawaii, and we stayed at the same resort. It was in Maui. And I saw this little Border Collie running around the resort. And the next day I saw him again, and his back leg was hanging off. And I thought, "Oh my god, that poor dog." But he was still bouncing around, and I asked the manager of the [resort], "What's the story with this dog?" He goes, "I think it belongs to the rancher down the street. He'll probably just shoot it, because they don't want to pay for vet bills." So we took the dog and brought it to the vet, got it dewormed, got rods in the leg, got it fixed, and we were going to take it home with us. And I called Gary from Hawaii. I said, "Gary, by the way we found this dog, this black-and-white Border Collie." And he goes, "Wait a minute. That sounds like the dog I saw when I was out there. In fact, I really had a connection with that dog. And right before I was going to leave I was chasing after him in the field and I stepped in a hole and I twisted my ankle and couldn't get the dog. Kevin, I think that's the dog. You're bringing him home?" I said, "Yeah, we're bringing him home. We're going to keep him. We're calling him 'Hana.'" Because we found him in Hana. And he goes, "Would you bring the dog over so I can see it? Because I think that's the dog that I was going to bring home."

Howard: No kidding.

Kevin: So we get the dog home and we bring it over, and sure enough that's the dog. That's the dog that he wanted. And I could tell he really wanted a dog, so I thought $500 was reasonable.

Howard: [*laughs*]

Kevin: So he kept that dog.

Howard: Is that really a true story?

Kevin: That's a true story. . . . And that dog became the best relationship he ever had—the longest.

Howard: Yeah, he didn't have successful relationships with women.

Kevin: No.

Howard: He never married, right?

Kevin: No, he didn't marry.

Howard: But that was so great for his comedy, because he would be on these talk shows talking about his lack of prowess with women, which was always such a great topic. And even back then no one ever talked about stuff like that.

Kevin: No.

Howard: Really, he was just something else. But when he came out with *The Larry*

Sanders Show, that did it for me.

Kevin: It was amazing. That broke so many barriers. Look at all the shows like *The Office* now. Well, *It's Garry Shandling's Show* [was] where he broke that fourth wall and started talking to the camera. But yeah, *The Larry Sanders Show* really made a big impact.

....

MARK RONSON ON AMY WINEHOUSE

Howard: Tell me how this works. This was [Amy's] second album, right?

Mark: This was her second album, yeah.

Howard: How do you meet? Does someone put you together?

Mark: Yeah, and I wasn't like a big-shot producer. She had been working on the record for a while, and somebody from her label in England said to me, "Do you want to work with Amy Winehouse?" And I was like, "I remember her. I liked some songs on her first record. Send her to my studio." So she comes to my studio, and we were actually coming in at the same time and I go—I recognized her 'cause she had the hair already, even then—and I was like, "You're Amy, right? I'm Mark." She goes, "Nice to meet you. I'm going up to see Mark Ronson." I'm like, "No, no, no, I'm Mark." She was like, "I thought you were going to be an old Jewish guy with a beard or something." Maybe 'cause she had heard my name for a while and she just pictured something different. Anyway, we got out, we started talking, we instantly got on like a house on fire. She was so funny.

Howard: Is there a certain thing with artists where you have to be—I don't want to use the word "cool," but there has to be a vibe, right? They've got to trust you. Probably 90 percent of your job is having the right personality, the right temperament, so that you don't get in her way but you also contribute. It's a weird line, right?

Mark: Yeah, you hear about famous producers throwing a chair at the drummer. Different things work for different people.

Howard: Pulling out a gun.

Mark: Exactly. For me, I found that [my role is] just being a good ear, open to anything, and getting the sense that, "Okay, I could actually do something musically that might be good for this person."

Howard: You have to have this meeting of the minds. There has to be this vibe. And Amy Winehouse to me is the representation of cool. I would worry the whole time I'm gonna say something wrong. I'm going to get on her bad side. And then you have artists that show up late, and you just have to be cool and go with it.

Mark: You gotta deal with a lot of shit, but you're working with really talented people who are essentially good people. You know, sometimes the better the artist, the more complex they are. But, yeah, Amy was so special, and right away we had this talk about music and she told me she wanted to make stuff that sounded like the sixties girl-group stuff, and

I'd never made anything like that but I was excited.

Howard: What about "Rehab" specifically? Did you work on this one with her?

Mark: Yeah. She had written a lot of songs before she got to New York. But we were walking down the street in SoHo. She wanted to go get a shirt. It was her boyfriend's birthday, and we were catching up, getting to know each other, and she was like, "You know, I used to be kind of fucked up, and there was this time when I was drinking a lot and my family and my manager and all these people came over to my house and they tried to make me go to rehab and I was like, 'Pssht, no, no, no.'" And she did the talk-to-the-hand gesture. And because she was talking about it in such a removed way and she was in such a good state when I met her, I was like, "Oh, this is a funny anecdote." And I was like, "I hate writing songs around a gimmick but there's something catchy about what you just said. You want to just go back to the studio and maybe try and turn that into a song?"

Howard: So she didn't recognize it necessarily as a song? She said, "They tried to make me go to rehab, and I said, 'No, no, no.'" And all of a sudden you look at each other and go, "Hey, maybe that's a lyric?" Is that how it works?

Mark: Yeah, 'cause she said it with rhythm and it sounded hook-y. I was like, "Let's just try it." So we went back to the studio. She was always so fast the way she wrote. She comes back in like thirty minutes and she's like, "I've got this song."

Howard: Just the music or the words?

Mark: She had the words and the music, and it was like a slow kind of blues. [*Ronson sings a slow version of the "Rehab" chorus.*] And I'm always thinking a little pop-y. Like, "Can we speed it up? Can we make it dance? You like 'Leader of the Pack.' Can we go [*handclaps*] boom-bapbap-bap." She was like, "All right, yeah, we can try it."

Howard: So what do you do? Do you lay down guitars and pianos?

Mark: I probably did a shitty little drum, 'cause I'm not a very good drummer, but a little [*handclaps*] boom-bapbap-bap. I would lay a little instrumental and say, "Does it work if you sing it over this?" 'Cause she had the whole song on the guitar. All I had to do was come up with a nice beat for it.

Howard: Was she tickled when this whole thing worked?

Mark: She [was]. We had such a good rhythm, because she would play me her songs, she would leave for the night, I would stay up all night trying different chords and beats.

··

LIL' KIM ON THE NOTORIOUS B.I.G.

Howard: The new album is called *The Notorious Kim*. Is that a play on Notorious B.I.G.?

Lil' Kim: Actually, it's a memorial to him. Because I loved him.

Howard: Because you were in love with him?

Lil' Kim: Yeah, I loved him.

Howard: You had sex with Notorious B.I.G.?

Lil' Kim: Yeah, I did.

Robin: Even though he was married?

Lil' Kim: Yeah. Sometimes in life—

Howard: Sometimes things happen. He's a very fat brother, if I may say. Not p-h-a-t, I mean f-a-t.

Lil' Kim: Well, he was phat to me, as in p-h-a-t.

Howard: I'm surprised you were attracted to such a heavyset man.

Lil' Kim: To me, he was gorgeous.

Howard: You liked the way he looked. You were always on top, right? Notorious B.I.G. never got on top of you?

Lil' Kim: I wanted him to. I wouldn't have minded. I'm a very strong woman.

Howard: But it would be difficult for him to breathe. Seriously, he was a very big brother. Most times he would lie on his back and you would climb on top of him during the lovemaking sessions, as they were?

Lil' Kim: I loved him so much, any position he wanted to try, I did. That's my baby. That was my baby.

Robin: That song was true. "Biggie, Biggie, Biggie."

Howard: "Biggie, Biggie, Biggie, can't you see?"

Lil' Kim: Can't you see I love you? I love you, Biggie. I know he's in this room right now.

Howard: Really?

Lil' Kim: If you knew Biggie, you would love him.

Howard: That's what everybody says.

Lil' Kim: You and Biggie would get along very well.

Howard: Well, let me tell you something, I'm going to channel Biggie. I'm getting a message from Biggie from heaven and he's saying, "Make love to Howard, Lil' Kim."

Lil' Kim: He's saying, "Cut it out." Biggie was everything. He was a musical genius and he was just a beautiful person.

Robin: Nobody ever says such nice things about you.

Howard: No.

Lil' Kim: You're great at what you do. You really are. You paved the way for me.

Howard: Really?

Lil' Kim: You talk dirty, just like me. I said [on the song "Who's Number One?"], "I'm nasty, worse than Howard Stern / This court is adjourned, now it's your turn."

····································

STEVEN VAN ZANDT ON CLARENCE CLEMONS

Howard: You're not going to try to replace Clarence with another sax player, are you?

Steven: I don't know. We just start our rehearsals this weekend. So we gotta talk about all this stuff. Obviously, you can't replace him, first of all. You know that. But it was terrible even with Danny [Federici].

Howard: Your keyboard player.

Steven: Yeah, we lost Danny. So we gotta talk about it this week and see what we're gonna do.

Howard: What is that like, when you talk about it? Is there a formal meeting where you go sit down and talk about Clarence?

Steven: No. Either before rehearsals or after rehearsals, we'll talk about it.

Howard: Should I be at the rehearsals to help you guys through this?

Steven: I think you should.

Robin: What do you think they should do?

Howard: What do I think they should do? I think they should do what I've seen Billy Joel do or McCartney do. You got a guy there who can play a lot of different things. He can do keyboard. He can stand up and play the sax. You have him there and you pay him a couple bucks. You know, he's not a band member. That's what you do. That's what we're gonna do, am I right, Steven? You're laughing 'cause I'm right. You get these pickup guys. They're not going anywhere. The guy already knows there's nothing happening for him. He's gonna get some solo deal that'll never go anywhere. Isn't that what you do, Steven?

Steven: You are funny. You are a funny guy.

Howard: That's gonna be it. Pick this guy up for a couple dollars. You're not gonna find a guy who had the presence of Clarence.

Clarence had the history with the band. You can't replace that.

Steven: That's it, that's it.

CEDRIC THE ENTERTAINER ON BERNIE MAC

Cedric: There used to be a big comedy competition Miller Genuine Draft used to do in Chicago. Chicago was another city where I would go and try to make it. I would drive up [from St. Louis]. And Bernie Mac was legendary even then. I just remember being in a club one night and he walks in and everybody goes, "There go Bernie Mac."

Howard: He was the greatest. We had him on the show many times, and he would give me the chills every time he walked in 'cause he was so fucking funny. The guy knew how to make people laugh, right? And he died so young.

Cedric: Yeah, yeah, he was, like, fifty-one.

Howard: Did you speak at his funeral?

Cedric: Yeah.

Howard: That had to be just so tragic, right?

Cedric: Well, you know, it was one of those things. It was very sad. 'Cause we were even thinking about doing *Kings of Comedy*. We were gonna try and go back out. A second tour. And he couldn't really travel 'cause of the lungs. The breathing thing. And so I said that onstage at the funeral. I was like, "People were literally asking me for Bernie Mac funeral tickets. He's that hot. 'Ced, I know you got two. Can you get me in?'"

Howard: I feel that Bernie Mac is one of the most underrated comics that ever lived. When people mention great comics, they'll mention Jerry Seinfeld. They'll mention Lenny Bruce. Pryor. Carlin. I don't hear Bernie Mac in those sentences. And he was. I don't know why.

Robin: Well, it was beginning to happen. He was making it in movies.

Cedric: Yeah, it was starting to be that rise. Bernie was underground for a long time. And he was actually comfortable with that.

Howard: And white America always confused you with Bernie Mac.

Cedric: Constantly. Somebody just said that on Twitter the other day. They saw me on a commercial, and they were like, "Oh, I thought Cedric the Entertainer was dead." I was like, "What?! Can I live? Can I live?"

Howard: Black America doesn't do that, do they?

Cedric: Not so much.

....

JADA PINKETT SMITH ON TUPAC SHAKUR

Howard: You were very close with Tupac Shakur.

Jada: Yes. I met Tupac at Baltimore School for the Arts. We went to high school together.

Howard: Tupac Shakur wasn't the gangster that we all think he was, right? His mother was a Black Panther, and he was sort of raised by the Black Panthers and all that.

Jada: Absolutely. He was a revolutionary without a revolution, if that makes any kind of sense. That kind of energy just transferred to a whole other thing.

Howard: And don't you believe that at that time he was in love with you? Because he would write poetry about you. You two weren't sexual with one another, but he said you could make him cum without sex, right?

Jada: It's so funny, because now being older I have more of an understanding of what that was between us. Because when you have two young people who have very strong feelings but there's no physical chemistry at all. It wasn't just for me. It was him too. There was a time when I was like, "Just kiss me. Let's just see how this goes." And I tell you, it had to be the most disgusting kiss for us both.

Howard: Explain that to me. Because it was so platonic, the relationship?

Jada: The only way I can put it is just—the higher power just did not want that. If Pac and I had any kind of sexual chemistry, we might have killed each other. Because we were both so passionate, and we love deeply. It was hard enough just being friends. We had a very volatile relationship.

Howard: Did you recognize him as a great talent at that point?

Jada: I did, I did.

Howard: Was it his poetry?

Jada: It was his poetry. It was his personality. I had never in my life met a person like Pac.

Howard: With that kind of charisma.

Jada: He had so much charisma. And he was poor. When I met Pac, he owned two pairs of pants and two sweaters, and that's it.

Howard: Were you shocked when he achieved the degree of fame that he did?

Jada: Absolutely not.

Howard: Really? Come on.

Jada: I knew that was going to happen.

Howard: For both of you to become famous out of the same shitty neighborhood in Baltimore is almost impossible.

Jada: It is. It's crazy. He used to tell me all the time, he was like, "Jada, you're a superstar. You're a superstar."

Howard: He didn't say it about himself?

Jada: He didn't say it about himself, no. He didn't. But he used to say it about me.

Howard: So you guys were these close friends. Really close. But then, as you go off to LA and pursue a career, and he goes off doing his thing, you guys are not friends. He went to jail. You've said when he went to jail for the first time, he called you after that, and that he changed. Jail changed him.

Jada: There was a lot of things that transpired once he went to jail. It was really once he came out that he changed quite a bit, which is understandable. Jail was a very difficult experience for him. And, of course, we were on two sides of the spectrum. Pac and I have always had very intense conversations. If we disagree with each other, we disagree hard-core. And we had a very hard-core disagreement.

Howard: What was the disagreement? What was the thing that broke you guys up in terms of a friendship?

Jada: I just wasn't in

agreement with the direction that he was taking, and I told him that it was a destructive direction.

Howard: A scary direction?

Jada: A very scary direction. And he felt as though I had changed. I got Hollywood, you know?

Robin: You had gone soft.

Jada: I had gone soft. And I understood all that. Looking back now, I totally understand where Pac was. Because at that particular point in time, that mentality was part of his survival for that moment. And it was actually a mentality he started to come out of before he was murdered.

Howard: And so you hadn't spoken to him for a couple of years. When he was murdered, you probably felt a lot of guilt that you hadn't been in touch, yes? Or were you guilt-free because you said to yourself, "Well, listen, I couldn't go in that direction. I didn't want to be friends with someone who was getting so hard-core angry"?

Jada: I don't think I was guilty as much as I felt just sadness for not having the opportunity to tell him that

I loved him. But I know he knew that. Because it wasn't the first time that we had had a bad argument and had stopped speaking and all that. That was kind of a constant in our relationship, so I didn't really look at it as a reason to feel guilty. But it definitely taught me a lesson, which is life is too short. Do not let disagreements stand in between you and people that you love and care about.

Howard: I can tell you're really emotional about him. I mean, you're crying.

Jada: Yes.

Howard: When you think of him, you have tears in your eyes.

Jada: I love him.

Howard: Terrible ending. Just so violent.

Jada: It was really tragic. But you know what? He left a very strong and powerful mark. People are still inspired by him.

Howard: Yes.

Jada: So he did his work.

Howard: Yes, he did.

Jada: He did his work, and that's what I'm happy about.

Howard: The thing I have

trouble with when someone dies that young is so much of their life is missed. And life is such a gift. Do you know what I mean?

Jada: Yes.

Howard: Even though it's hard and it's a struggle. Who knows what would have happened in that guy's life?

Jada: Oh, man, if he had reached this age, he'd have been something to reckon with.

Howard: You never know, but it sure seems like he would have been.

JUDD APATOW ON SAM KINISON

Judd: When I was doing stand-up originally, Kinison was the guy. And so when I'm in a club and Kinison's in the club, I'd just think, "I should stop being a comedian."

Howard: Right. It can actually defeat you to see somebody great at their craft. I sometimes would look at Kinison and go, "Oh my God, this guy's light-years ahead of everyone. How does anybody go into

stand-up comedy when there's Kinison?" I think about him every day. One of the most brilliant comic minds.

Judd: I used to see him when the crowd didn't know who he was. And that was a whole different thing. We did a Comic Relief benefit in '86, and no one really knew who Kinison was yet. Maybe he'd been on HBO a little bit. But at this charity event, he comes on and does the greatest hits of Kinison. The men lose their minds. Every woman in that room walks out. I've never seen a walkout situation where 125 women walk out the door and the guys are like, "Well, I'm staying." And then he tears the roof off the place.

Howard: And it didn't matter to him that he was polarizing. He just did his thing. It had to have been hard for you—it was for me—to see a great comedy mind like that, and I knew Sam pretty well, to see him destroy himself the way he did. Because I saw him go out many nights when he was drunk, and it really killed me.

I'd go, "God, to have those kind of gifts and to just abuse yourself." The abuse is crazy, right? I mean, it just doesn't make sense.

Judd: Especially when it's in slow motion. When somebody is struggling, and everyone knows he's struggling, and everyone's trying to help, and you realize, "Oh, at some point, people have to figure out how to do it." But I think he was sober at the end of his life.

Howard: Yeah, he was.

Judd: Which is really the tragedy of it—that he really got it together. What's weird about comedy now is that there really aren't any wild men anymore.

Howard: No.

Judd: There's no, like, insane people in comedy. Everyone is really good, and I think comedians are probably better for the most part. But where are the lunatics?

Howard: Insanity should be embraced. Like Andy Kaufman seemed insane. Kinison seemed insane. Dice seemed insane. Bob Goldthwait seemed crazy.

Even I remember the first time I saw Howie Mandel on *The Merv Griffin Show*, I thought he was mentally ill. It was great. The crazy guys. And everyone now wants to be the snarky Harvard-type guy.

DAN AYKROYD ON JOHN BELUSHI

Howard: You wrote *Ghostbusters* for Belushi.

Dan: I did. In fact, when the keyboard lit up at the office like a keno board telling me that he was gone, I was writing a line for him.

Howard: As you're writing the script, and you're writing John Belushi a line, you get the horrible news that John is gone?

Dan: Yeah. Then I had to go and tell Judy.

Howard: His wife.

Dan: Yeah. I had to get to her before it was public. So I ran from our office at 150 Fifth Avenue down to her place on Morton Street. I was passing a newsstand and they dropped the bundle off: "Belushi Dead at 33." So I just beat it to her place, before the headlines. And so, you know, I had to tell her.

Howard: Was it a shock to you, or was it something that you kind of expected? John partied hard. Every guy at *Saturday Night Live* was probably partying hard at that point. But he was really going hard.

Dan: We were afraid that it would happen. And we were very protective of him. I flushed a lot of coke down the toilet in those last days.

Howard: Would he get mad at you when you flushed it?

Dan: Oh yeah.

Howard: Did you hate his friends? I'm talking about these bad-influence-type friends. Was it impossibly difficult for you because you loved him so much?

Dan: Well, you know, the woman that put the needle in him. Cathy [Smith]. She didn't want to kill him any more than I did. She loved him. And I can't bear hate. You know, I can forgive, but I can't forget.

CHRIS CORNELL ON KURT COBAIN

Chris: I had friends die before [Kurt Cobain]. The way that he did it was kind of a twist. But other than that, I'd been through it before. And it was a shame. You know, it's a shame for his daughter, for one. It's a shame for fans. And . . . I don't know. It was a drag, and I wish it didn't happen. And I also think, like, if he would have just kind of hung on for six months, who knows? Six months later, he could've been a completely different guy.

Chris Rock

DECEMBER 8, 2014

I had the experience of doing stand-up once. It was in 1985. I was at WNBC, and things were not going well. Don, my agent, called and said, "You've got an offer for a one-off TV special. It's a stand-up comedy showcase. It's being filmed in a club in Hartford, Connecticut. It's only going to air in that area. They asked if you'd be the host and maybe do a little stand-up." Normally this is not something I would have said yes to. But (a) I needed the money; (b) I was insecure about the situation at NBC, so I figured I should try everything; and (c) except for promotional appearances, I hadn't done much TV. I asked Fred Norris to come with me. A limo picked us up. It was one of the first times I had ever been in one. Here's some trivia for my regular listeners: that's how I met Ronnie the Limo Driver. He was the driver that day.

I didn't have any material or jokes. I got up onstage and started telling stories. One of my advertising sponsors came to watch. He had a really hot girlfriend. I started picking on him. I said, "What's she doing with you?" Then I went and grabbed a couple bottles of liquor from the bar. I told the crowd, "They're not paying me much for this," and I started mixing drinks and selling them from the stage. After some more banter, I introduced the first comedian and sat down at our table.

"How'd I do, Fred?" I asked.

"I think you did really well!" he said.

We started scribbling down ideas for the next time I had to go up. Later in the night, I ran into a guy I'd grown up with in Roosevelt. He moved in the fourth grade. I hadn't seen him since.

"I didn't know you were a stand-up," he said. "You were really funny."

"I'm *not* a stand-up," I said.

When I saw the tape of the show, I was even more convinced. I was god-awful. I didn't think I was funny at all. I really didn't enjoy it. I was very uncomfortable in front of the audience. I feel the same way whenever I go on talk shows. Hearing that wave of laughter come back from the crowd breaks my rhythm. That's why radio is so perfect for me. I don't have to be swayed by getting a laugh every few seconds. The only person I'm performing for is Robin. As long as I'm making her laugh, that means I'm funny.

However, Chris Rock once said something to me that made me look differently at what I do. He has always viewed me as a stand-up comic. "You do a four-hour set every day," he told me, "and you never repeat yourself."

I've never forgotten those words. It felt like a really warm embrace. I genuinely believe that Chris is one of our greatest living comedians. Few performances have been funnier or more thought-provoking than his 1996 HBO special, *Bring the Pain*. The reason he's so good—as he explains in this interview—is that he works hard at it. Chris has never taken any shortcuts. He's always continued to work the clubs and refine his material. His wit has no off switch. I'll never forget the time he came in when I was getting ready to marry Beth, and he said, "I can't believe it. You're going back to Shawshank." His mind is always at work.

This interview is the perfect example of why I wanted to do this book. As much as I love radio, I've come to appreciate the written word. When I just listen to these interviews—maybe because of the pacing or because I'm caught up in the sound of the voices—I miss things. In the case of Chris Rock, whose mind moves at the speed of light, the potential for oversight is even greater.

There's material in this interview that you're about to read that, in my opinion, rates with the greatest stand-up Chris has ever performed. His takes on Leonardo DiCaprio's charmed life, Dave Chappelle's brilliance, the differing expectations of black and white families: for almost any other comedian, this would be career-highlight-reel stuff. For Chris, these were throwaway lines. It was just him riffing like a jazz musician. It came straight off the top of his head on a random weekday morning in a nearly empty radio studio. No preparation, no pen, no paper.

I had captured lightning in a bottle, but I missed it at the time. The conversation was happening too quickly for me to fully appreciate the brilliance of what Chris was saying. It deserved to be properly preserved. Written down. Like when Moses walked up Mount Sinai to talk to God. Rather than have Moses simply tell the Israelites the commandments and rely on oral tradition to pass them down, God inscribed them in stone so they could be examined for generations and have a uniquely powerful impact.

So like Moses walking down from the mountain, I present to you, my flock, the written word of Chris Rock. Amen.

Chris: Is this going to be a nice interview?

Howard: Yes, it will be nice.

Chris: We aren't going to do this thing where you kind of talk about other things and avoid my movie? That's your way of being nice.

Howard: No, we can talk about this one.

Chris: I have been listening. Your interviews are so freaking good now. It's a whole other level.

Robin: Has he never interviewed you in that way?

Chris: In depth? No, I don't think so.

Howard: Did you hear my Tan Mom interview?

Chris: No, I did not hear the Tan Mom interview.

Howard: I was hoping that you would listen to that.

Chris: I told my daughter I was doing *Howard Stern* this morning. She goes, "The guy from *America's Got Talent*?"

Howard: They have no idea I'm Fartman.

Chris: No idea.

Howard: No clue. How old is your oldest?

Chris: My oldest is twelve and she still likes to hang around me.

Howard: At what age does she realize her father is Chris Rock, and that sort of carries cachet with other kids?

Chris: When I'm at her school, I can tell the boys have seen every HBO special. The boys treat me like I'm Thelonious Monk or something.

Howard: They can quote every line?

Chris: They can quote every line. They are, like, "Mr. Rock." They're totally on it.

Howard: And that makes you proud, doesn't it?

Chris: That makes me proud. My daughter—literally the other day—goes, "Kevin Hart is funnier than you."

Howard: Really?

Chris: "Kevin Hart is much funnier. Dad, you need to watch Kevin Hart and study him because he works for the young people."

Howard: You have said in the past that you feel you suffer from dyslexia.

Chris: I do feel that I'm mildly dyslexic.

Howard: Have you ever been diagnosed?

Chris: I have never been diagnosed. I have never been tested. But even when I'm

> **MY DAUGHTER— LITERALLY THE OTHER DAY—GOES, "KEVIN HART IS FUNNIER THAN YOU."**

reading to my kids, when my daughter picks up a new book, I'm like, "Oh no."

Howard: You panic?

Chris: I'm so panicked.

Howard: Because when you read out loud, you have a problem?

Chris: I have a big problem reading out loud. Always have.

Howard: Were you embarrassed as a kid when they'd say, "Get up in front of the class and read"?

Chris: I was embarrassed as a kid. Even doing *SNL*, I'm like, "Oh no."

Howard: Was *Saturday Night* tough because everything was on cue cards?

Chris: Yes.

Howard: So when they would write a sketch and they put that up on cue cards, you were probably panicked inside?

Chris: I was always panicked inside. I'm always panicked to read aloud. Yes.

Howard: Now I have to go back and watch all the *Saturday Night Live* and watch you struggle with the cue cards.

Chris: I can *read*, Howard. I just have a problem reading aloud.

Howard: Okay, but it's still a problem.

Chris: That says "Howard Stern" right over there.

Howard: Very good.

Chris: "On air." I can read.

Howard: You're not retarded.

Chris: I'm not retarded. And I mean that in the nice way.

Howard: You were hysterically funny when you hosted *Saturday Night Live*. I really loved it. You did this material about the Boston Marathon and you got shit for it. I said on the air, "You've gotta fucking be kidding me." One of the jokes you said is, "Who the hell is gonna go in the Freedom Tower?" I've said this on the air myself. "I'm not going in the fucking Freedom Tower."

Chris: I'm not going in there.

Howard: Why was there this reaction?

Chris: I don't know. I mean, people laughed.

Howard: I laughed.

Chris: They laughed in the studio, so—I don't flip out on that stuff, man.

Howard: You didn't get affected by them being so negative?

Chris: No. Put it this way: I got a reaction out of them. They're talking about a monologue on *SNL*. How often does that happen? Never.

Howard: I remember the days when Sam Kinison hosted *Saturday Night Live*.

Chris: I was there. I was there a couple of times. Sam *took* me, when he was a comedian on *SNL*. And I watched him do coke right before he went on. Right before he went on he offered me some coke. I'm like, "Nah."

Howard: Isn't that mind-blowing to you? Could you do coke and then go out and do a set?

Chris: No.

Howard: No. You gotta be sharp, right? Razor-sharp.

Chris: Coke makes you sharp, though.

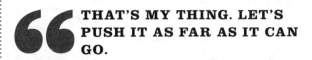

THAT'S MY THING. LET'S PUSH IT AS FAR AS IT CAN GO.

You'll cut yourself. That's how sharp you are.

Howard: I saw Sam pass out onstage. His second show. First show, sharp. And then all of a sudden fucked up and couldn't get through the second show. When you saw Sam Kinison go on *Saturday Night Live*, he used to get shit, because he would do his Jesus routine and America would go berserk. In a way, isn't that the badge of courage?

Chris: You got to piss off *somebody*. It's not good weed if you don't choke a little bit.

Howard: Did you clear this material with *Saturday Night Live* ahead of time?

Chris: No.

Howard: You didn't?

Chris: No. I never clear anything. I just go like this: "What *can't* I do?" And if nothing I'm going to do comes on that list, I'm going to do it. 'Cause anything I try to clear, they're gonna go, "Oh my God. You can't do that." Even when I hosted the Oscars, that was part of the deal. "Tell me what I can't say right now. You're not gonna hear this material until, like, five minutes before the show." 'Cause that's my thing. Let's push it as far as it can go.

Howard: You've said that you would host the Oscars again if they asked.

Chris: I was going to host the Oscars if

they asked. They didn't ask. Here is the weird thing I realized about the Oscars in retrospect: The Oscars is a religious ceremony, and people worship the statue. It's a big deal.

Howard: To the people sitting there.

Chris: Yes, and it is kind of not to be made fun of.

Howard: In other words, if you're going there, and you are going to be *Chris Rock*, the guy who is acerbic and really knows how to skewer someone, it's embarrassing. It's uncomfortable.

Chris: Yes. You hear reverends making jokes, but they don't joke about the religion.

Howard: And being Chris Rock, your fans then will skewer you because you *didn't* do all of that.

Chris: Exactly.

Howard: So why in God's name would you want to go and do that again?

Chris: Because it's the biggest audience a comedian can get. In the world. You got the Oscars and the Super Bowl, which I was offered one year.

Howard: To do the Super Bowl?

Chris: I was offered it the Janet Jackson nipple year. There was a bunch of acts, and Joel Gallen produced it. He was like, "I want you to do—" And I was like, "There's nothing for me to do on that show."

Howard: Yeah, what could you have done at the Super Bowl?

Chris: I don't know. I could have sucked. That's what I could have done.

Howard: He said to you, "Chris, what if you came out and did a minute?"

Chris: Like a minute or three minutes or whatever it was.

Howard: Was it tempting, though?

Chris: It *is* tempting. Just to be able to say it.

Howard: You would have been the first comic ever.

Chris: Just to get the stills. Just to have the pictures would have been amazing.

Howard: Do you have a million stories like that? Things you could have done that people would be shocked to know?

Chris: I got a few.

Howard: I do too. Why do we not tell those stories? Why do we not talk about the great things we've been offered? I'm guilty of this as well.

Chris: First of all, we've gotten enough anyway. No one wants to hear, "What? You could be *more* famous? You could have *more* money? Fuck you."

Howard: It's bragging, right?

Chris: Yeah. It's like, you don't want to hear Leo DiCaprio going, "You know who I *could have* fucked?" Stop it, Leo.

Howard: You fucked enough people.

Chris: You got enough, Leo.

Howard: That's right.

Chris: "You know what pussy I *turned down*?" Shut up, Leo. "Reese Witherspoon wanted me to lick her ass, but I said no." What? Leo, how'd you turn that down? "Halle Berry wanted me to cum in her face,

" I LOVE [LEONARDO DiCAPRIO]. . . . IF HE'S NOT DOING A MOVIE, HE'S FORTY POUNDS MORE WITH A BEARD AND A FUCKING MODEL. "FUCK Y'ALL. I'M EATING CHEESEBURGERS AND FUCKING FIVE BITCHES."

but I was busy." What? Notice how bad my Leo impression is.

Howard: It sounded just like him, actually.

Chris: I love the guy. The motherfucker— if he's not doing a movie, he's forty pounds more with a beard and a fucking model. "Fuck y'all. I'm eating cheeseburgers and fucking five bitches."

Howard: Don't you think that women would at some point say to themselves, "There is no shot with this guy because he's just gonna fuck me and leave me."

Chris: No woman thinks she has mediocre pussy. Every woman thinks she's got the greatest pussy in the world. "And if I could just get him to have *this* pussy, it will all change." I know I have a mediocre dick at best. On a good day, it's all right. No woman thinks her pussy is *okay*. "Once he gets a whiff of this, woo-hoo." Robin thinks, "If Leo got a little bit of Robin pussy—"

Howard: That would be it.

Chris: It's over.

Robin: No, I don't think that at all.

Chris: "It might be hard to get his attention, but if I can get him in here . . ." If you got to him, it will all change. That's what every woman thinks.

Howard: Is pussy overrated, though? Doesn't it just get you into tons of trouble?

Chris: It's all it ever does.

Howard: That's right. It only leads to aggravation.

Chris: It only leads to aggravation. I'm in the *People* magazine "sexiest" issue. I'm like, "What a fucking waste."

Howard: Don't give it to me.

Chris: Why now? What a fucking waste. If I was single, yes.

Howard: When you were single, they didn't tell you.

Chris: Why waste it on me? Give it to [David] Spade.

Howard: The new movie, by the way, is called *Top Five* and it opens this Friday. There are a lot of comedians you chose to be in the film. You got Whoopi [Goldberg] in there.

Chris: I got Whoopi, I got [Adam] Sandler, I got Seinfeld, I got J. B. Smoove, Cedric the Entertainer, Michael Che, Jay Pharoah, Brian Regan.

Howard: It sounds like you almost hit everybody.

Chris: I got a lot of guys. Couldn't get Chappelle.

Howard: Chappelle said no? What is it with Chappelle? Explain this whole

Chappelle thing to me. Why did he turn down $50 million? Is he having a nervous breakdown?

Chris: No.

Howard: I haven't seen him in years. I used to have him on all the time.

Chris: He was at Radio City. He did ten shows.

Howard: But I haven't seen him here. I used to have on Chappelle all the time before his TV show.

Chris: His kids are young, and you want to spend time with your kids while they're young. They're only young once. You were living in Long Island.

Howard: That's true. When my kids were young, that's what I did. Was Chappelle brilliant when you saw him?

Chris: He was brilliant. He's my favorite comedian.

Howard: Do you sit there and go, "Shit, I should have thought of that"?

Chris: Yes.

Howard: It's painful in a way to go see?

Chris: Sometimes it's painful, yeah. He's the only guy that does that to me.

Howard: And when you watch Chappelle or somebody who you admire, do you ever sit there and go, "Shit, I can't watch too closely, 'cause what if I accidentally take over something from him?"

Chris: Nah, guys like that—it's so good, you can't do anything with it. It would be like a bum finding a nuclear warhead.

Howard: "What do you do with this thing?"

Chris: It's only dangerous if a terrorist has it.

Howard: Tell me how hard it is to become a stand-up comic. Seriously, how many hours do you have to put in? I want to know the truth.

Chris: Ten thousand motherfucking hours. Malcolm Gladwell.

Howard: So he was right in *Outliers*?

Chris: Malcolm Gladwell is the closest I come to religion.

Howard: You have to go up there and bomb and just fucking just suck.

Chris: Ten thousand hours.

Howard: You started at Catch a Rising Star?

Chris: I started at Catch a Rising Star, but I really developed at the Comic Strip. Me and Sandler got the run. Me and Sandler and Colin Quinn and another guy named Jim Mendrinos. Richard Tienken, the owner of the Comic Strip, was off managing Eddie Murphy. This guy Lucien Hold just loved me and Sandler and Quinn and for whatever reason let us work every fucking night. Every show. Way too much.

Howard: When you say he let you work, he wouldn't pay you? He would just let you get up?

Chris: He'll pay five dollars a set or whatever. But he let us pass all the guys that were older than us. He broke the normal rules, and we got way more stage time.

Howard: This is before *Saturday Night Live*?

Chris: This is before *Saturday Night*.

We got so much more stage time than anybody else.

Howard: He wasn't doing that out of some sort of love of you. He just saw something in you.

Chris: He saw something. I do a set at Catch. I do a set at the Comic Strip. I do a set at the Improv. I do a set at the Cellar. Say you're going four times a night for six years straight.

Howard: Would you bomb?

Chris: Bomb a lot, yes. I bombed because I'm trying shit. I'd have material that worked, but I was always trying stuff.

Howard: How many times did you try to quit?

Chris: I never quit, man.

Howard: How did you make a living during all those years?

Chris: I lived with my parents until I was twenty-two.

Howard: When you were twenty-two and you're living with your parents and you're desperate for money, does the family look at you like you're the biggest piece of shit? Or are they banking on you to really make it?

Chris: The whole thing of me making it was so far-fetched.

Howard: How nice of your mother not to lay a trip on you. If I was twenty-two living at home, my parents would have just fucking booted me out.

Chris: Because you're white. The expectations are high. Me, everybody was just happy I wasn't a crackhead. "No crackhead. He's not dealing crack."

Howard: Was the lifestyle back then live with the parents and write material all day?

Chris: Work. I worked. I worked at Red Lobster. I worked at a halfway facility for mentally challenged adults. Making beds and making food and changing diapers on grown people and stuff.

Howard: Aren't you shocked that you had something inside you that your spirit didn't get crushed? Working at Red Lobster, waiting all day to get on, watching all those good people go, and then you have the nerve to get on the stage when you're not even really Chris Rock yet. When was the first time you knew you were really good at stand-up? When did it finally hit you that "I might be onto something"?

Chris: Two thousand eight.

Howard: Was it really?

Chris: At my third HBO special. I was like, "Maybe I got something there."

Howard: No, you felt you were really onto something when you did that HBO special. The one I love so much. "Books are like kryptonite."

Chris: Yes, *Bring the Pain.*

Howard: That's when you knew you were at the top of your game, right?

Chris: I was getting there. I was getting there.

Howard: And after *Saturday Night Live,* about which you say, "Hey, I should've worked harder. I should've been better at it."

Chris: I wasn't a big hitter on *SNL.* Even though Damon Wayans was before me, I was essentially the black guy after Eddie Murphy. So I was always going to get judged on that curve. *Saturday Night Live* is a great place to learn. Look at [Ben] Stiller. Stiller didn't get a lot of stuff on. Who's better than that guy? Rob Schneider did better on *SNL* than Ben Stiller? What sense does that fucking make? No disrespect to Rob, but Ben Stiller is a fucking monster.✦

Howard: But you said to yourself after *Saturday Night Live*, "You know what? Fuck this. I'm going back to stand-up, and I'm going to throw myself into it. Because if I'm ever going to make it big, that's where I'm going to make it." Right? That was the decision.

Chris: That was my thing. I wanted to be George Wallace. I wanted to be [Bobby] Slayton. I just want to be a really good comedian.

Robin: How did you find your voice? That's the thing.

Chris: You gotta be lucky enough. The same with you guys. You got on a radio show, and you were fortunate enough that no one was paying attention for a long period of time.

Howard: Ain't that the truth. You hit it right on the head.

Chris: You weren't making any money.

Howard: Right. Flying under the radar.

Chris: Then one day it clicked.

Howard: You're so right. I had so many friends who wanted to be on the radio, and they'd only work in big markets. If I figured out anything, it was, "I'm going to go to shithole radio markets and work this shit out until I get good enough that someone should want to hear me." At least I had that awareness.

Chris: You know what else, Robin?

Robin: What?

Chris: It was great coming up young, because everybody that was more famous than me, I actually agreed with it. I was all, "Yeah, Martin Lawrence is better than me. Yeah, Damon Wayans is better than me. Yeah, Sinbad's better." I didn't get frustrated until—I don't wanna say what name, but there came a point where I was like, "Okay, I'm better than this famous guy. Yeah, I should be up here right now." But I'd accepted my plight, like you did.

Howard: Yes, that makes a lot of sense to me.

Chris: A lot of guys don't accept their plight. They're unrealistic with where their talent is. And it's like, "Dude, you're not that good right now." That's what we have in common.

Howard: Right. We understood that we sucked.

✦ **For more on this from Ben Stiller, turn to page 547.**

Jon Stewart

NOVEMBER 15, 2017

I have a long history with Jon Stewart. When he got a late-night show on MTV, I was his first guest. Jon would often come on my show back when we were on terrestrial radio, but it was never a real interview. It was always just lighthearted joking around. One time we had a dance party in which the Goo Goo Dolls performed live while Gary, Fred, and some of the other staff slow-danced with each other dressed in thongs and *An Officer and a Gentleman*–style navy uniforms. Jon and I joined in wearing the dress whites and doing our best Richard Gere impersonations. I never got to talk about anything of real substance. One more example of a misguided notion that the audience wouldn't be interested in anything besides a goof.

In this interview, I wanted to go deeper with him. I never guessed how deep we'd get. We talked about his controversy with Trump while he was still on *The Daily Show*, and then we got into the Louis C.K. sexual harassment scandal. The news had only broken a day or two before. Jon was still processing it. He gave voice to that internal dialogue and the struggle he was having, and it was riveting. I am friendly with Louis C.K., and I was going through the same thing. We were both trying to work through our feelings right there on the air live.

Then we discussed Jon's relationship with his father, which was just heartbreaking. It got to the point where he even broke down a bit.

I'm so grateful to Jon for revealing himself to me and my listeners. We'd shared something truly remarkable. After the interview was over, I remember feeling a deep satisfaction. However, I also felt some sadness. Jon said he left *The Daily Show* because he knew it was a younger person's game, and he no longer had the insane energy necessary for the job. He discussed how he became too tired to even change his clothes to leave the office and shoot a street segment. I wanted to say, "No, Jon. You need to stay on the show. You need to stay in the fight. Just somehow find that energy. I don't want you to age out." Maybe I was sad because I was really talking to myself.

Howard: I want to talk about semiretirement. Because people—around here anyway—when I ask them, they always say, "Oh, Stewart's miserable now. He misses the limelight. He misses *The Daily Show*. He misses being on there." And I go, "I don't think he does."

Jon: No.

Howard: What John Oliver does is one day a week. I think if you had done that, you might have stayed in the game.

Jon: That's probably true. Although I think you'd also get tired of that. At a certain point, you have to evolve something. And I got to a point where I kind of didn't think I could do anything else with it. And thank God I did, because before Trump came, you need somebody who's thirty-two, thirty-three—who still has that type of energy, that type of stamina, that fire to go at it. I think I would have phoned it in. I was making decisions about bits toward the end of *The Daily Show* based on if I would have to change my clothes. That's how lazy I had gotten at that point.

> **IF THE LEFT WAS MAD AT ME, IT WAS ALWAYS "REMEMBER, THIS MAN IS A LITERAL PIECE OF SHIT." IF THE RIGHT WAS MAD AT ME, THEY WOULD ALWAYS USE MY BIRTH NAME. . . . "POOR JOHNNY LEIBOWITZ."**

Howard: You didn't want to go out on the street, let's say.

Jon: Right. "You're just doing an insert into this bit. We're just gonna throw your suit on and . . ." And I'm like, "Uh-huh. Is that downstairs?" And they're like, "Yeah, it's downstairs." And I'm like, "You know what? Why don't we do this in my office, and how about I wear a T-shirt?" So I felt like it was absolutely the right time. I was burnt on it. I was burnt on the system. Social media had just started to become a part of it, and sort of the weight of that, the churn of that.

Howard: I could imagine on social media, you must have gotten—well, not by liberals, obviously, but—

Jon: No, liberals too.

Howard: Liberals too. You get jumped on for everything, right?

Jon: Everything. And I could always tell. If the left was mad at me, it was always "Remember, this man is a literal piece of shit." If the right was mad at me, they would always use my birth name. Anytime you did something that angered the conservatives or the Right, it would always be like, "Poor Johnny Leibowitz."

Howard: Well, Trump started doing it.

Jon: Oh, he started doing that to me first, so they jumped on that.

Howard: I have always found, as a Jew, when someone wants to get to you—

Jon: Yup.

Howard: They go, "Oh, *Leibowitz*." What does that really mean? That does cut, right? It cuts into you.

Jon: Oh, I think it means—it plays into the conspiracy of "crypto-Jews." Jews that are passing but are actually working for the Bilderberg Group or the Illuminati and have placed out as sleeper cells into a variety of different—

Howard: Does that kind of attack work? Because a lot of Jewish people feel a sense of shame and guilt over all the anti-Semitism they've been whacked with, and somehow you start getting defensive. "What's wrong with saying 'Leibowitz'?" But yet it does. It's some sort of attack on you.

Jon: I think because it's not explicit. You can deal with people when they're being explicit. When there's passive-aggressive racism, you just want to say, "Just *say* it. Just say you think Jews are up to something." Don't make this implication. And it was surprising, because I couldn't figure out what Trump's motivation was for the attack. 'Cause generally he will attack if he feels—his whole thing is "I punch back." But sometimes people will just make even a constructive statement or a criticism that is legitimate and not below the belt, and he'll just come back with shit that's just—he'll burn the house down. That's what he does.

Howard: His punch back to you was calling you Leibowitz.

Jon: Yeah. "His real name is Jon Leibowitz. Why does he run from his heritage if he's so aboveboard?" Meanwhile, probably half the people on the show—you know, Steve

Carell was Steve Carelli. Aasif Mandvi was Aasif Mandviwala. Colbert was Col-*bert*.

Howard: People in show business do change their names.

Jon: And I didn't care for my father, so—

Howard: Right. Your parents divorced when you were young. It was not a pretty sight.

Jon: That's right. So we come back with, "Well, Donald Trump's real name is Fuckface Von Clownstick. And why does he run from the Von Clownstick heritage?" This sends him into a frenzy. And now the wasp hive of the Internet has just jumped on him with Fuckface Von Clownstick. So now he's in a position where he has to tweet out, "To all the losers and haters who are tweeting Fuckface Von Clownstick like it's so original . . ." So the whole Twitter war ultimately ends. Then three days later, at two-thirty in the morning—there's been nothing. I think the last tweet we sent out was, "I guess we hit a Fuckface Von Nervestick" or something like that. Two-thirty in the morning: "Little Jon Stewart is a pussy and would be helpless in a debate with me."

Howard: Is that what he said?

Jon: Yeah. Two-thirty in the morning.

Robin: It's like a sneak attack.

Jon: Yeah. And now he's the president. You imagine Lincoln at two-thirty in the morning being like [*imitates Abraham Lincoln voice*], "Little Robert E. Lee is a pussy."

Howard: The world has become such a dark place. I knew you were coming in, and then I saw you were on *The Today Show* and they of course ask you about Louis C.K.

Jon: Sure.

Howard: Because he's a friend of yours, and a friend of mine. But I thought, "Gee, this is so weird." It's almost like the question becomes an attack on you. "What are *you* gonna do now about your friend Louis C.K.?" And it's like, "I don't fucking know." The bottom line is this is all very fucking confusing.

Jon: Yes. That is correct. But it's also, I have a tendency—the way that I kind of work is, the first instinct you get on attack is a little defensive. Then it takes me a while to get over the defensiveness and try and close my eyes a little bit and, you know, rabbi it. That's why I grew the beard now.

Howard: What you mean by "rabbi" is, "try to consider other points of view about this."

Jon: Correct. I'll give you an example of this that happened, and it's in a similar lane. This was in the early two thousands, maybe mid–two thousands. A website called *Jezebel*, which is, like, a feminist-leaning website, they write a big exposé of *The Daily Show* and how it's a sort of "boys' club" mentality. And my first response is, like, "What the fu—no, no, no, no, no, no. I'm an OG feminist, man. I was raised by a single mother in the seventies. Like, she had a shirt that said, 'A woman needs a man like a fish needs a bicycle.' I felt like shit in my own house."

Howard: You were the enemy.

Jon: She referred to my father as Mister Wonderful. He died a while back; now she refers to him as Ex–Mister Wonderful. Except with, like, acid.

Howard: So you were very emotionally attached to your mother, and also considered her point of view a lot, and were raised by a very feminist-thinking, forward-thinking woman.

Jon: That's exactly right. So this thing comes out, and I'm like, "This is bullshit." I go back to the writers' room, and I'm like, "Can you fucking believe this? They're saying there's a boys' club. Steve, what do you think of that?" "No way!" "Matt?" "No way!" "Carl?" "No way!" Three guys with beards and glasses. And then I was like, "Ohhhh. *That's* what they meant." So the hardest part is to get over your defensiveness to find that kernel of constructive information that's in there. Now, we thought we were ahead of that, 'cause we do blind submissions so it's not sexist. But what you realize is, when you call agents—for writers, because that's the only way you get the submissions—they're only sending you white dudes from Harvard. And so you realize the system—the tributary that feeds the system—is actually where a lot of it lay. And to change that system takes actual effort. But they were right. The crux of the criticism—if I could get past my own defensiveness of it—was kind of right.

Howard: It's a hard thing to do, isn't it?

Jon: Nobody likes to be called on their bullshit. It's not a pleasant thing.

Howard: Yeah.

Jon: In this situation, the only reason that the Louis thing came up is I'm trying to promote an autism benefit.

Howard: That Louis was booked for.

Jon: And it is *the* story right now. I mean, look at the setup here [*indicating the studio*]. You and I sit, very comfortably, surrounded by water. The woman is in a terrarium—

Howard: That's right!

Jon: Where she's allowed to speak.

Robin: Howard, you're still trying to determine what my purpose is.

Howard: Right.

Jon: That's right. We're trying to determine it. She's not allowed to have *our* air.

Howard: She's in a protective booth.

Jon: That's right.

Howard: No one wants to be in my air.

Jon: We have the good air. She's over there in the ladies' air.

Robin: I'm hoping that they give me air.

Howard: But I guess my point was that it seemed like you are now getting attacked because you're supposed to come up with the perfect answer about Louis C.K.

Jon: Oh, no question.

Howard: And it's like, "Maybe I don't have the answer to everything. Maybe all of this is kind of new information, and I haven't had time to rabbi it."

Robin: Even Howard and I have been grappling with it and saying, "We don't know what to do about this."

Howard: Right.

Jon: You know, I do get that. I am defensive about it. When people have that certainty of "You knew." I know that I didn't know. You have to look at it in the context. My context is when I say, like, "Louis, my great friend." I have a lot of great friends that I started with and that I work with. I don't have their phone numbers. I don't have their e-mails. When we see each other, we fall back into—it's lovely to see them. I see guys that I haven't seen in twenty years that I worked with that I love, but we don't talk and communicate in that way. I consider Louis—and still do—a friend in that way. Whenever we saw each other, I was always . . . I love to see him. I love him as a comic. He was fun to work with when we worked together—this was, you know, twenty-five years ago.

Howard: Right.

Jon: But in *their* eyes, we all . . . the same way in my mother's eyes, when Woody Allen got in trouble, my mother said to me, "Did he ever tell you that?" And I'm like, "I don't know Woody Allen."

Howard: He doesn't talk to you?

Robin: There's no club?

Jon: What the Internet provides for folks is sort of an unrelenting certainty.

Howard: Right.

> ## "THE REAL PART THAT I CRITICIZE MYSELF ON IS, "WHAT WOULD I HAVE DONE IF I ACTUALLY HAD KNOWN?"

Jon: So what happens is, if you go on and you say, "I didn't know," the Internet, or those that are in the wasp hive for that one particular item—and there's different hives—just come flying in and go, "Fuck you. You're a piece of shit. I don't believe you."

Howard: Because you're a comedian and you know what every comedian's up to.

Jon: That's right. That's the part where you get defensive. Like a website that keeps writing articles putting the word *stunned* in quotations. They'll write, "Jon Stewart said he was 'stunned.'" You know, in quotations. Like, "Can you believe this asshole?" And then you feel like, "Well, you're a pretty reputable journalism website. Why didn't *you* write the article?" Like, everybody knew, but apparently they were waiting for me to kick him out of show business.

Robin: Why didn't *you* break this?

Howard: Walter Cronkite, yeah.

Jon: I think what they don't understand is—well, sometimes—I live a reclusive and somewhat oblivious life. And is that my fault? But the real question for me—here's the rabbi question.

Howard: Right.

Jon: I didn't know.

Howard: Right.

Jon: What if I did? That's the thing that bothers me. What if I did? What if I had known one of the women who was making the accusations? And I don't. I know they're in the comedy world, but I had not heard of them. But let's say I did, and one of them came to me and said, "Ten years ago or whatever, Louis did this."

Howard: What would you have done?

Jon: Would I still have worked with him? Would I still greet him? Like, that's the part—

Robin: You can't answer that question.

Jon: I can't honestly answer it, and that makes me feel shitty. That's the one thing that makes me feel—the real part that I criticize myself on is, "What would I have done if I actually had known?"

Howard: Yeah, I'm with you on that.

Jon: And my feeling is—and I'm trying to be as honest with myself as I can—I would . . . I would not have done something. I just don't think I would've. And, like, now I know John Quiñones is gonna come out with the cameras and be like, "You're a dick. You're never making my show." But I feel like I wouldn't have felt the urgency of it. Now, on the flip side of that, if they're gonna be rabbinical about it and look at it the other way, I'm an individual that—I still believe in my own decency. The Internet doesn't know who I am, and it doesn't shape the foundation of thinking I'm a decent person. I am fallible as fuck and make mistakes. But I can grow. I'm the type of person, hopefully, that can be helpful. I think I can still learn and still change behavior. It may take time, you know—

Howard: I think that's very fair. And *you* didn't do anything wrong.

Jon: I didn't do anything wrong explicitly. But I'm part of a system that does treat people poorly.

Howard: Right. But here's the thing. This is what I'm talking about: why you probably are enjoying not doing *The Daily Show* every day.

Jon: Completely.

Howard: You're a thoughtful guy. I know you to be—I don't know you super well, but I know you to be a decent guy. And it's gotta be fatiguing where everyone is saying, "Oh, Jon's a piece of shit." This has become so goddamn toxic. I'm talking about Twitter and the constant fucking, like, "I got you!"

Jon: Exactly. So here's where it gets really interesting. I feel like, in some respects, I *started* that. So now I'm being slightly hoisted on my own petard, because when I was doing the comedy—now, I would say we were very careful about context and we tried to layer our arguments fairly and smartly. But the Internet utilized that as *eviscerate*. Where we would think, you know, "Poke fun at this," it became "He eviscerated" or "He destroyed." So you became weaponized.

Howard: So here's something you did, *The Daily Show*, and now even you're

viewing it like, "Oh, I'm to blame." This was a great thing you did. You had a great accomplishment. It's so goddamn annoying and fatiguing—

Jon: But who am I to enjoy life?

Howard: Right. Have you talked to Letterman about retirement?

Jon: No.

Howard: Because you were able to walk away from a big show. A highly rated and highly respected and funny show. And you had the whole machine working for you. I admire that—walking away. I don't know . . . One day I guess I have to walk away from this, but—

Jon: But you found a balance.

Howard: Yeah.

Jon: First of all, you're in a different place in your life. Once your children are grown, it's a whole thing. So I have kids that are thirteen and eleven. And I was missing that. I saw them at crying times. You know, putting them to bed and just before school. I was so preoccupied when I was doing the show. It was all the time, and all day. I would go in, we'd sit—we had this very insular world where we would knock around these ideas. We would do that, and I'd get home at nine o'clock at night, and that was my whole life.

Howard: You know, when I think back on my life . . . My kids will always say to me, "Dad, you were *always* working." I didn't know how to function any other way. I had to make a living. I wanted to support the family.

Jon: What is your relationship like now with the kids? 'Cause you have the dual thing: you were working real hard, and also there's a divorce.

Howard: The divorce. Well, I've worked really hard on myself to be the best dad I could be. Which is not to say I'm the best dad. But I've really tried my best to be connected and communicate with them. And I gotta say, I feel like I'm in a really good place. I've had to sit and figure out: How can I make a relationship with my kids without my wife? In other words, so many guys depend on their wives to sort of, like, "Oh, Dad's busy working. Don't worry about it." They make all the excuses and they say, "Dad loves you."

Jon: Right.

Howard: When you're divorced, you either can check out—which is what your dad did—or you can say, "How do I make a relationship with the kids that's authentic and real?" Even while continuing working. And it's been really great. I feel closer to my kids than ever.

Jon: Will they ever raise with you frustrations, complaints that go down deep about that [the marriage] broke up, or that you weren't there?

Howard: Yes. All the time.

Jon: How old were they when that happened?

Howard: It started when they were young. You know, they really kind of sat me down and gave it to me. They didn't like the idea of divorce. They were miserable about it. But even now, we've done work in our relationships pertaining to that divorce—why it happened, how it affected our relationship. We talk about it all the time. I think it's the healthiest thing in the world. And I've learned not to be threatened by it. I used to get very—like what you said in the beginning. The defensiveness.

Jon: Yeah.

Howard: At first I'd be like, "You don't understand the reason, blah-blah-blah." And then I finally learned to shut the fuck up. Because this is how they feel. And why can't they express it? And why do I have to be threatened by it?

Jon: My relationship with my father ended not because of the divorce, but because of his behavior. I wouldn't even say in the immediate aftermath of the divorce, but down the road. And the problem happened because, as your relationship atrophies— as it can do in a divorce, especially with someone who was not available—you no longer have a strong enough foundation to weather bad behavior.

Howard: Right.

Jon: And so that's his inability. 'Cause I did get to a point where I understood marriages don't work sometimes. People fall out of love. But what I don't understand is what you just said, which is: "Why wouldn't you at least put in some work, for yourself, to help get in touch with some of the feelings that I might be having?"

Howard: If your father had been a strong

enough man, he would have been able to go somewhere, get some help and say, "Listen, I gotta figure out how to communicate with my son, how to make a relationship with him." And it is the most difficult thing in the world, to do that work. I'm actually moved when I talk about it, because I know how hard it is. I always say to guys who get divorced, "Get yourself into therapy." Like, with a really good therapist. Because you gotta learn how to connect.

Jon: Well, he had a good therapist. It was a Slivovitz—it's a brandy.

Howard: Your dad died in 2013?

Jon: Yeah.

Howard: Did you guys have a reconciliation of any kind?

Jon: No.

Howard: No.

Jon: It was very interesting. My father has never met my children.

Robin: Oh boy.

Howard: Jesus.

Jon: And now my kids are around the age that I was when my parents split up.

Howard: Did you go to his funeral?

Jon: I did go to his funeral. And I'll tell you . . . this is hard to talk about. . . . He was a depressed guy. I know now that in his family there's some mental illness. And he would drink. But when they got divorced, I was glad that he didn't live there anymore, because it was violent and it was terrible. And we went through a period where he lost his money. He'd been working as a scientist at RCA, and he hated it. He was a guy who

> **" I WAS SO PREOCCUPIED WHEN I WAS DOING THE SHOW. IT WAS ALL THE TIME, AND ALL DAY. . . . THAT WAS MY WHOLE LIFE.**

always did the right thing. You know, he was in the army, in Korea.

Howard: An accomplished guy.

Jon: An accomplished guy. But not as accomplished as he wanted to be, or as he thought he was. So there was a strange combination of arrogance and insecurity. They split up when I was very young, and he and I just never really connected. He connected a little better with my brother, because my brother is a smarter guy. They're both sort of brilliant in an analytical way.

Howard: Were you left with the feeling of "Why did he even have kids?" Like, "What was his thought process there?"

Jon: It's not that I was left with the feeling of "Why did he have kids?" It's that, "Why doesn't he like us more?" And now that I have children, it actually made me angrier. So what happened was, we don't have much of a relationship. Now I'm seventeen years old. Basically, it's been seven years. I had a grandmother who used to live in Brooklyn. He calls me up—it's about two weeks before I leave for college—and he goes, "Come with me. I need some help moving some of Grandma's stuff out of the house." Now, we have a relationship at this point. Basically

I see him once a month. Maybe a little bit less. He's closer to my brother. We don't really talk. We're in the car, and he says to me, "You know, I haven't been with your mother a long time. What do you think about if I got remarried?" And I'm like, "I don't care. Do whatever you want." "What do you think if I end up starting another family?" "Okay." "Um, I got married and I have a two-year-old."

Howard: Oh my God.

Jon: So I go, "Are you fucking kidding me?"

Howard: "Good thing I agreed."

Jon: Good thing I agreed. So then, like a week later, I'm off to college. My next interaction with them is, I worked for a landscaper. I was cutting the lawn at the little apartment complex that they lived in. It was bananas. The whole thing was—

Howard: Did you know he lived there?

Jon: Well, I did *then*. But I didn't before. He had this sort of fake little apartment that he had in Princeton that was like a hovel.

Howard: That's where he'd see you.

Jon: And the woman that he did it to was the woman he had an affair with. So it was all very complicated. And he never could cop to that. So when I got into this business, he was never supportive. He would just feed me a ton of shit. Always passive-aggressive. "When are you gonna get a real job?" I remember when I got *Letterman*, and he was like, "I thought they used experienced

people?" A lot of that shit. And it just sort of atrophied. Then one night, I can remember, it was after my grandfather died. I was very close to my grandfather. My mother's father. A couple days after that, he calls me up, and I'm thinking it's about that. And he's in a nostalgic mood. But I can tell he's drunk. And he goes, "I've been thinking about when you were born." So for me—

Howard: That's big.

Jon: It's big. He doesn't acknowledge any of the joy we may have had as a family. And I'm like, "So tell me about that." He goes, "Your mother was so bourgeois." I go, "What?" "She had to go to Doctors Hospital." Doctors Hospital no longer exists, but was in the Seventies on the East Side of Manhattan, and they lived in Washington Heights at that point. Or it might have been the Bronx. "She had to go to Doctors Hospital. She had to have that status."

Howard: So his memory was, "Your mother was such a pain in the ass."

Jon: Such a pain in the ass that we had to go to Doctors Hospital. "And I remember, on the day you were born, coming to the hospital, and you know who came out of the elevators?" I go, "What?" And he goes, "Gypsies. A Gypsy family." I'm like, "What?" And he's like, "Ha-ha, how 'bout that? You and your bourgeois. Guess who's in your hospital?"

Howard: Oh boy.

Jon: So that was the day that I decided, "This is over. That's it. We're done."

I REMEMBER THINKING, "THIS POOR MAN." I DIDN'T FEEL LIKE, "MY POOR FATHER." I FELT LIKE, "THIS . . . THIS POOR MAN. I'M SAD FOR THIS MAN—THAT THIS IS HOW IT ENDS."

Howard: What happened when you got really big? You'd think he would have tried to, like, weasel his way into his successful son's life.

Jon: Nah.

Howard: That couldn't even win him over.

Jon: There were moments. And by the way, if you talked to him, he'd be like, "I'm so proud. I was the proudest."

Howard: It's all bullshit.

Jon: He couldn't say it to me. When I went to visit him when he had dementia . . . because I wanted to be able to say to him, at least before he died—I don't know if he could hear anything—like, "I'm okay. I don't blame you, and I'm okay. I found joy and I found love and I found a family, and I'm okay." I remember my brother and I went, and we're sitting with his wife, who he's still married to. He had two kids. They're lovely enough people, but I don't have a relationship with them. I was watching him—they were feeding him, and he was out of it—and I remember thinking, "This poor man." I didn't feel like, "My poor father." I felt like, "This . . . this poor man. I'm sad for this man—that this is how it ends."

Howard: You know what's sad? Look what he missed out on. Having a son like you.

Jon: Not even having a son like me. 'Cause I was a pain in the ass. I had my problems. But what he missed out on was the unconditional love that you have for your family.

Howard: Do you think your whole drive to get famous or to be successful was to say "Fuck you"?

Jon: No. I think I wanted to do something I was passionate about. In terms of my drive, it came from my mother. 'Cause what happened was, she's a teacher, we don't have much money, and now he's gone. Now she's got two kids. And no money. She taught special ed at an elementary school. Or the gifted program. I just remember her students, they were in the garage. Like, she wasn't in the regular classroom. And she picked herself up by the bootstraps. At the time it was hard, 'cause she was gone a lot. So you were home alone a lot. Sometimes you would sleep in the house alone, 'cause she was working. But she did it. I don't even know how she did it. But she did it. She worked her ass off, and she did what she had to do, and she made sure that my brother and I were always taken care of. She was remarkable.

Howard: Is she the one who tells you you're funny?

Jon: She's the one who mostly tells me my sweaters look raggedy. And that the beard makes me look old.

Howard: Who told you you could be funny and make a living out of it?

Jon: My friends. They didn't tell me I could make a living, but my friends were the ones that I entertained. I didn't even consider something like that.

Howard: How old were you when you did stand-up for the first time?

Jon: I was probably twenty-three or twenty-four.

Howard: Were you good the first time you went up?

Jon: No.

Howard: Horrible?

Jon: Horrible. The Bitter End on Bleecker Street. My first joke? The punch line of my first joke—

Howard: I know it.

Jon: No, you don't.

Howard: If I know it, would that impress you?

Jon: That would impress me.

Howard: "Yid-lock."

Jon: Oh my God. That's *nuts*. That's nuts.

Howard: Tell the joke. This is your first joke.

Jon: First joke ever. "So I go down to the Diamond District in New York. And, you know, I'm just looking to be around my people, to absorb some of the

atmosphere. Plus, I like seeing men in hats. Just something I like. All of a sudden, lunchtime. Twelve-thirty, one. And all the doors to all the diamond stores open at once. And all the Hasidim rush out into the middle of the street to find their way to where they're going to eat lunch. And then suddenly, the whole thing comes to a complete, screeching halt. Yid-lock."

Howard: Big joke.

Jon: As you can imagine. Man, I would chew on that premise. I would paint this whole picture.

Howard: Make the buildup.

Jon: And then I would hit 'em with "Yid-lock." Every now and again, somebody would be like, "Oh, it's like *gridlock*."

Howard: "Oh yeah, we get it."

Jon: "Ohhh, that's interesting."

Howard: How many years does it take before you get good? Where people say, "Hey, that guy's pretty funny"?

Jon: That's hard, because you can get people to say that without being good.

Howard: But when did *you* start feeling good?

Jon: I started feeling good—what time is it? Probably around—

Howard: Ten minutes ago?

Jon: Yeah, it was probably about fifteen minutes ago.

Howard: I don't think you're kidding. 'Cause isn't it, like—

Jon: You never feel good.

> **IF YOU ASKED ME WHAT MADE ME FEEL THE BEST ABOUT SHOW BUSINESS, HONEST TO GOD, IT'S THAT I DID IT. IT'S THAT I MOVED. IT'S THAT I MUSTERED UP ENOUGH ENERGY TO PACK ALL MY SHIT INTO A U-HAUL, WITH NO JOB, AND DROVE TO NEW YORK. I HAD A SIX-WEEK SUBLET, AND I DID IT.**

Howard: When I hear our radio show, I go, "Ugh. It's horrible."

Jon: Do you know what I think it is? Here's what I feel good about. If you asked me what made me feel the best about show business, honest to God, it's that I did it. It's that I moved. It's that I mustered up enough energy to pack all my shit into a U-Haul, with no job, and drove to New York. I had a six-week sublet, and I did it.

Howard: The climb. The fact that you were successful and you worked at it and you constantly kept going and pushing yourself.

Jon: Yes. I can remember some nights . . . I was working at this place called Panchito's on Macdougal, doing the day bartending at a Mexican restaurant—which is truly the worst job. All you do all day is cut limes and make margarita mix for the night guy, who's gonna clean the fuck up and you're gonna walk out with a two-dollar tip-out. Then at night I would go to the Comedy Cellar. Back then, it wasn't what it is today. It was still a basement in the Village. The show would start at eight, and it would just roll all night. It was never packed, except on the weekends. And Manny Dworman, who ran the club, and Estee, who books it, put me on as the last guy. Every night. From Sunday through Thursday. Two o'clock in the morning.

Howard: That's the worst slot, I guess.

Jon: It's the slot that they give someone that for some reason they think, "Let's just see what happens to this guy. Let's just see what he uses this for." And so you develop your act for a jaundiced waitstaff and, like, drunk Dutch people who wandered in and actually thought there was gonna be music.

Howard: Right. Tough crowd.

Jon: But you learned how to be . . . yourself. And once you learn how to be yourself, *that's* when it opens up. You learn how to channel what you actually care about. And what you actually think about it. You find your voice.

Howard: That's true in radio.

Jon: Do you remember at what point in radio? 'Cause there was stuff for you too. You had this outsize personality.

Howard: You're right. There is a pressure, at least that I felt, that I had to be the most outrageous, that I had to have every single listener listening to me—which is an impossible, unrealistic, magical sort of fucking craziness. That somehow I can pull that off. So there was no time for anyone else. I just had to be fucking crazy.

Jon: But you did it.

Howard: Yeah.

Jon: But if you had done that in this environment, you would've stepped out over something. You would have burned out faster. I always felt like the turning point for you was the movie and book.

That's when I think you introspected in your career, and allowed us to see into it. And gave us a little bit of humanity. See, I feel like now you're doing your best Howard. I feel like this was you. The other stuff was performative. I'm gonna say this, and people don't know: you're a lovely man.

Howard: Thank you. I feel the same way about you.

Jon: Thank you, sir.

Howard: And we should end it.

Jon: Let's end it.

And Now a Word from Our President...

AUGUST 25, 2015

(1 year, 2 months, and 14 days until the election)

Howard: Mr. Trump.

Donald: Howard.

Howard: Can you believe how popular you are?

Donald: It's been crazy. Just this minute, a public policy polling came out in New Hampshire, and I'm 35 percent. And second place is 11. I'm sure it's only because over the years I've done your show.

Howard: You could actually be the president. This is starting to look like a reality.

Donald: Well, I'll tell you what, the country is doing very poorly, and we can make the country do well. One just came out in South Carolina where I'm in the mid-thirties.

Howard: You didn't expect this, did you? I mean, seriously. This big, this fast?

Donald: The intensity, the speed—a lot of things have happened. I'm very honored by it, to be honest with you.

Howard: Do you *really* want to be president? Because I look at your life, especially at what's going on at Mar-a-Lago. The White House is a horrible place to live compared to your Mar-a-Lago. Seriously.

Donald: Don't forget, Robin, Howard's been saying this to me for two years.

Robin: I know.

Donald: And you know what I want to do? I want to do a good job. There are so many things that can be straightened out so quickly. You talk about China, and how they've been ripping us off, and now they're taking us down with all the things they've done, and I can solve it. That's what I'm really good at. You understand. I can solve those problems.

Howard: And Melania will be the hottest first lady ever in the White House. Ever.

Donald: Well, she'll be a great first lady. She is a terrific person, as you know. You know, I'm having a lot of fun. I'm going to Iowa—

Howard: Have you given any thought to a vice president?

Donald: You know, I like to do one thing at a time. First thing I want to do is win, then I'll worry about it. There are a lot of good people around.

Howard: I was thinking, you might have to choose one of these guys like a [Marco] Rubio—someone you're not high on.

Donald: Well, some of them I respect. I don't respect everybody, but some of them I respect. Some of them are worthy, and some aren't. And there are a lot of good people around, frankly. And the vice president is actually a very important position. It's always been an underrated position.

Robin: Well, there are a lot of positions that need to be filled.

Donald: A lot. A lot.

Howard: I mean, the whole reason I'm bothering you was the whole Megyn Kelly thing, and where she is on a scale of one to ten, but I see you don't want to answer that.

Donald: Well, in the old days I wouldn't have minded answering that question, but today I think I'll pass.

Howard: Yeah, because now you're going to be president.

Donald: Today I'll take a pass. See, Robin, you learn with age. You become wise. You know it's fine, it's fine. And Fox has been fine. Roger Ailes is an amazing guy. They've been very fair.

Howard: What about me being a Supreme Court justice? Any thoughts about that? I mean, I am a judge on TV.

Donald: You would be—first of all, who knows Howard better than me, right? People don't know the real Howard, and people ask me what he's like. And, Howard, I'm going to ruin your reputation, in a very positive way.

Howard: Go ahead.

Donald: Howard is a much different person than people understand. He's the warmest, nicest guy. You deal with him in person, and you

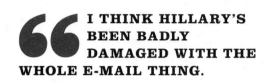

I THINK HILLARY'S BEEN BADLY DAMAGED WITH THE WHOLE E-MAIL THING.

leave and say, "What a nice guy." Then you hear him on the radio and think, "He's a total maniac." But Howard's the best guy in the world. He's a great guy.

Howard: But here's the one thing I want. If you really do pull this off, I want to go to Camp David. This is what you ought to do. You ought to open it up, so people can see what's going on there. There'd be a revolution, 'cause I think they've got something going on there, where all these guys check out. They get lazy.

Donald: You know what happens, Howard? These people go to Washington, and they become different people. They run, and they're going to do this, and they're going to do that. They're going to do everything. Then they get there, and they do nothing. I cannot let that happen to me.

Howard: Are you afraid of Joe Biden?

Donald: No. I think Joe Biden would be fun to run against, frankly.

Howard: Who would you rather run against? Hillary or Joe?

Donald: Well, I think it's irrelevant. I think Hillary's been badly damaged with the whole e-mail thing.

Howard: You think she's done.

Donald: I don't know. I've been saying General Petraeus did much less than her, and they destroyed his life. And she's done much more, far more. I mean, she wiped out a server after she got a subpoena from Congress. How much worse can you be than that? The documents were very classified, and it seems to me she has a lot of problems. Now, the only hope it seems to me is that the Democrats are running things now, so she won't get prosecuted. That's her only hope.

Howard: What are you going to do day one? Let's say you pull this off and become president. Day one, what do you do?

Donald: Hey, Howard, I have one big call coming in. Can I call you back?

Howard: Go ahead. Do your thing.

Donald: You know what I'm going to do as president? I'm going to do a great job. There's so many things we're going to do, we're going to do a great job. That I can tell you.

Howard: Talk to you later.

Donald: You're the best. Thanks, Howard.

David Letterman

AUGUST 16, 2017

Before I talk about David Letterman, I need to talk about my cat Leon. There is an important connection between the two.

Beth and I have fostered over eight hundred rescue cats since we were married in 2008. It has turned into her life's passion. She is busy with this twenty-four hours a day. If she isn't dishing out food or cleaning litter boxes, she is monitoring her Instagram account, which she uses to find homes for the cats. Sometimes we have as many as twenty-five foster cats in our house—everything from one-eyed cats to three-legged cats. Once in a while we will take one on permanently. Usually these are the most hard-luck cases. The first one was named Apple. She had some strange skin condition where she had lost all her fur. Fortunately, Beth managed to nurse her back to health and she regrew her coat. It was amazing. The vet said it was unlikely that Apple's fur would return.

Another cat we adopted was Leon. He was an eighteen-pound black Maine coon. We got him in 2010 from an animal shelter in Alabama that had been destroyed by a tornado. The North Shore Animal League America had gone down there to save as many animals as they could. Incredibly, Leon was the only survivor from that particular shelter. He had a bad infection, and it looked like he wasn't going to make it. Beth promised Leon that if he pulled through, she'd bring him home to live with us. Leon quickly recovered.

I knew nothing of their agreement. The first time I heard about Leon was when Beth showed up with him at the house. At that time, he didn't have a name. Coming up with names for the cats is always my job. For the ones Beth puts on Instagram, I try to come up with the cutest names possible to increase their chances of getting adopted, like Bella or JoJo or Pumpkin. I chose Leon just because I thought that was a funny name for a cat. That eventually morphed into Leon Bear, because he was the size of one.

I wanted nothing to do with Leon at first. Because I'm such a germophobe, all I could think about was that he had been sick in a tornado and could potentially infect me with whatever life-threatening bacteria remained in his system. That's my OCD kicking in big-time. It's also my way of protecting myself and not acknowledging my need to come in close.

I have always struggled with feeling emotional attachment to others. It's one of the most recurring topics I talk about in therapy. For much of my life, my attitude had been, "I don't need anyone. Screw 'em." That was my defense mechanism. It ensured I never got hurt or had to endure that powerless feeling of falling off a cliff that comes with caring deeply for another human being. It also ensured I didn't get close to many people. Even with Beth and my daughters—the people I loved most in the world—I could often be distant. I was so petrified of losing them that I would shut myself off. I would pull away. It was hard. Being afraid to love is a very sad lot in life.

My standoffishness didn't deter Leon. He followed me around everywhere. When I would be in my office painting or working on jokes for the radio show or even writing this book, he would sit on the couch and stare at me for hours. My sidekick annoyed me. He was the Garfunkel to my Simon. I wanted my space.

Then after a while he started to grow on me. I started calling him "My good boy." I would take a break from whatever I was doing and go sit on the couch next to him. I would have conversations with him. He would climb into my lap and start to purr. He got so excited to have me near him. I started to get excited too. I also started to get scared. Sometimes I couldn't handle how close I was getting to him. I would say, "Enough, Leon," and shoo him out of the office. That feeling of attachment was very uncomfortable for me. It was too much. It made me think of the old song "You Made Me Love You (I Didn't Want to Do It)."

Time kept passing, and our bond got stronger. We developed a nightly ritual. Leon would hop onto our bed—or as he got older I'd pick him up—and we would lay there watching TV while waiting for Beth to finish her nightly rounds with the other cats. Leon would curl up in the same spot on top of the sheet, turn his head toward the TV, and become engrossed in whatever was on the screen. He liked all the same shows I did, even *The Bachelor*. Leon wasn't afraid to show his feminine side.

Every night Beth would come into the bedroom and find us laying there and start laughing. She was so tickled by the sight of us. Beth has always known how hard it is for me to let my guard down. She was laughing because she was shocked that somehow, someway Leon had wormed his way into my life. I think she was proud of me. This was a huge breakthrough.

We had Leon for eight years. We were never sure how old he was. This past September, the vet found a large tumor. We had to get it removed or else Leon would die. The surgery was routine, we were told, and he was expected to come through it fine. I had this strange feeling. A few days before he went to the hospital, I had a long talk with him. I said, "Leon, you're going in for an operation. I can't lose you. You've been with me through thick and thin. Don't worry, you're going to be all right. We're going to be spending a lot more time together." But deep in my mind I knew this could be it.

Sadly, he died on the operating table. The tumor was even bigger than they thought, and he lost too much blood during the procedure. I was devastated. So was Beth. We sat in my office and cried. My life felt so empty without Leon sitting there on the couch next to me. I wrote a five-page love letter listing everything I cherished about him. I didn't want to forget a single detail of our time together. Little things, like how Leon only ate dry food and hated when I scratched his side. It was my way of paying tribute to him. I'm not sure when I'll be able to go back and read it. The pain is still too raw.

We had Leon cremated, and we put the small box containing his remains in a large Chinese vase in our bedroom. In that vase we keep the remains of our dog Bianca and all our resident cats who have passed away: Apple, Charlie, Sophia, and now Leon. Inside Leon's box is also his collar with contact information in case he ever got out of the house. "My name is Leon Bear Stern," it read. "Here is my phone number in case I am lost." I was the one who had been lost—lost until I found Leon.

There was a time when I would have been embarrassed to admit all of this. I would have never shared these feelings. Or if I did I would make some self-deprecating joke about it. Even now I'm tempted to do that—to say how lame or what a loser I am for feeling this way about a cat. I won't do that. I owe that to Leon. All my years of therapy have helped me be more vulnerable, but Leon was the secret ingredient. By opening myself up to him, I opened myself up to other people.

Which brings us to David Letterman.

For many years, I could never truly appreciate Dave. I could never admit how much I admired him, how close I felt to him, and how important he was to me. There has always been a special connection between us, going through similar phases of our lives at the same time. We both worked for NBC in New York in the eighties, creating loyal audiences. We both struggled with difficult management situations. We worked tirelessly throughout the next couple of decades, and our personal lives saw big changes: Dave having his first child at age fifty-six and me remarrying at fifty-four. By the 2000s and entering this decade we were both eager for a change. For Dave, that meant leaving his show. For me, that meant reinventing mine.

He had been a guest on my show a few times. He would come on to repay me for being on his show, which of course made me feel as if he was appearing solely out of obligation. It was always a little awkward. I was acting like a crazy person, Dave wasn't exactly thrilled to be in the studio, and the discussion just ended up being silly.

This interview was the first time that Dave without question wanted to be there. I was leaving the SiriusXM building one day, and he was standing in the lobby. He'd come by on some business of his own. We spotted each other, and he said he would like to do the show. I was ecstatic over the possibility. I thought, "I hope Dave isn't just saying that. Please let it be real. Please give me the chance to do this interview and finally show the respect and admiration I have for him."

I did even more preparation than I usually do. I kept a document open on my computer at all times so I could quickly write new questions. I would wake up in the middle of the night and jot down fifteen topics I wanted to raise with Dave. Between that and all my trips to the bathroom to address my enlarged prostate, I wasn't getting any sleep. Of course, there is always the risk of overpreparing. You don't want the interview to simply be a list of questions. However, I had to get this right. It felt important. I felt like this was my opportunity to get Dave on the record once and for all. This was an interview my audience had been waiting for as long as I had. I didn't want to leave anything out.

All my preparation paid off. I felt relaxed and easy, and we covered a lot of ground, including Dave's regrets about his show. He said he wished he could start the show over now because of how much he has changed and matured as a person. I can certainly relate to that. Robin Williams, Eminem, Carly Simon—I wish I could go back and do those interviews again. I wish I could get in a time machine and fix it. I wonder if that's why Dave wanted to come on. He understood that desire and remorse better than anyone, and if he couldn't get a do-over then at least he could give me the opportunity. We have both seen a lot of life, and we have both done a lot of reflecting. I think that comes through in this interview. It's one I can look at and see how far I've come, both professionally and personally.

Just like when I wrote that love letter to Leon, this is my love letter to Dave. I want him to know how much I care about him, and how grateful I am to have known him.

EVERYTHING WAS ALL RIGHT UNTIL I HAD A BIRTHDAY. . . . BECAUSE AT SEVENTY WHAT I'VE LEARNED IS OLD PEOPLE DROP DEAD.

Howard: When I look at you, I see a man who looks relaxed and younger. I fantasize that if I retired, I would have this youthful look. Now that you are retired—even though you're coming out of retirement—are you more relaxed and refreshed?

David: "Relaxed and refreshed"—both of which would need to be substantiated medically.

Howard: But how do you feel? Don't you feel this sense of, "I've accomplished everything I needed to accomplish"?

David: No. That's a myth.

Howard: Is it?

David: For me, it's a myth. Here's the thing: everything was all right until I had a birthday. I felt right up until my birthday. I felt relaxed and refreshed.

Howard: Right.

David: And then I had my birthday.

Howard: How long ago was this?

David: April.

Howard: Okay.

David: Seventy.

Howard: Wow.

David: Yeah. Wow. Exactly. So then I stopped feeling so relaxed and refreshed, because at seventy what I've learned is old people drop dead.

Howard: Can you still run? You're a big runner. Can you still run at seventy?

David: Yes.

Howard: Can you still go to the gym and work out? I find everything now hurts me for too long. There's no recovery.

David: You're right about that. But on my seventieth birthday, I ran ten miles.

Howard: Oh, no kidding?

David: Yeah, I've not finished yet, but— [*collective laughter*] by the way, I'm very happy to see you. When I left the show, I thought a lot of people will want me on shows. And no one wanted me on shows.

Howard: Is that really true? Jimmy Kimmel idolizes you.

David: Jimmy Kimmel has been very nice to me when I was on his show, and I'm going to be on it again in October. Unless, of course, I drop dead.

Howard: In all seriousness, is that one of your biggest fears? Your dad died young, right?

David: Yeah. Fifty-seven.

Howard: And had his first heart attack when he was thirty?

David: In his thirties, yeah.

Howard: And your dad—I didn't know this—was a florist, but he had fantasies of becoming a writer.

David: Right. I don't know if I told you

about it, but they used to, in the Sunday supplement in certain newspapers, you'd get *Parade* magazine. And you could take the Famous Writers test. They had an advertisement. You'd fill out the thing. They sent you a booklet to see if you were good enough to be a writer. My poor father sent off for the Famous Writers test booklet to see if he had what it takes to be a writer. And, lo and behold, turns out he had what it takes to be a writer, but couldn't afford the follow-up lessons to become a certified writer.

Howard: And as a kid, when you saw that, was it heartbreaking to you?

David: It's more heartbreaking now, as I think about it. Because at the time you just think, "Oh, that's what dads do," or "This is what my dad's doing."

Howard: Right. By the way, I'm sorry to hear about the death of your mother recently.

David: Ninety-six. She was going to be ninety-six. Died playing racquetball.

Howard: Is that true?

David: No.

Howard: But I would think maybe one of your sadnesses was your dad. Did your dad get to see your great success?

David: No.

Howard: Do you ever fantasize that he could have seen what became of you?

David: My mom lived so long that we once said, "Mom, you're not going to get the record." But she was such a fixture in my life. My father, conversely, was not, and I

always wondered what life would have been like the other way around: my mother sadly passed away at fifty-seven and my dad lived till he was ninety-six, or if they'd stayed together and been alive all those years. I wonder what that would have been. Your parents still alive?

Howard: Still alive.

David: What are their ages?

Howard: My father is ninety-four, my mother is eighty-nine.

David: Holy moly. And that's great, right?

Howard: Yeah, it's great to see. But it's also—because they have such a symbiotic relationship, I'm really worried if one of them gets ill, the other one is going to fall apart.

David: That's kind of the stereotype, isn't it?

Howard: Was your mom lonely?

David: No, I don't think she was lonely. Nothing killed her except the fact that she was ninety-six. She luckily did not have heart disease, did not have cancer, did not break a hip. She was not active but she could go out. She still liked to read. Some cognitive diminishment, but she was okay for ninety-six.

Howard: So it was kind of shocking in a way 'cause she was okay.

David: No, she wasn't one of those ninety-six-year-olds who are like, "I am ninety-six and I'm having the best sex of my life!" It wasn't one of those.

Howard: It's like my mom says, "Getting old isn't for wimps."

David: Yeah, that's what my mom would say too.

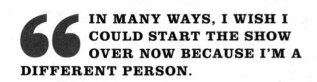

IN MANY WAYS, I WISH I COULD START THE SHOW OVER NOW BECAUSE I'M A DIFFERENT PERSON.

Howard: I know you loved Warren Zevon. He was a guest on the show. The man was dying.

David: Right.

Howard: And you have him on. It was amazing. The guy was making jokes about dying.

David: Yeah, it was very awkward.

Howard: You almost didn't know what to say. You were speechless about it. But you loved Warren Zevon, right?

David: I really did. I liked his lyrics. I thought it was rock-and-roll music in a different direction because the lyrics were literary, an allusion almost, and stories other people were not writing music about.

Howard: Do you have a love of music? I can never tell with you, because one time I was doing your show and you leaned into me. There was somebody—a musician—and you said something like, "Look at this guy." Like, almost with—

David: Disdain?

Howard: Yeah, disdain.

David: I was probably trying to impress you with being disdainful of life.

Howard: I wanted to say, "Look at me. I'm a mess. I can't laugh at that guy."

David: Well, you know, I'm a different person now. And you're a different person than you were then, I think.

Howard: Oh yeah. You know what I tried? Knowing you were coming in, I tried to go back and look at a lot of moments from the show.

David: Oh God.

Howard: I started looking at all the different episodes.

David: They're awful.

Howard: No, they're not. Mine were awful. I cringe when I see myself on your show. I go, "How the fuck did I do this show and make such an asshole out of myself?" I just cringe when I see it. One episode I kind of was able to watch for a little bit was when I came on dressed as a woman. I remember you were concerned. You were like, "What, I'm gonna interview Howard as some sort of character?" And I go, "No, I'll be Howard, but I just want to wear women's clothing." And it worked out just fine, in my mind at least. But the guy that I was most impressed with on your show was Chris Farley. He was absolutely delightful with you. There were certain people who vibed with you. Were you thrilled by Chris Farley?

David: Yeah, I don't know. In those days—that was back in NBC—I had so many other things on my mind that I don't know if I appreciated Chris Farley in a way that I would now. In many ways, I wish I could start the show over now because I'm a different person. I'm mature. I have a better understanding of the world around me and of the interaction with humans.

Howard: Is that why you can't watch the old shows? Because you look at the old you and go, "Jeez, I want to teach this guy something."

David: Perhaps that's one reason. But it isn't just that. I can't look through my high school yearbook. I can't look at the pictures of me when I was a kid.

Howard: Somebody the other night had a little game we were playing with the dice and they ask you questions—if you have any regrets.

David: Oh God.

Howard: And I went, "Oh, fuck." I said this is the only thing I want to admit: I did an interview once with Robin Williams a hundred years ago. And Will Ferrell. And I was such an asshole to these guys that a week before Robin Williams died, I said, "I want to call him and apologize to him 'cause I was such a fucking moron." I loved Robin Williams. And then, of course, what happened. There's a couple people I really feel this way about, and when I was watching your old clips—

David: Why would you watch the old clips?

Howard: Of you?

David: Yeah.

Howard: Because I want to remind myself of why I love you so much.

David: Oh, please.

Howard: You are such an innovator for late night. I just told the audience this this morning. Carson was doing it—and, yes, I know you worshipped him, but when he was doing it, it was feeling old. And you came in and something new happened. It was suddenly hip and cool.

David: For about three years.

Howard: No, it was very hip and cool. Like when Madonna would come on and curse. And she cursed, like, fourteen times. At the time, are you thinking, "This is the shittiest show ever, she's ruining this interview"? Or are you recognizing that this is going to be something they play over and over again for the rest of your career?

David: Sometimes. Again, I'm a completely different person now, and I would be so much better equipped to view the immediate surroundings of that show now than I was when Madonna was on. We used to have a guy on who was a cartoonist out of Cleveland. Very, very funny guy.

Howard: You're talking about Harvey Pekar?

David: Yeah, Harvey Pekar. He was great. He was tremendous. He would just go after stuff. He would whine. He would go after me. He would go after the network. He would go after everything in a very committed way. It wasn't a gag. It wasn't an act. He would really go to work on you.

Howard: He meant every word of what he was saying.

David: He was antiestablishment in a way you don't see guys like that anymore. And that used to really upset me, because I just thought, "Come on, Harvey, don't do this to us. Just play the game, blah-blah-blah-blah." Now I wish I could have had Harvey on every night, because that was tremendous.

Howard: Right. And it was something original. This kid, the actor—the one who put his foot in your face. You know who I'm talking about?

David: Joaquin Phoenix?

Howard: Not Joaquin Phoenix. I can't think of the guy's name.

David: Crispin Glover.

Howard: Yes, he came on and he was frantic. He was nuts. And then he did, like, a karate thing.

David: And he kicked me in the face.

Howard: You walked off the show. I believe you were genuinely nervous that this guy was going to actually go berserk.

David: That's right.

Howard: Now when you look at that, do you see that as great television, or do you still say there is something completely unhinged about this thing?

David: Again, now, yeah. You pray for something like that. But at the time, it was my career. I was so self-absorbed, needlessly self-absorbed. Because I'm following Johnny Carson. I don't know what's going to happen. There's a million guys lined up to take my job every night. It was life and death. And so I was just a dope.

Howard: Do you think you were insecure?

David: Oh God. In show business you think—'cause I had already blown one shot, the morning show—you think, "Okay, well, you can be done."

Howard: And this was your dream, to have a talk show. And finally got it. A lot of people don't realize—we know you had that plan to go do stand-up in Los Angeles. But while you were doing stand-up, you had some TV gigs. You did game shows. You did all that traditional stuff. And that probably killed you, because your dream was to have your own talk show, right?

David: Right, exactly.

Howard: It's frustrating when you have it in your head what you want to do and you can't get it.

David: Mm-hmm. And then when you do get it, you're scared silly that somebody's going to take it away from you.

Howard: Now, this is a very honest question. When you're sitting there doing the show and, you know, Charlize Theron is on. She looks magnificent, she's beautiful, she's being engaging, and you have this conversation. Do you start to think, "Oh my God, is there something going on between us?" I've had that. Sometimes I'm let down. A guest comes in, we seem like we're really close, and then it's over. Can you get deluded into thinking you have an actual friendship with this person?

David: Yeah, it'll happen to you later on today as well.

Howard: It will! But it will! I'm gonna go, "Wow, Dave and I are very close." You know what I mean? I think it's a mindfuck.

David: It didn't happen to me much. It happened to me occasionally. And then I always thought, "Of course this person acts like they're enjoying talking to me, because this person is an actor. There's no way in heck that they could actually be fond of this experience, 'cause they're just acting."

Howard: I guess they are. But when Drew Barrymore gets up on a desk and shows you her breasts . . . like, "Maybe she's into me?"

David: See, you make a good point. You make an awfully good point. Because at the end . . . I don't want to sound, and I probably will, but for a man, if a lovely woman—let's just say it wasn't a TV show, right? Let's just say I'm a guy in an office with a desk. And it's [*knocking sound*] "Drew Barrymore's here to see you." "Ah, yes, come in." And she jumps up on your desk and takes off her top. How could you not be affected by that?✦

Howard: I would get confused by everything. For you, did any real friendships come out of the show?

David: Yes. But only after years and years and years and years and years.

Howard: Of them being on the show?

David: Right. Because I just felt like they don't want me as a friend. And I don't know that I want *them* as a friend.

Howard: That's how I felt too.

David: But you became Mister Kiwanis Club at a certain point.

Howard: What do you mean?

David: When I first knew you, you had no friends.

Howard: I had no friends. All I thought about was work.

David: Yeah, me too. The same thing. That's all I wanted to think about. I was so self-centered, and the biggest mistake I made was delaying having a family, because I just didn't want anything to interfere with the show.

Howard: I sense you're a good dad around your son. You don't make it about you. That's always a temptation around your son, to say, "Look at what I've done. Come on, son, see? I'm the great David Letterman." We do all have those temptations.

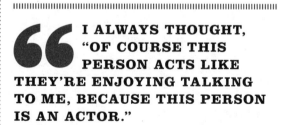

> **I ALWAYS THOUGHT, "OF COURSE THIS PERSON ACTS LIKE THEY'RE ENJOYING TALKING TO ME, BECAUSE THIS PERSON IS AN ACTOR."**

✦ **For more on this from Drew Barrymore, turn to page 548.**

THE BIGGEST MISTAKE I MADE WAS DELAYING HAVING A FAMILY.

David: Well—and you probably succumbed to this, as all parents do—I just love making him laugh. If I can genuinely make the kid spit stuff out his nose, then I feel like I'm a good dad.

Howard: I think you had kids at the right age.

David: Maybe.

Howard: I had kids when I was very young and was consumed with myself too much. And I say that to my kids in a very real way. I apologize to them.

David: How old are your kids?

Howard: My oldest daughter is thirty-four, and then I've got a thirty-one-year-old and a twenty-four-year-old.

David: That's fantastic, though. Aren't those relationships great?

Howard: They're wonderful. I love them. They're great people and they're doing wonderful things with their life. But boy oh boy, I wish I could have had some wisdom back then as a father. I wish I knew more, and I think having kids at an older age is probably better.

David: But on the other hand, I wish I had three kids. I just was so glued to the idea I've got to get this success of the show to the exclusion of everything else.

Howard: Your kids would have resented you for that attitude.

David: Who knows?

Howard: Or maybe they would have opened you up?

David: Life is life. You make it work, regardless, you know?

Ray Stern

JANUARY 12, 2000

What better way to end this book than with where I began?

I've been having my parents on the show since the very start, and they are hands-down the greatest guests in the history of radio. The reason why goes back to what I said earlier in the book about the first rule of being a successful radio personality: they both have very strong opinions. I can ask them about anything and they will give me an unfiltered response, an answer that is completely honest. If I had to teach a course on how to be a successful radio personality, that would be lesson number one: have a direct and clear point of view. Ask my mother about Johnny Carson: "I didn't like him. He was mean to his guests." Ask my father about his favorite animal: "An elephant. They live a long time, they are very high up on the food chain, and they have few natural predators." There is no hesitation. Definitive. Case closed. My parents do not mince words.

My audience loves them. Every time they appear on the show, the phone lines go crazy. They have no awareness of their genius. After my mom comes on the show, she will say to me, "Was I good? Do you think I was okay?" I'll say, "Are you kidding?" I could have done a show with my parents every day, or at least devoted an hour to them. "Let's check in on the Ben and Ray saga. . . . " Who knows how popular *Keeping Up with the Sterns* would be?

I'm not so willing to share the rest of my family with my listeners—not anymore. I used to bring my daughters on the show or have them call in. I stopped that after I began going to therapy. That was one of the first times that I said no to myself. As good as the radio was when the girls would come on, I realized that it stripped away our real relationship, and they were entitled to their anonymity. The most caring thing I could do was to keep them off the air. I suspect this was confusing for them when they were younger. I'm sure they wondered why suddenly I was no longer including them in this part of my life and if they'd done something wrong. I just thought it would be way more loving to let them have their separate identities and shine on their own. I've explained this to them now that they're grown, and I think they genuinely appreciate my decision. In fact, the main reason I started therapy was for them. Sure, I wanted to feel better and to understand why some things in my life weren't working, but my main purpose was to be able to develop a deeper connection with my kids. Similarly, while I used to have Beth on the show quite often, now she'll only come on when she has something to promote, usually related to animal rescue. Through therapy, I've learned that, tempting as it is to talk on the air about our private moments—to share stories that I know my listeners will find entertaining—in order to have a strong relationship with my wife, I have to be disciplined and keep certain special things just between the two of us. I've gotten much better at that. In my previous two books, I espoused the exact opposite approach—that to be a great radio personality you should scorch the earth looking for usable material and that every detail from your life as well as the lives of others is fair game. I now understand how wrong that is. There are some things more important than good radio.

To be perfectly honest, as loose and outrageous as the banter in the following interview is, when the microphone is turned off it is hard for me to dive deep and have an intensely emotional conversation with my mother. I have always been so concerned about her well-being. I feel protective of her. She has not had an easy life. Her mother died when she was nine years old, and she and her sister, Shirley—who was older by one year exactly, to the day—were passed around between several families. All of those situations were impoverished, as this was during the Depression. Later in life, when she was in her forties, she suffered another devastating loss with the death of Shirley. In the absence of their mother, my beautiful aunt had always filled that role. In my mind, my mother has always been like a delicate piece of china that needs to be handled with care. I'm afraid to sit down and have a conversation that might upset her.

To the listener, it might seem brave for me to talk so candidly with her about sex. You might even be jealous that you don't share this kind of looseness with your mom. This back-and-forth is easy for us. As I mentioned in the introduction to the "Sex & Relationships" section, our family always joked around about topics that were taboo. Nothing was off-limits. Brave would be forgetting the sex talk and having a deep, emotional dialogue. That is my true desire, but I'm too scared to do it—face-to-face, anyway. When I really think about it, I guess this book is a way of having that dialogue with my parents, of showing them who I am. I want them to be proud of me and what I've done in my career. I know they are, but this book is different. This is something new coming out of me, and I want to share it with them. In fact, that day a couple years ago when Simon & Schuster publisher Jonathan Karp came to my apartment and presented me with a finished book, I remember looking at it and thinking, "This is something I'd love my parents to see before they die."

My mother is now ninety-one and my father is ninety-five. When my wonderful sister, Ellen, and I get together—yes, Ellen, I did remember to put you in the book—we marvel at the fact we still have both of them. Quite frankly, watching them struggle with old age has been difficult. I'm grateful I can be there for them and hopefully make their lives a little easier. I've often given my parents a hard time on the radio for how they raised me, and sure, there are plenty of things I might have done differently as a parent, but I know they did the best they were capable of. With this book, I want to make it clear to them once and for all that I feel very lucky to have them as my parents and that I love them very much.

Howard: There's my mother on the phone. Hello, Mommy.

Ray: I wanted to wish you a happy birthday.

Robin: That's right. It's your big day.

Howard: Nineteen seventy-four. My mother was in a hospital.

Robin: Seventy-four? [*to Ray*] You're going along with that?

‟ IS THAT THE WAY I TALK? I DON'T TALK LIKE THAT, AND YOUR FATHER DOESN'T TALK THE WAY YOU PORTRAY HIM EITHER. HE MAY HAVE A LITTLE BIT OF A NEW YORK ACCENT, BUT CERTAINLY NOT THE ACCENT THAT YOU GIVE HIM.

Howard: She don't know dates. No, actually, 1954. My mother was in—where was I born? Mount Sinai?

Ray: Mount Sinai.

Howard: I didn't know that.

Ray: You don't know anything. You make up stories about everything. But they sound good.

Robin: What time was he born?

Howard: She doesn't even know.

Ray: In the evening.

Howard: These astrologers ask me what time I was born, and my mother goes [*imitates mother's voice*], "I don't know."

Ray: Is that the way I talk? I don't talk like that, and your father doesn't talk the way you portray him either. He may have a little bit of a New York accent, but certainly not the accent that you give him.

Howard: This isn't going well for a birthday greeting. Come on, let's review: 1954. It was a cold winter night. Was it snowing?

Ray: There was snow on the ground, but not snowing.

Howard: You lived in, what, Jackson Heights?

Ray: That's right.

Robin: In Queens.

Howard: You and Dad, of course, had a daughter. What was her name?

Ray: What do you mean, what was her name?

Howard: I forgot her name. For a second, I drew a blank. Ellen, right?

Ray: Right. That's right. You've got it.

Howard: You and Dad decided to have coitus.

Robin: Was he planned or was he an accident?

Howard: Did you guys regularly have sex with rubbers, and then one day Dad took his rubber off?

Ray: He was planned and he was loved.

Howard: In other words, Dad used to wear a rubber, and then he—

Ray: Pardon?

Howard: Dad used to wear a rubber when you guys had sex, I take it?

Ray: What's your business what he wore?

Howard: I want to know if I was really planned.

Ray: I called to wish you a happy birthday.

Howard: No, I'm asking you about my birth. I want to know about it. So, Dad said to you [*imitates father's voice*], "When we're going to have sex, I'm going to take off—"

Ray: How are we going to celebrate your birthday, Howard? I'm disappointed there is no party.

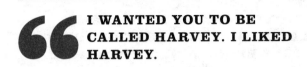

I WANTED YOU TO BE CALLED HARVEY. I LIKED HARVEY.

Robin: He could have thrown himself a party. He told everybody he didn't want parties.

Howard: But, Ma, you're the one who always said to me, "We don't celebrate birthdays. It's not a big deal."

Ray: Who said that? Whoever in this world said that?

Howard: You always told me as a kid. Once I turned, like, fourteen, "You're not going to have a birthday party anymore. You're too old."

Ray: You've got yourself a little mixed-up now.

Howard: I'm making all this up? You always told me that birthdays are all—

Ray: You had birthday parties.

Howard: You told me it was nonsense and that it was not a big deal.

Ray: I never told you it was nonsense. Never told you that.

Howard: You always said to me, "People make too big a deal out of it."

Ray: I never said that. I think it's a big deal.

Howard: Now you do. She's changed her tune over the years.

Ray: No, I haven't changed my tune.

Howard: She's trying to rewrite history. Okay, now, listen: Dad and you decided not to practice contraception and you were going to have a child.

Ray: We decided to have a baby.

Howard: Were you hoping it would be a boy?

Ray: I really thought it was a girl.

Howard: Because I wasn't hung that well. Were you planning a girl's name? What would my name have been?

Ray: I don't remember. I wanted you to be called Harvey. I liked Harvey. Dad said Howard, but I was set on Harvey and there was no phone in the hospital.

Howard: Wait, the reason you had to use an *h* is because Dad is Jewish and a lot of the people in the Jewish religion—

Ray: I'm Jewish too, right?

Howard: No, come on. Don't lie.

Robin: What? Did she convert?

Howard: Yes, she converted. She's Italian.

Ray: I converted from Judaism to Judaism.

Howard: I don't believe you. You have a thick Italian accent. No one's buying it. In other words, you had to use an *h*, so it was going to be Harvey but then Howard.

Ray: Yes, your father phoned the hospital and he told the nurse, "No Harvey."

Howard: "I'm going to take my rubber off now. I'm going to remove my rubber and make you a baby."

Ray: [*laughs*] He doesn't talk like that.

Howard: How many tries before you got pregnant? Did you get pregnant quickly with me?

Ray: No, I did not.

Howard: It took a while?

Ray: Yes.

Robin: You had to work on him.

Ray: [*laughs*] Yes.

Howard: In fact, your first attempt at having me failed. It was a miscarriage, right?

Ray: Yes.

Howard: She lost me. Thank God.

Robin: She didn't lose *you*. She lost whoever would've come before you.

Howard: After the miscarriage, you tried to have another child. You and Dad had to go at it a lot. That must have been horrible for you. I mean, to have that much sex.

Ray: We loved every minute of it.

Howard: You must have enjoyed not having to use a rubber, which is probably much better sex.

Ray: You are a love child.

Howard: I know that. I was made in love. At the time, you were a spring chicken. "Ray, I want you to spread your legs so we can make Howard. So we can raise a neurotic maniac."

Ray: That's what we raised, a neurotic maniac? You were a cute little boy and a sweet little boy.

Howard: And I was conceived in passion, is what you're saying.

Ray: Absolutely.

Howard: Dad kissed you, he caressed your breasts, and then began the actual sexual act.

Ray: If that's what you say, then that's what happened.

Howard: I want to know about my conception. Was I conceived in a missionary position? Doggy? What position was I conceived in?

Ray: In the best position.

Howard: Which is?

Ray: None of your business.

Howard: I was conceived in a bed?

Ray: Right.

Howard: You guys never would get wild.

Robin: It wasn't on the sink.

Howard: It wasn't on the sink or on the floor or in the backseat of the car. Nothing. Just right in the bed, I was conceived. Did you go to a doctor, and did he say to you, "Listen, in order to have a child, you should have sex three times a week"? Did you consult anyone?

Robin: Take your temperature?

Ray: I did.

Howard: You did? You did consult?

Ray: Yes. As a matter of fact, when your father brought the book home for me to take temperatures, that's when I conceived. I looked at the book and I said, "I'm not doing that."

Howard: Did you enjoy the sex? Because now there was no rubber involved, you must have enjoyed that more.

Ray: I don't recall.

Howard: You really don't.

Ray: I have amnesia.

Howard: What do you like better? Sex

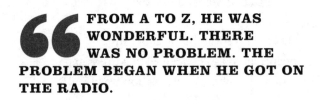

FROM A TO Z, HE WAS WONDERFUL. THERE WAS NO PROBLEM. THE PROBLEM BEGAN WHEN HE GOT ON THE RADIO.

with a rubber or without? Let's be adult about this.

Ray: Why do I have to discuss that?

Howard: Because it's my conception. I have a right to know. Did you squeal with delight?

Ray: I'm going to write a book.

Howard: Describe the noise you made when Dad would have sex with you.

Ray: I'm going to write a book and you'll pay for the book and then you'll know all that.

Howard: And would you go, like, "Oh, Ben. Oh my God. Oh, please, please, please. Oh, please give me a baby."

Ray: There you go.

Howard: Was it something like that?

Ray: There you go.

Howard: Would Pop ever do you twice in the same day?

Ray: Let's talk about your birthday.

Howard: Just a second. No, I want to know. You were so anxious to conceive me. Would Dad ever say, "All right, Ray. It's your temperature time. Let's do it twice." Did he ever say, "Let's do it twice on one day"?

Ray: No.

Howard: "You were so good, baby." "Oh, Ben, it's like steel."

Ray: Because I conceived the minute I looked at that book. That sobered me up.

Howard: How much weight did you gain with a young Howard Stern inside of you?

Ray: I was very small with you.

Howard: Really? You have big boobs, so I imagine they grew to monstrous proportions.

Ray: Monstrous.

Howard: Because my mother has gorgeous pumpkins. Did I make you sick? You didn't have any morning sickness?

Ray: No.

Howard: When I was born, was it a tough labor?

Ray: No. From A to Z, he was wonderful. There was no problem. The problem began when he got on the radio.

Howard: When you looked at me, when they put the baby in your arms—Dad wasn't with you in the delivery room, was he? Back then, they didn't do that.

Ray: No, they didn't.

Howard: You were unconscious and they drugged you and knocked you out. You don't even know what my birth was like because you were knocked out on drugs.

Robin: Were you cesarean?

Howard: No, I came out through my mother's vagina. Remember that, Ma? You could have shaved down. It made it a little rough. I thought I was lost in the forest. I couldn't find my way out.

Ray: You were fine.

Howard: I never suckled your breast, did I?

Ray: No.

Howard: You rejected me.

Robin: Straight to the bottle for you?

Howard: You rejected my mouth.

Ray: Which was wrong. In those days, the doctors did not encourage breastfeeding.

Howard: It's not too late, Ma. Just because I'm forty-five.

Robin: Do you think it would help right now?

Howard: Maybe we need to reenact that. You cradle me up in your arms and I'll suckle you. God, I'm going to throw up. Anyway, Mommy, how soon after did you wake up from your drug-induced nightmare stupor? They wake you up and they bring you the baby, right?

Ray: Yes.

Howard: I was wrapped in what? A blanket like Kal-El? [Superman's birth name]

Ray: A blanket.

Howard: Did you look at my whole body?

Ray: Of course I looked at your whole body.

Howard: Did you look at my penis? What did you think about the size of it?

Ray: I thought you were perfect.

Howard: It was small, right?

Ray: Nice, very nice. I was very satisfied.

Howard: Did you think I was wearing a Halloween mask? Because life has played a cruel trick on me, to this face. I could have been a gorgeous man. So when did Dad finally show up to see me? That night?

Ray: Yes. He never left the hospital. He was right outside.

Howard: "Ray, let's try to switch this baby. This one annoys me."

Ray: We had to own up to you, Howard.

Howard: Where's my foreskin? I want it back. Why did you circumcise me?

Ray: I have it for you.

Howard: Believe me, I want it.

Ray: That's what I'm leaving you in my will. It's wrapped up.

Howard: What would you have done with me if I was born retarded? Would you have raised me or would you have rejected me?

Ray: Howard.

Howard: You would have raised me. Thank you.

Robin: She *did* raise you.

Howard: Now, at what point in Dad's life and my life did he start yelling at me relentlessly about how stupid I was?

Ray: Your father didn't yell at you.

Howard: When was the first time Dad realized how stupid and annoying I was, and he began his relentless assault—

Ray: Your father supported you in every endeavor that you ever wanted. And you know that to be true.

Howard: Yes, that is true. There was no humiliation. He's a very warm guy, my dad.

Ray: He is.

Howard: He really is. He didn't call me an idiot right away.

Ray: He never called you an idiot.

Howard: Then you brought me home. How many days in the hospital before you brought me to the cockroach-infested apartment?

Ray: Not many. There were maybe two or three days.

Howard: When I slept, would the cockroaches and rats crawl all over me or would they—

Ray: There were no cockroaches and rats. We had a beautiful new apartment.

Howard: We didn't have rats?

Ray: No, we didn't have any rats.

Howard: You told me we had rats.

Ray: In Jackson Heights? No.

Howard: The other place, we had rats.

Ray: But you didn't live there, the Bronx.

Howard: Too bad. Would have made a better story. Were you anxious after you had me to get back into shape so Dad would have a sexy young wife? Did you have to diet down?

Ray: Your father accepted me any way I was. He never referred to me as not sexy or sexy.

Howard: You are a sexy woman. You have beautiful jugs.

Ray: Thank you. That's very nice of you.

Howard: Anyway, that was forty-six years ago that happened. Forty-six years ago.

Ray: I can't believe it, Howard.

Howard: Hard to believe, Mom. After me, you decided never to have children again. You closed up shop.

Ray: It was enough, Howard. You were enough.

Howard: Listen, Mom, I want to congratulate you. Really, it's not my birthday. It's your birthday. It's all about you.

Ray: It's for the both of us. I will allow you to get in on it.

Howard: You raised what the world now calls its worst nightmare.

Ray: But they all listen to the world's worst nightmare.

Howard: They all listen. I love you, Mommy.

Ray: I love you too.

For More on This . . .

Mike Tyson

OCTOBER 29, 2014

(from the Introduction, page 18)

Howard: When Robin Williams—I don't know if you were a fan of his.

Mike: I knew Robin.

Howard: You knew him personally?

Mike: Yeah.

Howard: How'd you meet him?

Mike: Trust me, people that deal with this situation, we know each other. We all know each other.

Howard: Were you at meetings with him?

Mike: I've been at a meeting with him, yeah.

Howard: And so when you were in a meeting with him, you knew he suffered from depression. Did you guys confide in one another?

Mike: Listen, this is very interesting. When I met him, he said, "I was waiting for you." And he started telling me about somebody I was purchasing from. And in my mind I'm saying—'cause you look up to Robin. He's high status. I say to myself, "How does he know this low-life dealer that I go to? They shouldn't even be in the same state together." You go to any measure to get high or to use when you're in that situation. So everybody knows everybody.

Howard: You're saying the world of drugs makes you go to the lowest common denominator.

Mike: Oh yes.

Howard: So when you wake up and you read that Robin Williams has killed himself, does it throw you into a tailspin? Does it make you think, "Oh shit, maybe I'm capable of this"?

Mike: One hundred percent. But more so when Mr. [Philip Seymour] Hoffman passed away. Because this is what you say—this is what my thick head says: "Wow, he was sober for twenty-something years and he died. What kind of chance do I stand?" You know what I mean? You think that he's clear and free. But we're never clear and free.

Howard: Do you ever have suicidal thoughts? Especially when a Robin Williams dies? Does that trigger it?

Mike: Listen, if you have a mental illness you're gonna think about suicide. Suicide is our comfort. He really killed the wrong person, you know what I mean? It was all about killing that disease that he possessed. It's not about killing yourself.

Howard: He was killing what? The voice in his head? Is that what it is? Is it a voice in your head or something? I don't understand.

Mike: Think of it like this. You're starving. You're absolutely famished. And that drug—heroin, cocaine—that's food.

Howard: You'll do anything to get it. So how the hell did you get off it?

Mike: Well, listen, I don't know if I'm off it. I'm clean now. This is a constant fight. And eventually that dark entity is gonna knock on the door. It's gonna come back. And we're gonna find out if all this training I've been doing is working. Am I gonna get knocked out and use? Or am I gonna raise my hand and go in the other direction? That's what it comes down to.

Howard: It seems insurmountable to me that you were able to kick it.

Mike: Well, for most people it is. But you have to be in the fight to even think about winning. You have to be in the fight. With everything you have.

Snoop Dogg

MAY 15, 2018

(from Madonna interview, page 28)

Snoop Dogg: Can I fuck you up real quick? One time, before [Tupac] was on Death Row Records, when he was just my homeboy, after we had met at the *Poetic Justice* wrap party, I was in New York and I was doing *Saturday Night Live*. And he was out here. And he was like, "Wassup, my nigga, where you at?" And I'm like, "I'm at *Saturday Night Live*. I ain't got no dope." That's when it was hard gettin' weed over here. I'm like, "Cuz, I ain't got no dope." He was like, "Don't worry about a mutherfuckin' thing, nigga. I'm comin' to *Saturday Night Live*. I'll be there in a minute." So he pulls up. But guess who he pulls up with?

Howard: Who?

Snoop Dogg: [*singing*] "Like a virgin, fucked for the very first time." He shows up with Madonna, man. And he comes in. He tells her, "Have a seat." She looks at me. I look at her. I say, "Oh wow. That's Madonna. But let me get that dope up out you." Showing me that he was [*clears throat*] elevated in the game.

Howard: He brought Madonna to *Saturday Night Live*.

Snoop Dogg: Man, please—to bring me some diz-nope. She was just along for the ride.

Howard: And think about it: bringing you diz-nope, as you say, was taking him away from fucking Madonna. What a man! That's a real brother.

Snoop Dogg: Say that.

Howard: I don't know if I'd do that for anybody. I'd stay home and fuck Madonna. I'm not bringing you weed.

Robin: You gotta find your own weed.

Snoop Dogg: I seen that with my own two eyes. And I've never spoke on it. I've been holding on to this shit for a long time. Man, he dicked her down. I seen it in her eyes.

Howard: You saw it in her eyes. She was in love.

Sharon Osbourne

SEPTEMBER 4, 2018

(from Ozzy Osbourne interview, page 52)

Howard: How are you and Ozzy doing? Everything okay?

Sharon: Great. Really, really good.

Howard: And he's behaving?

Sharon: He's so good. He is.

Howard: There was a manager of some kind who said [your separation] was all a publicity stunt because Ozzy was going on tour, that there was no trouble in the marriage.

Sharon: Oh, this was a guy who used to manage Black Sabbath in the early seventies. This was a guy who stole all their money.

Howard: Well, before you say anything—"allegedly."

Sharon: No, no, no, we went to court. He settled.

Howard: He did?

Sharon: Oh yeah.

Howard: Okay, just covering my own ass. So this guy came out and said you and Ozzy having marital problems was only a publicity stunt to sell tickets.

Sharon: First of all, we haven't seen this guy in a hundred fucking years.

Howard: So how would he know?

Sharon: How would he know? Does he come in our fucking house at night? I don't think so.

Howard: You know why I love your husband? I remember when I interviewed him years ago, and we were talking about how he went to rehab and he went to Betty Ford. In the early days.

Sharon: Yeah.

Howard: And he goes, "I went there to learn how to drink responsibly."

Sharon: That's what he thought.

Howard: And then he said, "I met with Betty Ford herself." I go, "You met with Betty Ford?" He goes, "I think I did." The guy is endlessly funny.

Sharon: So funny. One of the times he thought it was Betty Ford it was Elizabeth Taylor.

Howard: Was it really? So he said, "Hello, Mrs. First Lady. . . ."

Sharon: Yeah, and it's Elizabeth Taylor. She was there doing a speech, because she'd been there. She was there to encourage everybody.

Howard: How did Ozzy get back in your good graces? Did he come to you and say, "Listen, Sharon, I'm sober now. I'm not gonna fuck up."

Sharon: Yeah.

Howard: He did.

Sharon: Of course.

Howard: Did you record his speech to you? Because I would pay good money for that. You know I would. How long have you guys been married?

Sharon: Thirty-six years. But we've known each other forty-two. And we've been together as a couple thirty-eight.

Howard: Unbelievable.

Sharon: It's endless. My life has been with him.

Chevy Chase

SEPTEMBER 18, 2008

(from Bill Murray interview, page 90)

Howard: I thought you and Bill Murray were always at each other's throats. True or false?

Chevy: Not always. Once.

Howard: What happened? On the set of *Saturday Night Live*?

Chevy: Yeah. I went to host in 1978 or something. Bill had been my replacement when I left. I didn't know him well, but very funny. I went to the show and found out later from Lorne that John Belushi—who I'd known for years, even before *SNL*—had been quite jealous of my rise to fame. And maybe for good reason. The fact is that John was brilliant and by any real standard he should've been the big star.

Howard: For whatever reason, you charmed the American public. You became the face of *Saturday Night Live*.

Chevy: This ate a little bit at John. Enough so that, I found out later, John had said things to Bill about me that simply hadn't occurred. So he had already worked Bill up a little bit. And I was probably a little full of myself after a year of fame or whatever. And I have a sense that Billy probably wanted to knock me down a couple rungs. Billy also had a habit at the time of getting into fights with people. He liked it. Basically, words were said just before the show, in the makeup room. And he got me really pissed.

Howard: What did he say to you? Do you remember?

Chevy: Yeah, but I don't wanna.

Howard: What'd he say? Come on.

Chevy: I can't.

Howard: Share.

Chevy: No.

Howard: Share.

Chevy: Cher who?

Howard: Sonny and Cher.

Chevy: It's just not worth it. He's an older guy now and I think he's a little more mature than that. And I think I am too.

Howard: I don't think you're that mature.

Chevy: I don't either. But anyway, words were said. I finally went to his dressing room, just before the show, and opened the door and said, "You say something like that again, I'm gonna—" And John was there. They were both sitting there on a couch. And I realized in that instant that the total instigator was John. 'Cause he gave me a look. Which is kinda funny, really.

Howard: He was enjoying seeing the fruits of his labor. He'd laid the groundwork and here it was.

Chevy: I think so. But maybe a little guilty too, because what happened was Billy jumped up and charged me at the door. And I immediately got into a fight stance. 'Cause I boxed a lot. I had no problem with fights. I was ready to level him. And he was probably ready to scratch me up. At the same time John rushed to the door and put his hands on the door to block it off. As I remember I might have thrown a glancing punch off his forehead, and Billy I think might've hit him in the back of the head.

Howard: John broke it up.

Chevy: John broke his *head* up. And then also Brian Doyle-Murray, Billy's older brother, came behind me and grabbed my arms to stop me. He was strong as hell. Short guy, but these guys had obviously been in a few rumbles.

Howard: So you're not close with Bill Murray even to this day?

Chevy: Well, we've never been *close* but we've been very friendly. We play golf together. I don't play for crap. I don't like golf. Billy is a golf maven. And I think we've made an effort over the years to get to know each other better and to put that stuff behind us.

Gwyneth Paltrow

MAY 23, 2018

(from Harvey Weinstein interview, page 102)

Gwyneth: We had one instance in a hotel room where [Harvey Weinstein] made a pass at me. And then I really kind of stood up to him. I told my boyfriend at the time.

Howard: Brad Pitt.

Gwyneth: Brad Pitt.

Howard: By the way, I love him for this.

Gwyneth: I love him for this too.

Howard: You told him, "Harvey just did something really weird." And Harvey's moves are weird.

Gwyneth: It was weird. I was alone in a room with him.

Howard: Did you have any vibe leading up to it that he might be dangerous?

Gwyneth: Definitely not. It was out of the blue.

Howard: He felt like a father figure to you, probably.

Gwyneth: Yeah. I was blindsided.

Howard: And all of a sudden, "Let's go take a massage." That's the move.

Gwyneth: Yeah, that's the move.

Howard: He was naked?

Gwyneth: No, he was fully clothed. No bathrobe.

Howard: When you tell Brad, he says, "Fuck this guy. I'm gonna go over and confront him."

Gwyneth: So what happened was, I told him right away. I was very shaken by the whole thing. And I'd signed up to do two movies with him. I was afraid. We were at the opening of *Hamlet* on Broadway that Ralph Fiennes was in. Harvey was there. And Brad—it was like the equivalent of throwing him against the wall, you know? Energetically, it was like that.

Howard: Great guy, Brad Pitt, for doing that. But at the same time it's your story. It's your relationship with Harvey. As most guys do, he took action. Maybe you weren't even looking for that. He took it upon himself to confront Harvey.

Gwyneth: It was so fantastic, because what he did was he leveraged his fame and power to protect me at a time when I didn't have fame or power yet.

Howard: Did he ever tell you what he said?

Gwyneth: Yeah, he came back and told me exactly what he said. He said, "If you ever make her feel uncomfortable again, I'll kill you." Or something like that.

Howard: Wow. That's awesome.

Gwyneth: Yeah, it was great.

Howard: I would've done the same thing.

Gwyneth: Well, where the fuck were you then?

Ringo Starr

AUGUST 1, 2001

(from Paul McCartney interview, page 138)

Howard: Do you laugh at that guy Pete Best who left?

Ringo: Well, he didn't really leave. I don't laugh, no. Pete was doing the gig and then I got the gig.

Howard: Why did Pete leave the band?

Ringo: They asked him to. They asked him to leave and me to join. I had a gig already.

Howard: Did he ever come to see the Beatles?

Ringo: I don't know. I wouldn't think so, would you?

Howard: All the times I used to go see the Beatles movies—and I remember the first time I saw the first Beatles movie, *A Hard Day's Night*. I remember sitting in the theater and girls were screaming. I couldn't even hear the movie. If they put a close-up on one of you guys, girls would start screaming. And I was thinking of how great it was. But then I thought, "The movie I'd really wanna see is the Pete Best story." Like, where is he right now?

Ringo: Well, there you go. You could make it. You're in movies now, aren't you?

Howard: Yes, I am. I'm a big movie star. I'm a great actor. And did you ever expect anything like that in your life? I mean, could you have ever imagined?

Ringo: I loved the band, and we were big in Liverpool, and we thought we'd get big in Britain. And then we suddenly got big in Europe. And then we came to America. Which was, like, the place to be. If you're a musician, there's only America. And we go there with Murray the K and a number-one hit.

Howard: And when you stepped off the plane the first time—

Ringo: Fabulous.

Howard: You had no idea.

Ringo: No idea.

Howard: And it was a rush. You could really enjoy that.

Ringo: Oh yeah. I enjoyed it as we flew over. It's just one of those images that have always stayed with me. As we flew over New York—and this was America, and we'd never been before—it was like this big octopus pulling me down. It was fabulous.

Dave Grohl

MARCH 18, 1998

(from Courtney Love interview, page 146)

Howard: When Nirvana broke up, I figured, "Okay that's it. Won't hear from those guys again." Did you think that your musical career was over when Kurt was gone?

Dave: I knew that I could jump into a session with someone. The thing is, after you go through something like that, do you want to do it again?

Howard: When you hear that Kurt Cobain is dead, that's it, it's over, the band is gone?

Dave: Yeah.

Howard: Do you immediately get depressed and go, "That's the end of my musical career"?

Dave: You freak out.

Howard: First of all, it's somebody you know and somebody you love.

Dave: Right. And then you have to sit around, do nothing for a while.

Howard: Was the band on the verge of breaking up anyway?

Dave: Kind of, a little bit, sort of. It was just all too crazy. It was crazy. We're like dirtbags and, all of a sudden, we're knocking people out of the charts and then we're playing big shows and then we're making money. I just sat and laughed at the whole thing. I thought it was hilarious.

Howard: When you started shopping for a record deal after Nirvana and you had the Foo Fighters, probably a lot of people didn't want to talk to you, right?

Dave: The whole idea with this Foo Fighters stuff was that I just recorded it down the street and I just wanted to release it on my own label. Start a label, release the album, and not put any names or anything on it. Just call it Foo Fighters so people would think it was a band. What happened was I did this tape. I went and I recorded the first record I did in five days. I just went to the studio down the street from my house and I did it. And I went down to this tape duplication place, made a hundred tapes, and I was giving them to friends. This is what I'm doing and, all of a sudden, some record person got it and then another one got it, and then people were coming and asking us to go in to talk about signing with them and they hadn't even heard the tape yet.

Howard: What about the bass player from Nirvana?

Dave: Krist is in Seattle.

Howard: He's got to be pissed.

Dave: No, I don't think so. He does so much other stuff, man. He's got a farm. He's totally into living on his farm.

Howard: The poor bastard. He hit the bottom.

Dave: No, Krist is on the farm having a wonderful life.

Howard: What are all these rumors about Courtney Love? Dude, have you read this stuff?

Dave: No.

Howard: I went to research you yesterday. I wanted to see if I could find out stuff about you and it was all like, "Courtney Love killed Kurt."

Dave: That's been going on for a while.

Howard: Even this movie that they put out about Kurt Cobain's life and Nirvana and all that stuff, in it they implied that Courtney—

Dave: There was this private investigator that went out and, I guess, started this theory. Just like a conspiracy theory.

Howard: Totally slanderous.

Dave: Yeah, it's weird. I don't really pay attention to that stuff because it's too much of a headache.

Howard: Do you like Courtney?

Dave: We get along. I haven't talked to her in ages.

Pete Davidson

SEPTEMBER 24, 2018

(from Steve Rannazzisi interview, page 206)

Howard: I had on the comic Steve Rannazzisi.

Pete: Yeah.

Howard: Steve's whole story was that he had lied that he was at 9/11. He did it for a bunch of reasons, and some of them he still hasn't figured out why. But he told me in that interview that he went to you—he felt he owed you an apology for lying about 9/11. How did he line that up?

Pete: So, it was just, like, awkward. I was a fan of that show, *The League,* that he was on. I think it's a really funny show filled with funny guys. And I tweeted him, like, "I heard you got into comedy 'cause of 9/11. Me too." Maybe six years ago. And he wrote, "Something like that"—as a response. And I was like, "That's odd." And I never thought anything of it. And then that came out. And then I felt really bad, and I felt uncomfortable and in a weird position. Because for some reason I'm the mayor of 9/11.

Howard: Right.

Pete: I don't know what I did—I mean, I know I talk about it a lot. But for some reason they're like, "What does Pete think about this?" So I just tried to be funny. I was like, "Hey, we all make mistakes. I'm gonna go see my dad later." Like, "Ha, ha, ha." And then he, you know—he felt really bad. He reached out a bunch, and he was like, "I'm so sorry, man." And I was like, "Dude, it's whatever. It doesn't affect me. I feel bad for you actually." You know, whatever. And then this is the only thing I do want to clarify, 'cause I did see that. And then to fuck around and be, like, nice, I was like, "Hey, Steve . . . I'm the fuckin' 9/11 boy, okay? I'm the 9/11 boy not you." And he was like, "All right." And I was like, "All right, man, have a good one."

Howard: You were trying to release the tension.

Pete: And then he came on here and he was like, "He told me that he was the 9/11 guy, that this is his turf." And I was like, "Dude, what the—I'm not a fucking pussy."

Howard: I'm so glad I asked you that because I never understood—

Pete: Oh dude, it bothered me for years. I'm like, "People think I'm a fucking pussy now."

Howard: Oh, that's funny. Because when you said, "Hey, I want people to know I'm the 9/11 guy not you."

Pete: Ew.

Howard: I wasn't like, "Ew." I was just like, "Oh, that's interesting that that was important to Pete." But now that I'm talking to you, you were trying to release some of his guilt and try to be humorous and make light of the situation.

Pete: Yeah, I was just trying to fuck around. I knew it was a rough situation. But then he took it the wrong way, and I was like, "Oh no!"

Adam Carolla

APRIL 26, 2007

(from Jimmy Kimmel interview, page 294)

Howard: The way you met Jimmy Kimmel was he was on the radio and he was doing a celebrity boxing match?

Adam: Here's the story, and there's no hyperbole here. I was driving my truck over the hill to deliver a cabinet, an entertainment unit that I built for someone. I used to teach boxing classes in the morning and then I was a carpenter in the afternoon. I'm driving my beat-up pickup truck over Laurel Canyon and I'm listening to the morning radio out in Los Angeles. Jimmy's been on doing the sports for about two months. They just brought him out from Phoenix. And he says, "Bobby McFerrin injured himself on the ski slopes. He broke his leg." Then Jimmy goes on to say, "What kind of black guy skis? I've never seen a black guy on the ski slopes." Michael the maintenance man, the black man in the building, rushes in and starts yelling at Kimmel, "That's racist." An argument breaks out. Next thing you know—because you guys know radio—they say, "You guys are gonna have a boxing match. We need trainers. We need a venue." I'm driving my truck, I'm listening, and I'm thinking, "I could train one of these guys." Not Kimmel. Just "one of these guys." Because at the time Kimmel had been there for five or eight weeks. Michael the maintenance man had been there for five years. And of course you wanna train the brother over the fat Italian guy anyway—who, by the way, nobody liked at the time. And maybe still don't. So I said, "I'm gonna go over there and I'm gonna train Michael the maintenance man." I called ten times. Whoever their equivalent of Gary [Dell'Abate] was never called me back, of course.

Howard: Right.

Adam: So one day two weeks later, I literally drove to the building, got in, and stood out in the hallway when some UPS guy went in or some guy who changes the vending machine, and I said, "Tell 'em there's a boxing instructor out in the hall." Ten minutes later Jimmy comes waddling down the hall. I say, "My name's Adam. I'm a boxing instructor. I'm not a lunatic." I didn't tell him anything about comedy because I didn't want to freak him out. He said, "Fine. We'll get started today." So I started training him.

Howard: Was he horrible?

Adam: The first joke I told on radio was [when] they were interviewing me. You know, "How's he looking? How's the progress coming?" I said, "Well, first we were gonna call him the Italian Tornado. Then we were gonna call him the Brooklyn Assassin. But after seeing him move around in the ring we just settled on Jim. That or Kid Shits His Pants. It'll be a game-time decision." So I make friends with Jimmy, and first off he's driving a piece of shit. He's driving like an '82 RX-7 with a Bondo-covered fender. And I'm thinking, "This is radio? I gotta get back into carpentry."

Howard: How did he do in the fight?

Adam: He did nothing I told him to do, and he ended up getting the loss. But we became friends. And I asked him, "How do I get onto the radio? Can I drive the van? Can I answer the phones?"

Howard: So after hanging out with Jimmy, you said, "If he can do it, I can do it."

Adam: No, no, I said, "If he can do it, anyone can do it."

Howard: Had that not happened, do you think you ever would've gotten into radio?

Adam: I really don't know how I would've found my way in. I really don't.

Jason Alexander

JUNE 3, 2015

(from Larry David interview, page 323)

Howard: When you first took the role on *Seinfeld*, you didn't know you were playing Larry David.

Jason: No.

Howard: So you kind of played it like Woody Allen.

Jason: Yeah.

Howard: You did that for a while, and then you realized, "I'm playing Larry David, aren't I?"

Jason: We ran into an early episode where nothing made sense to me. The situation seemed ludicrous. I wish I could remember the episode—it was in the first eight, nine, ten of them. But I remember we did the table read and I went to Larry and said, "Larry, please help me. This would never happen to anybody. But if it did, no one on the planet would react like this."

Howard: And he said, "What are you talking about? This happened to me. And this is exactly what I did."

Jason: And then the bells went off. I went, "Ohhhh, okay." Then I just started really observing him and trying to pull as much of him into me as I could.

Howard: You were aggressive about getting that part.

Jason: They had apparently seen a lot of people in LA.

Howard: I have the list of people. Wanna hear it?

Jason: I've heard some. Some of them are pretty famous.

Howard: Larry Miller, excellent comedian. Brad Hall, who was on *Saturday Night Live*. David Alan Grier. Nathan Lane. And Steve Buscemi. They reportedly all auditioned for the role of George.

Jason: There are more. Paul Shaffer.

Howard: No kidding?

Jason: Danny DeVito was offered it at one point. Chris Rock was offered it at one point. But for whatever reason they didn't take it. So they had seen all these people, and couldn't quite find it, and they called a casting director and said, "Just put some theater actors on tape." All I had were a couple pages of the script, which read like a Woody Allen film. I had no context for it. Hence, I did the glasses and [*imitates Woody Allen*] as blatant a Woody Allen as I could do. I swear to God, I did Woody Allen. With the stuttering. And I said, "Oh, I'll never see it again. I made the tape and that was just an exercise." The truth was nobody from New York ever got a TV gig that way. You're not meeting the producers, you're not meeting the star. A couple weeks later I got a call from NBC. "Yes, please, we'd love to fly you out and screen-test you with Jerry."

John Stamos

JANUARY 4, 2016

(from Amy Poehler interview, page 372)

Howard: You went on a date with Amy Poehler, after her divorce.

John: Uh-huh.

Howard: You were into her. You were like, "I think she's attractive." Right?

John: Yes, yes.

Howard: You went on a date and nothing happened, 'cause she thought you were just a friend. She couldn't believe that you were into her. So nothing happened.

John: Yeah, we made a lot of plans that never happened. And then she e-mailed me and she was like, "Oh God, I might've talked about you on *Howard*." I was like, "Might've?"

Howard: But you were interested in Amy, right?

John: Yeah. She's supersmart and funny and cute.

Howard: She, I think, had the impression, "Oh, John Stamos would never be into me." I bet a lot of women go through that with you. It's about the fact that you're so good-looking. "He could have any woman he wants. He wouldn't be into me."

John: No, I have terrible game. I always think that I'm gonna be turned down. And that's the scariest thing.

Howard: Still?

John: Yeah.

Howard: Have you been turned down?

John: Yes.

Howard: I'm shocked.

John: That's why I think there's a fear to go for the right type of women. Because you're afraid.

Ben Stiller

MARCH 25, 2015

(from Chris Rock interview, page 490)

Howard: You've had a lot of integrity in your career. I didn't realize you were writing for *Saturday Night Live*, and you quit because they wouldn't put your sketches on TV. They wouldn't put your films on.

Ben: I wanted to direct, ever since I was a kid. I wanted to make short films for them like Albert Brooks did. That's what I wanted to do. And I didn't think I was very good as a live performer. I still don't.

Howard: You don't like acting, do you?

Ben: I like acting. I don't love live performing and sketch comedy live. I just don't feel that comfortable doing that.

Howard: When you did the *Madagascar* cartoons, you worked with Chris Rock. And you said it was intimidating because Chris is so fast.

Ben: Well, he's one of the funniest people of all time, yeah.

Howard: And you're standing there and you feel like a schlub, right?

Ben: Yes, for sure.

Howard: Because you're in the studio with him doing these voices, and they ask you to ad-lib.

Ben: Usually you're alone. You just do your thing on your own. Then every once in a while they put us together. Or I'd say, "Hey, let's get together so we can get some energy going." Because Chris and I have all these scenes together. And every time we'd get together I'd get very depressed because he'd improv and I'd go, "You know, let's not do this anymore."

Robin: What am I supposed to do while you're doing that?

Ben: I'm like watching him come up with, "Afro circus! Afro circus!" And I'm like, "Yep, there's the catchphrase. All right." And I'm like, "Marty! Marty!" Which is all I ever say in those movies.

Howard: Because you don't consider yourself this great wit. You work really hard at what you do, to be funny.

Ben: Yes. And I feel much more comfortable just being a director, honestly.

Howard: If you had your druthers, you would choose directing over acting.

Ben: Yeah, definitely.

Drew Barrymore

OCTOBER 27, 2015

(from David Letterman interview, page 517)

Howard: You inspired me. I went on *Letterman* and I danced on his desk in full drag and showed him my boobs.

Drew: [*laughs*]

Howard: When you did that, was that calculated?

Drew: No.

Howard: It wasn't.

Drew: So spontaneous. I mean, you can see me up there as if I am on a train that I don't know where it's going.

Howard: Is it like slow motion?

Drew: Yep. Completely out of body.

Howard: It was Dave's birthday, and you said, "Hey Dave, for your birthday"—which is a great moment of inspiration on talk shows. 'Cause it's hard to really make those things fly. And most people come on and say, "Hey, let me just talk about my project and get the hell out."

Drew: Yeah, yeah, yeah.

Howard: So you were having fun. You jump up on the desk, and you pick up your top, and you give Dave a topless dance.

Robin: It was a flash.

Drew: It was a quick flash. "The Blue Angel" chapter [in my book] is titled that after a place in the lower West Village where I did this funny little strip dance with my friend. And [Letterman's] producers got ahold of the information. This is before the Internet. How people found out anything at that point was a mystery. And he was like, "Can we talk about that on the show?" And I was like, "Sure, great." And so it just started . . . I don't know. It was just a runaway train.

Howard: It evolved. Now, when you're doing it, do you know it's going to become—it's a classic Letterman thing. They show it if there's ever a compilation video. It became a defining thing.

Drew: No, I had no idea. 'Cause I didn't even know what I was doing in the moment.

Howard: So did you get off and go, "Oh my god, I just killed it."

Drew: No, I got off and I was like, "Holy shit. What did I just do?" And when I watched it that night with friends, as I talk about in that chapter, I was like, "Okay. That was crazy. Fun. I think the tone came off okay. Thank God David Letterman didn't make me look bad in front of people." He could've. He could've sent me into a real bad place with disapproval in that moment. And instead he was charming and cute and let everybody know this was okay. And it *was* okay. And we got away with it. And that night I said to myself, "Okay, so next chapter you need to go and become a young lady. You're still a teenager, so this is okay. But you're about to be twenty and . . ." You know, I was right in that age gap where I was like, "I think that was the cap to your teens. What do you want your twenties to be?" And I immediately went out, and I know it's when I found [the film] *Ever After*. I found the path that I wanted to be on.

Howard: You mean that led to the path. Because you said, "That's the closing of a wild chapter."

Drew: Yeah. I was like, "I know what kind of kid and teenager I've been. What kind of woman am I going to become?" And I found this script that was a spin on the Cinderella tale, and it was about rescuing yourself. Sure, you want love at the end of the day. Get the prince, of course. But Jeanne Moreau in the beginning of the movie is like, "You Grimm Brothers got it wrong. This woman actually was smart and capable." It just blew my mind. 'Cause we're raised on fairy tales, and we're told to wait to be rescued. And it's like, "No. Rescue yourself."

Howard: So you were not upset about the Letterman thing. You saw it as a closing of a chapter.

Drew: It was the closing of a chapter.

Howard: Like a book.

Drew: The symphony ended.

This book is dedicated to all the animals
that my wife, Beth, and I have rescued over the years.
Here is a painting I did of one of them.
Her name was Sophia.

SOPHIA   STEVN 17